It's not unlike falling in love, reading the essays of Cynthia Ozick. Here is a mind as gentle and fierce all at once . . . A mind that embodies literature's finest potential. LOS ANGELES TIMES

The articles collected here do more than stand on their own. They jump up and down, they grab the reader by the shirt front. We may be living in 'an era when the notion of belles-lettres is profoundly dead' as Miss Ozick says in her Foreword, but it's thriving in *Art & Ardor*, which is by turns quarrelsome, quirky, unfair, funny and brilliant. KATHA POLLITT

I urge all lovers of American prose to read it . . . Cynthia Ozick is, for my money, the most accomplished and graceful literary stylist of our time.
JOHN SUTHERLAND

Splendid . . . Ozick relies on sensibility and intelligence to make their own way in the world . . . lyric grace under intellectual pressure gives her news its staying power. Her essays invite our admiration even as they challenge us to talk back.
DAVID LEHMAN

Even when you disagree with her, she electrifies your mind. NEW YORK TIMES

Brilliant . . . Ozick goes on being one of the most interesting minds at work in her Diaspora and our graven culture. JONATHAN LIEBERSON

As an essayist, Cynthia Ozick is a very good storyteller. Her arguments are plots . . . they twist and turn, digress, slow down and speed up, surprise with sudden illuminations . . . She likes to spin and sparkle . . .
THE NEW YORK TIMES BOOK REVIEW

Also by Cynthia Ozick

Nonfiction

Critics, Monsters, Fanatics and Other Literary Essays
The Din in the Head
Quarrel & Quandary
Fame & Folly
Metaphor & Memory
Art & Ardor

Fiction

Foreign Bodies
Collected Stories (UK)
Dictation: A Quartet
Heir to the Glimmering World
The Puttermesser Papers
The Shawl
The Messiah of Stockholm
The Cannibal Galaxy
Levitation: Five Fictions
Bloodshed and Three Novellas
The Pagan Rabbi and Other Stories
Trust

CYNTHIA OZICK

Letters of Intent

SELECTED ESSAYS

edited and introduced
by David Miller

Published in Great Britain in 2017 by Atlantic Books, an imprint of Atlantic Books Ltd.

Parts of this book previously appeared in the *New Yorker, New Republic,*
PEN, Standpoint (UK), *Paris Review* online, the *New York Times Book Review,*
Harper's Magazine and other publications.

10 9 8 7 6 5 4 3 2 1

A CIP catalogue record for this book is available from the British Library.

Hardback ISBN: 9781786491077

Printed in Great Britain by Bell & Bain Ltd, Glasgow

Atlantic Books
An Imprint of Atlantic Books Ltd
Ormond House
26–27 Boswell Street
London
WC1N 3JZ

www.atlantic-books.co.uk

"We make out of the quarrel with others, rhetoric,
But out of the quarrel with ourselves, poetry."

W. B. Yeats

IN MEMORIAM
David Miller
(1966–2016)
A jubilation and a blessing

Letters of Intent

Contents

Seizing Freedom

Introduction to this selection of
Cynthia Ozick's essays

Born in New York on 17 April 1928, Cynthia Ozick moved to the Bronx with her Russian-born parents, proprietors of the Park View Pharmacy in the Pelham Bay neighbourhood. She attended Hunter College High School in Manhattan, was awarded a B.A. from New York University and went on to study at Ohio State University, where she completed an M.A. in English literature, focusing on the novels of Henry James.

In 1971, Ozick received the Edward Lewis Wallant Award for her short story collection, *The Pagan Rabbi and Other Stories*. In 1997, she received the Diamonstein-Spielvogel Award for the Art of the Essay for the collection, *Fame and Folly*. In 2000, she won the National Book Critics Circle Award for *Quarrel & Quandary*.

Four of her stories have won first prize in the O. Henry competition. In 1986, she was selected as the first winner of the Rea Award for the Short Story. *Heir to the Glimmering World* (2004) – published as *The Bear Boy* in the United Kingdom – won high literary praise. She was on the shortlist for the 2005 Man Booker International Prize, and in 2008 was awarded the PEN/Nabokov Award and the PEN/Malamud Award, established by Bernard Malamud's family to celebrate excellence in the art of the short story. Her last novel *Foreign Bodies* was shortlisted for the Orange Prize (2012) and the Jewish Quarterly-Wingate Prize (2013).

The late David Foster Wallace called Ozick one of the greatest living American writers. She has been described by others as the Athena of America's literary pantheon, the Emily Dickinson of the Bronx, and one of the most accomplished and graceful literary stylists of her time. Only one volume of her essays has been published outside North America, under the title, *What Henry James Knew* (1993). With the publication of a new volume of essays by Houghton Mifflin in 2016, Atlantic now follows Weidenfeld & Nicolson, who published Ozick's *Collected Stories* in 2007 (revised 2008), by collecting Ozick's non-fiction in one volume, *Selected Essays*, something suggested to me by Karen Duffy in November 2015. My thanks are to Karen, and Will Atkinson, and also to Ravi Mirchandani, now at a different parish, who embraced Miss O with Sarah Castleton and all those at Atlantic Books, for ensuring the flame Ravi lit wasn't the usual Anglican effort, but a steady (perhaps even Roman) thing which might yet burn for a little longer. Melanie Jackson, and my colleagues at Rogers, Coleridge & White Ltd. continue to represent Cynthia with joy, because of her grace, and the miracle of her letters and emails – something else to be collected one day, if she lets us.

My real thanks are due to Miss O herself. I'm lucky to know her, to write, chat and infrequently challenge her, to have read her novels and her sublime stories but – above all – to have seen Miss O on her knees with my then toddler sons at the only publication party held for her. I have gossiped with, read because of, thought due to, laughed and argued with and questioned quite a lot of stuff with Miss O, usually on the phone (long conversations in the middle of someone's night) given there's a shrinking ocean between us: Tom Lehrer, Eliot (both George and T. S.), parodies, scandal, Updike, William Golding, God, Obama, Saul Bellow, James Wood (not the actor, or maybe so?), Philip Roth, Toni Morrison (a quick chat), Jonathan Franzen and more.

Our best meal together (so far) was in a hotel restaurant near Grand Central Station, overlooked by a 'doomed rose' (a rose which later appeared in something else), as Miss O nibbled cheese and fruit whilst I tore into my bloody steak. Or the one in her kitchen: no cheese, no steak. Just mental nibbling. Or the one with Laurence Laluyaux in Notting Hill when Laurence was questioned about her student life in Memphis, Tennessee. . . You get the point: curiosity abounds: it's (as I have said before to others) never dull.

Nearing the end of my reading for this volume, I told Miss O I had read, on a decently dull afternoon, her essay entitled 'Literature and The Politics of Sex', written in 1977 'when I was eleven,' when she wrote,

> 'What we ought to do, as writers, is seize freedom now, immediately, by recognizing that we already have it.'

In 2016, Miss O missed no beat and muttered about hearing one of those not even mentioned in her text as having been on NPR banging on about feminism and, said Miss O, "She sounded so dated." She also didn't like the title I suggested for this volume – as she states in the 'Forethoughts' to *Quarrel & Quandary*, "I resist the political, and am reluctant to take on its spots and stripes." She won.

Yet it remains the title of this introduction because I don't believe seizing the freedoms we have all grasped (since 1776 and before) have zilch to do with either creed or gender. There is nothing dated about what is included here: there never will be. It also seems to me in everything Cynthia Ozick has ever written, she's captured being free: if Conrad (rather than James) could have summarized her aims in one of his profitable Prefaces, it might be *to read others, write, see, think, just be.*

The essays selected here come from the six volumes published in the USA over the last thirty-three years. Given how we read now (by which of course I mean, *buy* – then read – books) here in your hands now is about half of Miss O: if you desire to read everything, you can.

Given her love of alliteration – Q & Q, M & M, F, & F, A & A – I have followed with Ls, as doing so made a case for itself, to me, and I hope to Miss O. The physical edition you may hold in your hand shall not be published digitally, become yawningly collectable – but yet sometimes a book should be a book, and a beautiful one. What is here is liberating: relish it.

All that is here is here because of love.

London
17 April 2016

LIVES

What Henry James Knew

✑

1. The Horrible Hours

As modernism sinks in, or fades out—as it recedes into a kind of latterday archaism, Cubism turned antiquated, the old literary avant-garde looking convincingly moth-eaten—certain writers become easier to live with. It is not only that they seem more accessible, less impenetrable, simpler to engage with, after decades of familiarity: the quality of mystery has (mysteriously) been drained out of them. Joyce, Proust, Woolf, surely Pound and Eliot— from all of these, and from others as well, the veil draws back. One might almost say, as the twentieth century shuts down, that they are objectively less "modern" than they once were. Their techniques have been absorbed for generations. Their idiosyncrasies may not pall, but neither do they startle. Their pleasures and their stings, while far from humdrum, nevertheless open out into psychological references that are largely recognizable. What used to be revelation (Proust's madeleine, the world that ends not with a bang but a whimper) is reduced to reflex. One reads these masters now with satisfac- tion—they have been ingested—but without the fury of early avarice.

Yet one of the great avatars of modernism remains immune to this curi- ous attrition: in the ripened Henry James, and in him almost alone, the sensation of mysteriousness does not attenuate; it thickens. As the years accumulate, James becomes, more and more compellingly, our contempo- rary, our urgency.

The author of *Daisy Miller* (1878), and of *Washington Square* (1880), and even of *The Portrait of a Lady* (1881), was a nineteenth-century writer of felicitous nuance and breadth. The earlier stories and novels are meant to be rooms with a view, thrown open to the light. If mysteries are gathered there, they are gathered to be dispelled. The entanglements of human nature, buf- feted by accident, contingency, mistaken judgment, the jarrings of the social web, the devisings of the sly or the cruel, are in any event finally transparent, rational. Isabel Archer's long meditation, in *The Portrait of a Lady*, on her marriage to Gilbert Osmond leads her to the unraveling—the clarification—

of her predicament. "They were strangely married," she perceives, "and it was a horrible life"—directly seen, understood, stated, in the manner of the fiction of realism. Like Catherine Sloper, the heroine of *Washington Square*, Isabel has known too little and now knows more. For the James of this mainly realist period, it is almost never a case of knowing too much.

After 1895, the veil thickens. Probably the most celebrated example of a darkening texture is the interpretive history of "The Turn of the Screw" (1898); what was once read wholly in the light of its surfaces can no longer sustain the innocence, or the obtuseness, of its original environment. The tale's first readers, and James himself, regarded this narrative of a frightened governess and her unusual young charges as primarily a ghost story, suitably shadowed in eerie riddle. In his Notebook sketch of 1895, James speaks of "apparitions," of "evil presences," of hauntings and their "strangely gruesome effect." In the Preface to "The Turn of the Screw" for the 1906 New York Edition of his work, he appears light-handedly to toss out the most conventional of these rumblings. "I cast my lot with pure romance," he insists, and calls "this so full-blown flower of high fancy" a "fairy-tale pure and simple." But also, and contradictorily, he assigns his apparitions "the dire duty of causing the situation to reek with the air of Evil," the specifications of which James admits he has left it to the reader to supply. "Make him *think* the evil, make him think it for himself," he asserts.

Since then, under the tutelage of Freud, later readers *have* thought it for themselves, and have named, on James's behalf, a type of horror he could not or would not have brought to his lips. What was implicit in james became overt in Freud. With time, and with renewed critical speculation, James's ghosts in "The Turn of the Screw" have swollen into the even more hideous menace of eros corrupted, including the forbidden, or hidden, sexuality of children. Whether James might have conceived explicitly of these images and hints of molestation is beside the point. There is, he contends in the Preface, "from beginning to end of the matter not an inch of expatiation," and evil's particulars are, on purpose, "positively all blanks," the better to delegate the imagination of terror to anyone but the author himself. Still, is it likely that the privacy of James's own imagination can be said to hold positively all blanks? Imagination works through exactitudes of detail, not through the abdication of its own authority. Whatever it was James thought, he thought something. Or, rather, he felt something: that gauzy wing that brushes the very pit of the mind even as the mind declares nothing is there. James is one of that handful of literary proto-inventors—ingenious intuiters—of the unconscious; it is the chief reason we count him among the imperial moderns.

The pivotal truth about the later Henry James is not that he chooses to tell too little—that now and then he deliberately fires blanks—but that he knows too much, and much more than we, or he, can possibly take in. It is as if the inklings, inferences, and mystifications he releases in his maturest fictions (little by little, like those medicinal pellets that themselves contain tinier pellets) await an undiscovered science to meet and articulate them. The Freud we already have may be insufficient to the James who, after 1895, became the recondite conjurer whom the author of *Daisy Miller* might not have recognized as himself.

In the fiction of realism—in the Jamesian tale before the 1895 crux—knowledge is the measure of what can be rationally ascertained, and it is almost never a case of knowing too much—i.e., of a knowledge beyond the reach not only of a narrative's dramatis personae but also of the author himself. The masterworks of modernism, however, nearly always point to something far more subterranean than simple ascertainment. *The Castle*, for example, appears to know more than Kafka himself knows about its own matter and mood, more about its remonstrances and motives, more about the thread of Kafka's mind. In the same way "The Turn of the Screw" and other Jamesian works of this period and afterward—*The Awkward Age* above all, as we shall see—vibrate with cognitions that are ultimately not submissive to their creator. It is as if from this time forward, James will write nothing but ghost stories—with the ghosts, those shadows of the unconscious, at the controls. Joyce in particular sought to delineate whatever demons beat below, to bring them into the light of day—to explain them by playing them out, to incarnate them in recognizable forms, or (as in *Finnegans Wake*) to re-incubate them in the cauldron of language. This was what the modernists did, and it is because they succeeded so well in teaching us about the presence of the unconscious that we find them more and more accessible today. But the later James—like Kafka, a writer seemingly as different from James as it is possible to be—is overridden by a strangeness that is beyond his capacity to domesticate or explicate. James, like Kafka, enters mazes and penetrates into the vortex of spirals; and, again like Kafka, the ghost in the vortex sometimes wears his own face.

The 1895 crux, as I have called it, was James's descent into failure and public humiliation. The story of that humiliation—a type of exposure that damaged James perhaps lastingly, and certainly darkened his perspectives—is brilliantly told in Leon Edel's consummate biography: a biography so psychologically discriminating that it has drawn generations of its readers into a powerful but curious sympathy with James. Curious, because an admirable genius is not nearly the same as a sympathetic one, an instruction James himself gives us in, to choose only two, Hugh Vereker and Henry St. George, the literary luminaries of a pair of tales ("The Figure in the Carpet," "The Lesson of the Master") bent on revealing the arrogance of art. Yet to approach James through Edel is, if not practically to fall in love with James, to feel the exhilarations of genius virtually without flaw. James, for Edel, is sympathetic and more; he is unfailingly and heroically civilized, selfless for art, gifted with an acuity of insight bordering on omniscience. He is—in James's own celebrated words—one of those upon whom nothing is lost. Edel's is a portrait that breaks through the frame of immaculate scholarship into generous devotion, a devotion that in the end turns on a poignant theory of James's fragility of temperament—and never so much as on the night of January 5, 1895, when James's play, *Guy Domville*, opening that evening, was jeered at and its author hissed.

Too nervous to sit through the rise of the curtain, James had gone down the street to attend Oscar Wilde's new work, *An Ideal Husband*. When it was over, scorning Wilde as puerile even as he made his way out through a wash of delighted applause, he returned to *Guy Domville* just as the closing lines were being spoken. Though the clapping that followed was perilously mixed with catcalls, the theater manager, misjudging, brought James out on the stage. "All the forces of civilization in the house," James described it afterward, "waged a battle of the most gallant, prolonged and sustained applause with the hoots and jeers and catcalls of the roughs, whose roars (like those of a cage of beasts at some infernal zoo) were only exacerbated by the conflict." George Bernard Shaw, who was in the audience as a reviewer, wrote of the "handful of rowdies" and "dunces" who sent out "a derisive howl from the gallery." James stumbled off the stage and walked home alone, brooding on "the most horrible hours of my life." The catastrophe of public rejection, James's biographer concludes, "struck at the very heart of his self-esteem, his pride and sovereignty as an artist."

It *had* been a sovereignty. In fact it had been an impregnability. He would not have been so damaged had he not had so far to fall. Literary embarrassment, to be sure, was familiar enough to James; it depressed him, as he grew older, that his novels were no longer widely read, and that his sales were often distressingly puny: but the assault on *amour-propre* that rocked James in the wake of his theater debacle was something else. It was a vulnerability as unprecedented as it was real—feelings of jeopardy, the first faint cracks of existential dread, the self's enfeeblement. He was unused to any of that; he had never been fragile, he had never been without the confidence of the self-assured artist, he had never been mistrustful. What he had been all along was magisterial. Admirers of Leon Edel's James may be misled by Edel's tenderness into imagining that some psychological frailty in James himself is what solicits that tenderness—but sovereign writers are not commonly both artistically vulnerable *and* sovereign.

And James's record of sovereignty—of tough impregnability—was long. He was fifty-two when the rowdies hissed him; he was twenty-one when he began publishing his Olympian reviews. To read these early essays is to dispel any notion of endemic hesitancy or perplexity: in 1866, at twenty-three, reviewing a translation of Epictetus, he speculates on the character of this philosopher of Stoicism with oracular force: "He must have been a wholesome spectacle in that diseased age, this free-thinking, plain-speaking old man, a slave and a cripple, sturdily scornful of idleness, luxury, timidity, false philosophy, and all power and pride of place, and sternly reverent of purity, temperance, and piety—one of the few upright figures in the general decline." This has the tone not simply of a prodigy of letters, but of large command, of one who knows the completeness of his powers. If anything can be said to be implicit in such a voice, it is the certainty of success; success on its own terms—those terms being the highest imaginable exchange between an elite artist and his elite readership. And the earlier these strenuous yet ultimately serene expectations can be established, the stronger the shield against vulnerability; mastery in youth arms one for life.

Or nearly so. On the night of January 5, 1895, when the virtuoso's offering was received like a fizzled vaudeville turn, the progress of unquestioned fame came to a halt. What was delicacy, what was wit, what was ardor, what was scrupulous insight? What, in brief, was the struggle for art if its object could be so readily blown away and trodden on? James might wrestle with these terrors till dawn, like that other Jacob, but his antagonist was more likely a messenger from Beelzebub than an angel of the Lord. Failure was an ambush, and the shock of it led him into an inescapable darkness.

He emerged from it—if he ever emerged from it at all—a different kind of writer. Defensively, he began to see in doubles. There was drama, and there was theater. And by venturing into the theater, he had to live up to—or down to—the theater's standards and assumptions. "I may have been meant for the Drama—God knows!—but I certainly wasn't meant for the Theater," he complained. And another time: "Forget not that you write for the stupid— that is, that your maximum of refinement must meet the minimum of intelligence of the audience—the intelligence, in other words, of the biggest ass it may contain. It is a most unholy trade." Yet in 1875, twenty years before the calamity, he exalted what had then seemed the holiest of trades, one that "makes a demand upon an artist's rarest gifts." "To work successfully beneath a few grave, rigid laws," he reflected, "is always a strong man's highest ideal of success." In 1881 he confided to his journal that "beginning to work for the stage" was "the most cherished of my projects."

The drama's attraction—its seductiveness—had its origin in childhood theater-going; the James children were introduced first to the New York stage, and then to the playhouses of London and Paris, of which they became habitues. But the idea of the *scene*—a passion for structure, trajectory; and revelation that possessed James all his life—broke on him from still another early source: the transforming ecstasy of a single word. On a summer night in 1854, in the young Henry's presence, a small cousin his own age (he was then eleven) was admonished by her father that it was time to go to bed, and ran crying to her mother for a reprieve. "Come now, my dear; don't make a scene—I *insist* on your not making a scene,' the mother reproved, and at that moment James, rapturously taking in the sweep of the phrase, fell irrevocably in love with the "witchcraft," as he called it, of the scene's plenitude and allure. "The expression, so vivid, so portentous," he said in old age, "was one I had never heard—it had never been addressed to us at home . . . Life at these intensities clearly became 'scenes'; but the great thing, the immense illumination, was that we could make them or not as we chose."

That, however, was the illumination of drama, not the actuality of theater managers, actors, audiences. The ideal of the stage—as a making, a kneading, a medium wholly subject to the artist's will—had become infected by its exterior mechanisms. "The dramatic form," he wrote in 1882, "seems to me the most beautiful thing possible; the misery of the thing is that the baseness of the English-speaking stage affords no setting for it." By 1886 he was driven to confess that the "very dear dream . . . had faded away," and that he now thought "less highly of the drama, as a form, a vehicle, than I did—compared with the novel which can do and say so much more." In James's novel of the theater, *The Tragic Muse*, begun in 1888, a character bursts out, "What crudity compared to what the novelist does!" And in 1894, in a letter to his brother William, James speculated that "unless the victory and the spoils have not . . . become more proportionate than hitherto to the humiliations and vulgarities and disgusts, all the dishonor and chronic insult," he intended "to chuck" the whole intolerable experiment and return to more elevated and independent courses. I have come to *hate* the whole theatrical subject."

It was a gradual but steady repudiation, repeatedly contradicted by James's continuing and zigzag pursuit of managers and productions. In the end, the theater repudiated him; but the distinction he insisted on between theater, that low endeavor, and drama, that "highest ideal," went on to serve him in what would become one of his strangest fictions. After *Guy Domville*, he undertook to imagine a novel which would have all the attributes of a theatrical production. The reader would be supplied with dialogue, sets, grand and ingenious costuming, gestures of the head and hand; there would be entrances and exits; there would be drawing rooms and wit. The "few grave, rigid laws" of the drama would wash away all the expository freedoms and flexibilities of the traditional novel—above all the chance to explain the action, to comment and interpret, to speak in metaphor. Narrative, and the narrator's guiding hum, would give way to the bareness of talk unaccoutered and unconstrued, talk deprived of authorial amplification; talk as *clue*.

The work that was to carry the burden of this lucidly calculated experiment was conceived on March 4, 1895, three months after the failure of *Guy Domville*. On that day James entered into his Notebook "the idea of the little London girl who grows up to 'sit with' the free-talking modern young mother . . . and, though the conversation is supposed to be expurgated for her, inevitably hears, overhears, guesses, follows, takes in, becomes acquainted with, horrors." The Notebook recorded nothing about any intention to mimic the form of a play: but in his Preface to the New York Edition (1908) of *The Awkward Age*, James stressed that, from the start, the story and its situation had presented itself to him "on absolutely scenic lines, and that each of these scenes in itself . . . abides without a moment's deflexion by the principle of the stageplay." Speaking of the "technical amusement" and "bittersweetness" arising from this principle, he reflected on the rich novelistic discursiveness he had early determined to do without: "Exhibition may mean in a 'story' twenty different ways, fifty excursions, alternatives, excrescences, and the novel, as largely practiced in English, is the perfect paradise of the loose end." The play, by contrast, "consents to the logic of but one way, mathematically right, and with the loose end as gross an impertinence on its surface, and as grave a dishonour, as the dangle of a snippet of silk or wool on the right side of a tapestry." Moreover, he pointed out, the play is committed to "objectivity," to the "imposed absence of that 'going behind,'" to eschewing the "storyteller's great property-shop of aids to illusion."

In choosing to write a novel confined to dialogue and scene; in deciding to shape *The Awkward Age* according to self-limiting rules of suppression and omission; in giving up the brilliant variety of the English novel's widest and lushest potential, an art of abundance that he had long ago splendidly perfected—what was James up to? What system of psychological opposition had he fallen into? On the one hand, a play in the form of a novel, or a novel in the form of a play, was a response to "the most horrible hours of my life." What the stage would not let him do, he would do in any case—on his own venerable turf, with no possibility of catcalls. An act of triumph, or contempt, or revenge; perhaps a reward for having endured so much shame. And on the other hand, a kind of penance: he was stripping himself clean, reducing a luxuriant craft to a monkish surrender of its most capacious instruments.

But penance for what? *The Awkward Age* represents an enigma. Though it intends unquestionably to be a comedy—a social comedy, a comedy of manners (as "The Turn of the Screw" unquestionably sets out to be a ghost story)—some enormous grotesquerie, or some grotesque enormity, insinuates itself into this ultimately mysterious work. Having straitjacketed his tale with the "few grave, rigid laws" of the stage, James resolved not to "go behind" its scenes with all those dozens of canny analyses and asides that are possible for the novel; yet on the whole it is as if proscenium and backdrop, and all the accouterments between them, have melted away, and nothing is left but what is "behind"—a "behind" any ordinary novelistic explication would not be equal to and could not touch. Paradoxically, the decision not to "go behind" put James squarely backstage, in the dark of the wings, in ill-lit and untidy dressing rooms among discarded make-up jars and their sticky filth—in the very place where there can be no explanation of the world on stage, because the world on stage is an invention and an untruth. James descended, in short, into an interior chaos; or to say it otherwise, with the composition of *The Awkward Age* he became, finally and incontrovertibly, a modernist. Like the modernists, he swept past the outer skin (the theater and its stage, the chatter of counterfeit drawing rooms, the comings and goings of actors and audiences, the coherent conscious machinery of things) to the secret life behind—glimmers of buried truths, the undisclosed drama of hint and inference.

The façade of comedy and the horror behind. And the penalty for "going behind"—while rigging up, via those "few grave, rigid laws," every obstacle to it—was the impenetrable blackness, the blankness, the *nox perpetua*, that gathered there, among the ropes and pulleys, where it is inevitable that one "hears, overhears, guesses, follows, takes in, becomes acquainted with, horrors." (The condition, one might note, of K. in *The Castle*.) And the horrors themselves? They cannot be named. It is their namelessness that defines them as horrors.

Yet James did give them a name—amorphous, suggestive, darkened by its imperial Roman origins, reminiscent of ancient clerical pageantry, more a riddle than a name: "the sacred terror." A translation, or, more likely a transmutation, of *sacro terrore*: the awe one feels in the presence of sacred or exalted personages, pope or emperor, before whom one may not speak; the dread one feels before the divine mysteries, or the head of Medusa. The face of a knowledge that is beyond our knowledge—intimations that cannot be borne. In the Preface to "The Turn of the Screw," James referred (handling it lightly so as not to be burned) to "the dear old sacred terror" as "the withheld glimpse" of "dreadful matter." The glimpse is withheld; to be permitted more than the glimpse would be to know too much. The sacred terror is, in fact, the sensation not simply fright, but a kind of revulsion—that comes when glimpse perilously lengthens into gaze.

2. The Sacred Terror

In 1894, the year before the idea of *The Awkward Age* materialized in his Notebook, and not long before *Guy Domville* went into rehearsals, two electrifying personal events brought James close to the sacred terror, far closer than he wished to be. In both instances he stopped at glimpse and contrived to shut himself away from gaze. The first event was the suicide, in Italy, of Constance Fenimore Woolson. A relation of James Fenimore Cooper, Fenimore (as she was called) was an American novelist who settled successively in Florence, Venice, and Rome. Bent on homage, she had first approached James in 1880, in Florence, with a letter of introduction from America. James found her intelligent and moderately engaging, and offered his assistance as an acutely sophisticated guide to Florentine art. But what was a cautious friendship on his part became, on hers, a worshipful love. James could not reciprocate. She was middle-aged, unmarried, deaf in one ear—an admirable companion whom he was learning to be wary of. He worried that she might mistake occasional camaraderie for an encouragement of the affections. The news of her death in 1894, after nearly a decade and a half of correspondence (her letters were very long, his very short) bewildered and initially misled him. He had the impression she had died of "pneumonia supervening on influenza," and prepared to journey from London to her funeral in Rome. "Poor isolated and fundamentally tragic being!" he summed her up. "She was intrinsically one of the saddest and least happy natures I have ever met; and when I ask myself what I *feel* about her death the only answer that comes to me is from what I felt about the melancholy, the limitations and the touching loneliness of her life. I was greatly attached to her and valued exceedingly her friendship." All that, however, was glimpse, not gaze. The moment James learned it was suicide that had removed Fenimore—she had leaped from a second-story window—he retreated quickly and decided against attending her burial. Leon Edel speculates that James felt some responsibility for the hopelessness that had led to what James termed her "suicidal mania." Whether that is so or not, it is certainly true that James came to rest in a conventional, and distancing, judgment—"fundamentally tragic being!"—and averted his eyes from any connection he might have had with Fenimore's dread, or her destruction. He would not seek to know too much. He would evade the sacred terror. He would not "go behind": the preparation for going behind—the horrible hours—had not yet occurred.

Two years before Fenimore's death, James's sister Alice died in London. The cause was breast cancer, but she had been strangely invalided since girl-hood, and was in the care of a young woman companion, Katharine Loring. Alice had followed James to London, or had at least followed his inclination to extract himself from America. Hers was an activist temperament (she interested herself in the hot politics of Irish Home Rule) that had chosen, for reasons neither her physicians nor her family could fathom, to go to bed for life. An 1889 photograph of her lodgings at Leamington—a health resort outside of London—survives: a capacious sick-room, high-ceilinged, with a single vast window, curtained and draperied; pictures dropped on long wires from the wainscoting; a chandelier sprouting fat globes; a tall carved mirror over a black fireplace; a round table with lamp, vase, flowers, books, magni-fying glass. The effect is of Victorian swathing—layers of cloth over every flat and vertical surface: the mantel hung with cloth, the table, the back of a chair. Lamps, jugs, flowers, photos parade across the mantel. The Persian hearthrug smothers still another carpet, splotched with large flowers. Alice James herself seems swathed, almost swaddled, half-erect on a kind of sofa muffled in voluminously sprawling bedclothes, pillows propping her shoulder and neck. Next to her, nearer the window, holding a book, sits Miss Loring, her throat and bosom lost in a flurry of scarves. Both women are severely buttoned to the chin. It is a photograph that incites the lungs to gulp air; if it were possible to step into this scene, though the looking glass is polished and clear, one might feel choked by too many flower-patterns, the mistiness of light incarcerated, the stale smells of unrelieved enclosure.

William James, in his farewell letter to his sister, wrote that "if the tumor should turn out to be cancerous, . . . then goodbye to neurasthenia and neu-ralgia and headache, and weariness and palpitation and disgust all at one stroke." To this physician brother, Alice had all along suffered from "the inscrutable and mysterious character of the doom of nervous weakness which has chained you down for all these years." Alice's illness, in short, was—until the advent of cancer—what we nowadays call "psychological." The genius sister of two genius brothers, she was self-imprisoned, self-restricted. Engulfed by cushions and shawls and wrappings at Leamington, in 1889 she began a diary: "I think that if I get into the habit of writing a bit about what happens, or rather what doesn't happen, I may lose a little of the sense of loneliness and desolation which abides with me."

She had had a history of terrors and nightmares. At twenty she had her first nervous breakdown (if that is what it was), at thirty her second, whereupon she was launched into an infinite series of undiagnosable ailments and their dubious, sometimes bizarre, remedies. She talked of suicide, and kept lists of contemporary suicides. She struggled for intellectual autonomy in an age when young women submitted, through marriage or otherwise, to the limitations of the domestic. Invalidism was, obliquely, one manner of solution: it yielded up an escape from ordinary female roles and contexts. At rest on her sofa, surrounded by heaps of books on every table-top, Alice lived in her head.

In her head she fought for Irish liberation; in her head she fought for her own. A famous sentence in her diary records a passionate revolution, in fantasy, of body and soul against a ruling class of one: "As I used to sit immovable reading in the library with waves of violent inclination suddenly invading my muscles, taking some one of their myriad forms such as throwing myself out of the window or knocking off the head of the benignant pater as he sat with his silver locks, writing at his table, it used to seem to me that the only difference between me and the insane was that I had not only all the horrors and suffering of insanity but the duties of doctor, nurse, and straitjacket upon me too."

In contrast to these dark recollections, Alice's diary offers a mellow view of Henry James, who often came to divert her and Miss Loring, bringing catty news and speculative gossip from his broader social world. "I have given him endless care and anxiety but notwithstanding this and the fantastic nature of my troubles I have never seen an impatient look upon his face or heard an unsympathetic or misunderstanding sound cross his lips. He comes at my slightest sign," she wrote, and spoke of a "pitch of brotherly devotion never before approached by the race." After Alice's death in 1892, Katharine Loring took away with her to Boston an urn containing Alice's ashes, and two thick notebooks; the latter were the pages of the diary. Two years later—in 1894, the year of Fenimore's suicide—Miss Loring arranged for the diary to be privately printed, and dispatched one copy to Henry, and another to William. Both brothers were impressed. Henry described his sister's literary claim—he recognized that the diary *was* a literary work—as "heroic in its individuality, its independence—its face-to-face with the universe for and by herself," and praised the "beauty and eloquence," the "rich irony and humor," of Alice's pen. William's own high pleasure—"a leaf in the family laurel crown"—was tempered by a graver evaluation: "personal power venting itself on no opportunity," he concluded.

But it was Henry who backed away from the diary much as he had had second thoughts about going to Fenimore's funeral. To begin with, he insisted that the diary not be published in his lifetime; and then he burned his copy—motivated, he said, by Alice's habit of setting down his sometimes unseemly accounts of friends and acquaintances. (Years later he made a bonfire of all the thousands of letters in his possession, obliterating the revelations of decades.) Amusement had become, in his sister's hands, document. James found himself shaken by "so many names, personalities, hearsays (usually, on Alice's part, through *me!*)"; he informed William that Alice's exposures made him "intensely nervous and almost sick with terror about possible publicity, possible accidents, reverberation etc.," and that he "used to say everything to Alice (on system) that could *egayer* [entertain] her bedside and many things in confidence. I didn't dream she wrote them down . . . It is a 'surprise' that is too much of a surprise." There was more for James to grapple with, though, than the mortification of stumbling on his own remarks. It might be disconcerting that Alice had mentioned a certain essayist's "self-satisfied smirk." Yet something else lay coiled at the bottom of his sister's diary, and James was unequipped to live with it.

He met there, in fact—side by side with the bits of raillery and the vehement Irish nationalism—terrifying resonances and reminiscent apparitions. After the death of the James paterfamilias at home in Massachusetts, the diary disclosed, Alice, desolate in an empty house, was assaulted by the vibrations of a voice: "In those ghastly days, when I was by myself in the little house on Mt. Vernon Street, how I longed to flee . . . and escape from the 'Alone, Alone!' that echoed thro' the house, rustled down the stairs, whispered from the walls, and confronted me, like a material presence, as I sat waiting, counting the moments." James himself, five years after the undoing of *Guy Domville*, grieved over "*the essential loneliness of my life*" (the emphasis is his own). "This loneliness," he put it, "what is it still but the deepest thing about one? Deeper, about me, at any rate, than anything else; deeper than my 'genius,' deeper than my 'discipline,' deeper than my pride, deeper, above all, than the deep counterminings of art."

Alice James's "Alone!" and Henry James's "deepest thing" had their antecedents in a phantasmagorical visitation endured by their father fifty years before. It was a vision, or a phantom, or an omen, so paralyzing to the spirit, so shocking in its horror, that Henry James Sr. was compelled to give it a name (seemingly a fusion of "devastation," "visitation," "vast") out of Swedenborgian metaphysics: *vastation*. One spring day after dinner, he testified, "feeling only the exhilaration incident to a good digestion," he was all at once flooded by panic: "To all appearance it was a perfectly insane and abject terror, without ostensible cause, and only to be accounted for, to my perplexed imagination, by some damned shape squatting invisible to me within the precincts of the room, and raying out from his fetid personality influences fatal to life. The thing had not lasted ten seconds before I felt myself a wreck; that is, reduced from a state of firm, vigorous, joyful manhood to one of almost helpless infancy." And another time he described himself as "inwardly shriveled to a cinder," altered to a "literal nest of hell within my own entrails."

The younger Henry James had turned away from Fenimore's suicide. In nearly the same moment he had turned away from his sister's diary. The suicide intimated influences fatal to life from a fetid personality. The diary was fundamentally a portrait of infantile helplessness, a shriveled soul, hell within the entrails. The elder James, with his damned shape; Fenimore, flinging herself to the pavement; Alice, listening to the ghostly susurrations of her abandonment—each had dared to look into the abyss of knowing too much; James would not look with them. It was not until he had himself succumbed to his own vastation—eye to eye with the sacred terror on the stage of the St. James Theater in 1895—that he was ready to exchange glimpse for gaze. The brawling pandemonium (it continued, in fact, for fifteen minutes) had not lasted ten seconds before he felt himself a wreck, reduced from a state of firm, vigorous, sovereign artistry to one of almost helpless infancy. Everything he had thought himself to be—a personage of majestic achievement—disintegrated in an instant. He could not go on as he had. Simply, he lost his nerve.

But he found, in the next work he put his hand to, not only a new way of imagining himself, but a new world of art. By paring away narrative rumination and exposition—by treating the novel as if it were as stark as a play-script—he uncovered (or invented) a host of labyrinthine depths and devices that have since been signally associated with literary modernism. For one thing, representation, while seeming to keep to its accustomed forms, took on a surreal quality, inscrutably off-center. For another, intent, or reason, gave way to the inchoate, the inexpressible. The narrative no longer sought to make a case for its characterizations; indirection, deduction, detection, inference proliferated. An unaccountable presence, wholly unseen, was at last let in, even if kept in the tale's dark cellar: the damned shape, the sacred terror. The tale began to know more than the teller, the dream more than the dreamer; and Henry James began his approach to the Kafkan. In those "most horrible hours of my life" after his inward collapse on the stage of the St. James, the curtain was being raised for *The Awkward Age*.

3. *The Awkward Age*

The Awkward Age is, ostensibly, a comedy of manners, and resembles its populous class in that it concerns itself with the marriageability of a young woman. Nearly a hundred years after James wrote, no theme may appear so moribund, so obsolete, as the notion of "marrying off" a daughter. Contemporary daughters (and contemporary wives) enter the professions or have jobs, and do not sit on sofas, month after month, to be inspected by possibly suitable young men who are themselves to be inspected for their incomes. The difference between late-Victorian mores and our own lies in female opportunity and female initiative, with freedom of dress and education not far behind. Yet the similarities may be stronger than the differences. It is still true that the term of marital eligibility for young women is restricted to a clearly specified span of years; it is still true that a now-or-never mentality prevails, and that young women (and often their mothers) continue to be stung by the risks of time. The gloves, parasols, boas, corsets, feathered hats, and floor-sweeping hems have vanished; the anxiety remains. A century ago, getting one's daughter appropriately married was a central social preoccupation, and, though marriage is nowadays not a young woman's only prescribed course in life, it is as much a gnawing preoccupation as it ever was. In this respect, no one can call the conditions of *The Awkward Age* dated.

In respect of sexual activity, those conditions are equally "modern." If sexual activity, in. habit and prospect, defines manners, then—as a comedy of manners—*The Awkward Age* is plainly not a period piece. To be sure, society no longer pretends, as the Victorians did, to an ideal of young virgins kept from all normal understanding until the postnuptial deflowering; but in *The Awkward Age*, which depicts a public standard of ineffable purity not our own, that standard is mocked with bawdy zest. (Henry James bawdy? Consider the scuffle during which little Aggie sets her bottom firmly down upon a salacious French novel.) *The Awkward Age*, as a matter of fact, teems with adultery and emblems of incest; what appears to be wholesome finally suggests the soiled and the despoiled.

Still, it is not sexual standards and their flouting that move this novel from its opening lightness toward the shadowed distortions that are its destination. Rather, it is the unpredictable allegiances of probity. Probity arrives in the shape of Mr. Longdon, who "would never again see fifty-five" but is rendered as an aged, even antediluvian, gentleman, complete with pince-nez, old-fashioned reticences, and touchy memories of his prime. In his prime, in a moral atmosphere he judges to be superior to that of the present, he (long ago) loved and lost Lady Julia. He has never married, and for years has lived away from London, in the country, in a house poignantly similar to James's own Lamb House in Rye. He is a meticulous watcher and silent critic, sensitive, upright, certainly elderly in his perception of himself; a man of the past. One might imagine at first that Mr. Longdon (he is always called "Mr.") is yet another incarnation of James's eager old gentlemen—the life-seeker Strether who, in *The Ambassadors*, opens himself to the seductions of Paris, or the thrill-thirsty John Marcher of "The Beast in the Jungle," who waits for some grand sensation or happening to befall him. Mr. Longdon, by contrast, is a backward-looker. Lady Julia was his Eden, and the world will never again be so bright or so right. "The more one thinks of it," he remarks, "the more one seems to see that society . . . can never have been anything but increasingly vulgar. The point is that in the twilight of time—and I belong, you see, to the twilight—it had made out much less how vulgar it *could* be."

He has come to London, then, as a kind of anthropologist (though his motives are never clarified), on the trail of Lady Julia's descendants, and is welcomed into the culture of the natives: the chief of the natives being Mrs. Brookenham, Lady Julia's daughter, who is at the hub of a fevered salon. All roads lead to Mrs. Brook's, and the travelers are encrusted with bizarre trappings. The Duchess, a callously opportunistic Englishwoman who is the widow of a minor Italian aristocrat, is rearing her Neapolitan ward, Agnesina ("Little Aggie"), as a snow-white slate on which "the figures were yet to be written." The hugely rich Mr. Mitchett, known as Mitchy, rigged out in unmatched merry-andrew gear and tolerant to the point of nihilism, is the zany but good-hearted son of a shoemaker become shoe mogul. Vanderbank, or Van—a handsome, winning, self-protective, evasive young man of thirty-five, impecunious on a mediocre salary; whom Mr. Longdon befriends—is Mrs. Brook's (relatively) secret lover. In and out of Mrs. Brook's salon flow schemers, snobs, faithless wives and husbands, jesters, idlers, fantastic gossips; even a petty thief, who happens to be Mrs. Brook's own son, Harold. And at the tea table in the center of it all sits (now and then) her daughter, Lady Julia's granddaughter, Fernanda—Nanda—who smokes, runs around London "squeezing up and down no matter whose staircase," and chooses as an intimate a married woman with an absent husband.

Nanda is fully aware of the corrupted lives of her mother's circle. Her father is indifferent, negligent, a cipher; her brother sponges on everyone who enters the house, and on every house he enters; her parents live enormously beyond their means; all relationships are measured by what can be gotten out of them. "Edward and I," Mrs. Brook declares to the Duchess, "work it out between us to show off as tender parents and yet to get from you everything you'll give. I do the sentimental and he the practical." With her "lovely, silly eyes," Mrs. Brook at forty-one is youthfully attractive, but cuts two years off her daughter's age in order to snip two years from her own. There is no shame, no guilt, no conscience; the intrinsic has no value.

All these people (but for the blunt Duchess, who is plain Jane) have names that are cursory, like their lives: Mrs. Brook, Van, Mitchy, Aggie, Tishy, Carrie, even Nanda; it is as if only Mr. Longdon troubles to take a long breath. "I've been seeing, feeling, thinking," he admits. He understands himself to be "a man of imagination," an observer, with a "habit of not privately depreciating those to whom he was publicly civil." (A habit that James himself, on the evidence of the embarrassments of Alice's diary, did not always live up to.) Mrs. Brook's salon, by contrast, feeds on conspiracy, on sublimely clever talk, on plots and outrageous calculations, on malice and manipulation, on exploitation, on matchmaking both licit and illicit; everyone is weighed for cash worth. Mitchy rates high on the money scale, low on social background. Vanderbank, with his beauty and cultivated charm, is the reverse. Mr. Longdon has money, judiciousness, and an unappeased and unfinished love for Lady Julia, whose memory serves as a standard for fastidious decorum and civilized reciprocity—none of it to be found in present-day London, least of all in Mrs. Brook's drawing room. Mr. Longdon despises Mrs. Brook and is almost preternaturally drawn to Nanda. Though Lady Julia was beautiful and Nanda is not, he is overcome by what he takes to be a magical likeness. In Nanda, Lady Julia is nearly restored for him— except that Nanda is a modern young woman with access to the great world; she knows what Lady Julia in her girlhood would never have been permitted (or perhaps would never have wished) to know.

The ground on which *The Awkward Age* is spread—and woven, and bound, and mercilessly knotted—is precisely this: what a young woman ought or ought not to know, in a new London that "doesn't love the latent or the lurking, had neither time nor sense for anything less discernible than the red flag in front of the steamroller," as Vanderbank cautions Mr. Longdon. "It wants cash over the counter and letters ten feet high. Therefore you see it's all as yet rather a dark question for poor Nanda—a question that in a way quite occupies the foreground of her mother's earnest little life. How *will* she look, what will be thought of her and what will she be able to do for herself?" Nanda at eighteen, having come of age (Mrs. Brook, for all her shaving of years, can no longer suppress this news), is ready to be brought down—from the schoolroom, so to speak—to mingle among the denizens and fumes of Mrs. Brook's nether realm. "I seem to see," James complained in his Notebook, ". . . English society before one's eyes—the great modern collapse of all the forms and 'superstitions' and respects, good and bad, and restraints and mysteries . . . decadences and vulgarities and confusions and masculinizations and femininizations—the materializations and abdications and intrusions, and Americanizations, the lost sense, the brutalized manner . . . the general revolution, the failure of fastidiousness." And he mourned the forfeiture "of nobleness, of delicacy, of the exquisite"—losses he connected with "the non-marrying of girls, the desperation of mothers, the whole alteration of manners . . . and tone, while our theory of the participation, the presence of the young, remains unaffected by it."

Nanda, in brief, still unmarried at twenty, becomes, by virtue (or, one might say, by vice) of her saturation in her mother's circle, unmarriageable. The Duchess has reared little Aggie on a different scheme—the strict continental preservation of her purity, mental and other. Little Aggie is consequently a marvel of protected innocence and ignorance, decorative and inutile, "like some wonderful piece of stitching." She is "really the sort of creature," Vanderbank offers, that Nanda "would have liked to be able to be." And Mrs. Brook lightly yet chillingly notes, "She couldn't possibly have been able . . . with so loose—or, rather, to express it more properly, so *perverse*—a mother."

Nanda's mother's looseness and perverseness is pointed enough: she knows her daughter is in love with Vanderbank, but means to keep hold of him for herself. Vanderbank, in any event, is useless as a potential husband—he has no money. Mitchy has both money and hope, and is perpetually in pursuit of Nanda. But fond though she is of him, Mitchy—a free balloon, a whimsical cynic, dotingly unconcerned, endlessly kind, all without being rooted in serious discrimination—is for Nanda literally untouchable. She will not so much as allow him to kiss her hand. Mitchy, she tells Mr. Langdon, is "impossible." Whom, then, will Nanda marry? In surroundings thickened by innuendo and conspiracy, Mr. Longdon, man of probity, himself descends to insinuation and plot—though he might think of these as inference and discretion. In combination with the Duchess, he cooks up the idea of inducing Vanderbank to marry Nanda. Despite the delicacy that veils his intent, it crudely comes down to money: Mr. Longdon will make it worth Vanderbank's while to propose to Nanda. After which, hearing of Mr. Longdon's scheme, Mitchy will relinquish Nanda (Nanda has herself urged Mitchy on Aggie), and the Duchess, finally, will have a clear field to sweep him up for her immaculate little ward. Shoemaker's offspring or no, Mitchy is a prize promising strings of pearls.

Aggie, wed to Mitchy, turns instantly wild. What was yesterday a *tabula rasa* grows hectic overnight with prurient scribblings. But under Mrs. Brook's reign (and London practice), a sullied Aggie is acceptable, predictable, even conventional. The Duchess is not simply calm. She is smug. Aggie, married, is promptly expected to know whatever there is to know of sexual heat, deceit, the denigration of husbands, the taking of lovers, the scufflings of wives. There is no surprise in any of it. English rules apply: abdications and intrusions, revolution and the failure of fastidiousness—as long as the wedding is past. Postnuptial contamination troubles no one.

Nanda's is a different case. She is tainted and unmarried. "If Nanda doesn't get a husband early in the business," the Duchess advises Mr. Longdon, "she won't get one at all. One, I mean, of the kind she'll take. She'll have been in it over-long for *their* taste." "Been in what?" Mr. Longdon asks. "Why in the air they themselves have infected for her!" the Duchess retorts. The infection is carried by the clever young men who, "with intellectual elbowroom, with freedom of talk," hang about Mrs. Brook's drawing room, putting their hostess "in a prodigious fix—she must sacrifice either her daughter or . . . her intellectual habits." And the Duchess crows: "You'll tell me we go farther in Italy, and I won't deny it, but in Italy we have the common sense not to have little girls in the room." Yet Nanda is far from being a little girl. "Of course she's supposedly young," the Duchess pursues, "but she's really any age you like: your London world so fearfully batters and bruises them."

In the end Vanderbank declines to marry Nanda, not even for profit. She delights him; he admires her; he may even adore her; and he is certainly not in love with her mother. Nanda, on her side, seemingly ignorant of Mr. Longden's bribe (though she is ignorant of nothing else), longs for Vanderbank's proposal. On a lyrical summer afternoon, it appears about to come; finally it does not. Nanda is "infected": she knows too much. Superficially, one may protest fashionable London's double standard—excessive worldliness does not interfere, after all, with the marital eligibility of young men. And the argument can be made—it *is* made—that if Vanderbank cannot marry without money, he cannot marry with it either: perhaps he scruples to wed on means not his own. But it is not Mr. Longden's bribe that Vanderbank finds impossible. It is Nanda herself, Nanda in her contamination. Nor is the infection he intuits in her merely social worldliness, however alarming that worldliness may be.

Nanda's infection is more serious than that. Her knowing pestilential things heard and seen in her mother's salon is not the whole source and sum of her malady. What might have stopped at taintedness through oversophistication has, since the arrival of Mr. Longdon—to whom she has passionately attached herself—deepened into another order of contagion. Behind the comedy, a seal lifts from over the void; the sacred terror is seeping into the tale. A gentleman of integrity, universally understood as such, Mr. Longdon begins to draw after him a gradual toxicity, screened by benevolence. Nanda speaks affectionately of his "curious infatuation." She is herself curiously infatuated: "I set him off—what do you call it?—I show him off," she tells Vanderbank, "by his going round and round as the acrobat on the horse in the circle goes round the clown." And she acknowledges that her conversations with Mr. Longdon explore "as far as a man and a woman can together." To her mother she explains, "I really think we're good friends enough for anything." "What do you call that then," Mrs. Brook inquires, "but his adopting you?" And another time Mrs. Brook wonders whether this "little fussy ancient man" is attempting to "make up to" her daughter.

But the bond between Mr. Longdon and Nanda is more mysterious than any December–May flirtation, and it is assuredly not an adoption. It is true that Mr. Longdon pursues, he courts, he possesses. He takes Nanda away to his country house for a long stay. And finally he takes her to live with him permanently: still, it is not an adoption, not a liaison, not anything like a marriage. It may be intended as a salvation: Nanda must be removed from Mrs. Brook's polluting household; Nanda, infected, is not marriageable. Mrs. Brook is privy to the fact of Mr. Longden's bribe (Vanderbank has tattled to her), and though it may (or may not) portend her losing Vanderbank as lover, nothing could gratify her more. "I can't help feeling," she observes, "that something possibly big will come of Mr. Longdon." "Big" means, in this lexicon, money; and when the bribe to Vanderbank fails, Nanda, for want of an alternative falling under Mr. Longden's protection, decidedly *does* fall into money.

She also falls into a peculiar aura: the aura of James's post-*Guy Domville* mood. James endowed Mr. Longdon not only with his own house, but with his own age, and with his own intimations of mortality and loss. To Nanda Mr. Longdon bursts out: "Oh, you've got time—you can come round again; you've a margin for accidents, for disappointments and recoveries: you can take one thing with another. But I've only my last little scrap." Mr. Longdon, one surmises, is here a mirror for certain darkening aspects of James himself. And so, interestingly, is Nanda, whose early self-recognition—"I shall never marry"—is a version of James's own youthful announcement: "I am too good a bachelor to spoil." The price of being so good a bachelor was a latterday profundity of loneliness, and in his later years—though there was no Lady Julia in James's past on which to hang a present attachment—there were sentimental yearnings toward a whole series of engaging and gifted young men. The journalist Morton Fullerton (who became Edith Wharton's lover for a time) was one of them; Hendrik Andersen, a sculptor, was another. A third, who struck James as especially endearing, was Jonathan Sturges. Sturges, crippled by polio in childhood, was an American residing in England, "full of talk and intelligence, and of the absence of prejudice . . . saturated with London, and with all sorts of contrasted elements in it, to which he has given himself up." This account of Sturges, appearing in one of James's letters, might easily be a portrait of Nanda. During the course of composition of *The Awkward Age*, which James was just then serializing for *Harper's*, Sturges was received with tender hospitality in Lamb House, and remained for many weeks. Nanda's visit to Mr. Longdon in his house in Suffolk (Lamb House is in Sussex) similarly lasts a number of weeks. The charming young men who so much appealed to James in this desolate period may have turned up, in Nanda, as a kind of imagined solution to isolation and despair. In real life, the charming young men came and went. In the novel, Nanda will move in and stay forever.

But *The Awkward Age* offers no solution after all. Nanda's ultimately going to live with Mr. Longdon is—for James's time and for our own—a serious anomaly. Nanda has twice been the subject of a bribe—once with Vanderbank, and again with her parents, who are only too glad to see that Mr. Longdon, by taking her in, really is doing something "big" for her. There is nothing honorable in Vanderbank's refusal of Mr. Longden's bribe, and there is nothing straightforward in that refusal, which is never directly spoken. Vanderbank, pleasing everyone and no one, simply drifts away. He has the carelessness of consummate indifference; what is too tangled, or too demanding, can have no claim on him. He will never come through. "There are things I ought to have done that I haven't," he reluctantly tells Nanda in their brief last meeting. "I've been a brute and I didn't mean it and I couldn't help it." Moments before this admission, he sums it all up: "The thing is, you see, that I haven't a conscience. I only want my fun."

Mr. Longdon himself, presumably a man of acute conscience, does not escape corruption. Entering a corrupt community—a bribable community—he uncovers in himself an inclination to offer bribes. For Nanda's parents, the thing is more flagrant than a bribe. Mrs. Brook has, beyond question, sold her daughter to a rich man who will undoubtedly make her his heir. Mrs. Brook's acquiescence in Nanda's removal confirms the smell of the marketplace: plainly she would have declared against Nanda's going off with a "little fussy ancient man" who was poor. Mr. Longdon, in consequence, has succeeded in buying for his empty house a young woman nearly a third his age—and no matter how benign, or rescuing, or salvational this arrangement may appear to him, it is at bottom a purchase transaction, intended to assuage his lonely need. The young woman he purposes to protect will be sequestered from society on the premise that she is anyhow unmarriageable; on his account (even if he supposes it to be on *her* account) she will be foreclosed from the turnings and chances of a life beyond his own elderly precincts.

But Nanda has been brought to Mr. Longden's house for still another reason: the revenge of love and the revenge of hate. Love of Lady Julia, hatred of Mrs. Brook. If Lady Julia in all her loveliness once passed him by; two generations afterward he is in possession of her grandchild. 'I'm a hater,' he says bluntly, reflecting on the decline of the standard that once made a "lady." In secluding Nanda from her mother's reach, he is trumpeting his contempt for Mrs. Brook: private hatred becomes public scorn. Nanda, for her part, goes with him willingly She is complicit in the anomaly of their connection; she is the instrument of her own retreat. It is not the money— the being provided for—that lures Nanda; it is the strangeness, and, above all, the surrender.

For Nanda, Mr. Longden's house holds out a suicidal peace: renunciation, a radical swerving from hope. Agreeing to enter that house of relinquishment (and moribund refinement)—this time never again to leave it—she is hurtled into a final storm of grief. Long ago, Mr. Longdon lost Lady Julia. Now Nanda has lost Vanderbank. They are matched in desolation.

> It burst from her, flaring up in a queer quaver that ended in something queerer still—in her abrupt collapse, on the spot, into the nearest chair, where she choked with a torrent of tears. Her buried face could only after a moment give way to the flood, and she sobbed in a passion as sharp and brief as the flurry of a wild thing for an instant uncaged; her old friend meantime keeping his place in the silence broken by her sound and distantly—across the room—closing his eyes to his helplessness and her shame. Thus they sat together while their trouble both conjoined and divided them.

Here James, in suddenly "going behind," momentarily abandons his "few grave, rigid laws" of dramatic restraint. It is as if, in this outburst of bereavement, the idea of helplessness and shame cannot be prevented from pressing forward, willy-nilly, from the cobwebbed backstage dark. The sacred terror is at last flung straight in the face of the tale. Not only helplessness and shame, but corruption; callousness; revenge; sexual displacement. Nanda displaces (or replaces) Lady Julia; beyond the novel's enclosure she may displace—or mask—James's endearing young men who come and go. There are, besides, incestuous hints: the young woman who might have been her protector's grandchild is intimately absorbed into the days and nights of his house. Her parents have abdicated. Her mother has sold her. The man she hoped to marry will not have her, even for a fortune. The man who takes her in, troubled by secret fevers and unthreshed motives, is sunk in a web of confusion; the young woman represents for him half a dozen identities, relations, unwholesome resolutions. And she, in joining him, has gone to bed, in effect, for life—as a penalty, or perhaps in penance, for knowing too much.

A panicked scenario. How much of it did James know? Did the teller penetrate to the bowels of the tale? The tale, in any case, penetrates—or decodes—the teller. The mosaic fly-eye of the narrative assembles all the shards and particles of James's chronicle of crisis, glimpse after glimpse, and sweeps them up, and compiles and conflates them into one horrendous *seeing*—James in his aging forlornness, in a house devoid of companionship and echoing with his sister's "Alone!"; Fenimore's wild crash; Alice's burial-in–life; the return of his father's "damned shape" and its fatal influences. And what was that shape if not James himself, at the crest of a life delivered over wholly to art, helpless on the stage on the evening of January 5, 1895, the crown of his genius thrown brutally down? "Thus they sat together while their trouble both conjoined and divided them." Divided, because James in his domicile, unlike Mr. Longdon, is alone, and will always be alone. Conjoined, because James is at once both Mr. Longdon and Nanda. But surely more than either or both. These two have been dropped into a pit. James is the pit's master, its builder and evoker.

After the cataclysmic turning point of *Guy Domville*, hidden knowings are everywhere in James—notably in *What Maisie Knew* (1897) and "The Turn of the Screw," and culminating in the last great pair of conspiratorial works, *The Wings of the Dove* (1902) and *The Golden Bowl* (1904). The recurrence, in his own sensibility, of the paternal vastarion, the recognition of an immutable deprivation ("*the essential loneliness of my life*"), the nearby explosions of suicide and self-immolation, the "horrible hours" themselves—all these pitchforked James out of the Victorian and into the modern novel. He broke down both social and narrative forms and plummeted, sans the old fastidiousness (and optimism), into the smoldering detritus of exhausted ways. It is probable that *The Awkward Age* is a novel that knows far more than its author knew, and holds more secrets of panic, shame, helplessness, and chaos than James could candidly face. But it was this work that crucially and decisively pried open the inmost door to the void. After which, released from glimpse into gaze, James could dare as Conrad dared, and as Kafka dared.

At the climax of his powers Henry James looked freely into the Medusan truth, he snared the unconsciousness. "Make him *think* the evil," he said, soliciting the unprepared nineteenth-century reader as the twentieth came near (a century that was to supply unthinkable evil), "make him think it for himself." And in the end—anarchy loosed upon the world, and pitilessness slouching toward him—James thought it for himself.

Henry James's Unborn Child

Henry James is the only American writer whom our well-ingrained democratic literary conventions have been willing to call Master. Not even Emerson, who as philosopher of individualism stands as a kind of Muse to all subsequent American culture and society, has been granted that title. It fell to James—this acknowledgment of magisterial illuminations—not simply because of his Balzacian amplitude, although that would have been reason enough. From the oceanic plenitude of James's imagination and genius there rode out, with the aristocratic majesty of great seagoing ships, a succession of novels (20 of these), short stories (112; some, by contemporary standards, the size of novels), biographies and autobiographies, critical and social essays (ranging from a book-length vision of Hawthorne to the 1905 Bryn Mawr College commencement speech), travel and museum impressions, a dozen plays, innumerable literary Notebooks, dazzling letters bearing both difficult truths and what James himself termed "the mere twaddle of graciousness."

Like the Cunarders of his day, James's ambition was intercontinental. An expatriate who came of age in Cambridge, Massachusetts, during the Civil War, he lived and wrote in hotels and lodgings in Rome, Venice, Florence, Paris. Eventually he took up residence in London, and finally he bought a house in the little English sea town of Rye. His themes too were international—Americans in Europe, Europeans in America. "Very special and very interesting," he once noted, "the state of being of the American who has bitten deep into the apple of 'Europe' and then been obliged to take his lips from the fruit." As it turned out, James never did take his lips from the fruit; he died an American bachelor who was also a patriotic British subject. Numbers of his short stories—like "Hugh Merrow"—are about English people in England.

Yet what marks James as Master is not his Europeanized cosmopolitan eye, or even the cornucopia of his cascading novels and tales—masterpiece after masterpiece. Well before the advent of what we now call modernism,

James's prose began to exhale the most refined and secret psychological processes and nuances; and it is these exquisite techniques of insight that distinguish him from other late-nineteenth-century writers. Mysteriously, with the passing of each new decade, James becomes more and more our contemporary—it is as if our own sensibilities are only just catching up with his. We can recognize him now as a powerful symbolist, one of the supreme literary innovators of consciousness.

"Hugh Merrow," an unfinished short story written in the densely reverberating style of James's "late manner," was discovered in 1937 by Leon Edel, James's unsurpassed interpreter and biographer, in an old sea chest at the bottom of Harvard's Widener Library. It lay there "neatly tied with red and blue cotton strips" among the last of the Notebooks and in the company of several commercial pocket diaries (in one of which James could view the Jewish liturgical calendar for the year 5671 amid the eclipses and tides of 1911). A fragment had, of course, no place in Edel's twelve-volume definitive edition of James's *Tales*. For fifty years—though "Hugh Merrow" was there for the asking, catalogued, readily accessible—no one came forward to publish it, comment on it, or even marvel at its uniquely truncated condition. An unaccountable absence of scholarly curiosity, given the always bustling university industry represented by Jamesian studies. (A Jamesian wonderment: is it only artists who are lured by the inchoate, and never scholars?) In bringing out *The Complete Notebooks of Henry James*—the sea-chest residue of James's pen—Leon Edel and his collaborator, Lyall H. Powers, have put into our hands the text of an acute psychological riddle: why did James, whose brilliant consummations did not fail him in 112 completed stories, break off in the middle of this one?

That he could have been discouraged by any falling off in tone or brio is unlikely. The style of "Hugh Merrow" is James at his steadiest and most assured. The comedy is burnished and fully self-aware. The progression of the plot is as finely calculated as anything James ever wrote. And it was not his habit, as the output of half a century testifies, to leave work unfinished. Nor was there anything casual about the design of "Hugh Merrow"—the Notebooks reveal at least six separate foreshadowings of this eccentric tale.

The first appears in the fall of 1895, in the form of a subject James calls "The Child," a story about a painter told to him thirdhand by friends of the Italian novelist Luigi Gualdo. In May of 1898, James begins to imagine a "woman who wants to have *been* married—to *have become* a widow," who approaches a painter for a portrait of the husband she has never had. A tendril of this motif turned into "The Tone of Time," chiefly about rival lovers—but what seems to have been brewing here, and to have kept on brewing, is the idea of the life never lived, the missed experience. (This was to become the reigning theme of *The Ambassadors*, a novel at the summit of James's art, also written during this period.) Two years later, in 1900, "the little 'Gualdo' notion" is still haunting James, and now he jots down the version he will finally pursue: "a young childless couple comes to a painter and asks him to *paint* them a little girl (or a child *quekonque*) whom they can have as their own—since they so want one and can't come by it otherwise. My subject is what I get out of *that*."

That same day, setting down a long row of names (over a hundred of them) for possible future use in stories, James lists "Archdean," which will emerge as Captain Archdean, the young would-be father in "Hugh Merrow." Two other names on that list—"Marcher" and "Bartram"—will empower one of James's most shocking psychological horror tales, "The Beast in the Jungle," published the following year: about a man whose life, tragically hollow, passes him by solely because he has wilfully missed the chance to live it. John Marcher does not marry May Bartram, and ends in devastating loneliness.

James was at this time preoccupied with his own loneliness. Not long after the names Archdean, Marcher, and Bartram were entered into his Notebook, he confessed, in a letter, to *"the essential loneliness of my life"*— the emphasis is his. "This loneliness," he inquired, "what is it still but the deepest thing about one? Deeper about *me*, at any rate, than anything else; deeper than my 'genius,' deeper than my 'discipline,' deeper than my pride, deeper, above all, than the deep counterminings of art." Loneliness, he said, was to be his final port. He was fifty-seven.

The bachelor painter Hugh Merrow is presented cheerfully as "our young man," and yet he too is described as ultimately solitary. "He was single, he was, behind everything, lonely, and it had been given him so little to taste of any joy of perfect union, that he was, as to many matters, not even at one with himself. The joy of perfect union, nevertheless, had hovered before him like a dream . . ." Again the theme of the missed experience. In the story's original scheme it was not to have been in the artist, this sense of the lost life, but rather in the childless couple. It is as if James had inadvertently sketched himself in: a fleeting self-portrait in a corner of the canvas.

On the other hand, James's self-scrutiny is everywhere on the canvas. Captain and Mrs. Archdean are hoping to commission a portrait of a child that doesn't exist, the child they cannot have. Adoption won't do; a real son or daughter will fall short of the ideal. "Hugh Merrow," from its confident start to its abrupt stop, is a meditation on the nature of imagination. How close to reality is the artist's invention? Can there be invention without at least partial grounding in actuality—some hint or model? Is there an ideal beauty that solid flesh can never duplicate? Can one live on fantasy just as well as on reality? Is there "such a drawback as [the artist's] having *too* free a hand?" Is imagination only a tricky disguise for the actual and the known? Is art the same as forgery?

But these questions point to only half the riddle of "Hugh Merrow." The other half may come nearer to the marrow of the self. (Is it unimportant, by the way, that "Hugh" can be heard as "you," and "Merrow" as "marrow"?) The other half is psychosexual. It is Mrs. Archdean's intelligence that Hugh Merrow draws close to; she asks him to combine with her in the making of her child. Looking around his studio at "things on easels, started, unfinished, but taking more or less the form of life," she vividly implores him to give birth to an imagined child on her account, in her place. And what is the sex of the child to be? Captain Archdean wants a boy who will look like his wife; Mrs. Archdean wants a girl in the image of her husband. Since they can't agree on which it is to be—*they* aren't a perfect union—they leave it up to Hugh Merrow: the sexual choice is his. Girl or boy? The painter must decide.

Here the fragment ends. There is no climax. "It was wonderful how he pleased them . . . If only he could keep it up!"

Yet James had often before made such choices. His novels and stories are full of little girls understood—and inhabited—from within. Sensitive little boys are somewhat fewer, but they are dramatically there. He continually chose one or the other—in effect he chose both. But in "Hugh Merrow" he was pressing the artist—himself—to give birth to pure imagining, roused from the artist's inmost being and equivalent to it. If the painting is the painter, then James was pressing the artist—he was pressing himself—to decide his own sex, a charge impossible to satisfy. James had never married; he had never achieved perfect union with anyone. He counted his solitude the deepest thing about him. As for sexual union, he was apparently wholly inexperienced, a true celibate. He was at various times attracted to artistic young men, and there has always been speculation about suppressed homoerotic inclinations. Some have even gone so far as to hint at a castrating accident, the notorious "obscure hurt" of James's youth.

James, for his part, burned all the papers and letters he wished to keep from us. He intended to close the door on his privacy. It is a door that we, out of respect for the Master, ought not to force. But "Hugh Merrow" may, after all, be a crack of light from under the door. If James did not go on with "Hugh Merrow," it may be that it required him to resolve, once and for all, the unspoken enigma of his sexual identity. And this, as protean artist, as imaginative tenant of the souls of both women and men, he could not do.

There is more. In the figurations of "Hugh Merrow," James put to himself in its most radical form the question of his own missed experience. In life he had chosen not to be husband or father. But "Hugh Merrow" demanded more than symbolic fatherhood. It demanded that the artist become, through the visionary organization of his art, a mother. It equated the artist with the embryo-bearing woman—while at the same time urging the substitution of art for life. The aesthetic birth was to be an explicit stand-in for an impossible biological fruition. And here the intrinsic contradictions may have grown too stressful for James; the metaphor burst and could not be sustained. He could not keep it up, he could not deliver. In "Hugh Merrow"—a tale seemingly easy and comic, and surely rich with the recognitions of its own bizarreness—James was flinging himself past the threshold of the erotic into the very birth canal itself. In the face of psychological pressure so plainly insupportable, he withdrew.

The question for us is whether *we* will withdraw. Given the enchantment of an unfinished story by Henry James brought to light almost a century after the Master first conceived "the little 'Gualdo' notion," how many writers and readers will be tempted to complete the artist's birth rites? Who now will dare to paint the unimaginable unborn Child?

The Selfishness of Art

1.

Biography, or call it life, attaches to certain writers—but only to certain writers—with the phantom tenacity of a Doppelgänger: history clouding into fable. Who can think of Scott Fitzgerald, say, without the leap into the Plaza fountain, or minus Zelda's madness and Scott's crackup? These emblematic truths are as indelible as the invented parties in the imaginary Gatsby's fictional mansion. And how to contemplate the Brontës in the absence of cramped parsonage, desolate heath, drunken Branwell? Bring George Eliot to mind, and you summon up the drama of her illicit "marriage" to George Henry Lewes. Here sits Jane Austen, eternally in her parlor, hiding her manuscript under her blotter when someone intrudes, as someone eternally does; and over there, in literary fame's more recent precincts, are Virginia and Vanessa and Leonard and Lytton and Clive, and Hemingway and his trophy mammals, including Gertrude Stein, and Alice Toklas, Gertrude's wife and slavey. Incidents, images, archival fragments dissolve into legend. The private life is rival to the work.

Among the great luminaries, Henry James has been relatively free—until lately—of the accretions of personal shock, underground gossip, and the speculations of academic sleuths; he is immaculately sealed, for the most part, within the enameled status of Master. The term Master, of course, is his own (as in "The Lesson of the Master"), but it is doubtful that he anywhere applied it to himself. It was Leon Edel, in his five-volume biography—a labor of decades—who gave this appellation its contemporary currency, and its lasting aura of literary heroism. Edel's James is heroic in art and heroic in virtue: the virtue of persistent aspiration; the transcendent courage of obsession. Two generations of writers (by now perhaps three) have turned to Edel for the model of an artist committed, through thick and thin, to what James named "our task," "our passion." The celebrated lines continue to reverberate: "We work in the dark—we do what we can—we give what we have. Our doubt is our passion and our passion is our task. The rest is the madness of art."

In his many tales of writers and painters, James was adamant in separating the deliberate and always sacral space of art from the vagaries, contingencies, and frustrations of the artist's life. He did not often speak in his own voice of this demarcation—but once, in the autumn of 1904, during a visit to America (from England, where he had long ago settled), he submitted to a journalist's interview. It was, she reported in the *New York Herald*, the first interview he had ever agreed to—"the marvel is how he has escaped"—and in her description of the "kindly if bewildered welcome from this man who is called intensely shy," we can glimpse him again looking to escape, or at least to elude his interlocutor's more intimate inquiries. "One's craft, one's art, is in his expression," he warned her, "not one's person, as that of some great actress or singer is hers. After you have heard a Patti sing why should you care to hear the small private voice of the woman?"

A credo can be a covert defense of a position not fully admitted to; and in this instance James's credo, despite its vocal flourish, was unmistakably a defense of covertness. He guarded his privacy with a ferocity that could sometimes startle, or even injure. When the invalided Alice James, his gifted and acerbic sister, died in England of breast cancer in 1892, leaving behind an extraordinary diary, Katharine Loring, her companion and caretaker, saw to the printing of four copies: two for herself, one for William—the renowned elder brother—and another for James. James read his copy, grew alarmed at his own role in it, and threw it in the fire; he was peremptory in forbidding publication. (The diary was published only in the following century.) And in 1909, when James was sixty-six, he made what he called a "gigantic bonfire" in the garden behind his house in Sussex and incinerated a lifetime's collection of letters. "I have been easier in my mind ever since," he announced. In an essay on George Sand composed a dozen years before this back-yard conflagration, he wrote with hot sympathy of the subversion of "the cunning of the inquirer" by "the pale forewarned victim, with every track covered, every paper burnt." What could be plainer than that? In 1915, a year before his death, he burned more papers; it took him a week. James intended to disappoint posterity, and to keep his secrets, whatever they were, from exposure.

His secrets, whatever they were, are consequently left to conjecture, whether ideological in the form of a definitive thesis (e.g., queer theory), or psychological in the way of an inspired hunch. Leon Edel fashioned James as a kind of sweeping literary conquistador ("The Conquest of London" is one of his rubrics)—except when Henry was in the presence of William, the brother who was older by two years and a luminary in his own right. Edel's disclosure of the fraternal tension—William superior and high-handedly critical, Henry subordinate and resentful, still struggling to assert against the favored first-born his own power and prestige—is far more the product of Edel's insight than of his research, though there is documentary force behind it. But Edel, in his warmly interpretive narrative of a generous and generously deserving James, did not venture much beyond this.

Edel's psychological forays generally follow an outward chronology (his speculations, for example, about the "obscure hurt," James's youthful back injury) and the more modest path of conventional literary criticism; he resists tampering with, or too zealously reconstructing, James's inmost psyche. In the expansive course of those magisterial five volumes, Edel remains a traditional biographer, not an infiltrator. Yet the restrained biographer had second thoughts. In a new preface prepared for an abridged and somewhat revised single-volume edition issued in 1985, he confessed that he was obliged "to keep constantly in mind the changes that have occurred in biographical writing and in social attitudes toward privacy and our sexual lives. These changes are profound . . . We are able to offer a more forthright record of personal relations, of deeper emotions and sexual fantasies." He added that though he continued to believe in James's lifelong celibacy, he would no longer hesitate to speak of the "homoerotic component." (The societal changes Edel alludes to are acute enough for Lionel Trilling to have acknowledged—looking back in late middle age on his early study of E. M. Forster—that at the time of writing he was entirely ignorant of Forster's homosexuality. It was not, he said, an issue in the culture.)

Eleven years after Edel gave the nod to sex, Sheldon Novick, author of a life of Oliver Wendell Holmes, Jr., brought out his controversial *Henry James: The Young Master*. Taking full advantage of those altered attitudes toward privacy, he challenged the celibacy premise with a spectacular claim. James, he noted, explicitly disapproved of celibacy: after a visit to a Shaker community in 1875, he condemned the Shakers' programmatic asexuality as a "lurking . . . asceticism" characterized by "the capacity for taking a grim satisfaction in dreariness."A comment on a social movement may or may not be personally revelatory; nevertheless Novick is persuaded of James's sexual activism. "I have taken it for granted," he writes, "that Henry James underwent the ordinary experiences of life," one of which he defines as "realized passion." And: "I have not made any discoveries about James's sexuality; James's sexual orientation, as we now say, has been an open secret for a hundred years." Even so, no biographer before Novick had ever suggested that Henry James and Oliver Wendell Holmes, the future Chief Justice of the

United States, went to bed together. Nor is this offered as speculation. "In that epochal spring, in a rooming house in Cambridge and in his own shuttered bedroom in Ashburton Place," Novick states, "Henry performed his first acts of love." James himself, reminiscing in his journal about those Cambridge days decades later, declared that "I knew there, *had* there . . . *l'initiation première* (the divine, the unique) there and in Ashburton Place . . . Ah, the 'epoch-making' weeks of the spring of 1865!" But whether this cry of remembered delight refers to first-time gay sex, or rather to the rapture of early literary success—James's first published story appeared in the *Atlantic Monthly* in March of that very spring—not even the most intuitive biographer can confirm.

James's bonfire is a blaze of aggressive reticence; it announces—and defends—the borders of the private life. And his admonition to his *New York Herald* interviewer (one imagines her as a type of Henrietta Stackpole, the peppy American journalist in *The Portrait of a Lady*) is a firmly shut gate: do not intrude on the small private life; the large coloratura of the diva's art is sufficient. In "The Private Life," a quasi-ghost story published in 1892, James closets his perpetually dedicated writer protagonist alone in a room with his pen, while a double—a light-minded social simulacrum—carries out the obligations of the public man. The tale is said to be based on Robert Browning, whose sequestered genius was never evident in his parlor manner; but it also describes James's impatience with "the twaddle of mere graciousness"—his term for the spirit and tone of much of his social correspondence.

T. S. Eliot, who consciously took James as his model in his own conquest of London, elevated Jamesian reticence to intractable dogma. His formulation of the objective correlative, which dominated an era with the unarguability of a papal bull, denied to poetry the presence or influence of any grain of autobiographical matter. Eliot issued a trinity of unassailable declarations: "The progress of an artist is a continual self-sacrifice, a continual extinction of personality"; "Emotion . . . has its life in the poem and not in the history of the poet"; "The more perfect the artist, the more completely separate in him will be the man who suffers and the mind which creates." What all this ideational superstructure actually meant, it turned out, was that Eliot the man had plenty to hide: an anguished personality, desolate emotions, and (especially) years of psychological suffering. The continual extinction of personality was not so much the artist's vaunted self-sacrifice as it was Eliot's attempt to escape from being truly known. A generation passed before his well-made bastion of secrecy was breached; Eliot's lofty strictures, reinforced by an unquestioned authority, held. Like some holy statue, he appeared to his public to have no private life at all; or, at least, nobody dared to inquire after one. It was not until Lyndall Gordon undertook to examine Eliot's experience—going beyond his career as a poet—that various half-concealed poisons (betrayal, misogyny, desertion, racism, anti-Semitism even post-Holocaust) began to spill out of the history of the man who suffered. *Eliot's Early Years* (1977) and *Eliot's New Life* (1988) are now combined, with additions, in Gordon's freshly issued one-volume *T. S. Eliot: An Imperfect Life*. Though she is unfailingly sympathetic to Eliot as an artist, to have read Gordon ten or even twenty years ago was (for those who once worshiped Eliot as literarily inviolable) akin to seeing the bronze monuments of Lenin pulled down after the demise of Communism in Russia. "Hatred is common; perfection rare. In him, the two were interfused" is Gordon's ultimate judgment on Eliot; but on the negative side she suppresses nothing. If others have followed her in forcing the inscrutable Eliot into the light, she was the first—the first relentless excavator into his private life.

In *A Private Life of Henry James: Two Women and His Art*, she is again first. It is possible—it has always been possible—to fall in love with Edel's tender James, and with the equally admirable genius in the biographies of R. W. B. Lewis, Frederick Kaplan, and Sheldon Novick. It is not possible to sink quite so gratifyingly into the private James (or, rather, the secret one) whom Gordon scrupulously deduces. "The deeper the silence, the more intently it speaks," she affirms; but unlike her predecessors, she is not drawn to "the homoerotic component." Her own project is more discriminating, and more labyrinthine in the tracing; it lies along the fault line between ambition and feeling. And in moving from Eliot to James, she turns from moral storm to moral nuance: where the private Eliot can be fiercely pitiless (after his first wife's permanent incarceration in a mental asylum, he never once went to see her—one instance among many), the private James is only selfish. Relying on Edel, and despite his candid account of James's defeats and depressions, we are made familiar with sweetness of temperament, courtliness, affection, humor, the benevolent beaming of a reserved figure who has learned the ways of an aristocrat. This is James as Edith Wharton knew him, according to Edel—close and warm as the drawing-room hearth, yet significantly distant; and all the same beloved. Yet the cause of art inevitably favors—promotes, urges—selfishness. James himself underlines this idea in tale after tale, where the artist is either shackled or doomed by "attachments." In "The Madonna of the Future," the attachment notably overwhelms the art, and the canvas remains blank. Elsewhere artists strain to break free of the claims of the natural. "One has no business to have children," the Master (who has them) declares in "The Lesson of the Master"; "I mean if one wants to do something good." Wife and offspring, he laments, are "an incentive to damnation, artistically speaking." And, as Gordon will take pains to show, so are friends and relations.

2.

A parenthetical reflection, for the moment, on writer's selfishness. From the very beginning James was what even in his own period was called a free-lance; he wrote for a living, and when he was not bringing out novels he was voluminously filling the magazines with long essays and stories. Between 1864 and 1910, one hundred and twelve tales—many of them, by our lights, actually novellas or short novels—appeared in the *Atlantic Monthly, Harper's,* the *North American Review,* the *Century,* the *Cornhill,* and numerous other periodicals. The novels themselves ran as serials. He lived in a magazine world, was tied to it, and had deadlines to meet and length requirements to abide by (which he habitually renegotiated and habitually exceeded). He worked, as we say, like a demon; and he was demonically driven by an ambition Balzacian in its appetite for majesty and abundance. One of the marvels of Edel's treatment—and the reason writers especially are magnetized—is its power to excite the reader with the sensation of single-minded literary ambition at its grandest, at the same time defining that sensation as an act of moral radiance. With the exception of James's comedic response to episodes of invasion by Edith Wharton, Edel has little to report about his subject's aversion to interruption. Wharton in her newfangled motor too often descended on James with her "eagle pounce," a terrifying firebird: "the whirr and wind of [her] great pinions is already cold on my foredoomed brow!" he cried. But he complained more gravely of his "inward ache" at the prospect of being swooped up and away from his work table. Edel supplies no further glimpse into that inward ache and what it might imply for an understanding of James's character in general. The fence James erected against intrusion into his private life was itself circumscribed by a second fence—or defense: an instinct to barricade against any distraction from the unrelenting pursuit of his life's appointed task. It made him into a secret monster—a monster on art's behalf; but he encased the monster in so many folds and ribbons and windings that this dissembling webwork of the creature's costume veiled him from easy recognition. As in the terrible metaphor of "The Private Life," the insatiable artist clung frenziedly to his desk, while Wharton and her chauffeur took the friendly gentleman, draped in his elaborate nineteenth-century manners, for a spin in her car. With writer's plentifulness comes writer's selfishness, James's sacred barrier against intrusion and distraction; the pairing of art and defense is ineluctable. For James, the barrier itself partook of the sacral because the exercise of art was acknowledged as holy: in his Notebooks he invokes Balzac and Maupassant with what can only be described as petitionary prayers to household gods.

James's age was submerged in a sea of letters. Literature mattered acutely, centrally, and was prized as a fundament of civilization. Even forty years ago we lived in the residue of that notion, and a new novel by a commanding writer galvanized the culture. All that has been eclipsed by film, TV, and dot-com, to say the obvious, and small note is taken nowadays of literary ambition, whether unobtrusively cloaked or savagely naked. Magazines—those with a reasonable circulation—commonly resist, and probably despise, stories; no more than a handful remain faithful, to a degree, to the old ideal of imaginative prose. Story may still retain its power in print, but only if (as in the name and nature of a long-ago pulp) it is True Story. The tales James published in his forties, saturated in the furiously free force and flow of language, patiently or impatiently sealing brick to telltale brick in the structure of character, above all heedlessly liberated to liberality—how to imagine narratives like these in our own magazines, which no longer welcome such imperiousness?

Current editorial inhibition is not so much a question of contemporary taste—the crucial changes of style, attitude, and attention since the premodern 1880s—as it is a revolutionary repudiation of the magazine as an arena for writer's sovereignty. In 1884, at forty-one—the same year he published "The Art of Fiction"—James brought to light, in serial form, two little-known tales, "Georgina's Reasons" and "A New England Winter." The first is an amazing human conundrum (postmodern, in our lingo); the second weaves an ingenious tissue of high comedy. Both display ambition metamorphosed into conscious sovereignty, the writer unimpeded, in full command, a thing inconceivable in popular late-twentieth-century periodicals. (Or, for that matter, in the late-twentieth-century academy, where writer's autonomy has long been undone by politics and deconstruction.) A comparable genius of our own time, if there were one, would not sail so easily with the wind. And since literary fiction is more and more unwanted, and the few writers who embrace it with old-fashioned lust grow more and more irrelevant, the issue of selfishness-for-the-sake-of-art begins to drift, more and more, into the fastness of a superannuated foreign psychology. The past: that alien bourne to which no traveler can return.

3.

Except the canny biographer. It is precisely James's selfishness that Lyndall Gordon meticulously teases out of the archive of extant letters, and out of her own insightful talent for making revelatory connections. As literary detective, she shuns the mischief that is motivated beforehand by what the excavator intends to find; it seems clear that she did not set out to uncover this aspect of James's character, and came upon it as a surprise. (It is certainly a surprise to the Edel-oriented.) Gordon's purpose was to learn more, much more, about two women in James's life—"female partners, posthumous partners," she calls them, "in that unseen space in which life is transformed into art." The two were Mary Temple, known as Minny, James's lively cousin, dead of tuberculosis at twenty-four, and Constance Fenimore Woolson, three years older than James, a successful novelist whose friendship with him was terminated by her suicide in Venice. Both figures have long been staples in all biographies of James. And while Woolson has had the status of a somewhat eccentric walk-on, Minny Temple has been granted the role of a pervasive minor goddess whose luminous influences touched several of James's American heroines. She can be traced most incisively in the dying Milly Theale of *The Wings of the Dove*, and even earlier in the dying Milly Theory of "Georgina's Reasons." Her living spirit animates the independent Daisy Miller, who succumbs to Roman fever, and also the freedom-claiming Isabel Archer of *The Portrait of a Lady*. Such intimations are hardly new; yet Gordon adds richly to what we already know of Minny Temple's variegated and enduring presence in James's imagination. (In the case of Woolson, much of what Gordon has to tell is altogether fresh disclosure.) But even if we are sufficiently informed of Minny Temple's phantomlike immanence, we have until now been in the dark about what the real Minny hoped for—and what she expected of—her cousin Harry.

There were six Temple cousins; four were girls. Minny was the youngest, James's junior by two years. Their parents had died of tuberculosis within months of each other, and the orphaned children were sent to live with the Edmund Tweedys, relatives of Henry James, Sr., who was their uncle. Minny was unconventional for her time; she might be unconventional for ours: once, on an impulse, she cut off all her hair. She had the recklessness of unfettered individuality; she was spontaneous, original, thoughtful, witty, passionate—"the amateur priestess of rash speculation," as James put it. In her teens she cultivated a fervent bond with Helena de Kay, a fellow school rebel (and future portraitist). At twenty, with the Civil War just over, she was surrounded by a body of intellectual young veterans who were drawn to her exuberance, among them Oliver Wendell Holmes and John Chipman Gray (a future professor of law whose correspondence with Minny was put to use by James in his late memoir). Though James's two younger brothers, Bob and Wilky, at sixteen and seventeen had been thrown into the fury of battle—Wilky with the first black regiment, led by Colonel Robert Shaw—James contrived to sit out the war at home. On the basis of a bad back (the legendary "obscure hurt," dismissed by a specialist as a temporary strain), he managed to dodge the draft, trying out an unsuccessful term or two at Harvard Law School, and devoting himself to turning out stories which he sent, unsigned, to magazines. William James, too, avoided army service, but Minny lost a brother to the war, and Bob and Wilky were permanently broken by it. When Wilky, severely wounded and hospitalized, pleaded for "a visit of 2 or 3 weeks" from James, he declined; he was preoccupied with the composition of a tale about murder. And there it was, the beginning of the deliberately blinding discipline of obsession: if a just war summoned, he would write tales; if a needy brother called out, he would write tales. It was not that he placed writing above life—he *used* life—but rather that he placed writing above compassion, and surely above danger. Compassion interrupts, danger interrupts absolutely.

With Minny, during and after the war, he walked, joked, talked seriously or playfully, meanwhile pursuing his "long and secret apprenticeship," as Gordon terms it, hiding his neophyte efforts from his family. In 1861 the Temple sisters settled with their guardians in Newport, an outpost of high-minded Boston. Julia Ward Howe was there, together with artists, historians, and assorted bluebloods and utopians; some, like the Jameses, came only for a season. It was here that James took in, for all the future, the quicksilver shimmer that was Minny—the ease, the freedom, the candor, the generous stride and the generous mind. James in old age remembered her, in the "pure Newport time," the "formative, tentative, imaginative Newport time," as "absolutely afraid of nothing." She, for her part, confided to Helena de Kay that her cousin Harry was "as *lovely* as ever, verily the *goodness* of that boy passeth human comprehension." Each discovered enchantment in the other, James in a sympathetic recognition of daring unbound by social constraint, Minny through sensing affectionate approval, as she had failed to feel it in the other Jameses. Minny reported that William, in fact, thought her "a *bad* thing." James relied on Minny to see as he saw, through the imagination; and Minny trusted Harry to be kind.

He was seventeen, she fifteen, when they began to roam the Newport landscape together; then he was twenty, she eighteen; and then he was twenty-six, ready to escape family and country for a life of autonomy—after which they never again met. He was on his way to London, with valuable letters of introduction in his pocket. He lunched with Leslie Stephen, and called on George Eliot, William Morris, Dante Gabriel Rossetti, and Charles Darwin; he was inching into the great world of letters. From England he went on to France, Switzerland, and Italy, heading for Rome. Minny, left behind, was compelled to exercise her own large ideas of autonomy within the walls of a society that confined young women to certain clear limits; pushing against commonly accepted restraints, she seemed oddball, a bad thing. She was restrained in still another way: she had contracted tuberculosis. Her sister Kitty, at twenty-five, had married Richard Stockton Emmet, a wealthy man of forty-seven. Minny, thin and ailing, went to live with the Emmets in Pelham, New York, where she was isolated and without real support. The Tweedys, her guardians, had in effect cast her off. As for her James relations,William, Alice, and Mrs. James openly disdained her, while the self-absorbed Henry, Sr., charged her with pride and conceit, and advised her to practice Christian humility. With her lungs hemorrhaging, it was plain to Minny (and to the medical wisdom of the period) that her only chance for improvement lay in a warm climate: "Rome, with its dry winter and cloudless skies, was the common hope of consumptives," Gordon explains. "Another winter in Pelham," Minny wrote to her cousin Harry in Rome, "might go far to finishing me up." In both social and medical terms, she was unable to travel alone, and the Tweedys, who went often to Italy, and who had reared the orphaned girl from the age of nine, never once invited her to go with them. A family proposal that would have taken her to the warmth of California in the company of her sister Elly fell through when Elly's husband, a railroad magnate, decided that remaining in the east was better for business. "The grand plan for Minny's recovery was incidental," Gordon concludes. Minny's recovery, it appeared, was incidental to nearly everyone close to her.

She did not believe it was incidental to cousin Harry. Rome was her coveted goal, and not only for the curative powers of its climate. Rome signified civilization, beauty, the American girl's dream of an idealized Europe; and Harry was there. "I am not very strong nowadays, altho' it is summer," she wrote to James. "I would give anything to have a winter in Italy." "I want to go abroad," she had pressed him earlier, "and I mean to think deeply about it, and try to get there." She went so far as to arrange for a chaperon to accompany and care for her, but soon withdrew from this scheme: she was not well enough. But there was a deeper obstacle. She was slowly growing aware of James's resistance to any tendril of a notion of dependence on him. Even relieved of physical responsibility for his cousin, he did not welcome her presence. He was at this time in a struggle with serious constipation and low spirits; he had fallen into a kind of invalidism. "To think that you should be ill and depressed so far away," she sympathized, "just when I was congratulating myself that you, at all events, were well and happy, even if nobody else was." "Nobody else" was Minny herself, but James was not responsive to this appeal or any other. The true blow came when he left Rome and returned to the dampness of England. She understood then— despite the old consolations of their longstanding intimacy—that she had no part at all in the principle that governed his being; her letters ceased. To William he confided his intention "to write as good a novel one of these days" as *The House of the Seven Gables*; his passions were overridingly directed to literary dominion. He may have cherished what he saw as Minny's "intellectual grace" and "moral spontaneity," but if she threatened, even at a distance, to distract his concentration and his will, he fled. Intellectual grace and moral spontaneity were not to intrude on his siege of the citadel of art—until, after Minny's death, they, and she, became the brightest stuff of his novels and tales.

4.

He had, then, the capacity to disappoint—to disappoint even the tenderest relation of his life. The tenderness, with Minny, was of a purity and a clarity; there might be a skein of romance thrown over their old walks and talks, but there was no question of marriage, no teasing sexuality. And James was still Harry.

Ten years later, at thirty-six, he had become Henry James, acclaimed man of letters, lionized author of the hugely popular *Daisy Miller*. It was at this time that he found himself pursued—at least he felt pursued—by Constance Fenimore Woolson, herself an American expatriate, who had traveled to London to present him with a letter of introduction. The letter wove together certain interesting connections. It had been given to Woolson by Henrietta, another of Minny Temple's sisters, who was now living in Cooperstown, New York—a village named for Woolson's great-uncle, James Fenimore Cooper, the famed novelist of the American frontier. Northern-born, Woolson moved south after the Civil War, visiting battlefields and military cemeteries, interviewing freed slaves, and publishing well-received fiction grounded in these explorations. When her mother died, she began a wandering Continental life, mainly in Italy, in hotels, pensions, or rented flats, industriously bringing out novels and stories. Her reputation grew sufficiently for the

Nation to charge her, in a swipe at literary women, with "infesting the magazines." She was, in short, a serious professional in an age when women who wrote were ferociously disparaged. "Women aren't literary in any substantial sense of the term," James complained, and produced the mocking tale of "Greville Fane" to prove the point. He called female reviewers "the hensex," and fumed at being seated at dinner with "a third-rate female novelist." Gordon slyly notes that even the monumental George Eliot did not escape diminishment: if she had seen and known more of life, James said, "she would have done greater things." This from a man who had avoided battle at home, frequented country houses abroad, and charted his characters' secret meditations when they were mostly indoors and sitting still.

Woolson and her letter of introduction missed James in London—he had already left for Paris—and caught him in Florence. It was a friendship that was destined to be unequal. She came to him as an adulator, defining herself—suitably—as the lesser writer; but he made her out to be less than she was. On one occasion he wounded her bitterly when he described her in a letter as "amiable," the kind of blandishment he applied to the generality of ladies whom he was an old hand at charming. She knew she was fiercer than that, and darker, and a hundred times more ambitious. He had met, Gordon tells us, "a writer absorbed in writing even more completely than himself." In their early acquaintance in Florence they made the rounds together of churches and galleries, paintings and sculptures, James leading and discoursing,Woolson rapturously attending. He had begun by thinking of her as a neatly dressed spinster, deaf in one ear, "a good little woman," "a perfect lady," "Miss Woolson." When her intellect and dedication showed themselves indefeasibly, he chose to call her Fenimore: an open recognition of sorts, which led to his talking over with her his current work. "I see her at discreet intervals," he admitted to William Dean Howells, editor of the *Atlantic*, who published both Woolson and James. "She is a very intelligent woman, and understands when she is spoken to." He had advanced, cautiously, to an appreciation of her—but she was always subordinate. She was, in his phrase, a "resource." He sent her his dramatization of *Daisy Miller* (it rankled him that it was never staged); she read and responded during an intense period when she was laboring thirteen hours a day to complete a manuscript of her own. One of her novels, serialized in *Harper's*, was so successful that she felt obligated to apologize to James. "Even if a story of mine should have a large 'popular' sale," she told him, she of course recognized that "the utmost best of my work cannot touch the hem of your first or poorest." And if he exploited her admiration and the usefulness of her literary scrutiny, she did not protest.

Nor did she protest that he hid their friendship; she colluded in his project of secrecy. Ten years of association were suppressed. "None of his London circle knew of her presence in his life," Gordon reveals. He rarely spoke or wrote of Woolson, and then only obliquely, masking the quality of their relationship. In 1886, on a visit to Florence, where she was then residing, he spent three weeks in rooms literally next door to hers, in a house she had rented. It had all the comforts of a private domesticity. A similar arrangement was undertaken the following year; again they divided the house, she on an upper floor, he on a lower. These prolonged occasions, with their meals and talks and inevitable familiarity, were kept carefully screened from James's usual society. And still he could disappear from her ken for eighteen months at a time. She may now and then have been a solace to him, but he dreaded being linked with her—he feared the publicity of an "attachment." As for Woolson, she not only understood when she was spoken to; she understood far more. A character in an 1882 story, "The Street of the Hyacinth," intimates her sense of James: "He was an excellent evader when he chose to exert himself, and he finally got away from the little high-up apartment . . . without any positive promise as to the exact date of his next visit." "My plans are uncertain," the Jamesian persona asserts. "I have a habit of not assuming responsibility, I suppose I have grown selfish."

James evaded Woolson whenever it pleased him. In January of 1894 she evaded him, and horribly: she threw herself from the window of her "little high-up apartment," this one in Venice, recently let. Like James himself (and like William and Alice), she was subject to periods of black depression. When the report of her death arrived, James at first thought it was from influenza, and prepared to go to the funeral. But when he learned she was a suicide, he recoiled, pronounced her "deranged," and insisted that she "was not, she was never, wholly sane." According to Gordon, this "slur of uncontrollable *dementia*" had a self-protective aim. "The coded message is plain: no one," she argues, "not the best of friends, could have prevented this death." The publicity James had always feared did, after all, explode around him. As long as three years after the event, the *New York Herald* was identifying him as "the principal mourner," and offering as "the truth about Mr. James's bachelorhood" his having been "this other author's devoted slave . . . Miss Woolson was not to be won."

Three months after Woolson's death, James committed himself to an extraordinarily uncharacteristic task. Woolson's sister and niece, Clara and Clare Benedict, were sailing from America to Venice to dismantle the little high-up apartment and all its accumulated treasures. James left London and eagerly joined them in the work of sorting and clearing—sacrificing five full weeks to manual drudgery in Woolson's memory. This seemingly charitable act had a deeply self-serving purpose. The continuing wet weather called for a daily fire, and into it—either trusted or unnoticed by his companions— James tossed every scrap that touched on himself or revealed anything that might cause him uneasiness.

Woolson served James ever afterward. A version of her turns up as the unnamed woman writer in "The Altar of the Dead"; as May Bartram in "The Beast in the Jungle"; as Miss Gostrey in *The Ambassadors*; and as Miss Staverton in "The Jolly Corner," a title derived from "Cheerful Corner," Woolson's childhood home. It was from a story of Woolson's that James took the phrase, and the metaphor, of "The Figure in the Carpet." Three times he visited her grave in the Protestant Cemetery in Rome. And, most mysteriously, in the autumn of 1894, in Oxford, he sought out the furnished flat she had occupied for the two preceding years and briefly let it; he slept in her bed.

Lyndall Gordon begins her remarkable study—intuitive, scholarly, novel-like, bold—with an amazing image. In 1956, four decades after James's death, a BBC program in his honor recorded, from Florence, the voice of an elderly woman who as a young girl had known James. She was remembering snatches of a scene he had related, all the while oddly laughing, about the death of "some very famous person" in Venice, about having to "do certain things," and about dresses, and a lagoon, and "horrible black balloons." Gordon opens her history with a reconstruction of this fantastic (and perhaps fantasized) memory, drawing also from a passage in "The Aspern Papers." A gentleman in a gondola in the middle of a Venetian lake is in the act of heaving into the water a bundle of lady's garments, all dark-colored and nicely tailored:

> The gondolier's pole would have been useful for pushing them under the still water. But the dresses refused to drown. One by one they rose to the surface, their busts and sleeves swelling like black balloons. Purposefully, the gentleman pushed them under, but silent, reproachful, they rose before his eyes.

It seems unlikely that James, with or without the Benedicts' leave, would have contrived so strange an expedition to dispose of Woolson's clothes. And yet the unlikely, the driven, the weird, were never foreign to his imagination. Gordon's picture of swollen sleeves and torsos resisting drowning, stubbornly bobbing, is as suggestive as she means it to be: a woman returning, a woman refusing to vanish. The two women, Minny Temple and Constance Woolson, whose phantoms took hold of James's vision, fevering and inflaming it, again and again replenish Gordon's thesis. Posthumously, they fed his genius. But when they were alive, his genius beat them off, defending itself with the isolating fortifications that alone sustain literary obsession. Before Harry turned his back on her, Minny believed her cousin's goodness passed comprehension. Woolson, older and worldlier, had a more sardonic view of what to expect. In a story about a literary lion, published a year after the start of her problematic friendship with James, she wrote: "Let us see a man of genius who is 'good' as well." The skeptical quotation marks emphasize her discernment: the ruthless sovereignty of the Master, the defensive selfishness of art.

Cinematic James

There appears to be no record of Henry James's ever having seen a movie. He died in London in 1916, at the age of seventy-three, a dozen years before the introduction of sound. The highbrow term "film" was decades in the future; what people went to was the picture show. And if Charlie Chaplin was deemed an artist by the discerning few, James was assuredly not among them. No one distinguished more stringently between High and Low than this acclaimed literary Master, author of matchless tales and architecturally resplendent novels. And wouldn't he think of movies as Low?

But James was enraptured by drama, and all his life tried to succeed in the theater, the only medium available to his era. "The dramatic form," he wrote in 1882, "seems to me the most beautiful thing possible." And another time: "An acted play is a novel intensified." He was single-mindedly obsessed by the notion of the scene. As a novelist, he explained, he worked on "absolutely scenic lines," and developed dialogue as it might be employed in a script, "with the loose end as gross an impertinence on its surface, and as grave a dishonor, as the dangle of a snippet of silk or wool on the right side of a tapestry." The evidence, then, is that James would have welcomed film, with its quicksilver dissolves, its ghostly special effects (he was in love with the ghost story), its lavish costumes and intensified color, its precision of landscape and weather and sky, and particularly its capacity for living portraiture through the technique of the closeup, rivaling in facial revelation anything he might have seen in the great galleries of Europe. He was, besides, sympathetically open to technical advance. When writer's cramp forced him to abandon his pen, he turned at once to the newfangled typewriter (the "typewriter" being, for James, the typist). Though still mainly in the period of the horse-drawn, he now and then enjoyed tooling up and down the countryside in Edith Wharton's chauffeur-driven motorcar. The progress of sophisticated film technology, had he lived to see it, would not have daunted or inhibited him.

Yet there was a Hollywood side, in the negative sense, to James's script-writing experience. Theater managers—who at that time were both producers and directors—got in the way of his purist ideas of dramatic art. Like many television and movie potentates nowadays, they were apt to fix solely and wholly on mass taste and mass profits, hoping to woo the trendiest and most sentimental audiences. After several unsatisfactory theatrical ventures, and especially after the humiliating failure of his 1905 play, *Guy Domville*, when he was subjected to jeers and howls from the pit, James gave up trying to please a larger public. In shame and fury he railed against show-biz, its "vulgarities and disgusts, all the dishonor and chronic insult," and said he intended "to chuck the whole intolerable experiment and return to more elevated and independent courses. I have come," he burst out, "to *hate* the whole theatrical subject."

And in *The Tragic Muse*, his 1888 theater novel, he has a character cry: "What crudity compared to what the novelist does!" There is a temptation to say the same about any film adaptation of a complex and nuanced work of fiction. A novel is, first of all, made out of language; it is language that determines whether a novel's storytelling trajectory will land it in the kingdom of art or in the rundown neighborhood of the hackneyed. *The Portrait of a Lady*, James's earliest full-scale masterpiece, is at its core an effective melodrama, chillingly equipped with an unsuspecting victim and sinister schemes and disclosures. What lifts it beyond melodrama is exactly what movies have no use for: acute, minute examination of motives; the most gossamer vibrations of the interior life; densely conceived villains and comic figures who cast unexpected shadows of self-understanding; a rich population of minor characters, each of whom has a history. And more: something atmospheric, something akin to what we might call a philosophy of the soul—a thing different from up-to-date sensibility.

A movie, by contrast, despite its all-encompassing arsenal of skills, probing angles, mood-inducing music, and miraculous technologies, is still a picture show. It shows us pictures above all, and Jane Campion's backgrounds and views in her film version of *The Portrait of a Lady* are immaculately beautiful—reminiscent of nineteenth-century canvases, and of the era of Beaux Arts. And if they breathe out a kind of museum insularity, that is what confirms their power: we know we are in another time, another and older England and Europe. Fabled sites become fresh pageants. An English country house, Rome and Florence, ancient churches and crypts and palaces and plazas, the Colosseum itself, all pass before us with the picturesque glow of authentic old lantern slides. But they are not sentimental; they convince.

At least three in Campion's cast[*] are unerringly persuasive in the same way. John Malkovich plays the callous, languorous dilettante, Gilbert Osmond, precisely as James imagined him: an aesthete devoted to objets d'art, for whom human beings too are objects to be turned in the hand at will. Martin Donovan, as Ralph Touchett, the heroine's consumptive cousin, sees omnisciently with eyes marvelously lit by both irony and longing. As Madame Merle, Barbara Hershey fully incarnates James's idea of the schemer, as vulnerable as she is dangerous, who lures Isabel Archer into a pitiless marriage with Osmond, Madame Merle's former lover and the father of her unacknowledged child.

But Nicole Kidman as Isabel Archer, Madame Merle's dupe, is far more Campion's creation than James's—even though, given the confinements of her medium, Campion keeps reasonably close to James's plot. Fatherless and motherless, a spirited young beauty, Isabel is plucked out of provincial Albany, New York, by her aunt, Mrs. Touchett (Shelley Winters, banally miscast), and brought into the wider opportunities of aristocratic England. There she enters the life of the grand country estates, and declines the offer of a brilliantly advantageous marriage to Lord Warburton, a member of Parliament (Richard E. Grant). Alone and dependent, she has seemingly given up her chance of access to a glittering society, and old Mr. Touchett, her wealthy banker uncle (John Gielgud), is bemused by such perversity. She has earlier refused a persistent American suitor, Caspar Goodwood (Viggo Mortensen)—she is ambitious beyond the velvet enclosures of marriage.

Just here is the conceptual spine of James's novel, its electrifying and chancy theory. Isabel Archer dreams of living hugely, of using her vivid capacities to take in the great and various world of boundless experience. Ralph Touchett, her admiring invalid cousin, sympathizes, understands, and makes it all possible. He persuades his dying father to leave Isabel a magnificent fortune. The Albany orphan is now an heiress, freed to infinite choice.

This is the point Campion unluckily loses sight of. She misses it both in detail and in scope. Isabel's first and buoyant choice is to voyage around the world, the bold outward sign of her valued new freedom—a freedom that Campion burlesques in a series of scenes (Isabel riding a camel, visiting the Pyramids) rendered playfully but reductively in silent-film style. Yet James recounts Isabel's worldly education as a serious enrichment: "She had ranged

---

[*] A film in a canister (and who today would dispute that movies are an art form?) is nevertheless not the same as a book in a library. The names of James's characters endure; nothing is more ephemeral than the names of the actors who portray them. The difference between characters in literature and actors in performance is the difference, say, between a waterfall and a drink of water. No matter how pretty the cup, the drink is short-lived.

. . . through space and surveyed much of mankind, and was therefore now, in her own eyes, a very different person from the frivolous young woman from Albany who had begun to take the measure of Europe."

And while Nicole Kidman is lovely, slender, and effectively winning, Campion has omitted the buoyancy and the ambition. Kidman's Isabel takes the measure mainly of herself, in erotic and autoerotic fantasies: Isabel caressing her own lips and cheek, Isabel prone in a vortex of three suitors who surround her like a whirligig, Isabel walking moodily through a landscape with a hand at her breast.

The film's opening moments startle with the faces and voices of a group of contemporary young women who comment on the act of kissing—and though such a prologue may seem extraneous to what follows, it is plainly offered as a key to the director's sensibility. Self-oriented eroticism (or call it, more generally, a circumscribed interest in one's body), a current theme of a certain order of feminism, here replaces James's searching idea of a large and susceptible imagination roiling with world-hunger. James describes Isabel, fresh from America, as "at all times a keenly-glancing, quickly-moving, completely animated young woman" who emits a "radiance, even a slight exaltation." No flicker of this expressive vitality can be glimpsed in Kidman's passive, morose, tearfully suffering Isabel.

This is partly because a film based on a novel is, perforce, essentially an excerpt, and Campion mostly gives us the climax and sorrowful denouement of Isabel's story, and little of its eagerly yearning premise. Of motives there is nothing. Isabel, who had earlier eschewed marriage as too narrow for her possibilities, marries after all, and discovers herself to be Gilbert Osmond's unsatisfactory, even inferior, bibelot. The palatial interiors darken, husband and wife turn bitter. The two old lovers, Madame Merle and Osmond, working together, have seized on Isabel only for her money, to assure their daughter's future. And the daughter, Pansy, a pitifully obedient child warehoused in a convent, is still another victim of this pair of polished plotters. (But Valentina Cervi, a robust young Italian actor, is irritatingly unsuited for the timorously fragile Pansy.)

Here, in these final concentrated scenes—trust tainted by malignancy—Campion is wholly faithful to the outer progress of James's narrative. Beyond this, her art supplies what no novel can: the direct sensation of voluptuous gazing—so many doors opening into spaciousness, objects, liveried servants, a boiling, dizzying ballroom.

Yet the aim of Campion's film is surely not a literal faithfulness to the crowded, chesslike movements of the original. A film strives to be, so to speak, a condensed *second* original, which means that it will fail if it strays from or perverts the discriminations of its source. Campion sets out to alter and coarsen those discriminations. Ralph Touchett on his deathbed is hurled, in Campion's hands, from deeply held cousinly love ("Oh my brother!" James has Isabel cry in her grief) to driven lover's love, in wholesale repudiation of James. It is as if he is not to be trusted to tell the truth about men and women, and about the justice of willed reticence. And if James's Isabel is generously and earnestly outward-turning, Campion's Isabel is just the opposite—fastened, as that mischievously anachronistic prologue warns, on the inner chamber of the sensual kiss.

James's Isabel, in the hope of freedom, looks to the broadening world. Campion's Isabel, all too programmatically, looks to the limits of self. That is why the novel is a tragedy—it enacts the defeat of freedom. And that is why the movie, through its governing credo, adds up to little more than a beautifully embroidered anecdote of a bad marriage.

What crudity compared to what the novelist saw!

The Lesson of the Master

There was a period in my life—to purloin a famous Jamesian title, "The Middle Years"—when I used to say, with as much ferocity as I could muster, "I hate Henry James and I wish he was dead."

I was not to have my disgruntled way. The dislike did not last and turned once again to adoration, ecstasy, and awe; and no one is more alive than Henry James, or more likely to sustain literary immortality. He is among the angels, as he meant to be.

But in earlier days I felt I had been betrayed by Henry James. I was like the youthful writer in "The Lesson of the Master" who believed in the Master's call to live immaculately, unspoiled by what we mean when we say "life"—relationship, family mess, distraction, exhaustion, anxiety, above all disappointment. Here is the Master, St. George, speaking to his young disciple, Paul Overt:

> "One has no business to have any children," St. George placidly declared. "I mean, of course, if one wants to do anything good."
> "But aren't they an inspiration—an incentive?"
> "An incentive to damnation, artistically speaking."

And later Paul inquires:

> "Is it deceptive that I find you living with every appearance of domestic felicity—blest with a devoted, accomplished wife, with children whose acquaintance I haven't yet had the pleasure of making, but who *must* be delightful young people, from what I know of their parents?"
> St. George smiled as for the candour, of his question. "It's all excellent, my dear fellow—heaven forbid I should deny it . . . I've got a loaf on the shelf; I've got everything in fact but the great thing."
> "And the great thing?" Paul kept echoing.

"The sense of having done the best—the sense which is the real life of the artist and the absence of which is his death, of having drawn from his intellectual instrument the finest music that nature had hidden in it, of having played it as it should be played. He either does that or he doesn't—and if he doesn't he isn't worth speaking of."

Paul pursues:

"Then what did you mean . . . by saying that children are a curse?"

"My dear youth, on what basis are we talking?" and St. George dropped upon the sofa at a short distance from him . . . "On the supposition that a certain perfection's possible and even desirable—isn't it so? Well, all I say is that one's children interfere with perfection. One's wife interferes. Marriage interferes."

"You think, then, the artist shouldn't marry?"

"He does so at his peril—he does so at his cost."

Yet the Master who declares all this is himself profoundly, inextricably, married; and when his wife dies, he hastens to marry again, choosing Life over Art. Very properly James sees marriage as symbol and summary of the passion for ordinary human entanglement, as experience of the most commonplace, most fated kind.

But we are also given to understand, in the desolation of this comic tale, that the young artist, the Master's trusting disciple, is left both perplexed and bereft: the Master's second wife is the young artist's first love, and the Master has stolen away his disciple's chance for ordinary human entanglement.

So the Lesson of the Master is a double one: choose ordinary human entanglement, and live; or choose Art, and give up the vitality of life's passions and panics and endurances. What I am going to tell now is a stupidity, a misunderstanding, a great Jamesian life-mistake: an embarrassment and a life-shame. (Imagine that we are in one of those lavishly adorned Jamesian chambers where intimate confessions not accidentally but suspensefully take place.) As I have said, I felt myself betrayed by a Jamesian trickery. Trusting in James, believing, like Paul Overt, in the overtness of the Jamesian lesson, I chose Art, and ended by blaming Henry James. It seemed to me James had left out the one important thing I ought to have known, even though he was saying it again and again. The trouble was that I was listening to the Lesson of the Master at the wrong time, paying powerful and excessive attention at the wrong time; and this cost me my youth.

I suppose a case can be made that it is certainly inappropriate for anyone to moan about the loss of youth and how it is all Henry James's fault. All of us will lose our youth, and some of us, alas, have lost it already; but not all of us will pin the loss on Henry James.

I, however, do. I blame Henry James.

Never mind the sublime position of Henry James in American letters. Never mind the Jamesian prose style—never mind that it too is sublime, nuanced, imbricated with a thousand distinctions and observations (the reason H. G. Wells mocked it), and as idiosyncratically and ecstatically redolent of the spirals of past and future as a garlic clove. Set aside also the Jamesian impatience with idols, the moral seriousness active in both the work and the life. (I am thinking, for example, of Edith Wharton's compliance in the face of their mutual friend Paul Bourget's anti-Semitism, and James's noble and definitive dissent.) Neglect all this, including every other beam that flies out from the stupendous Jamesian lantern to keep generations reading in rapture (which is all right), or else scribbling away at dissertation after dissertation (which is not so good). I myself, after all, committed a Master's thesis, long ago, called "Parable in Henry James," in which I tried to catch up all of James in the net of a single idea. Before that, I lived many months in the black hole of a microfilm cell, transcribing every letter James ever wrote to Mr. Pinker, his London agent, for a professorial book; but the professor drank, and died, and after thirty years the letters still lie in the dark.

All that while I sat cramped in that black bleak microfilm cell, and all that while I was writing that thesis, James was sinking me and despoiling my youth, and I did not know it.

I want, parenthetically, to recommend to the Henry James Society— there is such an assemblage—that membership be limited: no one under age forty-two and three-quarters need apply. Proof of age via birth certificate should be mandatory; otherwise the consequences may be harsh and horrible. I offer myself as an Extreme and Hideous Example of Premature Exposure to Henry James. I was about seventeen, I recall, when my brother brought home from the public library a science-fiction anthology, which, through an odd perspective that perplexes me still, included "The Beast in the Jungle." It was in this anthology, and at that age, that I first read James—fell, I should say, into the jaws of James. I had never heard of him before. I read "The Beast in the Jungle" and creepily thought: Here, here is my autobiography.

From that time forward, gradually but compellingly—and now I yield my scary confession—I became Henry James. Leaving graduate school at the age of twenty-two, disdaining the Ph.D. as an acquisition surely beneath the concerns of literary seriousness, I was already Henry James. When I say I "became" Henry James, you must understand this: though I was a near-sighted twenty-two-year-old young woman infected with the commonplace intention of writing a novel, I was also the elderly bald-headed Henry James. Even without close examination, you could see the light glancing off my pate; you could see my heavy chin, my watch chain, my walking stick, my tender paunch.

I had become Henry James, and for years and years I remained Henry James. There was no doubt about it: it was my own clear and faithful truth. Of course, there were some small differences: for one thing, I was not a genius. For another, even in my own insignificant scribbler class, I was not prolific. But I carried the Jamesian idea, I was of his cult, I was a worshiper of literature, literature was my single altar; I was, like the elderly bald-headed James, a priest at that altar; and that altar was all of my life. Like John Marcher in "The Beast in the Jungle," I let everything pass me by for the sake of waiting for the Beast to spring—but unlike John Marcher I knew what the Beast was, I knew exactly, I even knew the Beast's name: the Beast was literature itself, the sinewy grand undulations of some unraveling fiction, meticulously dreamed out in a language of masterly resplendence, which was to pounce on me and turn me into an enchanted and glorious Being, as enchanted and glorious as the elderly bald-headed Henry James himself.

But though the years spent themselves extravagantly, that ambush never occurred: the ambush of Sacred and Sublime Literature. The great shining Beast of Sacred and Sublime Literature did not pounce. Instead, other beasts, lesser ones, unseemly and misshapen, sprang out—all the beasts of ordinary life: sorrow, disease, death, guilt, responsibility, envy, grievance, grief, disillusionment—the beasts that are chained to human experience, and have nothing to do with Art except to interrupt and impede it, exactly according to the Lesson of the Master.

It was not until I read a certain vast and subtle book that I understood what had happened to me. The book was not by Henry James, but about him. Nowadays we give this sort of work a special name: we call it a nonfiction novel. I am referring, of course, to Leon Edel's ingenious and beautiful biography of Henry James, which is as much the possession of Edel's imagination as it is of the exhilaratingly reported facts of James's life. In Edel's rendering, I learned what I had never before taken in—but the knowledge came, in the Jamesian way, too late. What I learned was that Henry James himself had not always been the elderly bald-headed Henry James!—that he too had once been twenty-two years old.

This terrible and secret knowledge instantly set me against James. From that point forward I was determined to eradicate him. And for a long while I succeeded.

What had happened was this: in early young-womanhood I believed, with all the rigor and force and stunned ardor of religious belief, in the old Henry James, in his scepter and his authority. I believed that what he knew at sixty I was to encompass at twenty-two; at twenty-two I lived like the elderly bald-headed Henry James. I thought it was necessary—it was imperative, there was no other path!—to be, all at once, with no progression or evolution, the author of the equivalent of *The Ambassadors* or *The Wings of the Dove*, just as if "A Bundle of Letters," or "Four Meetings," or the golden little "The Europeans" had never preceded the great late Master.

For me, the Lesson of the Master was a horror, a Jamesian tale of a life of mishap and mistake and misconceiving. Though the Master himself was saying, in *The Ambassadors*, in Gloriani's garden, to Little Bilham, through the urgent cry of Strether, "Live, live!"—and though the Master himself was saying, in "The Beast in the Jungle," through May Bartram, how ghastly, how ghastly, it is to eschew, to evade, to turn from, to miss absolutely and irrevocably what is all the time there for you to seize—I mistook him, I misheard him, I missed, absolutely and irrevocably, his essential note. What I heard instead was: *Become a Master*.

Now the truth is it could not have been done, even by a writer of genius; and what a pitiful flicker of the flame of high ambition for a writer who is no more than the ordinary article! No one—not even James himself—springs all at once in early youth into full Mastery, and no writer, whether robustly gifted, or only little and pale, should hope for this implausible fate.

All this, I suppose, is not at all a "secret" knowledge, as I have characterized it, but is, rather, as James named it in the very person of his naive young artist, most emphatically *overt*—so obvious that it is a mere access of foolishness even to talk about it. Still, I offer the implausible and preposterous model of myself to demonstrate the proposition that the Lesson of the Master is not a lesson about genius, or even about immense ambition; it is a lesson about misreading—about what happens when we misread the great voices of Art, and suppose that, because they speak of Art, they mean Art. The great voices of Art never mean *only* Art; they also mean Life, they always mean Life, and Henry James, when he evolved into the Master we revere, finally meant nothing else.

The true Lesson of the Master, then, is, simply, never to venerate what is complete, burnished, whole, in its grand organic flowering or finish—never to look toward the admirable and dazzling end; never to be ravished by the goal; never to worship ripe Art or the ripened artist; but instead to seek to be young while young, primitive while primitive, ungainly when ungainly—to look for crudeness and rudeness, to husband one's own stupidity or ungenius.

There is this mix-up most of us have between ourselves and what we admire or triumphantly cherish. We see this mix-up, this mishap, this mishmash, most often in writers: the writer of a new generation ravished by the genius writer of a classical generation, who begins to dream herself, or himself, as powerful, vigorous and original—as if being filled up by the genius writer's images, scenes, and stratagems were the same as having the capacity to pull off the identical magic. To be any sort of competent writer one must keep one's psychological distance from the supreme artists.

If I were twenty-two now, I would not undertake a cannibalistically ambitious Jamesian novel to begin with; I would look into the eyes of Henry James at twenty-two, and see the diffident hope, the uncertainty, the marveling tentativeness, the dream that is still only a dream; the young man still learning to fashion the Scene. Or I would go back still further, to the boy of seventeen, misplaced in a Swiss Polytechnic School, who recalled in old age that "I so feared and abhorred mathematics that the simplest arithmetical operation had always found and kept me helpless and blank." It is not to the Master in his fullness I would give my awed, stricken, desperate fealty, but to the faltering, imperfect, dreaming youth.

If these words should happen to reach the ears of any young writer dumbstruck by the elderly bald-headed Henry James, one who has hungrily heard and ambitiously assimilated the voluptuous cathedral-tones of the developed organ-master, I would say to her or him: put out your lean and clumsy forefinger and strike your paltry, oafish, feeble, simple, skeletal, single note. Try for what Henry James at sixty would scorn—just as he scorned the work of his own earliness, and revised it and revised it in the manner of his later pen in that grand chastisement of youth known as the New York Edition. Trying, in youth, for what the Master in his mastery would condemn—that is the only road to modest mastery. Rapture and homage are not the way. Influence is perdition.

Justice (Again) to Edith Wharton

Nearly forty years ago, Edmund Wilson wrote a little essay about an under-rated American novelist and called it "Justice to Edith Wharton." She was in need of justice, he claimed, because "the more commonplace work of her later years had had the effect of dulling the reputation of her earlier and more serious work." During this last period—a stretch of about seventeen years, from (roughly) 1920 to her death in 1937—Edith Wharton's novels were bestsellers, her short stories commanded thousands of dollars; but both in mode and motivation she remained, like so many others in the twenties and thirties, a nineteenth-century writer. She believed in portraying charac-ter, her characters displayed the higher values, her prose was a platform for her own views. In 1937, when Wilson undertook to invigorate her reputa-tion, the machinery of nineteenth-century fiction was beginning to be judged not so much as the expression of a long tradition, or (as nowadays we seem to view it) as the exhausted practice of a moribund convention, but more bluntly as a failure of talent. Wilson accounted for that apparent failure in Edith Wharton by speculating on the psychological differences between male and female writers:

> It is sometimes true of women writers—less often, I believe, of men—that a manifestation of something like genius may be stimulated by some exceptional emotional strain, but will disappear when the stimu-lus has passed. With a man, his professional, his artisan's life is likely to persist and evolve as a partially independent organism through the vicis-situdes of his emotional experience. Henry James in a virtual vacuum continued to possess and develop his *métier*. But Mrs. Wharton had no *métier* in this sense.

What sort of "justice" is this? A woman typically writes best when her emo-tions are engaged; the barren female heart cannot seize the writer's trade?

57

Only a decade ago, such a declaration would have been derided by old-fashioned feminists as a passing insolence. But even the satiric reader, contending in one fashion or another with this passage, would have been able, ten years ago, to pluck the offending notion out as a lapse in the texture of a measured and generally moderating mind.

No longer. Wilson's idea returns only to hold, and it holds nowhere so much as among the literary proponents of the current women's movement: Wilson's lapse is exalted to precept. The idea of Edith Wharton as a "woman writer" in need of constantly renewable internal stimuli, whose gifts are best sustained by "exceptional emotional strain"—all this suits the newest doctrine of sexual exclusiveness in literature. Indeed, one of the outstanding tenets of this doctrine embraces Wilson unrelentingly. "Rarely in the work now being written by women," according to an article called "Toward a Definition of the Female Sensibility,"

> does one feel the presence of writers genuinely penetrating their own experience, risking emotional humiliation and the facing-down of secret fears, unbearable wisdoms . . . There are works, however . . . in which one feels the heroic effort stirring

and there follow numerous examples of women writing well because of the stimulus of some exceptional emotional strain.

Restitution, then (one supposes), is to come to Edith Wharton not from the old-fashioned feminists, but from the newer sort, who embrace the proposition that strong emotion in women, emotion uniquely female, is what will best nourish a female literature. What we are to look for next, it follows, is an ambitious new-feminist critical work studying Wharton's "vicissitudes of . . . emotional experience" and correlating the most fevered points with the most accomplished of the fictions.

Such a work, it turns out, more extensive and more supple than Wilson's pioneer brief would suggest, has just made its appearance: Ellen Moers's *Literary Women*. Like other new feminists, Moers believes that there is such an entity as the "history of women," that there are poetic images uniquely female; and even "landscapes charged with female privacy." She writes of "how much the freedom and tactile sensations of near-naked sea bathing has meant to modern women," and insists that a scene recounting the sensation of walking through a field of sea-like grass provides that "moment when Kate Chopin reveals herself most truly a woman writer." Edith Wharton's life—a buried life—ought, properly scrutinized, to feed such a set of sympathies, and to lure the attention of restitution. *Literary Women*, after all, is conceived of in part as a rescue volume, as a book of rehabilitation and justice: a number of writers, Moers explains, "came to life for me as women writers as they had not done before. Mrs. Gaskell and Anne Brontë had once bored me; Emily Dickinson was an irritating puzzle, as much as a genius; I could barely read Mary Shelley and Mrs. Browning. Reading them anew as women writers taught me how to get excited about these five, and others as well."

Others as well. But Edith Wharton is omitted from *Literary Women*. Her name appears only once, as an entry in an appendix. Only *The House of Mirth* is mentioned there, along with a reference, apparently by way of explanation of the larger omission, to the chapter on Edith Wharton in Alfred Kazin's *On Native Grounds*. Pursuing the citation, one discovers that Kazin, like Wilson, like the new feminists, speaks of "the need that drove her to literature." Whatever the need, it does not engage Moers; or Kazin. He advances the notion that "to Edith Wharton, whose very career as a novelist was the tenuous product of so many personal maladjustments, the novel became an involuted expression of self." Unlike the new feminists, Kazin will not celebrate this expression; it represents for him a "failure to fulfill herself in art." Wharton, he concludes, "remains not a great artist but an unusual American, one who brought the weight of her personal experience to bear upon a modern American literature to which she was spiritually alien."

Justice to Edith Wharton: where, then, is it to come from? Not taken seriously by the dominant criticism, purposefully ignored by the radical separatist criticism of the new feminists—she represents an antagonism. The antagonism is not new. Wharton describes it herself in her memoir, *A Backward Glance*:

> My literary success puzzled and embarrassed my old friends far more than it impressed them, and in my own family it created a kind of constraint which increased with the years. None of my relations ever spoke to me of my books, either to praise or blame—they simply ignored them; and among the immense tribe of my cousins, though it included many with whom I was on terms of affectionate intimacy, the subject was avoided as if it were a kind of family disgrace, which might be condoned but could not be forgotten. Only one eccentric widowed cousin, living a life of lonely invalidism, turned to my novels for occasional distraction, and had the courage to tell me so.

She continues: "At first I felt this indifference acutely; but now I no longer cared, for my recognition as a writer had transformed my life."

So it is here—in this uplifting idea, "my life," this teleological and novelistic idea above all—that one will finally expect to look for Wharton's restitution "as a writer." The justice that criticism perversely fails to bring, biography will achieve.

Perhaps. The biography of a novelist contains a wonderful advantage: it accomplishes, when well executed, a kind of mimicry. A good biography is itself a kind of novel. Like the classic novel, a biography believes in the notion of "a life"—a life as a triumphal or, tragic story with a shape, a story that begins at birth, moves on to a middle part, and ends with the death of the protagonist.

Despite the reliable pervasiveness of birth and death, hardly any "real" life is like that. Most simply unfold, or less than that, dream-walk themselves out. The middle is missing. What governs is not pattern but drift. Most American lives, moreover, fail to recognize that they are sticks in a stream, and are conceived of as novels-of-progress, as purposeful *Bildungsromane* saturated with an unending hopefulness, with the notion of infinite improvement on the way toward a salubrious goal; the frontier continues to inhabit the American mentality unfailingly.

And most American biographies are written out of this same source and belief. A biography that is most like a novel is least like a life. Edith Wharton's life, though much of it was pursued outside of America, is an American life in this sense: that, despite certain disciplines, it was predicated on drift, and fell out, rather than fell into place. If other American lives, less free than hers, drift less luckily between the Scylla and Charybdis of obligation and crisis, hers drifted in a setting all horizon, in a perpetual noncircumstance clear of external necessity. She had to invent her own environment and its conditions, and while this may seem the reverse of rudderlessness, what it signifies really is movement having to feign a destination. A life with a "shape" is occasioned by what is present in that life; drift grows out of what is absent, for Edith Wharton there was—outside the writing—no destination, and no obligation to get there. She had houses, she had wealth; she chose, rather than "had," friends. She had no family (she was estranged from her brothers, and we hear nothing further about the affectionate cousins), she had no husband (though she was married to one for more than half her life), she had no children. For a long time she resented and disliked children, and was obsessed by a love for small dogs. She was Henry James's ideal American heroine: she was indeed his very heiress of all the ages, she was "free," she was cultivated both in the conventional and the spiritual sense, she was gifted, acute, mobile; she appeared to be mistress of her destiny.

The destiny of such freedom is drift, and though her life was American in this, it was European in its resignation: she had no illusion that—outside

the writing—she was doing more than "filling in." Her one moment of elevated and secure purpose occurred when, inspired by the model of Walt
Whitman in the hospitals of the Civil War, she founded war relief agencies
in France during the First World War. She supervised brilliantly: she supervised her friendships, her gardeners, her guests, the particulars of her dinner
parties, her households; she even, to a degree, supervised the insurmountable Henry James—she took him for long rides in her car, she demanded
hours in London and tea at Lamb House, she finagled with his publisher to
provide him with a handsome advance (she herself was the secret philanthropist behind the scenes), she politicked to try and get him the Nobel
Prize in Literature. She supervised and commanded, but since no one
demanded anything of *her* (with a single exception, which, like the Gorgon's
head, was not to be gazed at), she was captain, on an uncharted deep, of a
ship without any imaginable port. She did everything on her own, to no real
end; no one ever asked her to accommodate to any pressure of need, she had
no obligations that she did not contrive or duty that she did not devise. Her
necessities were self-imposed. Her tub went round and round in a sea of
self-pleasing.

All this was outside the writing. One learns it from R. W. B. Lewis's
prize-winning biography, which is, like a posthumously uncovered Wharton
novel, sustained by the idea of "a life." It has the fecund progression, the
mastery of incident, the affectionate but balanced devotion to its protagonist, the power of suspenseful development, even the unraveling of a
mysterious love story, that the "old" novel used to deliver—the novel before
it became a self-referring "contemporary" art-object. In its own way it is a
thesis novel: it is full of its intention to bring justice to Edith Wharton. A
massive biography, almost by its weight, insists on the importance of its subject. Who would dare pass that writer by to whom a scholar-writer has
dedicated, as Lewis has, nearly a decade of investigation and discovery?
"They are among the handsomest achievements in our literature," he remarks
of her major fictions. And adds: "I have wondered, with other admirers of
Edith Wharton, whether her reputation might today stand even higher if she
had been a man."

If the last statement has overtones of the new feminism—glory but for
the impediment of sex—the book does not. Lewis sets out to render the life
of an artist, not of a "woman artist." Unexpectedly, though it is the artist he
is after, what he succeeds chiefly in giving us is the life of a woman. The
"chiefly" is no small thing: it is useful to have a documented narrative of an
exceptional upper-class woman of a certain American period. Still, without
romanticizing what is meant by the phrase "an artist's life," there is a differ-

ence between the biography of a writer and the mode of living of a narrow American class.

Can the life justify the writer then? Or, to put it otherwise, can biography take the place of literary judgment? Lewis's book is a straightforward "tale," not a critical biography. Nor is it "psychobiography": though it yields new and revealing information about Edith Wharton's sexual experience, it does not propose to illumine the hidden chambers of the writer's sentience—as, for example, Ruby V. Redinger's recent inquiry into George Eliot's relationship to her brother Isaac, with its hunches and conjectures, purports to do, or Quentin Bell's half-study, half-memoir of Virginia Woolf. Lewis has in common with these others the revelation of a secret. In the case of Quentin Bell, it is the exact extent of Virginia Woolf's insanity; in the volume on George Eliot, the secret is the dense burden of humiliation imposed by an adored brother more cruel and rigid than society itself. And in Lewis, the secret is an undreamed-of, now minutely disclosed, adulterous affair with a journalist. In all three accounts, the writer is on the whole not there. It is understandable that the writer is mainly absent for the psychobiographer; something else is being sought. It is even more understandable that the writer should be absent for a nephew-biographer, whose preoccupation is with confirming family stories.

But if, for Lewis, the writer is not there, it is not because he fails to look for her but because she is very nearly invisible. What, through luck and diligence, he causes to become visible is almost not the point, however unpredictable and startling his discoveries are. And they are two: the surprising place of Morton Fullerton in Edith Wharton's middle years, and the appearance of a candid manuscript, written in her seventies, describing, with the lyrical explicitness of an enraptured anatomist, a fictional incestuous coupling. The manuscript and the love affair are so contrary to the established Wharton legend of cold propriety that they go far to make us look again—but only at the woman, not at the writer.

The real secret in Lewis's biography is devoid of sex, lived or imagined, though its centerpiece is a bed; and it concerns not the woman but the writer. The secret is divulged on page 353, when Wharton is fifty-one, and occupies ten lines in a volume of nearly six hundred pages. The ten lines recount a perplexing incident—"a minor fit of hysterics." The occasion is mysterious: Edith Wharton and Bernard Berenson, touring the great cities and museums of Europe together, arrive at the Hotel Esplanade in Berlin. They check into their respective rooms, and Edith Wharton, ignoring the view of the city though she has never been there before, begins to rage because the bed in her hotel room was not properly situated; not until it had been moved to face the window did she settle down and begin to find Berlin "incomparable." Berenson thought this an absurd performance; but because Edith never harped upon the physical requirements of her literary life, he did not quite realize that she worked in bed every morning and therefore needed a bed which faced the light. It had been her practice for more than twenty years; and for a woman . . . who clung so tenaciously to her daily stint, the need was a serious one.

The fit and its moment pass; the ensuing paragraphs tell of German politics snubbed and German music imbibed—we are returned, in short, to the life of an upper-class American expatriate tourist, privileged to travel in the company of a renowned connoisseur. But the plangent moment—an outcry over the position of a bed—dominates the book: dominates what has gone before and what is to come, and recasts both. Either the biographer can stand up to this moment—the woman revealed *as writer*—or the book falls into the drifting ash of "a life."

It falls, but it is not the biographer's fault; or not his fault alone. Edith Wharton—as writer—is to blame. She put a veil over the bed that was her workplace, and screened away the real life that was lived in it. What moves like a long afterimage in the wake of reading Lewis is a procession of stately majesties: Edith Wharton always standing, always regal, always stiffly dressed and groomed, standing with her wonderfully vertical spine in the hall of one of her great houses, or in the drawing room of her Paris apartment, with her fine hand out to some equally resplendent guest, or in her gardens, not so much admiring her flowers as instructing or reprimanding the servants of her flowers; or else "motoring" through the dust of some picturesque lane in the French countryside, her chauffeur in peaked hat and leather goggles, like blinders, on a high seat in front of her, indistinguishable from the horse that still headed most vehicles on the road.

If this is the Wharton myth, she made it; she wove it daily. It winds itself out like a vivid movie, yet darkly; it leaves out the window-lit bed. What went on outside the bed does not account for what went on in it. She frequented literary salons, and on a smaller scale held them (after dinner, Henry James reading aloud in the library); she talked bookishly, and with fervor; she was an intellectual. But she was not the only brilliant woman of her time and status; all of that, in the biography of a writer, weighs little.

Visualize the bed: she used a writing board. Her breakfast was brought to her by Gross, the housekeeper, who almost alone was privy to this inmost secret of the bedchamber. (A secretary picked up the pages from the floor for typing.) Out of bed, she would have had to be, according to her code, properly dressed, and this meant stays. In bed, her body was free, and freed her pen.

There is a famous photograph of Edith Wharton seated at a desk; we know now, thanks to the "minor fit of hysterics" at the Hotel Esplanade, how the camera lies—even though it shows us everything we might want to know about a way of life. The time is in the 1890s, the writer is in her early thirties. The desk is vast, shining, with a gold-tooled leather top; at the rear of its far surface is a decorated rack holding half a dozen books, but these are point-less—not only because anyone using this desk would need an impossibly long reach, but because all the volumes are faced away from the writer, with their backs and titles to the open room. Two tall electrified candlestick-lamps (the wire drags awkwardly) stand sentinel over two smaller candlesticks; there is a single letter, already stamped; otherwise the desk is clear, except for a pair of nervous ringed hands fiddling with a bit of paper.

The hands belong to a young woman got up, to our eyes, as theatrically as some fanciful notion of royalty: she is plainly a lady of fashion, with a constricted waist and a constricting tall collar; her dress is of the whitest fabric, all eyeleted, embroidered, sashed; her hair is elaborately rolled and ringleted; an earring makes a white dot below the high dark eave of her hair; her back is straight, even as she leans forward with concentrated mouth and lost eyes, in the manner of a writer in trance. Mellifluous folds hide her feet; a lady has no legs. She is sitting on a graceful chair with whorled feet— rattan framed by the most beautiful carved and burnished wood. (A rattan chair with not a single hole? No one could ever have *worked* in such a chair; the photographer defrauds us—nothing more important than a letter will ever be written at this desk.) The Oriental carpet, with its curious and dense figures, is most explicitly in focus, and over the edge of it a tail of skirt spills, reflected white on a floor as sleek as polished glass. In the background, blurred to the camera's lens but instructive to ours: a broad-shouldered velvet chair, a marble bust on an ebony pedestal, a table with a huge porce-lain sculpture, a lofty shut oak or walnut door. In short, an "interior," reminding us that the woman at the unused desk has undertaken, as her first writing venture, a collaborative work called *The Decoration of Houses*.

There are other portraits in this vein, formal, posed, poised, "intellectual" (meaning the subject muses over a seeming letter or book), all jeweled clips and chokers and pearls in heavy rows, pendants, feathered hats, lapdogs, furs, statuesque burdens of flounced bosom and grand liquescent sleeve, queenly beyond our bourgeois imaginings. And the portraits of houses: mul-tiple chimneys, balconies, cupolas, soaring Romanesque windows, immense stone staircases, summer awnings of palatial breadth, shaped ivy, topiary like oversized chess pieces, walks, vistas, clouds of flower beds.

What are we (putting aside Marxist thoughts) to make of this avalanche of privilege? It is not enough to say: money. The class she derived from never talked of money; the money was invisible, like the writing in bed, and just as secret, and just as indispensable. The "love of beauty," being part of class habit, does not explain it; perhaps the class habit does. It was the class habit that kept her on the move: the class habit that is restlessness and drift. She wore out houses and places, or else her spirit wore out in them: New York, Newport, Lenox—finally America. In France there was the Paris apartment in the Rue de Varenne, then a small estate in St. Bricesous-Forêt, in the country north of Paris, then an old chateau in Hyères, on the warm Mediterranean coast. Three times in her life she supervised the total renovation of a colossal mansion and its grounds, in effect building and furnishing and landscaping from scratch; and once, in Lenox, she bought a piece of empty land and really did start from scratch, raising out of the earth an American palace called The Mount. All of this exacted from her the energy, attentiveness, and insatiable governing impulses of a corporation chief executive; or the head of a small state.

In an architectural lull, she would travel. All her life she traveled compulsively, early in her marriage with her husband, touring Europe from February to June, afterward with various male companions, with the sense, and with the propriety, of leading a retinue. Accumulating "scenes"—hotels, landscapes, seascapes, museums, villages, ruins—she saw all the fabled cities of Europe, the islands of the Aegean, Tunis, Algiers, Carthage, the Sahara.

And all the while she was surrounded by a crowd. Not simply while traveling: the crowd was part of the daily condition, of her houses and possessions. She had a household staff consisting of maids ("housemaids" and "chambermaids"—there appears to be a difference), a chief gardener and several under-gardeners, cook, housekeeper, major-domo, chauffeur, personal maid, "traveling" maid, secretary, "general agent," footmen. (One of the latter, accompanying her to I Tatti, the Berenson villa in Italy, inconveniently fell in love with a Berenson maid, and had to be surrendered.) These "establishments," Lewis remarks, "gave her what her bountiful nature desired: an ordered life, a carefully tended beauty of surroundings, and above all, total privacy." The "above all" engenders skepticism. Privacy? Surveying that mob of servants, even imagining them crossing silent carpets on tiptoe, one takes the impression, inevitably, of a hive. Her solitude was the congested solitude of a monarch; she was never, like other solitary-minded American writers (one thinks of Poe, or of course Emily Dickinson, or even Scott Fitzgerald), completely alone in the house. But these hectic movements of the hive were what she required; perhaps she would not have known how to do without them. Chekhov could sit at a table in the middle of the din of a large impoverished family, ignoring voices and footsteps in order to concentrate on the scratch of his pen. Edith Wharton sat up in bed with her writing board, in the middle of the active business of a house claiming her attention, similarly shutting out the only family she had. A hired family, an invented one. When she learned that her older brother Freddy, living not far away in Paris, had suffered a stroke, she was "unresponsive"; but when Gross, her housekeeper of long standing, and Elise, her personal maid, both grew fatally ill within a short space, she wrote in her diary, "All my life goes with those two dying women."

Nicky Mariano, in her memoir of her life as secretary-companion to Berenson, recalls how Edith Wharton treated her with indifference—until one day, aboard a yacht near Naples, she happened to ask after Elise. She was at once dispatched to the cabin below to visit with the maid. "From then on I became aware of a complete change in Edith's manner to me. There was a warmth, a tone of intimacy that I had never heard before." And again, describing how Wharton "looked after her servants with affectionate zeal and took a lively interest in all their joys and sorrows," she produces another anecdote:

> I remember how once during one of our excursions with her, she was deeply hurt and angry when on leaving a villa near Siena after a prolonged visit she discovered that neither her maid nor her chauffeur had been asked into the house.

What is the effect on a writer of being always encircled by servants? What we are to draw from this is not so much the sadness of purchased affections, or even the parasitism (once, left without much help for a brief period, she was bewildered about her daily survival), but something more perplexing: the moment-by-moment influence of continuous lower-class companionship. Room ought to be given to considering this; it took room in Wharton's life: she was with her servants all the time, she was with her friends and peers only some of the time. E. M. Forster sought out the common people in the belief that too much education atrophies the senses; in life and in art he went after the lower orders because he thought them the embodiment of the spontaneous gods of nature. In theory, at least—perhaps it was only literary theory—Forster wanted to become "instinctual," and instinct was with the working class. But Edith Wharton kept her distance even as she drew close; she remained mistress always. It made her a kind of double exile. As an expatriate settled in France, she had cut herself off from any direct infusion of the American sensibility and the American language. Through her attachment to her servants, she became intimately bound to illiterate lives remote from her mentality, preoccupations, habitual perceptions—a second expatriation as deliberate as the more obvious one. Nor did her servants give her access to "ordinary" life (she was no Lady Chatterley, there was no gamekeeper for her)—no one is "ordinary" while standing before the monarch of the house. Still, she fussed over her army of hirelings; it was a way of inventing claims. For her servants she provided pensions; she instituted a trust fund as a private charity for three Belgian children; she sent regular checks to her sister-in-law, divorced from her brother a quarter of a century and therefore clearly not to be taken for family. For family, in short, she substituted claims indisputably of her own making. She could feel responsible for servants and acquired dependents as others feel responsible for parents, brothers, children: but there was a tether made of money, and the power-end of the tether was altogether in her hand. With servants, there is no murkiness—as there sometimes is in friendship—about who is beholden to whom.

With her friends it was more difficult to invent claims; friendship has a way of resisting purchase, and she had to resort to ruses. When she wanted to release Morton Fullerton from the entangling blackmail of his former French mistress, she arranged with Henry James to make it seem as if the money were coming impersonally from a publisher. Fullerton having been, however briefly, her lover, it was hardly possible to hand over one hundred pounds and call it a "pension"; the object was not so much to keep Fullerton's friendship free as to establish the illusion of such freedom. It was enough for the controlling end of the money tether to know the tether was there; and anyhow the tether had a witness and an accomplice. "Please consider," James wrote, entering into the plot, "that I will play my mechanical part in your magnificent combination with absolute piety, fidelity, and punctuality."

But when it was James himself who came to be on the receiving end of the golden tether, he thundered against the tug of opulence, and the friendship was for a while impaired. The occasion was a proposal for his seventieth birthday: Edith Wharton, enlisting about forty moneyed Americans, thought to raise "not less than $5000," the idea being "that he should choose a fine piece of old furniture, or something of the kind"—but to James it all smelled blatantly of charity, meddling, pity, and cash. Once he got wind of the plan he called it a "reckless and indiscreet undertaking," and announced in a cable that he was beginning "instant prohibitive action. Please express to individuals approached my horror. Money absolutely returned."

It was returned, but within a few months James was hooked anyhow on that same line—hooked like Morton Fullerton, without being aware of it. This time the accomplice was Charles Scribner, who forwarded to James a phoney "advance" of eight thousand dollars intended to see him through the writing of *The Ivory Tower*—but the money was taken out of Wharton's own advance, from another publisher, of fifteen thousand dollars. The reluctant agent of the scheme, far from celebrating "your magnificent combination," saw it rather as "our fell purpose." "I feel rather mean and caddish and must continue so to the end of my days," Charles Scribner grumbled. "Please never give me away." In part this sullenness may have been guilt over not having himself volunteered, as James's publisher, to keep a master artist free from money anxiety, but beyond that there was a distaste for manipulation and ruse.

This moral confusion about proprieties—whom it is proper to tip, and whom not—expressed itself in other strange substitutions. It was not only that she wanted to pay her lover and her friend for services rendered, sexual or literary—clearly she had little overt recognition of the *quid pro quo* uses of philanthropy. It was not only that she loved her maid Gross more than her mother, and Arthur White her "man" more than her brother—it is understood that voluntary entanglements are not really entanglements at all. But there were more conspicuous replacements. Lacking babies, she habitually fondled small dogs: there is an absurd photograph of Edith Wharton as a young woman of twenty-eight, by then five years into her marriage, with an angry-looking Pekingese on each mutton-leg shoulder; the animals, pressed against her cheeks, nearly obscure her face; the face is cautious and contemplative, as of one not wanting to jar precious things. A similar photograph shows her husband gazing straight out at us with rather empty pale eyes over a nicely trimmed mustache and a perfect bow tie—on his lap, with no special repugnance, he is holding three small dogs, two of them of that same truculent breed, and though the caption reads "Teddy Wharton with his dogs," somehow we know better whose dogs they are. His body is detached; his expression, very correct and patient, barely hides—though Lewis argues otherwise—how he is being put upon by such a pose.

Until late in life, she never knew a child. Effie, the little girl in *The Reef*, is a child observed from afar—she runs, she enters, she departs, she is sent, she is summoned, at one moment she is presented as very young, at another she is old enough to be having lessons in Latin. She is a figment of a child. But the little dogs, up to the end of Edith Wharton's life, were always understood, always thought to have souls, always in her arms and in her bed; they were, Lewis says, "among the main joys of her being." Drawing up a list of her "ruling passions" at forty-four, she put "Dogs" second after "Justice and Order." At sixty-two she wrote in her journal of "the *us*ness" in the eyes of animals, "with the underlying *not-us*ness which belies it," and meditated on their "eternal inarticulateness and slavery. Why? their eyes seem to ask us."

The fellow feeling she had for the *not-us*ness of her Pekingese she did not have for her husband, who was, from her point of view, also "*not-us*." He too was inarticulate and mired in the slavery of a lesser intellect. He was a good enough man, interested (like his wife) in being perfectly clothed, vigorous and humorous and kind and compliant (so compliant that he once actually tried to make his way through James's *The Golden Bowl*)—undistinguished in any jot, the absolute product of his class. He had no work to do, and sought none. One of Edith Wharton's friends—a phrase instantly revealing, since her friends were practically never his; the large-hearted Henry James was nearly the only one to cross this divide—observed that Teddy Wharton's "idleness was busy and innocent." His ostensible employment was the management of his wife's trust funds, but he filled his days with sports and hunting, and his glass with fine wine. Wine was the one thing he had a connoisseur's familiarity with; and, of all the elegant good things of the world, wine was the one thing his wife disliked.

When he was fifty-three he began to go mad, chiefly, it would seem, because he had married the wrong wife, with no inkling that she would turn out to be the wrong wife. Edith Newbold Jones at twenty-three was exactly what Edward Wharton, a dozen years older, had a right to expect for himself: she had heritage (her ancestor, Ebenezer Stevens, was an enterprising artillery officer in the Revolutionary War), she had inheritance (the Joneses owned the Chemical Bank of New York and much of the West Side). In brief, family and money. The dominant quality—what he had married her for, with that same idle innocence that took note only of the pleasantly obvious—was what Edith Wharton was afterward to call "tribe." The Whartons and the Joneses were of the same tribe—old Protestant money—and he could hardly predict that his wife would soon replace him in the nuptial bed with a writing board. At first he was perplexed but proud: Louis Auchincloss quotes a description of Teddy Wharton from Consuelo Vanderbilt's memoirs as "more of an equerry than an equal, walking behind [his wife] and carrying whatever paraphernalia she happened to discard," and once (Lewis tells us), walking as usual behind her, Teddy exclaimed to one of her friends, "Look at that waist! No one would ever guess that she had written a line of poetry in her life." She, meanwhile, was driven to writing in her journal, "Oh, Gods of derision! And you've given me over twenty years of it!" This outcry occurred immediately after she had shown her husband, during a wearying train journey, "a particularly interesting passage" in a scientific volume called *Heredity and Variation*. His response was not animated. "I heard the key turn in my prison-lock," she recorded, in the clear metaphorical style of her fiction.

A case can be made that it was she who turned the key on him. His encroaching madness altered him—he began to act oddly, out of character; or, rather, more in character than he had ever before dared. The equerry of the paraphernalia undertook to behave as if he were master of the paraphernalia—in short, he embezzled a part of the funds it had been his duty to preserve and augment. And, having been replaced in bed by a writing board, he suddenly confessed to his wife (or perhaps feverishly bragged) that he had recently gone to live with a prostitute in a Boston apartment, filling its remaining rooms with chorus girls; the embezzled funds paid for the apartment. The story was in the main confirmed. His madness had the crucial sanity of needs that are met.

His wife, who—granted that philanthropy is not embezzlement—was herself capable of money ruse, and who had herself once rapturously fallen from merely spiritual friendship, locked him up for it. Against his protestations, and those of his sister and brother, he was sent to a sanitorium. Teddy had stolen, Teddy had fallen; he was an adulterer. She had never stolen (though there is a robust if mistaken critical tradition that insists she stole her whole literary outlook from Henry James); but she had fallen, she was an adulteress. Teddy's sexual disgrace was public; hers went undivulged until her biographer came upon it more than three decades after her death. But these sardonic parallels and opposites illumine little beyond the usual ironies of the pot and the kettle. What had all at once happened in Edith Wharton's life was that something *had* happened. Necessity intervened, her husband was irrefutably a manic-depressive. He had hours of excitement and accusation; more often he was in a state of self-castigation. He begged her for help, he begged to be taken back and to be given a second chance. ". . . when you came back last year," she told him, "I was ready to overlook everything you had done, and to receive you as if nothing had happened." This referred to the Boston apartment; she herself had been in a London hotel with Fullerton at nearly the same time. In the matter of her money she was more unyielding. Replying to his plea to be allowed to resume the management of her trusts and property, she took the tone of a mistress with a servant who has been let go, and who is now discovered still unaccountably loitering in the house. "In order that no further questions of this kind should come up, the only thing left for me to do is to suggest that you should resign your

Trusteeship . . . Your health unfortunately makes it impossible for you to take any active part in the management of my affairs." Gradually, over months, she evolved a policy: she did everything for him that seemed sensible, as long as it was cold-hearted. He was removed, still uncured, from the sanitorium, and subjected to a regime of doctors, trips, traveling companions, scoldings. In the end, when he was most sick and most desperate, she discarded him, handing him over to the doctors the way one hands over impeding paraphernalia to an equerry. She discarded him well before she divorced him; divorce, at that period and in her caste, took deliberation. She discarded him because he impeded, he distracted, he was a nuisance, he drained her, he wore her out. As a woman she was contemptuous of him, as a writer she fought off his interruptions. The doctors were more polite than Henry James, who characterized Teddy Wharton as able to "hold or follow no counter-proposal, no plan of opposition, of his own, for as much as a minute or two; he is immediately *off*—irrelevant and childish . . . one's pity for her is at the best scarce bearable."

She too pitied herself, and justly, though she forgot to pity *him*. He had lost all trust in himself, whatever he said he timidly or ingratiatingly or furiously took back. He was flailing vainly after the last flashes of an autonomy his wife had long ago stripped from him. And during all that angry space, when she was bitterly engaged in fending off the partisan ragings of his family, and coldly supervising his medical and traveling routines, she, in the stern autonomy of her morning bed, was writing *Ethan Frome*, finishing *The Reef*, bringing off short stories. She could do all this because she did not look into her husband's eyes and read there, as she had read in the eyes of her little dogs, the helpless pathos of "Why?" It was true that she did not and could not love him, but her virtue was always according to principle, not passion. Presumably she also did not love the French soldiers who were sick with tuberculosis contracted in the trenches of the First World War; nevertheless for them she organized a cure program, which she termed "the most vital thing that can be done in France now." Whatever the most vital thing for Teddy might have been—perhaps there was nothing—she relinquished it at last. The question of the tubercular soldiers was, like all the claims on her spirit that she herself initiated, volitional and opportune. She had sought out these tragedies, they were not implicated in the conditions of her own life, that peculiar bed she had made for herself—"such a great big uncompromising 4-poster," James called it. For the relief of tubercular soldiers and other good works, she earned a French medal, and was made a Chevalier of the Legion of Honor. An arena of dazzling public exertion. But in the lesser frame of private mess she did nothing to spare her husband the humiliation of his madness. It is one thing to go mad, it is another to be humiliated for it. The one time in her life drift stopped dead in its trackless spume, and a genuine claim made as if to seize her—necessity, redder in tooth and claw than any sacrifice one grandly chooses for oneself—she turned away. For her, such a claim was the Gorgon's head, to gaze on which was death.

Writer's death. This is something most writers not only fear but sweat to evade, though most do not practice excision with as clean a knife-edge as cut away "irrelevant and childish" Teddy from Edith Wharton's life. "Friend, client, child, sickness, fear, want, charity, all knock at once at thy closet door and say—'Come out unto us.' But keep thy state," Emerson advised, "come not into their confusion." And Mann's Tonio Kröger declaims that "one must die to life to be utterly a creator." This ruthless romantic idea—it cannot be lived up to by weaklings who succumb to conscience, let alone to love—is probably at bottom less romantic than pragmatic. But it is an idea very nearly the opposite of Wilson's and Kazin's more affecting view of Edith Wharton: that joylessness was her muse, that her troubles energized her for fiction—the stimulus of "some exceptional emotional strain," according to Wilson, "so many personal maladjustments," according to Kazin, which made the novelist possible. If anything made the novelist possible, it was the sloughing off of the sources of emotional strain and personal maladjustment. As for the parallel new-feminist opinion that a woman writes best when she risks "unbearable wisdoms," it does not apply: what wisdom Edith Wharton found unbearable she chose not to bear.

The rest was chatter. Having turned away from the Gorgon's head, she spent the remainder of her life—indeed, nearly the whole of it—in the mainly insipid, sometimes inspired, adventure of elevated conversation. She had her friends. There were few women—whether because she did not encounter her equals among women, or because she avoided them, her biographer yields no hint. The majority were men (one should perhaps say "gentlemen")—Lapsley, Lubbock, Berenson, Fullerton, Simmons, James, Bourget, D'Humières, Berry, Sturgis, Hugh-Smith, Maynard, Gregory, Grant, Scott . . . the list is longer still. Lewis fleshes out all these names brilliantly, particularly Berry and Fullerton; the great comic miraculous James needs no fleshing out. James was in a way afraid of her. She swooped down on him to pluck him away for conversation or sightseeing, and he matched the "commotion and exhaustion" of her arrivals against the vengeance of Bonaparte, Attila, and Tamerlane. "Her powers of devastation are ineffable," he reported, and got into the habit of calling her the Angel of Devastation. She interrupted his work with the abruptness of a natural force (she might occur at any time) and at her convenience (she had particular hours for her work, he had all hours for his). He read her novels and dispatched wondrous celebrating smokescreens of letters ("I applaud, I mean I value, I egg you on") to hide the insufficiency of his admiration. As for her "life," it was a spectacle that had from the beginning upset him: her "desolating, ravaging, burning and destroying energy." And again: "such a nightmare of perpetually renewable choice and decision, such a luxury of bloated alternatives." "*What* an incoherent life!" he summed it up. Lewis disagrees, and reproaches James for partial views and a probable fear of strong women; but it may be, on all the lavish evidence Lewis provides, that the last word will after all lie with drift, exactly as James perceived it in her rushing aimlessness aimed at him.

Before Lewis's landmark discovery of the Wharton-Fullerton liaison, Walter Van Rensselaer Berry—Wharton's distant cousin, an international lawyer and an aristocrat—was commonly regarded as the tender center and great attachment of her life. Lewis does not refute this connection, though he convincingly drains it of sexual particularity, and gives us the portrait of a conventionally self-contained dry-hearted lifelong bachelor, a man caught, if not in recognizable drift, then in another sort of inconclusiveness. But Walter Berry was Edith Wharton's first literary intellectual—a lightning bolt of revelation that, having struck early, never lost its electrical sting. Clearly, she fed on intellectuals—but in a withdrawn and secretive way: she rarely read her work aloud, though she rejoiced to hear James read his. She brooded over history and philosophy, understood everything, but was incapable in fiction or elsewhere of expressing anything but the most commonplace psychology. This was, of course, her strength: she knew how human beings behave, she could describe and predict and surprise. Beyond that, she had a fertile capacity for thinking up stories. Plots and permutations of plots teemed. She was scornful of writers who agonized after subject matter. Subjects, she said, swarmed about her "like mosquitoes," until she felt stifled by their multiplicity and variety.

The truth is she had only one subject, the nineteenth century's unique European literary subject: society. Standard American criticism, struggling to "place" Edith Wharton in a literary environment unused to her subject, has contrived for her the role of a lesser Henry James. This has served to indict her as an imitative figure. But on no significant level is the comparison with James pertinent, except to say that by and large they wrote about the same kinds of people, derived from the same class. Otherwise the difference can be seized in a breath: James was a genius, Wharton not. James invented an almost metaphysical art, Wharton's insights lay close against their molds: what she saw she judged. James became an American in the most ideal sense, Wharton remained an estranged New Yorker. James was an uncanny moralist, Wharton a canny realist. James scarcely ever failed—or, at least, his few failures when they occurred were nevertheless glorious in aspiration and seamless in execution. When Wharton failed, she fell into an embarrassing triteness of language and seeing.

It is a pity that her name is attached so unrelentingly—thanks to the American high school—to *Ethan Frome*, a desolate, even morbid, narrow, soft-at-the-center and at the last unsurprising novella not at all typical of her range. It is an outdoor book that ends mercilessly indoors; she was an indoor novelist. She achieved two permanent novels, one—*The House of Mirth*—a spoiled masterpiece, a kind of latterday reverse *Scarlet Letter*, very direct yet eerie; the other *The Age of Innocence*, a combination of ode and elegy to the New York of her childhood, affirmation and repudiation both. A good many of her short stories and some of the novellas ("The Old Maid," for instance) are marvels of shapeliness and pointedness. This applies also to stories written during her late period, when she is widely considered to have debased her gift. The common accusation—Wilson makes it—is that her prose finally came to resemble women's-magazine fiction. One can venture that she did not so much begin to sound like the women's magazines, as that they began to sound like her, a condition that obtains until this moment? No one has explored Wharton's ongoing subliminal influence on current popular fiction (see almost any issue of *Redbook*); such an investigation would probably be striking in its disclosure of the strength of her legacy. Like any hokey imitation long after the model is lost to consciousness, it is not a bad compliment, though it may be awkward to admit it. (One of the least likely tributes to the Roman Empire, after all, is the pervasiveness of nineteenth-century American civic architecture.) But *The House of Mirth* and *The Age of Innocence* are, like everything unsurpassable because deeply idiosyncratic, incapable of spawning versions of themselves; in these two novels she is in command of an inwardness commensurate with structure. In them she does not simply grab hold of society, or judge it merely; she turns society into an exulting bird of prey, with blood on its beak, steadily beating its wings just over our heads; she turns society into an untamable *idea*. The reader, apprehensive, yet lured by the bird's lyric form, covers his face.

She could do all that; she had that power. Lewis, writing to justify and defend, always her sympathetic partisan, nevertheless hedges. Having acknowledged that she had "begun to locate herself—with a certain assurance, though without vanity—in the developing course of American literature," he appends a doubt:

But in another part of her, there remained something of the conviction drilled into her in old New York that it was improper for a lady to write fiction. One could do so only if one joked about it—if one treated it, to borrow Lubbock's word, as "an amusement." She sometimes sounded as if her writing were her entertainingly guilty secret, and in her memoirs she referred to it (borrowing the title of a popular children's book of her own New York youth) as her "secret garden."

But in the winter of 1911 [she was then at work on *The Reef*], as on perhaps half a dozen other occasions, it was the believing artist that was in the ascendancy during the hard-driving morning hours.

Somehow it is easy to doubt that she had this doubt—or, if she once had it, that she held it for long. To believe in her doubt is to make the bad case of the orthodox critics who, unlike Lewis, have shrunk from taking her seriously as an artist because as an American aristocrat she was born shockingly appurtenanced, and therefore deserves to be patronized for her sorrows. To believe in her doubt is to make the bad case of the new feminists, for whom female sex is, always and everywhere, an impediment difficult to transcend—even when, for an obsessed writer of talent, there is nothing to transcend. To believe in her doubt is to reverse the terms of her life and her work. Only "half a dozen other occasions" when Wharton was a "believing artist"? Only so few? This would mean that the life outside her bed—the dressed life of conversation and travel, the matchstick life of drift—was the primary life, and the life with her writing board—the life of the believing artist—the deviation, the anomaly, the distraction.

But we know, and have always known (Freud taught us only how to reinforce this knowledge), that the secret self is the true self, that obsession is confession. For Edith Wharton that is the only acceptable evaluation, the only possible justice. She did not doubt her allegiance. The writing came first. That she kept it separate from the rest was a misrepresentation and a mistake, but it may also have been a species of holy instinct—it was the one uncontaminated zone of her being: the place unprofaned. Otherwise she can be defined only by the horrific gyrations of "a life"—by the spiraling solipsism and tragic drift that led her to small dogs instead of babies, servants instead of family, high-minded male distance instead of connubial friendship, public virtue instead of private conscience, infatuation instead of the love that sticks. Only the writing board could justify these ugly substitutions. And some would say—myself not among them—that not even the writing board justified them.

The Muse,
Postmodern and Homeless

If you're a writer and if you're by nature Sublime and
    Magisterial,
but you need cash—lots and lots—
don't try to change your literary spots.
Spot-changing won't get you any dough or even any cereal. You'll only
end up feeling gypped, not to mention funereal. So if you're a hifaluting
ineffable Artist of noble intent,
    you might as well stick to your last,
since nobody who reads for fun will read you for fun
    because it's impossible to read you fast.

These are lines Ogden Nash did not write. Henry James did, sort of, in the form of a melancholy comic tale called "The Next Time." Its hero is a genius novelist who, in the hope of making his fortune, attempts to become a popular hack. Again and again he feels sure he has finally gotten the hang of it—grinding out a best-selling quick read—but each time, to his disappointment, what emerges is only another masterpiece.

James himself once contrived to write a letter of Paris chat for the *New York Tribune*. He managed to keep it going for months, but the column was a failure. He could not "entertain." When the editor complained that James's themes were "too remote from popular interests," James snapped back: "If my letters have been 'too good' I am honestly afraid that they are the poorest I can do, especially for the money!" "I thought in all conscience," he said privately, "they had been flimsy enough."

"The Next Time" appeared in 1895; modernism was not yet born. But in his portrait (however teasing) of the artist as a sovereign and unbetrayable focus of authenticity, James had put his finger on what modernism was going to be mainly about.

"Things fall apart; the center cannot hold." That, we used to think, was the whole of modernism—Yeats mourning the irrecoverable old assurances while the surprising new shapes of things, symbols and fragments, flashed by in all their usurping alterations. Now we know better, and also, in a way, worse. Yeats hardly foresaw how our dissolutions would surpass his own—but where we are now is, after all, what he was describing.

And where we are now is the no-man's-land that more and more begins to inherit the name postmodern—atomized, leveled, thoroughly democratic turf where anything goes, everything counts, significance is what I say it is, literature is what's there for the exegetes: comic strips, 1950s sitcoms, fast-food hamburger ads. The elitism of High Art was vanquished long ago, and not only by the Marxists. The divide between Bob Dylan and Dylan Thomas is plugged by critical egalitarianism; so is the difference between poet and critic. *Allee samee*, as Allen Ginsberg once remarked of the great religions—as if wanting to repair the world and wanting to get out of it were indistinguishable. History is whatever selection most favors your cultural thesis. Movements move so rapidly that their direct ancestors are on to something else before they can be undermined and undone as rival precursors. Whether in painting or in literary theory, there is the glee of plenitude and proliferation along these postmodern boulevards, and a dogged pluralism, and individualism splintering off into idiosyncratic fits of unconventionality desperate to pass for original. With so much originality at hand (originality without an origin), and no center (or any number of centers, one to a customer), what's left to be called eccentric?

Modernism had its own widening gyres and ruptures—ruptures enough, hollow men and waste lands, the smashing of every rooted assumption and literary guaranty—but one center did hold, one pledge stuck. This was the artist's pledge to the self. Joyce, Mann, Eliot, Proust, Conrad (even with his furies): they *knew*. And what they knew was that—though things fall apart—the artist is whole, consummate. At bottom, in the deepest brain, rested the supreme serenity and masterly confidence of the sovereign maker.

Prior to modernism, genius scarcely needed to be centered—self-centered, "magisterial"—in this way. Jane Austen and Trollope had their village certainties to keep the balance, to pull toward the center: society, tradition, "realism," the solid verity of the vicar's wife. Even the Romantics, haunting the lonely periphery, deserting the matrix, still had a matrix to desert. The moderns looked all around, saw that nothing held, and began to make themselves up as law, and sometimes as religion. James, preparing in his Notebooks for a new piece of work, secretly crooned down at his pen: *mon bon, caro mio*. His dearest good angel, his faithful Muse, was housed in himself.

Almost no writer, not even the most accomplished, is like that now. Postmodernism, for writers, means fear and flux, unsureness, inward chaos, self-surprise. Virginia Woolf's *Common Reader* in full sail may suggest she is among the moderns, but her diaries show her trembling. Of contemporaries we read in English, only Nadine Gordimer, Joseph Brodsky, and V. S. Naipaul seem to own that central stillness, pride, and genuinely autocratic play of the humors that the moderns had; all three have been embattled by dislocations (Naipaul aggressively, by choice), and it is hard to tell whether it is the seizures of history we feel in these writers, or a true residue of modernist authority.

Those born into American indulgences are less flinty. John Updike in an interview last year spoke of the writer's work as "a little like handwriting. It comes out to be you no matter what you do. That is, it's recognizably Updike." A tendril of astonishment in that, as if there might reasonably have been an alternative. The moderns were unsurprised by their consistencies, and expected to come out what they were: inviolable. The characters in Philip Roth's *The Counterlife* are so wilily infiltrated by postmodernist inconstancy that they keep revising their speeches and their fates: you can't trust them even to stay dead. It goes without saying that we are forbidden to speculate whether the writer who imagined them is as anxiously protean, as cleft by doubt, as they.

Literary modernism, despite clangor and disjunction, was gilded by a certain voluptuousness: it came of the writer's self-knowledge—or call it selfanointment, a thing that properly embarrasses us today. But there was mettle in it; and also prowess, and defiance, and accountability. If the raggedy improvisations of postmodernism have killed off the idea of the Sublime and Magisterial Artist, it suits and gratifies our democratic temperament; the Sublime and the Magisterial were too long on their deathbeds anyhow.

Still, without modernism to give her shelter in the supernal confidence of genius, where can the Muse lodge now?

What Helen Keller Saw

Suspicion stalks fame; incredulity stalks great fame. At least three times—at ages eleven, twenty-three, and fifty-two—Helen Keller was assaulted by accusation, doubt, and overt disbelief. Though her luster had surpassed the stellar figures of generations, she was disparaged nearly as hotly as she was exalted. She was the butt of skeptics and the cynosure of idolators. Mark Twain compared her to Joan of Arc, and pronounced her "fellow to Caesar, Alexander, Napoleon, Homer, Shakespeare and the rest of the immortals." Her renown, he said, would endure a thousand years.

It has, so far, lasted more than a hundred, while steadily dimming. Fifty years ago, even twenty, nearly every ten-year-old knew who Helen Keller was. *The Story of My Life*, her youthful autobiography, was on the reading lists of most schools, and its author was popularly understood to be, if not the equal of Mark Twain's lavish exaggerations, a heroine of uncommon grace and courage, a sort of worldly saint. To admire her was an act of piety, and she herself, by virtue of the strenuous conquest of her limitations, was a living temple dedicated to the spirit of resurrection. Much of that worshipfulness has receded. Her name, if not entirely in eclipse, hardly elicits the awed recognition it once held. No one nowadays, without intending satire, would place her alongside Caesar and Napoleon; and in an era of earnest disabilities legislation, with wheelchair ramps on every street corner, who would think to charge a stone-blind, stone-deaf woman with faking her experience?

Yet as a child she was accused of plagiarism, and in maturity of "verbalism," illicitly substituting parroted words for firsthand perception. All this came about because she was at once liberated by language and in bondage to it, in a way few other human beings, even the blind and the deaf, can fathom. The merely blind have the window of their ears, the merely deaf listen through their eyes. For Helen Keller there was no partially ameliorating "merely." What she suffered was a totality of exclusion. Her early life was meted out in hints and inferences—she could still touch, taste, smell, and feel vibrations; but these were the very capacities that turned her into a wild creature, a kind of flailing animal in human form.

The illness that annihilated Helen Keller's sight and hearing, and left her mute, has never been diagnosed. In 1882, when she was four months short of two years, medical knowledge could assert only "acute congestion of the stomach and brain," though later speculation proposes meningitis or scarlet fever. Whatever the cause, the consequence was ferocity—tantrums, kicking, rages—but also an invented system of sixty simple signs, intimations of intelligence. The child could mimic what she could neither see nor hear: putting on a hat before a mirror, her father reading a newspaper with his glasses on. She could fold laundry and pick out her own things. Such quiet times were few. Frenzied, tempestuous, she was an uncontrollable barbarian. Having discovered the use of a key, she shut up her mother in a closet. She overturned her baby sister's cradle. Her wants were concrete, physical, impatient, helpless, and nearly always belligerent.

She was born in Tuscumbia, Alabama, fifteen years after the Civil War, when Confederate consciousness and mores were still inflamed. Her father, who had fought at Vicksburg, called himself a "gentleman farmer," and edited a small Democratic weekly until, thanks to political influence, he was appointed a United States marshal. He was a zealous hunter who loved his guns and his dogs. Money was usually short; there were escalating marital angers. His second wife, Helen's mother, was younger by twenty years, a spirited woman of intellect condemned to farmhouse toil. She had a strong literary side (Edward Everett Hale, the New Englander who wrote "The Man Without a Country," was a relative) and read seriously and searchingly. In Charles Dickens's *American Notes* she learned about Laura Bridgman, a deaf-blind country girl who was being educated at the Perkins Institution for the Blind, in Boston. Her savior was its director, Samuel Gridley Howe, humanitarian activist and husband of Julia Ward Howe, author of "The Battle Hymn of the Republic": New England idealism at its collective zenith.

Laura Bridgman was thirteen years old when Dickens met her, and was even more circumscribed than Helen Keller—she could neither smell nor taste. She was confined, he said, "in a marble cell, impervious to any ray of light, or particle of sound." But Laura Bridgman's cell could be only partly unlocked. She never mastered language beyond a handful of words unidiomatically strung together. Scientists and psychologists studied her almost zoologically, and her meticulously intricate lacework was widely admired and sold. She lived out her entire life in her room at the Perkins Institution; an 1885 photograph shows her expertly threading a needle with her tongue. She too had been a normal child, until scarlet fever ravaged her senses at the age of two.

News of Laura Bridgman ignited hope—she had been socialized into a semblance of personhood, while Helen remained a small savage—and hope led, eventually, to Alexander Graham Bell. By then the invention of the telephone was well behind him, and he was tenaciously committed to teaching the deaf to speak intelligibly. His wife was deaf; his mother had been deaf. When the six-year-old Helen was brought to him, he took her on his lap and instantly calmed her by letting her feel the vibrations of his pocket watch as it struck the hour. Her responsiveness did not register in her face; he described it as "chillingly empty." But he judged her educable, and advised her father to apply to Michael Anagnos, Howe's successor as director of the Perkins Institution, for a teacher to be sent to Tuscumbia.

Anagnos chose Anne Mansfield Sullivan, a former student at Perkins. "Mansfield" was her own embellishment; it had the sound of gentility. If the fabricated name was intended to confer an elevated status, it was because Annie Sullivan, born into penury, had no status at all. At five she contracted trachoma, a disease of the eye. Three years on, her mother died of tuberculosis and was buried in potter's field—after which her father, a drunkard prone to beating his children, deserted the family. The half-blind Annie and her small brother Jimmie, who had a tubercular hip, were tossed into the poorhouse at Tewksbury, Massachusetts, among syphilitic prostitutes and madmen. Jimmie did not survive the appalling inhumanity of the place, and decades later, recalling its "strangeness, grotesqueness and even terribleness," Annie Sullivan wrote, "I doubt if life or for that matter eternity is long enough to erase the terrors and ugly blots scored upon my mind during those dismal years from 8 to 14." She never spoke of them, not even to her intimates.

She was rescued from Tewksbury by a committee investigating its spreading notoriety, and was mercifully transferred to Perkins. There she learned Braille and the manual alphabet and came to know Laura Bridgman. At the Massachusetts Eye and Ear Infirmary she underwent two operations, which enabled her to read almost normally, though the condition of her eyes continued fragile and inconsistent over her lifetime. After six years she graduated from Perkins as class valedictorian; Anagnos recognized in her clear traces of "uncommon powers." His affectionate concern was nearly a flirtation (he had once teasingly caressed her arm), while she, orphaned and alone, had made certain to catch his notice and his love. When her days at Perkins were ended, what was to become of her? How was she to earn a living? Someone suggested that she might wash dishes or peddle needlework.

"Sewing and crocheting are inventions of the devil," she sneered. "I'd rather break stones on the king's highway than hem a handkerchief."

She went to Tuscumbia instead. She was twenty years old and had no experience suitable for what she would encounter in the despairs and chaotic defeats of the Keller household. She had attempted to prepare herself by studying Laura Bridgman's training as it was recorded in the Perkins archives. Apart from this, she had no resources other than the manual alphabet that enlivened her fingers, and the steely history of her own character. The tyrannical child she had come to educate threw cutlery, pinched, grabbed food off dinner plates, sent chairs tumbling, shrieked, struggled. She was strong, beautiful but for one protruding eye, unsmiling, painfully untamed: virtually her first act on meeting the new teacher was to knock out one of her front teeth. The afflictions of the marble cell had become inflictions. Annie demanded that Helen be separated from her family; her father could not bear to see his ruined little daughter disciplined. The teacher and her recalcitrant pupil retreated to a cottage on the grounds of the main house, where Annie was to be sole authority.

What happened then and afterward she chronicled in letter after letter, to Anagnos and, more confidingly, to Mrs. Sophia Hopkins, the Perkins housemother who had given her shelter during school vacations. Mark Twain saw in Annie Sullivan a *writer*: "How she stands out in her letters!" he exclaimed. "Her brilliancy, penetration, originality, wisdom, character and the fine literary competencies of her pen—they are all there." Her observations, both of herself and of the developing child, are kin, in their humanity, particularity, and psychological acumen, to philosophical essays. Jubilantly, and with preternatural awareness, she set down the progress, almost hour by hour, of Helen Keller's disentombment, an exuberant deliverance far more remarkable than Laura Bridgman's frail and inarticulate release. Howe had taught the names of things by attaching to them labels written in raised type—but labels on spoons are not the same as self-generated thoughts. Annie Sullivan's method, insofar as she recognized it formally as a method, was pure freedom. Like any writer, she wrote and wrote and wrote, all day long. She wrote words, phrases, sentences, lines of poetry, descriptions of animals, trees, flowers, weather, skies, clouds, concepts: whatever lay before her or came usefully to mind. She wrote not on paper with a pen, but with her fingers, spelling rapidly into the child's alert palm. Helen, quick to imitate yet uncomprehending, was under a spell of curiosity (the pun itself reveals the manual alphabet as magical tool). Her teacher spelled into her hand; she spelled the same letters back, mimicking unknowable configurations. But it was not until the connection was effected between finger-wriggling and its referent—the cognitive key, the insight, the crisis of discovery—that what we call mind broke free.

This was, of course, the fabled incident at the well pump, dramatized in film and (by now) collective memory, when Helen suddenly understood that the tactile pattern pecking at her hand was inescapably related to the gush of cold water spilling over it. "Somehow," the adult Helen Keller recollected, "the mystery of language was revealed to me." In the course of a single month, from Annie's arrival to her triumph in forcibly bridling the household despot, Helen had grown docile, eagerly willing, affectionate, and tirelessly intent on learning from moment to moment. Her intellect was fiercely engaged, and when language began to flood it, she rode on a salvational ark of words.

To Mrs. Hopkins Annie wrote ecstatically:

Something within me tells me that I shall succeed beyond my wildest dreams. I know that [Helen] has remarkable powers, and I believe that I shall be able to develop and mould them. I cannot tell how I know these things. I had no idea a short time ago how to go to work; I was feeling about in the dark; but somehow I know now, and I know that I know. I cannot explain it; but when difficulties arise, I am not perplexed or doubtful. I know how to meet them; I seem to divine Helen's peculiar needs . . .

Already people are taking a deep interest in Helen. No one can see her without being impressed. She is no ordinary child, and people's interest in her education will be no ordinary interest. Therefore let us be exceedingly careful in what we say and write about her . . . My beautiful Helen shall not be transformed into a prodigy if I can help it.

At this time Helen was not yet seven years old, and Annie was being paid twenty-five dollars a month.

The fanatical public scrutiny Helen Keller aroused far exceeded Annie's predictions. It was Michael Anagnos who first proclaimed her to be a miracle child—a young goddess. "History presents no case like hers," he exulted. "As soon as a slight crevice was opened in the outer wall of their twofold imprisonment, her mental faculties emerged full-armed from their living tomb as Pallas Athene from the head of Zeus." And again: "She is the queen of precocious and brilliant children, Emersonian in temper, most exquisitely organized, with intellectual sight of unsurpassed sharpness and infinite reach, a true daughter of Mnemosyne. It is no exaggeration to say that she is a personification of goodness and happiness." Annie, the teacher of a flesh-

and-blood earthly child, protested: "His extravagant way of saying [these things] rubs me the wrong way. The simple facts would be so much more convincing!" But Anagnos's glorifications caught fire: one year after Annie had begun spelling into her hand, Helen Keller was celebrated in newspapers all over the world. When her dog was inadvertently shot, an avalanche of contributions poured in to replace it; unprompted, she directed that the money be set side for the care of an impoverished deaf-blind boy at Perkins. At eight she was taken to visit President Cleveland at the White House, and in Boston was introduced to many of the luminaries of the period: Oliver Wendell Holmes, John Greenleaf Whittier, Edward Everett Hale, and Phillips Brooks (who addressed her puzzlement over the nature of God). At nine, saluting him as "Dear Poet," she wrote to Whittier:

> I thought you would be glad to hear that your beautiful poems make me very happy. Yesterday I read "In School Days" and "My Playmate," and I enjoyed them greatly . . . It is very pleasant to live here in our beautiful world. I cannot see the lovely things with my eyes, but my mind can see them all, and so I am joyful all the day long.
>
> When I walk out in my garden I cannot see the beautiful flowers, but I know that they are all around me; for is not the air sweet with their fragrance? I know too that the tiny lily-bells are whispering pretty secrets to their companions else they would not look so happy. I love you very dearly, because you have taught me so many lovely things about flowers, birds, and people.

Her dependence on Annie for the assimilation of her immediate surroundings was nearly total—hands-on, as we would say, and literally so—but through the raised letters of Braille she could be altogether untethered: books coursed through her. In childhood she was captivated by *Little Lord Fauntleroy*, Frances Hodgson Burnett's story of a sunnily virtuous boy who melts a crusty old man's heart; it became a secret template of her own character as she hoped she might always manifest it—not sentimentally, but in full awareness of dread. She was not deaf to Caliban's wounded cry: "You taught me language, and my profit on't / Is, I know how to curse." Helen Keller's profit was that she knew how to rejoice. In young adulthood, casting about for a faith bare of exclusiveness or harsh images, and given over to purifying idealism, she seized on Swedenborgian spiritualism. Annie had kept away from teaching any religion at all: she was a down-to-earth agnostic whom Tewksbury had cured of easy belief. When Helen's responsiveness to bitter social deprivation later took on a worldly strength, leading her to socialism, and even to unpopular Bolshevik sympathies, Annie would have no part of it, and worried that Helen had gone too far. Marx was not in Annie's canon. Homer, Virgil, Shakespeare, and Milton were: she had Helen reading *Paradise Lost* at twelve.

But Helen's formal schooling was widening beyond Annie's tutelage. With her teacher at her side, Helen spent a year at Perkins, and then entered the Wright-Humason School in New York, a fashionable academy for deaf girls; she was its single deaf-blind pupil. She also pleaded to be taught to speak like other people, and worked at it determinedly—but apart from Annie and a few others who were accustomed to her efforts, she could not be readily understood. Speech, even if imperfect, was not her only ambition: she intended to go to college. To prepare, she enrolled in the Cambridge School for Young Ladies, where she studied mathematics, German, French, Latin, and Greek and Roman history. In 1900 she was admitted to Radcliffe (then an "annex" to Harvard), still with Annie in attendance. Despite her necessary presence in every class, diligently spelling the lecture into Helen's hand, and hourly wearing out her troubled eyes as she transcribed text after text into the manual alphabet, no one thought of granting Annie a degree along with Helen. It was not uncommon for Annie Sullivan to play second fiddle to Helen Keller; the radiant miracle outshone the driven miracle worker. Not so for Mark Twain: he saw them as two halves of the same marvel. "It took the pair of you to make a complete and perfect whole," he said. Not everyone agreed. Annie was sometimes charged with being Helen's jailer, or harrier, or ventriloquist. During examinations at Radcliffe, she was not permitted to be in the building. For the rest, Helen relied on her own extraordinary memory and on Annie's lightning fingers. Luckily, a second helper, adept at the manual alphabet, soon turned up: he was John Macy, a twenty-five-year-old English instructor at Harvard, a writer and editor, a fervent socialist, and, eventually, Annie Sullivan's husband, eleven years her junior.

The money for all this schooling, and for the sustenance of the two young women (both enjoyed fine clothes and vigorous horseback riding), came in spurts from a handful of very rich men—among them John Spaulding, the Sugar King, and Henry Rogers, of Standard Oil. Helen charmed these wealthy eminences as she charmed everyone, while Annie more systematically cultivated their philanthropy. She herself was penniless, and the Kellers of Tuscumbia were financially useless. Shockingly, Helen's father had once threatened to put his little daughter on exhibit, in order to earn her keep. (Twenty years afterward, Helen took up his idea and went on the vaudeville circuit—she happily, Annie reluctantly—and even to Hollywood, where she starred in a silent movie, with the mythical Ulysses as her ecto-plasmic boyfriend.)

At Radcliffe Helen became a writer. She also became a third party to Annie's difficult romance: whoever wanted Annie inevitably got Helen too. Drawn by twin literary passions like his own, Macy was more than willing, at least at first. Charles Townsend Copeland—Harvard's illustrious "Copey," a professor of rhetoric—had encouraged Helen (as she put it to him in a grate-ful letter) "to make my own observations and describe the experiences peculiarly my own. Henceforth I am resolved to be myself, to live my own life and write my own thoughts." Out of this came *The Story of My Life*, the autobiography of a twenty-one-year-old, published while she was still an undergraduate. It began as a series of sketches for the *Ladies' Home Journal*; the fee was three thousand dollars. John Macy described the labori-ous process:

> When she began work at her story, more than a year ago, she set up on the Braille machine about a hundred pages of what she called "mate-rial," consisting of detached episodes and notes put down as they came to her without definite order or coherent plan. Then came the task where one who has eyes to see must help her. Miss Sullivan and I read the disconnected passages, put them into chronological order, and counted the words to make sure the articles should be the right length. All this work we did with Miss Keller beside us, referring everything, especially matters of phrasing, to her for revision . . .
>
> Her memory of what she had written was astonishing. She remem-bered whole passages, some of which she had not seen for many weeks, and could tell, before Miss Sullivan had spelled into her hand a half-dozen words of the paragraph under discussion, where they belonged and what sentences were necessary to make the connection clear.

This method of collaboration, essentially mechanical, continued throughout Helen Keller's professional writing life; yet within these con-straints the design, the sensibility, the cadences were her own. She was a self-conscious stylist. Macy remarked that she had the courage of her meta-phors—he meant that she sometimes let them carry her away—and Helen herself worried that her prose could now and then seem "periwigged." To the contemporary ear, many of her phrases are too much immersed in Victorian lace and striving uplift—but the contemporary ear has no entitlement, simply by being contemporary, to set itself up as judge: every period is marked by a prevailing voice. Helen Keller's earnestness is a kind of piety;

she peers through the lens of a sublimely aspiring poetry. It is as if Tennyson and the Transcendentalists had together got hold of her typewriter. At the same time, she is turbulently embroiled in the whole human enterprise—except, tellingly, for irony. She has no "edge," and why should she? Irony is a radar that seeks out the dark side; she had darkness enough. Her unfailing intuition was to go after the light. She flew toward it, as she herself said, in the hope of "clear and animated language." She knew what part of her mind was instinct and what part was information, and she was cautious about the difference; she was even suspicious, as she had good reason to be. "It is certain," she wrote, "that I cannot always distinguish my own thoughts from those I read, because what I read become the very substance and texture of my mind . . . It seems to me that the great difficulty of writing is to make the language of the educated mind express our confused ideas, half feelings, half thoughts, where we are little more than bundles of instinctive tendencies." She, who had once been incarcerated in the id, did not require knowledge of Freud to instruct her in its inchoate presence.

The Story of My Life was first published in 1903, with Macy's ample introduction. He was able to write about Helen nearly as authoritatively as Annie, but also—in private—more skeptically: after his marriage to Annie, the three of them set up housekeeping in rural Wrentham, Massachusetts. Possibly not since the Brontës had so feverishly literary a crew lived under a single roof. Of this ultimately inharmonious trio, one, internationally famous for decades, was catapulted now into still greater renown by the recent appearance of her celebrated memoir. Macy, meanwhile, was discovering that he had married not a woman, a moody one at that, but the indispensable infrastructure of a public institution. As Helen's secondary amanuensis, he continued to be of use until the marriage collapsed. It foundered on his profligacy with money, on Annie's irritability—she fought him on his uncompromising socialism, which she disdained—and finally on his accelerating alcoholism.

Because Macy was known to have assisted Helen in the preparation of *The Story of My Life*, the insinuations of control that often assailed Annie now also landed on him. Helen's ideas, it was said, were really Macy's; he had transformed her into a "Marxist propagandist." It was true that she sympathized with his political bent, but his views had not shaped hers. As she had come independently to Swedenborgian idealism, so had she come to societal utopianism. The charge of expropriation, of both thought and idiom, was old, and dogged her at intervals during much of her early and middle life: she was a fraud, a puppet, a plagiarist. She was false coin. She was "a living lie."

She was eleven when these words were first hurled at her, spewed out by a wrathful Anagnos. Not long before, he had spoken of Helen in celestial terms. Now he denounced her as a malignant thief. What brought on this defection was a little story she had written, called "The Frost King," which she sent him as a birthday present. In the voice of a highly literary children's narrative, it recounts how the "frost fairies" cause the season's turning.

> When the children saw the trees all aglow with brilliant colors they clapped their hands and shouted for joy, and immediately began to pick great bunches to take home. "The leaves are as lovely as flowers!" cried they, in their delight.

Anagnos—doubtless clapping his hands and shouting for joy—immediately began to publicize Helen's newest accomplishment. "The Frost King" appeared both in the Perkins alumni magazine and in another journal for the blind, which, following Anagnos, unhesitatingly named it "without parallel in the history of literature." But more than a parallel was at stake; the story was found to be nearly identical to "The Frost Fairies," by Margaret Canby, a writer of children's books. Anagnos was infuriated, and fled headlong from adulation and hyperbole to humiliation and enmity. Feeling personally betrayed and institutionally discredited, he arranged an inquisition for the terrified Helen, standing her alone in a room before a jury of eight Perkins officials and himself, all mercilessly cross-questioning her. Her mature recollection of Anagnos's "court of investigation" registers as pitiably as the ordeal itself:

> Mr. Anagnos, who loved me tenderly, thinking that he had been deceived, turned a deaf ear to pleadings of love and innocence. He believed, or at least suspected, that Miss Sullivan and I had deliberately stolen the bright thoughts of another and imposed them on him to win his admiration . . . As I lay in my bed that night, I wept as I hope few children have wept. I felt so cold, I imagined that I should die before morning, and the thought comforted me. I think if this sorrow had come to me when I was older, it would have broken my spirit beyond repairing.

She was defended by Alexander Graham Bell, and by Mark Twain, who parodied the whole procedure with a thumping hurrah for plagiarism, and disgust for the egotism of "these solemn donkeys breaking a little child's heart with their ignorant damned rubbish! A gang of dull and hoary pirates piously setting themselves the task of disciplining and purifying a kitten that they think they've caught pilfering a chop!" Margaret Canby's tale had been spelled to Helen perhaps three years before, and lay dormant in her prodigiously retentive memory; she was entirely oblivious of reproducing phrases not her own. The scandal Anagnos had precipitated left a lasting bruise. But it was also the beginning of a psychological, even a metaphysical, clarification that Helen refined and ratified as she grew older, when similar, if more subtle, suspicions cropped up in the press, compelling her to interrogate the workings of her mind. *The Story of My Life* was attacked in the *Nation* not for plagiarism in the usual sense, but for the purloining of "things beyond her powers of perception with the assurance of one who has verified every word . . . One resents the pages of second-hand description of natural objects." The reviewer blamed her for the sin of vicariousness: "all her knowledge," he insisted, "is hearsay knowledge."

It was almost a reprise of the Perkins tribunal: she was again being confronted with the charge of inauthenticity. Anagnos's rebuke—"Helen Keller is a living lie"—regularly resurfaced, sometimes less harshly, sometimes as acerbically, in the form of a neurologist's or a psychologist's assessment, or in the reservations of reviewers. A French professor of literature, who was himself blind, determined that she was "a dupe of words, and her aesthetic enjoyment of most of the arts is a matter of auto-suggestion rather than perception." A *New Yorker* interviewer complained, "She talks bookishly . . . To express her ideas, she falls back on the phrases she has learned from books, and uses words that sound stilted, poetical metaphors." A professor of neurology at Columbia University, after a series of tests, pooh-poohed the claim that her remaining senses might be in any way extraordinary—the acuity of her touch and smell, he concluded, was no different from that of other mortals. "That's a stab at my vanity," she joked.

But the cruelest appraisal of all came, in 1933, from Thomas Cutsforth, a blind psychologist. By this time Helen was fifty-three, and had published four additional autobiographical volumes. Cutsforth disparaged everything she had become. The wordless child she once was, he maintained, was closer to reality than what her teacher had made of her through the imposition of "word-mindedness." He objected to her use of images such as "a mist of green," "blue pools of dog violets," "soft clouds tumbling." All that, he protested, was "implied chicanery" and "a birthright sold for a mess of verbiage." He criticized

the aims of the educational system in which she has been confined during her whole life. Literary expression has been the goal of her formal education. Fine writing, regardless of its meaningful content,

89

has been the end toward which both she and her teacher have striven . . . Her own experiential life was rapidly made secondary, and it was regarded as such by the victim . . . Her teacher's ideals became her ideals, her teacher's likes became her likes, and whatever emotional activity her teacher experienced she experienced.

For Cutsforth—and not only for him—Helen Keller was the victim of language rather than its victorious master. She was no better than a copy; whatever was primary, and thereby genuine, had been stamped out. As for Annie, while here she was pilloried as the callous instrument of her pupil's victimization, elsewhere she was pitied as a woman cheated of her own life by having sacrificed it to serve another. Either Helen was Annie's slave, or Annie was Helen's.

Once again Helen had her faithful defenders. The philosopher Ernst Cassirer reflected that "a human being in the construction of his human world is not dependent upon the quality of his sense material." Even more trenchantly, a *New York Times* editor quoted Cicero: "When Democritus lost his sight he could not, to be sure, distinguish black from white; but all the same he could distinguish good from bad, just from unjust, honorable from disgraceful, expedient from inexpedient, great from small, and it was permitted him to live happily without seeing changes of color; it was not permissible to do so without true ideas."

But Helen did not depend on philosophers, ancient or modern, to make her case. She spoke for herself: she was nobody's puppet, her mind was her own, and she knew what she saw. Once, having been taken to the uppermost viewing platform of what was then the tallest building in the world, she defined her condition:

> I will concede that my guides saw a thousand things that escaped me from the top of the Empire State Building, but I am not envious. For imagination creates distances that reach to the end of the world . . . There was the Hudson—more like the flash of a swordblade than a noble river. The little island of Manhattan, set like a jewel in its nest of rainbow waters, stared up into my face, and the solar system circled about my head!

Her rebuttal to word-mindedness, to vicariousness, to implied chicanery and the living lie, was inscribed deliberately and defiantly in her daring images of swordblade and rainbow waters. That they were derived was no reason for her to be deprived—why should she alone be starved of enchantment? The deaf-blind person, she wrote, "seizes every word of sight and hearing, because his sensations compel it. Light and color, of which he has no tactual evidence, he studies fearlessly, believing that all humanly knowable truth is open to him." She was not ashamed of talking bookishly: it meant a ready access to the storehouse of history and literature. She disposed of her critics with a dazzling apothegm: "The bulk of the world's knowledge is an imaginary construction," and went on to contend that history itself "is but a mode of imagining, of making us see civilizations that no longer appear upon the earth." Those who ridiculed her rapturous rendering of color she dismissed as "spirit-vandals" who would force her "to bite the dust of material things." Her idea of the subjective onlooker was broader than that of physics, and while "red" may denote an explicit and measurable wavelength in the visible spectrum, in the mind it is flittingly fickle (and not only for the blind), varying from the bluster of rage to the reticence of a blush: physics cannot cage metaphor.

She saw, then, what she wished, or was blessed, to see, and rightly named it imagination. In this she belongs to a wider class than that narrow order of the tragically deaf-blind. Her class, her tribe, hears what no healthy ear can catch, and sees what no eye chart can quantify. Her common language was not with the man who crushed a child for memorizing what the fairies do, or with the carpers who scolded her for the crime of a literary vocabulary. She was a member of the race of poets, the Romantic kind; she was close cousin to those novelists who write not only what they do not know, but what they cannot possibly know.

And though she was early taken in hand by a writerly intelligence leading her purposefully to literature, it was hardly in the power of the manual alphabet to pry out a writer who was not already there. Laura Bridgman stuck to her lace making, and with all her senses intact might have remained a needlewoman. John Macy believed finally that between Helen and Annie there was only one genius—his wife. Helen's intellect, he asserted, was "stout and energetic, of solid endurance," able to achieve through patience and toil, but void of real brilliance. In the absence of Annie's inventiveness and direction, he implied, Helen's efforts would show up as the lesser gifts they were. This did not happen. Annie died, at seventy, in 1936, four years after Macy; they had long been estranged. By then her always endangered eyesight had deteriorated; depressed, obese, cranky, and inconsolable, she had herself gone blind. Helen came under the care of her secretary, Polly Thomson, a Scotswoman who was both possessively loyal and dryly unliterary: the scenes she spelled into Helen's hand never matched Annie's quicksilver evocations.

But even as she mourned the loss of her teacher, Helen flourished. Annie was dead; only the near-at-hand are indispensable. With the assistance of Nella Henney, Annie Sullivan's biographer, she continued to publish journals and memoirs. She undertook grueling visits to Japan, India, Israel, Europe, Australia, everywhere championing the blind, the deaf, the dispossessed. She was indefatigable until her very last years, and died in 1968 weeks before her eighty-eighth birthday.

Yet the story of her life is not the good she did, the panegyrics she inspired, or the disputes (genuine or counterfeit? victim or victimizer?) that stormed around her. The most persuasive story of Helen Keller's life is what she said it was: "I observe, I feel, I think, I imagine."

She was an artist. She imagined.

"Blindness has no limiting effect on mental vision. My intellectual horizon is infinitely wide," she was impelled to argue again and again. "The universe it encircles is immeasurable." And like any writer making imagination's mysterious claims before the material-minded, she had cause enough to cry out, "Oh, the supercilious doubters!"

But it was not herself alone she was shielding from these skirmishes: she was a warrior in a wide and thorny conflict. Helen Keller, if we are presumptuous enough to reduce her so, can be taken to be a laboratory for empirical demonstration. Do we know only what we see, or do we see what we somehow already know? Are we more than the sum of our senses? Does a picture—whatever strikes the retina—engender thought, or does thought create the picture? Can there be subjectivity without an object to glance off from? Metaphysicians and other theorists have their differing notions, to which the ungraspable organism that is Helen Keller is a retort. She is not an advocate for one side or the other in the ancient debate concerning the nature of the real. She is not a philosophical or neurological or therapeutic topic. She stands for enigma, and against obtuseness; there lurks in her still the angry child who demanded to be understood, yet could not be deciphered. She refutes those who cannot perceive, or do not care to value, what is hidden from sensation.

Against whom does she rage, whom does she refute? The mockers of her generation and ours. The psychiatrist Bruno Bettelheim, for instance. "By pretending to have a full life," he warned in a 1990 essay, "by pretending that through touch she knew what a piece of sculpture, what flowers, what trees were like, that through the words of others she knew what the sky or clouds looked like, by pretending that she could hear music by feeling the vibrations of musical instruments," she fooled the world into thinking the "terribly handicapped are not suffering deeply every moment of their lives." Pretender, trickster: this is what the notion of therapy makes of "the words of others," which we more commonly term experience; heritage; literature. At best the therapist pities, at worst he sees delusion. Perhaps Helen Keller did suffer deeply. Then all the more honor to the flashing embossments of the artist's mask. Oddly, practitioners of psychology—whom one would least expect to be literalists—have been quickest to blame her for imposture. Let them blame Keats, too, for his delusionary "Heard melodies are sweet, but those unheard are sweeter," and for his phantom theme of negative capability, the poet's oarless casting about for the hallucinatory shadows of desire.

Helen Keller's lot, it turns out, was not unique. "We work in the dark," Henry James affirmed, on behalf of his own art, and so did she. It was the same dark. She knew her Wordsworth: "Visionary power / Attends the motions of the viewless winds / Embodied in the mystery of word: / There, darkness makes abode." She fought the debunkers who, for the sake of a spurious honesty, would denude her of landscape and return her to the marble cell. She fought the iron pragmatists who meant to disinherit her, and everyone, of poetry. She fought the tin ears who took imagining to be mendacity. Her legacy, after all, is an epistemological marker of sorts: proof of the real existence of the mind's eye.

In one respect, though, she was incontrovertibly as fraudulent as the cynics charged. She had always been photographed in profile: this hid her disfigured left eye. In maturity she had both eyes surgically removed and replaced with glass—an expedient known only to those closest to her. Everywhere she went, her sparkling blue prosthetic eyes were admired for their living beauty and humane depth.

The Impossibility of Being Kafka

Franz Kafka is the twentieth century's valedictory ghost. In two incomplete yet incommensurable novels, *The Trial* and *The Castle*, he submits, as lingering spirits will, a ghastly accounting—the sum total of modern totalitarianism. His imaginings outstrip history and memoir, incident and record, film and reportage. He is on the side of realism—the poisoned realism of metaphor. Cumulatively, Kafka's work is an archive of our era: its anomie, depersonalization, afflicted innocence, innovative cruelty, authoritarian demagoguery, technologically adept killing. But none of this is served raw. Kafka has no politics; he is not a political novelist in the way of Orwell or Dickens. He writes from insight, not, as people like to say, from premonition. He is often taken for a metaphysical or even a religious writer, but the supernatural elements in his fables are too entangled in concrete everydayness, and in caricature, to allow for any incandescent certainties. The typical Kafkan figure has the cognitive force of a chess master—which is why the term "Kafkaesque," a synonym for the uncanny, misrepresents at the root. The Kafkan mind rests not on unintelligibility or the surreal, but on adamantine logic—on the sane expectation of rationality. A singing mouse, an enigmatic ape, an impenetrable castle, a deadly contraption, the Great Wall of China, a creature in a burrow, fasting as an art form, and, most famously, a man metamorphosed into a bug—all these are steeped in reason; and also in reasoning. "Fairy tales for dialecticians," the critic Walter Benjamin remarked. In the two great zones of literary susceptibility—the lyrical and the logical—the Kafkan "K" attaches not to Keats, but to Kant.

The prose that utters these dire analytic fictions has, with time, undergone its own metamorphosis, and only partly through repeated translations into other languages. Something—fame—has intervened to separate Kafka's stories from our latter-day reading of them two or three generations on. The words are unchanged; yet those same passages Kafka once read aloud, laughing at their fearful comedy, to a small circle of friends, are now markedly altered under our eyes—enameled by that labyrinthine process through which a literary work awakens to discover that it has been transformed into a classic. Kafka has taught us how to read the world differently: as a kind of decree. And because we have read Kafka, we know more than we knew before we read him, and are now better equipped to read him acutely. This may be why his graven sentences begin to approach the scriptural; they become as fixed in our heads as any hymn; they seem ordained, fated. They carry the high melancholy tone of resignation unabraded by cynicism. They are stately and plain and full of dread.

And what is it that Kafka himself knew? He was born in 1883; he died, of tuberculosis, in 1924, a month short of his forty-first birthday. He did not live to see human beings degraded to the status and condition of vermin eradicated by an insecticidal gas.* If he was able to imagine man reduced to insect, it was not because he was prophetic. Writers, even the geniuses among them, are not seers. It was his own status and condition that Kafka knew. His language was German, and that, possibly, is the point. That Kafka breathed and thought and aspired and suffered in German—in Prague, a German-hating city—may be the ultimate exegesis of everything he wrote.

The Austro-Hungarian monarchy, ruled by German-speaking Habsburgs until its dissolution in the First World War, was an amalgam of a dozen national enclaves. Czech-speaking Bohemia was one of these, restive and sometimes rebellious under Habsburg authority. Since the time of Joseph II, who reigned between 1780 and 1790, the imperial parliament—centered in Vienna—had governed in German; all laws were published in German; all outlying bureaucracies and educational systems were conducted in German; German was the language of public offices and law courts; all official books and correspondence were kept in German. Though later rulings ame-liorated these conditions somewhat, the struggle for Czech language rights

---

*His three sisters, Ottla, Valli, and Elli, who survived him, perished at Auschwitz and Lodz between 1941 and 1943. And suppose Kafka had not died of tuberculosis in 1924? Of all the speculations and hypotheses about Kafka, this may be the most significant. In 1940 he would have been fifty-seven. If only he had lived that long—*The Castle* and other works would have been completed, and how many further masterpieces would now be in our possession! Yet what would those extra years have meant for Kafka? By 1940, the Jews of Prague were forbidden to change their addresses or leave the city. By 1941, they could not walk in the woods around Prague, or travel on trolleys, buses, and subways. Telephones were ripped out of Jewish apartments, and public telephones were off-limits to Jews. Jewish businesses were confiscated; firms threw out their Jewish employees; Jewish children were thrown out of school. And so on and so on and so on, until ghettoization, degradation, deportation, and murder. That is how it was for Ottla, Valli, and Elli, and for all of Kafka's tedious and unliterary relatives ("The joys and sorrows of my relatives bore me to my soul," he complained in his diary); and that is how it would have been for Kafka. The work he left behind was at first restricted to Jewish readers only, and then banned as "harmful and undesirable." Schocken, his publisher, escaped to Tel Aviv. It remains doubtful that Kafka would have done the same.

was on-going, determined, and turbulent. Prague's German-speaking minority, aside from the official linguistic advantage it enjoyed, was prominent both commercially and intellectually. Vienna, Berlin, Munich—these pivotal seats of German culture might be far away, but Prague reflected them all. Here, in Bohemia's major city, Kafka attended a German university, studied German jurisprudence, worked for a German insurance company, and published in German periodicals. German influence was dominant; in literature it was conspicuous.

That the Jews of Prague were German-identified, by language and preference—a minority population within a minority population—was not surprising. There were good reasons for this preference. Beginning with the Edict of Toleration in 1782, and continuing over the next seventy years, the Habsburg emperors had throughout their territories released the Jews from lives of innumerable restrictions in closed ghettos; emancipation meant civil freedoms, including the right to marry at will, to settle in the cities and enter the trades and professions. Among Bohemia's Jews of Kafka's generation, ninety percent were educated in German. Kafka was privately tutored in Czech, but in his academically rigorous German elementary school thirty of the thirty-nine boys in his class were Jews. For Bohemian patriots, Prague's Jews bore a double stigma: they were Germans, resented as cultural and national intruders, and they were Jews. Though the Germans were as unfriendly to the German-speaking Jews as the Czechs were, militant Czech nationalism targeted both groups.

Nor was modern Czech anti-Semitism without its melancholy history. With the abolition of the ghettos and the granting of civil rights, anti-Jewish demonstrations broke out in 1848, and again in 1859, 1861, and 1866. In neighboring Hungary in 1883, the year of Kafka's birth, a blood-libel charge—a medieval canard accusing Jews of the ritual murder of a Christian child—brought on renewed local hostility. In 1897, the year after Kafka's bar mitzvah observance, when he was fourteen, he was witness to a ferocious resumption of anti-Jewish violence that had begun as an anti-German protest over the government's denial of Czech language rights. Mark Twain, reporting from Vienna on the parliamentary wrangling, described conditions in Prague: "There were three or four days of furious rioting . . . the Jews and Germans were harried and plundered, and their houses destroyed; in other Bohemian towns there was rioting—in some cases the Germans being the rioters, in others the Czechs—and in all cases the Jew had to roast, no matter which side he was on." In Prague itself, mobs looted Jewish businesses, smashed windows, vandalized synagogues, and assaulted Jews on the street. Because Kafka's father, a burly man, could speak a little Czech and had Czech employees—he called them his "paid enemies," to his son's cha-grin—his sundries shop was spared. Less than two years later, just before Easter Sunday in 1899, a teenage Czech girl was found dead, and the blood libel was revived once more; it was the future mayor of Prague who led the countrywide anti-Jewish agitation. Yet hatred was pervasive even when vio-lence was dormant. And in 1920, when Kafka was thirty-seven, with only three years to live and *The Castle* still unwritten, anti-Jewish rioting again erupted in Prague. "I've spent all afternoon out in the streets," Kafka wrote in a letter contemplating fleeing the city, "bathing in Jew-hatred. *Prašivo ple-meno*—filthy brood—is what I heard them call the Jews. Isn't it only natural to leave a place where one is so bitterly hated? . . . The heroism involved in staying put in spite of it all is the heroism of the cockroach, which also won't be driven out of the bathroom." On that occasion, Jewish archives were destroyed and the Torah scrolls of Prague's ancient Altneu synagogue were burned. Kafka did not need to be, in the premonitory sense, a seer; as an observer of his own time and place, he saw. And what he saw was that, as a Jew in Central Europe, he was not at home; and though innocent of any wrongdoing, he was thought to deserve punishment.

Inexplicably, it has become a commonplace of Kafka criticism to over-look nearly altogether the social roots of the psychological predicaments animating Kafka's fables. To an extent there is justice in this disregard. Kaf-ka's genius will not lend itself to merely local apprehensions; it cannot be reduced to a scarring by a hurtful society. At the other extreme, his stories are frequently addressed as faintly christological allegories about the search for "grace," in the manner of a scarier *Pilgrim's Progress*. It is true that there is not a word about Jews—and little about Prague—in Kafka's formal writ-ing, which may account for the dismissal of any inquisitiveness about Kafka's Jewishness as a "parochialism" to be avoided. Kafka himself is said to have avoided it. But he was less assimilated (itself an ungainly notion) than some of his readers wish or imagine him to have been. Kafka's self-made, coarsely practical father was the son of an impoverished kosher butcher, and began peddling in peasant villages while he was still a child. His middle-class mother was descended from an eminent Talmud scholar. Almost all his friends were Jewish literati. Kafka was seriously attracted to Zionism and Pal-estine, to Hebrew, to the pathos and inspiration of an East European Yiddish theater troupe that had landed in Prague: these were for him the vehicles of a historic transcendence that cannot be crammed into the term "parochial." Glimmerings of this transcendence seep into the stories, usually by way of their negation. "We are nihilistic thoughts that come into God's head," Kafka told Max Brod, the dedicated friend who preserved the unfinished body of his work. In all of Kafka's fictions the Jewish anxieties of Prague press on, invisibly, subliminally; their fate is metamorphosis.

But Prague was not Kafka's only subterranean torment. His harsh, crushing, uncultivated father, for whom the business drive was everything, hammered at the mind of his obsessively susceptible son, for whom literature was everything. Yet the adult son remained in the parental flat for years, dreading noise, interruption, and mockery, writing through the night. At the family table the son sat in concentration, diligently Fletcherizing his food, chewing each mouthful a hundred times, until it liquified. He experimented with vegetarianism, gymnastics, carpentry, and gardening, and repeatedly went on health retreats, once to a nudist spa. He fell into a stormy, fitfully interrupted but protracted engagement to Felice Bauer, a pragmatic manufacturing executive in Berlin; when he withdrew from it he felt like a felon before a tribunal. His job at the Workers' Accident Insurance Institute (where he was a token Jew) instructed him in the whims of contingency and in the mazy machinery of bureaucracy. When his lungs became infected, he referred to his spasms of cough as "the animal." In his last hours, pleading with his doctor for morphine, he said, "Kill me, or else you are a murderer"— a final conflagration of Kafkan irony.

Below all this travail, some of it self-inflicted, lay the indefatigable clawings of language. In a letter to Max Brod, Kafka described Jews who wrote in German (he could hardly exclude himself) as trapped beasts: "Their hind legs were still stuck in parental Judaism while their forelegs found no purchase on new ground." They lived, he said, with three impossibilities: "the impossibility of not writing, the impossibility of writing German, the impossibility of writing differently. You could add," he concluded, "a fourth impossibility, the impossibility of writing."

The impossibility of writing *German*? Kafka's German—his mother tongue—is spare, somber, comic, lucid, pure; formal without being stilted. It has the almost platonic purity of a language unintruded on by fads or slang or the street, geographically distanced from the tumultuous bruisings of the mean vernacular. The Hebrew poetry written by the Jews of medieval Spain was similarly immaculate; its capital city was not Córdoba or Granada but the Bible. In the same way Kafka's linguistic capital was not German-speaking Prague on the margins of empire, but European literature itself. Language was the engine and chief motive of his life: hence "the impossibility of not writing." "I've often thought," he ruminated to Felice Bauer, "that the best way of life for me would be to have writing materials and a lamp in the innermost room of a spacious locked cellar." When he spoke of the impossibility of writing German, he never meant that he was not master of the language; his wish was to be consecrated to it, like a monk with his beads. His fear was that he was not entitled to German—not that the language did not belong to him, but that he did not belong to it. German was both hospitable and inhospitable. He did not feel innocently—uncomplicatedly, unself-consciously—German. Put it that Kafka wrote German with the passion of an ingenious yet stealthy translator, always aware of the space, however minute, between his fear, or call it his idea of himself, and the deep ease of at-homeness that is every language's consolation. *Mutter*, the German word for "mother," was, he said, alien to him: so much for the taken-for-granted intimacy and trust of *die Muttersprache*, the mother tongue. This crevice of separation, no thicker than a hair, may underlie the estrangement and enfeebling distortions that shock and ultimately disorient every reader of Kafka.

But if there is, in fact, a crevice—or a crisis—of separation between the psyche and its articulation in Kafka himself, what of the crevice that opens between Kafka and his translators? If Kafka deemed it impossible to be Kafka, what chance can a translator have to snare a mind so elusive that it escapes even the comprehension of its own sensibility? "I really am like rock, like my own tombstone," Kafka mourned. He believed himself to be "apathetic, witless, fearful," and also "servile, sly, irrelevant, unsympathetic, untrue . . . from some ultimate diseased tendency." He vowed that "every day at least one line shall be directed against myself." "I am constantly trying to communicate something incommunicable, to explain something inexplicable," he wrote. "Basically it is nothing other than . . . fear spread to everything, fear of the greatest as of the smallest, paralyzing fear of pronouncing a word, although this fear may not only be fear but also a longing for something that is greater than any fear." A panic so intuitional suggests—forces on us—still another Kafkan impossibility: the impossibility of translating Kafka.

There is also the impossibility of *not* translating Kafka. An unknown Kafka, inaccessible, mute, secret, locked away, may now be unthinkable. But it was once thinkable, and by Kafka himself. At the time of his death the bulk of his writing was still unpublished. His famous directive (famously unheeded) to Max Brod to destroy his manuscripts—they were to be "burned unread"—could not have foreseen their canonization, or the near-canonization of their translators. For almost seventy years, the work of Willa and Edwin Muir, a Scottish couple self-taught in German, has represented Kafka in English; the mystical Kafka we are long familiar with—and whom the Muirs derived from Max Brod—reflects their voice and vision. It was they who gave us *Amerika, The Trial, The Castle,* and nine-tenths of the stories.

And it is because the Muirs toiled to communicate the incommunicable that Kafka, even in English, stands indisputably among the few truly indelible writers of the twentieth century—those writers who have no literary progeny, who are *sui generis* and cannot be echoed or envied.

Yet any translation, however influential, harbors its own dissolution. Literature endures; translation, itself a branch of literature, decays. This is no enigma. The permanence of a work does not insure the permanence of its translation—perhaps because the original remains fixed and unalterable, while the translation must inevitably vary with the changing cultural outlook and idiom of each succeeding generation. Then are the Muirs, in their several redactions, dated? Ought they to be jettisoned? Is their "sound" not ours? Or, more particularly, is their sound, by virtue of not being precisely ours, therefore not sufficiently Kafka's? After all, it is Kafka's sound we want to hear, not the 1930s prose effects of a couple of zealous Britishers.

Notions like these, and also the pressures of renewal and contemporaneity, including a concern for greater accuracy, may account for a pair of fresh English renderings published in 1998: *The Trial*, translated by Breon Mitchell, and *The Castle*, the work of Mark Harman. (Both versions have been brought out by Schocken, an early publisher of Kafka. Formerly a Berlin firm that fled the Nazi regime for Palestine and New York, it is now returned to its origin, so to speak, through its recent purchase by Germany's Bertelsmann.) Harman faults the Muirs for theologizing Kafka's prose beyond what the text can support. Mitchell argues more stringently that "in attempting to create a readable and stylistically refined version" of *The Trial*, the Muirs "consistently overlooked or deliberately varied the repetitions and interconnections that echo so meaningfully in the ear of every attentive reader of the German text." For instance, Mitchell points out, the Muirs shy away from repeating the word "assault" ("*überfallen*"), and choose instead "seize," "grab," "fall upon," "overwhelm," "waylay"—thereby subverting Kafka's brutally intentional refrain. Where Kafka's reiterated blow is powerful and direct, Mitchell claims, theirs is dissipated by variety.

But this is not an argument that can be decided only on the ground of textual faithfulness. The issues that seize, grab, fall upon, waylay, etc., translation are not matters of language in the sense of word-for-word. Nor is translation to be equated with interpretation; the translator has no business sneaking in what amounts to commentary. Ideally, translation is a transparent membrane that will vibrate with the faintest shudder of the original, like a single leaf on an autumnal stem. Translation is autumnal; it comes late, it comes afterward. Especially with Kafka, the role of translation is not to convey "meaning," psychoanalytical or theological, or anything that can be summarized or paraphrased. Against such expectations, Walter Benjamin magisterially notes, Kafka's parables "raise a mighty paw." Translation is transmittal of that which may be made out of language, but is a condition beyond the grasp of language.

The Trial is just such a condition. It is a narration of being and becoming. The title in German, *Der Prozess*, expresses something ongoing, evolving, unfolding, driven on by its own forward movement—a process and a passage. Joseph K., a well-placed bank official, a man of reason, sanity, and logic, is arrested, according to the Muirs, "without having done anything wrong"—or, as Breon Mitchell has it, "without having done anything truly wrong." At first K. feels his innocence with the confidence, and even the arrogance, of self-belief. But through the course of his entanglement with the web of the law, he drifts sporadically from confusion to resignation, from bewilderment in the face of an unnamed accusation to acceptance of an unidentifiable guilt. The legal proceedings that capture K. and draw him into their inescapable vortex are revealed as a series of implacable obstacles presided over by powerless or irrelevant functionaries. With its recondite judges and inscrutable rules, the "trial" is more tribulation than tribunal. Its impartiality is punishing; it tests no evidence; its judgment has no relation to justice. The law ("an unknown system of jurisprudence") is not a law that K. can recognize, and the court's procedures have an Alice-in-Wonderland arbitrariness. A room for flogging miscreants is situated in a closet in K.'s own office; the court holds sessions in the attics of rundown tenements; a painter is an authority on judicial method. Wherever K. turns, advice and indifference come to the same.

"It's not a trial before the normal court," K. informs the out of-town uncle who sends him to a lawyer. The lawyer is bedridden and virtually useless. He makes a point of displaying an earlier client who is as despairing and obsequious as a beaten dog. The lawyer's maidservant, seducing K., warns him, "You can't defend yourself against this court, all you can do is confess." Titorelli, the painter who lives and works in a tiny bedroom that proves to be an adjunct of the court, is surrounded by an importuning chorus of phantomlike but aggressive little girls; they too "belong to the court." The painter lectures K. on the ubiquity and inaccessibility of the court, the system's accumulation of files and its avoidance of proof, the impossibility of acquittal. "A single hangman could replace the entire court," K. protests. "I'm not guilty," he tells a priest in a darkened and empty cathedral. "That's how guilty people always talk," the priest replies, and explains that "the proceedings gradually merge into the judgment." Yet K. still dimly hopes: perhaps the priest will "show him . . . not how to influence the trial, but how to break out of it, how to get around it, how to live outside the trial."

Instead the priest recites a parable: Kafka's famed parable of the door-keeper. Behind a door standing open is the Law; a man from the country asks to be admitted. (In Jewish idiom, which Kafka may be alluding to here, a "man from the country"—*am ha'aretz*—connotes an unrefined sensibility impervious to spiritual learning.) The doorkeeper denies him immediate entrance, and the man waits stoically for years for permission to go in. Finally, dying, still outside the door, he asks why "no one but me has requested admittance." "No one else could gain admittance here," the door-keeper answers, "because this entrance was meant solely for you. I'm going to go and shut it now." Torrents of interpretation have washed over this fable, and over every other riddle embedded in the body of *The Trial*. The priest himself, from within the tale, supplies a commentary on all possible com-mentaries: "The commentator tells us: the correct understanding of a matter and misunderstanding the matter are not mutually exclusive." And adds: "The text is immutable, and the opinions are often only an expression of despair over it." Following which, K. acquiesces in the ineluctable verdict. He is led to a block of stone in a quarry, where he is stabbed, twice, in the heart—after feebly attempting to raise the knife to his own throat.

Kafka's text is by now held to be immutable, despite much posthumous handling. Translations of the work (supposing that all translations are indis-tinguishable from opinions) are often only expressions of despair; understanding and misunderstanding may occur in the same breath. And *The Trial* is, after all, not a finished book. It was begun in 1914, two weeks after the outbreak of the First World War. Kafka recorded this cataclysm in his diary, in a tone of flat dismissal: "2 August. Germany has declared war on Russia—Swimming in the afternoon," and on August 21 he wrote, "I start 'The Trial' again." He picked it up and left it off repeatedly that year and the next. Substantial fragments—unincorporated scenes—were set aside, and it was Max Brod who, after Kafka's death, determined the order of the chapters and appended the allegorical reflections which so strongly influenced the Muirs. Discussion continues about the looseness of Kafka's punctuation—commas freely and unconventionally scattered. (The Muirs, following Brod, regulate the liberties taken in the original.) Kafka's translators, then, are confronted with textual decisions large and small that were never Kafka's. To these they add their own.

The Muirs aim for a dignified prose, unruffled by any obvious idio-syncrasy; their cadences lean toward a formality tinctured by a certain soulfulness. Breon Mitchell's intent is radically other. To illustrate, let me try a small experiment in contrast and linguistic ambition. In the novel's penultimate paragraph, as K. is brought to the place of his execution, he sees a window in a nearby building fly open, and a pair of arms reach out. The Muirs translate: "Who was it? A friend? A good man? Someone who sympathized? Someone who wanted to help? Was it one person only? Or was it mankind? Was help at hand?" The same simple phrases in Mitchell's rendering have a different timbre, even when some of the words are identical: "Who was it? A friend? A good person? Someone who cared? Someone who wanted to help? Was it just one person? Was it everyone? Was there still help?" The Muirs' "Was help at hand?" has a Dickensian flavor: a touch of nineteenth-century purple. And "mankind" is not what Kafka wrote (he wrote "*alle*," everyone), though it may be what he meant; in any case it is what the Muirs, who look to symbolism, distinctly do mean. To our contemporary ears, "Was it one person only?"—with "only" placed after the noun—is vaguely stilted. And surely some would find "a good man" (for "*ein guter Mensch*," where "*Mensch*" signifies the essential human being) sexist and ideologically wanting. What we hear in the Muirs' language, overall, is something like the voice of Somerset Maugham: British, cultivated, cautiously genteel even in extremis; middlebrow.

Breon Mitchell arrives to sweep all that Muirish dustiness away, and to refresh Kafka's legacy by giving us a handier Kafka in a vocabulary close to our own—an American Kafka, in short. He has the advantage of working with a restored and more scholarly text, which edits out many of Brod's interferences. Yet even in so minuscule a passage as the one under scrutiny, a telltale syllable, therapeutically up-to-date, jumps out: Americans may be sympathetic ("*teilnahm*"), but mainly they care. Other current Americanisms intrude: "you'd better believe it" (the Muirs say tamely, "you can believe that"); "without letting myself be thrown by the fact that Anna didn't appear" (the Muirs: "without troubling my head about Anna's absence"); "I'm so tired I'm about to drop"; "you'd have to be a serious criminal to have a commission of inquiry come down on you"; "You're not mad at me, are you?"; "fed up"; and so forth. There is even a talk-show "more importantly." Mitchell's verb contractions ("isn't," "didn't") blanket Kafka's grave exchanges with a mist of Seinfeld dialogue. If the Muirs sometimes write like sticks, Mitchell now and then writes shtick. In both versions, the force of the original claws its way through, despite the foreign gentility of the one and the colloquial unbuttonedness of the other. Unleashed by Kafka's indefinable genius, unreason-thwarting-reason slouches into view under a carapace of ill-fitting English.

Of the hundred theories of translation, some lyrical, some stultifyingly academic, others philologically abstruse, the speculations of three extraordinary literary figures stand out: Nabokov, Ortega y Gasset, and Walter Benjamin. Nabokov, speaking of Pushkin, demands "translations with copious footnotes, footnotes reaching up like skyscrapers . . . I want such footnotes and the absolutely literal sense." This, of course, is pugnaciously anti-literary—Nabokov's curmudgeonly warning against the "drudge" who substitutes "easy platitudes for the breathtaking intricacies of the text." It is, besides, a statement of denial and disbelief: no translation is ever going to work, so please don't try. Ortega's milder disbelief is finally tempered by aspiration. "Translation is not a duplicate of the original text," he begins; "it is not—it shouldn't try to be—the work itself with a different vocabulary." And he concludes, "The simple fact is that the translation is not the work, but a path toward the work"—which suggests at least the possibility of arrival.

Benjamin withdraws altogether from these views. He will believe in the efficacy of translation as long as it is not of this earth, and only if the actual act of translation—by human hands—cannot be accomplished. A German Jew, a contemporary of Kafka, a Hitler refugee, a suicide, he is eerily close to Kafka in mind and sensibility; on occasion he expresses characteristically Kafkan ideas. In his remarkable 1923 essay, "The Task of the Translator," he imagines a high court of language that has something in common with the invisible hierarchy of judges in *The Trial*. "The translatability of linguistic creations," he affirms, "ought to be considered even if men should prove unable to translate them." Here is Platonism incarnate: the non-existent ideal is perfect; whatever is attempted in the world of reality is an imperfect copy, falls short, and is useless. Translation, according to Benjamin, is debased when it delivers information, or enhances knowledge, or offers itself as a trot, or as a version of Cliffs Notes, or as a help to understanding, or as any other kind of convenience. "Translation must in large measure refrain from wanting to communicate something, from rendering the sense," he maintains. Comprehension, elucidation, the plain import of the work—all that is the goal of the inept: "Meaning is served far better—and literature and language far worse—by the unrestrained license of bad translators."

What is Benjamin talking about? If the object of translation is not meaning, what is it? Kafka's formulation for literature is Benjamin's for translation: the intent to communicate the incommunicable, to explain the inexplicable. "To some degree," Benjamin continues, "all great texts contain their potential translation between the lines; this is true to the highest degree of sacred writings." And yet another time: "In all language and linguistic creations there remains in addition to what can be conveyed something that cannot be communicated . . . that very nucleus of pure language." Then woe to the carpentry work of real translators facing real texts! Benjamin is scrupulous and difficult, and his intimations of ideal translation cannot easily be paraphrased: they are, in brief, a longing for transcendence, a wish equivalent to the wish that the translators of the Psalmist in the King James version, say, might come again, and in our own generation. (But would they be fit for Kafka?)

Benjamin is indifferent to the exigencies of carpentry and craft. What he is insisting on is what Kafka understood by the impossibility of writing German: the unbridgeable fissure between words and the spells they cast. Always for Kafka, behind meaning there shivers an intractable darkness, or (rarely) an impenetrable radiance. And the task of the translator, as Benjamin intuits it, is not within the reach of the conscientious if old-fashioned Muirs, or the highly readable Breon Mitchell, whose *Trial* is a page-turner (and whose glistening contemporaneity may cause his work to fade faster than theirs). Both the superseded Muirs and the eminently useful Mitchell convey information, meaning, complexity, "atmosphere." How can one ask for more, and, given the unparalleled necessity of reading Kafka in English, what, practically, is "more"? Our debt to the translators we have is unfathomable. But a look into Kafka's simplest sentences—*"Wer war es? Ein Freund? Ein guter Mensch? . . . Waren es alle?"*—points to Benjamin's nearly liturgical plea for "that very nucleus of pure language" which Kafka called the impossibility of writing German; and which signals also, despairingly, the impossibility of translating Kafka.

Transcending the Kafkaesque

How, after all, does one dare, how can one presume? Franz Kafka, named for the fallen crown of a defunct empire, has himself metamorphosed into an empire of boundless discourse, an empire stretched out across a firmament of interpretation: myth, parable, allegory, clairvoyance, divination; theory upon thesis upon theophany; every conceivable incarnation of the sexual, the political, the psychological, the metaphysical. Another study of the life? Another particle in the deep void of a proliferating cosmos. How, then, does one dare to add so much as a single syllable, even in the secondary exhalation of a biography?

One dares because of the culprits. The culprits are two. One is "Kafkaesque," which buries the work. The other is "transcend," which buries the life. A scrupulous and capacious biography may own the power to drive away these belittlements, and Reiner Stach's mammoth three volumes (only the second and third have appeared in English so far) are superbly tempered for exorcism. With its echo of "grotesque," the ubiquitous term "Kafkaesque" has long been frozen into permanence, both in the dictionary and in the most commonplace vernacular. Comparative and allusive, it has by now escaped the body of work it is meant to evoke. To say that such and such a circumstance is Kafkaesque is to admit to the denigration of an imagination that has burned a hole in what we take to be modernism—even in what we take to be the ordinary fabric and intent of language. Nothing is "like" "The Hunger Artist." Nothing is "like" "The Metamorphosis." Whoever utters "Kafkaesque" has neither fathomed nor intuited nor felt the impress of Kafka's devisings. If there is one imperative that ought to accompany any biographical or critical approach, it is that Kafka is not to be mistaken for the Kafkaesque. The Kafkaesque is what Kafka presumably "stands for"—an unearned and usurping explication. And from the very start, serious criticism has been overrun by the Kafkaesque, the lock that portends the key: homoeroticism for one maven, the father-son entanglement for another, the theological uncanny for yet another. Or else it is the slippery commotion of time; or of messianism; or of Thanatos as deliverance. The Kafkaesque, finally, is reductiveness posing as revelation.

The persistence of "transcend" is still more troublesome. What is it that Kafka is said to transcend? Every actual and factual aspect of the life he lived, everything that formed and informed him, that drew or repelled him, the time and the place, the family and the apartment and the office—and Prague itself, with its two languages and three populations fixed at the margins of a ruling sovereignty sprawled across disparate and conflicting nationalities. Kafka's fictions, free grains of being, seem to float, untethered and self-contained, above the heavy explicitness of a recognizable society and culture. And so a new and risen Kafka is born, cleansed of origins, unchained from the tensions, many of them nasty, of Prague's roiling German-Czech-Jewish brew, its ambient anti-Semitism and its utopian Zionism, its Jewish clubs and its literary stewpot of Max Brod, Oskar Baum, Franz Werfel, Otto Pick, Felix Weltsch, Hugo Bergmann, Ernst Weiss. In this understanding, Kafka is detached not from the claims of specificity—what is more strikingly particularized than a Kafka tale?—but from a certain designated specificity.

In an otherwise seamless introduction to Kafka's *Collected Stories,* John Updike takes up the theme of transcendence with particular bluntness: "Kafka, however unmistakable the ethnic source of his 'liveliness' and alienation, avoided Jewish parochialism, and his allegories of pained awareness take upon themselves the entire European—that is to say, predominantly Christian—malaise." As evidence, he notes that the Samsas in "The Metamorphosis" make the sign of the cross. Nothing could be more wrong-headed than this parched Protestant misapprehension of Mitteleuropa's tormented Jewish psyche. (Danilo Kiš, Isaac Babel, Elias Canetti, Walter Benjamin, Gershom Scholem, Stefan Zweig, Josef Roth: from these wounded ghosts, a chorus of knowing laughter.) The idea of the parochial compels its opposite: what is not parochial must be universal. And if the parochial is deemed a low distraction from the preponderant social force—"that is to say, predominantly Christian"—then what is at work is no more than supercilious triumphalism. To belittle as parochial the cultural surround ("the ethnic source") that bred Kafka is to diminish and disfigure the man—to do to him what so many of Kafka's stories do to their hapless protagonists.

As biographer, Reiner Stach will have none of this. Nowhere in *The Decisive Years* nor in *The Years of Insight* does he impose on Kafka an all-encompassing formula. He offers no key, no code, no single-minded interpretive precept: the Kafkaesque is mercifully missing. Instead, he allows

Kafka's searing introspections, as they emerge from the letters and diaries, to serve as self-defining clues. Kafka saw his stories not as a reader or critic will, but *from the inside,* as the visceral sensations of *writing.* "I am made of literature; I am nothing else and cannot be anything else," he announced to Felice Bauer, the woman he would never marry. It was a statement meant not so much metaphorically as bodily. At twenty-nine, on September 23, 1912, he exulted in his diary as an exhausted but victorious long-distance swimmer, on completing a marathon, might:

> The story, "The Judgment," I wrote during the night of the 22nd, from 10 P.M. to 6 A.M., in one sitting. I could hardly pull my legs out from under the desk; they had become stiff from sitting. The frightful exertion and pleasure of experiencing how the story developed right in front of me, as though I were moving forward through a stretch of water. Several times during the night I lugged my own weight on my back. How everything can be hazarded, how for everything, even for the strangest idea, a great fire is ready in which it expires and rises up again . . . At 2 A.M. I looked at the clock for the last time. As the maid came through the front room in the morning, I was writing the last sentence. Turning off the lamp, the light of day. The slight pains in my chest. The exhaustion that faded away in the middle of the night . . . Only in this way can writing be done, only in a context like this, with a complete opening of body and soul.

Stach will go no further than Kafka's own reflections and admissions. In this restraint he follows Kafka himself: on no account, he instructed the publisher of "The Metamorphosis," should the insect be pictured. He saw explication as intrusion, and willful interpretation as a false carapace. A premonitory authorial warning: he was already warding off the Kafkaesque.

In refusing the critic's temptation, Stach is freed as biographer. Open to him is the limitless web of the societal, the political, the historical, the customary, the trivial; everything material, explicit, contemporaneous—sometimes day by day, on occasion even hour by hour; the trains and the telephones; the offices and the office machines; the bureaucrats and their litigations; the apartment and the family's noises. In brief: the parochial, in all its dense particularity. The biographer excavates, he does not transcend, and through this robustly determined unearthing he rescues Kafka from the unearthliness of his repute.

Foremost is the question of language. In Prague, Czechs spoke Czech, Germans spoke German, Jews spoke German. Kafka's ruminations on his relation to the language he was born into are by now as familiar (or as over-familiar) as his face in the photographs, and equally revealing of shrouded pain. Jews who wrote in German, he lamented, resembled trapped beasts, neither at home in their native idiom nor alien to it. They lived, moreover, with three impossibilities: "the impossibility of not writing, the impossibility of writing German, the impossibility of writing differently." To which he added a fourth, "the impossibility of writing."

Kafka's prose has been universally lauded as spare, somber, comic, lucent, almost platonically pure; but many of those who acclaim it are compelled to read through the art of the translator. Shelley Frisch, Stach's heroic American translator, movingly reproduces his intended breadth and pace and tone, though now and again she is tempted to transmute the biographer's turns of phrase into popular local catchwords ("tickled pink," "thrown for a loop," "let off steam," "went to temple," "right off the bat," and many more). This is not altogether a failing, since it is Stach, not Kafka, whom these displaced Americanisms represent; but at the same time they serve to remind us that the biographer, whose *Muttersprache* is German, comes to Kafka's idiom with the deep linguistic affinities that only a native German, one who is also a literary writer, can assert. It is with such felt authority that Stach looks back at Kafka's writing—not to say how and what it is, but rather how and what it is not: "There were no empty phrases, no semantic impurities, no weak metaphors—even when he lay in the sand and wrote postcards." Yet there is another side to Stach's closeness to Kafka's rhetoric. When Kafka declared the impossibility of writing German, it was plainly not the overriding mastery of his language that was in doubt, but its ownership—not that German did not belong to him, but that he did not belong to it. German was unassailably at the root of his tongue; might he claim it societally, nationally, as a natural inheritance, as an innate entitlement? The culture that touched him at all points had a prevailing Jewish coloration. Family traditions, however casually observed, were in the air he breathed, no matter how removed he was from their expression. His most intimate literary friendships consisted entirely of writers of similar background; at least two, Max Brod and Hugo Bergmann, were seriously committed to Zionism. He studied Hebrew, earnestly if fitfully, at various periods of his life, and he attended Martin Buber's lectures on Zionism at the meetings of Bar Kochba, the Association of Jewish University Students. Unlike the disdainful Jewish burghers of Prague, who had long ago shed what they dismissed as an inferior *zhargón,* he was drawn to a troupe of Yiddish-speaking players from Poland and their lively but somewhat makeshift theater. He was a warm proponent of the work of Berlin's Jewish Home, which looked after the welfare and education of impoverished young immigrants from Eastern Europe. He read Heinrich Graetz's massive *History of the Jews;* he read *Der Jude,* the monthly founded by Buber; he read *Die Jüdische Rundschau,* a Zionist weekly; he read *Selbstwahr,* yet another Zionist periodical, whose editor and all of its contributors he knew. He also read *Die Fackel,* Karl Kraus's scourging satiric journal.

If Kafka's profoundest conviction ("I am made of literature") kept its distance from these preoccupations and influences, he nevertheless felt their pressure in the way of an enveloping skin. His commanding conundrums, including the two opposing impossibilities—writing and not-writing—are almost suffocatingly knotted into Jewish insecurities. Zionism was one symptom of this powerful unease; and so was Kraus's repudiation of Zionism, and his furious advocacy of radically self-obscuring assimilation.

It is difficult to refrain from pondering how a biographer (and a biographer is inevitably also a historian) will confront these extremes of cultural tension. Every biography is, after all, a kind of autobiography: it reveals predispositions, parallels, hidden needs; or possibly an unacknowledged wish to take on the subject's persona, to become his secret sharer. The biographer's choice of subject is a confession of more than interest or attunement. The desire to live alongside another life, year by year, thought for thought, is what we mean by possession. And for Stach to be close, both as a given and as a fortuity, to Kafka's language can hardly reflect the full scope of his willed immersion. He must also come close to Jewish foreboding—a foreboding marinated in the political and tribal and linguistic complexities of Austria-Hungary at the turbulent crux of its demise. Much of Kafka's fiction—*The Trial, The Castle,* "In the Penal Colony"—has too often made of him a prognosticator, as if he could intuit, through some uncanny telescope, the depredations that were soon to blacken Europe in the middle of the twentieth century. But the times required no clairvoyance; Jewish disquiet was an immediacy. At fourteen, Kafka witnessed anti-Semitic rioting that had begun as an anti-German protest against the Habsburg government's denial of Czech language rights. At thirty-seven, three years before his death, and with *The Castle* still unwritten, he saw Prague's historic Altneu synagogue attacked and its Torah scrolls torched. "I've been spending every afternoon outside on the streets, wallowing in anti-Semitism," he recounted. "The other day I heard the Jews called *Prasivé plenemo* [mangy brood]. Isn't it natural to leave a place where one is so hated? . . . The heroism of staying on nevertheless is the heroism of cockroaches that cannot be exterminated even from the bathroom."

Post-Holocaust, all this must sting a susceptible German ear; note that Zyklon B, the genocidal gas of the extermination camps, was originally used as an insecticide. Yet there are reminders still more unsettling. Because a biography of Kafka will perforce include minor characters—his sisters Elli, Valli, and Ottla, for instance—it must finally arrive at Kafka's afterlife, the destiny he did not live long enough to suffer: that zone of ultimate impossibility wherein all other impossibilities became one with the impossibility of staying alive. Between 1941 and 1943, all three sisters perished, Elli and Valli in Chelmno, Ottla in Auschwitz. They hover over Kafka's biographies—this one, and all the rest—like torn and damaged Fates. Stach is never unaware of these points of connection; at first, uninvited, *sotto voce,* behind the scenes, in quiet recognition, they pierce the weave of his narrative. But by the time he attains his coda, Stach's watchful voicing of the fraught history of the Jews of central Europe during the passage of Kafka's life will have risen to a thunder.

And while a biographer may be willy-nilly a historian, and subliminally an autobiographer, he is, even more so, a species of novelist—of the nineteenth-century, loose-baggy-monster variety. He is in pursuit of the whole trajectory of a life, beginning, middle, end: chronology is king, post-modern fragmentation unwelcome, landscapes lavish, rooms and furnishings the same, nothing goes unnoticed. The biographer is a simulacrum, say, of George Eliot, who places her characters against the background of a society rendered both minutely and expansively, attending to ancestry, religion, economic standing, farming, banking, business, reading, travel, and more. Stach, in this vein, is doubtless the first to give so plentiful an account of the activities of the Prague Workers' Accident Insurance Company, the government agency where Kafka was employed as a lawyer from 1908 until 1918, when advancing tuberculosis forced his retirement. That he divided his day into office and work—by declaring them antithetical—is itself a type of credo; but Kafka's exalted literary image has too readily obscured the press of the quotidian. What did Kafka *do,* what were his everyday responsibilities? Stach lifts the dry-as-dust veil:

> If an industrialist submitted an appeal, the office had to establish proof that the safety precautions of the firm in question were not up to the latest standards. But what were the latest standards? They could not be definitively stipulated with ordinances; they had to be continually re-established, if possible by personal observation. Kafka, who already had legal expertise, quickly acquired the technical know-how; he attended courses and traveled through northern Bohemian industrial cities. Next to the swaying stacks of appeals on his huge office desk there was an

array of journals on accident prevention . . . in the areas in which he specialized—particularly the woodworking industry and quarries.

And so on and so on. An annual report, ostensibly submitted by Kafka, is titled "Accident Prevention Rules for Wood Planing Machines," and recommends the use of a cylindrical spindle. It is accompanied by illustrations of mutilated hands. In the wake of World War I, with its tens of thousands of maimed and shell-shocked soldiers, he was to see far worse.

For Kafka, none of these lawyerly obligations, however demanding, counted as work. No matter that his acumen and skills were regularly rewarded with promotion by the pair of bookish and obliging men who were his superiors, and though he was deemed so valuable that they contrived to have him exempted from military service, he felt depleted, and even assaulted, by the very papers his own hand produced. Of this necessarily official language he wrote bitterly, "I am still holding all of it in my mouth with revulsion and a feeling of shame, as though it were raw flesh cut out of me (that is how much effort it cost me) . . . everything in me is ready for lyrical work, and a work of that kind would be a heavenly resolution and a real coming alive for me, while here, in the office, because of such a wretched document I have to tear from a body capable of such happiness a piece of its flesh." And again, with the emphasis of despair: *"Real hell is there in the office; I no longer fear any other."* And yet another tightening of the vise: "For me it is a horrible double life from which there is probably no way out except insanity."

At two o'clock in the afternoon, at the close of the six tormenting hours in the office, he escaped to the family apartment, a noisy and crowded habitat that was less a refuge than a second entrapment. Seven persons occupied these cramped and untranquil rooms: the blustering bullying paterfamilias, the compliant mother, the three daughters, the discontented son yearning for privacy and quiet, and a live-in maid. Kafka's bedroom, the burning vortex of his nocturnal writing, lay between the parlor and his parents' room; it was a passageway for his father's comings and goings, early and late, trailing his bathrobe. And the apartment, like the office, had its own distinct raison d'être: it was the ground, the support, and the indispensable source of administrative personnel for the family shop, a successful fancy-goods emporium with numerous employees. Since both parents put in many hours there, and all family members were obliged to do the same, in this way the shop fed the apartment, and the apartment fed the shop. Hermann Kafka, the son of a *shochet*—a ritual butcher—had risen from a burdened childhood in a backward rural village to bourgeois respectability, and was impatient with any deviation from conventional expectations. Ottla, the youngest daughter, was attracted to the countryside and aspired to farming—a far cry from her duties in the shop. Franz was still another riddle. At the dinner table he confined himself to an ascetic diet of mainly fruits and nuts, masticating each mouthful thirty-two times, according to the nutritional tenets of Fletcherism. But his most controversial habit was sleeping in the afternoon after leaving the office: this was to secure a usable wakefulness for the sake of his work—his true work—in the apartment's welcome middle-of-the-night silence. Sleeping in the afternoon, during shop hours? To the business-minded father, this was incomprehensible; it was delinquent.

Kafka's delinquency became still more scandalous when he was recruited to take on the ownership and management of an asbestos factory, in partnership with the ambitious husband of his newly married sister Elli. Hermann Kafka approved of his son-in-law's entrepreneurial plans, but since family money was being dedicated to this enterprise, and the young man was an untried stranger, it was imperative that a blood relation contribute to the stability and probity of the business. At first Kafka attempted to fulfill a commitment he had never sought—the literature-besotted son as industrialist!—and grudgingly gave his afternoons to the factory, which meant sacrificing his nights. Despite his father's irritable proddings, he could not keep up even a pretense of interest (he was at this time far more absorbed in the precarious fortunes of the Yiddish players he had befriended), and at length the business failed. The record Kafka left of it is oblivious to product and profit-and-loss; and though conceivably he might have appraised the factory and its perilously superannuated machines through the eyes of the workers' accident official, it was instead the fevered midnight writer who observed "the girls in their absolutely unbearably dirty and untailored clothing, their hair unkempt, as though they had just got out of bed, their facial expressions set by the incessant noise of the transmission belts and by the separate machine that is automatic but unpredictable, stopping and starting. The girls," he went on,

are not people—you don't say hello to them, you don't apologize for bumping into them; when you call them over to do something, they do it but go right back to the machine; with a nod of the head you show them what to do; they stand there in petticoats; they are at the mercy of the pettiest power . . . When six o'clock comes, however, and they call it out to one another, they untie their kerchiefs from around their necks and hair, dust themselves off with a brush that is passed around the room and is demanded by the ones that are impatient, they pull their skirts over their heads and wash their hands as well as they can,

they are women, after all; . . . you can no longer bump into them, stare
at them, or ignore them; . . . and you do not know how to react when
one of them holds your winter coat for you to put on.

The kerchiefs, the skirts, the brush, the washing, the coat: Walter Benjamin, in his discriminating musings on Kafka, concludes that "the gesture remains the decisive thing." "Each gesture," he writes, "is an event—one might even say, a drama—in itself." And it is the factory girl's simple act of helping with a coat that has the power to embarrass, perhaps even to shame, the owner.

This drama of the minutely mundane was what Kafka demanded of Felice Bauer; it was an inquisition of the humdrum, a third degree of her every movement and choice. He wanted a description of her blouse, her room, her reading, her sleeping; what her employment entailed; how she was occupied when at leisure (she liked to go dancing, she practiced gymnastics). He wanted to claim and envelop her altogether. He repeatedly asked for her photograph, and he repeatedly sent his own. When in their accelerating daily—sometimes hourly—correspondence she abandoned the formal *Sie* and addressed him familiarly as *Du,* he fell into a trance of happiness.

Felice, a distant relation of Max Brod's visiting from Berlin, was introduced to Kafka at the Brod family dinner table. It was, apart from Brod's parents, a meeting of young people. Felice was twenty-five, Max twenty-eight, Kafka twenty-nine. Stach announces this unwittingly portentous occasion with a trumpet blast: "The history of human events, like intellectual and literary history, highlights certain dates; these are engraved in the cultural formation of future generations . . . The evening of August 13, 1912 . . . changed the face of German language literature, of world literature." These grand phrases might have been applied to the somewhat more modest purpose of Kafka's presence that night: he and Brod had planned to look over a collection of sketches that Brod had long been urging his reluctant friend to agree to publish. The final decision about the order of the pieces was consummated in a colloquy after dinner, and what was to become Kafka's earliest publication, *Meditation,* was at last ready to be sent off. From the point of view of Kafka's biographers, though, what changed the face of world literature was not this small book by a little-known writer too perfectionist to release his work without lacerating self-doubt; it was the face of Felice Bauer. If not for the blizzard of revelatory letters that swept over her, enraptured and entreating to begin with, and then dismissive and retreating, Kafka's ponderings and sufferings during five crucially introspective years would have remained a vacuum: cries unheard, crises unrecorded.

Hers was a wholly ordinary face. Kafka, sitting across from the young woman from Berlin, at first mistook her for the maid. "Bony empty face," he later wrote, looking back at his initial impression, "displaying its emptiness openly. A bare throat. Her blouse tossed on . . . A nose almost broken. Blond, somewhat stiff, unappealing hair, and a strong chin." He did not note the two black moles that are prominent in one of her photos, though absent in others, or, in nearly all of these, the bad teeth masked by closed lips. He learned that she worked for Parlograph, a firm selling dictation machines, having risen from typist to managerial status, and often traveling to trade fairs as company representative. If her looks and dress failed to attract him, her independence, reflected in her conversation, did. That she frequently read through the night impressed him. When she mentioned that she was studying Hebrew, he was captivated, and before the evening was over, the two of them were planning a journey to Palestine together—after which Kafka did not set eyes on her again for the next seven months. When he began to write to her, it was as a smitten and instantly possessive lover.

The Felice of Kafka's tumultuous letters was an imagined—a wished-for—figure. The actual Felice was an intelligent, practical, reasonable, efficient, problem-solving, generous woman who very soon recognized that she had been singled out by an uncommon rapture stirred by an uncommon nature. She was more than willing to respond, but every accommodating attempt resulted in a setback. He complained that she was not open enough; yet according to the standards and constraints of the proper middle-class background that defined her, how could she be? Her father was living apart from his family, her unmarried sister was suddenly pregnant, her brother had to be shipped off to America to escape reckless money entanglements. When these secret shames were finally disclosed, they were scarcely what put off Kafka; her habit of silence would bring him a deeper dismay. He had sent her an inscribed copy of *Meditation,* and though he appealed to her, piteously, for a comment ("Dearest, look, I want to have the feeling that you turn to me with everything; nothing, not the slightest thing should be left unsaid"), she never replied. Perhaps she could not: what was she to make of writing so enigmatic? She went to the theater, she read Ibsen; still, what was she to make of, say, "Trees," a story, if that is what it was, of four perplexing sentences? How was she to fathom such a thing?

For we are like tree trunks in the snow. In appearance they lie sleekly and a little push should be enough to set them rolling. No, it can't be done, but they are firmly wedded to the ground. But see, even that is only appearance.

His passionate explanation—"I am made of literature and nothing else"—led to misunderstanding. Pragmatist that she was, she counseled moderation. And worse yet: it led to what she took to be understanding—she had begun to sense in him "seeds of greatness." And with all the sympathetic warmth of wishing to please him, she stumbled into a critical misjudgment (she offered to be close to him while he wrote) and lost him altogether. His shock at this innocent proposal turned into vehement resentment, bordering even on revulsion, as if she were intending to fleece him of his survival as a writer; and shock, resentment, revulsion culminated in one of his most wrenchingly monastic images of artistic self-entombment:

> Once you wrote that you wanted to sit by my side as I write; just keep in mind that I cannot write like that (even so I cannot write much), but in that case I would not be able to write at all. Writing means revealing oneself to excess, the utmost candor and surrender, in which a person would feel he is losing himself in his interaction with other people and from which he will always shy away as long as he hasn't taken leave of his senses—because everyone wants to live as long as he is alive . . . Anything that writing adopts from the surface of existence . . . is nothing, and caves in on itself at the moment that a truer feeling rattles this upper ground. That is why one cannot be alone enough when one is writing; that is why it cannot be quiet enough around one; the night is not night enough . . . I have often thought that the best kind of life for me would be to stay in the innermost room of an extended locked cellar with my writing materials and a lamp . . . What I would write! From what depths I would draw it up!

Here he was assuring the woman who trusted she would soon become his wife that the prospect of her coming near would threaten his capacity to live, and that rather than have her sit beside him, he would prefer to be immured underground. This ruthless detachment continued through two painful official engagements (the later embroiling him in the off-putting ritual of choosing the marital furniture and the conjugal apartment), until he had depleted Felice down to the very lees of her usable sustenance.

In the vista of Kafka's life, Felice is a promontory, partly because she occupied so large a tract of it, but also because of a simple bibliographical datum: she kept his letters. (He did not preserve hers.) She kept them through her marriage, and through her emigration to America in 1936, when escape from Nazi Germany became imperative, until her unremarked death in 1960 in a New York suburb. Beyond—or below—the promontory are the foothills, lesser outcroppings that reflect the configuration of the greater. Or put it that the letters to Felice expose the template, the very genome, of Kafka's character as it has revealed itself to biographers, and to Stach in particular; and by now they are seen to be *literature* as much as the canonical work itself. They underlie a binding continuum: from the diaries to the letters to Felice to the letters to Milena Jesenská to the letters to Max Brod to the prodigious one-hundred-page letter to Kafka's father—and even to a single sketch, ink on paper, drawn by Kafka. A stark black stick figure, stick elbows bent, stick legs outstretched among stick legs of table and chair, all of it spider-like. The spider's body—a human head—rests on the table. It is an image of defeat, surrender, despair, submission.

Milena Jesenská came to Kafka as a translator; in every way she was what Felice was not. Her eyes were as pale as Felice's, but rounder, and her nose was round, and her chin, and her mouth. Felice was a conformist: the furniture must be heavy and ornate, signaling a settled and prosperous marriage. Milena was a rebel, and to earn money in a lean time she was not above carrying luggage for travelers in the Vienna train station. She was a nimble writer and an ardent if contrarian spirit: "a living fire," as Kafka described her to Brod. Her mother was long dead, and her father, an eminent professor of dentistry, recognizing her exceptional gifts, sent her to an elite high school for Czech girls, where the classics and modern languages were taught and the arts were encouraged and cultivated. She and a handful of like-minded classmates made it a habit to loiter in Prague's literary cafés, where she encountered Ernst Pollak, ten years her senior, whom she eventually married. From her father's standpoint it was an insurrectionist act that estranged him from his daughter. The professor was a Czech nationalist, hostile to Germans, and especially averse to their Prague subdivision, German-identified Jews. After futilely confining Milena in a mental institution for some months, he dispatched her and the social embarrassment of her Jewish husband to Vienna—where, in a period of serious postwar scarcity, food was even harder to come by than in Prague. Only yesterday the capital of an empire, Vienna was now a weakened and impoverished outlier, despite its lively literary scene. It turned out to be an uneasy match: Pollak was a persistent philanderer and a dissatisfied writer *manqué,* impressively voluble in bookish circles but stymied on the page. It was he who introduced Milena to Kafka's still sparse publications, which inspired her to render "The Stoker" into Czech—the story that was to become the opening chapter of *The Man Who Disappeared,* his abandoned early novel. Kafka was admiring and gratified ("I find there is constant powerful and decisive understanding," he told her), and their correspondence began, rapidly turning intimate: Kafka's second limitless outpouring of letters to a young woman who kindled his longings and embodied his subterranean desires.

But if Felice had been a fabricated muse, as unresponsively remote from his *idée fixe* as a muse ought not to be, Milena was no muse at all. She provoked and importuned him from a position of equality; she was perceptive and quick and blunt and forward. Almost instantly she startled him: "Are you a Jew?" And though he had rarely spoken to Felice of the disquieting Jewish consciousness that perpetually dogged him (a self-punishing sensitiveness he and Brod had in common), to Milena he unburdened himself with a suicidal bitterness that in one ferocious stroke reviled and mocked the choking anti-Semitism he knew too well:

> I could sooner reproach you for having much too high an opinion of the Jews (me included) . . . at times I'd like to stuff them all, as Jews (me included) into, say, the drawer of the laundry chest, wait, open the drawer a little to see if they've all suffocated, and if not, shut the drawer again, and keep doing this until the end.

She had to put up with this; yet she summoned him, and he came, and in the Vienna woods one afternoon they lived out an idyll, the two of them lying on the forest floor, he with his head on her half-exposed breast. Together they schemed how she might leave Pollak; in the end she could not. He was himself not free; he was at this time engaged to be married to Julie Wohryzek, a young woman whom Hermann Kafka, threatening and berating, disapproved of as déclassée; unlike Felice, she was not suitably respectable. Her father was a penniless cobbler and the *shammes* of a synagogue—worse, she occasionally fell into a low Yiddish phrase, and still worse, she had a "loose" reputation. Kafka had met her at a boardinghouse passing for a tuberculosis sanitorium; like him, she was there to convalesce. When Milena swept in, he disposed of this inflamed but short-lived attachment as no better than a dalliance, to be blown away like a stray straw. A space, then, was cleared for Milena: a landscape wherein the intellectual could be joined to the erotic. She filled it with her certainties and uncertainties, her conviction too often erased by ambivalence. Kafka's uncertainties ran deeper, and his mode of retreat was well practiced: "We are living in misunderstandings; our questions are rendered worthless by our replies. Now we have to stop writing to one another and leave the future to the future." To Brod, Milena sent an epitaph to the marriage that both she and Kafka had evaded. "He always thinks that he himself is the guilty and weak one," she wrote. "And yet there is not another person in the world who has his colossal strength: that absolutely unalterable necessity for perfection, purity, and truth." Milena outlived Kafka by twenty years. In 1944, she was arrested for sheltering Jews and aiding their flight; she perished in Ravensbrück.

Despite three failed engagements, Kafka never married. Yet he was not without such confidential support; there were, in fact, three loyally solicitous persons who took on a wifely role: his sister Ottla, Max Brod, and, at the close of his life, Dora Diamant. Ottla and Kafka had, early on, an obstacle in common—Hermann Kafka and his resistance to their independence. The monstrous (in size and in force) *J'accuse* that the son addressed, though never delivered, to the father now stands as yet another canonical work. Ottla's more quiet eruption came through stubborn acts of autonomy; unlike Kafka, she left behind both the family apartment and her role in the family economy. Hermann Kafka might mock his Czech employees as "my paid enemies," but Ottla chose to marry a Czech. And when the domestic commotion became unsustainable for Kafka's work, she gave him the use of the little neighborhood hideaway she had privately acquired. When his tuberculosis began to advance, and he declined to be admitted to yet another sanitorium (there were many such recuperative sojourns), with wifely devotion she cared for him at the longed-for farm she finally secured in the remote village of Zürau, where Kafka felt uncommonly serene. "I live with Ottla in a good little marriage," he assured Brod.

Brod was Kafka's confidant and champion, first reader, and also first listener: despite reticence and self-denigration, Kafka relished reading his work to friends. It was Brod who pushed Kafka to publish, pursuing skeptical editors on his behalf. "I personally consider Kafka (along with Gerhart Hauptmann and Hamsun) the greatest living writer!" he exclaimed to Martin Buber. "What I wouldn't do to make him more active!" Brod was himself energetic on many fronts: he turned out novels, plays, polemics, political broadsides; he ran to meetings for this cause and that; he labored to bridge the divide between Germans and Czechs; he promoted Czech writers and composers; and with Kafka (though not so diligently) he studied Hebrew. The two friends traveled to Weimar to visit Goethe's house, where each drew a sketch of the house and garden, and Kafka was all at once infatuated with the caretaker's young daughter.

But increasingly, Kafka's excursions away from Prague were solitary journeys to health resorts and tuberculosis sanitoriums; and inexorably in step with these, Stach's later chapters hurtle through harrowing episodes of fever, relentless coughing, days forcibly spent in bed, and finally, when the disease spread to the larynx, the threat of suffocation. Brod, always Kafka's anxious guardian, pressed him from the first to see the proper specialist and under-take the proper treatment. Kafka himself was oddly unperturbed: he believed that a psychosomatic element was the cause, and that, as he wrote to Ottla, "there is undoubtedly justice in this illness." As his condition worsened, he was compelled to give up his position at the Workers' Accident Insurance Company—which, like much of postwar Europe, was undergoing a political transformation. Habsburg officialdom was now replaced by Czech official-dom, in Munich swastikas were flying, and in Prague the decibels of anti-Semitism rang shriller. Hermann Kafka, uneasy in the company of his paid enemies, closed up his shop.

In the summer of 1923, Kafka—already seriously beginning to fail—entered into what can only be called a marriage, even if it had no official sanction and may never have been sexually consummated. It was his most daring personal commitment, and the only one untroubled by vacillation or doubts. Dora Diamant was twenty-five years old, the daughter of a rigidly observant Polish Hasidic family loyal to the dynastic rebbe of Ger. Though Zionism was frowned on as dangerously secular, Dora found her way to the writings of Theodor Herzl, broke from the constrictions of her background, and settled in Berlin. Here she worked with the children of the Jewish Home, the very institution Kafka had been so moved by in the past (and had pressed hard for Felice to support as a volunteer). Berlin was in chaos, reel-ing under strikes, riots, food shortages, and massive inflation. Despite every predictable discomfort and gravely diminishing funds, it was into this mael-strom that Kafka came to join Dora for one of the most tranquil intervals of his life. Half earnestly, half fancifully, they spoke of a future in Palestine, where, to make ends meet, together they would open a little restaurant. But the fevers continued to accelerate, and while Dora nursed him with singular tenderness, it became clear, especially under pressure from the family in Prague, that he was in urgent need of professional care. Another sanitorium followed, and then a hospital specializing in diseases of the larynx, always with Dora hovering protectively near. By now Kafka's suffering had intensi-fied: unable to speak, he communicated on slips of paper; unable to swallow food, he was facing actual starvation, even as he struggled over proofs of "The Hunger Artist." At the last he pleaded for a lethal dose of morphine, warning—Kafka's deliberate paradox of the final paroxysm—that to be deprived of his death would count as murder. With Tolstoyan power, Stach carries us through these sorrowful cadences; the reader is left grieving.

Ottla; Hermann Kafka; Felice; Milena; Dora. They are, ultimately, no more than arresting figures in a biography. When the book is shut, their life-shaping influences evaporate. Not so Max Brod. He became—and remains—a lasting force in Kafka's posthumous destiny. In disobeying his friend's firm request to destroy the existing body of his unpublished manuscripts and to prevent further dissemination of those already in print, Brod assured the survival of the work of an unparalleled literary master. Solely because of this proprietary betrayal, *The Trial, The Castle,* and *Amerika* (Brod's title for *The Man Who Disappeared*) live on; had there been no Brod, there would be no Kafka as we now read him. (And had Brod not fled German-occupied Prague for Tel Aviv in 1939, there would today not be a substantial cache of still unvetted manuscripts preserved in an Israeli national archive. It is from this trove that Stach's yet-to-be-published final volume will be drawn.) Savior though he was, Brod also manipulated whatever came into his hands. He invented titles for what was left untitled. He organized loose chapters into a sequence of his own devising. Having taken on the role of Kafka's authentic representative, he argued for what he believed to be the authoritative interpretation of Kafka's inmost meanings.

Stach ventures no such defining conviction. Instead, he ruminates and speculates, not as a zealously theorizing critic, but as a devoted literary sympathizer who has probed as far as is feasible into the concealments of Kafka's psyche. Often he stops to admit that "we cannot know." In contemplating the work, he tentatively supposes and experientially exposes. He eschews the false empyrean, and will never look to transcend the ground that both moored and unmoored his subject. In this honest and honorable biography there is no trace of the Kafkaesque; but in it you may find a crystal granule of the Kafka that was.

Mrs. Virginia Woolf:
A Madwoman and Her Nurse

No recent biography has been read more thirstily by readers and writers of fiction than Quentin Bell's account of the life of his aunt, Virginia. Reviewing it, Elizabeth Hardwick speaks of "the present exhaustion of Virginia Woolf," and compares the idea of Bloomsbury—it "wearies"—to a pond run out of trout. But for most American writers, bewildered by the instability of what passes for culture and literature, envious of the English sense of place and of being placed, conscious of separations that yet lack the respectability of "schools" or even the interest of alien perspectives, stuck mainly with the crudity of being either For or Against Interpretation, the legend of Bloomsbury still retains its inspiriting powers. Like any Golden Age, it promises a mimetic future: some day again, says Bloomsbury of 1905, there will be friends, there will be conversation, there will be moods, and they will all again *really matter*, and fall naturally, in the way of things that matter, into history.

Part of the special history of the Bloomsbury of mood is pictorial—and this has nothing to do with the art critic Roger Fry, or the painter Duncan Grant. It is not what the painters painted or what the writers wrote about painting that hangs on: it is the photographs, most of them no more official than snapshots, of the side of a house, two people playing checkers on an old kitchen chair set out in the yard, three friends and a baby poking in the sand. The snapshots are all amateur. Goblets of brightness wink on eaves, fences, trees, and wash out faces in their dazzle; eyes are lost in blackened sockets. The hem of a dress is likely to be all clarity, but the heads escape—under hat brims, behind dogs, into mottled leaf-shade. And out of the blur of those hopeless poses, cigarettes, hands on knees, hands over books, anxious little pups held up to the camera, walking sticks, long grotesque nose-shadows, lapels, outdoor chairs and tables, there rises up—no, leaks down—so much tension, so much ambition, so much fake casualness, so much heartbreaking attention to the momentariness of the moment. The

people in the snapshots knew, in a way we do not, who they were. Bloomsbury was self-conscious in a way we are not. It sniffed at its own perceptions,
even its own perceived posterity. Somewhere early in the course of her diaries, Virginia Woolf notes how difficult it would be for a biographer to
understand her—how little biographers can know, she said—only from the
evidence of her journals. Disbelieving in the probity of her own biography,
she did not doubt that she would have her own biographer.

She did not doubt; she knew; they knew. Hatched from the last years of
the reign of Victoria, Bloomsbury was still a world where things—if not
people, then ideas—could be said to reign. Though old authority might be
sneered at (or something worse even than a sneer—Virginia Woolf declared
her certainty that she could not have become a writer had her father lived),
though proprieties might be outrageously altered ("Semen?" asked Lytton
Strachey, noticing a stain on Vanessa Bell's skirt one afternoon), though sex
was accessible and often enough homoerotic, though freedom might be proclaimed on Gordon Square, though livings were earned, there was
nonetheless a spine of authority to support Bloomsbury: family, descent,
class and community—the sense of having-in-common. Bloomsbury, after
all, was an inheritance. Both E. M. Forster's and Virginia Woolf's people
were associated with the liberal and intellectual Clapham Sect of the century before. Cambridge made a kind of cousinship—the staircase at Trinity
that drew together Clive Bell, Saxon Sydney-Turner, and Virginia Woolf's
brother Thoby Stephen was the real beginning of the gatherings at Gordon
Square. Bloomsbury was pacifist and busy with gossip about what it always
called "buggery," but it was not radical and it did not harbor rebels. Rebels
want to make over; the Bloomsburyites reinforced themselves with their like.
The staircase at Trinity went on and on for the rest of their lives, and even
Virginia Woolf, thinking to make over the form of the novel, had to have each
newly completed work ratified by Morgan Forster and sometimes Maynard
Keynes before she could breathe at ease again. The authority of one's closest
familiars is the unmistakable note of Bloomsbury. It was that sure voice she
listened for. "Virginia Woolf was a Miss Stephen," Quentin Bell begins, in
the same voice; it is an opening any outsider could have written, but not in
that sharp cadence. He is not so much biographer as a later member of the
circle—Virginia Woolf's sister's son, the child of Vanessa and Clive Bell. He
knows, he does not doubt. It is the note of self-recognition; of confidence; of
inheritance. Everything is in his grip.

And yet—as she predicted—Virginia Woolf's biographer fails her. He
fails her, in fact, more mournfully than any outsider could. It is his grip that
fails her. This is not only because, sticking mainly to those matters he has

sure authority over, he has chosen to omit a literary discussion of the body of work itself. "I have found the work of the biographer sufficiently difficult without adventuring in other directions," he tells us, so that to speak of Quentin Bell's "sure authority" is not to insinuate that all his data are, perhaps, out of childhood memory or family reminiscence, or that he has not mined library after library, and collection after collection of unpublished papers. He is, after all, of the next generation, and the next generation is always in some fashion an outsider to the one before. But what *is* in his grip is something more precise, curiously, than merely data, which the most impersonal research can reliably throw up: it is that particular intimacy of perspective—of experience, really—which characterizes not family information, but family bias. Every house has its own special odor to the entering guest, however faint—it sticks to the inhabitants, it is in their chairs and in their clothes. The analogy of bias to scent is chiefly in one's unconsciousness of one's own. Bell's Woolf is about Virginia, but it has the smell of Vanessa's house. The Virginia Woolf that comes off these pages is a kind of emanation of a point of view, long settled, by now, into family feeling. Stephens, Patties, Fishers—all the family lines—each has its distinct and legendary scent. The Stephens are bold, the Patties are fair, the Fishers are self-righteous. And Virginia is mad.

She was the family's third case of insanity, all on the Stephen side. Leslie Stephen, Virginia Woolf's celebrated father—a man of letters whose career was marked not least by the circumstance that Henry James cherished him—was married twice, the second time to Julia Duckworth, a widow with children. Together they produced Vanessa and Virginia, Thoby and Adrian. A child of Leslie Stephen's first marriage, the younger of Virginia's two half-sisters, was born defective—it is not clear whether backward or truly insane—and was confined to an asylum, where she died old. Virginia's first cousin—the child of her father's brother—went mad while still a young man, having struck his head in an accident. But one wonders, in the retrograde and rather primitive way one contemplates families, whether there might not have been a Stephen "taint." In a family already accustomed to rumor of aberration, Virginia Woolf, in any case, was incontrovertibly mad. Her madness was distinguished, moreover, by a threatening periodicity: at any moment it could strike, disabling everyone around her. Vanessa had to leave her children and come running, nurses had to be hired, rest homes interviewed, transport accomplished. The disaster was ten times wider than its victim.

And just here is the defect in writing out of family authority. The odor is personal, hence partial. Proust says somewhere that the artist brings to the work his whole self, to his familiars only those aspects that accommodate them. The biographer close to his subject has the same difficulty; the aspect under which Quentin Bell chiefly views his aunt Virginia is not of accommodation but of a still narrower partiality: discommodity, the effect on family perspective of Virginia Woolf's terrible and recurrent insanity. It was no mere melancholia, or poetic mooning—as, reading Leonard Woolf's deliberately truncated edition of her diary, we used to guess. A claustrophilic though inspired (also self-inspiring) document, it made us resent the arbitrary "personal" omissions: was it the madness he was leaving out? Certainly we wanted the madness too, supposing it to be the useful artistic sort: grotesque moods, quirks—epiphanies really. But it was not that; it was the usual thing people get put away for, an insanity characterized by incoherent howling and by violence. She clawed her attendants and had to be restrained; she would not touch food; she was suicidal. Ah, that cutting difference: not that she longed for death, as poets and writers sometimes do for melancholy's sake, but that she wanted, with the immediacy of a method, to be dead.

Bell's Woolf, then, is not about the Virginia Woolf of the diaries, essays, and novels—not, in the Proustian sense, about the writer's whole self. And surely this is not simply because literary criticism is evaded. Bell's Woolf is not about a writer, in fact; it is about the smell of a house. It is about a madwoman and her nurse.

The nurse was Leonard Woolf. Upon him Quentin Bell can impose no family aspects, rumors, characteristics, old experience, inherited style. He does not trail any known house-scent, like Stephens, Patties, Fishers. Though he shared the Cambridge stairs—Thoby Stephen, Saxon Sydney-Turner, Clive Bell, Lytton Strachey, and Leonard Woolf together briefly formed the Midnight Society, a reading club that met on Saturday evenings in Clive Bell's rooms—he was not an inheritor of Cambridge. Cambridge was not natural to him, Bloomsbury was not natural to him, even England was not natural to him—not as an inheritance; he was a Jew. Quentin Bell has no "authority" over Leonard Woolf, as he has over his aunt; Leonard is nowhere in the biographer's grip.

The effect is unexpected. It is as if Virginia Woolf escapes—possessing her too selectively, the biographer lets her slip—but Leonard Woolf somehow stays to become himself. Which is to say, Bell's Virginia Woolf can be augmented by a thousand other sources—chiefly by her own work—but we learn as much about Leonard Woolf here as we are likely to know from any other source. And what we learn is a strange historical judgment, strange but unfragmented, of a convincing wholeness: that Leonard Woolf was a family sacrifice. Without him—Quentin Bell's clarity on this point is ineffaceable—

Virginia Woolf might have spent her life in a mental asylum. The elder Stephens were dead, Thoby had died at twenty-six, Adrian married a woman apparently indifferent to or incompatible with the Bloomsburyites; it was Vanessa on whom the grimness fell. Leonard Woolf—all this is blatant—got Vanessa off the hook. He was, in fact, deceived: he had no inkling he was being captured for a nurse.

> Neither Vanessa nor Adrian gave him a detailed and explicit account of Virginia's illnesses or told him how deadly serious they might be . . . Her insanity was clothed, like some other painful things in that family, in a jest . . . Thus, in effect if not in intention, Leonard was allowed to think of Virginia's illnesses as something not desperately serious, and he was allowed to marry her without knowing how fearful a care such a union might be. In fairness to all parties it must be said that, even if Virginia's brother and sister had been as explicit and circumstantial as they ought to have been, Leonard would certainly not have been deflected from his purpose of marrying Virginia . . . As it was, he learnt the hard way and one can only wonder, seeing how hard it was, and that he had for so long to endure the constant threat of her suicide, to exert constant vigilance, to exercise endless persuasive tact at mealtimes and to suffer the perpetual alternations of hope and disappointment, that he too did not go mad.
>
> In fact he nearly did, although he does not mention it.

"He does not mention it." There was in Leonard Woolf an extraordinary silence, a containment allied to something like concealment, and at the same time open to a methodical candor. This is no paradox; candor is often the mode of the obtuse person. It is of course perilous to think of Leonard Woolf as obtuse: he was both activist and intellectual, worldly and introspective; his intelligence, traveling widely and serenely over politics and literature, was reined in by a seriousness that makes him the most responsible and conscientious figure among all the Bloomsburyites. His seriousness was profound. It was what turned a hand press "small enough to stand on a kitchen table" into the Hogarth Press, an important and innovative publishing house. It was what turned Leonard Woolf himself from a highly able agent of colonialism—at the age of twenty-four he was an official of the British ruling apparatus in Ceylon—into a convinced anti-imperialist and a fervent socialist. And it was what turned the Jew into an Englishman.

Not that Leonard Woolf is altogether without ambivalence on this question; indeed, the word "ambivalence" is his own. Soon after his marriage to

Virginia Stephen, he was taken round on a tour of Stephen relations—among them Virginia's half-brother, Sir George Duckworth, in his large house in Dalingridge Place, and "Aunt Anny," who was Lady Ritchie, Thackeray's daughter, in St. George's Square. He suffered in these encounters from an "ambivalence in my attitude to the society which I found in Dalingridge Place and St. George's Square. I disliked its respectability and assumptions while envying and fearing its assurance and manners." And: "I was an outsider to this class, because, although I and my father before me belonged to the professional middle class, we had only recently struggled up into it from the stratum of Jewish shopkeepers. We had no roots in it." This looks like candor—"we had no roots"—but it is also remarkably insensible. Aware of his not belonging, he gives no evidence anywhere that the people he moved among were also aware of it. It is true that his own group of self-consciously agnostic Cambridge intellectuals apparently never mentioned it to his face. Thoby Stephen in a letter to Leonard in Ceylon is quick enough to speak of himself, mockingly, as a nonbelieving Christian—"it's no good being dainty with Christians and chapel's obviously rot"—but no one seems ever to have teased Leonard about his being an agnostic Jew. In the atmosphere of that society, perhaps, teasing would have too dangerously resembled baiting; levity about being a Christian was clearly not interchangeable with levity about being a Jew. Fair enough: it never is. But Virginia, replying to a letter in which Leonard implores her to love him, is oddly analytical: ". . . of course, I feel angry sometimes at the strength of your desire. Possibly, your being a Jew comes in also at this point. You seem so foreign." Was he, like all those dark lubricious peoples whose origins are remote from the moderating North, too obscurely other? She corrects herself at once, with a kind of apology: "And then I am fearfully unstable. I pass from hot to cold in an instant, without any reason; except that I believe sheer physical effort and exhaustion influence me." The correction—the retraction—is weak, and fades off; what remains is the blow: "You seem so foreign."

We do not know Leonard's response to this. Possibly he made none. It would have been in keeping had he made none. Foreignness disconcerted him—like Virginia he was at moments disturbed by it and backed away—and if his own origins were almost never mentioned to his face, his face was nevertheless *there*, and so, in those striking old photographs, were the faces of his grandparents. Leonard Woolf is bemused in his autobiography by his paternal grandfather, "a large, stern, black-haired, and black-whiskered, rabbinical Jew in a frock coat." Again he speaks of this "look of stern rabbinical orthodoxy," and rather prefers the "round, pink face of an incredibly old Dutch doll," which was the face of his Dutch-born maternal grandmother—

about whom he speculates that it was "possible that she had a good deal of non-Jewish blood in her ancestry. Some of her children and grandchildren were fair-haired and facially very unlike the 'typical' Jew." Her husband, however, was a different case: "No one could have mistaken him for anything but a Jew. Although he wore coats and trousers, hats and umbrellas, just like those of all the other gentlemen in Addison Gardens, he looked to me as if he might have stepped straight out of one of those old pictures of caftaned, bearded Jews in a ghetto . . ." Such Jews, he notes, were equipped with "a fragment of spiritual steel, a particle of passive and unconquerable resistance," but otherwise the character, and certainly the history, of the Jews do not draw him. "My father's father was a Jew," he writes, exempting himself by two generations. "I have always felt in my bones and brain and heart English and, more narrowly, a Londoner, but with a nostalgic love of the city and civilization of ancient Athens." He recognizes that his "genes and chromosomes" are something else; he is a "descendant" of "the world's official fugitives and scapegoats."

But a "descendant" is not the same as a member. A descendant shares an origin, but not necessarily a destiny. Writing in his eighties, Leonard Woolf recollects that as a schoolboy he was elected to an exclusive debating society under the thumb of G. K. Chesterton and his brother, and "in view of the subsequent violent anti-Semitism of the Chestertons" he finds this "amusing"; he reports that he was "surprised and flattered." Sixty-three years afterward he is still flattered. His description of the public school that flattered him shows it to be a detestable place, hostile to both intellect and feeling: "I got on quite well with the boys in my form or with whom I played cricket, football, and fives, but it would have been unsafe, practically impossible, to let them know what I really thought or felt about anything which seemed to me important." *Would have been unsafe.* It was a risk he did not take—unlike Morgan Forster, who, in the same situation in a similar school, allowed himself to be recognized as an intellectual and consequently to suffer as a schoolboy pariah. Leonard Woolf did not intend to take on the role of pariah, then or later. Perhaps it was cowardice; or perhaps it was the opposite, that "fragment of spiritual steel" he had inherited from the ghetto; or perhaps it was his sense of himself as exempt from the ghetto.

Certainly he always thought of himself as wholly an Englishman. In the spring of 1935 he and Virginia drove to Rome. "I was astonished then (I am astonished still)," Quentin Bell comments, "that Leonard chose to travel by way of Germany." They were on German soil three days; near Bonn they encountered a Nazi demonstration but were unharmed, and entered Italy safely. What prompted Leonard Woolf to go into Germany in the very hour

Jews were being abused there? Did he expect Nazi street hoodlums to distinguish between an English Jewish face and a German Jewish face? He carried with him—it was not needed and in the event of street hoodlumism would anyhow have been useless—a protective letter from an official of the German embassy in London. More than that, he carried—in his "bones and brain and heart"—the designation of Englishman. It was a test, not of the inherited fragment of spiritual steel, but of the strength of his exemption from that heritage. If Quentin Bell is twice astonished, it may be because he calculated the risk more closely than Leonard; or else he is not quite so persuaded of the Englishness of Leonard Woolf as is Leonard Woolf.

And, superficially at least, it is difficult to be persuaded of it. One is drawn to Leonard's face much as he was drawn to his grandfather's face, and the conclusion is the same. What Leonard's eyes saw was what the eyes of the educated English classes saw. What Leonard felt on viewing his grandfather's face must have been precisely what Clive Bell and Thoby Stephen would have felt. There is an arresting snapshot—still another of those that make up the pictorial history of Bloomsbury—of Leonard Woolf and Adrian Stephen. They are both young men in their prime; the date is 1914. They are standing side by side before the high narrow Gothic-style windows of Asham House, the Sussex villa Leonard and Virginia Woolf owned for some years. They are dressed identically (vests, coats, ties) and positioned identically—feet apart, hands in pockets, shut lips gripping pipe or cigarette holder. Their shoes are lost in the weedy grass, and the sunlight masks their faces in identical skull-shadows. Both faces are serene, holding back amusement, indulgent of the photographer. And still it is not a picture of two cultivated Englishmen, or not only that. Adrian is incredibly tall and Vikinglike, with a forehead as broad and flat as a chimney tile; he looks like some blueblood American banker not long out of Princeton; his hair grows straight up like thick pale straw. Leonard's forehead is an attenuated wafer under a tender black forelock, his nose is nervous and frail, he seems younger and more vulnerable than his years (he was then thirty-four) and as recognizably intellectual as—well, how does one put the contrast? Following Leonard, one ought to dare to put it with the clarity of a certain cultural bluntness: he looks like a student at the yeshiva. Leonard has the unmistakable face of a Jew. Like his grandfather—and, again like him, despite his costume—Leonard Woolf might have stepped out of one of those pictures of caftaned Jews in the ghetto.

The observation may be obvious and boring but it is not insignificant, if only because it is derived from Leonard himself; it is his own lesson. What can be learned from it is not merely that he was himself conscious of all that curious contrast, but that his fellows could not have been indifferent to it. In a 1968 review of the penultimate volume of Leonard Woolf's memoirs, Dan Jacobson wonders, "Did his being a Jew never affect . . . his career or social life in the several years he spent as a colonial officer in Ceylon, his only companions during that time being other colonial civil servants—not in general the most enlightened, tolerant, or tactful of British social groups? Did it not arise in the political work he carried out later in England, especially during the rise of Nazism?" On all these matters Leonard is mute; he does not mention it. Not so Virginia. "He's a penniless Jew," she wrote in a letter to a friend announcing her marriage, and we know that if she had married a poor man of her own set she would not have called him a penniless Englishman. She called Leonard a Jew not to identify or explain him, but because, quite simply, that is how she saw him; it was herself she was explaining. And if she wrote light-heartedly, making a joke of marriage without inheritance, it was also a joke in general about unaccoutered Jews—from her point of view, Leonard had neither inheritance nor heritage. He was—like the Hogarth Press later on—self-created.

Of course, in thinking about Leonard Woolf, one is plainly not interested in the question of the acculturated Jew (". . . nearly all Jews are both proud and ashamed of being Jews," Leonard writes—a model of the type); it is not on the mark. What *is* to the point is the attitude of the class Leonard aspired to join. "Virginia for her part," Quentin Bell notes—and it is unnecessary to remind oneself that he is her nephew—

> had to meet the Woolf family. It was a daunting experience. Leonard himself was sufficiently Jewish to seem to her disquietingly foreign; but in him the trait was qualified. He had become so very much a citizen of her world . . . But Leonard's widowed mother, a matriarchal figure living with her large family in Colinette Road, Putney, seemed very alien to Virginia. No place could have been less like home than her future mother-in-law's house.
>
> And how did the Woolfs regard her? Did they perceive that she thought their furniture hideous? Did she seem to them a haughty goy thinking herself too good for the family of their brilliant son? I am afraid that they probably did.
>
> [Here follows an account of Virginia's response—aloof and truculent—upon learning the character of the dietary laws, which Mrs. Woolf observed.]
>
> Virginia was ready to allow that Mrs. Woolf had some very good

qualities, but her heart must have sunk as she considered what large opportunities she would have for discovering them.

"Work and love and Jews in Putney take it out of me," she wrote, and it was certainly true.

This aspect of Virginia Stephen's marriage to Leonard Woolf is usually passed over in silence. I have rehearsed it here at such length not to emphasize it for its own sake—there is nothing novel about upper-class English distaste for Jews—but to make a point about Leonard. He is commonly depicted as, in public, a saintly socialist, and, in private, a saintly husband. He was probably both; but he also knew, like any percipient young man in love with a certain segment of society, how to seize vantage ground. As a schoolboy he was no doubt sincerely exhilarated by the playing field, but he hid his intellectual exhilarations to make it look as if the playing field were all there was to esteem; it was a way, after all, of buying esteem for himself. And though he was afterward no doubt sincerely in love with Virginia Stephen (surely a woman less intelligent would not have satisfied him), it would be a mistake to suppose that Virginia herself—even given her brilliance, her splendid head on its splendid neck, the radiance of her first appearance in Thoby's rooms in Cambridge wearing a white dress and round hat and carrying a parasol, astonishing him, Leonard says, as when "in a picture gallery you suddenly come face to face with a great Rembrandt or Velasquez"—it would be ingenuous, not to say credulous, to think that Virginia alone was all there was to adore. Whether Leonard Woolf fell in love with a young woman of beauty and intellect, or more narrowly with a Stephen of beauty and intellect, will always be a formidable, and a necessary, question.

It is a question that, it seems to me, touches acutely on Leonard Woolf in his profoundly dedicated role as nurse. He was dedicated partly because he was earnestly efficient at everything, and also because he loved his wife, and also because he was a realist who could reconcile himself to any unlooked-for disaster. He came to the situation of Virginia's health determinedly and unquestioningly, much as, years later, when the German bombings had begun, he joined up with the Local Defence Volunteers: it was what had to be done. But in the case of Virginia more than merely courage was at issue; his "background" had equipped him well to be Virginia Stephen's nurse. When things were going badly he could take on the burden of all those small code-jottings in his diary—"V.n.w.," "b.n.," "V.sl.h."—and all the crises "Virginia not well," "bad night," "Virginia slight headache" horrendously implied, for the simple reason that it was worth it to him. It was worth it because she was a genius; it was worth it because she was a Stephen.

The power and allure of the Stephen world lay not in its distance from the Jews of Putney—Bloomsbury was anyhow hardly likely to notice the Jews of Putney, and if Virginia did notice, and was even brought to tea there, it was through the abnormal caprice of a freakish fate—but in its illustriousness. Virginia was an illustrious young woman: had she had no gift of her own, the luster of her father's situation, and of the great circle of the aristocracy of intellect into which she was born, would have marked her life. It was additionally marked by her double fortune of genius and insanity, and though her primary fortune—the circle into which she was born—attracted, in the most natural way, other members of that circle, the biting and always original quality of her mind put the less vivid of them off. Her madness was not public knowledge, but her intellect could not be hidden. Her tongue had a fearful and cutting brilliance. "I was surprised to find how friendly she made herself appear," said Walter Lamb, another of Thoby Stephen's Cambridge friends, amazed on one occasion to have been undevoured. He courted her for a time, pallidly, asking frightened questions: "Do you want to have children and love in the normal way?"—as if he expected nothing usual from Virginia Stephen. "I wish," she wrote to Lytton Strachey, after reporting Lamb's visits, "that earth would open her womb and let some new creature out." The courtship was brief and ended in boredom. Lamb's offer was one of at least four proposals of marriage from differing sources; Strachey himself had tendered her one. Since he preferred stableboys to women, a fact they both understood very well, it was a strange mistake. Sydney Waterlow, still another Cambridge name, was a suitor; she regarded him as "amiable." Hilton Young, a childhood friend—cast, says Quentin Bell, from a "smooth and well-proportioned mould"—might have been an appropriate match, mixing politics with poetry and gaining a peerage; he was merely "admirable." Meanwhile, Virginia was thoughtfully flirting with her sister's husband. At twenty-nine, despite all these attentions, she was depressed at being still unmarried; she was despondent, as she would be for the rest of her life, over her childlessness. Not one of those triflings had turned to infatuation, on either side.

It was fortunate. There was lacking, in all these very intelligent men, and indeed in their type in general, the kind of sexual seriousness that is usually disparaged as uxoriousness. It was a trait that Leonard invincibly possessed and that Clive Bell despised as "provincial and puritanical, an enemy to all that was charming and amusing in life." Clive was occupied by a long-standing affair and lived apart from Vanessa, who, at various times, lived with Roger Fry and with Duncan Grant—who was (so closely was this group tied) Lytton Strachey's cousin, and who may have been (so Quentin Bell allows us to conjecture) the father of Quentin's sister, Angelica. Vanessa typed and distributed copies of Lytton Strachey's indecent verse; once at a party she did a topless dance; it was legendary that she had at another party fornicated with Maynard Keynes *"coram publico"*—the whole room looking on. It may have been in honor of these last two occasions that Virginia Woolf, according to Quentin Bell, pronounced human nature to have been "changed in or about December 1910."

It was not a change Leonard Woolf approved of. Four years after this crucial date in human history he published a novel critical of "unnatural cultured persons" given to "wild exaggerated talk" and frivolous behavior; it was clearly an assault on Vanessa and Clive Bell and their circle. The novel, called *The Wise Virgins*, was about *not* marrying Virginia. Instead the hero is forced to marry a Putney girl, and lives unhappily ever after—only because, having been infected with Bloomsbury's licentious notions, he has carelessly gotten her with child. The fictional Leonard loses the heroine who represents Virginia, and is doomed to the drabness of Putney; in the one act he both deplores Bloomsbury and laments his deprivation of it. The real Leonard tried to pick his way between these soul-cracking contradictions. He meant to have the high excitement of Bloomsbury—and certainly "frivolity" contributed to Bloomsbury's dash and eclat—without the frivolity itself. He meant to be master of the full brilliant breadth of all that worldliness, and at the same time of the more sober and limiting range of his native seriousness.

That he coveted the one while requiring the other was—certainly in her biographer's eyes—the salvation of Virginia. No one else in that milieu could have survived—surely not as husband—her illnesses. Roger Fry, for instance, put his own mad wife away and went to live with Vanessa. As for Lamb, Waterlow, Young—viewed in the light of what Virginia Woolf's insanity extracted from her caretaker, their possibilities wither. Of all her potential husbands, only Leonard Woolf emerged as fit. And the opposite too can be said: of Bloomsbury's potential wives, only Virginia emerged as fit for Leonard. He was fit for her because her madness, especially in combination with her innovative genius, demanded the most grave, minutely persevering and attentive service. She was fit for him not simply because she represented Bloomsbury in its most resplendent flowering of originality and luminousness; so, after all, did Vanessa, an accomplished painter active with other painters in the revolutionary vitality of the Post-Impressionists. But just as no marriage could survive Vanessa for long, so Leonard married to Vanessa would not have survived Bloomsbury for long. What Leonard needed in

Virginia was not so much her genius as her madness. It made possible for him the exercise of the one thing Bloomsbury had no use for: uxoriousness. It allowed him the totality of his seriousness unchecked. It *used* his seriousness, it gave it legitimate occupation, it made it both necessary and awesome. And it made *her* serious. Without the omnipresent threat of disintegration, freed from the oppression of continuous vigil against breakdown, what might Virginia's life have been? The flirtation with Clive hints at it: she might have lived, at least outwardly, like Vanessa. It was his wife's insanity, in short, that made tenable the permanent—the secure—presence in Bloomsbury of Leonard himself. Her madness fed his genius for responsibility; it became for him a corridor of access to her genius. The spirit of Bloomsbury was not Leonard's, his temperament was against it—Bloomsbury could have done without him. So could a sane Virginia.

The whole question of Virginia's sexuality now came into Leonard's hands. And here too he was curiously ambivalent. The honeymoon was not a success; they consulted Vanessa, Vanessa the sexual creature—when had she had her first orgasm? Vanessa could not remember. "No doubt," she reflected, "I sympathised with such things if I didn't have them from the time I was 2." "Why do you think people make such a fuss about marriage & copulation?" Virginia was writing just then; ". . . certainly I find the climax immensely exaggerated." Vanessa and Leonard put their heads together over it. Vanessa said she believed Virginia "never had understood or sympathised with sexual passion in men"; this news, she thought, "consoled" Leonard. For further consolation the two of them rehearsed (and this was before England had become properly aware of Freud) Virginia's childhood trauma inflicted by her elder half-brother George Duckworth, who had, under cover of big-brotherly affection, repeatedly entered the nursery at night for intimate fondlings, the nature of which Virginia then hardly comprehended; she knew only that he frightened her and that she despised him. Apparently this explanation satisfied Leonard—the "consolation" worked—if rather too quickly; the ability to adjust speedily to disappointment is a good and useful trait in a colonial officer, less so in a husband. It does not contradict the uxorious temperament, however, and certainly not the nursing enterprise: a wife who is seen to be frigid as well as mad is simply taken for that much sicker. But too ready a reconcilement to bad news is also a kind of abandonment, and Leonard seems very early to have relinquished, or allowed Virginia to relinquish, the sexual gratifications of marriage. All the stranger since he repeatedly speaks of himself as "lustful." And he is not known to have had so much as a dalliance during his marriage.

On the other hand, Quentin Bell suggests—a little coyly, as if only blamelessly hinting—that Virginia Woolf's erotic direction was perhaps toward women rather than men. The "perhaps" is crucial: the index to the first volume lists "passion for Madge Vaughan," "passion for Violet Dickinson," but the corresponding textual passages are all projections from the most ordinary sort of data. Madge Vaughan was a cousin by marriage whom Virginia knew from the age of seven; at sixteen she adored her still, and once stood in the house paralyzed by rapture, thinking, "Madge is here; at this moment she is actually under this roof"—an emotion, she once said, that she never equaled afterward. Many emotions at sixteen are never equaled afterward. Of Virginia's intense letter-writing to Violet Dickinson—a friend of her dead half-sister—Quentin Bell says: ". . . it is clear to the modern reader, though it was not at all clear to Virginia, that she was in love and that her love was returned." What is even clearer is that it is possible to be too "modern," if that is what enables one to read a sensual character into every exuberant or sympathetic friendship between women. Vita Sackville-West, of course, whom Virginia Woolf knew when both writers were already celebrated, was an established sapphist, and was plainly in pursuit of Virginia. Virginia, she wrote, "dislikes the quality of masculinity," but that was the view of one with a vested interest in believing it. As for Virginia, she "felt," according to her biographer, "as a lover feels—she desponded when she fancied herself neglected, despaired when Vita was away, waited anxiously for letters, needed Vita's company and lived in that strange mixture of elation and despair which lovers—and one would have supposed only lovers—can experience." But all this is Quentin Bell. Virginia herself, reporting a three-day visit from Sackville-West, appears erotically detached: "These Sapphists *love* women; friendship is never untinged with amorosity . . . I like her and being with her and the splendour—she shines in the grocer's shop . . . with a candle lit radiance." She acknowledged what she readily called Vita's "glamour," but the phrase "these Sapphists" is too mocking to be lover's language. And she was quick to criticize Vita (who was married to Harold Nicolson) as a mother: ". . . she is a little cold and off-hand with her boys." Virginia Woolf's biographer nevertheless supposes—he admits all this is conjecture—"some caressing, some bedding together." Still, in the heart of this love, if it was love, was the ultimate withdrawal: "In brain and insight," Virginia remarked in her diary, "she is not as highly organised as I am." Vita was splendid but "not reflective." She wrote "with a pen of brass." And: "I have no enormous opinion of her poetry." Considering all of which, Quentin Bell notes persuasively that "she could not really love without feeling that she was in the presence of a superior intellect." Sackville-West, for her part, insisted that not only did Virginia not like the quality of masculinity, but also the "possessiveness and love of domination in men."

Yet Leonard Woolf dominated Virginia Woolf overwhelmingly—nor did she resist—not so much because his braininess impressed her (his straightforwardly thumping writing style must have claimed her loyalty more than her admiration), but because he possessed her in the manner of—it must be said again—a strong-minded nurse with obsessive jurisdiction over a willful patient. The issue of Virginia Woolf's tentative or potential lesbianism becomes reduced, at this point, to the merest footnote of possibility. Sackville-West called her "inviolable"; and the fact is she was conventionally married, and had conventional expectations of marriage. She wanted children. For a wedding present Violet Dickinson sent her a cradle. "My baby shall sleep in [it]," she said at thirty. But it stood empty, and she felt, all her life, the ache of the irretrievable. "I don't like the physicalness of having children of my own," she wrote at forty-five, recording how "the little creatures"—Vanessa's children—"moved my infinitely sentimental throat." But then, with a lurch of candor: "I can dramatise myself a parent, it is true. And perhaps I have killed the feeling instinctively; or perhaps nature does." Two years after declaring the feeling killed, during a dinner party full of worldly conversation with the Webbs and assorted eminences, she found herself thinking: "L. and myself . . . the pathos, the symbolical quality of the childless couple."

The feeling was not killed; it had a remarkable durability. There is no record of her response to the original decision not to have children. That decision was Leonard's, and it was "medical." He consulted three or four people variously qualified, including Vanessa's doctor and the nurse who ran the home to which Virginia was sent when most dangerously disturbed (and to whom, according to Bell, Leonard ascribed "an unconscious but violent homosexual passion for Virginia"—which would, one imagines, make one wonder about the disinterestedness of her advice). Leonard also requested the opinion of Dr. George Savage, Virginia's regular physician, whom he disliked, and was heartily urged to have babies; soon after we find him no longer in consultation with Dr. Savage. Bell tells us that "in the end Leonard decided and persuaded Virginia to agree that, although they both wanted children, it would be too dangerous for her to have them." The "too dangerous" is left unexplained; we do not even know Leonard's ostensible reason. Did he think she could not withstand pregnancy and delivery? She was neither especially frail nor without energy, and was a zealous walker, eight miles at a time, over both London and countryside; she hefted piles of books and packed them for the Hogarth Press; she had no organic impediments. Did he believe she could not have borne the duties of rearing? But in that class there was no household without its nanny (Vanessa had two), and just as she never had to do a housekeeping chore (she never laid a fire, or made a bed, or washed a sock), she need not have been obliged to take physical care of a child. Did he, then, fear an inherited trait—diseased offspring? Or did he intend to protect the phantom child from distress by preventing its birth into a baleful household? Or did he mean, out of some curious notion of intellectual purity, not to divide the strength of Virginia's available sanity, to preserve her undistracted for her art?

Whatever the reason, and to spare her—or himself—what pains we can only guess at, she was in this second instance released from "normality." Normality is catch-as-catch-can. Leonard, in his deliberateness, in his responsibility, was more serious than that, and surrendered her to a program of omissions. She would be spared the tribulations both of the conjugal bed and of childbed. She need not learn ease in the one; she need not, no, must not, venture into the other. In forbidding Virginia maternity, Leonard abandoned her to an unparalleled and unslakable envy. Her diary again and again records the pangs she felt after visits with Vanessa's little sons—pangs, defenses, justifications: she suffered. Nor was it a social suffering—she did not feel deprived of children because she was expected to. The name "Virginia Woolf" very soon acquired the same resonance for her contemporaries ("this celebrity business is quite chronic," she wrote) as it has for us—after which she was expected to be only Virginia Woolf. She learned, after a while, to be only that (which did not, however, prevent her from being an adored and delightful aunt), and to mock at Vanessa's mothering, and to call it obsessive and excessive. She suffered the envy of the childless for the fruitful, precisely this, and nothing societally imposed; and she even learned to transmute maternal envy into a more manageable variety—literary begrudging. This was directed at Vanessa's second son, Julian Bell, killed in the Spanish Civil War, toward whose literary ambitions Virginia Woolf was always ungenerous, together with Leonard; a collection of Julian's essays, prepared after his death, Leonard dubbed "Vanessa's necrophily." Vanessa-envy moved on into the second generation. It was at bottom a rivalry of creatureliness, in which Virginia was always the loser. Vanessa was on the side of "normality," the placid mother of three, enjoying all the traditional bourgeois consolations; she was often referred to as a madonna; and at the same time she was a thorough-going bohemian. Virginia was anything but placid, yet lived a sober sensible domestic life in a marriage stable beyond imagining, with no trace of bohemianism. Vanessa the bohemian madonna had the best of both hearth-life and free life. Virginia was barred from both.

Without the authoritative domestic role maternity would have supplied, with no one in the household dependent on her (for years she quarreled with her maid on equal or inferior terms), and finding herself always—as potential patient—in submission, Virginia Woolf was by degrees nudged into a position of severe dependency. It took odd forms: Leonard not only prescribed milk at eleven in the morning, but also topics for conversation in the evening. Lytton Strachey's sister-in-law recalls how among friends Leonard would work up the "backbone" of a subject "and then be happy to let [Virginia] ornament it if she wanted to." And he gave her pocket money every week. Her niece Angelica reports that "Leonard kept Virginia on very short purse-strings," which she exercised through the pleasures of buying "coloured string and sealing-wax, notebooks and pencils." When she came to the end of writing a book, she trembled until Leonard read it and gave his approval. William Plomer remembers how Leonard would grow alarmed if, watching Virginia closely, he saw her laugh a little too convulsively. And once she absent-mindedly began to flick bits of meat off her dinner plate; Leonard hushed the company and led her away.

All of which has given Leonard his reputation for saintliness. A saint who successively secures acquiescence to frigidity, childlessness, dependency? Perhaps; probably; of course. These are, after all; conventual vows—celibacy, barrenness, obedience. But Leonard Woolf was a socialist, not an ascetic; he had a practical political intelligence; he was the author of books called *Empire and Commerce in Africa* and *Socialism and Co-operation;* he ran the Hogarth Press like a good businessman; at the same time he edited a monthly periodical, *The International Review;* he was literary editor of *The Nation.* He had exactly the kind of commonsensical temperament that scorns, and is repelled by, religious excess. And of Virginia he made a shrine; of himself, a monk. On the day of her death Virginia walked out of the house down to the river Ouse and drowned herself; not for nothing was that house called Monk's House. The letter she left for Leonard was like almost every other suicide note, horribly banal, not a writer's letter at all, and rich with guilt—"I feel certain I am going mad again. I feel we can't go through another of those terrible times . . . I can't go on spoiling your life any longer." To Vanessa she wrote, "All I want to say is that Leonard has been so astonishingly good, every day, always; I can't imagine that anyone could have done more for me than he has . . . I feel he has so much to do that he will go on, better without me . . ."

Saints make guilt—especially when they impose monkish values; there is nothing new in that. And it was the monk as well as her madness she was fleeing when she walked into the Ouse, though it was the saint she praised.

"I don't think two people could have been happier than we have been," the note to Leonard ended. A tragic happiness—such a thing is possible: cheerful invalids are commonplace, and occasionally one hears of happy inmates. A saintly monk, a monkish nurse? All can be taken together, and all are true together. But the drive toward monkishness was in Leonard. What was natural for himself he prescribed for Virginia, and to one end only: to prevent her ongoing nervous crises from reaching their extreme state; to keep her sane. And to keep her sane was, ultimately, to keep her writing. It is reasonable to imagine that without Leonard Woolf there would have been very little of that corpus the name Virginia Woolf calls to mind—there would have been no *Mrs. Dalloway*, no *To the Lighthouse*, no *The Waves*, no *Common Reader*. And it may be that even the word Bloomsbury—the redolence, the signal—would not have survived, since she was its center. "She would not have been the symbol" of Bloomsbury, T. S. Eliot said, "if she had not been the maintainer of it." For Bloomsbury as an intellectual "period" to have escaped oblivion, there had to be at least one major literary voice to carry it beyond datedness. That voice was hers.

The effort to keep her sane was mammoth. Why did Leonard think it was worth it? The question, put here for the second time, remains callous but inevitable. Surely it would have been relieving at last (and perhaps to both of them) to let her slide away into those rantings, delusions, hallucinations; she might or might not have returned on her own. It is even possible that the nursing was incidental, and that she recovered each time because she still had the capacity to recover. But often enough Leonard—who knew the early symptoms intimately—was able to prevent her from going under; each pulling-back from that brink of dementia gained her another few months of literary work. Again and again he pulled her back. It required cajolery, cunning, mastery, agility, suspiciousness, patience, spoon-feeding, and an overwhelming sensitiveness to every flicker of her mood. Obviously it drained him; obviously he must have been tempted now and then to let it all go and give up. Almost anyone else would have. Why did he not? Again the answer must be manifold. Because she was his wife; because she was the beloved one to whom he had written during their courtship, "You don't know what a wave of happiness comes over me when I see you smile"; because his conscience obliged him to; because she suffered; because—this before much else—it was in his nature to succor suffering. And also: because of her gift; because of her genius; for the sake of literature; because she was unique. And because she had been a Miss Stephen; because she was Thoby Stephen's sister; because she was a daughter of Leslie Stephen; because she was, like Leonard's vision of Cambridge itself, "compounded of . . . the atmosphere of long years of history and great traditions and famous names [and] a profoundly civilized life"; because she was Bloomsbury; because she was England.

For her sake, for art's sake, for his own sake. Perhaps above all for, his own sake. In her he had married a kind of escutcheon; she represented the finest grain of the finest stratum in England. What he shored up against disintegration was the life he had gained—a birthright he paid for by spooning porridge between Virginia Woolf's resisting lips.

Proust is right to tell us to go to a writer's books, not to his loyalties. Wherever Leonard Woolf is, there Virginia Woolf is not. The more Leonard recedes or is not present, the more Virginia appears in force. Consequently Quentin Bell's biography—the subversive strength of which is Leonard—demands an antidote. The antidote is, of course, in the form of a reminder—that Virginia Woolf was a woman of letters as well as a patient; that she did not always succumb but instead could be an original fantasist and fashioner of an unaccustomed way of seeing; that the dependency coincided with a vigorous intellectual autonomy; that together with the natural subordination of the incapacitated she possessed the secret confidence of the innovator.

Seen through Leonard's eyes, she is, in effect, always on the verge of lunacy. "I am quite sure," he tells us in his autobiography, "that Virginia's genius was closely connected with what manifested itself as mental instability and insanity. The creative imagination in her novels, her ability to 'leave the ground' in conversation, and the voluble delusions of the breakdown all came from the same place in her mind—she 'stumbled after her own voice' and followed 'the voices that fly ahead.'" At the same time her refusal to eat was associated with guilt—she talked of her "faults"—and Leonard insists that "she remained all through her illness, even when most insane, terribly sane in three-quarters of her mind. The point is that her insanity was in her premises, in her beliefs. She believed, for instance, that she was not ill . . ."

Seen through the books, she is never "ill," never lunatic. Whether it was mental instability or a clear-sighted program of experiment in the shape of the novel that unhinged her prose from the conventional margins that had gone before is a question not worth speculating over. Leonard said that when mad she heard the birds sing in Greek. The novels are not like that: it is not the data that are altered, but the sequence of things. When Virginia Woolf assaulted the "old" fiction in her famous *Mr. Bennett and Mrs. Brown*, she thought she was recommending getting rid of the habit of data; she thought this was to be her Active platform. But when she grappled with her own inventions, she introduced as much data as possible and strained to express it all under the pressure of a tremendous simultaneity. What she was getting rid of was consecutiveness; precisely the habit of premises. If clinging to premises was the sanity of her insanity, then the intent of her fiction was not an extension of her madness, as Leonard claimed, but its calculated opposite. The poetry of her prose may have been like the elusive poetry of her dementia, but its steadfast design was not. "The design," she wrote of *Mrs. Dalloway*, "is so queer and so masterful"; elated, she saw ahead. She was an artist; she schemed, and not through random contractions or inflations of madness, but through the usual methods of art: inspired intellection, the breaking down of expectation into luminous segments of shock.

A simpler way of saying all this is that what she achieved as a stylist cannot really be explained through linking it with madness. The diaries give glimpses of rationalized prefigurations; a letter from Vanessa suggests moths, which metamorphosed into *The Moths*, which became *The Waves*. She knew her destination months before she arrived; she was in control of her work, she did what she meant to do. If the novels are too imaginatively astonishing to be persuasive on this point, the essays will convince. They are read too little, and not one of them is conceptually stale, or worn in any other way. In them the birds do not sing in Greek either, but the Greek—the sign of a masterly nineteenth-century literary education—shows like a spine. In the essays the control of brilliant minutiae is total—historical and literary figures, the particulars of biography, society, nationality, geography. She is a courier for the past. In Volume III of the *Collected Essays*, for instance, the range is from Chaucer through Montaigne through some Elizabethans major and minor, through Swift and Sterne and Lord Chesterfield, Fanny Burney and Cowper. She was interested also in the lives of women, especially writers. She studies Sara Coleridge, the poet's daughter; Harriette Wilson, the mistress of the Earl of Craven; Dr. Johnson's Mrs. Thrale; and Dorothy Osborne, a talented letter-writer of the seventeenth century. The language and scope of the essays astound. If they are "impressionistic," they are not self-indulgent; they put history before sensibility. When they are ironic, it is the kind of irony that enlarges the discriminatory faculty and does not serve the cynical temper. They mean to interpret other lives by the annihilation of the crack of time: they are after what the novels are after, a compression of then and now into the simultaneity of a singular recognition and a single comprehension. They mean to make every generation, and every instant, contemporaneous with every other generation and instant. And yet—it does not contradict—they are, taken all together, the English Essay incarnate.

The autonomous authority of the fiction, the more public authority of the essays, are the antidotes to Bell's Woolf, to Leonard's Virginia. But there is a third antidote implicit in the whole of the work, and in the drive behind the work, and that is Virginia Woolf's feminism. It ought to be said at once that it was what can now be called "classical" feminism. The latter-day choice of Virginia Woolf, on the style of Sylvia Plath, as a current women's-movement avatar is inapposite and mistaken. Classical feminism is inimical to certain developing strands of "liberation." Where feminism repudiates the conceit of the "gentler sex," liberation has come to reaffirm it. Where feminism asserts a claim on the larger world, liberation shifts to separatism. Where feminism scoffs at the plaint of "sisters under the skin," and maintains individuality of condition and temperament, liberation reinstates sisterhood and sameness. Where feminism shuns self-preoccupation, liberation experiments with self-examination, both psychic and medical. Classical feminism as represented by Virginia Woolf meant one thing only: access to the great world of thinking, being, and doing. The notion of "male" and "female" states of intellect and feeling, hence of prose, ultimately of culture, would have been the occasion of a satiric turn for Virginia Woolf; so would the idea of a politics of sex. Clive Bell reports that she licked envelopes once or twice for the Adult Suffrage League, but that she "made merciless fun of the flag-waving fanaticism" of the activists. She was not political—or, perhaps, just political enough, as when Chekhov notes that "writers should engage themselves in politics only enough to protect themselves from politics." Though one of her themes was women in history (several of her themes, rather; she took her women one by one, not as a race, species, or nation), presumably she would have mocked at the invention of a "history of women"—what she cared for, as *A Room of One's Own* both lucidly and passionately lays out, was access to a unitary culture. Indeed, *Orlando* is the metaphorical expression of this idea. History as a record of division or exclusion was precisely what she set herself against: the Cambridge of her youth kept women out, and all her life she preserved her resentment by pronouncing herself undereducated. She studied at home, Greek with Janet Case, literature and mathematics with her father, and as a result was left to count on her fingers forever—but for people who grow up counting on their fingers, even a Cambridge education cannot do much. Nevertheless she despised what nowadays is termed "affirmative action," granting places in institutions as a kind of group reparation; she thought it offensive to her own earned prestige, and once took revenge on the notion. In 1935 Forster, a member of the Committee of the London Library, informed her that a debate was under way concerning the admission of women members. No women were admitted. Six years later Virginia Woolf was invited to serve; she said she would not be a "sop"—she ought to have been invited years earlier, on the same terms as Forster, as a writer; not in 1941, when she was already fifty-nine, as a woman.

Nor will she do as martyr. Although Cambridge was closed to her, literary journalism was not; although she complains of being chased off an Oxbridge lawn forbidden to the feet of women, no one ever chased her off a page. Almost immediately she began to write for the *Times Literary Supplement* and for *Cornhill;* she was then twenty-two. She was, of course, Leslie Stephen's daughter, and it is doubtful whether any other young writer, male or female, could have started off so auspiciously: still, we speak here not of "connections" but of experience. At about the same time she was summoned to teach at Morley, a workers' college for men and women. One of her reports survives, and Quentin Bell includes it as an appendix. "My four women," she writes, "can hear eight lectures on the French Revolution if they wish to continue their historical learning"—and these were working-class women, in 1905. By 1928, women had the vote, and full access to universities, the liberal professions, and the civil service. As for Virginia Woolf, in both instances, as writer and teacher, she was solicited—and this cannot be, after all, only because she was Leslie Stephen's daughter. She could use on the spot only her own gifts, not the rumor of her father's. Once she determined to ignore what Bell calls the "matrimonial market" of upper-class partying, into which for a time her half-brother George dragooned her, she was freed to her profession. It was not true then, it is not true now, that a sublime and serious pen can be circumscribed.

Virginia Woolf was a practitioner of her profession from an early age; she was not deprived of an education, rather of a particular college; she grew rich and distinguished; she developed her art on her own line, according to her own sensibilities, and was acclaimed for it; though insane, she was never incarcerated. She was an elitist, and must be understood as such. What she suffered from, aside from the abysses of depression which characterized her disease, was not anything like the condition of martyrdom—unless language has become so flaccid that being on occasion patronized begins to equal death for the sake of an ideal. What she suffered from really was only the minor inflammations of the literary temperament. And she was not often patronized: her fame encouraged her to patronize others. She could be unkind, she could be spiteful, she could envy—her friendship with Katherine Mansfield was always unsure, being founded on rivalry. Mansfield and her husband, the journalist John Middleton Murry, "work in my flesh," Virginia Woolf wrote, "after the manner of the jigger insect. It's annoying, indeed degrading, to have these bitternesses." She was bitter also about James Joyce; she thought him, says Bell, guilty of "atrocities." Her diary speaks of "the damned egotistical self; which ruins Joyce," and she saw *Ulysses* as "insistent, raw, striking and ultimately nauseating." But she knew Joyce to be moving in the same direction as herself; it was a race that, despite her certainty of his faults, he might win. By the time of her death she must have understood that he *had* won. Still, to be outrun in fame is no martyrdom. And her own fame was and is in no danger, though, unlike Joyce, she is not taken as a fact of nature. Virginia Woolf's reputation in the thirty and more years since her death deepens; she becomes easier to read, more complex to consider,

To Charlotte Brontë, born sixty-six years before Virginia Woolf, Robert Southey, then Poet Laureate, had written, "Literature cannot be the business of a woman's life, and it ought not to be." No one addressed Virginia Woolf of Bloomsbury in this fashion; she was sought out by disciples, editors, litterateurs; in the end Oxford and Cambridge asked her to lecture before their women's colleges. If the issue of martyrdom is inappropriate (implying as it does that a woman who commits suicide is by definition a martyr), what of heroism? Virginia Woolf's death was or was not heroic, depending on one's view of suicide by drowning. The case for Leonard's heroism is more clear-cut: a saint is noble on behalf of others, a hero on behalf of himself. But if Virginia Woolf is to be seen as a heroine, it must be in those modes outside the manner of her death and even the manner of her life as a patient in the house.

If she is to be seen as a heroine, it must be in the conjuring of yet another of those Bloomsbury photographs—this time one that does not exist. The picture is of a woman sitting in an old chair holding a writing board; the point of her pen touches a half-filled page. To gaze at her bibliography is, in a way, to conjure this picture that does not exist—hour after hour, year after year, a life's accumulation of stupendous visionary toil. A writer's heroism is in the act of writing; not in the finished work, but in the work as it goes.

Vanessa's son gives us no heroine: only this stubborn and sometimes querulous self-starving madwoman, with so stoic, so heroic, a male nurse. And when she runs away from him to swallow the Ouse, the heroism of both of them comes to an end.

Diary-Keeping

Again these lyrical, allusive, and alluring names! Lytton, Carrington, Clive, Roger, Vanessa, Duncan, Leonard, Maynard, Gertler, Ka, Kot, Janet, Aldous, Bob, Arnold, Ottoline, Morgan, Logan, Katherine, Desmond, Murry, Nick, Saxon, Alix . . . Miniaturized by the Cyclops eye of hindsight, with the gold dust shaken out of them, one or two have broken out of legend to survive— E. M. Forster solidly and on his own, also the economist Keynes; the rest shakily and in shadow, reduced to "period" names: the polemicist Toynbee rapidly growing quaint, Aldous Huxley's novels long ago turned problematical, Katherine Mansfield fallen even out of the anthologies, Sidney and Beatrice Webb fixed in Fabian caricature. The "men of letters"—Robert Trevelyan, John Middleton Murry, Desmond MacCarthy, Logan Pearsall Smith: how far away and small they now seem! And the painters, Vanessa Bell, Duncan Grant, Mark Gertler, and the art critics, Clive Bell and Roger Fry—lost molecules in the antiquity of modernism. And Saxon Sydney-Turner? Less than a molecule; a civil servant in the British Treasury. Lytton Strachey? A minor psychological historian given to phrasing both fustian and trite; he had his little vogue. Leonard Woolf? An ungainly writer and social reformer active in anticolonial causes, an early supporter of the League of Nations—who thinks of him as anything other than Virginia Woolf's husband?

Merited fame, when it outlives its native generation (we may call this genius if we wish), is the real Midas touch. "Bloomsbury" means Virginia Woolf and her satellites. The men and women she breathed on shine with her gold. She did not know she was their sun, they did not know they were her satellites; but it is easy now, seventy years after they all seemed to glitter together, to tell the radiance from the penumbra. Even now—she is still ascending—she is not a genius to everyone; Lionel Trilling dismissed her, probably for her purported "subjectivity," and the women's movement claims but distorts her, for the same reason. Her genius does no one any good, has no social force or perspective, and—like most literature—is not needed: it is the intolerant genius of riddle. But not the sort of riddle-of-the-absurd that is left there, amorphous and mystical on the page. She will not fail to deliver. Her riddles are all concretely and dazzlingly solved by organization into ingenious portraiture. Hers is a beaklike and unifying imagination, impatient (unlike Forster's) with muddle or puzzle; she will seize any loose flying cloth and make it over for a Jolly Roger. Identity discovered in flux is all. So the mystery of her own mother was deciphered through Mrs. Ramsay in *To the Lighthouse;* and so the stippled occasions of daily life are drawn into coherency through the device of a secret diary.

This first volume, covering the years of the Great War, tells of shortages and moonlit air raids, of strikes and huddling in cellars, of frustrations with servants and in-laws; it is also the period of the founding of the Hogarth Press, the acquisition of Monk's House, and the publication of Virginia Woolf's earliest novels, *The Voyage Out* and *Night and Day;* it is the time when many of the remarkable essays that became *The Common Reader* were beaten out under the guise of journalism written against a deadline. All these matters amaze because they are familiar; we know them from a dozen other sources; we are already in possession of Virginia Woolf, after all—and yet how shocking to peer through her window at last, how astounding to hear her confirm everything in her own voice! A diary is a time machine; it puts us not simply on the doorstep but inside the mind, and yields to curiosity its ultimate consummation.

Yet Virginia Woolf's diary is not (to stumble on that perilous word again) "subjective." There are few psychological surprises. A Freudianly-inclined reader might be interested in the juxtaposition, in a single paragraph, of a memory of a childhood fear of "being shut in"; zoo animals that "grunt and growl"; and a visit to an "invalid" just emerged from a healthy childbirth. But there is no intent to record moods. Learning that Lady Ottoline Morrell keeps a diary, Virginia notes with light contempt that it is "devoted however to her 'inner life'; which made me reflect that I haven't an inner life." By and large, this is an accurate enough description of her own diary-keeping. It eschews "feelings"; it is dense with happenings: visits, party-goings, walks, scenery and season, political meetings, concerts, conversations; the purchase of a wristwatch, a pen (the dipping kind), a glass bottle, new spectacles. It is built not on sensibility but on the *pointillisme* of chronicle.

Chronicle is the foundation, but the structure is all explicit portraiture, and each portrait is fixed, final, locked into its varnish for ever. If she begins in murk, with hints and signs, she carries her inquisitiveness into graphic intelligibility.

Of Robert Trevelyan, poet and classicist:

. . . he manages to be more malevolent than anyone I know, under a cover of extreme good nature. He reminds me of the man with the pointed stick, who picks up scraps of paper. So Bob collects every scrap of gossip within reach.

Of Beatrice Webb:

She has no welcome for one's individuality . . . Marriage [she said] was necessary as a waste pipe for emotion, as a security in old age . . . & as a help to work. We were entangled at the gates of the level crossing when she remarked, "Yes, I daresay an old family servant would do as well."

Of Sidney Webb:

. . . one could even commit the impropriety of liking him personally, which one can hardly do in the case of Mrs. Webb.

Of Lytton Strachey's fame:

How did he do it, how is he so distinct & unmistakable if he lacks originality & the rest? Is there any reputable escape from this impasse in saying that he is a great deal better than his books?

Of the painter Mark Gertler:

He is a resolute young man; & if good pictures can be made by willing them to be good, he may do wonders. No base motive could have its way with him; & for this reason I haven't great faith in him. Its too moral and intellectual an affair I advised him, for arts sake, to keep sane; to grasp, & not exaggerate, & put sheets of glass between him & his matter . . . But he can think pianola music equal to hand made, since it shows the form, & the touch & the expression are nothing.

Of Lytton's brother James Strachey (whom Freud later analyzed):

He has all the right books, neatly ranged, but not interesting in the least—not, I mean, all lusty & queer like a writer's books.

They parade by, these portraits, by the dozens, then by the hundreds; they cascade and grow orchestral; the diary, as she acknowledges, begins to comprehend its own meaning. The portraits are extraordinary not only for the power of their penetration, but for language as strong and as flexible and as spontaneous as that of any of the English masters, including Dickens. And they have the gift of seeing through the flummery of their moment: though Lytton Strachey is a more significant friend to the style of Virginia Woolf's imagination than Leonard Woolf (whose comings and goings to reformers' meetings criss-cross these pages), though they converse in the bliss of perfect rapport, she judges him with the dispassion of posterity. Nearly all the portraits have this singular contemporary balance—contemporary, that is, with *us*.

But she is also malicious in the way of the class she was born into. She calls the common people "animals," "a tepid mass of flesh scarcely organized into human life." Unlike the majority of her class, she mocked the war; but the celebrations that mark its end she ridicules as "a servants peace." Of famine following massacre: "I laughed to myself over the quantities of Armenians. How can one mind whether they number 4,000 or 4,000,000? The feat is beyond me." She has no piety or patriotism, but retains the Christian bias of the one, and the Imperial bias of the other. "I do not like the Jewish voice; I do not like the Jewish laugh," she writes of Leonard's sister, and the two visiting Ceylonese with whom Leonard is forming committees on colonial oppression she refers to as "persistent darkies." In all these instances there may be the little devil's-tail flick of self-derision; still, the spite stands. Though hospitality is constant, her sister Vanessa is not much on her mind, but she misses no opportunity to disparage Leonard's family; and perhaps, one discovers, even Leonard himself. In an ominous sentence seemingly directed at a speech by the socialist theosophist Annie Besant, but more dangerously at the principled Leonard, she comments, "It seems to me more & more clear that the only honest people are the artists, & that these social reformers & philanthropists get so out of hand, & harbour so many discreditable desires under the guise of loving their kind, that in the end there's more to find fault with in them than in us." In all Leonard's plethora of meeting after meeting, there is no way that "us" can be made to include Virginia Woolf's husband.

Yet, for all that, the social distaste and the portraits—those astonishing projections into the long view—are not what the diary is about, or for. Why does she keep it, and keep it up? How to explain the compulsion to write nearly every day, from New Year's Day 1915 until the onset of mental illness in February; then again from August 1917 unceasingly until December 1919? To write through bombings, flu, strikes, Leonard's malaria, changes of residence (the Woolfs voyaged continually between London and the country), house-buying, hand-printing? Above all, to write while writing? It was a discipline she admits to wanting to be only a pleasure, but clearly she needed to do it. The reasons she gives are various: to interpret the thirty-seven-year-old Virginia to the "old Virginia" of fifty; or "my belief that the habit of writing thus for my own eye only is good practice" for writing well; and sometimes one sees how it is a "therapy journal" for writer's depression, in which the terror of self-doubt is ministered to again and again by the furious craving for praise. Now and then a future reader twinkles in these private pages—why else would she meticulously speak of "my father Sir Leslie," and is it for herself she notes that "almost always the afternoon is dry in England"? On occasion the diary serves as a pouch for leakings of unwritten essays—energetic readings of Byron and Milton. And of course it is nice to know that Virginia Woolf, catered to by two servants—how easy it was for her to have crowds of friends for dinner and tea and weekends!—once lost her underpants in the street in the middle of winter. (She lets this pass without comment; the sneer comes two entries later, when women get the vote.)

But all these useful reasons, pretexts, needs—her eye sidelong on us, more directly on her own intelligence—are not to the point, and especially do not explain the explosions of portraiture. "I might in the course of time [she tells herself in a meditation on the "kind of form which a diary might attain to"] learn what it is that one can make of this loose, drifting material of life; finding another use for it than the use I put it to, so much more consciously & scrupulously, in fiction." That was April 1919. Two months earlier, she had already made that find, but failed to recognize it. On February 5, adopting the tone of a governess, she scolds, "What a disgraceful lapse! nothing added to my disquisition, & life allowed to waste like a tap left running. Eleven days unrecorded."

Life allowed to waste, and still she did not see what she meant. The following October 7, during a railway strike that "broke in to our life more than the war did," the riddle begins to unravel: "Is it [the diary] worth going on with? . . . I wonder why I do it. Partly, I think, from my old sense of the race of time 'Time's winged chariot hurrying near'—Does it stay it?"

In the end she knew what she meant, and what keeping the diary was for. It was literally a keeping—not for disclosure, but for "staying," for making life stay, for validating breath. Her diary, though it is a chronicle and a narrative, is all the same not intended solely for a "record." A record is a hound padding after life. But a diary is a shoring-up of the ephemeral, evidence that the writer takes up real space in the world. For Virginia Woolf, as these incandescent streams of language show, the life she lived and the people she knew did not become real until they were written down.

Morgan and Maurice: A Fairy Tale

Possibly the most famous sentence in Forster's fiction is the one that comes out of the blue at the start of Chapter Five of *The Longest Journey*: "Gerald died that afternoon." The sentence is there with no preparation whatever—no novelistic "plant," no hidden tracks laid out in advance. Just before the turning of the page we have seen Gerald resplendent in his sexual prime, "with the figure of a Greek athlete and the face of an English one," a football player of no special distinction but the fact of his glorious aliveness. Then, without warning, he is "broken up."

The suddenness of Gerald's death has been commented on almost too often by Forster seminarians; it is, after all, a slap in the reader's face, and must be accounted for. Asked about it in a 1952 interview (it was then forty-five years since the book had first appeared), Forster would only say, "It had to be passed by." An insulting answer. Forster is a gentleman who never insults unintentionally; he also intends to shock, and he never shocks inadvertently. Shock is the nearest he can come to religious truths. If you are reading a Forster story about a vigorous young man and happen, in the most natural way, to forget for just that moment how Death lies in ambush for all of us, Forster will rub your nose in reminders. How dare you forget that Death is by, how dare you forget Significance? Like those medieval monks who kept a skull on their desks, Forster believes in the instructiveness, the salubriousness, of shock. He believes that what is really important comes to us as a shock. And like nature (or like religion bereft of consolation), he withholds, he is unpredictable, he springs, so as to facilitate the shock.

That is in the fiction. His own life seemed not like that. He endured the mildest of bachelor lives, with, seen from the outside, no cataclysms. He was happiest (as adolescents say today, he "found himself") as a Cambridge undergraduate, he touched tenuously on Bloomsbury, he saw Egypt and India (traveling always, whether he intended it or not, as an agent of Empire), and when his mother died returned to Cambridge to live out his days among the undergraduates of King's. He wrote what is called a "civilized" prose, sometimes too slyly decorous, occasionally fastidiously poetic, often enough as direct as a whip. His essays, mainly the later ones, are especially direct: truth-telling, balanced, "humanist"—kind-hearted in a detached way, like, apparently, his personal cordiality. He had charm: a combination of self-importance (in the sense of knowing himself to be the real thing) and shyness. In tidy rooms at King's (the very same College he had first come up to in 1897), Forster in his seventies and eighties received visitors and courtiers with memorable pleasantness, was generous to writers in need of a push (Lampedusa among them), and judiciously wrote himself off as a pre-1914 fossil. Half a century after his last novel the Queen bestowed on him the Order of Merit. Then one day in the summer of 1970 he went to Coventry on a visit and died quietly at ninety-one, among affectionate friends.

That was the life. That none of this was meant to be trusted, not, certainly, to be taken at face value—least of all the harmonious death—suddenly came clear last year, when the British Museum let it be known it was in possession of an unpublished Forster novel, written in 1913, between the two masterpieces *Howards End* and *A Passage to India;* and that the novel was about homosexual love. Biographically, the posthumous publication of *Maurice* is the precise equivalent of "Gerald died that afternoon." (Trust the fiction, not the life.) It was to be sprung on us in lieu of a homily, and from the grave itself—another audacious slap in the face.

But literary shock, especially when it is designed to be didactic, has a way of finally trivializing. The suddenness of Gerald's death presses so hard for Significance that Significance itself begins to give way, and wilts off into nothing more impressive than a sneer. Forster, prodding the cosmos to do its job of showing us how puny we are, is left holding his little stick—the cosmos has escaped him, it will not oblige. Gerald's death may surprise, but the teaching fails: death qua death is not enough. We must have grief to feel death, and Forster did not give us enough Gerald to grieve over. We were never allowed to know Gerald well, or even to like him a little; he is an unsympathetic minor character, too minor to stand for the abyss. Shock does not yield wisdom on short acquaintance.

Maurice is meant to convey wisdom on longer acquaintance: here is a full-scale history of a homosexual from earliest awakening to puzzlement to temporary joy to frustration to anguish, and at last to sexual success. In *Maurice* it is society Forster prods, not the cosmos; it is one of Forster's few books in which death does not reverberate in any major way. But like the cosmos in *The Longest Journey*, society in *Maurice* eludes Forster's stick. In *Howards End* it did not: he impaled English mores in the house-renting habits of Mr.

Wilcox, and wrote of the money-and-property mentality in such a way as to dishevel it permanently. *Howards End* is, along with *Middlemarch* thirty-odd years before, the prototypical English Wisdom Novel—wisdom in the category of the-way-things-really-are, the nest of worms exposed below the surface of decency. *Maurice* is even more ambitious: it appears not merely to attack and discredit society, but to outwit it. How? By spite; by spitting in the eye of conventional respectability; by inventing a triumphant outcome against the grain of reality and (then) possibility. "A happy ending was imperative," Forster explained in a message that accompanies the novel in the manner of a suicide note (and is, in fact, styled by him a "Terminal Note"); like a suicide note it represents defense, forethought, revenge—the culmination of extensive fantasizing. "I shouldn't have bothered to write otherwise. I was determined that in fiction anyway two men should fall in love and remain in it for the ever and ever that fiction allows."

The key words are: in fiction. *Maurice*, in short, is a fairy tale. I don't choose this term for the sake of an easy pun, or to take up the line of ribaldry, and certainly not to mock. I choose it because it is the most exact. *Maurice* is not merely an idyll, not merely a fantasy, not merely a parable. It is a classical (though flawed and failed) fairy tale in which the hero is stuck with an ineradicable disability. In the standard fairy tale he may be the youngest of three, or the weakest, or the poorest and most unlikely—in Maurice's instance he is the oddest, and cannot love women. In the prescribed manner he encounters sinister advice and dissembling friends and gets his profoundest wish at the end, winning—as a reward for the wish itself—the hand of his beloved. The essence of a fairy tale is that wishing *does* make it so: the wish achieves its own fulfillment through its very steadfastness of desire. That is why fairy tales, despite their dark tones and the vicissitudes they contain so abundantly, are so obviously akin to daydreams—daydreaming is a sloughing-off of society, not an analysis of it. To wish is not to explain; to wish is not to reform. In real life wishing, divorced from willing, is sterile and begets nothing. Consequently *Maurice* is a disingenuous book, an infantile book, because, while pretending to be about societal injustice, it is really about make-believe, it is about wishing; so it fails even as a tract. Fairy tales, though, are plainly literature; but *Maurice* fails as literature too. In a fairy or folk tale the hero, even when he is a trickster, is a model of purity and sincerity. What is pure and sincere in him is the force of his wish, so much so that his wish and his nature are one. But Maurice as hero has a flaw at the center of him; he is conceived impurely and insincerely.

This impurity Forster himself appears to concede. "In Maurice," the

Terminal Note explains further, "I tried to create a character, who was completely unlike myself or what I supposed myself to be: someone handsome, healthy, bodily attractive, mentally torpid, not a bad business man and rather a snob. Into this mixture I dropped an ingredient that puzzles him, wakes him up, torments him and finally saves him." The impurity, then, is the ingredient of homosexuality dropped into a man who is otherwise purely Mr. Wilcox, lifted temperamentally intact out of *Howards End:* a born persecutor whom fear of persecution "saves" from the practice of his trait.

But whatever Forster's hope for Maurice was, this is not the sensibility he has rendered. It is impossible to believe in Maurice as a businessman or a jock (in Cambridge vocabulary, a "blood"). He is always Ricky of *The Longest Journey* (which means he is always Morgan Forster) got up in a grotesque costume—The Sensitive Hero as Callous Philistine—and wearing a wobbly wig. Whenever Maurice is most himself, the prose gives a lurch: it is Forster remembering, with a mindful shudder, to throw in a liter of mental torpidity here, a kilo of investment shrewdness there. But all that is artifice and sham. Forster loves music; Maurice is ignorant of it; consequently Maurice's self-knowledge occurs partly through Tchaikovsky. Forster at school recoiled from games and fell in love with Hellenism; Maurice has "physical pluck" and is an indifferent scholar (his "Greek was vile"); consequently on Prize Day he delivers a Greek Oration. No matter how Forster sidesteps it, Maurice keeps coming out Forster. After a while the absurdity of the effort to coarsen Maurice—to de-Morgan him, so to speak—fatigues; Forster's pointless toil at this impossibility becomes, for the reader, an impatience and an embarrassment. It is embarrassing to watch a writer cover his tracks in the name of exploring them. Purporting to show a hard man turn soft under the pressure of alienation from the general run of society, Forster instead (and without admitting it) shows a soft man turn softer—so soft he slides off into the teleology of the fairy tale. This falsification is the real impurity of the novel. Its protagonist falls apart at the marrow, like a book left outdoors overnight in the rain. *Maurice* cannot hold because Maurice is made of paper and breaks like dough at the first moist lover's squeeze.

One suspects Forster knew this. How could he not? He had already published three nearly perfect minor novels and one extraordinary major one. He had already created the Schlegels and the Wilcoxes. Written in his own handwriting across the top of the British Museum's typescript of *Maurice*, and put there possibly as late as 1960, were the Delphic words: "Publishable, but is it worth it?" The ambiguity is typical. Is the reference to the homosexual theme—or to the level of craftsmanship? That Forster was distinctly capable of detecting a falling-off from his own standard we know from his account of *Arctic Summer*, a work he abandoned midway because of "fiction-technicalities." Comparing the texture of his unfinished novel with the "density" of *A Passage to India*, he explained, "There must be something, some major object toward which one is to approach . . . What I had in *Arctic Summer* was thinner, a background and color only." If he was able to sense the thinness of one novel and then let it go, why did he preserve *Maurice*, which he must surely have perceived as at least equally thin? In 1960, the date of the Terminal Note, thirty-three years had already passed since Forster's invention (in *Aspects of the Novel*) of the terms "flat" and "round" to describe the differences between characters in novels. A flat character is always predictable; a round character is not. Maurice is neither flat nor round, but something else—a ghost—and Forster must have known it. How could he not? What made him want to hang on to a protagonist so dismally flawed? The answer may be in the "something, some major object toward which one is to approach." In *Maurice* it is painfully easy to see what that major object is: sex, overt and unfudged. Forster preserved the approach but did not arrive. "There is no pornography," the Terminal Note scrupulously reports. So much the worse for Maurice. He is there—he was put to paper neither flat nor round—only for the sake of the sex scenes; and the sex scenes are hardly there at all. Maurice—neither flat nor round—is the ghost of undepicted, inexplicit coitus, of the missing "pornography."

Except for those absent sex scenes—one feels them struggling to be born, and Forster stamping them regretfully out at their earliest gasp—*Maurice* has no reason to be. It is a novel, if one can say such a thing, without a cause. Or, rather, the only genuine cause for it, the force that got it written, was a fresh and potent interest in all those matters that did *not* get written: the caresses in detail, the embraces, the endearments precisely depicted. Instead we are only handed plot. And to be handed plot is, in the case of *Maurice*, to be handed something worn out almost to risibility. It is not that *Maurice* has no plot; it does, and I suppose I am bound to recount a little of it; but it is a plot that Forster has dealt with at least twice before in the two novels of which *Maurice* is the shadow-novel, and, in fact, in what may have been the very first short story he ever wrote.

In all of these—"Albergo Empedocle," *The Longest Journey, A Room with a View*—a poetic but naive hero (or heroine) falls in love with a woman (or man) who appears at first to be even more sensitive and poetic, but who betrays by turning out to be unable to love with equal tenderness or sincerity. In *The Longest Journey* Ricky, charmed by the ecloguelike scene he witnesses of the "Greek athlete" Gerald kissing Agnes in the dell, marries Agnes and finds instead that he has surrendered his spirit to coldness and cynicism. In

A Room with a View Lucy, whose poetic nature is expressed in music, becomes engaged to Cecil; Cecil is brilliant, and therefore seems to be in love with art, Leonardo, and Italy, but is in reality "like a Gothic statue," which "implies celibacy, just as a Greek statue implies fruition." "Albergo Empedocle" describes the breakup of an engagement between Mildred, a young woman intellectually immersed in Hellenism, and Harold, who suddenly feels himself to be the reincarnation of a Greek youth. For the moment Mildred is romantically enraptured at the notion. But she ends up thinking her fiancé mad—whereupon he displays his love for another youth, ancient Greek-style. All these tender lovers, genuinely won to the Greek ideal of the body, are betrayed by a capricious and false Hellenism.

Maurice too finds his hard-earned Hellenism betrayed. In the joyfully liberating atmosphere of Cambridge he is introduced to music, Plato, and Clive Durham, a worshiper of Greece and a lapsed Christian. Like the others, they have their day in the dell and become lovers, though mainly sentimentally (Clive "abstained . . . almost from caresses"). Then Clive goes on a pilgrimage to Greece, and there—in Greece; irony!—"becomes normal." He has "turned to women," and enters the life of conventional county society, marrying coldly and growing more and more worldly and opportunistic. Maurice's outlook darkens. He too tries to "become normal." There follow relatively good, though thin, Forsterian scenes with a doctor (who can only say "Rubbish" to the idea of homosexuality) and a hypnotist (who decides the case is hopeless). Then comes the happy ending. Just as Lucy in *A Room with a View* flees from Cecil to marry the Panlike figure of George Emerson, Maurice flees his family, his work, and society altogether, going off to live tenderly ever after with a rough-mannered but loving gamekeeper.

"There is no pornography." In short, a daydream without pictures. But what *Maurice* lacks, and what is necessary to it because it belongs at the heart of its imagining, *is* the pictures, *is* the "pornography"—or what Forster significantly continued to think of as pornography. What surely was not necessary was the reflex of Forster's ineluctable plot—the same story of compulsive attraction and callous faithlessness that he was driven to manipulate again and again, looking for some acceptable means to tell what he *really* wanted to tell about the importance of the body. It was pointless to write a book like *Maurice* unless the body in its exact—not implied, not poeticized—male lineaments could be truly shown. Forster did not show it truly. It is clear enough that he longed to show it truly—he lingers over those blurry passages in which he might have shown it truly, and instead reaches desperately for the expedient of poetry. "And their love scene drew out . . . Something of exquisite beauty arose in the mind of each at last, something unforgettable and eternal, but built of the humblest scraps of speech and from the simplest emotions." And of the flesh. But it is the flesh that Forster omits.

The reason for this omission, it seems to me, is not that in the England of 1913 Forster still did not dare to put it explicitly in (Gide in France had already launched *Corydon*, but that was France), and not even that Forster still belonged mentally to the England of 1897. No. The reason—unlikely though it may appear at first hearing—is that Forster thought homosexuality wrong: naturally wrong, with the sort of naturalness that he did not expect to date. (The Terminal Note admits that *Maurice* "certainly dates" in other respects, and mentions its "half-sovereign tips, pianola-records, norfolk jackets.") But if *Maurice* is a fairy tale, it is not because two men do not ever, then or now, out of fiction as well as in, live together happily and permanently, but because Forster himself believed that except in fiction and daydream they ought not to. Against his deepest wish he set his still deeper belief. *They ought not to:* despite the fact that he was always openly in favor of the liberalization in England of laws concerning homosexuality, despite the fact that as early as 1928, beginning with the *Well of Loneliness* case, he went to court to testify against the suppression of a homosexual novel, the first of a succession of such books he publicly defended and praised.

Forster's own books are full of veiled portraits of repressed or hidden or potential homosexuals, from Ansell in *The Longest Journey* to Tibby in *Howards End* (who warms the teapot "almost too deftly," is called "Auntie Tibby" for fun, and is declared not to be "a real boy"). The description of Cecil in *A Room with a View* fits not only what the young Tibby will become, but what Maurice's lover Clive already is: "He is the sort who are all right as long as they keep to things—books, pictures—but kill when they come to people." Many of Forster's clergymen are seen to be embittered ascetics who, had they not suppressed the body, would have loved men. Mr. Borenius, the rector in *Maurice*, jealously accuses the gamekeeper of being "guilty of sensuality." It is because Forster himself is always on the side of sensuality, of "fruition" as against "celibacy," that all his spokesmen-characters, with profound sadness, eventually yield up their final judgment—on moral and natural grounds, and despite Forster's renowned liberalism—against homosexuality. *Maurice*, where the wish for lasting homoerotic bliss is allowed to come true, is no exception to Forster's moral conviction.

It is precisely on this issue of sensuality that Forster's reservations rest. Forster believes, with Christianity, that the opposite of sensuality is sterility. And not sterility in any metaphorical sense—not in the meaning of an empty or unused life. With Christianity, Forster believes that sensuality is designed to beget progeny. The most melancholy passage in *Maurice* occurs at Maurice's most ecstatic moment—when he is at last physically in possession of Clive:

> An immense sadness—he believed himself beyond such irritants—had risen up in his soul. He and the beloved would vanish utterly—would continue neither in Heaven nor on Earth. They had won past the conventions, but Nature still faced them, saying with even voice, "Very well, you are thus; I blame none of my children. But you must go the way of all sterility." The thought that he was sterile weighed on the young man with a sudden shame. His mother or Mrs. Durham might lack mind or heart, but they had done visible work; they had handed on the torch their sons would tread out.

And it is Ansell in *The Longest Journey* who gives the homosexual's view of progeny, which is renunciation. He is strolling in the British Museum talking of "the Spirit of Life" when he is told that Ricky and Agnes are expecting a child. His response: "I forgot that it might be." Then: "He left the Parthenon to pass by the monuments of our more reticent beliefs—the temple of the Ephesian Artemis, the statue of the Cnidian Demeter. Honest, he knew that here were powers he could not cope with, nor, as yet, understand." Artemis the protectress of women, Demeter the goddess of fertility. Thus Ansell. And thus Auden. Somewhere Auden has written that homosexual men do not love their sterility; that homosexuals too would welcome parenthood; but out of decency and selflessness forgo it.

"Be fruitful and multiply." That Forster alone perhaps of all homosexual writers is willing to take seriously the biblical injunction, and is left feeling desolated by it, is a measure of how attached he remained to Christian morals. In this attachment he was unlike any homosexual in his Cambridge generation, and possibly unlike any English-speaking homosexual in the generations afterward, Auden excepted. The Gay Liberation argument that homosexual activity is a positive good in a world afflicted by overpopulation would not have won Forster over.

Homosexuality did not begin with Lytton Strachey, but homosexual manners did. All those habits and signals that we now associate with the educated homosexual sensibility can be said to have had their start in Cambridge when Strachey was an undergraduate; and Strachey set the style for them. Sects and persuasions, like nationalities, have their forerunners and traditions: presumably Franciscans still strive to retain the mind-set of Saint

Francis, Quakers recall George Fox, the white American South continues to feel itself patrician. Forster himself was influenced in liberal thinking by his ancestors in the Clapham Sect, an abolitionist group. The recollection need not be conscious; we inherit, rather than mimic, style. So with educated homosexual manners. The passion for beauty and distinction, the wit with its double bur of hilarity and malice, the aesthetic frame of mind, even the voice that edges thinly upward and is sometimes mistaken for "effeminacy"—all these are Stracheyisms. Strachey at Cambridge and afterward was so forceful in passing on Stracheyism that he founded a school, active to this day. It had, and has, two chief tenets: one was antiphilistinism expressed as elitism (one cannot imagine Strachey making a hero of a gamekeeper with no grammar, or addressing, as Forster did, a Working Men's College); the other was a recoil from Christianity. In these tenets especially Forster did not acquiesce.

Though Forster knew Strachey well at Cambridge (he even confesses that a Cambridge character in *Maurice* was modeled on Strachey), he remained peripheral to the Strachey set. This astounding group was concentrated in the Cambridge Conversazione Society, better known as the Apostles, which mingled older alumni and undergraduates, never much more than a dozen at a time, and was devoted to intellectual wrangling, high wit, snobbery toward "bloods," and, in an underground sort of way, homosexuality: its brilliant members kept falling in and out of love with one another. At one time Strachey and John Maynard Keynes were both furious rivals for the love of one Duckworth; afterward Keynes, like Clive Durham, "became normal" and married a ballerina. Through all this Forster kept himself apart and remote, "the elusive colt of a dark horse," as Keynes called him. The Apostles churned out barristers, chief justices, governors of outlying parts of the Empire, dons, historians, economists, mathematicians, philosophers, many of them with family attachments to one another: in short, the ruling intellectual class of England more or less reproducing itself. The smaller "aesthetic" section of this privileged and brainy caste withdrew to become Bloomsbury; but from Bloomsbury too Forster held himself in reserve. One reason was his temperamental shyness, his inclination toward an almost secretive privateness. The more compelling reason was that he did not think or feel like the Apostles, or like Bloomsbury. He was more mystical than skeptical. The ideal of freedom from all restraint made him uncomfortable in practice. Unlike Strachey, he did not scoff easily or vilify happily (though it ought to be noted that there is a single radiant "Balls" in *Maurice*), and did not use the word "Christian" as a taunt. To the Apostles—self-declared "immoralists," according to Keynes—and to Bloomsbury he must have seemed a little out of date. He never shared their elation at smashing conventional ideas; though himself an enemy of convention, he saw beyond convention to its roots in nature. Stracheyan Bloomsbury assented to nothing, least of all to God or nature, but Forster knew there were "powers he could not cope with, nor, as yet, understand." Bloomsbury was alienated but not puzzled; Forster was puzzled but not alienated. His homosexuality did not divide him from society, because he saw that society in the largest sense was the agent of nature; and when he came to write *A Passage to India* he envisioned culture and nature as fusing altogether. Homosexuality led him not away from but toward society. He accepted himself as a man with rights—nature made him—but also very plainly as a deviant—nature would not gain by him. It is no accident that babies are important in his books.

The shock of the publication of *Maurice*, then, is not what it appears to be at first sight: Forster as Forerunner of Gay Lib. Quite the opposite. He used his own position as an exemplum, to show what the universe does not intend. If that implies a kind of rational martyrdom, that is what he meant; and this is what shocks. We had not thought of him as martyr. For Forster, "I do not conform" explains what does conform, it does not celebrate nonconformity. He was a sufferer rather than a champion. Now suddenly, with the appearance of *Maurice*, it is clear that Forster's famous humanism is a kind of personal withdrawal rather than a universal testimony, and reverberates with despair. Christopher Lehmann-Haupt in a recent *Times* review remarks that Maurice's homosexuality is "a symbol of human feelings." But Forster would disagree that homosexuality stands for anything beyond what it is in itself, except perhaps the laying-waste of the Cnidian Demeter. Homosexuality to Forster signified sterility; he practiced it like a blasphemer, just as he practiced his humanism like a blasphemer. There is no blasphemy where there is no belief to be betrayed; and Forster believes in the holiness of the goddess of fertility: Demeter, guardian of the social order and marriage. The most dubious social statement Forster ever made is also his most famous one: if I had to choose between betraying my country or my friend, I hope I would have the guts to betray my country. He says "I"; the note is personal, it is not an injunction to the rest of us. *Maurice* instructs us explicitly in what he understands by "friend"; in Maurice's boyhood dream the word "friend" foretells the love of a man for a man. We have encountered that charged word in Forster before. The statement about betrayal cannot be universalized, and Forster did not mean it to be. Declarations about bedmates do not commonly have general application.

Does it devalue the large humanistic statement to know that its sources are narrowly personal? Yes. And for Forster too: he does not ask society to conform to him, because he believes—he says it again and again everywhere in his books, but nowhere more poignantly than in his novel about homosexual love—he believes in the eternal stream. He died among affectionate friends, but not harmoniously; he was not content to go the way of all sterility, to vanish utterly. Books are not progeny, and nature does not read.

I append to my observations about Forster's *Maurice* a reply to a correspondent who charged me with not loving Forster enough.

Forster as Moralist:
A Reply to Mrs. A. F.

Lionel Trilling begins his book about Forster with this observation: "E. M. Forster is for me the only living novelist who can be read again and again and who, after each reading, gives me what few writers can give us after our first days of novel-reading, the sensation of having learned something." To this statement another can be added, virtually a corollary: Forster is also one of those very few writers (and since Forster's death, there is none now living) who excite competitive passions—possessive rivalries, in fact—among serious readers, each of whom feels uniquely chosen to perceive the inner life of the novels.

In recent years Forster has grown thinner for me, especially as essayist. Not that I would now deny Forster's powers or his brilliance, or claim that the masterpieces are not masterpieces, still giving out, as Trilling said almost thirty years ago, "the sensation of having learned something." But what we learn from the novels is not what we learn from the essays. The novels do not preach morality and the essays, in their way, do. Or, to put it differently, the novels preach a novelistic morality—in the early ones, the ethics of Spontaneity; in *A Passage to India*, the anti-ethics of a mystical nihilism. But the essays—pre-eminently "What I Believe," which Mrs. F. cites—tell us how we are to go about living from moment to moment. "Where do I start?" Forster asks. And answers: "With personal relationships." Of this approach Mrs. F. says: "I like it well."

I do not, because it strikes me as incomplete and self-indulgent. Nevertheless I recognize Mrs. F.'s tone—it was once mine, and I think we can spot our erstwhile psychological twins—at the end of her letter, when she concludes that I do "not love [Forster] enough—for what he *did* do." I withdraw from the contest and agree that Mrs. F. is right. She *does* love Forster's ideas and qualities, if not more than I once did, certainly more than I do now.

And the reasons I have, so to speak, fallen out of love with Forster are the very reasons she is still in thrall to him. A novelist, as she says, is both psychologist and metaphysician (and social historian). That is why we become most attached to those novels which give us an adequate account of the way the world seems to us. Novelists interpret us, and when we "choose" a novelist we are really choosing a version of ourselves. The same is true of essayists. What I no longer choose to choose among Forster's ideas is "Only Connect," which signifies, of course, "personal relationships." When I said in my remarks on *Maurice* that it devalued "the large humanistic statement to know that its sources are narrowly personal," I was not referring to Forster's novelistic imagination (of course the women in his novels are women and not disguised male homosexuals), but to his liberalism. We are now unambiguously apprised of Forster's homosexuality, and *Maurice* makes it shudderingly plain that Forster considered homosexuality to be an affliction, the ineradicable mark of a fated few. To use language grown shabby from repetition, he regarded himself as part of an oppressed minority; and, applying Only Connect, he could stand in for and champion other oppressed minorities—Indians under English colonialism, for instance, who suffered from the English public-school mentality precisely as he had suffered from it. But this, after all, is a compromised liberalism. There is nothing admirable in it; it is devalued by the presence of the vested interest. It is no trick, after all, for a Jew to be against anti-Semitism, or for a homosexual to be against censorship of homosexual novels. The passion behind the commitment may be pure, but the commitment is not so much a philosophy of liberalism as it is of self-preservation. Morality must apply some more accessible standard than personal hurt. In *Howards End* Mr. Wilcox, disapproving of Helen's affair with Leonard Bast, gets his nose rubbed in a reminder of his own affair, long ago, with Mrs. Bast: what's sauce for the goose is sauce for the gander. But suppose the gander has had no sauce? I am not a homosexual; if I had been in England in 1935, should I not have been disturbed by the law that interfered with the untrammeled publication of *Boy*, as Forster was? (See his essay "Liberty in England.") Liberalism, to be the real thing, ought to be disinterested.

But the inadequacy of Only Connect—that it is *not* disinterested—is not the whole of my charge against "personal relationships" as the ultimate moral standard. Deciding your behavior person by person (Forster was apparently the inventor of an early form of situation ethics) seems to me a localized, partial, highly contingent, catch-as-catch-can sort of morality. "This is my friend; I love him; therefore I will not kill him" is, in my view, inferior to saying, once and for all, "Thou shalt not kill." The reason is not simply that the overall Commandment is relatively more efficient than figuring it out one person at a time as you go along, but also that it is more reliable. "This is my friend; I love him" can too easily turn into "This was my friend; now I hate him." And if that is all there is to it, if there is no larger motive than "personal relationships" to govern human behavior, one might as well kill him. It is not only that "Love and loyalty to an individual can run counter to the claims of the State" (though the single example Forster can think of to illustrate this possibility is Brutus and Cassius vis-à-vis Caesar, not exactly the sort of situation that one is likely to encounter on an everyday basis)—it is also, as Forster himself recognizes, that love and loyalty can run counter to themselves; in short, they rot. They are "a matter for the heart, which signs no documents." That is why, taking up—as Forster himself does—the question of reliability, and writing about these matters on stone some four thousand years before Forster, Moses thought that having it down on a document might not be a bad idea. "But reliability," Forster sensibly answers Moses, "is not a matter of contract—that is the main difference between the world of personal relationships and the world of business relationships." It is also one of the differences between personal relationships and universal ethics. To Forster, Moses comes out a businessman with a contract, and in the same essay (we are still in "What I Believe") he says he prefers Montaigne and Erasmus. "My temple stands," he asserts, "not upon Mount Moriah but in that Elysian Field where even the immoral are admitted." It is not a very great distance from an Elysian Field that makes no distinction between innocents and murderers (for we have a right to take the persons Forster calls "immoral" at their most extreme) to the *ou-boum* of the Marabar Caves, which swallows up both good and evil into one of the unknown black holes of the universe, similarly without distinction. The problem with Forster's "personal relationships"—or, to use Mrs. F.'s term, his personal loyalties—is that they tend to slip away at the first intrusion of something spooky or ineffably cosmic—of something, in brief, that suggests his notion of Religion, which is pagan in the sense of fearfulness, imbued with the uncanniness of *lacrimae rerum*, un-human, without relation to the world of men. When Mrs. Moore in the cave hears the *ou-boum* of nothingness, she "lost all interest, even in Aziz [who had become her good friend], and the affectionate and sincere words that she had spoken to him seemed no longer hers but the air's."

Mrs. Moore in the Marabar Caves is obviously an extreme example of the dissolution of a friendship. But Forster, as we know, is fond of extremes, so it is not too much to say that Mrs. Moore is also an extreme example of someone who—quoting Mrs. F. quoting Forster—"hate[s] the idea of causes." Her hatred of causes does not strengthen her in friendship. She betrays her friend by losing interest in him, because the universe has shown her that it is impersonal, and that friendship and betrayal and loss are all the same to it. She has no "cause"—no motivation, no ideal contract—that restricts her from betraying her friend. Forster's dedication to personal relationships without contract is doomed to work only very rarely, not only because friendship succeeds only very rarely, but because it is, in a world of friends and non-friends, not enough. "Do not lie about your friend, whom you love" is, in moral distance, a light-year from "Do not tell lies about anyone at all"—or, as it is more commonly formulated, "Do not bear false witness." A contractual, or communal, ethics, when violated, at least leaves the standard intact. A catch-as-catch-can ethics, based on your feelings for your friend, leaves everything in a shambles when it is violated.

A case can of course be made that Forster's ethics of privacy derives through Romanticism with its discovery of the Individual from Nonconformism with its emphasis on regulating personal morality through conscience. Whatever their sources, though, the moral and political positions that emerge from "What I Believe" seem to me to be disturbingly partial. They may do a certain credit to the sensibility of a hurt man who knows enough to be thoughtful about the hurts of others, but they fail of universal application. Forster never comes head-on against the problem of how to get the "bloods" to behave less callously. Or, rather, he dodges the problem by loading it: by giving Mr. Wilcox an old affair to hide, by making Maurice a homosexual. His whole men turn out not to be whole at all; Forster appears incapable of accepting the *principle* of not hurting without first making a hurt felt. His humanity goes from wound to wound. His politics, his morality, ultimately his liberalism, all signify the humanism of cripples. It is too thin. The thugs escape.

The difficulty, I think, is that Mrs. F. mixes up these specific questions raised by Forster's political and moral positions with a general analysis of the novelistic imagination. Her description of the "miracle" of the Active imagination is superb and very nearly complete, but I am puzzled about why she has introduced it. My judgment on Forster's humanism does not lead logically to any judgment on his capacity to imagine. If I believe, as I do, that Forster's sense of himself as a kind of martyr taints the candor of his liberalism with a hidden self-interest, how does this relate to Mrs. F.'s notion that I somehow also believe the novels to be homosexual disguises? They are obviously not homosexual disguises. Nothing in what I wrote suggested they might be. That there are in Forster's fiction men with homosexual tendencies has always been clear and is now clearer. A pair of obvious examples: Ricky and Ansell, Aziz and Fielding. Revisited in the aftermath of *Maurice* (I have, for instance, been rereading *A Passage to India*), they have new resonances;

so does the passionate "friend" in the essay called "Notes on the English Character" (1920), who is an adumbration of Aziz as Forster himself in that essay is an adumbration of Fielding. As for Forster's use of the word "friend": until some industrious clod of a graduate student gives us the definitive concordance for that word in Forster's *oeuvre,* we shall not know how often he intended it wistfully and how often straightforwardly. But until we get the concordance, we will have to rely on impressions—and my impression is that it is a word Forster most often uses wistfully. I feel certain—it is an impression—that the friend for whom Forster would betray his country is thought of wistfully. When you betray your country, that is treason, a capital offense. Betraying your country for your friend, you die. I quote Mrs. F. quoting Maurice in a passage she herself calls "the epitome of the homosexual 'friend' "He could die for such a friend . . . they would make any sacrifice for each other, and count the world nothing." Maurice would betray his country for such a friend; Forster is largely indistinguishable from Maurice; and yet Mrs. F. writes, "I don't believe you can imagine him to mean by 'friend' anything different from what you or I or anyone would mean by it." My impression is otherwise.

But all this is about friendship between men. Against the rest—Mrs. F.'s catalogue of "love, courtship, marriage, sisterhood, fatherhood, sonhood"— nothing can be insinuated. Forster believed, as I have said, in Demeter, the most domestic of all the goddesses.

So two cheers for Forster's Friendship. "Two cheers are quite enough," Forster remarked of Democracy, saving his third for "Love the Beloved Republic." If, as Mrs. F. asserts, I do not love Forster enough for what he has done, it is not because I fail to celebrate his novelistic imagination, but rather because I would dislike living in his Republic, where personal relationships govern (one might dare to say seethe) and there are no communal contracts. I save half my third cheer for the Covenant; and the other half, following Forster in all his novels but the last, for Demeter.

The Phantasmagoria
of Bruno Schulz

Thirty-five years ago, Bruno Schulz, a fifty-year-old high-school art teacher in command of one of the most original literary imaginations of modern Europe, was gunned down by a Jew-hunting contingent of SS men in the streets of an insignificant provincial town in eastern Galicia. On the map of Poland the town hides itself from you; you have to search out the tiniest print to discover Drogobych. In this cramped crevice of a place Schulz too hid himself—though not from the Nazis. Urged on by a group of writers, the Polish underground devised a means of escape—false papers and a hiding place. Schulz chose to die unhidden in Drogobych. But even before the German storm, he had already chosen both to hide and to die there. He knew its streets, and their houses and shops, with a paralyzed intimacy. His environment and his family digested him. He was incapable of leaving home, of marrying, at first even of writing. On a drab salary, in a job he despised, he supported a small band of relatives, and though he visited Warsaw and Lvov, and once even went as far as Paris, he gave up larger places, minds, and lives for the sake of Drogobych—or, rather, for the sake of the gargoylish and astonishing map his imagination had learned to draw of an invisible Drogobych contrived entirely out of language.

In English there is virtually no biographical information to be had concerning Schulz. It is known that his final manuscript, a novel called *The Messiah*, was carried for safekeeping to a friend; both friend and manuscript were swallowed up by the sacrificial fires of the Europe of 1942. All of Schulz's letters, and two-thirds of the very small body of his finished work—two novels, one novella—remain untranslated and, so far, inaccessible to American readers. It is a powerful omission. Think what our notion of the literature of the Dark Continent of Europe would be like if we had read our way so late into the century without the most renowned of the stories in *Red Cavalry*, or without "Gimpel the Fool," or without *The Metamorphosis*. A verbal landscape stripped of Babel or Singer or Kafka is unimaginable to us now, and it may turn out, in the wake of *The Street of Crocodiles*, that Schulz can stand naturally—or unnaturally—among those writers who break our eyes with torches, and end by demonstrating the remarkable uses of a purposeful dark.

In this dark the familiar looms freakish, and all of these—Babel as Cossack Jew, Singer purveying his imps and demiurges, Kafka with his measured and logical illogic—offer mutations, weird births, essences and occasions never before suspected. *The Street of Crocodiles*, at one with that mythic crew, is a transmogrified Drogobych: real town and real time and real tasks twisted and twisted until droplets of changed, even hateful, even hideous, beauty are squeezed out of bolts of cloth, ledgers, tailors' dummies, pet birds, a row of shops, a puppy, a servant girl. As in Kafka, the malevolent is deadpan; its loveliness of form is what we notice. At the heart of the malevolent—also the repugnant, the pitiless—crouches the father: Schulz's own father, since there is an inviolable autobiographical glaze that paints over every distortion. The father is a shopkeeper, the owner of a dry-goods store. He gets sick, gives up work, hangs around home, fiddles with his account books, grows morbid and sulky, has trouble with his bowels, bursts out into fits of rage. All this is novelist's material, and we are made to understand it in the usual way of novels.

But parallel with it, engorging it, is a running flame of amazing imagery—altogether exact and meticulous—that alters everything. The wallpaper becomes a "pullulating jungle . . . filled with whispers, lisping and hissing." Father "sitting clumsily on an enormous china chamberpot" turns into a prophet of "the terrible Demiurge," howling with "the divine anger of saintly men." Father shrinks, hides in closets, climbs the curtains and perches there like a baleful stuffed vulture, disappears "for many days into some distant corner of the house." Schulz's language is dense with disappearances, losses, metamorphoses. The dry-goods shop is flooded by a "cosmogony of cloth." Crowded streets become "an ultra-barrel of myth." The calendar takes on a thirteenth month. Rooms in houses are forgotten, misplaced. A bicycle ascends into the zodiac. Even death is somehow indefinite; a murk, a confusion. Father "could not merge with any reality and was therefore condemned to float eternally on the periphery of life, in half-real regions, on the margins of existence. He could not even earn an honest citizen's death." Father, alive, lectures on manikins: "There is no dead matter . . . lifelessness is only a disguise behind which hide unknown forms of life." A dog represents "the most essential secret of life, reduced to this simple, handy, toy-like form." Wallpapers become bored; furniture, "unstable, degenerate," breaks out into rashes. The maid rules the master with ominous and magisterial positions of her fingers—she points, waggles, tickles. She is a kind of proto-Nazi. Father takes up ornithology and hatches a condor like "an emaciated ascetic, a Buddhist lama," an idol, a mummy—it resembles father himself. (A fore-echo of Kosinski, another Pole obsessed by fearful birds.) Father loathes cockroaches, violently pursues them, and is transformed, undertaking at last their "ceremonial crawl."

> He lay on the floor naked, stained with black totem spots, the lines of his ribs heavily outlined, the fantastic structure of his anatomy visible through the skin; he lay on his face, in the grip of an obsession of loathing which dragged him into the abyss of its complex paths. He moved with the many-limbed, complicated movements of a strange ritual in which I recognized with horror an imitation of the ceremonial crawl of a cockroach.

In Kafka's myth, it is the powerless son who turns into a cockroach; here it is the father who has lost control. Everything is loosened; it is not that the center does not hold; there never was a center. "Reality is as thin as paper and betrays with all its cracks its imitative character." "Our language has no definitions which would weigh, so to speak, the grade of reality." Given these hints, it may be misleading to anticipate *The Street of Crocodiles* with so "normal" a signal as *novel*: it is a thick string of sights and sinuosities, a cascade of flashes, of extraordinary movements—a succession of what television has taught us to call "film clips," images in magnetic batches, registered storms, each one shooting memories of itself into the lightnings of all the others. What is being invented in the very drone of our passive literary expectations is Religion—not the taming religion of theology and morality, but the brute splendors of rite, gesture, phantasmagoric transfiguration, sacrifice, elevation, degradation, mortification, repugnance, terror, cult. The religion of animism, in fact, where everything comes alive with an unpredictable and spiteful spirit-force, where even living tissue contains ghosts, where there is no pity.

Such metaphysical specters have their historical undersides. Home shifts, its forms are unreliable, demons rule. Why should these literary Jews of twentieth-century Slavic Europe—Babel, whose language was Russian, two years younger than Schulz; Kafka, who wrote in German, seven years older; Singer, a Yiddish writer, a dozen years younger; and finally (one is tempted to enter the next generation) the American Kosinski—why should these cultivated Slavic Jews run into the black crevices of nihilism, animalism, hollow riddle? Why, indeed, should these writers be the very ones almost to invent the literary signposts of such crevices? Gogol came first, it is true; but it is the Slavic Jews who have leaped into the fermenting vat. The homelessness and ultimate pariahship felt by Schulz—an assimilated, Polish-speaking Jew, not so much a Jew as a conscious Pole—in the years before the fiery consummation of the Final Solution may explain why the real Drogobych took on the symbolic name Crocodile Street, and became the place where "nothing ever succeeds . . . nothing can ever reach a definite conclusion." But it did, in gunshot, on the streets of Drogobych in 1942. "Over the whole area," Schulz writes of his visionary town, "there floats the lazy licentious smell of sin."

The shock of Schulz's images brings us the authentic bedevilment of the Europe we are heir to. Schulz's life was cut short. His work, a small packet, reminds us of father: "the small shroud of his body and the handful of nonsensical oddities." Some of the packet was lost in the human ash heap. As for the little that remains: let us set it beside Kafka and the others and see how it measures up for truth-telling.

"Please, Stories Are Stories":
Bernard Malamud

Hart and Schaffner are dead; Marx, ringed round with laurels, has notoriously retired. But the firm itself was dissolved long ago, and it was Saul Bellow who, with a sartorial quip, snipped the stitches that had sewn three acclaimed and determinedly distinct American writers into the same suit of clothes, with its single label: "Jewish writer." In Bellow's parody, Bellow, Malamud, and Roth were the literary equivalent of the much-advertised men's wear company—but lighthearted as it was, the joke cut two ways: it was a declaration of imagination's independence of collective tailoring, and it laughingly struck out at the disgruntlement of those who, having themselves applied the label in pique, felt displaced by it.

Who were these upstarts, these "pushy intruders" (as Gore Vidal had it), who were ravishing readers and seizing public space? Surveying American publishing, Truman Capote railed that "the Jewish mafia has systematically frozen [Gentiles] out of the literary scene." In a 1968 essay, "On Not Being a Jew," Edward Hoagland complained that he was "being told in print and sometimes in person that I and my heritage lacked vitality . . . because I could find no ancestor who had hawked copper pots in a Polish shtetl." Katherine Anne Porter, describing herself as "in the direct, legitimate line" of the English language, accused Jewish writers of "trying to destroy it and all other living things they touch." More benignly, John Updike invented Bech, his own Jewish novelist, and joined what he appeared to regard as the dominant competition.

Yet it was not so much in response to these dubious preconceptions as it was to a rooted sense of their capacious American literary inheritance that all three unwillingly linked novelists were reluctant to be defined by the term "Jewish writer." "I am not a Jewish writer, I am a writer who is a Jew," Philip Roth announced in Jerusalem in 1963. And Bellow, pugnaciously in a 1988 lecture: "If the WASP aristocrats wanted to think of me as a Jewish poacher on their precious cultural estates then let them."

Bernard Malamud sorted out these contentious impulses far more circumspectly. "I am a writer," he said in an interview on his sixtieth birthday, "and a Jew, and I write for all men. A novelist has to, or he's built himself a cage. I write about Jews, when I write about Jews, because they set my imagination going. I know something about their history, the quality of their experience and belief . . . The point I am making is that I was born in America and respond, in American life, to more than Jewish experience."

Though unexpressed, there lurks in all these concurring animadversions a fear of the stigma of the "parochial"—a charge never directed (and why not?) against Cather's prairie Bohemians, or the denizens of Updike's Brewer or Faulkner's Yoknapatawpha. Still, it is not through sober public rhetoric but in the wilder precincts of fiction that Malamud discloses his animating credo. It emerges in the clear voice of Levitansky, the antihero of "Man in the Drawer," a harried Soviet-Jewish writer whose work is barred from publication because it speaks human truths inimical to Stalinist policy. The American journalist who has worriedly befriended Levitansky asks whether he has submitted any Jewish stories, to which the writer retorts: "Please, stories are stories, they have not nationality . . . When I write about Jews comes out stories, so I write about Jews." It is this unanchored drive to create tales, Malamud implies, that generates subject matter—the very opposite of Henry James's reliance on the story's "germ," the purloinings and devisings of the observed world. "Stories are stories" is Malamud's ticket to untrammeled writerly freedom. Except to Scheherazade, he owes no social debts.

Despite this purist manifesto, Malamud is in fact steeped everywhere in social debt; his aesthetic is instinct with the muted pulse of what used to be called moral seriousness, a notion gone out of fashion in American writing, where too often flippancy is mistaken for irony. Malamud, a virtuoso of darkest irony, refuses the easy conventions of cynicism and its dry detachment. His stories know suffering, loneliness, lust, confinement, defeat; and even when they are lighter, they tremble with subterranean fragility. Older readers who were familiar with the novels and stories in the years of their earliest publication will recall the wonderment they aroused, beginning with the fables of *The Magic Barrel,* as each new tale disrupted every prevailing literary expectation. The voice was unlike any other, haunted by whispers of Hawthorne, Babel, Isak Dinesen, even Poe, and at the same time uniquely possessed: a fingerprint of fire and ash. It was as if Malamud were at work in a secret laboratory of language, smelting a new poetics that infused the inflections of one tongue into the music of another. His landscapes, nature's and the mind's, are inimitable; the Malamudian sensibility, its wounded openness to large feeling, has had no successors.

When the ambient culture changes, having moved toward the brittleness of wisecrack and indifference, and the living writer is no longer present, it can happen that a veil of forgetfulness falls over the work. And then comes a literary crisis: the recognition that a matchless civilizational note has been muffled. A new generation, mostly unacquainted with the risks of uncompromising and hard-edged compassion, deserves Malamud even more than the one that made up his contemporary readership. The idea of a writer who is intent on judging the world—hotly but quietly, and aslant, and through the subversions of tragic paradox—is nowadays generally absent: who is daring enough not to be cold-eyed? For Malamud, trivia has no standing as trivial, everything counts, everything is at stake—as in "The Jewbird," where a bossy crow-like intruder named Schwartz invades a family, refuses birdseed in favor of herring, and to ingratiate himself tutors the dull son. But the father, sensing a rival for domination, is enraged, and this fanciful comedy ends in primal terror and murder. Pity leaves its signature even in farce.

"The Jewbird" is one of thirty-six stories in the Library of America's definitive three-volume publication (the third is forthcoming) honoring Malamud's work on the hundredth anniversary of his birth; six of these Malamud himself never saw in print. Also included in the pair of volumes are five novels: *The Natural, The Assistant, A New Life, The Fixer,* and *Pictures of Fidelman.*

A New Life may be the most overlooked of Malamud's long fictions, perhaps because it has been mistaken for yet another academic novel. But the sheath is not the sword, and *A New Life* is as exquisite in its evocation of American transformation as Gatsby himself. Reversing the classic theme of the young-man-from-the-provinces, S. Levin, incipient wife stealer, "formerly a drunkard," is a refugee from the New York tenements who leaves behind the grit of urban roil to be absorbed by village ways. Cascadia, the unprepossessing northwestern college he joins as a low-ranking teacher, turns out to be precisely that: a provincial village of the kind we might read of in an English novel of rural life, with its petty hierarchies and spites and rivalries. Yet the local terrain—trees, flowers, green hills, pristine vistas—is intoxicating to the city dweller, and here Malamud, whose impoverished outer-borough warrens are uniformly grim, writes peerlessly, as nowhere else, of proliferating natural beauty. And in the vein of Huck Finn, who chooses damnation over the lies of conventional morality, he casts a redemptive radiance on the fraught flight of an adulterous woman and her fornicating lover. In its tormented, satiric, and startling underminings, *A New Life*—which, like *The Natural,* stands tonally apart from Malamud's other work—is one of those rare transfiguring American novels that turn wishing into destiny.

The Assistant and *The Fixer* are closer to the stories in their melancholy texture and feverish desperation. And as in the stories, a man's labor becomes his identity. Morris Bober tends a precarious grocery store, where his assistant hungers after love. The fixer, Yakov Bok, a worker in a brickyard, is unjustly imprisoned, walled in by an anti-Semitic blood-libel charge. Each person's fate pursues him: Fidelman in Rome, "a self-confessed failure as a painter," is stalked by the elusive Susskind, who covets Fidelman's suit. Leo Finkle, a rabbinical student, is hounded by Salzman the marriage broker. Alexander Levine, "a black Jew and an angel to boot," appears to Manischevitz, a tailor mired in suffering. Rosa, a maid in thrall to her lover, wheedles a pair of shoes out of the dignified professor whose rooms she cleans. Apparitions, stalkings, houndings, claims and demands: unbidden, duties and obligations fall on Malamud's characters with the power of commandments. The pursuer and the quarry are each other's double; through self-recognition, repugnance is conjured into acquiescence. In the shifting kaleidoscope of all these whirling tales, Malamud's quest is for renewal—freedom from the shackled self. Some have argued, not unpersuasively, that his humble Jews are stand-ins for universal suffering: in fiction as in life, living human beings ought not to be thrust into the annihilating perils of metaphor. Malamud easily escapes these transgressive erasures—the allegorical Jew, the Jew-as-symbol—through the blunt and earthy specificity of his ordinary Jews: census taker, shoemaker, bookseller, night school student, baker, egg candler, peddler, janitor, tailor (several), grocer (several, failing), taxi driver, actor, painter (failed), writer (several, failed). Wrenched into life by a master fabulist, they breathe, feel, yearn, struggle.

Then with all these believable Jews on hand, is Malamud a "parochial" writer, after all? Yes, blessedly so, as every sovereign imaginative artist is obliged to be, from Dickens to Nabokov to Flannery O'Connor to Malamud himself: each one the sole heir to a singular kingdom.

W. H. Auden at the 92nd Street Y

There must be sorrow if there can be love.
—FROM "CANZONE"

Ah, the fabled sixties and seventies! Jack Kerouac and William Burroughs! The glorious advent of Howling! Of Getting Stoned! The proliferation of Ginsbergian Exclamation Points!

To secure the status of their literary subversion, these revolutionary decades were obliged, like the cadres of every insurrection, to denigrate and despise, and sometimes to blow up, their immediate predecessor, the Fifties—the middling middle, the very navel, of the twentieth century. The fifties, after all, were the Eisenhower years, stiff and small like Mamie's bangs (and just as dated), dully mediocre, constrained, consumerist, car-finned, conformist, forgettable, and stale as modernism itself. Randall Jarrell, one of its leading poets and critics, named this midcentury epoch "the Age of Criticism"—and what, however he intended it, could suggest prosiness more? And what is prosiness if not the negation of the lively, the living, the lasting, the daring, the true and the new?

The reality was sublimely opposite. It was, in fact, the Age of Poetry, a pinnacle and an exaltation; there has not been another since. Its poets were more than luminaries—they were colossi, their very names were talismans, and they rose before us under a halo of brilliant lights like figures in a shrine. It *was* a kind of shrine: the grand oaken hall, the distant stage and its hallowed lectern, the enchanted voices with their variegated intonations, the rapt listeners scarcely breathing, the storied walls themselves in trance—this was the Poetry Center of the 92nd Street Y in the heart of the twentieth century.

And bliss was it to be young and enraptured in the dusk of that cavernous arena, at $20 per season ticket! It was the Age of Poetry precisely because it was still the age of form, when form, even when abandoned, was there to *be* abandoned. (Wild child Allen Ginsberg knew and revered his progenitors, even as he tossed them to the winds.) And form, in those disparaged fifties, meant difficulty in the doing; meant the hard practice of virtuosity; meant the plumbing of language for all its metamorphoses and undiscovered metrics; meant the heritage of knowledge; meant, in order to aspire to limitlessness, the pressure of limits—rhyme, even rhyme, a thing of wit and brio, never an archaism. Poetry then had not yet fallen into its present slough of trivia and loss of encompassment, the herding of random images of minuscule perspective leading to a pipsqueak epiphany, a delirium of incoherence delivered, monotone upon monotone, in the cacophony of a slam.

Instead, a procession of giants. Their names are lasting, their lines permanent, and their voices (fortunately) recorded—voices idiosyncratic, distinct, and so luxuriant in their unlikeness that it is an astonishment to see so many so large all alive at once. They have nothing in common but their dazzling mastery. And behold, on this selfsame platform, T. S. Eliot—a sacerdotal figure, the era's reigning literary pope, fake-Brit sonorities reverberating like a cathedral organ, grim and tragic, and as funereal as a marble tomb. And then W. H. Auden, capaciously contrapuntal, though they lived in consonance, Eliot born in 1888, Auden in 1907, Eliot an American who chose England, Auden an Englishman turned American. They died eight years apart, and knew the same world, the same political dooms, and the same return to the metaphysics of Christianity. On that broad stage Auden seemed at the time a lesser god: only Eliot could fill, as he once did, a football stadium. The public Eliot was a venerated monument that loomed unforgivingly, while Auden, even in public, had an air of plainness. Auden's reading was *spoken;* it had almost a casualness, a flatness, a matter-of-factness. He read poetry as if he were reading prose. He refused the vatic and the flamboyant. "I must try to eliminate from my own poetry false emotion, inflated rhetoric, empty sonorities," he once wrote. And in an interview: "Poetry is not self-expression." Eliot's thundering fame has since shrunk to a period datum, or, as in *The Four Quartets,* a mystical haze. But Auden, the most copious poet in English of the last century, unequaled for variety and scope—drama, lyric, ballad, sonnet, libretto, villanelle, and more—is the touchstone for all serious poets writing now.

And more: he is the necessary antithesis of Eliot: how clearly, two or three generations on, we can feel this! When the Twin Towers were felled by jihadist terror, and the world of American self-confidence ended not with a whimper but with a civilization-shattering bang, it was not "The Waste Land" that was invoked to toll the bell of mourning. Not "London Bridge is falling down falling down falling down . . . *shantih shantih shantih,*" that melancholic jigsaw of allusions, but the hard mundane despairing concrete *presentness* of Auden's "September 1, 1939":

I sit in one of the dives
On Fifty-second Street
Uncertain and afraid
As the clever hopes expire
Of a low dishonest decade:
Waves of anger and fear
Circulate over the bright
And darkened lands of the earth,
Obsessing our private lives;
The unmentionable odor of death
Offends the September night.

Here there are no symbols, no arcane "objective correlative." Invasion and war, violence and dread, horizon and olfactory nerve, place and time—the kernel of the hour, its history and politics—are intimately knotted in these plainspoken lines, open and direct and quick with fury. And never portentous in the way of a shrouded haruspex.

Elsewhere, Auden's dry satiric voice can seize boisterously and shamelessly on the vernacular, capsizing the lyrical with a trickster's parodic quip:

Goddess of bossy underlings, Normality!
What murders are committed in thy name!
Totalitarian is thy state Reality,
Reeking of antiseptics and the shame
Of faces that all look and feel the same.
Thy Muse is one unknown to classic histories,
The topping figure of the hockey mistress.

(FROM "LETTER TO LORD BYRON")

Though it may require a British staccato to rhyme "mistress" with "histories," the syncopated excitement of such a mélange of constructs, balanced by modulating couplets and quatrains, is Auden's signature; or call it the audaciously conflicting cadences of his breathing. His politics is metaphysics, his metaphysics is history, his history is humanity adrift in a labyrinth of its own making. In his heroic abundance he will catch hold of any form—or invent a new one—to assess, judge, condemn, praise, ruminate, fulminate, love; and once, in the name of literature, forgive:

Time that is intolerant
Of the brave and innocent,
And indifferent in a week
To a beautiful physique,

Worships language and forgives
Everyone by whom it lives;
Pardons cowardice, conceit,
Lays its honours at their feet.

Time that with this strange excuse
Pardoned Kipling and his views,
And will pardon Paul Claudel,
Pardons him for writing well.

(FROM "IN MEMORY OF W. B. YEATS")

No thought or feeling or concept eludes Auden: death, dream, doubt, loss, beauty, sex, love, fear, appetite, flight, wrath, hope, yearning, refuge, bliss, catastrophe, homage, savagery, pity, heritage, exile, nightmare—every motion, motive, and emotion of the range and plethora of human endurance. In one of his most impassioned elegies, addressed in supplication to the spirit of Henry James—"O stern proconsul of intractable provinces, / O poet of the difficult, dear addicted artist"—he contemplates the flooding in of all that the world contains or intimates, its "hinted significant forms":

As I stand awake on our solar fabric,
That primary machine, the earth, which gendarmes, banks,
      And aspirin pre-suppose,
On which the clumsy and sad may all sit down, and any who will
Say their a-ha to the beautiful, the common locus
Of the master and the rose.

Our theatre, scaffold, and erotic city
And all the infirm species and partners in the act
      Of encroachment bodies crave
Though solitude in death is de rigueur for their flesh
And the self-denying hermit flies as it approaches
      Like the carnivore to a cave.

That its plural numbers may unite in meaning,
Its vulgar tongues unravel the knotted mass
    Of the improperly conjunct,
Open my eyes to all its hinted significant forms,
Sharpen my ears to detect amid its brilliant uproar
    The low thud of the defunct.
    . . .
All will be judged. Master of nuance and scruple,
Pray for me and for all writers living and dead;
    Because there are many whose works
Are in better taste than their lives; because there is no end
To the vanity of our calling; make intercession
    For the treason of all clerks.

These are verses that can be understood, beyond the literary invocation that is their conceit, as philosophical advocacy, or even as a kind of crooked incantation, forsaking easy eloquence. They decline to chant or sing, and never has rhyme been so inconspicuous, while at the same time insinuating its sly and stealthy beat. Auden is a poet—no, *the* poet—of unembarrassed intellect. Ideas are his emotions, emotions are his ideas. His successors and inheritors can be named in an uncommonly short list—contemporary poets for whom the lyrical ear and the all-seeing eye and the mind in fever are entwined with the breath and bread of the world; and to whom history, that multitudinous ghost, is no stranger.

Perhaps there is no extant recording of Auden reading "At the Grave of Henry James" on the august stage of the 92nd Street Y half a century ago. Or perhaps there is. Still, whatever it was that we anointed listeners were once blessed to hear, the timbre and the rasp, and the Hurrah and the Alas, of the poet's voice can be found again in these plain lines:

    . . . Only the past
Is present, no one about but the dead as,
Equipped with a few inherited odds and ends,
    One after another we are
Fired into life to seek the unseen target where all
Our equivocal judgments are judged and resolved in
    One whole Alas or Hurrah.

Fanatics

Milena Jesenská, Kafka's translator and lover, has left us a useful and persuasive definition of fanaticism: "that absolute, unalterable necessity for perfection, purity, and truth." It was Kafka she meant.

Then let us now praise fanaticism, how it binds the like and the unlike, how it aspires to purity, how it engenders art at its most sublime, seeking the visionary and the inescapable; and how it reveres the ascendancy of its desires.

Kafka, a fanatic of language, was not alone. America had its own language fanatics, of which he was unaware. In the novel we know as *Amerika* (*The Man Who Disappeared*, also called *The Stoker*), anomalous characters populating his American scenes are rife; but Kafka's imagination, capaciously strange though it was, could not have conceived of the American Hebraists, as prodigiously single-minded as himself, who were thriving in the very years he was at work on *Amerika*.

That Kafka contended with his native German even as he powerfully embraced it is one of the salient keys to his character: the key is in hand, but there is no lock for it to fit into. German was his, ineradicably, yet insecurely. His famously self-lacerating lament—that Jews who wrote in German had "their hind legs stuck in parental Judaism while their forelegs found no purchase on new ground"—suggests some small helpless underground animal futilely attempting to escape its burrow. But when he crucially, even triumphantly, announced, "I am made of literature and nothing else," it could only mean that it was German idiom and essence, German root and rootedness, that had formed and possessed him.

Why, then—early in life until late, and with strenuous diligence—did he pursue the study of Hebrew? The notebooks that survive (archived in the National Library of Israel) are redolent of an ironic pathos: an earnest schoolboy's laboriously inked vocabulary lists, Hebrew into German, in the very hour that the world's most enduring masterworks were spilling from this selfsame pen. When at twenty-nine Kafka was first introduced to Felice Bauer, the young woman to whom he would be twice engaged but would never marry, he thought her unprepossessing, but was nevertheless instantly drawn to her talk: she was, she told him, studying Hebrew.

The American Hebraists, poets who in their youth had emigrated from Eastern Europe, were Kafka's contemporaries. They were also his peers in language fanaticism: they too were made of language and nothing else—but the language that formed and possessed them was Hebrew. Unlike Kafka's feverish wrestling with the fraught and unseemly question of hind legs and forelegs, they were consumed, body and soul, with no ambivalence of belonging, by Hebrew. Not only were they fanatics in their claim of intimately ingrained ownership of Hebrew, its godlike guardians and creators, they were fanatics in their relation to their new environment. English was all around them, awaiting their mastery; and they did become masters of English, and still it was Hebrew that inflamed them. Nor were they—unlike Kafka—torn by incessant doubt and self-repudiation. Scattered in cities all over America, they sat in tranquil rooms, on new ground, immersed in the renewing sublimity of the ancient alphabet.

No Hebraist poets inhabit Kafka's *Amerika*, but we can try to imagine, had he journeyed, like his protagonist Karl, to the real America, and encountered one or two of these psalm-besotted obsessives, would they recognize one another as equally eaten by that glorious but perilous worm, literary fanaticism?

Lionel Trilling and the Buried Life

Half a century ago, Lionel Trilling summoned me into his office at Columbia University to be interviewed for admission to his renowned graduate seminar. For ten minutes or so I sat fixed under his gray prosecutorial eye; he seemed gray all over—his suit, his tie, the level line of his hair, his nostrils with their monarchical arches. His manner was reticent, hiddenly mocking, almost inviolable. I saw him as a kind of monument, and I hoped for access to his seminar less for the sake of what I would study there than for proximity to his fame. It was the Age of Criticism—the marmoreal tag given to it by Randall Jarrell, one of its poet-critics—and Trilling was its most eminent literary intellectual. *The Liberal Imagination*, his landmark work—a collection of sixteen essays previously published mainly in literary quarterlies—had appeared only the year before, in 1950; it had catapulted an already vigorous reputation into something hierarchical: rank, influence, authority.

From the 1940s on, the Age of Criticism had been especially fruitful, and had multiplied so many literary exegetes and ruminators that, with all their differences, they had come to constitute an establishment. They might call themselves Southern Agrarians, like Allen Tate and John Crowe Ransom, or Neo-Thomists, like Eliseo Vivas, or formalists, like Cleanth Brooks—but whatever the rubric and whatever the tendency, the mantle of New Criticism fell over all of them. Their essays had a formidable resonance in the literature departments of universities in both England and America, though nowhere so impressively as in the American academy. Nowadays the jingling mantra of their illustrious names—I. A. Richards, William Empson (whose Seven *Types of Ambiguity* was once reigning doctrine), René Wellek, W. K. Wimsatt, Kenneth Burke, Yvor Winters—is a faded archaism, together with the monastic tenets of New Criticism itself. In its ascendancy the chief dogma of New Criticism, irresistible and indisputable, was *explication de texte*, or close reading, which meant the exclusion of all external interpretive biases: no politics, no past, no social forms, no ethics. Instead, the isolated purity of metaphor, image, "tension," irony—absolutist elements that were said to be objectively inherent in the work, which was looked on as a self-enclosed artifact. In the most up-to-date graduate schools of the time (I was fresh from one of these), all this was felt not as a literary movement, but as a theology linked to eternity. It was with such a credo—New Criticism as sacrosanct truth—that I arrived at Trilling's office door.

His ridicule, courteous and restrained, was direct enough. "You don't really believe," he asked—it was accusation rather than question—"that literature has nothing to do with psychology, with biography or society or history?" I did believe it; I had been trained to believe it. Who of my generation was not susceptible to that aesthetic casuistry? But it was instantly plain that to admit to adherence to New Critical precepts would shut me out from the seminar; so, just as instantly, I switched allegiance to the other side, though five minutes before I had scarcely known that there was another side. It was the seminar I coveted—not the substance of the seminar (Victorian social theorists), but some unfathomable emanation of the mind that presided over it. I wanted to witness the enigma of fame.

The seminar turned out to be a disappointment. In one respect it confirmed everything Trilling had heralded in those electrifying ten minutes in his office: it was saturated in social and historical issues. New Criticism had no status here and was altogether shunned; after all, Trilling in *The Liberal Imagination* had assailed what he called the New Critics' pervasive "anxiety lest the work of art be other than totally self-contained." In this self-contained room of ambitious young scholars—headed almost universally for academic careers—there were more personal anxieties. Trilling was disconsolate and irritable. He was impatient; often he seemed fatigued. He had one or two favorites, whom he would praise profusely—but he was sarcastic or indifferent to others. If a comment struck him as inadequate, his lantern-like eyes would silence the speaker with barely disguised dismissal; his gray back was a wall of contempt, of wishing to be elsewhere.

Trilling did wish to be elsewhere, and had already taken steps to effect it. While the semester was running its course, and I sat cowed and bewildered by fame's unexpected face, he was setting down in his private notebooks an account of his disgust for the seminar and his relief in his coming release from it. The seminar, he wrote,

> needs a total intellectual and emotional involvement that I shld never want to make . . . And then the students dismay me . . . But then all graduate students trouble & in a way repel me and I must put down here the sensation of liberation I experienced when I arranged for my

withdrawal from the graduate school, from seminars . . . For one thing I became a public character and always on view, having to live up to the demands made upon a public character, & finding that the role seemed to grow inward . . . And here I should set down my ever-growing dislike of teaching & the systematic study of literature more and more it goes against the grain.

These extraordinary thoughts were recorded in 1951. Trilling would continue to teach for the next quarter century, until his death in 1975, and his position as "public character" would grow in prominence and distinction. But eleven years later, in 1962, after confessing his admiration for a novel by Sartre, he was lamenting (again in the seclusion of his notebooks), "Nothing has so filled me with shame and regret at what I have not done." A hollow introspection, secretly whispered while standing in the very palm of literary fame. ("I hear on all sides," he had written some years earlier, "of the extent of my reputation—which some call 'fame' . . . It is the thing I have wanted from childhood on—although of course in much greater degree.") By 1962, Trilling had published a major work on Matthew Arnold, a vanguard study of E. M. Forster, and more than fifty consummately original essays collected in three highly influential volumes. He had also written a novel. He was, by any standard, a "figure," and by his own standard especially. Assessing George Orwell —"He is not merely a writer, he is a figure"— he attached this term to those who "are what they write, whom we think of as standing for something as men because of what they have written in their books. They preside, as it were, over certain ideas and attitudes."

Trilling's ideas, particularly his political ideas, evolved from decade to decade, but his attitudes remained consistent. He stood for—he presided over—a disposition toward the claims of morality. "My own interests," he said in a 1961 essay on teaching, "lead me to see literary situations as cultural situations, and cultural situations as great elaborate fights about moral issues, and moral issues as having something to do with gratuitously chosen images of personal being, and images of personal being as having something to do with literary style." This was unmistakably the portrait of a figure, the man who is what he writes; the tone is a public one of self-knowledge and confidence. Yet in July of that same year Trilling was privately regretting what he had made of his life, and grieving that he was not someone else:

— Death of Ernest Hemingway . . .—who would suppose how much he has haunted me? How much he existed in my mind—as a reproach?

He was the only writer of our time I envied. I respected him in his most foolish postures and in his worst work.

Haunted by Hemingway? Envy? Reproach? Trilling was fifty-six when he sequestered these emotions in his notebooks. But in 1933, at twenty-eight, his Columbia position still provisional and no permanent appointment in sight, he was reproaching himself still more vehemently.

Saw a letter Hemingway wrote to Kip [Clifton Fadiman]—a crazy letter, written when he was drunk—self-revealing, arrogant, scared, trivial, absurd; yet felt from reading it how right such a man is compared to the "good minds" of my university life—how he will produce and mean something to the world . . . how his life which he could expose without dignity and which is anarchic and "childish" is a better life than anyone I know could live, and right for his job. And how far-far-far I am going from being a writer—how less and less I have the material and the mind and the will. A few—very few—more years and the last chance will be gone.

The surprisingly incongruous attraction to Hemingway, the envy, the reproach, the regret, the dark intimations of something irretrievable: none of this moodiness was visible in the public character. That Trilling—the incarnation of dignity, discipline, moderation—should look wistfully to the heedlessness and anarchy he saw in Hemingway is on the face of it unimaginable. In the corpus of the masterful essays this underground desire to shed or oppose civilization can be glimpsed only once or twice, and then mainly through peepholes in the prose. Writing of the stories in Isaac Babel's *Red Cavalry* (a Jew riding with the Red Army's Cossacks), Trilling exposed the skeleton of his internal antithesis: "The Jew conceived his own ideal character to consist in his being intellectual, pacific, humane. The Cossack was physical, violent, without mind or manners." By inheritance and temperament, Trilling was the first. He understood the writer (by which he meant the novelist) to be a type radically different from himself: instinctual, a reckless darer, a hero. Paraphrasing Henry James, he agreed that "the artist quite as much as any man of action carries his ultimate commitment and his death warrant in his pocket." As a teacher of literature, as the kind of honored public character he had become, he was immured in the intellectual, the pacific, the humane; there was no risk, no death warrant, in the reflective life of the literary essayist. Musing harshly on his Columbia colleagues, he deplored "such people as Mark VD [Van Doren], who yearly seems to me to grow weaker and weaker, more academic, less a person." As for Trilling himself: "My being a professor and a much respected and even admired one is a great hoax . . . Suppose I were to dare to believe that one could be a professor and a man! and a writer!" Here was bitterness, here was regret: he did not believe that a professor could be truly a man; only the writer, with his ultimate commitment to the wilderness of the imagination, was truly a man.

In approaching such ironies—Trilling as self-repudiator, Trilling as failed writer—one ought to be warned. Journal entries, those vessels of discontent, are notoriously fickle, subject to the torque of mutable feeling, while power flourishes elsewhere. Even if a thread of constancy appears to run through years of an interior record, it is useful to be tentative. Without caution, speculation falls into usurpation. Though the living Trilling was valued and acclaimed, the dead Trilling has been made into a puppet, violated by at least two memoirists: his wife and his son. Diana Trilling, in her 1993 account of their marriage, insisted that she taught him how to write. "He had been writing and publishing for some years before we met," she admitted, "but I helped him to write more attractively, with more clarity and rigor both of thought and expression. His prose had hitherto tended to laxness. Itself not disciplined, it could allow for undisciplined thinking . . . I was relentless in my editorial address to every word he wrote." If this seems unlikely—and more than that, injurious—James Trilling's claim (in a polemic in the *American Scholar*) that his father suffered from attention deficit disorder is still more troubling. Diana Trilling names herself the bestower of style. James Trilling presumes to account for the properties of that style. By insinuating weakness where there was sovereignty, both tend to undermine Trilling's public standing from a private vantage. Inevitably, the malicious dust of a colossus pulled down fills the nostrils.

Trilling's capacious prose was complex and scrupulous. It qualified, weighed, probed; it was the opposite of lax, merging taut lines of thought from disparate starting points. It was a manner that had been moved to fine discriminations ever since, at twenty-one, Trilling began to write for the *Menorah Journal*, a Jewish literary and cultural periodical edited by Elliot Cohen (who later founded *Commentary*). Years afterward, Trilling wrote lovingly of Cohen as "the only great teacher I have ever had," a man who owned "the unremitting passion of genius." With Cohen's encouragement (and Cohen was himself still in his twenties), Trilling reviewed novels by such contemporary luminaries as Ludwig Lewisohn, Robert Nathan, and Lion Feuchtwanger; poetry by Charles Reznikoff and Louis Untermeyer ("Mr. Untermeyer is not a good poet, American or Jewish"), and translations from the Yiddish. He published essays both historical and speculative, ranging from "A Friend of Byron" to "The Changing Myth of the Jew," and though over the decades his style grew more elaborately nuanced, its distinction, and the reach and versatility that defined it, was brilliantly evident from the first. His colleagues on the magazine included Clifton Fadiman, Lewis Mumford, Charles Beard, and Mark Van Doren—essayists all; but Trilling had a more crucial ambition. *The Menorah Journal* became the depository of story after story; he wrote more short fiction now than at any other time in his life. His last labor of fiction was quietly consummated in 1947, when he was forty-two, with the publication of *The Middle of the Journey*, his only novel—and from the point of view of the academy, where he seemed so much at home, it came unexpectedly.

Yet all along, confessional sighs of loss and competitiveness had been turning up in the notebooks: "Story of a university teacher who never got to write"—an idea for a story that never got written. After a visit from Allen Ginsberg, a former student: "We spoke of Kerouac's book. I predicted that it would not be good & insisted. But later I saw with what bitterness I had made the prediction—not wanting K's book to be good." These are the ruminations not of a teacher or a critic, but of a writer of fiction desperate to be in the running. "The attack on my novel," he recorded, "that it is gray, bloodless, intellectual, without passion, is always made with great personal feeling, with anger.—How dared I presume?"

He did not presume again. There were no other novels. By 1945 the stories, and the ideas for stories, had trickled to a stop. That stricken cry of his middle age, mourning the death of Hemingway, was also a lamentation for the death of another novelist—himself.

In his study of Matthew Arnold—a majestic work begun at twenty-three and submitted as his doctoral dissertation a decade later—Trilling spoke of a "feeling of intimacy" with his subject. The attachment was lifelong. He described Arnold's style as "subtle critical dialectic" and his method as requiring "that we suspend our absolute standards and look at events and ideas, past or present, in the light of their historical determinants." These Arnoldian leitmotifs became Trilling's own critical instruments, reflecting the veiled melancholia and austerity of Arnold's famed "high seriousness." But there was something else the young Trilling took from Arnold—a strangely predictive force embedded in a single poem. Twice in the course of his biography of a mind, as he called it, Trilling quotes phrases—the same phrases—from "The Buried Life," Arnold's dejected stanzas on the diminution of his poetic stream:

And we have been on many thousand lines,
And we have shown, on each, spirit and power,

But hardly have we, for one little hour,
Been on our own line, have we been ourselves.

. . .

And long we try in vain to speak and act
Our hidden self, and what we say and do
Is eloquent, is well—but 'tis not true!

"The Muse has gone away," Trilling comments. "Men feel, as they leave youth, that they have more or less consciously assumed a role by excluding some of the once-present elements from themselves. But ever after they are haunted by the fear that they might have selected another, better, role, that perhaps they have made the wrong choice." Even as Trilling was penning these relentless words, he was howling in his journal their anguished echo: *how far-far-far I am going from being a writer . . . A few—very few—more years and the last chance will be gone*. Before he was thirty, he was already seeing Arnold as the prophet of his own buried life. The public character he would acquire, his status as a figure, was eloquent, was well; but the Muse who lights the hidden self had gone away.

Since Trilling's death in 1975, the literary culture he espoused and embodied has itself gone away. English departments today harbor few defenders of literary high seriousness as Trilling conceived and felt it. In an unfinished essay truncated by his final illness—"Why We Read Jane Austen"—Trilling set out to explain "the aim of traditional humanistic education." Its purpose, he said, was to read "about the conduct of other people as presented by a writer highly endowed with moral imagination" and "to see this conduct as relevant to [our] own . . . in that it redeems the individual from moral torpor; its communal effect," he concluded, "is often said to be decisive in human existence." He went on to modify and modulate and reconsider, bringing in contradictory examples from history and ethnology, and offering "at least a little complication to humanism's rather simple view of the relation in which our moral lives stood to other cultures"—but the argument against moral torpor held. Twenty years earlier, musing on Jane Austen's *Mansfield Park*, he had written, "Never before had the moral life been shown as she shows it to be, never before had it been conceived to be so complex and difficult and exhausting," and, shockingly, he announced, "She is the first to be aware of the Terror which rules our moral situation, the ubiquitous anonymous judgment to which we respond. . . . She herself is an agent of the Terror." He said the same of Robert Frost, in a notoriously revisionist speech at a dinner honoring Frost's eighty-fifth birthday.

Almost no one nowadays comes to literary criticism with these premises and intonations. Little of Trilling's intellectual cosmos survives, having been displaced by a perfervid and constantly evanescing succession of rapidly outmoded theoretical movements: structuralism, deconstruction, cultural studies, gender studies, queer studies, postcolonialism. It is Trilling himself who represents the buried life of American literary culture—the brooding body of his essays, their opalescent criss-cross of clauses, the minute waverings of his oscilloscopic mind, above all his now nearly incomprehensible influence. His name has dimmed. In the graduate schools his work is mostly unread, and his ideas undiscussed. His ideas were large and cumulative and, knot by knot, unnerving: his method was not to knit up but to unravel. Rather than zero in on a single aspect of human life and examine it as if it were an entire civilization (a current academic tendency), he did the opposite. In the broad imprint of any social period he read something of exigent present need or taste, enacted against the hot concerns of the past, but nearly always with contemporary habits of thought at the forefront. In pondering the place of "duty" in the Victorian novel, for instance, and more generally in the England of the nineteenth century, he set out to counter the cant of the middle of the twentieth:

> Such figures as the engineer Daniel Doyce of *Little Dorrit* or Dr. Lydgate of *Middlemarch* represent the developing belief that a man's moral life is bound up with his loyalty to the discipline of his calling . . . The Church, in its dominant form and characteristic virtue, was here quite at one with the tendency of secular feeling; its preoccupation may be said to have been less with the achievement of salvation than with the performance of duty.
>
> The word grates upon our moral ear. We do what we should do, but we shrink from giving it the name of duty. "Cooperation," "social-mindedness," the "sense of the group," "class solidarity"—these locutions do not mean what duty means. They have been invented precisely for the purpose of describing right conduct in such a way as not to imply what duty implies—a self whose impulses and desires are very strong, and a willingness to subordinate those impulses and desires to the claim of some external nonpersonal good. The new locutions are meant to suggest that right action is typically to be performed without any pain to the self.
>
> The men of the nineteenth century did not imagine this possibility. They thought that morality was terribly hard to achieve, at the cost of renunciation and sacrifice. We of our time often wonder what could

have made the difficulty . . . That the self may destroy the self by the very energies that define its being, that the self may be preserved by the negation of its own energies—this, whether or not we agree, makes a paradox, makes an irony, that catches our imagination. Much of the nineteenth-century preoccupation with duty was not love of law for its own sake, but rather a concern with the hygiene of the self.

"The hygiene of the self": the phrase is Trilling distilled. From the tangled English garden of an intricate foreign culture—a culture long gone—he plucked the one telling thorn, the thorn most likely to draw blood from the living.

"Trilling was our last Victorian sage," Mark Krupnick, author of a book-length consideration of Trilling's career, wrote from the perspective of 1986. It was a judgment designed to suggest not mustiness but something more pressing and expansive: what contemporary critic will speak, directly and repeatedly, as Trilling did, of "the contradictions, paradoxes and dangers of the moral life"? These stringent words appear in the introduction to Trilling's 1943 study of E. M. Forster, where the term "liberal imagination" first crops up. Some time later, in his rebuke to Stalinism in *The Liberal Imagination*, Trilling proposed contradiction and paradox as an antidote to ideology, which he saw as simple, utopian, and authoritarian. "The job of criticism," he insisted, was "to recall liberalism to its first essential imagination of variousness and possibility, which implies the awareness of complexity and difficulty." All this was a response to the pervasive politics of the thirties and forties. Trilling himself had been, briefly, an active radical, a member of the Communist-led National Committee for the Defense of Political Prisoners; he resigned in 1933. Youthful associations of this kind were widespread among intellectuals in that fermenting period of Depression and the rise of fascism in Europe. In Chicago, Saul Bellow and Isaac Rosenfeld were in an identical fever of radical world upheaval. "Politics was everywhere," Rosenfeld recalled, looking back. "One ate and drank it." Trilling was quicker than most to fall away.

But when he advised the liberals of the forties to turn from "agencies, and bureaus, and technicians," and to cultivate instead a "lively sense of contingency and possibility," and when he was troubled by his complacent students of the fifties who glibly accepted antithetical ideas without resistance or perturbation—who were, in fact, bored by the subversive and the antisocial—how could he have foreseen the riotous campus demonstrations of 1968? In connecting politics with literature—"the politics of culture," he called it—he was unwittingly entering the vestibule of the politicization of literature, a commonplace in today's universities. Unwitting or not, Trilling was bemused to see how the impulse of unrestraint that inflamed the modern masters—Conrad, Mann, Lawrence, Kafka, Nietzsche—was beginning to infiltrate, and finally take over, popular thought and style. These writers, he pointed out, with all their relentless counterminings, asked "every question that is forbidden in polite society." By the 1970s, no question remained that was forbidden in polite society, and no answer, either; there was little left of the notion of polite society altogether. What was liberty for Lawrence became libertinism in the streets. The bold contrariness of the moderns had succeeded so well that Trilling starchily named its dominance in the country at large "the adversary culture." Babbitt and H. L. Mencken's booboisie were routed. Conrad's heart of darkness—the instinctual storm—that had once been the esoteric province of modernist high art had gone public. First the professors, then the rappers; or vice versa. The Cossacks were astride the politics of culture.

Such were Trilling's ultimate convictions, hidden under the ornate historical scaffolding of *Sincerity and Authenticity*, the Charles Eliot Norton Lectures he delivered at Harvard in 1970. In language grown more and more imbricated, more and more allergic to self-disclosure, he indicted the empty sentimentality of "egalitarian hedonism." Outside the lecture hall, the indictment was muted, and so oblique as to seem equivocal. In 1974, Norman Podhoretz, who headed *Commentary* (where Trilling had long published), faulted his former teacher for his hesitations and charged him with a failure of nerve in the face of "a resurgence of philistinism, very often of simple cultural barbarism." Trilling's response was that he had been overtaken by fatigue. "One's reaction was likely to be a despairing shrug," he said. On the Vietnam issue he remained unengaged. But hesitation and ambivalence had been in the grain of his literary temperament from the beginning; they lurked in the short stories he wrote in his twenties. He preferred ambiguity to resolution. He was attracted to the indeterminacies of negative capability, Keats's gauzy formula for "remaining content with half-knowledge," "being in uncertainties, mystery, doubts." In essay after essay he alluded to contingency, the conditioned life, the limits of the unavoidable and the unchangeable. Freud's *Civilization and Its Discontents*, with its bleak recognitions, was a touchstone; he came back to it again and again.

Probably no literary critic of Trilling's standing, with a history of so enduring and authoritative a presence, is in greater eclipse than Lionel Trilling. Edmund Wilson may no longer be widely read, but he survives as a vivid cultural witness, perhaps because of his connection with the clouds of legend that continue to trail Scott Fitzgerald and Hemingway; he was almost the last of the thoroughgoing generalists. (The very last may be Trilling's friend and Columbia colleague Jacques Barzun, whose *From Dawn to Decadence* is an excursion through five hundred years of Western history.) The patrician Wilson, whom Trilling admired and hoped to emulate, was also among the last of the independent men of letters—a genuine free lance of uncompromised autonomy. Trilling, though, needed the security of a steady job. As a young college instructor he was for a time supporting both his ailing wife and his impoverished parents; even so, he aspired to Wilson's princely freedom. The prestige he craved, and the lusts of his ambition, were not to be satisfied by a professorship, however elevated his position eventually became. Though he did not have Wilson's elasticity—Trilling might have been incurious about the Iroquois—the mettle of his literary scrutiny, and his excavations into the meaning of culture, surpassed the scope of the academy. He was in it and yet seemed to loom somewhere beyond it. Erudition enriched his thinking, but it was intuition more than learning that pressed his sentences forward from loop to loop. He was an intellectual who wanted to be an artist.

The eclipse of an artist can sometimes be reversed (Melville and Dickinson are the famous American examples); the eclipse of an intellectual, almost never. When a society changes—and from generation to generation society always changes—art trumps time. That Anna Karenina's divorce troubles would not be likely to lead to her suicide in the twenty-first century hardly invalidates the purity of Tolstoy's masterwork. Literary intellectuals, by contrast, are singularly chained to the mood and condition of their given decades. Time may turn novels into classics; critical essays it turns into symptomatic documents of an era. In our own era, no one has supplanted Trilling, and it is easy to understand why. The study of literature no longer strives for what Trilling (in language that might invite scoffing) dared to call "moral realism." Today there is a well-known critic celebrated for aesthetic rhapsody, and countless minor zealots enmeshed in the vines of ri-varous ideologies, from which too many English-department Tarzans swing. But there is no grand cultural explicator and doubter, no serious traveler to the most exalted, and often the most problematical, stations of art and ideas and manners, no public mind contemplating the transcendent through the gritty resistances of human vulnerability. Trilling was conscious of a complexity of earthbound ironies: he saw that despite the loftiness of one's will or desire, the gross and the immediate impose themselves.

"The kind of critical interest I am asking the literary intellectual to take in the life around him is a proper interest of the literary mind," he stated in 1952, in one of his more roundabout sentences, five years after he had stopped writing fiction. This was not the bright and malleable sentence of a fiction writer; it was the utterance of a figure. "Art," he ended, with his most Arnoldian gesture, "strange and sad as it may be to have to say it again, really is the criticism of life."

Criticism is the watchword. It is sad though not strange that, in the thin stream of his fiction, Trilling's narrative vigor was constrained partly by the emotionally pruned-down Hemingway example, but mainly through the absence of that tumultuous and wingèd strain that animates character and lubricates it and gives it the quiver of being. All the same, Trilling was a novelist. Or, with more novels than one to his name, could have been; and perhaps should have been. He had the psychological equipment for it. His social and historical shrewdness was steeped in experience (Whittaker Chambers was the model for Gifford Maxim of *The Middle of the Journey*), and he had, in his storytelling, a lucidly objective American voice. With a body of work behind him, the novelist he most might have resembled was William Dean Howells—of whom Trilling wrote, "we expect of him that he will involve us in the enjoyment of moral activity through the medium of a lively awareness of manners, that he will delight us by touching on high matters in the natural course of gossip." And what is this if not a sketch of Trilling's own lone novel? Defending Howells, he notes that critics have judged Howells's fiction to be "bloodless"—the very word, bitterly recorded in the notebooks, that had been applied to The *Middle of the Journey*.

Four years before his death, Trilling was invited to give a talk at Purdue University. Uncharacteristically, he chose to speak of himself:

> I am always surprised when I hear myself referred to as a critic. After some thirty years of having been called by that name, the role and the function it designates seems odd to me.
>
> I do not say alien, I only say odd. With the passing years I have learned to accept the name—to live with it, as we say—and even to be gratified by it. But it always startles me, takes me a little back . . .
>
> If I ask myself why this is so, the answer would seem to be that in some sense I did not ever undertake to be a critic . . . The plan that did please my thought was certainly literary, but what it envisaged was the career of a novelist. To this intention, criticism, when eventually I began to practice it, was always secondary, an afterthought: in short, not a vocation but an avocation.

An astonishing public confession: the years of teaching, the years of writing, the honor and the fame that accrued in its wake—all this no more than an avocation! And the vocation? Buried.

Sad and strange as it may be to have to say it again (and who can help echoing and re-echoing Trilling's blue notes?), the whole of it, vocation and avocation, is by now defeated, buried, lost. The imposing stuff of Trilling's literary temperament, resplendent in its intellect and subtlety and style— and, dare one say, its nobility—may turn out to be no more than a reminder and a marker: a necessary headstone. Criticism of life is not seen to be the business of criticism. The demarcations of high culture have given way to the obliteration of boundaries. The figure has given way to the performer.

But suppose vocation and avocation had really been transposed, and Trilling had fulfilled his intention, leaving behind a long row of novels— novels of manners, of social observation, and (as he once characterized Howells's novels) of moderate sentiments and the sense of things? In 1976, Jacques Barzun, thinking back to the figure that was already fading a year after Trilling's death, regretted his friend's "unwarrantedly subdued reputation." If there had been more novels, he agreed (perhaps he was privy to Trilling's more intimate reflections), "or if he had spoken as a free lance instead of from an academic platform, the response might have been different—not wiser, perhaps, but louder and nearer the mark."

There is no long row of novels: they once existed in Trilling's fantasy; they may dimly glimmer in ours. Still, in the shoreless precincts of the essays one can hear the call, desolate but urgent, of the thinker and the teacher—and never mind that behind the scenes he disowned teaching. He may have despaired of his students, but not of ideas. What he was after, in the classroom and in the world, was the "power of supposing that ideas are real"; he was persuaded that only an "intense and ambivalent sense of history" could fuel that power. He condemned fashionable self-consciousness and self-pity, which he identified as false virtue and light resolve. He eschewed softness. He saw through "the political awareness that is not aware, the social consciousness which hates full consciousness, the moral earnestness which is moral luxury." He saw through his own time, and perhaps through ours.

Then is it possible, after all, that it is not Lionel Trilling who is buried and lost, but rather ourselves, we who relinquish his austere searchings for the sake of angry academic piddlings and ephemeral public trivia?

An inexorable postscript. Any mention of Trilling's name today instantly elicits the recognition that he was the first Jew appointed to Columbia

University's permanent English faculty—as if this were the only significant relic of an eminent career. Trilling's triumph erupted on the heels of a humiliating dismissal; he had been fired on the grounds that he was a Jew and a Marxist. Attempting to fight back, he secured painful interviews with the men who had ejected him; it was for his own good, they told him, he would not fit in. In desperation he sent a copy of his dissertation to Nicholas Murray Butler, Columbia's president. Butler chose merit over bigotry—but the harsh peril of this history left Trilling wary ever after. The young writer who was drawn to the *Menorah Journal* for its intellectual and literary standards rose to be the edgy critic who later denigrated that journal as "sterile." He was concerned with reputation and how to achieve it—how to avoid eclipse. It was lasting fame he had in mind. "I know of no writer in English," he insisted, "who has added a micromillimeter to his stature by 'realizing his Jewishness,' although I know of some who have curtailed their promise by trying to heighten their Jewish consciousness." Trilling wrote these words in 1944, when the German ovens were at full blast and European Jewish consciousness was, in the most literal sense, unrealized. He was then thirty-nine; his stature was already assured. He could not have imagined that he would come to be remembered largely, if not chiefly, as Columbia's first Jew.

T. S. Eliot at 101

∽

"The Man Who Suffers and the Mind Which Creates"

Thomas Stearns Elliot, poet and pre-eminent modernist, was born one hundred and one years ago. His centennial in 1988 was suitably marked by commemorative reporting, literary celebrations in New York and London, and the publication of a couple of lavishly reviewed volumes: a new biography and a collection of the poet's youthful letters. Probably not much more could have been done to distinguish the occasion; still, there was something subdued and bloodless, even superannuated, about these memorial stirrings. They had the quality of a slightly tedious reunion of aging alumni, mostly spiritless by now, spurred to animation by old exultation recollected in tranquility. The only really fresh excitement took place in London, where representatives of the usually docile community of British Jews, including at least one prominent publisher, condemned Eliot for anti-semitism and protested the public fuss. Elsewhere, the moment passed modestly, hardly noticed at all by the bookish young—who, whether absorbed by recondite theorizing in the academy, or scampering after newfangled writing careers, have long had their wagons hitched to other stars.

In the early seventies it was still possible to uncover, here and there, a tenacious English department offering a vestigial graduate seminar given over to the study of Eliot. But by the close of the eighties, only "The Love Song of J. Alfred Prufrock" appears to have survived the indifference of the schools—two or three pages in the anthologies, a fleeting assignment for high school seniors and college freshmen. "Prufrock," and "Prufrock" alone, is what the latest generations know—barely know: not "The Hollow Men," not "La Figlia che Piange," not "Ash-Wednesday," not even "The Waste Land". Never *Four Quartets*. And the mammoth prophetic presence of T. S. Eliot himself—that immortal sovereign rock—the latest generations do not know at all.

To anyone who was an undergraduate in the forties and fifties (and possibly even into the first years of the sixties), all that is inconceivable—as if a part of the horizon had crumbled away. When, four decades ago, in a literary period that resembled eternity, T. S. Eliot won the Nobel Prize in Literature, he seemed pure zenith, a colossus, nothing less than a permanent luminary fixed in the firmament like the sun and the moon—or like the New Criticism itself, the vanished movement Eliot once magisterially dominated. It was a time that, for the literary young, mixed authority with innovation: authority was innovation, an idea that reads now, in the wake of the anti-establishment sixties, like the simplest contradiction. But modernism then was an absolute ruler—it had no effective intellectual competition and had routed all its predecessors; and it was modernism that famously carried the "new."

The new—as embodied in Eliot—was difficult, preoccupied by parody and pastiche, exactingly allusive and complex, saturated in manifold ironies and inflections, composed of "layers," and pointedly inaccessible to anybody expecting run-of-the-mill coherence. The doors to Eliot's poetry were not easily opened. His lines and themes were not readily understood. But the young who flung themselves through those portals were lured by unfamiliar enchantments and bound by pleasurable ribbons of ennui. "April is the cruellest month," Eliot's voice, with its sepulchral cadences, came spiraling out of 78 r.p.m. phonographs, "breeding / Lilacs out of the dead land, mixing / Memory and desire . . ." That toney British accent—flat, precise, steady, unemotive, surprisingly high-pitched, bleakly passive—coiled through awed English departments and worshipful dormitories, rooms where the walls had pin-up Picassos, and Pound and Eliot and *Ulysses* and Proust shouldered one another higgledy-piggledy in the rapt late-adolescent breast. The voice was, like the poet himself, nearly sacerdotal, impersonal, winding and winding across the country's campuses like a spool of blank robotic woe. "Shantih shantih shantih," "not with a bang but a whimper," "an old man in a dry month," "I shall wear the bottoms of my trousers rolled"—these were the devout chants of the literarily passionate in the forties and fifties, who in their own first verses piously copied Eliot's tone: its restraint, gravity, mystery; its invasive remoteness and immobilized disjointed despair.

There was rapture in that despair. Wordsworth's nostalgic cry over the start of the French Revolution—"Bliss was it in that dawn to be alive, / But to be young was very heaven!"—belongs no doubt to every new generation; youth's heaven lies in its quitting, or sometimes spiting, the past, with or without a historical crisis. And though Eliot's impress—the bliss he evoked— had little to do with political rupture, it was revolutionary enough in its own way. The young who gave homage to Eliot were engaged in a self-contradictory double maneuver: they were willingly authoritarian even as they jubilantly rebelled. On the one hand, taking on the puzzlements of modernism, they were out to tear down the Wordsworthian tradition itself, and on the other they were ready to fall on their knees to a god. A god, moreover, who despised free-thinking, democracy, and secularism: the very conditions of anti-authoritarianism.

How T. S. Eliot became that god—or, to put it less extravagantly, how he became a commanding literary figure who had no successful rivals and whose formulations were in fact revered—is almost as mysterious a proposition as how, in the flash of half a lifetime, an immutable majesty was dismantled, an immutable glory dissipated. It is almost impossible nowadays to imagine such authority accruing to a poet. No writer today—Nobel winner or no—holds it or can hold it. The four* most recent American Nobel laureates in literature—Czeslaw Milosz, Saul Bellow, Isaac Bashevis Singer, and Joseph Brodsky (three of whom, though citizens of long standing, do not write primarily in English)—are much honored, but they are not looked to for manifestos or pronouncements, and their comments are not studied as if by a haruspex. They are as far from being cultural dictators as they are from filling football stadiums.

Eliot *did* once fill a football stadium. On April 30, 1956, fourteen thousand people came to hear him lecture on "The Frontiers of Criticism" at the University of Minnesota, in Minneapolis. By then he was solidly confirmed as "the Pope of Russell Square," as his London admirer Mary Trevelyan began to call him in 1949. It was a far-reaching papacy, effective even among students in the American Midwest; but if the young flocked to genuflect before the papal throne, it was not they who had enthroned Eliot, nor their teachers. In the Age of Criticism (as the donnish "little" magazines of the time dubbed the forties and fifties), Eliot was ceded power, and accorded veneration, by critics who were themselves minor luminaries. "He has a very penetrating influence, perhaps not unlike an east wind," wrote William Empson, one of whose titles, *Seven Types of Ambiguity*, became an academic catchphrase alongside Eliot's famous "objective correlative." R. P. Blackmur said of "Prufrock" that its "obscurity is like that of the womb"; Eliot's critical essays, he claimed, bear a "vital relation" to Aristotle's *Poetics*. Hugh Kenner's comparison is with still another monument: "Eliot's work, as he once noted of Shakespeare, is in important respects one continuous poem," and for Kenner the shape of Eliot's own monument turns out to be "the Arch which stands when the last marcher has left, and endures when the last centurion or sergeant-major is dust." F. R. Leavis, declaring Eliot "among the greatest poets of the English language," remarked that "to have gone seriously into

---

* There is, of course, now a fifth: Toni Morrison.

the poetry is to have had a quickening insight into the nature of thought and language." And in Eliot's hands, F. O. Matthiessen explained, the use of the symbol can "create the illusion that it is giving expression to the very mystery of life."

These evocations of wind, womb, thought and language, the dust of the ages, the very mystery of life, not to mention the ghosts of Aristotle and Shakespeare: not since Dr. Johnson has a man of letters writing in English been received with so much adulation, or seemed so formidable—almost a marvel of nature itself—within his own society.

Nevertheless there was an occasional dissenter. As early as 1929, Edmund Wilson was complaining that he couldn't stomach Eliot's celebrated conversion to "classicism, royalism, and Anglo-Catholicism." While granting that Eliot's essays "will be read by everybody interested in literature," that Eliot "has now become the most important literary critic in the English-speaking world," and finally that "one can find no figure of comparable authority," it was exactly the force of this influence that made Wilson "fear that we must give up hope." For Wilson, the argument of Eliot's followers "that, because our society at the present time is badly off without religion, we should make an heroic effort to swallow medieval theology, seems . . . utterly futile as well as fundamentally dishonest." Twenty-five years later, when the American intellectual center had completed its shift from free-lance literary work like Wilson's—and Eliot's—to the near-uniformity of university English departments, almost no one in those departments would dare to think such unfastidious thoughts about Eliot out loud. A glaze of orthodoxy (not too different from the preoccupation with deconstructive theory currently orthodox in English departments) settled over academe. Given the normal eagerness of succeeding literary generations to examine new sets of entrails, it was inevitable that so unbroken a dedication would in time falter and decline. But until that happened, decades on, Eliot studies were an unopposable ocean; an unstoppable torrent; a lava of libraries.

It may be embarrassing for us now to look back at that nearly universal obeisance to an autocratic, inhibited, depressed, rather narrow-minded and considerably bigoted fake Englishman—especially if we are old enough (as I surely am) to have been part of the wave of adoration. In his person, if not in his poetry, Eliot was, after all, false coinage. Born in St. Louis, he became indistinguishable (though not to shrewd native English eyes), in his dress, his manners, his loyalties, from a proper British Tory. Scion of undoctrinaire rationalist New England Unitarianism (his grandfather had moved from Boston to Missouri to found Washington University), he was possessed by guilty notions of sinfulness and martyrdom and by the monkish disciplines of asceticism, which he pursued in the unlikely embrace of the established English Church. No doubt Eliot's extreme self-alterations should not be dismissed as ordinary humbug, particularly not on the religious side; there is a difference between impersonation and conversion. Still, self-alteration so unalloyed suggests a hatred of the original design. And certainly Eliot condemned the optimism of democratic American meliorism; certainly he despised Unitarianism, centered less on personal salvation than on the social good; certainly he had contempt for Jews as marginal if not inimical to his notions of Christian community. But most of all, he came to loathe himself, a hollow man in a twilight kingdom.

In my undergraduate years, between seventeen and twenty-one, and long after as well, I had no inkling of any of this. The overt flaws—the handful of insults in the poetry—I swallowed down without protest. No one I knew protested—at any rate, no professor ever did. If Eliot included lines like "The rats are underneath the piles. / The jew [sic] is underneath the lot," if he had his Bleistein, "Chicago Semite Viennese," stare "from the protozoic slime" while elsewhere "The jew squats on the windowsill, the owner" and "Rachel *née* Rabinovitch / Tears at the grapes with murderous paws"—well, that, sadly, was the way of the world and to be expected, even in the most resplendent poet of the age. The sting of those phrases—the shock that sickened—passed, and the reader's heart pressed on to be stirred by other lines. What was Eliot to me? He was not the crack about "Money in furs," or "Spawned in some estaminet in Antwerp." No, Eliot was "The Lady is withdrawn / In a white gown, to contemplation, in a white gown" and "Then spoke the thunder/ DA / *Datta*: what have we given?" and "Afternoon grey and smoky, evening yellow and rose"; he was incantation, mournfulness, elegance; he was liquescence, he was staccato, he was quickstep and oar, the hushed moan and the sudden clap. He was lyric shudder and rose-burst. He was, in brief, poetry incarnate; and poetry was what one lived for.

And he was something else beside. He was, to say it quickly, absolute art: high art, when art was at its most serious and elitist. The knowledge of that particular splendor—priestly, sacral, a golden cape for the initiate—has by now ebbed out of the world, and many do not regret it. Literary high art turned its back on egalitarianism and prized what is nowadays scorned as "the canon": that body of anciently esteemed texts, most of them difficult and aristocratic in origin, which has been designated Western culture. Modernism—and Eliot—teased the canon, bruised it, and even sought to astonish it by mocking and fragmenting it, and also by introducing Eastern infusions, such as Eliot's phrases from the Upanishads in "The Waste Land" and Pound's Chinese imitations. But all these shatterings, dislocations, and idiosyncratic juxtapositions of the old literary legacies were never intended to abolish the honor in which they were held, and only confirmed their centrality. Undoing the canon is the work of a later time-of our own, in fact, when universal assent to a central cultural standard is almost everywhere decried. For the moderns, and for Eliot especially, the denial of permanently agreed-on masterworks—what Matthew Arnold, in a currency now obsolete beyond imagining, called "touchstones"—would have been unthinkable. What one learned from Eliot, whose poetry skittered toward disintegration, was the power of consolidation: the understanding that literature could genuinely *reign*.

One learned also that a poem could actually be penetrated to its marrow—which was not quite the same as comprehending its meaning. In shunting aside or giving up certain goals of ordinary reading, the New Criticism installed Eliot as both teacher and subject. For instance, following Eliot, the New Criticism would not allow a poem to be read in the light of either biography or psychology. The poem was to be regarded as a thing-in-itself; nothing environmental or causal, including its own maker, was permitted to illuminate or explain it. In that sense it was as impersonal as a jar or any other shapely artifact that must be judged purely by its externals. This objective approach to a poem, deriving from Eliot's celebrated "objective correlative" formulation, did not dismiss emotion; rather, it kept it at a distance, and precluded any speculation about the poet's own life, or any other likely influence on the poem. "The progress of an artist is a continual self-sacrifice, a continual extinction of personality," Eliot wrote in his landmark essay, "Tradition and the Individual Talent." "Emotion . . . has its life in the poem and not in the history of the poet." And, most memorably: "The more perfect the artist, the more completely separate in him will be the man who suffers and the mind which creates." This was a theory designed to prevent old-fashioned attempts to read private events into the lines on the page. Artistic inevitability, Eliot instructed, "lies in this complete adequacy of the external to the emotion" and suggested a series of externals that might supply the "exact equivalence" of any particular emotion: "a set of objects, a situation, a chain of events." Such correlatives—or "objective equivalences"—provided, he insisted, the "only way of expressing emotion in the form of art." The New Criticism took him at his word, and declined to admit any other way. Not that the aesthetic scheme behind Eliot's formulation was altogether new. Henry James, too, had demanded—"Dramatize, dramatize!"—that the work of art resist construing itself in public. When Eliot, in offering his objective correlative, stopped to speak of the "*données* of the problem"—*donnée* was one of James's pet Gallicisms—he was tipping off his source. No literary figure among James's contemporaries had paid any attention to this modernist dictum, often not even James himself. Emerging in far more abstruse language from Eliot, it became a papal bull. He was thirty-five at the time.

The method used in digging out the objective correlative had a Gallic name of its own: *explication de texte*. The sloughing off of what the New Criticism considered to be extraneous had the effect of freeing the poem utterly—freeing it for the otherwise undistracted mind of the reader, who was released from "psychology" and similar blind alleys in order to master the poem's components. The New Criticism held the view that a poem could indeed be mastered: this was an act of trust, as it were, between poem and reader. The poem could be relied on to yield itself up to the reader—if the reader, on the other side of the bargain, would agree to a minutely close "*explication*," phrase by phrase: a process far more meticulous than "interpretation" or the search for any identifiable meaning or definitive commentary. The search was rather for architecture and texture—or call it resonance and intricacy, the responsive web-work between the words. *Explication de texte*, as practiced by the New Critics and their graduate-student disciples, was something like watching an ant maneuver a bit of leaf. One notes first the fine veins in the leaf, then the light speckled along the veins, then the tiny glimmers charging off the ant's various surfaces, the movements of the ant's legs and other body parts, the lifting and balancing of the leaf, all the while scrupulously aware that ant and leaf, though separate structures, become—when linked in this way—a freshly imagined structure.

A generation or more was initiated into this concentrated scrutiny of a poem's structure and movement. High art in literature—which had earlier been approached through the impressionistic "appreciations" that commonly passed for critical reading before the New Criticism took hold—was seen to be indivisible from *explication de texte*. And though the reverence for high art that characterized the Eliot era is now antiquated—or dead—the close reading that was the hallmark of the New Critics has survived, and remains the sine qua non of all schools of literary theory. Currently it is even being applied to popular culture; hamburger advertisements and television sitcoms can be serious objects of up-to-date critical examination. Eliot was hugely attracted to popular culture as an innovative ingredient of pastiche— "Sweeney Agonistes," an unfinished verse drama, is saturated in it. But for Eliot and the New Critics, popular culture or "low taste" contributed to a literary technique; it would scarcely have served as a literary subject, or "text," in its own right. Elitism ruled. Art was expected to be strenuous, hard-earned, knotty. Eliot explicitly said so, and the New Critics faithfully concurred. "It is not a permanent necessity that poets should be interested in philosophy," Eliot wrote (though he himself had been a graduate student in philosophy at Harvard and Oxford, and had completed a thesis on F. H. Bradley, the British idealist). "We can only say that it appears likely that poets in our civilization, as it exists at present, must be *difficult*. Our civilization comprehends great variety and complexity, and this variety and complexity, playing upon a refined sensibility, must produce various and complex results. The poet must become more and more comprehensive, more allusive, more indirect, in order to force, to dislocate if necessary, language into his meaning."

He had another requirement as well, and that was a receptiveness to history. Complexity could be present only when historical consciousness prevailed. He favored history over novelty, and tradition over invention. While praising William Blake for "a remarkable and original sense of language and the music of language, and a gift of hallucinated vision," Eliot faulted him for his departures from the historical mainstream. "What his genius required, and what it sadly lacked, was a framework of accepted and traditional ideas which would have prevented him from indulging in a philosophy of his own." And he concluded, "The concentration resulting from a framework of mythology and theology and philosophy is one of the reasons why Dante is a classic, and Blake only a poet of genius." Genius was not enough for Eliot. A poet, he said, in "Tradition and the Individual Talent," needs to be "directed by the past." The historical sense "compels a man to write not merely with his own generation in his bones, but with the feeling that the whole of the literature of Europe from Homer and within it the whole of the literature of his own country has a simultaneous existence and composes a simultaneous order."

A grand view; a view of grandeur; high art defined: so high that even the sublime Blake fails to meet its measure. It is all immensely elevated and noble—and, given the way many literary academics and critics think now, rare and alien. Aristocratic ideas of this kind, which some might call eurocentric and obscurantist, no longer engage most literary intellectuals; nor did they, sixty years ago, engage Edmund Wilson. But they were dominant for decades, and in the reign of Eliot they were law. Like other postulates, they brought good news and bad news; and we know that my good news may well be your bad news. Probably the only legacy of the Eliot era that everyone can affirm as enduringly valuable is the passionate, yet also disinterested, dissection of the text, a nuanced skill that no critical reader, taking whatever ideological stand, can do without. This exception aside, the rest is all disagreement. As I see it, what appeared important to me at twenty-one is still important; in some respects I admit to being arrested in the Age of Eliot, a permanent member of it, unregenerate. The etiolation of high art seems to me to be a major loss. I continue to suppose that some texts are worthier than other texts. The same with the diminishment of history and tradition: not to incorporate into an educable mind the origins and unifying principles of one's own civilization strikes me as a kind of cultural autolobotomy. Nor am I ready to relinquish Eliot's stunning declaration that the reason we know so much more than the dead writers knew is that "they are that which we know." As for that powerful central body of touchstone works, the discredited "canon," and Eliot's strong role in shaping it for his own and the following generation, it remains clear to me—as Susan Sontag remarked at the 1986 International PEN Convention—that literary genius is not an equal opportunity employer; I would not wish to drop Homer or Jane Austen or Kafka to make room for an Aleutian Islander of lesser gifts, however unrepresented her group may be on the college reading list.

In today's lexicon these are no doubt "conservative" notions, for which Eliot's influence can be at least partly blamed or—depending on your viewpoint—credited. In Eliot himself they have a darker side—the bad news. And the bad news is very bad. The gravity of high art led Eliot to envision a controlling and exclusionary society that could, presumably, supply the conditions to produce that art. These doctrinal tendencies, expressed in 1939 in a little book called *The Idea of a Christian Society*, took Eliot—on the eve of Nazi Germany's ascendancy over Europe—to the very lip of shutting out, through "radical changes," anyone he might consider ineligible for his "Community of Christians." Lamenting "the intolerable position of those who try to lead a Christian life in a non-Christian world," he was indifferent to the position of those who would try to thrive as a cultural minority within his contemplated Utopia. (This denigration of tolerance was hardly fresh. He had argued in a lecture six years before that he "had no objection to being called a bigot.") In the same volume, replying to a certain Miss Bower, who had frowned on "one of the main tenets of the Nazi creed—the relegation of women to the sphere of the kitchen, the children, and the church," Eliot protested "the implication that what is Nazi is wrong, and need not be discussed on its own merits." Nine years afterward, when the fight against Germany was won, he published *Notes Toward the Definition of Culture*, again proposing the hegemony of a common religious culture. Here he wrote—at a time when Hitler's ovens were just cooled and the shock of the Final Solution just dawning—that "the scattering of Jews amongst peoples holding the Christian faith may have been unfortunate both for these peoples and for the Jews themselves," because "the effect may have been to strengthen the illusion that there can be culture without religion." An extraordinary postwar comment. And in an Appendix, "The Unity of European Culture," a radio lecture broadcast to Germany in 1946, one year after the Reich was dismantled, with Europe in upheaval, the death camps exposed, and displaced persons everywhere, he made no mention at all of the German atrocities. The only reference to "barbarism" was hypothetical, a worried projection into a potentially barren future: "If Christianity goes, the whole of our culture goes," as if the best of European civilization (including the merciful tenets of Christianity) had not already been pulverized to ash throughout the previous decade. So much for where high art and traditional culture landed Eliot.

There is bad news, as it happens, even in the objective correlative. What was once accepted as an austere principle of poetics is suddenly decipherable as no more than a device to shield the poet from the raw shame of confession. Eliot is now unveiled as a confessional poet above all—one who was driven to confess, who *did* confess, whose subject was sin and guilt (his own), but who had no heart for the act of disclosure. That severe law of the impersonality of the poem—the masking technique purported to displace emotion from its crude source in the poet's real-life experience to its heightened incarnation in "a set of objects, a situation, a chain of events"—turns out to be motivated by something less august and more timorous than pure literary theory or a devotion to symbol. In the name of the objective correlative, Eliot had found a way to describe the wound without the embarrassment of divulging who held the knife. This was a conception far less immaculate than the practitioners of the New Criticism ever supposed; for thirty years or more Eliot's close readers remained innocent of—or discreet about—Eliot's private life. Perhaps some of them imagined that, like the other pope, he had none.

The assault on the masking power of the objective correlative—the breach in Eliot's protective wall—came about in the ordinary way: the biographies began. They began because time, which dissolves everything, at last dissolved awe. Although the number of critical examinations of Eliot, both book-length and in periodicals, is beyond counting, and although there are a handful of memoirs by people who were acquainted with him, the first true biography did not appear until a dozen years after his death. In 1977 Lyndall Gordon published *Eliot's Early Years*, an accomplished and informative study taking Eliot past his failed first marriage and through the composition of "The Waste Land." Infiltrated by the familiar worshipfulness, the book is a tentativehybrid, part dense critical scrutiny and part cautious narrative— self-conscious about the latter, as if permission has not quite been granted by the author to herself. The constraints of awe are still there. Nevertheless the poetry is advanced in the light of Eliot's personal religious development, and these first illuminations are potent. In 1984 a second biography arrived, covering the life entire; by now awe has been fully dispatched. Peter Ackroyd's *T. S. Eliot: A Life* is thorough, bold, and relaxed about its boldness—even now and then a little acid. Not a debunking job by any means, but admirably straightforward. The effect is to bring Eliot down to recognizably human scale—disorienting to a reader trained to Eliot-adulation and ignorant until now of the nightmare of Eliot's youthful marriage and its devastating evolution. Four years on, Eliot's centenary saw the publication of *Eliot's New Life*, Lyndall Gordon's concluding volume, containing augmented portraits—in the nature of discoveries—of two women Ackroyd had touched on much less intensively; each had expected Eliot to marry her after the death of his wife in a mental institution. Eliot was callous to both. Eleven years following her first study, Gordon's manner continues respectful and her matter comprehensive, but the diffidence of the narrative chapters is gone. Eliot has acquired fallibility, and Gordon is not afraid to startle herself, or the long, encrusted history of deferential Eliot scholarship. Volume Two is daring, strong, and psychologically brilliant. Finally, 1988 also marked the issuance of a fat book of letters, *The Letters of T. S. Eliot, Vol. I: 1898–1922*, from childhood to age thirty-five (with more to come), edited by Eliot's widow, Valerie Eliot, whom he married when she was thirty and he sixty-eight.

"The man who suffers and the mind which creates"—these inseparables, sundered long ago by Eliot himself, can now be surgically united.

If Eliot hid his private terrors behind the hedge of his poetry, the course of literary history took no notice of it. Adoration, fame, and the Nobel Prize came to him neither in spite of nor because of what he left out; his craft was in the way he left it out. And he had always been reticent; he had always hidden himself. It can even be argued that he went to live in England in order to hide from his mother and father.

His mother, Charlotte Stearns Eliot, was a frustrated poet who wrote religious verse and worked for the civic good. His father, Henry Ware Eliot, was an affluent businessman who ran a St. Louis brick-manufacturing company. Like any entrepreneur, he liked to see results. His father's father, an intellectual admired by Dickens, was good at results—though not the conventional kind. He had left the family seat in blueblood Boston to take the enlightenment of Unitarianism to the American West; while he was at it he established a university. Both of Eliot's parents were strong-willed. Both expected him to make a success of himself. Both tended to diminish his independence. Not that they wanted his success on any terms but his own—it was early understood that this youngest of six siblings (four sisters, one of whom was nineteen years older, and a brother almost a decade his senior) was unusually gifted. He was the sort of introspective child who is photographed playing the piano or reading a book or watching his girl cousins at croquet (while himself wearing a broad-brimmed straw hat and a frilly dress, unremarkable garb for upper-class nineteenth-century male tots). His mother wrote to the headmaster of his prep school to ensure that he would not be allowed to participate in sports. She wrote again to warn against the dangers of swimming in quarry ponds. She praised Eliot's schoolboy verse as better than her own, and guaranteed his unease. "I knew what her verses meant to her. We did not discuss the matter further," he admitted long afterward. At his Harvard commencement in 1910, the same year as the composition of "Portrait of a Lady" and a year before "Prufrock," he delivered the farewell ode in a style that may have been a secret parody of his mother's: "For the hour that is left us Fair Harvard, with thee, / Ere we face the importunate years . . ." His mother was sympathetic to his ambitions as a poet—too sympathetic: it was almost as if his ambitions were hers, or vice versa. His father took a brisk view of Eliot's graduate studies in philosophy: they were the ticket to a Harvard professorship, a recognizably respectable career.

But Eliot would not stay put. To the bewilderment of his parents—the thought of it gave his mother a "chill"—he ran off to Paris, partly to catch the atmosphere of Jules Laforgue, a French poet who had begun to influence him, and partly to sink into Europe. In Paris he was briefly attracted to Henri Bergson, whose lectures on philosophy he attended at the College de France, but then he came upon Charles Maurras; Maurras's ideas— "*classique, catholique, monarchique*"—stuck to him for life, and were transmuted in 1928 into his own "classicist, royalist, Anglo-Catholic." In 1910 the word "fascist" was not yet in fashion, but that is exactly what Maurras was: later on he joined the pro-Nazi Vichy regime, and went to jail for it after World War II. None of this dented Eliot's enduring admiration; *Hommage a Charles Maurras* was written as late as 1948. When Eliot first encountered him, Maurras was the founder of an anti-democratic organization called Action Française, which specialized in student riots and open assaults on free-thinkers and Jews. Eliot, an onlooker on one of these occasions, did not shrink from the violence. (Ackroyd notes that he "liked boxing matches also.")

After Paris he obediently returned to Harvard for three diligent years, doing some undergraduate teaching and working on his doctoral degree. One of his courses was with Bertrand Russell, visiting from England. Russell saw Eliot at twenty-five as a silent young dandy, impeccably turned out, but a stick without "vigour or life—or enthusiasm." (Only a year later, in England, the diffident dandy—by then a new husband—would move with his bride right into Russell's tiny flat.) During the remainder of the Harvard period, Eliot embarked on Sanskrit, read Hindu and Buddhist sacred texts, and tunneled into the investigations that would culminate in his dissertation, *Experience and the Objects of Knowledge in the Philosophy of F. H. Bradley.* Screened by this busy academic program, he was also writing poetry. When Harvard offered him a traveling scholarship, he set off for Europe, and never again came back to live in the country of his birth. It was the beginning of the impersonations that were to become transformations.

He had intended an extensive tour of the Continent, but, in August of 1914, when war broke out, he retreated to England and enrolled at Oxford, ostensibly to continue his studies in philosophy. Oxford seemed an obvious way station for a young man headed for a professorial career, and his parents, shuttling between St. Louis and their comfortable New England summer house, ineradicably American in their habits and point of view, could not have judged otherwise, or suspected a permanent transatlantic removal. But what Eliot was really after was London: the literary life of London, in the manner of Henry James's illustrious conquest of it three decades before. He was quiet, deceptively passive, always reserved, on the watch for opportunity. He met Ezra Pound almost immediately. Pound, a fellow expatriate, was three years older and had come to London five years earlier. He had already published five volumes of poetry. He was idiosyncratic, noisy, cranky, aggressive, repetitively and tediously humorous as well as perilously unpredictable, and he kept an eye out for ways to position himself at the center of whatever maelstrom was current or could be readily invented. By the time he and Eliot discovered each other, Pound had been through imagism and was boosting Vorticism; he wanted to shepherd movements, organize souls, administer lives. He read a handful of Eliot's Harvard poems, including "Portrait of a Lady" and "Prufrock," and instantly anointed him as the real thing. To Harriet Monroe in Chicago, the editor of *Poetry*, then the most distinguished—and coveted—American journal of its kind, he trumpeted Eliot as the author of "the best poem I have yet had or seen from an American," and insisted that she publish "Prufrock." He swept around London introducing his new protégé and finding outlets for his poems in periodicals with names like *Others* and *BLAST* (a Vorticist effort printed on flamingo-pink paper and featuring eccentric typography).

Eliot felt encouraged enough by these successes to abandon both Oxford and Harvard, and took a job teaching in a boy's secondary school to support the poet he was now heartened to become. His mother, appalled by such recklessness, directed her shock not at Eliot but at his former teacher, Bertrand Russell (much as she had gone to the headmaster behind the teenage Eliot's back to protest the risks of the quarry pond): "I hope Tom will be able to carry out his purpose of coming on in May to take his degree. The Ph.D. is becoming in America . . . almost an essential condition for an Academic position and promotion therein. The male teachers in our secondary schools are as a rule inferior to the women teachers, and they have little social position or distinction. I' hope Tom will not undertake such work another year—it is like putting Pegasus in harness." Eliot's father, storming behind the scenes, was less impressed by Pegasus. The appeal to Russell concluded, "As for 'The *BLAST*,' Mr. Eliot remarked when he saw a copy he did not know there were enough lunatics in the world to support such a magazine."

Home, in short, was seething. Within an inch of his degree, the compliant son was suddenly growing prodigal. A bombardment of cables and letters followed. Even the war conspired against the prodigal's return; though Pound was already preparing to fill Eliot's luggage with masses of Vorticist material for a projected show in New York, the danger of German U-boats made a journey by sea unsafe. Russell cabled Eliot's father not to urge him to sit for his exams "UNLESS IMMEDIATE DEGREE IS WORTH RISKING LIFE." "I was not greatly pleased with the language of Prof. Russell's telegram," Eliot's father complained in a letter to Harvard. "Mrs. Eliot and I will use every effort to induce my son to take his examinations later. Doubtless his decision was much influenced by Prof. Russell." Clearly the maternal plea to Russell had backfired. Meanwhile Harvard itself, in the person of James H. Woods, Eliot's mentor in the philosophy department, was importuning him; Woods was tireless in offering an appointment. Eliot turned him down. Three years on, the family campaign to lure him home was unabated: the biggest gun of all was brought out—Charles W. Eliot, eminent educational reformer, recently President of Harvard, architect of the "five-foot shelf" of indispensable classics, and Eliot's grandfather's third cousin once removed. "I conceive that you have a real claim on my attention and interest," he assured his wayward young relative.

It is, nevertheless, quite unintelligible to me how you or any other young American scholar can forego the privilege of living in the genuine American atmosphere—a bright atmosphere of freedom and hope. I have never lived long in England-about six months in all—but I have never got used to the manners and customs of any class in English society, high, middle, or low. After a stay of two weeks or two months in England it has been delightful for me to escape . . .

Then, too, I have never been able to understand how any American man of letters can forego the privilege of being of use primarily to Americans of the present and future generations, as Emerson, Bryant, Lowell, and Whittier were. Literature seems to me highly climatic and national . . . You mention in your letter the name of Henry James. I knew his father well, and his brother William very well; and I had some conversation with Henry at different times during his life. I have a vivid remembrance of a talk with him during his last visit to America. It seemed to me all along that his English residence for so many years contributed neither to the happy development of his art nor to his personal happiness.

. . . My last word is that if you wish to speak through your work to people of the "finest New England spirit" you had better not live much longer in the English atmosphere. The New England spirit has been nurtured in the American atmosphere.

What Eliot thought—three years before the publication of "The Waste Land"—of this tribal lecture, and particularly of its recommendation that he aspire to the mantle of the author of "Thanatopsis," one may cheerfully imagine. In any case it was too late, and had long been too late. The campaign was lost before the first parental shot. Eliot's tie to England was past revocation. While still at Oxford he was introduced to Vivien Haigh-Wood, a high-spirited, high-strung, artistic young woman, the daughter of a cultivated upper-class family; her father painted landscapes and portraits. Eliot, shy and apparently not yet relieved of his virginity, was attracted to her rather theatrical personality. Bertrand Russell sensed in her something brasher, perhaps rasher, than mere vivaciousness—he judged her light, vulgar, and adventurous. Eliot married her only weeks after they met. The marriage, he knew, was the seal on his determination to stay in England, the seal his parents could not break and against which they would be helpless. After the honeymoon, Russell (through pure chance Eliot had bumped into him on a London street) took the new couple in for six months, from July to Christmas—he had a closet-size spare room—and helped them out financially in other ways. He also launched Eliot as a reviewer by putting him in touch with the literary editor of the *New Statesman*, for whom Eliot now began to write intensively. Probably Russell's most useful service was his arranging for Eliot to be welcomed into the intellectual and literary circle around Lady Ottoline Morrell at Garsington, her country estate. Though invitations went to leading artists and writers, Garsington was not simply a salon: the Morrells were principled pacifists who provided farm work during the war for conscientious objectors. Here Eliot found Aldous Huxley, D. H. Lawrence,

Lytton Strachey, Katherine Mansfield, the painter Mark Gertler, Clive Bell, and, eventually, Leonard and Virginia Woolf. Lady Ottoline complained at first that Eliot had no spontaneity, that he barely moved his lips when he spoke, and that his voice was "mandarin." But Russell had carried him—in his arms, as it were—into the inmost eye of the most sophisticated whorl of contemporary English letters. The American newcomer who had left Harvard on a student fellowship in 1914 was already, by the middle of 1915, at the core of the London literary milieu he had dreamed of. And with so many models around him, he was working on disposing of whatever remnants of St. Louis remained lodged in his mouth, and perfecting the manner and accent of a high-born Englishman. (If he was grateful to Russell for this happy early initiation into precisely the society he coveted, by 1931—in "Thoughts After Lambeth," an essay on the idea of a national English church—he was sneering, in italics, at Russell's *gospel of happiness.*")

Meanwhile his parents required placating. A bright young man in his twenties had gone abroad to augment his studies; it was natural for him to come home within a reasonable time to get started on real life and his profession. Instead, he had made a precipitate marriage, intended to spend the rest of his days in a foreign country, and was teaching French and arithmetic in the equivalent of an American junior high school. Not surprisingly, the brick manufacturer and his piously versifying wife could not infer the sublime vocation of a poet from these evidences. Eliot hoped to persuade them. The marriage to Vivien took place on June 26, 1915; on June 28 Ezra Pound wrote a very long letter to Eliot's father. It was one of Eliot's mother's own devices—that of the surrogate pleader. As his mother had asked Russell to intervene with Eliot to return him to Harvard, so now Eliot was enlisting Pound to argue for London. The letter included much information about Pound's own situation, which could not have been reassuring, since—as Pound himself remarked—it was unlikely that the elder Eliot had ever heard of him. But he sweetened the case with respectable references to Edgar Lee Masters and Robert Browning, and was careful to add that Robert Frost, another American in London, had "done a book of New England eclogues." To the heartbroken father who had looked forward to a distinguished university career for his son, Pound said, "I am now much better off than if I had kept my professorship in Indiana"—empty comfort, considering it was Fair Harvard that was being mourned; what Pound had relinquished was Wabash College in a place called Crawfordsville. What could it have meant to Eliot's father that this twenty-nine-year-old contributor to the lunatic *BLAST* boasted of having "engineered a new school of verse now known in England, France and America," and insisted that "when I make a criticism of your son's work it is not an amateur criticism"? "As to his coming to London," Pound contended,

> anything else is a waste of time and energy. No one in London cares a
> hang what is written in America. After getting an American audience a
> man has to begin all over again here if he plans for an international
> hearing . . . The situation has been very well summed up in the sen-
> tence: "Henry James stayed in Paris and read Turgenev and Flaubert,
> Mr. Howells returned to America and read Henry James." . . . At any
> rate if T.S.E. is set on a literary career, this is the place to begin it and
> any other start would be very bad economy.

"I might add," he concluded, "that a literary man's income depends very much on how rigidly he insists on doing exactly what he himself wants to do. It depends on his connection, which he makes himself. It depends on the number of feuds that he takes on for the sake of his aesthetic beliefs. T.S.E. does not seem to be so pugnacious as I am and his course should be smoother and swifter."

The prediction held. The two-year eruption that was Vorticism waned, and so did Pound's local star; he moved on to Paris—leaving London, as it would turn out, in Eliot's possession. Pound's letter to the elder Eliot was not all bluster: he may have been a deft self-promoter, but he was also a pro- moter of literary ideas, and in Eliot's work he saw those ideas made flesh. The exuberance that sent Pound bustling through London to place Eliot here and there was the enthusiasm of an inventor whose thingamajig is just beginning to work in the world at large, in the break-through spirit of Alex- ander Graham Bell's "Mr. Watson, come here." In Pound's mind Eliot was Pound's invention. Certainly the excisions he demanded in "The Waste Land" radically "modernized" it in the direction of the objective correlative by keep- ing in the symbols and chopping out context and narrative, maneuvering the poem toward greater obliqueness and opacity. He also maneuvered Eliot. A determined literary man must go after his own "connection," he had advised Eliot's father, but the boisterous Pound served the reticent Eliot in a network of useful connections that Eliot would not have been likely to make on his own including John Quinn, a New York literary philanthropist who became his (unpaid) agent in America and shored him up from time to time with generous money contributions.

Eliot was dependent on Pound's approval, or for a long while behaved as if he was. It was Pound who dominated the friendship, periodically shooting out instructions, information, scalawag counsel and pontification. "I value his verse far higher than that of any other living poet," Eliot told John Quinn in 1918. Gradually, over a span of years, there was a reversal of authority and power. Eliot rose and Pound sank. Under the pressure of his marriage (Vivien never held a job of any kind, nor could she have, even if it had been expected of her), Eliot ascended in the pragmatic world as well. He gave up teaching secondary school—it required him to supervise sports—and tried evening adult extension-course lecturing. The preparation was all-consuming and the remuneration paltry. Finally he recognized—he was, after all, his father's son—that this was no way to earn a living. A friend of Vivien's family recommended him to Lloyds Bank, where he turned out to be very good at the work—he had a position in the foreign department—and was regularly praised and advanced. Eventually he joined Faber & Gwyer, the London publishing house (later Faber & Faber), and remained associated with it until the end of his life. And then it was Pound who came to Eliot with his manuscripts. Eliot published them, but his responses, which had once treated Pound's antics with answering foolery, became heavily businesslike and impatient. As founder and editor of a literary journal Vivien had named *The Criterion*, Eliot went on commissioning pieces from Pound, though he frequently attempted to impose coherence and discipline; occasionally he would reject something outright. In 1922 Pound had asserted that "Eliot's *Waste Land* is I think the justification of the 'movement,' of our modern experiment, since 1900," but by 1930 he was taunting Eliot for having "arrived at the supreme Eminence among English critics largely through disguising himself as a corpse." Admiration had cooled on both sides. Still, Eliot's loyalty remained fundamentally steadfast, even when he understood that Pound may have been approaching lunacy. After the Second World War, when Pound was a patient in St. Elizabeth's Federal Hospital for the Insane in Washington, D.C.—the United States government's alternative to jailing him for treason—Eliot signed petitions for his release and made sure to see him on visits to America. Eliot never publicly commented on the reason for Pound's incarceration: Pound had supported the Axis and had actively aided the enemy. On Italian radio, in Mussolini's employ, he had broadcast twice-weekly attacks on Roosevelt, Churchill, and the Jews (whom he vilified in the style of Goebbels).

Though in the long run the friendship altered and attenuated—especially as Eliot grew more implicated in his Christian commitment and Pound in his self-proclaimed paganism—Eliot learned much from Pound. He had already learned from Laforgue the technique of the ironically illuminated persona. The tone of youthful ennui, and the ageless though precocious recoil from the world of phenomena, were Eliot's own. To these qualities of negation

Pound added others: indirection, fragmentation, suggestibility, the force of piebald and zigzag juxtaposition—what we have long recognized as the signs of modernism, that famous alchemy of less becoming more. But even as he was tearing down the conventional frame of art, Pound was instructing Eliot in how to frame a career: not that Eliot really needed Pound in either sphere. Poets and critics may fabricate "movements," but no one can invent the Zeitgeist, and it was the Zeitgeist that was promulgating modernism. Eliot may well have been headed there with or without Pound at the helm. That Pound considered Eliot a creature of his own manufacture—that he did in fact tinker with the design—hardly signifies, given that Eliot's art was anyhow likely to fall into the rumbling imperatives of its own time. As for Eliot's advancement into greater and greater reputation, even pushy Pound could not push a miracle into being. Still, it was evident early on that Pound's dictates were in full operation. "Now I am going to ask you to do something for me," Eliot informs his brother Henry in 1915,

> in case you are in Boston or New York this summer. These are suggestions of Ezra Pound's, who has a very shrewd head, and has taken a very great interest in my prospects. There will be people to be seen in Boston and New York, editors with whom I might have some chance . . . As you are likeliest to be in Boston, the first thing is the *Atlantic Monthly*. Now Pound considers it important, whenever possible, to secure introductions to editors from people of better social position than themselves,

and he goes on to propose that Isabella Stewart Gardner, an influential blueblood connection of his, be dragooned into sending a note to the editor of the *Atlantic* on Eliot's behalf. A few days later he is writing to Mrs. Gardner herself, announcing the imminent arrival of his brother, "in order that he may get your advice." To Henry he admits he has only a handful of poems to show, including "some rather second rate things," but anyhow he asks him to try for an opening at *Harper's, Century, Bookman*, and the *New Republic*. "Nothing needs to be done in Chicago, I believe."

Thus, Pound's training in chutzpah. Yet much of it was native to Eliot, picked up at the parental knee. Not for nothing was he the offspring of a mother who was a model of the epistolary maneuver, or of a father who demanded instant success. He had been reared, in any event, as one of the lords of creation in a conscious American aristocracy that believed in its superior birthright—a Midwestern enclave of what Cousin Charles Eliot had called "the finest New England spirit." In the alien precincts of London, where his credentials were unknown or immaterial, the top could not be so easily guaranteed; it would have to be cajoled, manipulated, seduced, dared, commanded, now and then dodged; it would have to be pressed hard, and cunningly. All this Eliot saw for himself, and rapidly. Reserve shored up cunning. It scarcely required Pound to teach him how to calculate the main chance, or how to scheme to impose his importance. He was actually better at it than Pound, because infinitely silkier. Whereas Pound had one voice to assault the barricades with—a cantankerous blast in nutty frontiersman spelling ("You jess set and hev a quiet draw at youh cawn-kob") that was likely to annoy, and was intended to shake you up—Eliot had dozens of voices. His early letters—where he is sedulously on the make—are a ventriloquist's handbook. To Mrs. Gardner he purrs as one should to a prominent patroness of the arts, with friendly dignity, in a courteously appreciative tone, avoiding the appearance of pursuit. Addressing the irascibly playful Pound, he is irascibly playful, and falls into identical orthographical jokiness. To his benefactor John Quinn he is punctiliously—though never humbly—grateful, recording the state of his literary barometer with a precision owed to the chairman of the board; nor does he ever fail to ask after Quinn's health. To his father he writes about money, to his mother about underwear and overcoats. Before both of them, anxiety and dutifulness prevail; he is eager to justify himself and to tot up his triumphs. He means to show them how right he was in choosing a London life; he is not a disappointment after all. "I am staying in the bank," he reports (he had been offered an editorship on a literary journal)—this alone will please his father, but there is much more:

> As it is, I occupy rather a privileged position. I am out of the intrigues and personal hatreds of journalism, and everyone respects me for working in a bank. My social position is quite as good as it would be as editor of a paper. I only write what I want to—now—and everyone knows that anything I do write is good. I can influence London opinion and English literature in a better way. I am known to be disinterested. Even through the Egoist I am getting to be looked up to by people who are far better known to the general public than I. There is a small and select public which regards me as the best living critic, as well as the best living poet, in England. I shall of course write for the *Ath*. [*The Athenaeum*] and keep my finger in it. I am much in sympathy with the editor, who is one of my most cordial admirers. With that and the Egoist and a young quarterly review which I am interested in, and which is glad to take anything I will give, I can have more than enough power to satisfy me. I really think that I have far more *influence* on

English letters than any other American has ever had, unless it be Henry James. I know a great many people, but there are many more who would like to know me, and I can remain isolated and detached.

All this sounds very conceited, but I am sure it is true, and as there is no outsider from whom you would hear it, and America really knows very little of what goes on in London, I must say it myself. Because it will give you pleasure if you believe it, and it will help to explain my point of view.

This was surely the voice of a small boy making his case to his skeptical parents: *it will give you pleasure if you believe it.* He was thirty years old. The self-assurance—or call it, as others did, the arrogance—was genuine, and before his father and mother he was unashamed of speaking of the necessity of power. Such an aspiration was axiomatic among Eliots. What he had set himself to attain was the absolute pinnacle—a place inhabited by no one else, where he could "remain isolated and detached." Fate would give him his wish exactly and with a vengeance, though not quite yet. If he was puffing London to St. Louis, and representing himself there as "the best living critic, as well as the best living poet, in England," two months later he was telling Lytton Strachey that he regarded "London with disdain," and divided "mankind into supermen, termites, and wireworms. I am sojourning among the termites."

In all this there is a wonder and an enigma: the prodigy of Eliot's rocket-like climb from termite to superman. London (and New York and Boston) was swarming with young men on a course no different from Eliot's. He was not the only one with a hotly ambitious pen and an appetite for cultivating highly-placed people who might be useful to him. John Middleton Murry and Wyndham Lewis, for example, both of whom were in Eliot's immediate circle, were equally striving and polished, and though we still know their names, we know them more in the nature of footnotes than as the main text. All three were engaged in the same sort of essayistic empire-building in the little magazines, and at the same time. Lewis published Eliot in *BLAST*, Murry published him in *The Athenaeum*, and later Eliot, when he was editing *The Criterion*, published Lewis. Yet Eliot very quickly overshadowed the others. The disparity, it can be argued, was that Eliot was primarily a poet; or that Eliot's talent was more robust. But even if we believe, as most of us do, that genius of its own force will sooner or later leap commandingly out (Melville's and Dickinson's redemption from obscurity being our sacred paradigms), the riddle stands: why, for Eliot, so soon? His termite days were a brevity, a breath; he was superman in an instant. What was it that singled

Eliot out to put him in the lead so astoundingly early? That he ferociously willed it means nothing. Nearly all beginning writers have a will for extreme fame; will, no matter how resilient, is usually no more efficacious in the marketplace than daydream.

If there is any answer to such questions—and there may not be—it may lie hidden in one of Eliot's most well-appointed impersonations: the voice he employed as essayist. That charm of intimacy and the easy giving of secrets that we like to associate with essayists—Montaigne, Lamb, Hazlitt, George Orwell, Virginia Woolf when the mood struck her—was not Eliot's. As in what is called the "familiar" essay, Eliot frequently said "I"—but it was an "I" set in ice cut from the celestial vault: uninsistent yet incontestable, serenely sovereign. It seemed to take its power from erudition, and in part it did; but really it took it from some proud inner figuration or incarnation—as if Literature itself had been summoned to speak in its own voice:

> I am not considering whether the language of Dante or Shakespeare is superior, for I cannot admit the question: I readily affirm that the differences are such as make Dante easier for a foreigner. Dante's advantages are not due to greater genius, but to the fact that he wrote when Europe was still more or less one. And even had Chaucer or Villon been exact contemporaries of Dante, they would still have been farther, linguistically as well as geographically, from the center of Europe than Dante.

Who could talk back to that? Such sentences appear to derive from a source of knowledge—a congeries of assumptions—indistinguishable from majesty. In short, Eliot would not *permit* himself to be ignored, because it was not "himself" he was representing, but the very flower of European civilization. And there may have been another element contributing to the ready acceptance of his authority: as a foreigner, he was drawn to synthesizing and summarizing in a way that insiders, who take their context for granted, never do. He saw principles where the natives saw only phenomena. Besides, he had a clear model for focused ascent: Henry James. Knowing what he meant to become, he was immune to distraction or wrong turnings. "It is the final perfection, the consummation of an American," Eliot (in one of his most autobiographical dicta) wrote of James, "to become, not an Englishman, but a European—something which no born European, no person of any European nationality, can become."

So much for the larger trajectory. He had mapped out an unimpeded ideal destination. In the lesser geography of private life, however, there was

an unforeseen impediment. Henry James had never married; Eliot had married Vivien. In 1915 she was twenty-seven, slender, lively, very pretty, with a
wave in her hair and a pleasant mouth and chin. By 1919, Virginia Woolf
was describing her as "a washed out, elderly and worn looking little woman."
She complained of illness from the very first, but otherwise there were few
immediate hints of the devastation to come. She was absorbed in Eliot's
career. He brought his newest work to her for criticism; she read proofs; she
assisted in preparing the *Criterion*. She also did some writing of her own—
short stories, and prose sketches that Eliot admired and published in *The
Criterion*. She had energy enough at the start: there were excursions, dinners, visits to Garsington, dance halls, dance lessons, theater, opera; even a
flirtation with Bertrand Russell that turned into a one-night stand. ("Hellish
and loathsome," Russell called it.) A month after the wedding she told Russell that she had married Eliot because she thought she could "stimulate"
him, but that it could not be done. She began to suffer from headaches,
colitis, neuralgia, insomnia. "She is a person who lives on a knife edge," Russell said. Eliot himself often woke at night feeling sick. He was plagued by
colds, flu, bronchial problems; he smoked too much and he consistently
drank too much, though he held it well. Retreating from Vivien, he threw
himself into the work at the bank and into developing his literary reputation.
Vivien had nowhere to go but into resentment, ill-will, hysteria. In the morn-
ings the bed linens were frequently bloody—she menstruated excessively,
and became obsessed with washing the sheets. She washed them herself
even when they stayed in hotels. Morphine was prescribed for her various
symptoms; also bromides and ether (she swabbed her whole body with ether,
so that she reeked of it), and mercilessly bizarre diets—a German doctor
combined starvation with the injection of animal glands. She collapsed into
one nervous illness after another. Eliot repeatedly sent her to the country to
recuperate while he remained in town. When his mother, now an elderly
widow, and one of his sisters came on a visit from America, Vivien was
absent, and Eliot was obliged to manage the complications of hospitality on
his own. Anxiety over Vivien crept into all his business and social correspondence: "my wife has been very ill"; "she is all right when she is lying
down, but immediately she gets up is very faint"; "wretched today—another
bad night"; "Have you ever been in such incessant and extreme pain that you
felt your sanity going, and that you no longer knew reality from delusion?
That's the way she is. The doctors have never seen so bad a case, and hold
out no definite hope, and have so far done her no good. Meanwhile she is in
screaming agony . . ."

She brought out in him all his responsibility, vigilance, conscientiousness, troubled concern; in brief, his virtue. Her condition bewildered him; nothing in his experience, and certainly nothing in his upbringing, had equipped him for it; her manifold sicknesses were unpredictable, and so was she. Her sanity was in fact going. Daily she made him consider and reconsider his conduct toward her, and her ironic, clever, assaultive, always embarrassing responses ran tumbling over his caution. He dreaded dinner parties in her company, and went alone or not at all. It became known that Eliot was ashamed of his wife. But he was also ashamed of his life. Little by little he attempted to live it without Vivien, or despite Vivien, or in the few loopholes left him by Vivien. She was in and out of sanitoria in England, France, and Switzerland; it was a relief to have her away. What had once been frightened solicitude was gradually transmuted into horror, and horror into self-preservation, and self-preservation into callousness, and callousness into a kind of moral brutality. She felt how, emotionally and spiritually, he was abandoning her to her ordeal. However imploringly she sought his attention, he was determined to shut her out; the more he shut her out, the more wildly, dramatically, and desperately she tried to recapture him. He was now a man hunted—and haunted—by a mad wife. He saw himself transmogrified into one of the hollow men of his own imagining, that scarecrow figure stuck together out of "rat's coat, crowskin, crossed staves":

> The eyes are not here
> There are no eyes here
> In this valley of dying stars
> In this hollow valley
> This broken jaw of our lost kingdoms

He carried this Golgothan self-portrait with him everywhere; his lost kingdoms were in the stony looks he gave to the world. Virginia Woolf was struck by "the grim marble face . . . mouth twisted and shut; not a single line free and easy; all caught, pressed, inhibited." "Humiliation is the worst thing in life," he told her. Vivien had humiliated him. Torment and victimization— she of him, and he of her—had degraded him. Bouts of drink depleted him. At times his behavior was as strange as hers: he took to wearing pale green face powder, as if impersonating the sickly cast of death. Virginia Woolf thought he painted his lips. In 1933, after eighteen years of accelerating domestic misery, he finally broke loose: he went to America for a series of angry lectures (published later as *After Strange Gods: A Primer of Modern*

Heresy) in which he attacked Pound, D. H. Lawrence, liberalism, and "free-thinking Jews," complaining that the United States had been "invaded by foreign races" who had "adulterated" its population. In London, meanwhile, a remorseful Vivien was refurbishing the flat for his homecoming; she even offered to join him overseas. In the black mood of his lectures her letter shocked him into a quick cruel plan. Writing from America, he directed his London solicitors to prepare separation documents and to deliver them to Vivien in his absence. When he arrived back in England, the deed was done. Vivien in disbelief continued to wait for him in the reupholstered flat. He moved instead into the shabby guest rooms of the parish house of St. Stephen's, an Anglican congregation with a high-church bent. There, subdued and alone among celibate priests, he spent the next half-dozen years in penance, suffering the very isolation and detachment he had once prized as the influential poet's reward.

Yet Vivien was in pursuit. Though he kept his lodgings secret from her, with fearful single-mindedness she attempted to hunt him down, turning up wherever there might be a chance of confronting him, hoping to cajole or argue or threaten him into resuming with her. He contrived to escape her time after time. By now he had left the bank for Faber; she would burst into the editorial offices without warning, weeping and pleading to be allowed to talk to him. One of the staff would give some excuse and Eliot would find a way of sneaking out of the building without detection. She carried a knife in her purse—it was her customary flamboyance—to alarm him; but it was a theater knife, made of rubber. She sent Christmas cards in the name of "Mr. and Mrs. T. S. Eliot," as if they were still together, and she advertised in *The Times* for him to return. She called herself sometimes Tiresias, and sometimes Daisy Miller, after the doomed Jamesian heroine. In a caricature of what she imagined would please him, she joined the newly formed British Union of Fascists. One day she actually caught him; she went up to him after a lecture, handed him books to sign as if they were strangers, and begged him to go home with her. He hid his recoil behind a polite "How do you do?" When she got wind of a scheme to commit her to a mental hospital, she fled briefly to Paris. In 1938 she was permanently institutionalized, whether by her mother or her brother, or by Eliot himself, no one knows; but Eliot had to have been consulted, at the very least. When her brother visited her in 1946, a year before her death, he reported that she seemed as sane as he was. She had tried on one occasion to run away; she was captured and brought back. She died in the asylum a decade after her commitment. Eliot never once went to see her.

Out of this brutalizing history of grieving and loss, of misalliance, misfortune, frantic confusion, and recurrent panic, Eliot drew the formulation of his dream of horror—that waste land where

> *. . . I Tiresias have foresuffered all*
> *. . . and walked among the lowest of the dead*
> *Here is no water but only rock . . .*
> *If there were only water amongst the rock*
> *Dead mountain mouth of carious teeth that cannot spit*
>
> *. . . blood shaking my heart*
> *The awful daring of a moment's surrender*
> *Which an age of prudence can never retract*
> *By this, and this only, we have existed*
> *Which is not to be found in our obituaries*
> *Or in memories draped by the beneficent spider*
> *Or under seals broken by the lean solicitor*
> *In our empty rooms*

He might have regarded his marriage and its trials as a regrettable accident of fallible youth—the awful daring of a moment's surrender—compounded by his initial sense of duty and loyalty. But he was shattered beyond such realism, and finally even beyond stoicism. He felt he had gazed too long on the Furies. The fiery brand he had plucked out of his private inferno seemed not to have been ignited in the ordinary world; it blackened him metaphysically, and had little to do with fractured expectations or the social difficulties of mental illness. What he knew himself to be was a sinner. The wretchedness he had endured was sin. Vivien had been abused—by doctors and their scattershot treatments, and by regimens Eliot could not have prevented. The truth was she had been drugged for years. And he had abused her himself, perhaps more horribly, by the withdrawal of simple human sympathy. It was she who had smothered his emotional faculties, but reciprocal humiliation had not earned reciprocal destinies. Vivien was confined. He was freed to increase his fame. Nevertheless—as if to compensate her—he lived like a man imprisoned; like a penitent; like a flagellant. He was consumed by ideas of sin and salvation, by self-loathing. The scourge that was Vivien had driven him to conversion: he entered Christianity seriously and desperately, like a soul literally in danger of damnation, or as though he believed he was already half-damned. The religiosity he undertook was a kind of brooding medieval monkishness: ascetic, turned altogether inward, to the sinful self. Its work was the work of personal redemption. In "Ash-Wednesday" he exposed the starting point, the beginning of abnegation and confession:

> *Because these wings are no longer wings to fly*
> *But merely vans to beat the air*
> *The air which is now thoroughly small and dry*
> *Smaller and dryer than the will*
> *Teach us to care and not to care*
> *Teach us to sit still.*

And in a way he did learn to sit still. He was celibate. He was diligent and attentive in his office life while conducting an orderly if lonely domestic routine. He was at Mass every morning, and frequently went on retreat. During the night blitz of London in 1939, he served for a time as an air raid warden, often staying up till dawn. Then, to escape the exhausting bombings, like so many others he turned to commuting from the far suburbs, where he became the paying guest of a family of gentlewomen. In 1945, at the war's end, he made another unusual household arrangement, one that also had its spiritual side: he moved in with John Hayward, a gregarious wit and bookish extrovert whom disease had locked in a wheelchair. Eliot performed the necessary small personal tasks for his companion, wheeled him to the park on pleasant afternoons, and stood vigilantly behind his chair at the parties Hayward liked to preside over—Eliot reserved and silent under the burden of his secret wounds and his eminence, Hayward boisterous, funny, and monarchically at ease. In the evenings, behind the shut door of the darkest room at the back of the flat, Eliot recited the rosary, ate his supper from a tray, and limited himself to a single game of patience. This odd couple lived together for eleven years, until Eliot suddenly married his young secretary, Valerie Fletcher. She offered him the intelligent adoration of an infatuated reader who had been enchanted by his poetry and his fame since her teens; she had come to Faber & Faber with no other motive than to be near him. Vivien had died in 1947; the marriage to Valerie took place in 1957. After the long discipline of penance, he opened himself to capacious love for the first time. As he had known himself for a sinner, so now he knew himself for a happy man.

But the old reflex of recoil—and abandonment—appeared to have survived after all. From youth he had combined ingrained loyalty with the contrary habit of casting off the people who seemed likely to impede his freedom. He had fled over an ocean to separate himself from his demanding parents—though it was his lot ultimately to mimic them. He was absorbed by religion like his mother, and ended by writing, as she did, devotional poetry. Like his father, he was now a well-established businessman, indispensable to his firm and its most influential officer. (It developed that he copied his father even in trivia. The elder Eliot was given to playful doodlings of cats. The son—whose knack for cartooning exceeded the father's—wrote clever cat verses. These, in the form of the long-running Broadway musical, are nearly the whole sum of Eliot's current American renown: if today's undergraduates take spontaneous note of Eliot at all, it will be *Cats* on their tape cassettes, not "The Waste Land.") Still, despite these evolving reversions, it was the lasting force of his repudiations that stung: his scorn for the family heritage of New England Unitarianism, his acquisition in 1927 of British citizenship. He had thrown off both the liberal faith of his fathers—he termed it a heresy—and their native pride of patriotism. He had shown early that he could sever what no longer suited. The selfless interval with John Hayward was cut off overnight: there is a story that Eliot called a taxi, told Hayward he was going off to be married, and walked out. After so prolonged a friendship—and a dependence—Hayward felt cruelly abandoned. He never recovered his spirit. Eliot was repeatedly capable of such calculated abruptness. His abandonment of Vivien—the acknowledged sin of his soul, the flaming pit of his exile and suffering—was echoed in less theological tones in his careless dismissal of Emily Hale and Mary Trevelyan, the wounded women whose loving attachment he had welcomed for years. When Vivien died, each one—Emily Hale in America and Mary Trevelyan close at hand in London—believed that Eliot would now marry her.

Miss Hale—as she was to her students—was a connection of the New England cousins; Eliot had known her since her girlhood. Their correspondence, with its webwork of common associations and sensibilities, flourished decade after decade—she was a gifted teacher of drama at various women's colleges and private schools for girls, with a modest but vivid acting talent of her own. Eliot's trips to America always included long renewing visits with her, and she in turn traveled to England over a series of summer vacations to be with him. One of their excursions was to the lavish silent gardens of Burnt Norton, the unoccupied country mansion of an earl. (That single afternoon of sunlight and roses was transformed by "a grace of sense, a white light still and moving," into the transcendent incantations of "Burnt Norton," the first of the *Quartets*.) In America she waited, in tranquil patience and steady exultation, for the marriage that was never to come: generations of her students were informed of her friendship with the greatest of living poets. Eliot found in her, at a distance, unbodied love, half-elusive nostalgia, the fragility of an ideal. When she threatened, at Vivien's death, to become a real-life encumbrance, he diluted their intimacy; but when he married Valerie Fletcher he sloughed Emily off altogether—rapidly and brutally. Stunned and demoralized—they had been friends for fifty years—she gave up teaching and spiralled into a breakdown. She spent the rest of her life in the hope that her importance to Eliot would not go unrecognized. Her enormous collection of his letters (more than a thousand) she donated to Princeton University, and—Eliot-haunted and Eliot-haunting—she asked him to return hers. He did not reply; he had apparently destroyed them. The "man I loved," she wrote to Princeton, "I think, did not respond as he should have to my long trust, friendship and love." She stipulated that the Princeton repository not be opened until 2019; she looked to her vindication then. Having been patient so long, she was willing to be patient even beyond the grave. Eliot may have bestowed his infirm old age on Miss Fletcher, but the future would see that he had loved Miss Hale in his prime.

As for Mary Trevelyan, she was a hearty pragmatist, a spunky activist, a bold managerial spirit. For nineteen years she was a prop against Eliot's depressions, a useful neighbor—she drove him all over in her car—and, to a degree, a confidante. From the beginning of Vivien's incarceration until his marriage to Valerie—i.e., from 1938 until 1957—Eliot and Mary were regularly together at plays, at parties, and, especially, at church. Their more private friendship centered on lunches and teas, domestic evenings cooking and listening to music in Mary's flat, her matter-of-fact solicitude through his illnesses and hypochondria. They made a point of mentioning each other in their separate devotions. Mary was at home in the pieties Eliot had taken on—she came of distinguished High Anglican stock, the elite of government, letters, and the cloth, with a strong commitment to public service. Her father was a clergyman who erected and administered churches; the historian G. M. Trevelyan was a cousin; her relatives permeated Oxford and Cambridge. (Humphrey Carpenter, author of a remarkably fine biography of Ezra Pound—fittingly published in Eliot's centenary year—represents the newest generation of this family.)

With Mary, Eliot could unbutton. He felt familiar enough to indulge in outbursts of rage or contemptuous sarcasm, and to display the most withering side of his character, lashing out at the people he despised. Through it all she remained candid, humorous, and tolerant, though puzzled by his unpredictable fits of withdrawal from her, sometimes for three months at a time.

He drew lines of conduct she was never permitted to cross: for instance, only once did he agree to their vacationing together, and that was when he needed her—and the convenience of her driving—to help entertain his sister, visiting from America. Mary was accommodating but never submissive. During the war she organized a rest hostel in Brussels for soldiers on leave from the front; in 1944 she nursed hundreds of the wounded. After the war she traveled all over Asia for UNESCO, and founded an international house in London for foreign students. Plainly she had nothing in common with the wistful and forbearing Miss Hale of Abbot Academy for girls. But her expectations were the same. When Vivien died, Mary proposed marriage to Eliot—twice. When he refused her the first time, he said he was incapable of marrying anyone at all; she thought this meant his guilt over Vivien. The second time, he told her about his long attachment to Emily Hale, and how he was a failure at love; she thought this meant psychological exhaustion. And then he married Valerie. Only eight days before the wedding—held secretly in the early morning at a church Eliot did not normally attend—he and Mary lunched together for hours; he disclosed nothing. On the day of the wedding she had a letter from him commemorating their friendship and declaring his love for Valerie. Mary sent back two notes, the earlier one to congratulate him, the second an unrestrained account of her shock. Eliot responded bitterly, putting an end to two decades of companionship.

But all this—the years of self-denial in the parish house, the wartime domesticity among decorous suburban ladies, the neighborly fellowship with John Hayward and Mary Trevelyan, the break with Hayward, the break with Emily Hale, the break with Mary Trevelyan, the joyous denouement with Valerie Fletcher—all this, however consecrated to quietism, however turbulent, was aftermath and postlude. The seizure that animated the poetry had already happened—the seizure was Vivien. Through Vivien he had learned to recognize the reality of sin in all its influences and phases; she was the turning wind of his spiritual storm. Vivien herself understood this with the canniness of a seer: "As to Tom's *mind*," she once said, "I am his mind." The abyss of that mind, and its effect on Eliot as it disintegrated, led him first through a vortex of flight, and then to tormented contemplation, and finally to the religious calm of "Burnt Norton":

> *Time present and time past*
> *Are both perhaps present in time future.*
> *And time future contained in time past.*

Time past marked the psychological anarchy of his youthful work, that vacuous ignorance of sin that had produced "Prufrock," "Gerontion," "The Hollow Men," "The Waste Land". Not to acknowledge the real presence of sin is to be helpless in one's degradation. Consequently Prufrock is a wraith "pinned and wriggling on the wall," uncertain how to "spit out all the butt-ends of my days and ways"; Gerontion is "a dry brain in a dry season"; the hollow men "filled with straw" cannot falter through to the end of a prayer—"For Thine is / Life is / For Thine is the"; the voice of "The Waste Land"—"burning burning burning burning"—is unable to imagine prayer. And the chastening "future contained in time past" is almost surely the inferno that was Vivien: what else could that earlier hollowness have arrived at if not a retributive burning? The waste land—a dry season of naked endurance without God—had earned him the ordeal with Vivien; but the ordeal with Vivien was to serve both time past and time future. Time past: he would escape from the formless wastes of past metaphysical drift only because Vivien had jolted him into a sense of sin. And time future: only because she had jolted him into a sense of sin would he uncover the means to future absolution—the genuine avowal of himself as sinner. To the inferno of Vivien he owed clarification of what had been. To the inferno of Vivien he owed clarification of what might yet be. If Vivien was Eliot's mind, she had lodged Medusa there, and Medusa became both raging muse and purifying savior. She was the motive for exorcism, confession, and penitence. She gave him "Ash-Wednesday," a poem of supplication. She gave him *Four Quartets*, a subdued lyric of near-forgiveness, with long passages of serenely prosaic lines (occasionally burned out into the monotone of philosophic fatigue), recording the threshold of the shriven soul:

> . . . *music heard so deeply*
> *That it is not heard at all, but you are the music*
> *While the music lasts. These are only hints and guesses,*
> *Hints followed by guesses; and the rest*
> *Is prayer, observance, discipline, thought and action.*
> *The hint half guessed, the gift half understood, is Incarnation.*

What makes such "reading backward" possible, of course, is the biographies. (I have relied on Peter Ackroyd and Lyndall Gordon for much of the narrative of Eliot's life.) Knowledge of the life interprets—decodes—the poems: exactly what Eliot's theory of the objective correlative was designed to prevent. Occasionally the illuminations cast by reading backward provoke the uneasy effect of looking through a forbidden keyhole with a flashlight:

> *"My nerves are bad tonight. Yes, bad. Stay with me.*
> *"Speak to me. Why do you never speak? Speak.*
> > *"What are you thinking of? What thinking? What?*
> *"I never know what you are thinking. Think."*
>
> *I think we are in rats' alley*
> > *Where the dead men lost their bones.*

That, wailing out of a jagged interval in "The Waste Land", can only be Vivien's hysteria, and Eliot's recoil from it. But it hardly requires such explicitness (and there is little else that is so clearly explicit) to recognize that his biographers have broken the code of Eliot's reticence—that programmatic reticence embodied in his doctrine of impersonality. The objective correlative was intended to direct the reader to a symbolic stand-in for the poet's personal suffering—not Vivien but Tiresias. Secret becomes metaphor. Eliot's biographers begin with the metaphor and unveil the secret. When the personal is exposed, the objective correlative is annihilated.

And yet the objective correlative has won out, after all, in a larger way. If "The Waste Land" can no longer hide its sources in Eliot's private malaise, it has formidably sufficed as an "objective equivalence" for the public malaise of generations. Its evocations of ruin, loss, lamentation, its "empty cisterns and exhausted wells," are broken sketches of the discontents that remain when the traditional props of civilization have failed: for some (unquestionably for Eliot), a world without God; for others, a world without so much as an illusion of intelligibility or restraint. In 1867, contemplating the Victorian crisis of faith, Matthew Arnold saw "a darkling plain . . . where ignorant armies clash by night," but in Eliot's echoing "arid plain" there is nothing so substantial as even a clash—only formlessness, "hooded hordes swarming," "falling towers"; hallucination succeeds hallucination, until all the crowns of civilization—"Jerusalem Athens Alexandria / Vienna London"—are understood to be "unreal."

In 1922 (a postwar time of mass unemployment, economic disintegration and political uncertainty), "The Waste Land" fell out upon its era as the shattered incarnation of dissolution, the very text and texture of modernism—modernism's consummate document and ode. In the almost seventy years since its first publication, it has taken on, as the great poems do (but not the very greatest), a bloom of triteness (as ripe truth can overmature into truism). It is no more "coherent" to its newest readers than it was to its astonished earliest readers, but it is much less difficult; tone and technique no longer startle. Post-Bomb, post-Holocaust, pos-moonwalk, it may actually be too tame a poem to answer to the mindscape we now know more exhaustively than Eliot did. Professor Harry Levin, Harvard's eminent pioneer promulgator of Proust, Joyce, and Eliot, quipped a little while ago—not altogether playfully—that modernism "has become old-fashioned." "The Waste Land" is not yet an old-fashioned poem, and doubtless never will be. But it does not address with the same exigency the sons and daughters of those impassioned readers who ecstatically intoned it, three and four decades ago, in the belief that infiltration by those syllables was an aesthetic sacrament. Even for the aging generation of the formerly impassioned, something has gone out of the poem—not in "The Waste Land" proper, perhaps, but rather in that parallel work Eliot called "Notes on *The Waste Land.*" This was the renowned mock-scholarly apparatus Eliot tacked on to the body of the poem, ostensibly to spell out its multiple allusions—a contrivance that once seemed very nearly a separate set of modernist stanzas: arbitrary, fragmented, dissonant, above all solemnly erudite. "The whole passage from Ovid," drones the sober professorial persona of the "Notes," "is of great anthropological interest." There follow nineteen lines of Latin verse. The procession of brilliantly variegated citations—Augustine, the Upanishads, Verlaine, Baudelaire, Hermann Hesse, Shakespeare, Tarot cards, the Grail legend—suggests (according to Professor Levin) that context was to Eliot what conceit was to the metaphysical poets. A fresh reading of the "Notes" admits to something else—the thumbed nose, that vein in Eliot of the practical joker, released through Macavity the Mystery Cat and in masses of unpublished bawdy verses (nowadays we might regard them as more racist than bawdy) starring "King Bolo's big black bassturd kween." In any case, whatever pose Eliot intended, no one can come to the "Notes" today with the old worshipful gravity. They seem drained of austerity—so emphatically serious that it is hard to take them seriously at all.

The same with the plays. With the exception of the first of the five, *Murder in the Cathedral*—a major devotional poem of orchestral breadth—the plays are all collapsed into curios. From our perspective, they are something worse than period pieces, since that is what they were—Edwardian drawing room dramas-when they were new. They hint at (or proclaim) a failure of Eliot's public ear. His aim was to write popular verse plays for the English stage—an aim worthy (though Eliot never had the hubris to say this) of Shakespeare. George Bernard Shaw had been content with prose—and the majestically cunning prose speeches in *Murder in the Cathedral* are reminiscent of nothing so much as Shaw's *Saint Joan*, including Shaw's preface to that play. The dialogue of enjambment that is the style and method of *The Cocktail Party*, *The Confidential Clerk*, and *The Elder Statesman*, never attains the sound of verse, much less poetry. That was precisely Eliot's hope: he considered *Murder in the Cathedral* too blatantly poetic, a "dead end." His goal was to bury the overt effects of poetry while drawing out of ordinary speech and almost ordinary situations a veil of transcendence—even, now and then, of mystical horror, as when (in *The Family Reunion*) the Furies suddenly appear, or when (in *The Cocktail Party*) a character we are meant to imagine as a saint and a martyr goes off to be a missionary among the "natives" and is eaten by ants. (Having first been crucified, it ought to be added. And though there are farcical moments throughout, the devouring anthill is not intended as one of them.) Nevertheless, nothing transcendent manages to rise from any printed page of any of the last four plays—almost nothing suggestive of poetry, in fact, except an occasional "wisdom" patch in the semi-lyrical but largely prosy manner of the philosophical lines in *Four Quartets*. Possibly this is because the printed page is perforce bare of technical stagecraft, with its color and excitement. Yet—similarly unaccoutered— Shakespeare, Marlowe, and Shaw, in their greater and lesser written art, send out language with presence and power enough to equal absent actors, sets, lighting, costumes. Much of Eliot's dialogue, rather than achieving that simplicity of common speech he aspired to, plummets to the stilted, the pedestrian, the enervated:

> *Oh, Edward, when you were a little boy!*
> *I'm sure you were always getting yourself measured*
> *To prove how you had grown since the last holidays.*
> *You were always intensely concerned with yourself;*
> *And if other people grow, well, you want to grow too.*

Given only the text and nothing else, a reader of *The Cocktail Party*, say, will be perplexed by its extravagant performing history: in London and New York in the fifties, it filled theaters and stunned audiences. Read now, these later plays are unmistakably dead, embalmed, dated beyond endurance— dated especially in the light of the vigorous fifties, when the energetic spokesmen of the Angry Young Men were having their first dramatic hearing. As playwright, Eliot inexplicably eschewed or diluted or could not pull off his theory of demarcation between "the man who suffers and the mind which creates," so the plays are surprisingly confessional—the Furies harbor Vivien, a character is tormented by thinking he has killed his wife, Valerie turns up as a redemptive young woman piously named Monica, etc. Since Eliot's private life was not only closed but unguessed at in those years, gossip could not have been the lure for theater-goers. The lure was, in part, skillful production: on the page, the Furies when they pop up seem as silly as the news of the hungry anthill, but their theatrical embodiment was electrifying. Fine performances and ingenious staging, though, were at bottom not what brought overflowing audiences to see Eliot's plays. They came because of the supremacy of Eliot's fame. They came because verse drama by T. S. Eliot was the most potent cultural vitamin of the age.

Inevitably we are returned to the issue (there is no escaping it at any point) of Eliot's renown. As a young man, he had hammered out the prestige of a critical reputation by means of essay after essay. By the time of the later plays he had become a world celebrity, an international feature story in newspapers and magazines. But neither the essays by themselves, nor (certainly) the plays—always excepting *Murder in the Cathedral*, which ought to count among the most lastingly resonant of the poems—could have won for Eliot his permanent place in English letters. The fame belongs to the poems. The rest, however much there might be of it, was spinoff. Yet the body of poems is amazingly small in the light of Eliot's towering repute. In 1958, for example, invited to Rome for an honorary degree, he was driven through streets mobbed with students roaring "*Viva* Eliot!" Mass adulation of this sort more often attaches to presidents and monarchs—or, nowadays, to rock stars. What did that roar rest on? Leaving aside the early Bolo ribaldry (which in any case never reached print), the fourteen cat verses, and the contents of a little posthumous collection called *Poems Written in Early Youth* (from ages sixteen to twenty-two), but not omitting two unfinished works—"Sweeney Agonistes" and "Coriolan"—Eliot's entire poetic oeuvre comes to no more than fifty-four poems. England, at least, is used to more abundant output from the poets it chooses to mark with the seal of permanence. My copy of Wordsworth's *Poetical Works* adds up to nine hundred and sixty-six pages of minuscule type, or approximately a thousand poems. The changes in the written culture between, say, the "Ode on Intimations of Immortality," published in 1807, and Eliot's "Waste Land", published one hundred and fifteen years later, speak for themselves. Still, granting the impertinence of measuring by number, there remains something extraordinary—even uncanny—about the torrent of transoceanic adoration that, for Eliot, stemmed from fifty-four poems.

Eliot may have supposed himself a classicist, but really he is in the line of the Romantics: subjective, anguished, nostalgic, mystical, lyrical. The critic Harold Bloom's mild view is that he "does not derive from Dante and Donne, as he thought, but from Tennyson and Whitman"—a judgment that might have stung him. For Eliot to have believed himself an offspring of the cosmic Dante and the precision-worker Donne, and to end, if Professor

Bloom is correct, as a descendant of the softer, lusher music of Tennyson, is no serious diminishment (Tennyson is permanent too)—though it is a diminishment. Lord Tennyson, the British Empire's laureate, may have seemed a weighty and universal voice to the Victorians. For us he is lighter and more parochial. It is in the nature of fame to undergo revision: Eliot appears now to be similarly receding into the parochial, even the sectarian (unlike the all-embracing Whitman, with whom he shares the gift of bel canto). His reach—once broad enough to incorporate the Upanishads—shrank to extend no farther than the neighborhood sacristy, and to a still smaller space: the closet of the self. His worship was local and exclusionary not simply in the limited sense that it expressed an astringent clerical bias, or that he observed the forms of a narrow segment of the Church of England—itself an island church, after all, though he did his best to link it with what he termed "the Universal Church of the World." What made Eliot's religiosity local and exclusive was that he confined it to his personal pain and bitterness: he allowed himself to become estranged from humanity. Feeling corrupt in himself, he saw corruption everywhere: "all times are corrupt," he wrote; and then again, "the whole of modern literature is corrupted by what I call Secularism." Demanding that faith—a particular credo—be recognized as the foundation of civilization, he went on to define civilization as extraneous to some of its highest Western manifestations—the principles of democracy, tolerance, and individualism. Despite his youthful study of Eastern religion and his poet's immersion in Hebrew scripture, he was finally unable to imagine that there might be rival structures of civilization not grounded in the doctrine of original sin, and yet intellectually and metaphysically exemplary. Even within the familial household of Christendom, he was quick to cry heretic. In any event, the style of his orthodoxy was, as Harry Levin put it, "a literary conception." As a would-be social theorist he had a backward longing for the medieval hegemony of cathedral spires—i.e., for a closed society. It was a ruefulness so poignant that it preoccupied much of the prose and seeped into the melancholy cadences of the poetry. As a modernist, Eliot was the last of the Romantics.

In the end he could not disengage the mind that created from the man who suffered; they were inseparable. But the mind and the man—the genius and the sufferer—had contributed, in influence and authority, more than any other mind and man (with the exception perhaps of Picasso) to the formation of the most significant aesthetic movement of the twentieth century. It was a movement so formidable that its putative successor cannot shake off its effects and is obliged to carry on its name; helplessly, we speak of the "postmodern." Whether postmodernism is genuinely a successor, or merely an updated variant of modernism itself, remains unresolved. Yet whichever it turns out to be, we do know for certain that we no longer live in the literary shadow of T. S. Eliot. "Mistah Kurtz—he dead"—the celebrated epigraph Eliot lifted from Conrad's *Heart of Darkness* and affixed to "The Hollow Men"—applies: the heart has gone out of what once ruled. High art is dead. The passion for inheritance is dead. Tradition is equated with obscurantism. The wall that divided serious high culture from the popular arts is breached; anything can count as "text." Knowledge-saturated in historical memory—is displaced by information, or memory without history: data. Allusiveness is crosscultural in an informational and contemporary way (from, say, bee-keeping to film-making), not in the sense of connecting the present with the past. The relation of poets to history is that they can take it or leave it, and mostly they leave it, whether in prosody or in the idea of the venerable. If it is true that "The Waste Land" could not be written today because it is too tame for the savagery we have since accumulated, there is also a more com-pelling truth: because we seem content to live without contemplation of our formal beginnings, a poem like "The Waste Land", mourning the loss of an integral tradition, is for us inconceivable. For the modernists, the center notoriously did not hold; for us (whatever we are), there is no recollection of a center, and nothing to miss, let alone mourn.

Was it the ever-increasing rush to what Eliot called "Secularism" that knocked him off his pinnacle? Was it the vague nihilism of "modern life" that deposed modernism's prophet? Was Eliot shrugged off because his pessimis-tic longings were ultimately judged to be beside the point? The answer may not be as clearcut as any of that. The changes that occurred in the forty years between the Nobel award in 1948 and Eliot's centennial in 1988 have still not been assimilated or even remotely understood. The Wordsworth of the "Ode to Duty" (composed the same year as "Intimations of Immortality") has more in common with the Eliot of *Four Quartets*—the differing idioms of the poetry aside—than Eliot has with Allen Ginsberg. And yet Ginsberg's "Howl," the single poem most representative of the break with Eliot, may owe as much, thematically, to "The Waste Land" as it does to the bardic Whitman, or to the opening of the era of anything-goes. Ginsberg belongs to the generation that knew Eliot as sanctified, and, despite every irruption into indiscipline, Eliot continues alive in Ginsberg's ear. For the rest, a look at the condition of most poetry in America today will disclose how far behind we have left Eliot. William Carlos Williams, a rival of Eliot's engaged in another vein of diction and committed to sharply contrasting aesthetic goals ("no ideas but in things"), said of the publication of "The Waste Land" that he "felt at once it had set me back twenty years," largely because of its European gravity of erudition. The newest generation in the line of descent from Williams, though hardly aware of its own ancestry, follows Williams in repudiating Eliot: music is not wanted, history is not wanted, idea is not wanted. Even literature is not much wanted. What *is* wanted is a sort of verbal snapshot: the quick impression, the short flat snippet that sounds cut from a sentence in a letter to a friend, the casual and scanty "revelation." As Eliot in his time spurned Milton's exalted epic line as too sublime for his need, so now Eliot's elegiac fragments appear too arcane, too aristocratic, and too difficult, for contemporary ambition. Ironic allusiveness—Eliot's inspired borrowing—is out of the question: there is nothing in stock to allude to. Now and then there are signs—critical complaints and boredom— that the school of pedestrian verse-making is nearly exhausted, and more and more there are poets who are venturing into the longer line, the denser stanza, a more intense if not a heightened diction.

But the chief elements of the Age of Eliot are no longer with us, and may never return: the belief that poetry can be redemptive, the conviction that history underlies poetry. Such notions may still be intrinsic to the work of Joseph Brodsky and Czeslaw Milosz—Europeans resident in America. Eliot was an American resident in Europe. Even as he was exacting from both poetry and life a perfected impersonation of the European model, he was signing himself, in letters, *Metoikos*, the Greek word for resident alien. He knew he was a contradiction. And it may simply be that it is in the renunciatory grain of America to resist the hierarchical and the traditional. Eliot's "high culture" and its regnancy in and beyond the American university may have been an unsuccessful transplant that "took" temporarily, but in the end would be rejected by the formation of natural tissue. Or, as Eliot himself predicted in the "Dry Salvages" section of *Four Quartets*,

> *We had the experience but missed the meaning.*

For the generation for whom Eliot was once a god (my own), the truth is that we had the experience and were irradiated by the meaning. Looking back over the last forty years, it is now our unsparing obligation to disclaim the reactionary Eliot. What we will probably go on missing forever is that golden cape of our youth, the power and prestige of high art.

LITERATURE

The Impious Impatience of Job

ↂ

The riddles of God are more satisfying than the
solutions of men.
—G. K. CHESTERTON

1. What the Scholars Say

Twenty-five centuries ago (or perhaps twenty-four or twenty-three), an unnamed Hebrew poet took up an old folk tale and transformed it into a sacred hymn so sublime—and yet so shocking to conventional religion—that it agitates and exalts us even now. Scholars may place the Book of Job in the age of the Babylonian Exile, following the conquest of Jerusalem by Nebuchadnezzar—but to readers of our own time, or of any time, the historicity of this timeless poem hardly matters. It is timeless because its author intended it so; it is timeless the way Lear on the heath is timeless (and Lear may owe much to Job). Job is a man who belongs to no known nation; despite his peerless Hebrew speech, he is plainly not a Hebrew. His religious customs are unfamiliar, yet he is no pagan: he addresses the One God of monotheism. Because he is unidentified by period or place, nothing in his situation is foreign or obsolete; his story cannot blunder into anachronism or archaism. Like almost no other primordial poem the West has inherited, the Book of Job is conceived under the aspect of the universal—if the universal is understood to be a questioning so organic to our nature that no creed or philosophy can elude it.

That is why the striking discoveries of scholars—whether through philological evidences or through the detection of infusions from surrounding ancient cultures—will not deeply unsettle the common reader. We are driven—we common readers—to approach Job's story with tremulous palms held upward and unladen. Not for us the burden of historical linguistics, or the torrent of clerical commentary that sweeps through the centuries, or the dusty overlay of partisan interpretation. Such a refusal of context, historical and theological, is least of all the work of willed ignorance; if we choose to turn from received instruction, it is rather because of an intrinsic knowledge—the terror, in fact, of self-knowledge. Who among us has not been tempted to ask Job's questions? Which of us has not doubted God's justice? What human creature ever lived in the absence of suffering? If we, ordinary clay that we are, are not equal to Job in the wild intelligence of his cries, or in the unintelligible wilderness of his anguish, we are, all the same, privy to his conundrums.

Yet what captivates the scholars may also captivate us. A faithful English translation, for instance, names God as "God," "the Lord," "the Holy One," "the Almighty"—terms reverential, familiar, and nearly interchangeable in their capacity to evoke an ultimate Presence. But the author of Job, while aiming for the same effect of incalculable awe, has another resonance in mind as well: the dim tolling of some indefinable aboriginal chime, a suggestion of immeasurable antiquity. To achieve this, he is altogether sparing in his inclusion of the Tetragrammaton, the unvocalized YHVH (the root of which is "to be," rendered as "I am that I am"), which chiefly delineates God in the Hebrew Bible (and was later approximately transliterated as Yahweh or Jehovah). Instead, he sprinkles his poem, cannily and profusely, with pre-Israelite God-names: El, Eloah, Shaddai—names so lost in the long-ago, so unembedded in usage, that the poem is inevitably swept clean of traditional pieties. Translation veils the presence—and the intent—of these old names; and the necessary seamlessness of translation will perforce paper over the multitude of words and passages that are obscure in the original, subject to philological guesswork. Here English allows the common reader to remain untroubled by scholarly puzzles and tangles.

But how arresting to learn that Satan appears in the story of Job not as that demonic figure of later traditions whom we meet in our translation, but as *ha-Satan*, with the definite article attached, meaning "the Adversary"—the counter-arguer among the angels, who is himself one of "the sons of God." Satan's arrival in the tale helps date its composition. It is under Persian influence that he turns up—via Zoroastrian duality, which pits, as equal contenders, a supernatural power for Good against a supernatural power for Evil. In the Book of Job, the scholars tell us, Satan enters Scripture for the first time as a distinct personality and as an emblem of destructive forces. But note: when the tale moves out of the prose of its fablelike frame into the sovereign grandeur of its poetry, Satan evaporates; the poet, an uncompromising monotheist, recognizes no alternative to the Creator, and no opposing might. Nor does the poet acknowledge any concept of afterlife, though

Pharisaic thought in the period of his writing is just beginning to introduce that idea into normative faith.

There is much more that textual scholarship discloses in its search for the Job-poet's historical surround: for example, the abundance of words and phrases in Aramaic, a northwestern Semitic tongue closely related to Hebrew, which was rapidly becoming the lingua franca of the post-Exilic Levant. Aramaic is significantly present in other biblical books as well: in the later Psalms, in Ecclesiastes, Esther, and Chronicles—and, notably, in the Dead Sea Scrolls. The Babylonian Talmud is written in Aramaic; it is the language that Jesus speaks. Possibly the Job-poet's everyday speech is Aramaic—this may account for his many Aramaisms—but clearly, for the literary heightening of poetry, he is drawn to the spare beauty and noble diction of classical Hebrew (much as Milton, say, in constructing his poems of Paradise, invokes the cadences of classical Latin).

And beyond the question of language, the scholars lead us to still another enchanted garden of context and allusion: the flowering, all over the ancient Near East, of a form known as "wisdom literature." A kind of folk-philosophy linking virtue to prudence, and pragmatically geared to the individual's worldly success, its aim is instruction in level-headed judgment and in the achievement of rational contentment. The biblical Proverbs belong to this genre, and, in a more profoundly reflective mode, Ecclesiastes and portions of Job; but wisdom literature can also be found in Egyptian, Babylonian, Ugaritic, and Hellenistic sources. It has no overriding national roots and deals with personal rather than collective conduct, and with a commonsensical morality guided by principles of resourcefulness and discretion. A great part of the Book of Job finds its ancestry in the region's pervasive wisdom literature (and its descendants in today's self-improvement bestsellers). But what genuinely seizes the heart are those revolutionary passages in Job that violently contradict what all the world, yesterday and today, takes for ordinary wisdom.

2. What the Reader Sees

However seductive they are in their insight and learning, all these scholarly excavations need not determine or deter our own reading. We, after all, have in our hands neither the Hebrew original nor a linguistic concordance. What we do have—and it is electrifying enough—is the Book of Job as we readers of English encounter it. And if we are excluded from the sound and texture of an elevated poetry in a tongue not ours, we are also shielded from problems of structure and chronology, and from a confrontation with certain endemic philological riddles. There is riddle enough remaining—a riddle that is, besides, an elemental quest, the appeal for an answer to humankind's primal inquiry. So there is something to be said for novice readers who come to Job's demands and plaints unaccoutered: we will perceive God's world exactly as Job himself perceives it. Or put it that Job's bewilderment will be ours, and our kinship to his travail fully unveiled, only if we are willing to absent ourselves from the accretion of centuries of metaphysics, exegesis, theological polemics. Of the classical Jewish and Christian theologians (Saadia Gaon, Rashi, ibn Ezra, Maimonides, Gersonides, Gregory, Aquinas, Calvin), each wrote from a viewpoint dictated by his particular religious perspective. But for us to be as (philosophically) naked as Job will mean to be naked of bias, dogma, tradition. It will mean to imagine Job solely as he is set forth by his own words in his own story.

His story, because it is mostly in dialogue, reads as a kind of drama. There is no proscenium; there is no scenery. But there is the dazzling spiral of words—extraordinary words, Shakespearean words; and there are the six players, who alternately cajole, console, contradict, contend, satirize, fulminate, remonstrate, accuse, deny, trumpet, succumb. Sometimes we are reminded of Antigone, sometimes of Oedipus (Greek plays that are contemporaneous with Job), sometimes of Othello. The subject is innocence and power; virtue and injustice; the Creator and His Creation; or what philosophy has long designated as theodicy, the Problem of Evil. And the more we throw off sectarian sophistries—the more we attend humbly to the drama as it plays itself out—the more clearly we will see Job as he emerges from the venerable thicket of theodicy into the heat of our own urgency. Or call it our daily breath.

3. Job's Story

Job's story—his fate, his sentence—begins in heaven, with Satan as prosecuting attorney. Job, Satan presses, must be put to trial. Look at him: a man of high estate, an aristocrat, robust and in his prime, the father of sons and daughters, respected, affluent, conscientious, charitable, virtuous, God-fearing. God-fearing? How effortless to be always praising God when you are living in such ease! Look at him: how he worries about his lucky children and their feasting, days at a time—was there too much wine, did they slide into blasphemy? On their account he brings sacred offerings in propitiation. His possessions are lordly, but he succors the poor and turns no one away;

his hand is lavish. Yet look at him—how easy to be righteous when you are carefree and rich! Strip him of his wealth, wipe out his family, afflict him with disease, and *then* see what becomes of his virtue and his piety!

So God is persuaded to test Job. Invasion, fire, tornado, destruction, and the cruelest loss of all: the death of his children. Nothing is left. Odious lesions creep over every patch of Job's skin. Tormented, he sits in the embers of what was once his domain and scratches himself with a bit of shattered bowl. His wife despairs: after all this, he still declines to curse God! She means for him to dismiss God as worthless to his life, and to dismiss his ruined life as worthless. But now a trio of gentlemen from neighboring lands arrives—a condolence call from Eliphaz, Bildad, and Zophar, Job's distinguished old friends. The three weep and are mute—Job's broken figure appalls: pitiable, desolate, dusted with ash, scraped, torn.

All the foregoing is told in the plain prose of a folk tale: a blameless man's undoing through the conniving of a mischievous sprite. A prose epilogue will ultimately restore Job to his good fortune, and, in the arbitrary style of a fable, will even double it; but between the two halves of this simple narrative of loss and restitution the coloration of legend falls away, and a majesty of outcry floods speech after speech. And then Job's rage ascends—a rage against the loathsomeness of "wisdom."

When the horrified visitors regain their voices, it is they who appear to embody reasonableness, logic, and prudence, while Job—introduced in the prologue as a man of steadfast faith who will never affront the Almighty—rails like a blasphemer against an unjust God. The three listen courteously as Job bewails the day he was born, a day that "did not shut the doors of my mother's womb, nor hide trouble from my eyes." In response to which, Eliphaz begins his first attempt at solace: "Can mortal man be righteous before God? Can a man be pure before his Maker? . . . Behold, happy is the man whom God reproves; therefore despise not the chastening of the Almighty." Here is an early and not altogether brutal hint of what awaits Job in the severer discourse of his consolers: the logic of punishment, the dogma of requital. If a man suffers, it must be because of some impiety he has committed. Can Job claim that he is utterly without sin? And is not God a merciful God, "for He wounds, but binds up; He smites, but His hands heal"? In the end, Eliphaz reassures Job, all will be well.

Job is not comforted; he is made furious. He has been accused, however obliquely, of having sinned, and he knows with his whole soul that he has not. His friends show themselves to be as inconstant as a torrential river, icy in winter, vanishing away in the heat. Rather than condole, they defame. They root amelioration in besmirchment. But if Job's friends are no friends, then what of God? The poet, remembering the Psalm—"What is man that thou are mindful of him?"—has Job echo the very words. "What is man," Job charges God, that "thou dost set thy mind upon him, dost visit him every morning, and test him every moment? . . . If I sin, what do I do to thee, thou watcher of men?" And he dreams of escaping God in death: "For now I shall lie in the earth; thou wilt seek me, but I shall not be."

Three rounds of increasingly tumultuous debate follow, with Eliphaz, Bildad, and Zophar each having a turn, and Job replying. Wilder and wilder grow the visitors' accusations; wilder and wilder grow Job's rebuttals, until they are pitched into an abyss of bitterness. Job's would-be comforters have become his harriers; men of standing themselves, they reason from the conventional doctrines of orthodox religion, wherein conduct and consequence are morally linked: goodness rewarded, wickedness punished. No matter how hotly Job denies and protests, what greater proof of Job's impiety can there be than his deadly ordeal? God is just; he metes out just deserts. Is this not the grand principle on which the world rests?

Job's own experience refutes these arguments; and his feverish condemnation of God's injustice refutes religion itself. "I am blameless!" he cries yet again, and grimly concludes: "It is all one: therefore I say, He destroys both the blameless and the wicked. When disaster brings sudden death, He mocks the calamity of the innocent. The earth is given into the hand of the wicked; He covers the face of its judges." Here Job, remarkably, is both believer and atheist. God's presence is incontrovertible; God's moral integrity is nil. And how strange: in the heart of Scripture, a righteous man impugning God! Genesis, to be sure, records what appears to be a precedent. "Wilt thou destroy the righteous with the wicked?" Abraham asks God when Sodom's fate is at stake; but that is more plea than indictment, and anyhow there is no innocence in Sodom. Yet how distant Job is from the Psalmist who sings "The Lord is upright . . . there is no unrighteousness in Him," who pledges that "the righteous shall flourish like the palm tree," and "the workers of iniquity shall be destroyed forever." The Psalmist's is the voice of faith. Job's is the voice of a wounded lover, betrayed.

Like a wounded lover, he envisions, fleetingly, a forgiving afterlife, the way a tree, cut down to a stump, can send forth new shoots and live again— while man, by contrast, "lies down and rises not again." Or he imagines the workings of true justice: on the one hand, he wishes he might bring God Himself to trial; on the other, he ponders manmade law and its courts, and declares that the transcript of his testimony ought to be inscribed permanently in stone, so that some future clansman might one day come as a vindicator, to proclaim the probity of Job's case. (Our translation famously—

and not disinterestedly—renders the latter as "I know that my Redeemer lives," a phrase that has, of course, been fully integrated into Christian hermeneutics.) Throughout, there is a thundering of discord and clangor. "Miserable comforters are you all!" Job groans. "Surely there are mockers about me"—while Eliphaz, Bildad, and Zophar press on, from pious apologias to uncontrolled denunciation. You, Job, they accuse, you who stripped the naked of their clothing, gave no water to the weary, withheld bread from the hungry!

And Job sees how the tenets of rectitude, in the mouths of the zealous, are perverted to lies.

But now, abruptly, a new voice is heard: a fifth and so far undisclosed player strides onstage. He is young, intellectually ingenious, confident, a bit brash. Unlike the others, he bears a name with a Hebrew ring to it: Elihu. "I also will declare my opinion," he announces. He arrives as a supplanter, to replace stale wisdom with fresh, and begins by rebuking Job's haranguers for their dogma of mechanical tit-for-tat. As for Job: in his recalcitrance, in his litanies of injured innocence, in his prideful denials, he has been blind to the *uses* of suffering; and doesn't he recognize that God manifests Himself in night visions and dreams? Suffering educates and purifies; it humbles pride, tames the rebel, corrects the scoffer. "What man is like Job, who drinks up scoffing like water?" Elihu points out—but here the reader detects a logical snag. Job has become a scoffer only as a result of gratuitous suffering: then how is such suffering a "correction" of scoffing that never was? Determined though he is to shake Job's obstinacy, Elihu is no wiser than his elders. Job's refusal of meaningless chastisement stands.

So Elihu, too, fails as comforter—but as he leaves off suasion, his speech metamorphoses into a hymn in praise of God's dominion. "Hear this, O Job," Elihu calls, "stop and consider the wondrous work of God"—wind, cloud, sky, snow, lightning, ice! Elihu's sumptuous limning of God's power in nature is a fore-echo of the sublime climax to come.

4. The Voice Out of the Whirlwind

Job, gargantuan figure in the human imagination that he is, is not counted among the prophets. He is not the first to be reluctant to accept God's authority: Jonah rebelled against sailing to Nineveh in order to prophesy; yet he did go, and his going was salvational for a people not his own. But the true prophets are self-starters, spontaneous fulminators against social inequity, and far from reluctant. Job, then, has much in common with Isaiah,

Jeremiah, Micah and Amos: he is wrathful that the wicked go unpunished, that the widow and the orphan go unsuccored, that the world is not clothed in righteousness. Like the noblest of the prophets, he assails injustice; and still he is unlike them. They accuse the men and women who do evil; their targets are made of flesh and blood. It is human transgression they hope to mend. Job seeks to rectify God. His is an ambition higher, deeper, vaster, grander than theirs; he is possessed by a righteousness more frenzied than theirs; the scale of his justice-hunger exceeds all that precedes him, all that was ever conceived; he can be said to be the consummate prophet. And at the same time he is the consummate violator. If we are to understand him at all, if we are rightly to enter into his passions at their pinnacle, then we ought to name him prophet; but we may not. Call him, instead, antiprophet—his teaching, after all, verges on atheism: the rejection of God's power. His thesis is revolution.

Eliphaz, Bildad, and Zophar are silenced. Elihu will not strut these boards again. Job's revolution may be vanity of vanities, but his adversaries have lost confidence and are scattered. Except for Job, the stage is emptied.

Then God enters—not in a dream, as Elihu theorized, not as a vision or incarnation, but as an irresistible Eloquence.

Here I am obliged to remark on the obvious. In recapitulating certain passages, I have reduced an exalted poem to ordinary spoken sentences. But the ideas that buttress Job are not merely "expressed in," as we say, language of high beauty; they are inseparable from an artistry so far beyond the grasp of mind and tongue that one can hardly imagine their origin. We think of the Greek plays; we think of Shakespeare; and still that is not marvel enough. Is it that the poet is permitted to sojourn, for the poem's brief life, in the magisterial Eye of God? Or is it God who allows Himself to peer through the poet's glass, as through a gorgeously crafted kaleidoscope? The words of the poem are preternatural, unearthly. They may belong to a rhapsodic endowment so rare as to appear among mortals only once in three thousand years. Or they may belong to the Voice that hurls itself from the whirlwind.

5. The Answer

God has granted Job's demand: "Let the Almighty answer me!" Now here at last is Job's longed-for encounter with that Being he conceives to be his persecutor. What is most extraordinary in this visitation is that it appears to be set apart from everything that has gone before. What is the Book of Job *about*? It is about gratuitous affliction. It is about the wicked who escape whipping. It is about the suffering of the righteous. God addresses none of this. It is as if He has belatedly stepped into the drama without having consulted the script—none of it: not even so much as the prologue. He does not remember Satan's mischief. He does not remember Job's calamities. He does not remember Job's righteousness.

As to the latter: Job will hardly appeal for an accounting from God without first offering one of his own. He has his own credibility to defend, his own probity. "Let me be weighed in a just balance," he insists, "and let God know my integrity!" The case for his integrity takes the form of a bill of particulars that is unsurpassed as a compendium of compassionate human conduct: no conceivable ethical nuance is omitted. It is as if all the world's moral fervor, distilled from all the world's religions, and touching on all the world's pain, is assembled in Job's roster of loving kindness. Job in his confession of integrity is both a protector and a lover of God's world.

But God seems alarmingly impatient; His mind is elsewhere. Is this the Lord whom Job once defined as a "watcher of men"? God's answer, a fiery challenge, roils out of the whirlwind. "Where were *you*," the Almighty roars, in supernal strophes that blaze through the millennia, "when I laid the foundation of the earth?" And what comes crashing and tumbling out of the gale is an exuberant ode to the grandeur of the elements, to the fecundity of nature: the sea and the stars, the rain and the dew, the constellations in their courses, the lightning, the lion, the raven, the ass, the goat, the ostrich, the horse, the hawk—and more, more, more! The lavishness, the extravagance, the infinitude! An infinitude of power; an infinitude of joy; an infinitude of love, even for the ugly hippopotamus, even for the crocodile with his terrifying teeth, even for creatures made mythical through ancient lore. Even for Leviathan! Nothing in the universe is left unpraised in these glorious stanzas—and one thinks: had the poet access to the electrons, had he an inkling of supernovas, had he parsed the chains of DNA, God's ode to Creation could not be richer. Turn it and turn it —God's ode: everything is in it.

Everything but the answer to the question that eats at Job's soul: why God permits injustice in the fabric of a world so resplendently woven. Job is conventionally judged to be a moral violator because he judges God Himself to be a moral violator. Yet is there any idea in the history of human thought more exquisitely tangled, more furiously daring, more heroically courageous, more rooted in spirit and conscience than Job's question? Why does God |not praise the marrow of such a man as Job at least as much as He praises the intricacy of the crocodile's scales? God made the crocodile; He also made Job.

God's answer to Job lies precisely in His not answering; and Job, with lightning insight, comprehends. "I have uttered what I did not understand," he acknowledges, "things too wonderful for me, which I did not know."

His new knowledge is this: that a transcendent God denies us a god of our own devising, a god that we would create out of our own malaise, or complaint, or desire, or hope, or imagining; or would manufacture according to the satisfaction of our own design. We are part of God's design: can the web manufacture the spider? The Voice out of the whirlwind warns against god-manufacture—against the degradation of a golden calf surely, but also against god-manufacture even in the form of the loftiest visions. Whose visions are they? Beware: they are not God's; they are ours. The ways of the true God cannot be penetrated. The false comforters cannot decipher them. Job cannot uncover them. "The secret things belong to the Lord our God," Job's poet learned long ago, reading Deuteronomy. But now: see how Job cannot draw Leviathan out with a hook—how much less can he draw out God's nature, and His purpose!

So the poet, through the whirlwind's answer, stills Job.

But can the poet still the Job who lives in us? God's majesty is eternal, manifest in cell and star. Yet Job's questions toil on, manifest in death camp and hatred, in tyranny and anthrax, in bomb and bloodshed. Why do the wicked thrive? Why do the innocent suffer? In brutal times, the whirlwind's answer tempts, if not atheism, then the sorrowing conviction of God's indifference.

And if we are to take the close of the tale as given, it is not only Job's protests that are stilled; it is also his inmost moral urge. What has become of raging conscience? What has become of loving kindness? Prosperity is restored; the dead children are replaced by twice the number of boys, and by girls exceedingly comely. But where now is the father's bitter grief over the loss of those earlier sons and daughters, on whose account he once indicted God? Cushioned again by good fortune, does Job remember nothing, feel nothing, see nothing beyond his own renewed honor? Is Job's lesson from the whirlwind finally no more than the learning of indifference?

So much for the naked text. Perhaps this is why—century after century—we common readers go on clinging to the spiritualizing mentors of traditional faith, who clothe in comforting theologies this God-wrestling and comfortless Book.

Yet how astoundingly up-to-date they are, those ancient sages—redactors and compilers—who opened even the sacred gates of Scripture to philosophic doubt!

Existing Things

❧

First inkling. If I were to go back and back—*really* back, to earliest consciousness—I think it would be mica. Not the prophet Micah, who tells us that our human task is to do justly, and to love mercy, and to walk humbly with our God; but that other still more humble mica—those tiny glints of isinglass that catch the sun and prickle upward from the pavement like shards of star-stuff. Sidewalks nowadays seem inert, as if cement has rid itself for ever of bright sprinklings and stippled spangles. But the pavement I am thinking of belongs to long ago, and runs narrowly between the tall weeds of empty lots, lots that shelter shiny green snakes.

The lots are empty because no one builds on them; it is the middle of the summer in the middle of the Depression, childhood's longest hour. I am alone under a slow molasses sun, staring at the little chips of light flashing at my feet. Up and down the whole length of the street there is no one, not a single grownup, and certainly, in that sparse time, no other child. There is only myself and these hypnotic semaphores signaling eeriness out of the ground. But no, up the block a little way, a baby carriage is entrusted to the idle afternoon, with a baby left to sleep, all by itself, under white netting.

If you are five years old, loitering in a syrup of sunheat, gazing at the silver-white mica-eyes in the pavement, you will all at once be besieged by a strangeness: the strangeness of understanding, for the very first time, that you are really alive, and that the world is really true; and the strangeness will divide into a river of wonderings.

Here is what I wondered then, among the mica-eyes:

I wondered what it would be like to become, for just one moment, every kind of animal there is in the world. Even, I thought, a snake.

I wondered what it would be like to know all the languages in the world.

I wondered what it would be like to be that baby under the white netting.

I wondered why, when I looked straight into the sun, I saw a pure circle.

I wondered why my shadow had a shape that was me, but nothing else; why my shadow, which was almost like a mirror, was not a mirror.

I wondered why I was thinking these things; I wondered what wondering was, and why it was spooky, and also secretly sweet, and amazingly interesting. Wondering felt akin to love—an uncanny sort of love, not like loving your mother or father or grandmother, but something curiously and thrillingly other. Something that shone up out of the mica-eyes.

Decades later, I discovered in Wordsworth's *Prelude* what it was:

> . . . *those hallowed and pure motions of the sense*
> *Which seem, in their simplicity, to own*
> *An intellectual charm;*
> . . . *those first-born affinities that fit*
> *Our new existence to existing things.*

And those existing things are all things, everything the mammal senses know, everything the human mind constructs (temples or equations), the unheard poetry on the hidden side of the round earth, the great thirsts everywhere, the wanderings past wonderings.

First inkling, bridging our new existence to existing things. Can one begin with mica in the pavement and learn the prophet Micah's meaning?

Ruth

↬

For
Muriel Dance, in New York;
Lee Gleichmann, in Stockholm;
Sarah Halevi, in Jerusalem; and
Inger Mirsky, in New York

1. Flowers

There were only two pictures on the walls of the house I grew up in. One
was large, and hung from the molding on a golden cord with a full golden
tassel. It was a painting taken from a photograph—all dark, a kind of grayish-
brown; it was of my grandfather Hirshl, my father's father. My grandfather's
coat had big foreign-looking buttons, and he wore a tall stiff square yarmulke
that descended almost to the middle of his forehead. His eyes were severe,
pale, concentrated. There was no way to escape those eyes; they came after
you wherever you were. I had never known this grandfather: he died in
Russia long ago. My father, a taciturn man, spoke of him only once, when
I was already grown: as a boy, my father said, he had gone with his father on
a teaching expedition to Kiev; he remembered how the mud was deep in the
roads. From my mother I learned a little more. Zeyde Hirshl was frail. His
wife, Bobe Sore-Libe, was the opposite: quick, energetic, hearty, a skilled
zogerke—a women's prayer leader in the synagogue—a whirlwind who kept a
dry-goods store and had baby after baby, all on her own, while Zeyde Hirshl
spent his days in the study-house. Sometimes he fainted on his way there.
He was pale, he was mild, he was delicate, unworldly; a student, a *melamed*,
a fainter. Why, then, those unforgiving stern eyes that would not let you go?

My grandfather's portrait had its permanent place over the secondhand
piano. To the right, farther down the wall, hung the other picture. It was
framed modestly in a thin black wooden rectangle, and was, in those spare
days, all I knew of "art." Was it torn from a magazine, cut from a calendar?

A barefoot young woman, her hair bound in a kerchief, grasping a sickle, stands alone and erect in a field. Behind her a red sun is half-swallowed by the horizon. She wears a loose white peasant's blouse and a long dark skirt, deeply blue; her head and shoulders are isolated against a limitless sky. Her head is held poised: she gazes past my gaze into some infinity of loneliness stiller than the sky.

Below the picture was its title: *The Song of the Lark*. There was no lark. It did not come to me that the young woman, with her lifted face, was straining after the note of a bird who might be in a place invisible to the painter. What I saw and heard was something else: a scene older than this French countryside, a woman lonelier even than the woman alone in the calendar meadow. It was, my mother said, Ruth: Ruth gleaning in the fields of Boaz.

For many years afterward—long after *The Song of the Lark* had disappeared from the living room wall—I had the idea that this landscape (a 1930s fixture, it emerged, in scores of American households and Sunday-school classrooms) was the work of Jean-François Millet, the French painter of farm life. "I try not to have things look as if chance had brought them together," Millet wrote, "but as if they had a necessary bond between them. I want the people I represent to look as if they really belonged to their station, so that imagination cannot conceive of their ever being anything else."

Here is my grandfather. Imagination cannot conceive of his ever being anything else: a *melamed* who once ventured with his young son (my blue-eyed father) as far as Kiev, but mainly stayed at home in his own town, sometimes fainting on the way to the study-house. The study-house was his "station." In his portrait he looks as if he really belonged there; and he did. It was how he lived.

And here is Ruth, on the far side of the piano, in Boaz's field, gleaning. Her mouth is remote: it seems somehow damaged; there is a blur behind her eyes. All the sadness of the earth is in her tender neck, all the blur of loss, all the damage of rupture: remote, remote, rent. The child who stands before the woman standing barefoot, sickle forgotten, has fallen through the barrier of an old wooden frame into the picture itself, into the field; into the smell of the field. There is no lark, no birdcall: only the terrible silence of the living room when no one else is there. The grandfather is always there; his eyes keep their vigil. The silence of the field swims up from a time so profoundly lost that it annihilates time. There is the faint weedy smell of thistle: and masses of meadow flowers. In my childhood I recognized violets, lilacs, roses, daisies, dandelions, black-eyed Susans, tiger lilies, pansies (I planted, one summer, a tiny square of pansies, one in each corner, one in the middle), and no more. The lilacs I knew because of the children who brought them to school in springtime: children with German names, Koech-ling, Behrens, Kuntz.

To annihilate time, to conjure up unfailingly the fragrance in Boaz's field (his field in *The Song of the Lark*), I have the power now to summon what the child peering into the picture could not. "Tolstoy, come to my aid," I could not call then: I had never heard of Tolstoy: my child's Russia was the grandfather's portrait, and stories of fleeing across borders at night, and wolves, and the baba yaga in the fairy tales. But now: "Tolstoy, come to my aid," I can chant at this hour, with my hair turned silver; and lo, the opening of *Hadji Murad* spills out all the flowers in Boaz's field:

> It was midsummer, the hay harvest was over and they were just begin-ning to reap the rye. At that season of the year there is a delightful variety of flowers—red, white, and pink scented tufty clover; milk-white ox-eye daisies with their bright yellow centers and pleasant spicy smell; yellow honey-scented rape blossoms; tall campanulas with white and lilac bells, tulip-shaped; creeping vetch; yellow, red, and pink scabi-ous; faintly scented, neatly arranged purple plantains with blossoms slightly tinged with pink; cornflowers, the newly opened blossoms bright blue in the sunshine but growing paler and redder towards evening or when growing old; and delicate almond-scented dodder flowers that withered quickly.

Dodder? Vetch? (Flash of Henry James's Fleda Vetch.) Scabious? Rape and campanula? The names are unaccustomed; my grandfather in the study-house never sees the flowers. In the text itself—in the Book of Ruth—not a single flower is mentioned. And the harvest is neither hay nor rye; in Boaz's field outside Bethlehem they are cutting down barley and wheat. The flowers are there all the same, even if the text doesn't show them, and we are obliged to take in their scents, the weaker with the keener, the grassier with the meatier: without the smell of flowers, we cannot pass through the frame of history into that long ago, ancientness behind ancientness, when Ruth the Moabite gleaned. It is as if the little spurts and shoots of fragrance form a rod, a rail of light, along which we are carried, drifting, into that time before time "when the judges ruled."

Two pictures, divided by an old piano—Ruth in *The Song of the Lark*, my grandfather in his yarmulke. He looks straight out; so does she. They sight each other across the breadth of the wall. I stare at both of them. Even-tually I will learn that *The Song of the Lark* was not painted by Millet, not at all; the painter is Jules Breton—French like Millet, like Millet devoted to rural scenes. *The Song of the Lark* hangs in the Art Institute of Chicago; it is possible I will die without ever having visited there. Good: I never want to see the original, out of shock at what a reproduction now discloses: a mistake, everything is turned the other way! On our living room wall Ruth faced right. In the Art Institute of Chicago she faces left. A calendar reversal!—but of course it feels to me that the original is in sullen error. Breton, unlike Millet, lived into our century—he died in 1906, the year my nine-year-old mother came through Castle Garden on her way to framing *The Song of the Lark* two decades later. About my grandfather Hirshl there is no "eventually"; I will not learn anything new about him. He will not acquire a different maker. Nothing in his view will be reversed. He will remain a dusty indoor *melamed* with eyes that drill through bone.

Leaving aside the wall, leaving aside the child who haunts and is haunted by the grandfather and the woman with the sickle, what is the connection between this dusty indoor *melamed* and the nymph in the meadow, standing barefoot amid the tall campanula?

Everything, everything. If the woman had not been in the field, my grandfather, three thousand years afterward, would not have been in the study-house. She, the Moabite, is why he, when hope is embittered, murmurs the Psalms of David. The track her naked toes make through spice and sweetness, through dodder, vetch, rape, and scabious, is the very track his forefinger follows across the letter-speckled sacred page.

2. Mercy

When my grandfather reads the Book of Ruth, it is on Shavuot, the Feast of Weeks, with its twin furrows: the text's straight furrow planted with the alphabet; the harvest's furrow, fuzzy with seedlings. The Feast of Weeks, which comes in May, is a reminder of the late spring crops, but only as an aside. The soul of it is the acceptance of the Torah by the Children of Israel. If there is a garland crowning this festival of May, it is the arms of Israel embracing the Covenant. My grandfather will not dart among field flowers after Ruth and her sickle; the field is fenced round by the rabbis, and the rabbis—those insistent interpretive spirits of Commentary whose arguments and counter-arguments, from generation to generation, comprise the Tradition—seem at first to be vexed with the Book of Ruth. If they are not actually or openly vexed, they are suspicious; and if they are not willing to be judged flatly suspicious, then surely they are cautious.

The Book of Ruth is, after all, about exogamy, and not simple exogamy—

marriage with a stranger, a member of a foreign culture: Ruth's ancestry is hardly neutral in that sense. She is a Moabite. She belongs to an enemy people, callous, pitiless; a people who deal in lethal curses. The children of the wild hunter Esau—the Edomites, who will ultimately stand for the imperial oppressors of Rome—cannot be shut out of the family of Israel. Even the descendants of the enslaving Egyptians are welcome to marry and grow into intimacy. "You shall not abhor an Edomite, for he is your kinsman. You shall not abhor an Egyptian, for you were a stranger in his land. Children born to them may be admitted into the congregation of the Lord in the third generation" (Deut. 2 3: 8–9). But a Moabite, never: "none of their descendants, even in the tenth generation, shall ever be admitted into the congregation of the Lord, because they did not meet you with food and water on your journey after you left Egypt, and because they hired Balaam . . . to curse you" (Deut. 23: 4–5). An abyss of memory and hurt in that: to have passed through the furnace of the desert famished, parched, and to be chased after by a wonder-worker on an ass hurling the king's maledictions, officially designed to wipe out the straggling mob of exhausted refugees! One might in time reconcile with Esau, one might in time reconcile with hard-hearted Egypt. All this was not merely conceivable—through acculturation, conversion, family ties, and new babies, it could be implemented, it *would* be implemented. But Moabite spite had a lasting sting.

What, then, are the sages to do with Ruth the Moabite as in-law? How account for her presence and resonance in Israel's story? How is it possible for a member of the congregation of the Lord to have violated the edict against marriage with a Moabite? The rabbis, reflecting on the pertinent verses, deduce a rule: Moabite, not *Moabitess*. It was customary for men, they conclude, not for women, to succor travelers in the desert, so only the Moabite males were guilty of a failure of humanity. The women were blameless, hence are exempt from the ban on conversion and marriage.

Even with the discovery of this mitigating loophole (with its odd premise that women are descended only from women, and men from men; or else that all the women, or all the men, in a family line are interchangeable with one another, up and down the ladder of the generations, and that guilt and innocence are collective, sex-linked, and heritable), it is hard for the rabbis to swallow a Moabite bride. They are discomfited by every particle of cause-and-effect that brought about such an eventuality. Why should a family with a pair of marriageable sons find itself in pagan Moab in the first place? The rabbis begin by scolding the text—or, rather, the characters and events of the story as they are straightforwardly set out.

Here is how the Book of Ruth begins:

In the days when the judges ruled, there was a famine in the land; and a man of Bethlehem in Judah, with his wife and two sons, went to reside in the country of Moab. The man's name was Elimelech, his wife's name was Naomi, and his two sons were named Mahlon and Chilion—Ephrathites of Bethlehem in Judah. They came to the country of Moab and remained there.

Elimelech, Naomi's husband, died; and she was left with her two sons. They married Moabite women, one named Orpah and the other Ruth, and they lived there about ten years. Then those two—Mahlon and Chilion—also died; so the woman was left without her two sons and without her husband.

Famine; migration; three deaths in a single household; three widows. Catastrophe after catastrophe, yet the text, plain and sparse, is only matter-of-fact. There is no anger in it, no one is condemned. What happened, happened—though not unaccoutered by echo and reverberation. Earlier biblical families and journeys-toward-sustenance cluster and chatter around Elimelech's decision: "There was a famine in the land, and Abram went down to Egypt to sojourn there, for the famine was severe in the land" (Gen. 12: 10). "So ten of Joseph's brothers went down to get rations in Egypt . . . Thus the sons of Israel were among those who came to procure rations, for the famine extended to the land of Canaan" (Gen. 42: 3,5). What Abraham did, what the sons of Jacob did, Elimelech also feels constrained to do: there is famine, he will go where the food is.

And the rabbis subject him to bitter censure for it. The famine, they say, is retribution for the times—"the days when the judges ruled"—and the times are coarse, cynical, lawless. "In those days there was no king in Israel; everyone did what he pleased" (Judges 17:6). Ironic that the leaders should be deemed "judges," and that under their aegis the rule of law is loosened, each one pursuing "what is right in his own eyes," without standard or conscience. Elimelech, according to the rabbis, is one of these unraveled and atomized souls: a leader who will not lead. They identify him as a man of substance, distinguished, well-off, an eminence; but arrogant and selfish. Even his name suggests self-aggrandizement: *to me shall kingship come.* Elimelech turns his back on the destitute conditions of hungry Bethlehem, picks up his family, and, because he is rich enough to afford the journey, sets out for where the food is. He looks to his own skin and means to get his own grub. The rabbis charge Elimelech with desertion; they accuse him of running away from the importunings of the impoverished, of provoking discouragement and despair; he is miserly, there is no charitableness in him, he is ungenerous. They call him a "dead stump"—he attends only to his immediate kin and shrugs off the community at large. Worse yet, he is heading for Moab, vile Moab! The very man who might have heartened his generation in a period of upheaval and inspired its moral repair leaves his own country, a land sanctified by Divine Covenant, for a historically repugnant region inhabited by idolators—and only to fill his own belly, and his own wife's, and his own sons'.

Elimelech in Moab will die in his prime. His widow will suffer radical denigration—a drop in status commonly enough observed even among independent women of our era—and, more seriously, a loss of protection. The rabbis will compare Naomi in her widowhood with "the remnants of the meal offerings"—i.e., with detritus and ash. Elimelech's sons—children of a father whose example is abandonment of community and of conscience—will die too soon. Already grown men after the death of Elimelech, they have themselves earned retribution. Instead of returning with their unhappy mother to their own people in the land dedicated to monotheism, they settle down to stay, and marry Moabite women. "One transgression leads to another," chide the rabbis, and argue over whether the brides of Mahlon and Chilion were or were not ritually converted before their weddings. In any case, a decade after those weddings, nothing has flowered for these husbands and wives, fertility eludes them, there will be no blossoming branches: the two young husbands are dead—dead stumps—and the two young widows are childless.

This is the rabbis' view. They are symbolists and metaphor-seekers; it goes without saying they are moralists. Punishment is truthful; punishment is the consequence of reality, it instructs in what happens. It is not that the rabbis are severe; they are just the opposite of severe. What they are after is simple mercy: where is the standard of mercy and humanity in a time when careless men and women follow the whim of their own greedy and expedient eyes? It is not merciful to abandon chaos and neediness; chaos and neediness call out for reclamation. It is not merciful to forsake one's devastated countrymen; opportunism is despicable; desertion is despicable; derogation of responsibility is despicable; it is not merciful to think solely of one's own family: if I am only for myself, what am I? And what of the hallowed land, that sacral ground consecrated to the unity of the Creator and the teaching of mercy, while the babble and garble of polymyth pullulate all around? The man who throws away the country of aspiration, especially in a lamentable hour when failure overruns it—the man who promotes egotism, elevates the material, and deprives his children of idealism—this fellow, this Elimelech, vexes the rabbis and afflicts them with shame.

Of course there is not a grain of any of this in the text itself—not a word about Elimelech's character or motives or even his position in Bethlehem. The rabbis' commentary is all extrapolation, embroidery, plausible invention. What is plausible in it is firmly plausible: it stands to reason that only a wealthy family, traveling together *as* a family, would be able to contemplate emigration to another country with which they have no economic or kinship ties. And it follows also that a wealthy householder is likely to be an established figure in his home town. The rabbis' storytelling faculty is not capricious or fantastic: it is rooted in the way the world actually works, then and now.

But the rabbis are even more interested in the way the world *ought* to work. Their parallel text hardly emerges ex nihilo. They are not oblivious to what-is: they can, in fact, construct a remarkably particularized social density from a handful of skeletal data. Yet, shrewd sociologists though they are, it is not sociology that stirs them. What stirs them is the aura of judgment—or call it ethical interpretation—that rises out of even the most comprehensively imagined social particularity. The rabbis are driven by a struggle to uncover a moral immanence in every human being. It signifies, such a struggle, hopefulness to the point of pathos, and the texture and pliability of this deeply embedded matrix of optimism is more pressing for the rabbis than any other kind of speculation or cultural improvisation. Callousness and egotism are an affront to their expectations. What are their expectations in the Book of Ruth? That an established community figure has an obligation not to demoralize his constituency by walking out on it. And that the Holy Land is to be passionately embraced, clung to, blessed, and defended as the ripening center and historic promise of the covenanted life. Like the Covenant that engendered its sanctifying purpose, Israel cannot be "marginalized." One place is not the same as another place. The rabbis are not cultural relativists.

From the rabbis' vantage, it is not that their commentary is "implicit" in the plain text under their noses; what they see is not implicit so much as it is fully intrinsic. It is there already, like invisible ink gradually made to appear. A system of values produces a story. A system of values? Never mind such Aristotelian language. The rabbis said, and meant, the quality of mercy: human feeling.

3. Normality

I have been diligent in opening the first five verses of the Book of Ruth to the rabbis' voices, and though I am unwilling to leave their voices behind—

they painstakingly accompany the story inch by inch, breath for breath— I mean for the rest of my sojourn in the text (perforce spotty and selective, a point here, a point there) to go on more or less without them. I say "more or less" because it is impossible, really, to go on without them. They are (to use an unsuitable image) the Muses of exegesis: not the current sort of exegesis that ushers insights out of a tale by scattering a thousand brilliant fragments, but rather the kind that ushers things *toward*: a guide toward principle. The Book of Ruth presents two principles. The first is what is normal. The second is what is singular.

Until Elimelech's death, Naomi has been an exemplum of the normal. She has followed her husband and made no decisions or choices of her own. What we nowadays call feminism is of course as old as the oldest society imaginable; there have always been feminists: women (including the unsung) who will allow no element of themselves—gift, capacity, natural authority— to go unexpressed, whatever the weight of the mores. Naomi has not been one of these. Until the death of her husband we know nothing of her but her compliance, and it would be foolish to suppose that in Naomi's world a wife's obedience is not a fundamental social virtue. But once Naomi's husband and sons have been tragically cleared from the stage, Naomi moves from the merely passive virtue of an honorable dependent to risks and contingencies well beyond the reach of comfortable common virtue. Stripped of every social support, isolated in a foreign land, pitifully unprotected, her anomalous position apparently wholly ignored by Moabite practices, responsible for the lives of a pair of foreign daughters-in-law (themselves isolated and unprotected under her roof), Naomi is transformed overnight. Under the crush of mourning and defenselessness, she becomes, without warning or preparation, a woman of valor.

She is only a village woman, after all. The Book of Ruth, from beginning to end, is played out in village scenes. The history of valor will not find in Naomi what it found in another village woman: she will not arm herself like a man or ride a horse or lead a military expedition. She will never cross over to another style of being. The new ways of her valor will not annul the old ways of her virtue.

And yet—overnight!—she will set out on a program of autonomy. Her first act is a decision: she will return to Bethlehem, "for in the country of Moab she had heard that the Lord had taken note of His people and given them food." After so many years, the famine in Bethlehem is spent—but since Naomi is cognizant of this as the work of the Lord, there is a hint that she would have gone back to Bethlehem in Judah in any event, even if that place were still troubled by hunger. It is no ordinary place for her: the Lord hovers over Judah and its people, and Naomi in returning makes restitution for Elimelech's abandonment. Simply in her determination to go back, she rights an old wrong.

But she does not go back alone. Now, willy-nilly, she is herself the head of a household bound to her by obedience. "Accompanied by her two daughters-in-law, she left the place where she had been living; and they set out on the road back to the land of Judah." On the road, Naomi reflects. What she reflects on—only connect! she is herself an exile—is the ache of exile and the consolations of normality.

> Naomi said to her two daughters-in-law, "Turn back, each of you to her mother's house. May the Lord deal kindly with you, as you have dealt with the dead and with me! May the Lord grant that each of you find security in the house of a husband!" And she kissed them farewell. They broke into weeping and said to her, "No, we will return with you to your people."
>
> But Naomi replied, "Turn back, my daughters! Why should you go with me? Have I any more sons in my body who might be husbands for you? Turn back, my daughters, for I am too old to be married. Even if I thought there was hope for me, even if I were married tonight and I also bore sons, should you wait for them to grow up? Should you on their account debar yourselves from marriage? Oh no, my daughters!"

In a moment or so we will hear Ruth's incandescent reply spiraling down to us through the ardors of three thousand years; but here let us check the tale, fashion a hiatus, and allow normality to flow in: let young stricken Orpah not be overlooked. She is always overlooked; she is the daughter-in-law who, given the chance, chose not to follow Naomi. She is no one's heroine. Her mark is erased from history; there is no Book of Orpah. And yet Orpah is history. Or, rather, she is history's great backdrop. She is the majority of humankind living out its usualness on home ground. These young women—both of them—are cherished by Naomi; she cannot speak to them without flooding them in her fellow feeling. She *knows* what it is to be Orpah and Ruth. They have all suffered and sorrowed together, and in ten years of living in one household much of the superficial cultural strangeness has worn off. She pities them because they are childless, and she honors them because they have "dealt kindly" with their husbands and with their mother-in-law. She calls them—the word as she releases it is accustomed, familiar, close, ripe with dearness—*b'notai*, "my daughters," whereas the voice of the narrative is careful to identify them precisely, though neutrally, as *khalotekha*, "her daughters-in-law."

Orpah is a loving young woman of clear goodness; she has kisses and tears for the loss of Naomi. "They broke into weeping again, and Orpah kissed her mother-in-law farewell." Her sensibility is ungrudging, and she is not in the least narrow-minded. Her upbringing may well have been liberal. Would a narrow-minded Moabite father have given over one of his daughters to the only foreign family in town? Such a surrender goes against the grain of the ordinary. Exogamy is never ordinary. So Orpah has already been stamped with the "abnormal"; she is already a little more daring than most, already somewhat offbeat—she is one of only two young Moabite women to marry Hebrews, and Hebrews have never been congenial to Moabites. If the Hebrews can remember how the Moabites treated them long ago, so can the Moabites: traditions of enmity work in both directions. The mean-spirited have a habit of resenting their victims quite as much as the other way around. Orpah has cut through all this bad blood to plain humanity; it would be unfair to consider her inferior to any other kindhearted young woman who ever lived in the world before or since. She is in fact superior; she has thrown off prejudice, and she has had to endure more than most young women of her class, including the less spunky and the less amiable: an early widowhood and no babies. And what else is there for a good girl like Orpah, in her epoch, and often enough in ours, but family happiness?

Her prototype abounds. She has fine impulses, but she is not an iconoclast. She can push against convention to a generous degree, but it is out of the generosity of her temperament, not out of some large metaphysical idea. Who will demand of Orpah—think of the hugeness of the demand!—that she admit monotheism to the concentration and trials of her mind? Offer monotheism to almost anyone—offer it as something to take seriously—and ninety-nine times out of a hundred it will be declined, even by professing "monotheists." A Lord of History whose intent is felt, whose Commandments stand with immediacy, whose Covenant summons perpetual self-scrutiny and a continual Turning toward moral renewal, and yet *cannot, may not, be physically imagined*? A Creator neither remote and abstract like the God of the philosophers, nor palpable like the "normal" divinities, both ancient and contemporary, both East and West? Give us (cries the nature of our race) our gods and goddesses, give us the little fertility icons with their welcoming breasts and elongated beckoning laps, give us the resplendent Virgin with her suffering brow and her arms outstretched in blessing, give us the Man on the Cross through whom to learn pity and love, and sometimes brutal exclusivity! Only give us what our eyes can see and our understanding understand: who can imagine the unimaginable? That may be for the philosophers; *they* can do it; but then they lack the imagination of the Covenant. The philosophers leave the world naked and blind and deaf and mute and relentlessly indifferent, and the village folk—who refuse a lonely cosmos without consolation—fill it and fill it and fill it with stone and wood and birds and mammals and miraculous potions and holy babes and animate carcasses and magically divine women and magically divine men: images, sights, and swallowings comprehensible to the hand, to the eye, to plain experience. For the nature of our race, God is one of the visual arts.

Is Orpah typical of these plain village folk? She is certainly not a philosopher, but neither is she, after ten years with Naomi, an ordinary Moabite. Not that she has altogether absorbed the Hebrew vision—if she had absorbed it, would she have been tempted to relinquish it so readily? She is somewhere in between, perhaps. In this we may suppose her to be one of us: a modern, no longer a full-fledged member of the pagan world, but always with one foot warming in the seductive bath of those colorful, comfortable, often beautiful old lies (they can console, but because they are lies they can also hurt and kill); not yet given over to the Covenant and its determination to train us away from lies, however warm, colorful, beautiful, and consoling.

Naomi, who is no metaphysician herself, who is, rather, heir to a tradition, imposes no monotheistic claim on either one of her daughters-in-law. She is right not to do this. In the first place, she is not a proselytizer or polemicist or preacher or even a teacher. She is none of those things: she is a bereaved woman far from home, and when she looks at her bereaved daughters-in-law, it is home she is thinking of, for herself and for them. Like the rabbis who will arrive two millennia after her, she is not a cultural relativist: God is God, and God is One. But in her own way, the way of empathy—three millennia before the concept of a democratic pluralist polity—she is a kind of pluralist. She does not require that Orpah accept what it is not natural for her, in the light of how she was reared, to accept. She speaks of Orpah's return not merely to her people but to her gods. Naomi is the opposite of coercive or punitive. One cannot dream of Inquisition or jihad emerging from her loins. She may not admire the usages of Orpah's people—they do not concern themselves with the widow and the destitute; no one in Moab comes forward to care for Naomi—but she knows that Orpah has a mother, and may yet have a new husband, and will be secure where she is. It will not occur to Naomi to initiate a metaphysical discussion with Orpah! She sends her as a lost child back to her mother's hearth. (Will there be idols on her mother's hearth? Well, yes. But this sour comment is mine, not Naomi's.)

So Orpah goes home; or, more to the point, she goes nowhere. She stays home. She is never, never, never to be blamed for it. If she is not extraordinary, she is also normal. The extraordinary is what is not normal, and it is no fault of the normal that it does not, or cannot, aspire to the extraordinary. What Orpah gains by staying home with her own people is what she always deserved: family happiness. She is young and fertile; soon she will marry a Moabite husband and have a Moabite child.

What Orpah loses is the last three thousand years of being present in history. Israel continues; Moab is not. Still, for Orpah, historic longevity—the longevity of an Idea to which a people attaches itself—may not be a loss at all. It is only an absence, and absence is not felt as loss. Orpah has her husband, her cradle, her little time. That her gods are false is of no moment to her; she believes they are true. That her social system does not provide for the widow and the destitute is of no moment to her; she is no longer a widow, and as a wife she will not be destitute; as for looking over her shoulder to see how others fare, there is nothing in Moab to require it of her. She once loved her oddly foreign mother-in-law. And why shouldn't openhearted Orpah, in her little time, also love her Moabite mother-in-law, who is as like her as her own mother, and will also call her "my daughter"? Does it matter to Orpah that her great-great-great-grandchildren have tumbled out of history, and that there is no Book of Orpah, and that she slips from the Book of Ruth in only its fourteenth verse?

Normality is not visionary. Normality's appetite stops at satisfaction.

4. Singularity

No, Naomi makes no metaphysical declaration to Orpah. It falls to Ruth, who has heard the same compassionate discourse as her sister-in-law, who has heard her mother-in-law three times call out "Daughter, turn back"—it falls to Ruth to throw out exactly such a declaration to Naomi.

Her words have set thirty centuries to trembling: "Your God shall be my God," uttered in what might be named visionary language. Does it merely "fall" to Ruth that she speaks possessed by the visionary? What is at work in her? Is it capacity, seizure, or the force of intent and the clarity of will? Set this inquiry aside for now, and—apart from what the story tells us she really did say—ask instead what Ruth might have replied in the more available language of pragmatism, answering Naomi's sensible "Turn back" exigency for exigency. What "natural" reasons might such a young woman have for leaving her birthplace? Surely there is nothing advantageous in

Ruth's clinging to Naomi. Everything socially rational is on the side of Ruth's remaining in her own country: what is true for Orpah is equally true for Ruth. But even if Ruth happened to think beyond exigency—even if she were exceptional in reaching past common sense toward ideal conduct—she need not have thought in the framework of the largest cosmic questions. Are we to expect of Ruth that she be a prophet? Why should she, any more than any other village woman, think beyond personal relations?

In the language of personal relations, in the language of pragmatism and exigency, here is what Ruth might have replied:

> Mother-in-law, I am used to living in your household, and have become accustomed to the ways of your family. I would no longer feel at home if I resumed the ways of my own people. After all, during the ten years or so I was married to your son, haven't I flourished under your influence? I was so young when I came into your family that it was you who completed my upbringing. It isn't for nothing that you call me daughter. So let me go with you.

Or, higher on the spectrum of ideal conduct (rather, the conduct of idealism), but still within the range of reasonable altruism, she might have said:

> Mother-in-law, you are heavier in years than I and alone in a strange place, whereas I am stalwart and not likely to be alone for long. Surely I will have a second chance, just as you predict, but you—how helpless you are, how unprotected! If I stayed home in Moab, I would be looking after my own interests, as you recommend, but do you think I can all of a sudden stop feeling for you, just like that? No, don't expect me to abandon you—who knows what can happen to a woman of your years all by herself on the road? And what prospects can there be for you, after all this long time away, in Bethlehem? It's true I'll seem a little odd in your country, but I'd much rather endure a little oddness in Bethlehem than lose you fo rever, not knowing what's to become of you. Let me go and watch over you.

There is no God in any of that. If these are thoughts Ruth did not speak out, they are all implicit in what has been recorded. Limited though they are by pragmatism, exigency, and personal relations, they are already anomalous. They address extraordinary alterations—of self, of worldly expectation. For Ruth to cling to Naomi as a daughter to her own mother is uncommon enough; a universe of folklore confirms that a daughter-in-law is not a daughter. But for Ruth to become the instrument of Naomi's restoration to safekeeping within her own community—and to prosperity and honor as well—is a thing of magnitude. And, in fact, all these praiseworthy circumstances do come to pass: though circumscribed by pragmatism, exigency, and personal relations. And without the visionary. Ideal conduct—or the conduct of idealism—is possible even in the absence of the language of the visionary. Observe:

> They broke into weeping again, and Orpah kissed her mother-in-law farewell. But Ruth clung to her. So she said, "See, your sister-in-law has returned to her people. Go follow your sister-in-law."
>
> But Ruth replied: "Do not urge me to leave you, to turn back and not follow you. For wherever you go, I will go; wherever you lodge, I will lodge; your people shall be my people. Where you die, I will die, and there I will be buried. Only death will part me from you." When Naomi saw how determined she was to go with her, she ceased to argue with her, and the two went on until they reached Bethlehem.

Of course this lovely passage is not the story of the Book of Ruth (any more than my unpoetic made-up monologues are), though it might easily have been Ruth's story. In transcribing from the text, I have left out what Ruth passionately put in: God. And still Ruth's speech, even with God left out, and however particularized by the personal, is a stupendous expression of loyalty and love.

But now, in a sort of conflagration of seeing, the cosmic sweep of a single phrase transforms these spare syllables from the touching language of family feeling to the unearthly tongue of the visionary:

> "See, your sister-in-law has returned to her people and her gods. Go and follow your sister-in-law." But Ruth replied, "Do not urge me to leave you, to turn back and not follow you. For wherever you go, I will go; wherever you lodge, I will lodge; your people shall be my people, and your God my God. Where you die, I will die, and there I will be buried. Thus and more may the Lord do to me if anything but death parts me from you."

Your God shall be my God: Ruth's story is kindled into the Book of Ruth by the presence of God on Ruth's lips, and her act is far, far more than a ringing embrace of Naomi, and far, far more than the simple acculturation it resembles. Ruth leaves Moab because she intends to leave childish ideas behind. She is drawn to Israel because Israel is the inheritor of the One Universal Creator.

Has Ruth "learned" this insight from Naomi and from Naomi's son? It may be; the likelihood is almost as pressing as evidence: how, without assimilation into the life of an Israelite family, would Ruth ever have penetrated into the great monotheistic cognition? On the other hand: Orpah too encounters that cognition, and slips back into Moab to lose it again. Inculcation is not insight, and what Orpah owns is only that: inculcation without insight. Abraham—the first Hebrew to catch insight—caught it as genius does, autonomously, out of the blue, without any inculcating tradition. Ruth is in possession of both inculcation *and* insight.

And yet, so intense is her insight, one can almost imagine her as a kind of Abraham. Suppose Elimelech had never emigrated to Moab; suppose Ruth had never married a Hebrew. The fire of cognition might still have come upon her as it came upon Abraham—autonomously, out of the blue, without any inculcating tradition. Abraham's cognition turned into a civilization. Might Ruth have transmuted Moab? Ruth as a second Abraham! We see in her that clear power; that power of consummate clarity. But whether Moab might, through Ruth, have entered the history of monotheism, like Israel, is a question stalled by the more modest history of kinship entanglement. In Ruth's story, insight is inexorably accompanied by, fused with, inculcation; how can we sort out one from the other? If Ruth had not been married to one of Naomi's sons, perhaps we would have heard no more of her than we will hear henceforth of Orpah. Or: Moab might have ascended, like Abraham's seed, from the gods to God. Moab cleansed and reborn through Ruth! The story as it is given is perforce inflexible, not amenable to experiment. We cannot have Ruth without Naomi; nor would we welcome the loss of such loving-kindness. All the same, Ruth may not count as a second Abraham because her tale is enfolded in a way Abraham's is not: she has had her saturation in Abraham's seed. The ingredient of inculcation cannot be expunged: there it is.

Nevertheless it seems insufficient—it seems askew—to leave it at that. Ruth marries into Israel, yes; but her mind is vaster than the private or social facts of marriage and inculcation; vaster than the merely familial. Insight, cognition, intuition, religious genius—how to name it? It is not simply because of Ruth's love for Naomi—a love unarguably resplendent-that Naomi's God becomes Ruth's God. To stop at love and loyalty is to have arrived at much, but not all; to stop at love and loyalty is to stop too soon.

Ruth claims the God of Israel out of her own ontological understanding.

She knows—she knows directly, prophetically—that the Creator of the Universe is One.

5. Unfolding

The greater part of Ruth's tale is yet to occur—the greater, that is, in length and episode. The central setting of the Book of Ruth is hardly Moab; it is Bethlehem in Judah. But by the time the two destitute widows, the older and the younger, reach Bethlehem, the volcanic heart of the Book of Ruth— the majesty of Ruth's declaration—has already happened. All the rest is an unfolding.

Let it unfold, then, without us. We have witnessed normality and we have witnessed singularity. We will, if we linger, witness these again in Bethlehem; but let the next events flash by without our lingering. Let Naomi come with Ruth to Bethlehem; let Naomi in her distress name herself Mara, meaning bitter, "for the Lord has made my lot very bitter"; let Ruth set out to feed them both by gleaning in the field of Elimelech's kinsman, Boaz— fortuitous, God-given, that she should blunder onto Boaz's property! He is an elderly landowner, an affluent farmer who, like Levin in *Anna Karenina*, works side by side with his laborers. He is at once aware that there is a stranger in his field, and is at once solicitous. He is the sort of man who, in the heat of the harvest, greets the reapers with courteous devoutness: "The Lord be with you!" A benign convention, perhaps, but when he addresses Ruth it is no ordinary invocation: "I have been told of all that you did for your mother-in-law after the death of her husband, how you left your father and mother and the land of your birth and came to a people you had not known before. May the Lord reward your deeds. May you have a full recompense from the Lord, the God of Israel, under whose wings you have sought refuge!" Like Naomi, he calls Ruth "daughter," and he speaks an old-fashioned Hebrew; he and Naomi are of the same generation.

But remember that we are hurrying along now; so let Naomi, taking charge behind the scenes, send Ruth to sleep at Boaz's feet on the threshing floor in order to invite his special notice—a contrivance to make known to Boaz that he is eligible for Ruth's salvation within the frame of the levirate code. And let the humane and flexible system of the levirate code work itself out, so that Boaz can marry Ruth, who will become the mother of Obed, who is the father of Jesse, who is the father of King David, author of the Psalms.

The levirate law in Israel—like the rule for gleaners—is designed to redeem the destitute. The reapers may not sweep up every stalk in the meadow; some of the harvest must be left behind for bread for the needy. And if a woman is widowed, the circle of her husband's kin must open their homes to her; in a time when the sole protective provision for a woman is marriage, she must have a new husband from her dead husband's family— the relative closest to the husband, a brother if possible. Otherwise what will become of her? Dust and cinders. She will be like the remnants of the meal offerings.

Boaz in his tenderness (we have hurried past even this, which more than almost anything else merits our hanging back; but there it is on the page, enchanting the centuries—a tenderness sweetly discriminating, morally meticulous, wide-hearted and ripe)—Boaz is touched by Ruth's appeal to become her husband-protector. It is a fatherly tenderness, not an erotic one—though such a scene might, in some other tale, burst with the erotic: a young woman, perfumed, lying at the feet of an old man at night in a barn. The old man is not indifferent to the pulsing of Eros in the young: "Be blessed of the Lord, daughter! Your latest deed of loyalty is greater than the first, in that you have not turned to younger men." The remark may carry a pang of wistfulness, but Boaz in undertaking to marry Ruth is not animated by the lubricious. He is no December panting after May. A forlorn young widow, homeless in every sense, has asked for his guardianship, and he responds under the merciful levirate proviso with all the dignity and responsibility of his character, including an ethical scruple: "While it is true that I am a redeeming kinsman, there is another redeemer closer than I"—someone more closely related to Elimelech than Boaz, and therefore first in line to assume the right, and burden, of kinship protection.

In this closer relative we have a sudden pale reminder of Orpah. Though she has long vanished from the story, normality has not. Who conforms more vividly to the type of Average Man than that practical head of a household we call John Doe? And now John Doe (the exact Hebrew equivalent is Ploni Almoni) briefly enters the narrative and quickly jumps out of it; averageness leaves no reputation, except for averageness. John Doe, a.k.a. Ploni Almoni, is the closer relative Boaz has in mind, and he appears at a meeting of town elders convened to sort out the levirate succession in Naomi's case. The hearing happens also to include some business about a piece of land that Elimelech owned; if sold, it will bring a little money for Naomi. Naomi may not have known of the existence of this property—or else why would she be reduced to living on Ruth's gleaning? But Boaz is informed of it, and immediately arranges for a transaction aimed at relieving both Naomi and Ruth. The sale of Elimelech's property, though secondary to the issue of marital guardianship for Naomi's young daughter-in-law, is legally attached to it: whoever acquires the land acquires Ruth. The closer relative, Ploni Almoni (curious how the text refuses him a real name of his own, as if it couldn't be bothered, as if it were all at once impatient with averageness), is willing enough to buy the land: John Doe always understands money and property. But he is not at all willing to accept Ruth. The moment he learns he is also being asked to take on the care of a widow—one young enough to bear children, when very likely he already has a family to support—he changes his mind. He worries, he explains, that he will impair his estate. An entirely reasonable, even a dutiful, worry, and who can blame him? If he has missed his chance to become the great-grandfather of the Psalmist, he is probably, like Ploni Almoni everywhere, a philistine scorner of poetry anyhow.

And we are glad to see him go. In this he is no reminder of Orpah; Orpah, a loving young woman, is regretted. But like Orpah he has only the usual order of courage. He avoids risk, the unexpected, the lightning move into imagination. He thinks of what he has, not of what he might do: he recoils from the conduct of idealism. He is perfectly conventional, and wants to stick with what is familiar. Then let him go in peace—he is too ordinary to be the husband of Ruth. We have not heard him make a single inquiry about her. He has not troubled over any gesture of interest or sympathy. Ruth is no more to him than an object of acquisition offered for sale. He declines to buy; he has his own life to get on with, and no intention of altering it, levirate code or no levirate code. "You do it," he tells Boaz.

Boaz does it. At every step he has given more than full measure, whether of barley or benevolence. We have watched him load Ruth's sack with extra grain to take back to Naomi. He has instructed the reapers to scatter extra stalks for her to scoop up. He has summoned her to his own table for lunch in the field. He is generous, he is kindly, he is old, and in spite of his years he opens his remaining strength to the imagination of the future: he enters on a new life inconceivable to him on the day a penniless young foreigner wandered over his field behind the harvest workers. *Mercy, pity, peace, and love*: these Blakean words lead, in our pastoral, to a beginning.

The beginning is of course a baby, and when Naomi cradles her grandchild in her bosom, the village women cry: "A son is born to Naomi!" And they cry: "Blessed be the Lord, who hath not withheld a redeemer from you today! May his name be perpetuated in Israel! He will renew your life and sustain your old age; for he is born of your daughter-in-law, who loves you and is better to you than seven sons."

Only eighty-five verses tell Ruth's and Naomi's story. To talk of it takes much longer. Not that the greatest stories are the shortest—not at all. But a short story has a stalk—or shoot—through which its life rushes, and out of which the flowery head erupts. The Book of Ruth—wherein goodness grows out of goodness, and the extraordinary is found here, and here, and here—is sown in desertion, bereavement, barrenness, death, loss, displacement, destitution. What can sprout from such ash? Then Ruth sees into the nature of Covenant, and the life of the story streams in. Out of this stalk mercy and redemption unfold; flowers flood Ruth's feet; and my grandfather goes on following her track until the coming of Messiah from the shoot of David, in the line of Ruth and Naomi.

A Short Note on "Chekhovian"

"Chekhovian." An adjective that had to be invented for the new voice Chekhov's genius breathed into the world—elusive, inconclusive, flickering; nuanced through an underlying disquiet, though never morbid or disgruntled; unerringly intuitive, catching out of the air mute inferences, glittering motes, faint turnings of the heart, tendrils thinner than hairs, drift. But Chekhov's art is more than merely Chekhovian. It is dedicated to explicit and definitive portraiture and the muscular trajectory of whole lives. Each story, however allusive or broken off, is nevertheless exhaustive—like the curve of a shard that implies not simply the form of the pitcher entire, but also the thirsts of its shattered civilization.

And yet it is an odd misdirection that we have come to think of Chekhov mainly as a writer of hints and significant fragments, when so much of his expression is highly colored and abundant, declaratively open, even noisy. He is not reticent, and his people are often charged with conviction, sometimes ludicrously, sometimes with the serious nobility of Chekhov himself. But even when his characters strike us as unwholesome, or exasperating, or enervated, or only perverse (especially then), we feel Chekhov's patience, his clarity—his meticulous humanity, lacking so much as a grain of malevolence or spite. At bottom Chekhov is a writer who has flung his soul to the side of pity, and sees into the holiness and immaculate fragility of the hidden striver below. Perhaps this is why we know that when we are with Chekhov, we are with a poet of latency. He is an interpreter of the underneath life, even when his characters appear to be cut off from inwardness.

He is also an artist of solidity and precision. Here is Aksinya (from "In the Ravine"): "a handsome woman with a good figure, who wore a hat and carried a parasol on holidays, got up early and went to bed late, and ran about all day long, picking up her skirts and jingling her keys, going from the granary to the cellar and from there to the shop." That is the vigor of outerness; Chekhov is as much a master of the observed as he is of the unobserved. And he is, besides, the source of unusual states of wisdom, astonishing psychological principles. He can transfigure latency into drama, as in "Ward No. Six," which belongs with Conrad's "The Secret Sharer" among the great expositions of self-disclosure. And this too is Chekhov: he teaches us us.

And God Saw Literature,
That It Was Good:
Robert Alter's Version

In the Third Century B.C.E., Ptolemy Philadelphus, ruler of Alexandria, Egypt's most Hellenized and sophisticated city, determined that a Greek rendering of the Torah should be included in the Great Library of that famed metropolis. To that end, he sent lavish gifts to Eleazar, the high priest of the Temple in Jerusalem, who reciprocated by dispatching to Alexandria seventy-two sages, six from each of the twelve biblical tribes, to begin the work of translation. Ptolemy greeted the visitors with a banquet lasting seven days, after which they were taken to the island of Pharos. Here each man was shut up in his own cell, in strictest seclusion, each toiling separately over the Hebrew original, in order to perfect its transcription into the lingua franca of the age. Seventy days later, when the scribes emerged from their labors, it was revealed that the seventy-two individually calculated translations were identical, each to the other, varying not by a jot or a tittle. Hence the name Septuagint (meaning seventy), immemorially given to the miraculous Greek text: a book divine in its essence, and thereby divine in its production. When heaven has a hand in translation, it is bound to be immaculate. God, who is One, sees to the oneness—the indivisibility—of His word. Many scribes, but one authentic Voice.

Thus the legend. Yet stripped of the sacral, it encapsulates the most up-to-date thesis concerning the nature of the Hebrew Bible: that it can, after all, be read as a unity, indivisibly, like any literary work. The contemporary idea of reading the Bible as literature comes after two hundred years of strenuous philological sorting out, the purpose of which was to unravel what tradition had always held to be a tightly textured whole. Scholars, minutely excavating linguistic layers and Ugaritic cognates, pulled out disparate threads, and identified each according to its purported source and time. Instead of one Author, there were now several: the J writer, for whom God bore the name Yahweh (the German philologists' J Englished to our Y); the E writer, who invoked not Yahweh but Elohim; the P writer, a priest, or circle of priests, absorbed by the formalities of cult and rite; and finally D, the Deuteronomist. But even for the unravelers, who had zealously quartered the singularity of Transcendence, there was a unifier. This was the unknown Redactor, who, shrewdly concealing the seams, had spliced all four strands into canonical coherence. It was the Redactor whom the philologists sought to undermine. Below his work lay the multifaceted hidden truth.

For the ascendant Bible-as-literature movement—a movement, if it can sustain the term, confined mostly to university classes and those common readers drawn to Scripture for reasons other than pious belief—the Redactor returns not simply as an implied collator or pragmatic editor, but as a conscious literary mind, alert to every nuance of trope and type, whether verse or prose, from storytelling and the drama of character to national epic, from monotheistic grandeur to homely lentil stew. The Bible, then, can be read not for its authority (or not for its authority alone), but for its fastidious and deliberate art. But since Scriptural artfulness is also moral art, a potency of precept adheres to it nonetheless. The literary approach, writes Robert Alter, "directs attention to the moral, psychological, political, and spiritual realism of the biblical texts, which is a way of opening ourselves to something that deserves to be called their authority, whether we attribute that authority solely to the power of human imagination or to a transcendent source of illumination that kindled the imagination of the writers to express itself through these particular literary means."

The quotation is from Alter's 1991 volume, *The World of Biblical Literature*, which—along with *The Art of Biblical Narrative*, *The Art of Biblical Poetry*, and related earlier works—can, in retrospect, be seen as the arduously analytic preparation for an undertaking of such ambitiousness that to call it uncommon hardly suggests how very rare it really is. "Ethical monotheism," Alter sums up, "was delivered to the world not as a series of abstract principles but in cunningly wrought narratives, poetry, parables, and orations, in an intricate patterning of symbolic language and rhetoric that extends even to the genealogical tables and the laws." And in the most succinct summary of all, he cites the Talmudic view: "The Torah speaks in human language." Human language, yes, but who would dare to render Scripture single-handedly, all on one's own? In fact, in the entire history of biblical translation, there have been only three daredevil intellects, each inspired by profound belief, who have achieved one-man renditions: the Latin of Jerome, the German of Luther, and the English of William Tyndale. Tyndale, who was burned at the stake for his presumption in desiring the Bible to be accessible in the vernacular, is generally regarded as the forerunner of, or influence on, the King James Version—a work that is distinctly a committee enterprise. Though Jerome and Luther each had occasional rabbinic consultants, and Luther was advised also by Melancthon, a Reformist scholar, their translations stand as monuments to the power of individual rhetoric and intent. Luther in particular impressed on German as inexhaustible a linguistic force as the King James Version left on English. In English, notably, all significant biblical translation since Tyndale's sixteenth-century version, without exception, has been by committee. Until now.

That is why Robert Alter's intrepid Englishing of the Pentateuch, *The Five Books of Moses: A Translation with Commentary*, can be called historically astounding: with a gap of four hundred years, it comes directly after Tyndale. It will be seen to differ from standard American translations, whether it is the Anchor Bible, or the Revised English Bible, or the Jewish Publication Society's *Tanakh*, or any other significant collective project that may come to mind. Though not without manifold influences and appreciations (the medieval Ibn Ezra, for instance, or E. A. Speiser, a contemporary philological exegete), Alter aspires beyond erudition to the kind of sensibility a reader might bring to James or Proust. In this he scarcely means to reduce the hallowed stature of the biblical narratives, but the very opposite. Close attention to "the literary miracle of the stories," he points out in an introductory essay, will emphasize and intensify the rhetorical ingenuities by which "the chief personages are nevertheless imagined with remarkable integrity and complexity as individual characters . . . growing and changing through long stretches of life-experience." At the same time, he reminds us, the Hebrew Bible, unlike the novel of character and personal vicissitudes, "has been shaped to show forth God's overwhelming power in history, exerted against one of the great ancient kingdoms, and the forging of the nation through a spectacular chain of divine interventions that culminates in the spectacle of the revelation on the mountain of God's imperatives to Israel." So it is no wonder that previous translators, trembling before the transcendent majesty of the Hebrew text, have huddled together in protective consultative committees.

In one striking case, the consultants have not been present at the table. Everett Fox, relying on the work of the German-Jewish luminaries Martin Buber and Franz Rosenzweig, and adopting their approach of etymological mimesis—Hebrew roots cast as German roots—attempted a similar effect in English. Useful as a study guide and as a trot, it is not quite what we mean by translation, if translation is taken to be the avoidance of awkwardness. Fox's awkwardness is purposeful: "YHWH will pass over the entrance, / and will not give the bringer-of-ruin (leave) to come into your house to deal-the-blow" (Exodus 12:23). Helpful though this may be to the beginning student peering into the Hebrew, it is scarcely normative English.

Isaac Leeser, it ought to be noted, an eminent nineteenth-century German-born American rabbi, might have been able to claim the mantle of one-man translation (his was published in 1853) had he not clung so closely to the King James Version, faithful to its diction in general, and differing only in an occasional well-argued word: in Genesis, for instance, choosing "expansion" for "firmament."

So the opportunity for modern singularity, post-Tyndale, remains open to Alter. Yet what he has undertaken is not an act of hubris; it is a work of conviction. His conviction is twofold: first, the unextraordinary recognition that all translation is of its time, steeped in an impermanent idiom, ultimately to be superseded by the more familiar lingo of ongoing generations. The language of the King James Version is poetically enthralling and rightly revered, but our daily tongues no longer traffic in "walketh" and "shalts" (and we may be impatient with its deliberate, if only occasional, christological inaccuracies). It goes without saying that the foundational document of our civilization, as the Bible is often termed, needs to be understood in the language of its period; the drive toward the vernacular that defines Luther, Tyndale, and the King James Version is as urgent today as it was then, and perhaps more so now, when Scriptural references are alien to most undergraduates, and the majority of American synagogue congregations turn from the Hebrew text to the facing page, where the English translation resides.

If the necessity of contemporary usage were all that motivated Alter, he might have been content with the existing collective translations, despite their lack of stylistic force. But the second element drawing him to this mammoth work—he calls it "an experiment"—is the belief that it is precisely the discoveries of philological scholarship that have distanced readers through their preoccupation with lexical components and syntactical forms at the expense of insight, metaphor, tone, imagery, cadence, all spilling from the cornucopia of literary virtuosity. In short, the obstacle of philology's tin ear. Citing still another objection to contemporary modes of translation, Alter condemns "the heresy of explanation": as when, for example, the ubiquitous word "hand" (*yad* in Hebrew, a similarly strong monosyllable), a stoutly visual and flexible noun capable of multiple figurative effects, is "clarified" abstractly as "trust" or "care." ("And he left all that he had in Joseph's hands," Genesis 39:6.)

Alter also faults the common reliance on subordinate clauses to avoid parataxis, the distinctive biblical repetition of "and . . . and . . . and." Here we may recall E. M. Forster's witty formulation, in *Aspects of the Novel*, of plot as opposed to story: "'The king died and then the queen died' is a story. 'The king died, and then the queen died of grief' is a plot. The time-sequence is preserved, but the sense of causality overshadows it." Biblical narrative will have none of this. A typical series of statements connected by "and" complicates, it does not simplify, the reader's comprehension; implied causality haunts the chain of events through rhythmic repetition directed, in the way of a musical composition, at the interpretive ear. The Bible is all plot, all causality: its substance derives, after all, from the First Cause.

In arguing for the Bible's literary status, or standard, Alter maintains that "the language of biblical narrative in its own time was stylized, decorous, dignified," yet was never "a lofty style, and was certainly neither ornate nor euphemistic . . . a formal literary language but also, paradoxically, a plain-spoken one." And again: "A suitable English version should avoid at all costs the modern abomination of elegant synonymous variation, for the literary prose of the Bible turns everywhere on significant repetition, not variation." Finally, he insists that "the mesmerizing effect of these ancient stories will scarcely be conveyed if they are not rendered in a cadenced English prose that at least in some ways corresponds to the powerful cadences of Hebrew."

This, then, is the prescription: the task, the aim, the experiment Alter has set for himself. The heresy of explanation will be repudiated. The sound and sense of the original will be honored. Contemporary English will be employed, but not slavishly: "a limited degree of archaizing is entirely appropriate," he warns. And clearly Alter's vision includes the sweeping moral horizon that is the Bible's raison d'être. In addition, all this is to be accomplished while traversing vastly disparate regions of text and idea: the thematic and psychological Patriarchal Tales, the ritual instructions, the communal imperatives, and ultimately the pervasive assurance that the God of the Bible directs the course of history through an interdependent compact with humankind, and particularly with humankind's biblical stand-in, the nation of Israel.

Can Alter, working alone—sans colleagues, relying solely on his own instinct for the impress and idiom of two unrelated linguistic strands, as isolated in his toil as any of the fabled seventy-two—can he pull it off?

One might as well begin before the beginning, with pre-existence, before there was anything. Here are the first four verses of the profoundly familiar King James Version:

> In the beginning God created the heaven and the earth. And the earth was without form, and void; and darkness was upon the face of the deep. And the Spirit of God moved upon the face of the waters. And

God said, Let there be light: and there was light. And God saw the light, that it was good; and God divided the light from the darkness.

And now Alter:

When God began to create heaven and earth, and the earth then was welter and waste and darkness over the deep and God's breath hovering over the waters, God said, "Let there be light." And God saw the light, that it was good, and God divided the light from the darkness.

What can be discerned in these nearly identical passages? A syntactical disagreement over the first word, *b'reshit*: does the particle *b'* represent a prepositional phrase ("In the beginning") or a clause ("When God began")? Together with current scholarship, Alter votes for the clause. Where the King James Version introduces stops, breaking up the Hebrew into recognizable English sentences, Alter follows the uninterrupted flow of the original, subverting conventional English grammar, so that for a moment we are borne along with Joycean rapidity. For *ruah*, which can mean breath or wind or spirit, Alter chooses breath, the more physical—the more anthropomorphic—word. These in themselves are small and unsurprising innovations. What genuinely startles is the inspired coupling of "welter and waste," with its echoes of *Beowulfian* alliteration perfectly conjoined, in sound and intent, with the Hebrew *tohu-vavohu*. A happening of this kind is one translator's own little miracle; no committee could hope to arrive at it.

But Alter's choice of "hovering," and especially the evocative footnote it triggers, may possibly lead to a muddling of one of his salient principles of translation. "*Hovering*," Alter notes, "the verb attached to God's breath-mind-spirit, elsewhere describes an eagle fluttering over its young and so might have a connotation of parturition or nurture as well as rapid back-and-forth movement." There is nothing to complain of in this valuable footnote; quite the opposite. It deepens, it enlarges, it leaps to associative imagery in the intuitive manner of poetry, and it is one of hundreds of equally illuminating glosses in a volume of more than a thousand pages. Nor are these copious amplifications all that Alter supplies for the sake of enriching the pristine text; besides the overall introductory essay, each of the Five Books has its own prefatory exposition.

Leviticus, for instance, lacking appealing human characters and a story, is often classed as an arid collection of rites and legalisms. But after reminding us that "small Jewish boys were introduced to the Torah not through the great story of creation and the absorbing tales of the patriarchs in Genesis but through Leviticus," Alter drills through this off-putting customary view to a distilling insight central to understanding the Hebrew Bible. "There is a single verb," he tells us, "that focuses the major themes of Leviticus—'divide' (Hebrew, *hivdil*) . . . What enables existence and provides a framework for the development of human nature, conceived in God's image, and of human civilization is a process of division and insulation—light from darkness, day from night, the upper waters from the lower waters, and dry land from the latter. That same process is repeatedly manifested in the ritual, sexual, and dietary laws of Leviticus." And he concludes: "God's holiness, whatever else it may involve and however ultimately unfathomable the idea may be, implies an ontological division or chasm between the Creator and the created world, a concept that sets off biblical monotheism from the worldview of antecedent polytheisms." This is why tradition required little children to begin with Leviticus. Here Alter cites Rashi, a seminal exegete of the eleventh century: "Let the pure ones come and study the laws of purity."

In the light of Alter's declared opposition to "the heresy of explanation," what are we to infer from his vast and formidable critical engines? He has not chosen to publish his translation in the absence of embellishing footnotes and conceptual elaborations. He cleaves to interpretation, he does not eschew imaginative commentary, explication is zealously welcomed. Yet what is amply permitted outside the text is considered heresy within the text. This makes a muddle of sorts. Every translator knows, often despairingly, that accommodation must be allowed for, simply because the *ruah*—the spirit, indeed the respiratory apparatus—of each language is intrinsic and virtually unduplicable. Even when there are cognates (and there are none between Hebrew and English), the related words have their own distinctive character. In fact, not to accommodate can sometimes set off misdirection toward an implausible meaning.

Alter objects to the Revised English Bible's substitution of "offspring" for "seed" in God's promise to Abraham (Genesis 22:17): "I will greatly bless you and will greatly multiply your seed, as the stars in heaven and as the sand on the shore of the sea, and your seed shall take hold of its enemies' gate." (Both the Revised Standard Version and the Jewish Publication Society's *Tanakh* give "descendants.") If selecting the stronger noun were the only consideration, there could be no demurral. "Seed" yields a concrete image; it is of the earth; it includes, in the most literal way, the generative function (*semen*, Latin for seed); and it denotes the multiplicity of generations. "Offspring" is clumsy, even ugly, and is as far from God's dazzling stretches of stars and sand as this morning's newspaper is from William Blake. The difficulty is that the contemporary reader's linguistic expectations, long estranged from biblical idiom, is more attuned to the *New York Times* than to the "Songs of Innocence"; and if seed is not readily understood to mean progeny, who can make sense of "his seed shall take hold of his enemies' gate"? ("His enemies' gate" may be bewildering enough: to capture a "gate," the approach to a city, was to subjugate the city itself.) Despite Alter's reasoned liking for "a limited degree of archaization," his purpose in bringing ancient Hebrew into American English is, after all, to decrease the distance between Scripture and our quotidian lives. A modicum of textual accommodation—Alter's "heresy"—may cause poets and sticklers to sigh; but there are instances when a sigh must trump a muddle. And if Alter did not believe in enlightening twenty-first-century readers, he would have given us a translation as bare of the interpretive luxuriance of his scholia as a tree denuded of its innate verdancy.

On the other hand, Alter's determination to replicate the original as closely as possible, while it will surely satisfy the sticklers, will do more than that for the poets. The poets will rejoice. Alter's language ascends to a rare purity through a plainness that equals the plainness of the Hebrew. To achieve this, he has had to come to a clear decision about the nature of English, with its two sources, or etymological strands: the florid Latinate and the spare Germanic; or call it Dr. Johnson versus Lincoln. The voice of Alter's Hebrew-in-English is Lincoln's voice, whose words and meter resonate in American ears with biblical gravity and biblical promise. It is in this plainspeaking, quickly accessible Anglo-Saxon prose, simple monosyllable following simple monosyllable, that Alter lets us hear God's imperatives, pleas, hopes, and elations:

> . . . for the Lord shall turn back to exult over you for good as He exulted over your fathers, when you heed the voice of the Lord your God to keep His commands and his statutes written in this book of teaching, when you turn back to the Lord your God with all your heart and with all your being. For this command which I charge you today is not too wondrous nor is it distant. It is not in the heavens, to say, "Who will go up for us to the heavens and take it for us and let us hear it, that we may do it?" And it is not beyond the sea, to say, "Who will cross over for us beyond the sea and take it for us and let us hear it, that we may do it?" But the word is very close to you, in your mouth and in your heart, to do it. See, I have set before you today life and good and death and evil, that I charge you today to love the Lord your God, to go in His ways and to keep His commands and His statutes and laws. . . . Life and death I set before you, the blessing and the curse, and you shall choose life . . . (Deuteronomy 30:9–19)

Alter's gloss looks past this passage to the kind of world that surrounded it:

> The Deuteronomist, having given God's teaching a local place and a habitation in a text available to all, proceeds to reject the older mythological notion of the secrets or wisdom of the gods. It is the daring hero of the pagan epic who, unlike ordinary men, makes bold to climb the sky or cross the great sea to bring back the hidden treasures of the divine realm—as Gilgamesh crosses the sea in an effort to bring back immortality. This mythological and heroic era, the Deuteronomist now proclaims, is at an end, for God's word, inscribed in a book, has become the intimate property of every person.

To which we might add, a book that is "not wondrous" requires no sacred mysteries, no sacred mediators, no sacred hierarchies. All the same, God's commands, statutes, and laws are not easy; they are grounded in self-restraint. Seven of the Ten Commandments begin with "Do not." And insofar as the overarching vision of monotheism encompasses ritual, it is as "a battle against the inchoate," Alter argues. "Authorized ritual is in all respects the exact opposite of ecstatic orgy (another departure in principle from the pagan world)."

Remarks like these—informational, historical, pedagogical—have a secularized socio-anthropological flavor so radically different in tone from the diction of the translation itself that we need to be reminded that Alter has crafted both. The text breathes out power and truth. The footnote is instructional. The one carries divine authority, the other carries . . . what? The authority of a teachers' manual, perhaps, the kind with the answers at the back of the book. But if the Bible in all the purity of its expression is genuinely and wholly intended to be read as *literature*, its prerogatives will descend to the level merely of prestige: the prestige of literature, which, as Alter has already defined it, derives its authority solely from "the power of human imagination." Literary prestige, though, tends to have a weak hold on authority, as the immemorial shufflings of the canon show us; otherwise the work of Virgil would still be as revered today as it was when the Latin spelling, Vergil, was deposed in favor of its Marian echo. The necessity of Virgil diminished when he came to be seen as Vergil the poet, not Virgil the prophet.

The necessity of the Bible, if it is to be seen solely as poetry and story, may flatten in the same way. All sacred books contain the wise or stirring pleasures of narrative: the Bhagavad-Gita tells stories, the Taoist scriptures of Chuang-Tsu tell stories, the Zoroastrian Zend-Avesta tells stories, the

Koran tells stories, Confucius and Mencius tell stories, the Buddha tells stories; African and American Indian sacred tales abound. The earth is flooded with stories, hymns, and parables regarded as holy in their origins. The literary approach can deflate them all. The short story writer Flannery O'Connor, an intransigent believer, said of the Christian mysteries that if they were not true, "then the hell with them." A skilled teller of tales, she insisted on a distinction between imagination of the kind she herself could wield and what she took to be divine revelation. And it may be that if all the world's scriptures had long ago been flattened into literature, and packed side by side, despite their dissimilarities and divergences, into a single bookshelf—much as *Madame Bovary*, say, can stand in civil proximity to *Crime and Punishment*, and Joyce cheek by jowl with Proust—all our habitations and histories might have been far more pacific. Novels and stories do not war with one another; neither, *pace* Harold Bloom, do they always engage in supersessionism (at least not of the jihadist variety).

But stories, though they influence and enlarge us, do not deliver Commandments. The Bible cannot be pumped up from literary prestige to divine prerogative through arguing from the power of human imagination, even when that power is "kindled" by positing measureless structures of transcendent dominion. What, then, are unbelieving readers of the Five Books left with? Unless they happen to be moral philosophers who will deduce law and right conduct from reason, it is stories they are left with, and—for nonphilosophers—isn't that enough? On their face, the Patriarchal Tales, like all literature that endures, touch on everything recognizable in ordinary human life: crises between parents and children, between siblings, between husbands and wives; hunger and migration, jealousy and reconciliation, sudden ascent and sudden subjugation, great love and great hatred. Universally felt, they are family annals in a family album. The Joseph narrative is doubtless the most moving story of all: here stands Joseph, Pharaoh's mighty viceroy, interrogating the humbly petitioning brothers who in the past flung him into a pit and sold him to traders on their way to Egypt. Catching sight of Benjamin, the tender younger son of Rachel, their mother, "Joseph hurried out, for his feelings for his brother overwhelmed him and he wanted to weep, and he went into the chamber and wept there. And he bathed his face and came out and held himself in check and said, 'Serve bread.'"

In this enclosed fraternal scene, God is not needed, and seems not to be present. So far, the drama of Joseph appears to resemble the stories we call literature; and yet it does not, because Joseph will not permit God to be exiled out of his world. When, bowing before Pharaoh's deputy, the brothers plead for forgiveness, Joseph is again swept into weeping, and invokes not only God, but God's design: "And Joseph said, 'Fear not, for am I instead of God? While you meant evil for me, God meant it for good.'" And further: "Do not be pained and do not be incensed with yourselves that you sold me down here, because for sustenance God has sent me before you . . . to make you a remnant on earth and to preserve life, for you to be a great surviving group. And so, it is not you who sent me here but God." A few verses on, Joseph dies, at one hundred and ten, and is embalmed according to Egyptian custom. And now, portentously, the Book of Genesis ends: "He was put in a coffin in Egypt."

That coffin signifies more than a human story. It is God's story: Egypt will become a coffin for the Hebrews until God redeems them. God in the Hebrew Bible is Causality, and Causality, unlike Joseph or Benjamin, cannot be a character in a tale—an assertion that has been broadly contradicted, or at least qualified, in formulations by both Harold Bloom and Jack Miles. In his winning and ingenious *God: A Biography*, Miles is moved to ask, "How did all this feel to God?" and sets out to see Him as a "character who 'comes to life' in a work of literary art." Miles's God has an indelible, even a familiar, human personality, not unlike the mercurial protagonist of an epic, or an opera, or a labyrinth of motives by Henry James. And while it may be possible to transmute aspects of Scripture into literature by means of the fictive imagination—certainly Thomas Mann succeeded in turning the Joseph chronicle into a massive and masterly novel—finally Scripture itself rebels against it. Mann's fiction can claim no greater authority than writerly genius.

Just here is the nub and the rub of it: if the God of the Bible is not "real," then—in creative-writing-course argot—the Bible's stories won't and don't *work*. For the faithless skeptic or rationalist confronting Scripture (a category of modernity that includes, I suppose, most of us), there is nothing more robust to lean on than suspension of disbelief, the selfsame device one brings to Jane Austen. Mr. Darcy and Mr. Knightly, salvational creations both, are not real; we believe in them anyway. Causality deserves better. Causality escapes the mere "comes to life" of character.

It is the directness and consummate clarity of Alter's rendering that forces this conclusion. The translator's richly developed notes and reflections are informed by scholarship, wit, and intuition; without the intrusions of didacticism, they educate. But the antique words, on their own power, and even in a latter-day language, draw us elsewhere, to that indeterminate place where God is not a literary premise but a persuasive certainty—whether or not we are willing to go there.

LETTERS

Dostoyevsky's Unabomber

1.

Soon after dawn on a very cold winter morning in 1849, fifteen Russian criminals, in groups of three, were led before a firing squad. They were all insurgents against the despotism of Czar Nicholas I. They were mostly educated men, idealists in pursuit of a just society. They felt no remorse. Several were professed atheists. All were radicals. A priest carrying a cross and a Bible accompanied them. The first three were handed white gowns and shapeless caps and ordered to put these on; then they were tied to posts. The rest waited their turn. Each man in his own way prepared to die. The sun was beginning to brighten; the firing squad took aim. At just that moment there was a signal—a roll of drums—and the rifles were lowered. A galloping horseman announced a reprieve. Although the condemned were unaware of it, the execution was staged, and the reprieve was designed to demonstrate the merciful heart of the Czar. Instead of being shot, the criminals were to be transported in shackles to a Siberian penal colony.

One of the men went permanently mad. Another, fifteen years afterward, wrote *Crime and Punishment*, an impassioned assault on exactly the kind of radical faith that had brought its author to face the Czar's riflemen that day. It was a work almost in the nature of double jeopardy: as if Fyodor Dostoyevsky in middle age—a defender of the Czar, the enemy of revolutionary socialism—were convicting and punishing his younger self yet again for the theories the mature novelist had come to abhor.

2.

A new type of crime is on the American mind—foreign, remote, metaphysical, even literary; and radically different from what we are used to. Street crime, drunken crime, drug-inspired crime, crimes of passion, greed, revenge, crimes against children, gangster crime, white-collar crime, break-ins, car thefts, holdups, shootings—these are familiar, and to a degree nearly expected. They shake us up without disorienting us. They belong to our civilization; they are the darker signals of home. "Our" crime has usually been local—the stalker, the burglar, the mugger lurking in a doorway. Even Jeffrey Dahmer, the cannibal sadist who kept boys' body parts in his kitchen refrigerator, is not so very anomalous in the context of what can happen in ordinary neighborhoods—a little girl imprisoned in an underground cage; children tormented, starved, beaten to death; newborns bludgeoned; battered women, slain wives, mutilated husbands. Domesticity gone awry.

All that is recognizable and homespun. What feels alien to America is the philosophical criminal of exceptional intelligence and humanitarian purpose who is driven to commit murder out of an uncompromising idealism. Such a type has always seemed a literary construct of a particular European political coloration (*The Secret Agent, The Princess Casamassima*), or else has hinted at ideologies so removed from tame Republicans and Democrats as to be literally outlandish. Then came the mysterious depredations of the Unabomber. Until the melodramatic publication of his manifesto in major newspapers, the Unabomber remained an unpredictable riddle, unfathomable, sans name or habitation. In garrulous print his credo revealed him to be a visionary. His dream was of a green and pleasant land liberated from the curse of technological proliferation. The technical élites were his targets: computer wizards like Professor David Gelernter of Yale, a thinker in pursuit of artificial intelligence. Maimed by a package bomb, Gelernter escaped death; others did not.

In the storm of interpretation that followed the Unabomber's public declaration of principles, he was often mistaken for a kind of contemporary Luddite. This was a serious misnomer. The nineteenth-century Luddites were hand weavers who rioted against the introduction of mechanical looms in England's textile industry; they smashed the machines to protect their livelihoods. They were not out to kill, nor did they promulgate romantic theories about the wholesome superiority of hand looms. They were selfish, ruthlessly pragmatic, and societally unreasonable. By contrast, Theodore Kaczynski—the Unabomber—is above all a calculating social reasoner and messianic utopian. His crimes, for which he was found guilty as charged, were intended to restore us to cities and landscapes clear of digital complexities; he meant to clean the American slate of its accumulated technostructural smudges. At the same time, we can acknowledge him to have been selfless and pure, loyal and empathic, the sort of man who befriends, without condescension, an uneducated and impoverished Mexican laborer. It is easy to think of the Unabomber, living out his principles in his pollution-free mountain cabin, as a Thoreauvian philosopher of advanced environmentalism. The philosopher is one with the murderer. The Napoleonic world-improver is one with the humble hermit of the wilderness.

In the Unabomber, America has at last brought forth its own Raskolnikov—the appealing, appalling, and disturbingly visionary murderer of *Crime and Punishment*, Dostoyevsky's masterwork of 1866. But the Unabomber is not the only ideological criminal (though he may be the most intellectual) to burst out of remoteness and fantasy onto unsuspecting native grounds. It was a political conviction rooted in anti-government ideas of liberty suppressed that fueled the deadly bombing of a Federal building in Oklahoma City. God's will directed the bombing of the World Trade Center, and the Muslim zealots who devised the means are world-improvers obedient to the highest good; so are the bombers of abortion clinics. The Weathermen of the sixties, who bombed banks and shot police in order to release "Amerika" from the tyranny of a democratic polity, are close ideological cousins of the Russian nihilists who agitated against Alexander II, the liberalizing Czar of a century before. That celebrated 1960s mantra—to make an omelet you need to break eggs—had its origin not in an affinity for violence, but in the mouth-watering lure of the humanitarian omelet. It was only the gastronomic image that was novel. In the Russian sixties, one hundred years earlier—in 1861, the very year Alexander II freed the serfs—a radical young critic named Dimitry Pisarev called for striking "right and left" and announced, "What resists the blow is worth keeping; what flies to pieces is rubbish." Here was the altruistic bomber's dogma, proclaimed in the pages of a literary journal—and long before *The New York Review of Books* published on its front cover a diagram of how to construct a Molotov cocktail.

Like the Unabomber, Raskolnikov is an intellectual who publishes a notorious essay expounding his ideas about men and society. Both are obscure loners. Both are alienated from a concerned and affectionate family. Both are tender toward outcasts and the needy. Both are élitists. Both are idealists. Both are murderers. Contemporary America, it seems, has finally caught up with czarist Russia's most argumentative novelist.

And in *Crime and Punishment* Dostoyevsky was feverishly pursuing an argument. It was an argument against the radicals who were dominant among Russian intellectuals in the 1860s, many of them espousing nihilist views. In the universities especially, revolutionary commotion was on the rise. Yet there was an incongruity in the timing of all these calls for violent subversion. St. Petersburg was no longer the seat of the old Czar of the repressive 1840s, the tyrannical Nicholas I, against whose cruelties convulsive outrage might be justly presumed. Paradoxically, under that grim reign even the most fiery radicals were at heart gradualists who modeled their hopes on Western reformist ideas. By the incendiary sixties, the throne was held by Nicholas's moderate son and successor, whose numerous democratic initiatives looked to be nudging Russia toward something that might eventually resemble a constitutional monarchy. The younger revolutionary theorists would have none of it. It was incomplete; it was too slow. Liberalism, they roared, was the enemy of revolution, and would impede a more definitive razing of evil.

The first installments of *Crime and Punishment* had just begun to appear in *The Russian Messenger*, a Slavophile periodical, when a student revolutionary made an attempt on the life of the Czar as he was leaving the gardens of the Winter Palace to enter his carriage. The government responded with a draconian crackdown on the radicals. "You know," Dostoyevsky wrote cuttingly to his publisher in the wake of these events, "they are completely convinced that on a *tabula rasa* they will immediately construct a paradise." But he went on to sympathize with "our poor little defenseless boys and girls" and "their enthusiasm for the good and their purity of heart." So many "have become nihilists so purely, so unselfishly, in the name of honor, truth, and genuine usefulness! You know they are helpless against these stupidities, and take them for perfection." And though in the same letter he spoke of "the powerful, extraordinary, sacred union of the Czar with the people," he objected to the increase in repression. "But how can nihilism be fought without freedom of speech?" he asked.

This mixture of contempt for the radicals and solicitude for their misguided, perplexed, and perplexing humanity led to the fashioning of Raskolnikov. Pisarev striking right and left was one ingredient. Another was the appeal of self-sacrificial idealism. And a third was the literary mode through which Dostoyevsky combined and refined the tangled elements of passion, brutishness, monomaniacal principle, mental chaos, candor, mockery, fury, compassion, generosity—and two brutal ax-murders. All these contradictory elements course through Raskolnikov with nearly a Joycean effect; but if stream of consciousness flows mutely and uninterruptedly, assimilating the outer world into the inner, Raskolnikov's mind—and Dostoyevsky's method—is zigzag and bumpy, given to rebellious and unaccountable alterations of purpose. Raskolnikov is without restraint—not only as an angry character in a novel, but as a reflection of Dostoyevsky himself, who was out to expose the entire spectrum of radical thought engulfing the writers and thinkers of St. Petersburg.

This may be why Raskolnikov is made to rush dizzyingly from impulse to impulse, from kindliness to withdrawal to lashing out, and from one underlying motive to another—a disorderliness at war with his half-buried and equivocal conscience. Only at the start is he seen, briefly, to be deliberate and in control. Detached, reasoning it out, Raskolnikov robs and murders a pawnbroker whom he has come to loathe, an unpleasant and predatory old woman alone and helpless in her flat. He hammers her repeatedly with the heavy handle of an ax:

> Her thin hair, pale and streaked with gray, was thickly greased as usual, plaited into a ratty braid and tucked under a piece of horn comb that stuck up at the back of her head . . . he struck her again and yet again with all his strength, both times with the butt-end, both times on the crown of the head. Blood poured out as from an overturned glass.

Unexpectedly, the old woman's simple-minded sister just then enters the flat; she is disposed of even more horribly: "The blow landed directly on the skull, with the sharp edge, and immediately split the whole upper part of the forehead, almost to the crown."

The second slaying is an unforeseen by-product of the first. The first is the rational consequence of forethought. What is the nature—the thesis—of this forethought? Shortly before the murder, Raskolnikov overhears a student in a tavern speculating about the pawnbroker: she is "rich as a Jew," and has willed all her money to the Church. "A hundred, a thousand good deeds and undertakings . . . could be arranged and set going by the money that old woman has doomed to the monastery!" exclaims the student.

> Hundreds, maybe thousands of lives put right; dozens of families saved from destitution, from decay, from ruin, from depravity, from the venereal hospitals—all on her money. Kill her and take her money, so that afterwards with its help you can devote yourself to the service of all mankind and the common cause . . . One death for hundreds of lives— it's simple arithmetic! And what does the life of this stupid, consumptive, and wicked old crone mean in the general balance? No more than the life of a louse, a cockroach.

Startled by this polemic, Raskolnikov admits to himself that "*exactly the same thoughts* had just been conceived in his own head"—though not as harmless theoretical bombast.

The theory in Raskolnikov's head—Benthamite utilitarianism, the greatest good for the greatest number, with its calibrated notions of what is useful and what is expendable—had been current for at least a decade among the

Westernizing majority of the Russian intelligentsia, especially the literati of the capital. In supplying Bentham with an ax, Dostoyevsky thought to carry out the intoxications of the utilitarian doctrine as far as its principles would go: brutality and bloodletting would reveal the poisonous fruit of a political philosophy based on reason alone.

A fiercely sardonic repudiation of that philosophy—some of it in the vocabulary of contemporary American controversy—is entrusted to Raskolnikov's affectionate and loyal comrade, Razumikhin:

> It started with the views of the socialists . . . Crime is a protest against the abnormality of the social set-up—that alone and nothing more, no other causes are admitted—but nothing! . . . With them one is always a "victim of the environment"—and nothing else! . . . If society itself is normally set up, all crimes will at once disappear, because there will be no reason for protesting . . . Nature isn't taken into account, nature is driven out, nature is not supposed to be! . . . On the contrary, a social system, coming out of some mathematical head, will at once organize the whole of mankind and instantly make it righteous and sinless . . . And it turns out in the end that they've reduced everything to mere brickwork and the layout of corridors and rooms in a phalanstery!

The phalanstery, a cooperative commune, was the brainchild of Charles Fourier, who, along with the political theorist Saint-Simon (and well before Marx), was an enduring influence on the Francophile Russian radical intelligentsia. But Razumikhin's outcry against the utopian socialists who idealize the life of the commune and fantasize universal harmony is no more than a satiric rap on the knuckles. Dostoyevsky is after a bloodier and more threatening vision—nihilism in its hideously perfected form. This is the ideological cloak he next throws over Raskolnikov; it is Raskolnikov's manifesto as it appears in his article. The "extraordinary man," Raskolnikov declaims, has the right to "step over certain obstacles" in order to fulfill a mission that is "salutary for the whole of mankind."

> In my opinion, if, as the result of certain combinations, Kepler's or Newton's discoveries could become known to people in no other way than by sacrificing the lives of one, or ten, or a hundred or more people who were hindering the discovery, or standing as an obstacle in its path, then Newton would have the right, and it would even be his duty . . . to *remove* those ten or a hundred people, in order to make his discoveries known to all mankind.

Every lawgiver or founder of a new idea, he goes on, has always been a criminal—"all of them to a man . . . from the fact alone that in giving a new law they thereby violated the old one . . . and they certainly did not stop at shedding blood either, if it happened that blood . . . could help them." Such extraordinary men—Lycurgus, Solon, Napoleon—call for "the destruction of the present in the name of the better," and will lead the world toward a new Jerusalem.

To which Razumikhin, recoiling, responds: "You do finally permit bloodshed *in all conscience.*" And just here, in the turbulence of Razumikhin's revelation—and prefiguring Sakharov, Solzhenitsyn, and Sharansky—Dostoyevsky makes his case for the dismantling of the Soviet state half a century before the revolutionary convulsion that brought it into being.

3.

Yet the mammoth irony of Dostoyevsky's life remains: the writer who excoriated the radical theorists, who despised the nihilist revolutionaries, who wrote novel after novel to defy them, once belonged to their company.

It is easy to dislike him, and not because the spectacle of a self-accusing apostate shocks. He ended as a Slavophile religious believer; but in his twenties he was what he bitterly came to scorn—a Westernizing Russian liberal. Nevertheless a certain nasty consistency ruled. At all times he was bigoted and xenophobic: he had an irrational hatred of Germans and Poles, and his novels are speckled with anti-Semitism. He attacked Roman Catholicism as the temporal legacy of a pagan empire, while extolling Russian Orthodoxy. He was an obsessive and deluded gambler scheming to strike it rich at the snap of a finger: he played madly at the roulette tables of Europe, and repeatedly reduced himself and his pregnant young second wife to actual privation. Escaping debtors' prison in Russia, he was compelled for years to wander homelessly and wretchedly through Germany and Switzerland. In Wiesbaden he borrowed fifty thalers from Turgenev and took ten years to repay him. He held the rigidly exclusionary blood-and-soil tenet that the future of civilization lay with Russia alone. He was seriously superstitious and had a silly trust in omens and dreams. He was irritable, sometimes volcanically so, and inordinately vain. And if all these self-inflicted debilities of character were not ugly enough, he suffered from a catastrophic innate debility: he was subject, without warning, to horrifying epileptic seizures in a period when there were no medical controls.

Though not quite without warning. Dostoyevsky's fits were heralded by a curious surge of ecstasy—an "aura" indistinguishable from religious exalta-tion. He underwent his first seizure, he reported, on Easter morning in 1865, when he was forty-four years old: "Heaven had come down to earth and swallowed me. I really grasped God and was penetrated by Him." But there may have been unidentified earlier attacks, different in kind. At the age of ten he experienced an auditory hallucination; he thought he heard a voice cry "A wolf is on the loose!" and was comforted by a kindly serf who belonged to his father.

Later fits uniformly triggered the divine penumbra. He was well pre-pared for it. From childhood he had been saturated in a narrow household piety not unlike the unquestioning devoutness of the illiterate Russian peas-ant. Prayers were recited before icons; a clergyman came to give lessons. The Gospels were read, and the *Acta Martyrum*—the lives of the saints—with their peculiarly Russian emphasis on passive suffering. No Sunday or reli-gious holiday went unobserved, on the day itself and at vespers the evening before. Rituals were punctiliously kept up. Dostoyevsky's father, a former army doctor on the staff of a hospital for the poor outside Moscow, fre-quently led his family on excursions to the great onion-domed Kremlin cathedrals, where religion and nationalism were inseparable. Every spring, Dostoyevsky's mother took the children on a pilgrimage to the Monastery of St. Sergey, sixty miles from Moscow, where they kneeled among mobs of the faithful before an imposing silver reliquary said to contain the saint's miracu-lous remains. None of this was typical of the Russian gentry of the time. Neither Tolstoy nor Turgenev had such an upbringing. Joseph Frank, Dos-toyevsky's superb and exhaustive biographer, explains why. "Most upper-class Russians," he recounts, "would have shared the attitude exemplified in Her-zen's anecdote about his host at a dinner party who, when asked whether he was serving Lenten dishes out of personal conviction, replied that it was 'simply and solely for the sake of the servants.'"

There is speculation that Dostoyevsky's father may himself have had a mild form of epilepsy: he was gloomy, moody, and unpredictably explosive, a martinet who drank too much and imposed his will on everyone around him. In his youth he had completed his studies at a seminary for non-monastic clergy, a low caste, but went on instead to pursue medicine, and eventually elevated himself to the status of the minor nobility. His salary was insuffi-cient and the family was not well off, despite the doctor's inheritance of a small and scrubby estate, along with its "baptized property"—the serfs attached to the land. When Dostoyevsky was sixteen, his father dispatched him and his older brother Mikhail, both of whom had literary ambitions, to the Academy of Military Engineers in St. Petersburg, in preparation for government careers. But the doctor's plan for his sons came to nothing. Less than two years later, in a season of drought, bad crops, and peasant resentment, Dostoyevsky was informed that his father had been found dead on the estate, presumably strangled by his serfs. Killings of this kind were not uncommon. In a famous letter to Gogol (the very letter that would ultimately send Dostoyevsky before the firing squad), the radical critic Vissarion Belinsky wrote that the Czar was "well aware of what landowners do with their peasants and how many throats of the former are cut every year by the latter."

Freed from engineering (and from a despotic father), Dostoyevsky went flying into the heart of St. Petersburg's literary life. It was the hugely influential Belinsky who catapulted him there. Dostoyevsky's first novel, *Poor Folk*—inspired by the social realism of Balzac, Victor Hugo, and George Sand, and published in 1846—was just the sort of fiction Belinsky was eager to promote. "Think of it," he cried, "it's the first attempt at a social novel we've had." Belinsky was a volatile man of movements—movements he usually set off himself. He was also quickly excitable: he had leaped from art-for-art's-sake to a kind of messianic socialism (with Jesus as chief socialist) to blatant atheism. In literature he espoused an ardent naturalism, and saw Dostoyevsky as its avatar. He instantly proclaimed the new writer to be a genius, made him famous overnight, and admitted him, at twenty-four, into St. Petersburg's most coveted intellectual circle, Belinsky's own "pléiade." Turgenev was already a member. The talk was socialist and fervent, touching on truth and justice, science and atheism, and, most heatedly, on the freeing of the serfs. Here Christianity was not much more than a historical metaphor, a view Dostoyevsky only briefly entered into; but he was fiery on the issue of human chattel.

Success went to his head. "Everywhere an unbelievable esteem, a passionate curiosity about me," he bragged to his brother. "Everyone considers me some sort of prodigy . . . I am now almost drunk with my own glory." The pléiade responded to this posturing at first with annoyance and then with rough ribbing. Belinsky kept out of it, but Turgenev took off after the young prodigy with a scathing parody. Dostoyevsky walked out, humiliated and enraged, and never returned. "They are all scoundrels and eaten up with envy," he fumed. He soon gravitated to another socialist discussion group, which met on Friday nights at the home of Mikhail Petrashevsky, a twenty-six-year-old aristocrat. Petrashevsky had accumulated a massive library of political works forbidden by the censors, and was even less tolerant of Christianity than the pléiade: for him Jesus was "the well-known demagogue." To improve the miserable living conditions of the peasants on his land, Petrashevsky had a commodious communal dormitory built for them, with every amenity provided. They all moved in, and the next day burned down the master's paternalistic utopia. Undaunted, Petrashevsky continued to propagandize for his ideas: the end of serfdom and censorship, and the reform of the courts. His commitment was to gradualism, but certain more impatient members of the Petrashevsky circle quietly formed a secret society dedicated to an immediate and deeply perilous activism.

It was with these that Dostoyevsky aligned himself; he joined a scheme to print and disseminate the explosive manifesto in the form of the letter to Gogol, which Belinsky had composed a year or so earlier, protesting the enslavement of the peasants. Russia, Belinsky wrote, "presents the dire spectacle of a country where men traffic in men, without ever having the excuse so insidiously exploited by the American plantation owners who claim that the Negro is not a man." Dostoyevsky gave an impressive reading of this document at one of Petrashevsky's Friday nights. His audience erupted into an uproar; there were yells of "That's it! That's it!" A government spy, unrecognized, took notes, and at four in the morning Dostoyevsky's bedroom was invaded by the Czar's secret police. He was arrested as a revolutionary conspirator; he was twenty-seven years old.

Nicholas I took a malicious interest in the punishment for this crime against the state—the Czar *was* the state—and personally ordered the mock execution, the last-minute reprieve, the transport to Siberia. Dostoyevsky's sentence was originally eight years; he served four at forced labor in a prison camp at Omsk and the rest in an army regiment. In Siberia, after his release from the camp, he married for the first time—a tumultuous widow with worsening tuberculosis. His own affliction worsened; seizure followed on seizure. For the remainder of his life he would not be free of the anguish of fits. He feared he would die while in their grip.

The moment of cataclysmic terror before the firing squad never left him. He was not so much altered as strangely—almost mystically—restored: restored to what he had felt as a child, kneeling with his mother at the reliquary of St. Sergey. He spoke circumspectly of "the regeneration of my convictions." The only constant was his hatred of the institution of serfdom—but to hate serfdom was not to love peasants, and when he began to live among peasant convicts (political prisoners were not separated from the others), he found them degraded and savage, with a malignant hostility toward the gentry thrown into their midst. The agonies of hard labor, the filth, the chains, the enmity, the illicit drunkenness, his own nervous disorders—all these assailed him, and he suffered in captivity from a despondency nearly beyond endurance.

And then—in a metamorphosis akin to the Ancient Mariner's sudden love for the repulsive creatures of the sea—he was struck by what can only be called a conversion experience. In the twisted and branded faces of the peasant convicts—men much like those who may have murdered his father—he saw a divine illumination; he saw the true Russia; he saw beauty; he saw the kind-hearted serf who had consoled him when the imaginary wolf pursued. Their instinctive piety was his. Their soil-rootedness became a precept. He struggled to distinguish between one criminal motive and another: from the viewpoint of a serf, was a crime against a hardened master really a crime? Under the tatters of barbarism, he perceived the image of God.

The collective routine of the stockade drove him further and further from the socialist dream of communal living. "To be alone is a normal need," he railed. "Otherwise, *in this enforced communism one turns into a hater of mankind.*" And at the same time he began to discover in the despised and brutalized lives of the peasant convicts a shadow of the redemptive suffering that is the Christian paradigm. More and more he inclined toward the traditional Orthodoxy of his upbringing. He fought doubt with passionate unreason: "If someone proved to me that Christ is outside the truth, then I should prefer to remain with Christ than with the truth." This set him against his old associates, both radicals and liberals. It set him against Petrashevsky and Belinsky, whose highest aspiration had been a constitutional republic in league with a visionary ethical socialism. It set him against illustrious literary moderates and Westernizers like Turgenev and Alexander Herzen. Emerging from his Siberian ordeal, he thundered against "the scurvy Russian liberalism propagated by good-for-nothings." Years later, when Belinsky was dead, Dostoyevsky was still sneering at "shitheads like the dung-beetle Belinsky," whom he would not forgive because "that man reviled Christ to me in the foulest language."

The culmination of these renunciations was a white-hot abomination of radicalism in all its forms—from the Western-influenced gentry-theorists of the 1840s to the renegade *raskolniki* (dissenters) who burst into nihilism in the sixties, when student revolutionaries radicalized the universities. With his brother Mikhail, Dostoyevsky founded *Vremya (Time)*, a literary-political periodical intended to combat the socialist radicals. Their immediate target was *The Contemporary*, an opposing polemical journal; it was in the arena of the monthlies that the ideological fires, under literary cover to distract the censors, smoldered. Though *Vremya* was a success, a misunderstanding led the censorship to close it down. Soon afterward, Dostoyevsky's wife died of consumption; then Mikhail collapsed and died. The grieving Dostoyevsky attempted to revive the magazine under another name, but in the absence of his brother's business management he fell into serious debt, went bankrupt, and in 1867 fled to the hated West to escape his creditors.

With him went Anna, the worshipful young stenographer to whom he had begun to dictate his work, and whom he shortly married. Four enforced years abroad took on the half-mad, hallucinatory frenzy of scenes in his own novels: he gambled and lost, gambled and wrote, pawned his wife's rings and gambled and lost and wrote. His work was appearing regularly in the reactionary *Russian Messenger*. Dostoyevsky had now altogether gone over to the other side. "All those trashy little liberals and progressives," he mocked, "find their greatest pleasure and satisfaction in criticizing Russia . . . everything of the slightest originality in Russia [is] hateful to them." It was on this issue that he broke with Turgenev, to whom words like "folk" and "glory" smelled of blood. Turgenev, for his part, thought Dostoyevsky insane. And yet it was Turgenev's *Fathers and Sons*, with its ambiguous portrait of a scoffing nihilist, that was Raskolnikov's sensational precursor.

Turgenev's novel was dedicated to Belinsky. Dostoyevsky broke with Belinsky, he broke with Turgenev, he broke with Petrashevsky, he broke with Herzen—not only because of their liberalism, but because he believed that they did not love Russia enough. To love Russia was to love the Czar and the debased peasant (who, debased by the Czar, also loved the Czar); it was to see human suffering as holy and the peasant as holy; it was to exalt the *obshchina*, the Russian village commune, while condemning the French philosophic cooperative; it was to love the Russian Church largely through the vilification of all other churches; it was to press for the love of God with a hateful ferocity.

Joseph Frank seems certain that Dostoyevsky's conversion "should not be seen as that of a strayed ex-believer returning to Christ," since he had "always remained in some sense a Christian." But the suggestion of a continuum of sensibility may be even stronger than that. After a plunge into the period's dominant cultural milieu, the son of an authoritarian father—authoritarian personally, religiously, nationally—returns to the father. It is common enough that an intellectual progression will lead to a recovery of the voices around the cradle.

In January of 1881, Dostoyevsky, now an honored literary eminence more celebrated than Turgenev, died of a hemorrhage of the throat. Two months later, Czar Alexander II—Russia's earnest liberalizer and liberator—was assassinated. From the last half of the nineteenth century until the Bolshevik defeat of the liberal Kerensky government in the second decade of the twentieth, revolution continued to overcome reform. In this guise—

injury for the sake of an ideal—Raskolnikov lives on. For seventy years he was victorious in Russia. And even now, after the death of the Soviet Union, auguring no one knows what, his retributive figure roves the earth. If he is currently mute in Russia, he remains restive in Northern Ireland, and loud in the Middle East; he has migrated to America. He survives in the violence of humanitarian visionaries who would seize their utopias via ax, Molotov cocktail, or innocent-looking packages sent through the mail.

4.

Raskolnikov as monster of ruination, reason's avenging angel: here speaks the ideologue Dostoyevsky, scourge of the radicals. But this single clangorous note will not hold. Dostoyevsky the novelist tends toward orchestration and multiplicity. Might there be other reasons for the murder of the old woman? Raskolnikov has already been supplied with messianic utilitarianism, a Western import, carried to its logical and lethal end. On second thought (Dostoyevsky's second thought), the killing may have a different and simpler source—family solidarity. A university dropout, unable to meet his tuition payments, Raskolnikov, alienated and desperate, has been guiltily taking money from his adoring mother and sister in the provinces. At home there is crisis: Dunya, his sister, has been expelled from her position as governess in the Svidrigailov household, where the debauched husband and father had been making lecherous advances. To elude disgrace and to ease her family's poverty—but chiefly to secure a backer for her brother's career—Dunya becomes engaged to a rich and contemptible St. Petersburg bureaucrat. In this version of Raskolnikov's intent, it is to save his sister from a self-sacrificial marriage that he robs the old woman and pounds her to death.

Dostoyevsky will hurry the stealing-for-sustenance thesis out of sight quickly enough. As a motive, it is too narrow for his larger purpose, and by the close of the novel it seems almost forgotten, and surely marginal—not only because Raskolnikov hides the stolen money and valuables and never touches them again, but because such an obvious material reason is less shattering than what Dostoyevsky will soon disclose. He will goad Raskolnikov to a tempestuousness even past nihilism. Past nihilism lies pure violence—violence for is own sake, without the vindication of a superior future. The business of revolution is only to demolish, the anarchist theorist and agitator Mikhail Bakunin once declared. But in Raskolnikov's newest stand, not even this extremist position is enough:

Then I realized . . . that power is given only to the one who dares to reach down and take it. Here there is one thing, one thing only: one has only to dare! . . . I wanted to *dare*, and I killed . . . that's the whole reason! . . . I wanted to kill without casuistry . . . to kill for myself, for myself alone! I didn't want to lie about it even to myself! It was not to help my mother that I killed—nonsense! I did not kill so that, having obtained means and power, I could become a benefactor of mankind. Nonsense! . . . And it was not money above all that I wanted when I killed . . . I wanted to find out then, and find out quickly, whether I was a louse like all the rest, or a man? . . . Would I dare to reach down and take, or not?

A rapid shuttling of motives, one overtaking the other: family reasons, societal reasons, altruism, utilitarianism, socialism, nihilism, Napoleonic raw domination. Generations of readers have been mystified by this plethora of incitements and explanations. Why so many? One critic, the Russian Formalist Mikhail Bakhtin, analyzing Dostoyevsky's frequent ellipses and the back-and-forth interior dialogue of characters disputing with themselves— each encompassing multiple points of view—concludes that Dostoyevsky was the inventor of a new "multivoice" genre, which Bakhtin calls the "polyphonic novel." Some simply assume that Dostoyevsky changed his mind as he went along, and since he was unable to revise what was already in print— the novel appeared in installments written against deadlines—he was compelled to stitch up the loose ends afterward as best he could. (This sounds plausible enough; if true, it would leave most serious Dostoyevsky scholars of the last century with egg on their faces.)

A British academic, A. D. Nuttall, offers a psychiatric solution: Raskolnikov is in a state of self-hypnotic schizophrenia. Walter Kaufmann invokes existentialism, drawing Dostoyevsky into Nietzsche's and Kierkegaard's web. Freud speculates that Dostoyevsky expresses "sympathy by identification" with criminals as a result of an Oedipal revolt against his father. Harold Bloom, sailing over Raskolnikov's inconsistencies, sees in him an apocalyptic figure, "a powerful representative of the will demonized by its own strength." "The best of all murder stories," says Bloom, *Crime and Punishment* seems to me beyond praise and beyond affection." For Vladimir Nabokov, on the other hand, the novel is beyond contempt; he knew even in his teens that it was "long-winded, terribly sentimental, and badly written." Dostoyevsky is "mediocre," and his "gallery of characters consists almost exclusively of neurotics and lunatics." As for Dostoyevsky's religion, it is a "special lurid brand of the Christian faith." "I am very eager to debunk Dostoyevsky," Nabokov assures us.

Is this a case of the blind men and the elephant? Or the novel as Rorschach test? There is something indeterminate in all these tumbling alternatives—in Raskolnikov's changing theories, in the critics' clashing responses. Still, all of them taken together make plain what it is that Dostoyevsky's novel turns out not to be. It is not, after all, a singlemindedly polemical tract fulminating against every nineteenth-century radical movement in sight—though parts may pass for that. It is not a detective thriller, despite its introduction of Porfiry, a crafty, nimble-tongued, penetratingly intuitive police investigator. It is not a social protest novel, even if it retains clear vestiges of an abandoned earlier work on alcoholism and poverty in the forlorn Marmeladovs, whom Raskolnikov befriends: drunken husband, unbalanced tubercular wife, daughter driven to prostitution.

And it is not even much of what it has often been praised for being: a "psychological" novel—notwithstanding a startling stab, now and then, into the marrow of a mind. George Eliot is what we mean, in literature, by psychological; among the moderns, Proust, Joyce, James. Dostoyevsky is not psychological in the sense of understanding and portraying familiar human nature. *Crime and Punishment* is in exile from human nature—like the deeply eccentric 'Notes from Underground', which precedes it by a year. The underground man, Raskolnikov's indispensable foreshadower, his very embryo, revels in the corrupt will to seek out extreme and horrible acts, which gladden him with their "shameful accursed sweetness." But Raskolnikov will in time feel suffocated by the mental anguish that dogs his crime. Suspicions close in on him; a room in a police station seems no bigger than a cupboard. And soon suffering criminality will put on the radiant robes of transcendence. Led by the saintly Sonya Marmeladova, who has turned harlot to support her destitute family, Raskolnikov looks at last to God. The nihilist, the insolent Napoleon, is all at once redeemed—implausibly, abruptly—by a single recitation from the Gospels, and goes off, docile and remorseful, to serve out his sentence in Siberia.

Nabokov gleefully derides Dostoyevsky's sentimental conventions: "I do not like this trick his characters have of 'sinning their way to Jesus.'" Ridiculing Raskolnikov's impetuous "spiritual regeneration," Nabokov concedes that "the love of a noble prostitute . . . did not seem as incredibly banal in 1866 . . . as it does now when noble prostitutes are apt to be received a little cynically." Yet the doctrine of redemption through suffering came to be the bulwark of Dostoyevsky's credo. He believed in spiritual salvation. He had been intimate with thieves and cutthroats; he had lived among criminals. He had himself been punished as a criminal. Even as he was writing *Crime and Punishment*, he was under the continuing surveillance of the secret police.

The secret police, however, are not this novel's secret. Neither are the *ukases* and explosives of that Czarist twilight. Murder and degradation; perversity, distortion, paralysis, abnormal excitation, lightning conversion; dive after dive into fits of madness (Raskolnikov, his mother, Svidrigailov, Katerina Marmeladova); a great imperial city wintry in tone, huddled, frozen in place, closeted, all in the heart of summertime—these are not the usual characteristics of a work dedicated to political repudiations. *Crime and Punishment* is something else, something beyond what Dostoyevsky may have plotted and what the scholars habitually attend to. Its strangeness is that of a galloping centaur pulling a droshky crowded with groaning souls; or else it is a kaleidoscopic phantasmagoria, confined, churning, stuttering. St. Petersburg itself has the enclosed yet chaotic quality of a perpetual dusk, a town of riverbank and sky, taverns, tiny apartments cut up into rented cabins and cells, mazy alleys, narrow stairways, drunks, beggars, peddlers, bedraggled students, street musicians, whores—all darkened and smudged, as if the whole of the city were buried in a cellar, or in hell.

This irresistible deformation of commonly predictable experience is what fires Dostoyevsky's genius. Nabokov dislikes that genius (I dislike it too) because its language is a wilderness and there are woeful pockets of obscurantist venom at its center. But in the end *Crime and Punishment* is anything but a manifesto. Citizenly rebuttal is far from its delirious art. In the fever of his imagining, it is not the radicals Dostoyevsky finally rebukes, but the Devil himself, the master of sin, an unconquerable principality pitted against God.

Young Tolstoy: An Apostle of Desire

Contemplating the unpredictable trajectory of Tolstoy's life puts one in mind of those quizzical Max Beerbohm caricatures, wherein an old writer confronts—with perplexity, if not with contempt—his young self. So here is Tolstoy at seventy-two, dressed like a *muzhik* in belted peasant tunic and rough peasant boots, with the long hoary priestly beard of a vagabond pilgrim, traveling third class on a wooden bench in a fetid train carriage crowded with the ragged poor. In the name of the equality of souls he has turned himself into a cobbler; in the name of the pristine Jesus he is estranged from the rites and beliefs of Russian Orthodoxy; in the name of Christian purity he has abandoned wife and family. He is ascetic, celibate, pacifist. To the multitude of his followers and disciples (Gandhi among them), he is a living saint.

And over here—in the opposite panel—is Tolstoy at twenty-three: a dandy, a horseman, a soldier, a hunter, a tippler, a gambler, a wastrel, a frequenter of fashionable balls, a carouser among gypsies, a seducer of servant girls; an aristocrat immeasurably wealthy, inheritor of a far-flung estate, master of hundreds of serfs. Merely to settle a debt at cards, he thinks nothing of selling (together with livestock and a parcel of land) several scores of serfs.

In caricature the two—the old Tolstoy, the young Tolstoy—cannot be reconciled. In conscience, in contriteness, they very nearly can. The young Tolstoy's diaries are self-interrogations that lead to merciless self-indictments, pledges of spiritual regeneration, and utopian programs for both personal renewal and the amelioration of society at large. But the youthful reformer is also a consistent backslider. At twenty-six he writes scathingly, "I am ugly, awkward, untidy and socially uncouth. I am irritable and tiresome to others; immodest, intolerant and shy as a child. In other words, a boor . . . I am excessive, vacillating, unstable, stupidly vain and aggressive, like all weaklings. I am not courageous. I am so lazy that idleness has become an ineradicable habit with me." After admitting nevertheless to a love of virtue, he confesses: "Yet there is one thing I love more than virtue: fame. I am so ambitious, and this craving in me has had so little satisfaction, that if I had to choose between fame and virtue, I am afraid I would very often opt for the former."

A year later, as an officer stationed at Sevastopol during the Crimean War, he is all at once struck by a "grandiose, stupendous" thought. "I feel capable of devoting my life to it. It is the founding of a new religion, suited to the present state of mankind: the religion of Christ, but divested of faith and mysteries, a practical religion, not promising eternal bliss but providing bliss here on earth. I realize," he acknowledges, "that this idea can only become a reality after several generations have worked consciously toward it," but in the meantime he is still gambling, losing heavily, and complaining of "fits of lust" and "criminal sloth." The idealist is struggling in the body of the libertine; and the libertine is always, at least in the diaries, in pursuit of self-cleansing.

It was in one of these recurrent moods of purification in the wake of relapse that Tolstoy determined, in 1851, to go to the Caucasus, an untamed region of mountains, rivers, and steppes. He had deserted his university studies; he was obsessed by cards, sex, illusory infatuation; he was footloose and parentless. His mother had died when he was two, his father seven years later. He had been indulged by adoring elderly aunts, patient tutors, obsequious servants (whom he sometimes had flogged). When the family lands fell to him, he attempted to lighten the bruised and toilsome lives of his serfs; the new threshing machine he ordered failed, and behind his back they called him a madman. Futility and dissatisfaction dogged him. Once more a catharsis was called for, the hope of a fresh start innocent of salons and balls, in surroundings unspoiled by fashion and indolence, far from the silks and artifice of Moscow and St. Petersburg. Not fragile vows in a diary, but an act of radical displacement. If Rousseau was Tolstoy's inspiration—the philosopher's dream of untutored nature—his brother Nicholas, five years his senior, was his opportunity. Nicholas was an officer at a *stanitsa*, a Cossack outpost, in the Caucasus. Tolstoy joined him there as a zealous cadet. The zeal was for the expectation of military honors, but even more for the exhilaration of seeing Cossack life up close. The Cossacks, like their untrammeled landscape, were known to be wild and free; they stood for the purity of natural man, untainted by the affectations of an overrefined society.

So thinks Olenin, the young aristocrat whose sensibility is the motivating fulcrum of *The Cossacks*, the novel Tolstoy began in 1852, shortly after his arrival in the Caucasus. Like Tolstoy himself, Olenin at eighteen:

had been free as only the rich, parentless young of Russia's eighteen-forties could be. He had neither moral nor physical fetters. He could do anything he wanted . . . He gave himself up to all his passions, but only to the extent that they did not bind him . . . Now that he was leaving Moscow he was in that happy, youthful state of mind in which a young man, thinking of the mistakes he has committed, suddenly sees things in a different light—sees that these past mistakes were incidental and unimportant, that back then he had not wanted to live a good life, but that now, as he was leaving Moscow, a new life was beginning in which there would be no mistakes and no need for remorse. A life in which there would be nothing but happiness.

But the fictional Olenin is Tolstoy's alter ego only in part. After months of dissipation, each comes to the Caucasus as a volunteer soldier attached to a Russian brigade; each is in search of clarity of heart. Olenin, though, is a wistful outsider who is gradually drawn into the local mores, while his creator is a sophisticated and psychologically omniscient sympathizer with the eye of an evolving anthropologist.

After starting work on *The Cossacks*, Tolstoy soon set it aside and did not return to finish it until an entire decade had elapsed. In the interval, he continued to serve in the military for another three years; he published stories and novels; he traveled in Europe; he married. Still, there is little evidence of a hiatus; the narrative of *The Cossacks* is nearly seamless. It pauses only once, of necessity, in chapter four—which, strikingly distanced from character and story, and aiming to explain Cossack culture to the uninitiated, reads much like an entry in a popular encyclopedia. Terrain and villages are minutely noted; also dress, weapons, songs, shops, vineyards, hunting and fishing customs, the status and behavior of girls and women. "At the core of [Cossack] character," Tolstoy writes, "lies love of freedom, idleness, plunder, and war . . . A Cossack bears less hatred for a Chechen warrior who has killed his brother than for a Russian soldier billeted with him. . . . A dashing young Cossack will flaunt his knowledge of Tatar, and will even speak it with his brother Cossacks when he drinks and carouses with them. And yet this small group of Christians, cast off on a distant corner of the earth, surrounded by Russian soldiers and half-savage Mohammedan tribes, regard themselves as superior, and acknowledge only other Cossacks as their equals." On and on, passage after descriptive passage, these living sketches of Cossack society accumulate—so much so, that a contemporary critic observed, "A score of ethnological articles could not give a more complete, exact, and colorful picture of this part of our land."

303

Cynthia Ozick

The name "Cossack" appears to derive from a Turkic root meaning free-booter, or, in a milder interpretation, adventurer. As a distinct population group, the Cossacks grew out of a movement of peasants escaping serfdom, who in the fifteenth century fled to the rivers and barren plains of Ukraine and southeastern Russia, seeking political autonomy. Having established self-governing units in areas close to Muslim-dominated communities, whose dress and outlook they often assimilated, the Cossacks were eventually integrated into the Russian military; their villages became army outposts defending Russia against the furies of neighboring Chechen fighters. It is into this history—that of an admirable, courageous, independent people, in gaudy Circassian costume, the women as splendidly self-reliant as the men—that Tolstoy sets Olenin, his citified patrician. And it is vital for Tolstoy to halt his story before it has barely begun—momentarily to obliterate it from view—in order to supply his readers in Moscow and St. Petersburg with a geographical and sociological portrait of the land Olenin is about to encounter. For such readers, as for Olenin, the Cossacks are meant to carry the romantic magnetism of the noble primitive.

But there is a different, and far more sinister, strain of Cossack history, which Tolstoy omits, and which later readers—we who have passed through the bloody portals of the twentieth century—cannot evade. Tolstoy saw, and survived, war. We too have seen war; but we have also seen, and multitudes have not survived, genocide. The most savage of wars boasts a cause, or at least a pretext; genocide pretends nothing other than the lust for causeless slaughter. And it is genocide, it must be admitted, that is the ineluctable resonance of the term "Cossacks." Writing one hundred and fifty years ago, Tolstoy registers no consciousness of this genocidal association—the long trail of Cossack pogroms and butcheries; hence the Cossacks of his tale are merely conventional warriors. Lukashka, a young fighter, coldly fells a Chechen enemy; his companions vie for possession of the dead man's coat and weapons. Afterward they celebrate with pails of vodka. A flicker of humane recognition touches the killer, but is quickly snuffed: "'He too was a man,' Lukashka said, evidently admiring the dead Chechen." To which a fellow Cossack replies, "Yes, but if it had been up to him, he wouldn't have shown you any mercy." It is the language of war, of warriors, heinous enough, and regrettable—still, nothing beyond the commonplace.

Then is it conceivable that we know more, or wish to know more, than the majestic Tolstoy? Along with Shakespeare and Dante, he stands at the crest of world literature: who can own a deeper sensibility than that of Tolstoy, who can know more than he? But we do know more: through the grimness of time and the merciless retina of film, we have been witness to

304

indelible scenes of genocide. And it is because of this ineradicable contemporary knowledge of systematic carnage that Cossack history must now, willy-nilly, trigger tremor and alarm. Fast-forward from Tolstoy's 1850s to the year 1920: Isaac Babel, a Soviet reporter, is riding with the Red Cossacks (a brigade that has made common cause with the Bolsheviks); they are hoping forcibly to bring Poland to Communism. Babel, like Olenin, is a newcomer to the ways of the Cossacks, and he too is entranced by nature's stalwarts. In his private diary he marvels at these skilled and fearless horsemen astride their thundering mounts: "inexplicable beauty," he writes, "an awesome force advancing . . . red flags, a powerful, well-knit body of men, confident commanders, calm and experienced eyes." And again, describing a nocturnal tableau: "They eat together, sleep together, a splendid silent companionship . . . they sing songs that sound like church music in lusty voices, their devotion to horses, beside each man a little heap—saddle, bridle, ornamental saber, greatcoat."

But there is a lethal underside to this muscular idyll. Daily the Cossacks storm into the little Jewish towns of Polish Galicia, looting, burning, torturing, raping, branding, desecrating, murdering: they are out to slaughter every living Jew. Babel, a Jew who will become one of Russia's most renowned writers (and whom the Soviet secret police will finally execute), conceals his identity: no Jew can survive when Cossacks are near. (My own mother, who emigrated from Czarist Russia in 1906 at the age of nine, once confided, in a horrified whisper, how a great-uncle, seized in a Cossack raid, was tied by his feet to the tail of a horse; the Cossack galloped off, and the man's head went pounding on cobblestones until the skull was shattered.)

Tolstoy did not live to see the atrocities of 1920; he died in 1910, and by then he had long been a Christian pacifist; but surely he was aware of other such crimes. The Cossack depredations of the nineteenth century are infamous; yet these, and the mass killings Babel recorded, hardly weigh at all in comparison with the Chmielnicki massacres that are the bloodiest blot on Cossack history. In a single year, between 1648 and 1649, under the leadership of Bogdan Chmielnicki, Cossacks murdered three hundred thousand Jews, a number not exceeded until the rise of the genocidal Nazi regime.

None of this, it goes without saying, forms the background of Tolstoy's novel; *The Cossacks*, after all, is a kind of love story: its theme is longing. The seventeenth century is buried beyond our reach, and already the events of the middle of the twentieth have begun to recede into forgetfulness. All the same, the syllables of "Cossacks" even now retain their fearful death toll, and a reader of our generation who is not historically naïve, or willfully amnesiac, will not be deaf to their sound.

Yet Tolstoy's stories are above all always humane, and his depiction of his Cossacks is vigorously individuated and in many ways unexpectedly familiar. They are neither glorified nor demeaned, and they are scarcely the monsters of their collective annals; if they are idiosyncratic, it is only in the sense of the ordinary human article. *The Cossacks* was immediately acclaimed. Turgenev, older than Tolstoy by ten years, wrote rapturously, "I was carried away." Turgenev's colleague, the poet Afanasy Fet, exclaimed, "The ineffable superiority of genius!" and declared *The Cossacks* to be a masterpiece; and so it remains, validated by permanence. Then what are we to do with what we know? How are we to regard Tolstoy, who, though steeped in principles of compassion, turned away from what he knew?

The answer, I believe, lies in another principle, sometimes hard to come by. Not the solipsist credo that isolates literature from the world outside itself, but the idea of the sovereign integrity of story. Authenticity in fiction depends largely on point of view—so it is not Tolstoy's understanding of the shock of history that must be looked for; it is Olenin's. And it is certain that Olenin's mind is altogether bare of anything that will not stir the attention of a dissolute, rich, and copiously indulged young man who lives, like most young men of his kind, wholly in the present, prone to the prejudices of his class and time. Tolstoy means to wake him up—not to history, not to pity or oppression, but to the sublimeness of the natural world.

So come, reader, and never mind!—set aside the somber claims of history, at least for the duration of this airy novel. *A Midsummer Night's Dream* pays no heed to the Spanish Armada; *Pride and Prejudice* happily ignores the Napoleonic Wars; *The Cossacks* is unstained by old terrors. A bucolic fable is under way, and Olenin will soon succumb to the mountains, the forest, the village, the spirited young men, the bold young women. His first view of the horizon—"the massive mountains, clean and white in their gentle contours, the intricate, distinct line of the peaks and the sky"—captivates him beyond his stale expectations, and far more genuinely than the recent enthusiasms of Moscow: "Bach's music or love, neither of which he believed in."

> All his Moscow memories, the shame and repentance, all his foolish and trivial dreams about the Caucasus, disappeared forever. It was as if a solemn voice told him: "Now it has begun!". . . Two Cossacks ride by, their rifles in slings bouncing lightly on their backs, and the brown and gray legs of their horses blur—again the mountains. Across the Terek [river], smoke rises from a village—again the mountains. The sun rises and sparkles on the Terek, shimmering through the weeds—again the

mountains. A bullock cart rolls out of a Cossack village, the women are walking, beautiful young women—the mountains.

And almost in an instant Olenin is transformed, at least outwardly. He sheds his formal city clothes for a Circassian coat to which a dagger is strapped, grows a Cossack mustache and beard, and carries a Cossack rifle. Even his complexion alters, from an urban pallor to the ruddiness of clear mountain air. After three months of hard bivouac living, the Russian soldiers come flooding into the village, stinking of tobacco, their presence and possessions forced on unwilling Cossack hosts. Olenin is no ordinary soldier—his servant has accompanied him from Moscow, and he is plainly a gentleman who can pay well for his lodging, so he is quartered in one of the better accommodations, a gabled house with a porch, which belongs to the cornet, a man of self-conscious status: he is a teacher attached to the regiment. To make room for him, the cornet and his family must move into an adjacent thatch-roofed cabin: Olenin, like every Russian billeted in the village, is an unwelcome encroachment. "You think I need such a plague? A bullet into your bowels!" cries Old Ulitka, the cornet's wife. Maryanka, the daughter, gives him silent teasing hostile glances, and Olenin yearns to speak to her: "Her strong, youthful step, the untamed look in the flashing eyes peering over the edge of the white kerchief, and her strong, shapely body struck Olenin . . . 'She is the one!' he thought." And again:

He watched with delight how freely and gracefully she leaned forward, her pink smock clinging to her breasts and shapely legs, and how she straightened up, her rising breasts outlined clearly beneath the tight cloth. He watched her slender feet lightly touch the ground in their worn slippers, and her strong arms with rolled-up sleeves thrusting the spade into the dung as if in anger, her deep black eyes glancing at him. Though her delicate eyebrows frowned at times, her eyes expressed pleasure and awareness of their beauty.

But he cannot approach her. He is solitary, watchful, bemused by everything around him. He sits on his porch, reading, dreaming; alone and lost in the woods, he is overpowered by a spurt of mystical idealism. More and more the abandoned enticements and impressions of Moscow ebb, and more and more he immerses himself in Cossack habits. He befriends a garrulous, grizzled old hunter, Eroshka, a drunkard and a sponger, who teaches him the secrets of the forest and introduces him to *chikhir*, the local spirits. In and out of his cups, Eroshka is a rough-cut philosopher, ready to be blood brother to all—Tatars, Armenians, Russians. He mocks the priests, and believes that "when you croak, grass will grow over your grave, and that will be that." "There's no sin in anything," he tells Olenin. "It's all a lie!"

And meanwhile Maryanka continues elusive. She is being courted by Lukashka, whom Olenin both admires and envies. Lukashka is all that Olenin is not—brash, reckless, wild, a fornicator and carouser, fit for action, at one with the life of a fighter. He is a Cossack, and it is a Cossack—not Olenin—that is Maryanka's desire. Even when Olenin is finally and familiarly accepted by Old Ulitka, Maryanka resists. At bottom, *The Cossacks* is an old-fashioned love triangle, as venerable as literature itself; yet it cannot be consummated, on either man's behalf. Maryanka may not have Lukashka— violence destroys him. And she must repudiate Olenin: he is a stranger, and will always remain so. Despite the Circassian coat, despite Eroshka's embraces, despite the merrymaking *chikhir*, he is, unalterably, a Russian gentleman. He will never be a Cossack. In the end Moscow will reclaim him.

But Tolstoy's art has another purpose, apart from the regretful realism of the tale's denouement and its understated psychological wisdom. It is, in this novel, a young man's art, instinct with ardor—an ardor lacking any tendril of the judgmental. By contrast, the old Tolstoy, at seventy, pledged to religio-political issues of conscience, nevertheless declined to lend his moral weight to a manifesto seeking a reprieve for Dreyfus, the French Jewish officer falsely accused of treason. Though this was the cause célèbre of the age, Tolstoy was scornful: Dreyfus was hardly a man of the people; he was not a *muzhik*; he was not a pacifist believer. "It would be a strange thing," he insisted, "that we Russians should take up the defense of Dreyfus, an utterly undistinguished man, when so many exceptional ones have been hanged, deported, or imprisoned at home." His polemical engines charged instead into a campaign on behalf of the Dukhobors, an ascetic communal sect that refused to bear arms and, like Tolstoy himself, preached nonresistance to evil. A brutal initiative urged by the Czar had exiled the group to the Caucasus, where at the government's behest bands of Cossack horsemen surrounded the sectarians, whipped and maimed them, and pillaged their houses. Tolstoy was outraged, and in a letter to the Czar protested that such religious persecutions were "the shame of Russia." That among the agents of persecution were the selfsame Cossack daredevils about whom he had written so enchantingly forty years before will perhaps not escape notice.

And again: never mind! The young Tolstoy is here possessed less by social commitment than by the sensory. His visionary lyricism exults in Maryanka's strong legs, and in the mountains, woods, and sparkling rivers of the Caucasus. The Caucasus is his motive and his message. Natural beauty is his lure. Tolstoy's supremacy in capturing heat, weather, dust, the thick odors of the vineyard, culminates in a voluptuous passage:

> The villagers were swarming over the melon fields and over the vine-
> yards that lay in the stifling shade, clusters of ripe black grapes
> shimmering among broad translucent leaves. Creaking carts heaped high
> with grapes made their way along the road leading from the vineyards,
> and grapes crushed by the wheels lay everywhere in the dust. Little
> boys and girls, their arms and mouths filled with grapes and their shirts
> stained with grape juice, ran after their mothers. Tattered laborers car-
> ried filled baskets on powerful shoulders. Village girls, kerchiefs wound
> tightly across their faces, drove bullocks harnessed to local carts. Sol-
> diers by the roadside asked for grapes, and the women climbed into the
> rolling carts and threw bunches down, the men holding out their shirt
> flaps to catch them. In some courtyards the grapes were already being
> pressed, and the aroma of grape-skin leavings filled the air. . . . Laugh-
> ter, song, and the happy voices of women came from within a sea of
> shadowy green vines, through which their smocks and kerchiefs peeked.

The scene is Edenic, bursting with fecundity, almost biblical in its over-flowingness. Scents and juices spill out of every phrase: it is Tolstoy's sensuous genius at its ripest. Olenin will return to Moscow, yes; but his eyes have been dyed by the grape harvest, and he will never again see as he once saw, before the Caucasus, before Maryanka, before the mountains. The novel's hero is the primordial earth itself, civilization's dream of the pastoral. The old Tolstoy—that crabbed puritanical sermonizing septuagenarian who wrote *What Is Art?*, a tract condemning the pleasures of the senses—might wish to excoriate the twenty-something author of *The Cossacks*. The old Tol-stoy is the apostle of renunciation. But the young Tolstoy, who opens Olenin to the intoxications of the natural world, and to the longings of love, means to become, at least for a time, an apostle of desire.

I. B. Singer's Book of Creation

Some time ago, when Isaac Bashevis Singer first mounted the public platform to speak in English, he was asked whether he really believed in *sheydim*—in imps and demons, ghosts and spirits. The response, partly a skip and partly a glint, followed considerable playful pondering and ended in a long shrug: "Yes and no." The rebuke of an imp guarding secrets, one might judge—but surely a lesser imp, capable mainly of smaller mischiefs: the knotting of elflocks in the audience's hair, perhaps.

Years pass; the astonishing stories accumulate; the great Nobel is almost upon Singer, and the question reliably recurs. Now the answer is direct and speedy: "Yes, I believe there are unknown forces." This is no longer the voice of a teasing imp. Never mind that its tone clearly belongs to an accustomed celebrity who can negotiate a question period with a certain shameless readiness; it is also a deliberate leaning into the wind of some powerful dark wing, fearsomely descried.

Whether the majesty of the Nobel Prize in Literature has since altered Singer's manipulation of this essential question, I do not know. Nevertheless the question remains central, though not quite so guileless as it appears. Should we believe that Singer believes in the uncanny and the preternatural? Is there ever a trustworthy moment when a storymonger is not making things up, especially about his own substance and sources? Doesn't an antic fancy devoted to cataloguing folly always trifle with earnest expectation? And what are we to think of the goblin cunning of a man who has taken his mother's given name—Bashevis (i.e., Bathsheba)—to mark out the middle of his own? Singer's readers in Yiddish call him, simply, "Bashevis." A sentimental nom de plume? His is anything but a nostalgic imagination. Does the taking-on of "Bashevis" imply a man wishing to be a woman? Or does it mean that a woman is hiding inside a man? Or does Singer hope somehow to entangle his own passions in one of literature's lewdest and nastiest plots: King David's crafty devisings concerning the original Bathsheba? Or does he dream of attracting to himself the engendering powers of his mother's soul through the assumption of her name? Given the witness of the tales themselves, we are obliged to suspect any or all of these notions, as well as others we have not the wit of fantasy to conjure up.

Accordingly, nearly every one of the forty-seven stories in The *Collected Stories of Isaac Bashevis Singer* is a snail-whorl narrative grown out of similar schemings, impersonations, contrivances, devices, and transmutations. The story of David and Bathsheba is, without fail, one that Singer's plot-fecundity might have churned up, though it would likely be a demon that dispatches Uriah the Hittite. The story of a woman taking on the semblance of a man, Singer has in fact already invented, in "Yentl the Yeshiva Boy," a remarkable fable about a girl who lusts after scholarship. In "The Dead Fiddler," coarse Getsel, in the form of a dybbuk, hides inside a woman, causing the delicate Liebe Yentle to swig and swear. As for the acquisition of names that confer eccentric or arrogant ambitions, there is Zeidel Cohen, a descendant of the exegete Rashi, who prepares to become Zeidlus the First, Pope of Rome; and Alchonon the teacher's helper, a plain fellow who succeeds in passing himself off, in "Taibele and Her Demon," as the lecherous Hurmizah, step-nephew of Asmodeus, King of the Demons.

On one flank Singer is a trickster, a prankster, a Loki, a Puck. His themes are lust, greed, pride, obsession, misfortune, unreason, the oceanic surprises of the mind's underside, the fiery cauldron of the self, the assaults of time and place. His stories offer no "epiphanies" and no pious resolutions; no linguistic circumscriptions or Heming-wayesque self-deprivations. Their plenitudes chiefly serve undefended curiosity, the gossip's lure of what-comes-next. Singer's stories have plots that unravel not because they are "old-fashioned"—they are mostly originals and have few recognizable modes other than their own—but because they contain the whole human world of affliction, error, quagmire, pain, calamity, catastrophe, woe: things happen; life is an ambush, a snare; one's fate can never be predicted. His driven, mercurial processions of predicaments and transmogrifications are limitless, often stupendous. There are whole fistfuls of masterpieces in this one volume: a cornucopia of invention.

Because he cracks open decorum to find lust, because he peers past convention into the pit of fear, Singer has in the past been condemned by other Yiddish writers outraged by his seemingly pagan matter, his superstitious villagers, his daring leaps into gnostic furies. The moral grain of Jewish feeling that irradiates the mainstream aspirations of Yiddish literature has always been a kind of organic extension of Talmudic ethical ideals: family devotion, community probity, *derekh erets*—self-respect and respect for others—the stringent expectations of high public civility and indefatigable integrity, the dream of messianic betterment. In Singer, much of this seems absent or overlooked or simply mocked; it is as if he has willed the crashing-down of traditional Jewish sanity and sensibility. As a result, in Yiddish literary circles he is sometimes viewed as—it is the title of one of these stories—"The Betrayer of Israel."

In fact, he betrays nothing and no one, least of all Jewish idealism. That is the meaning of his imps and demons: that human character, left to itself, is drawn to cleanliness of heart; that human motivation, on its own, is attracted to clarity and valor. Here is Singer's other flank, and it is the broader one. The goblin cunning leads straight to this: Singer is a moralist. He tells us that it is natural to be good, and unholy to go astray. It is only when Lilith creeps in, or Samael, or Ketev Mriri, or the sons of Asmodeus, that evil and impurity are kindled. It is the inhuman, the antihuman, forces that are to blame for harms and sorrows. Surely these imps must be believed in; they may have the telltale feet of geese—like Satan, their sire—but their difficult, shaming, lubricious urges are terrestrially familiar. Yet however lamentably known they are, Singer's demons are intruders, invaders, no true or welcome part of ourselves. They are "psychology"; and history; and terror; above all, obsessive will. If he believes in them, so, unwillingly but genuinely, do we.

And to understand Singer's imps is to correct another misapprehension: that he is the recorder of a lost world, the preserver of a vanished sociology. Singer is an artist and transcendent inventor, not a curator. His tales—though dense with the dailiness of a God-covenanted culture, its folkways, its rounded sufficiency, especially the rich intensities of the yeshiva and its bottomless studies—are in no way documents. The Jewish townlets that truly were are only seeds for his febrile conflagrations: where, outside of peevish imagination, can one come on the protagonist of "Henne Fire," a living firebrand, a spitfire burning up with spite, who ultimately, through the spontaneous combustion of pure fury, collapses into "one piece of coal"? Though every doorstep might be described, and every feature of a head catalogued (and Singer's portraits are brilliantly particularized), parables and fables are no more tied to real places and faces than Aesop's beasts are beasts.

This is not to say that Singer's stories do not mourn those murdered Jewish townlets of Poland, every single one of which, with nearly every inhabitant, was destroyed by the lords and drones of the Nazi Gehenna. This volume includes a masterly memorial to that destruction, the broken-hearted testimony of "The Last Demon," which begins emphatically with a judgment on Europe: "I, a demon, bear witness that there are no more demons left. Why demons, when man himself is a demon?" And sums up:

> I've seen it all . . . the destruction of Poland. There are no more Jews, no more demons. The women don't pour out water any longer on the night of the winter solstice. They don't avoid giving things in even numbers. They no longer knock at dawn at the antechamber of the synagogue. They don't warn us before emptying the slops. The rabbi was martyred on a Friday in the month of Nissan. The community was slaughtered, the holy books burned, the cemetery desecrated. *The Book of Creation* has been returned to the Creator . . . No more sins, no more temptations! . . . Messiah did not come for the Jews, so the Jews went to Messiah. There is no further need for demons.

This tenderness for ordinary folk, their superstitions, their folly, their plainness, their lapses, is a classical thread of Yiddish fiction, as well as the tree trunk of Singer's own hasidic legacy—love and reverence for the down-to-earth. "The Little Shoemakers" bountifully celebrates the Fifth Commandment with leather and awl; the hero of "Gimpel the Fool," a humble baker, is endlessly duped and stubbornly drenched in permanent grace; the beautiful story "Short Friday" ennobles a childless old couple who, despite privation and barrenness, turn their unscholarly piety into comeliness and virtue. Shmuel-Leibele's immaculate happiness in prayer, Shoshe's meticulous Sabbath meal, shine with saintliness; Singer recounts the menu, "chicken soup with noodles and tiny circlets of fat . . . like golden ducats," as if even soup can enter holiness. Through a freakish accident—snow covers their little house and they are asphyxiated—the loving pair ascend in death together to paradise. When the demons are stilled, human yearning aspires toward goodness and joy. (Singer fails to note, however, whether God or Samael sent the pure but deadly snow.)

In Singer the demons are rarely stilled, and the luminous serenity of "Short Friday" is an anomaly. Otherwise pride furiously rules, and wild-hearted imps dispose of human destiny. In "The Unseen," a prosperous and decent husband runs off with a lusty maidservant at the urging of a demon; he ends in destitution, a hidden beggar tended by his remarried wife. "The Gentleman from Cracow" corrupts a whole town with gold; he turns out to be Ketev Mriri himself. In "The Destruction of Kreshev," a scholar who is a secret Sabbatian and devil-worshiper induces his wife to commit adultery with a Panlike coachman. Elsewhere, excessive intellectual passion destroys genius. An accomplished young woman is instructed by a demon to go to the priest, convert, and abandon her community; the demon assumes the voice of the girl's grandmother, herself the child of a Sabbatian. A rabbi is "plagued by something new and terrifying: wrath against the Creator," and struggles to fashion himself into an atheist. Character and motive are turned inside out at the bidding of imps who shove, snarl, seduce, bribe, cajole. Allure ends in rot; lure becomes punishment.

This phantasmagorical universe of ordeal and mutation and shock is, finally, as intimately persuasive as logic itself. There is no fantasy in it. It is the true world we know, where we have come to expect anguish as the consequence of our own inspirations, where we crash up against the very circumstance from which we had always imagined we were exempt. In this true world suffering is endemic and few are forgiven. Yet it may be that for Singer the concrete presence of the unholy attests the hovering redemptive holy, whose incandescence can scatter demons. *Yes, I believe in unknown forces.*

Not all the stories in this collection emerge from the true world, however. The eerie authority of "The Cabbalist of East Broadway" is a gripping exception, but in general the narratives set in the American environment are, by contrast, too thin. Even when intentionally spare—as in the marvelous "Vanvild Kava," with its glorious opening: "If a Nobel Prize existed for writing little, Vanvild Kava would have gotten it"—the European settings have a way of turning luxuriantly, thickly coherent. Presumably some of these American locales were undertaken in a period when the fertile seed of the townlets had begun to be exhausted; or else it is the fault of America itself, lacking the centrifugal density and identity of a yeshiva society, the idea of community as an emanation of God's gaze. Or perhaps it is because many of these American stories center on Singer as writer and celebrity, or on someone like him. It is as if the predicaments that fly into his hands nowadays arrive because he is himself the centrifugal force, the controlling imp. And an imp, to have efficacy, as Singer's genius has shown, must be a kind of dybbuk, moving in powerfully from outside; whereas the American narratives are mainly inside jobs, about the unusual "encounters" a famous writer meets up with.

The Collected Stories is supplied with a sparse author's note (misleadingly called an Introduction on the book jacket), but it is unsatisfyingly patched, imbalanced, cursory; anyone trusting imps will fail to trust the note. Apparently Singer thinks fiction is currently under a threat from "the zeal for messages." I wish it were possible to list every translator's name, from Saul Bellow, Isaac Rosenfeld, Dorothea Strauss, Mirra Ginsburg, and Joseph Singer to the less renowned Ruth Schachner Finkel, Evelyn Torton

Beck, Herbert Lottman, Rosanna Gerber, Elizabeth Schub, and all the rest. It is interesting that there are so many, and that there are always new ones. Singer has not yet found his Lowe-Porter or Scott Moncrieff. Still, the voice is steady and consistent, as if there were only one voice; undoubtedly it is the imposition of Singer's own. After all these years, the scandalous rumors about Singer's relation to his changing translators do not abate: how they are half-collaborators, half-serfs, how they start out sunk in homage, accept paltry fees, and end disgruntled or bemused, yet transformed, having looked on Singer plain. One wishes Singer would write their frenzied tale, set it in Zamość, and call it "Rabbi Bashevis's Helpers." In any event, his helpers cannot reach the deep mine and wine of Singer's mother tongue, thronged (so it was once explained to me by a Tel Aviv poet accomplished in Hebrew, Yiddish, and English) with that unrenderable Hebrew erudition and burnished complexity of which we readers in English have not an inkling, and are permanently deprived. Deprived? Perhaps. *The Collected Stories*, when all is said and done, is an American master's Book of Creation.

The Sister Melons of J. M. Coetzee

The literature of conscience is ultimately about the bewilderment of the naive. Why do men carry guns and build prison camps, when the nurturing earth is made for freedom? To the outcast, the stray, the simpleton, the unsuspecting—to the innocent–the ideologies that order society are inane, incomprehensible. Comprehension comes unaccoutered, stripped, uninstructed—like Huck Finn on the loose, who merely knows what he knows. And what the pariah Huck knows, against the weight and law and common logic of his slaveholding "sivilization," is that the black man is whole, the rightful owner of his life and times.

In *Life & Times of Michael K*, J. M. Coetzee, a South African born in 1940, has rewritten the travail of Huck's insight, but from the black man's point of view, and set in a country more terrible—because it is a living bitter hardhearted contemporary place, the parable-world of an unregenerate soon-after-now, with little pity and no comedy. Conscience, insight, innocence: Michael K cannot aspire to such high recognitions—he is "dull," his mind is "not quick." He was born fatherless and with a disfigurement: a harelip that prevented him from being nourished at his mother's breast. When he needs some tools to make a cart to transport his dying mother, he breaks into a locked shed and takes them. The smallest transgression, undetected and unpunished, the single offense of his life; yet nearly every moment of his life is judged as if he were guilty of some huge and undisclosed crime—not for nothing is his surname resonant with the Kafkan "K." His crime is his birth. When as a schoolchild he is perplexed by long division, he is "committed to the protection" of a state-run orphanage for the "variously afflicted." From then on he is consistently protected—subject to curfews, police permits, patrols, convoys, sentries, guns, a work camp with wire fences, a semi-benevolent prison hospital: tyranny, like his school, "at the expense of the state."

Though a mote in the dustheap of society, he is no derelict. From the age of fifteen he has worked as a gardener in a public park in Cape Town. His worn and profoundly scrupulous mother also lives honorably; she is a domestic servant for a decent enough elderly couple in a posh seaside apartment house. They have gone to the trouble of keeping a room for her—an unused basement storage closet without electricity or ventilation. Her duties end at eight o'clock at night six days a week. When she falls ill, she is dependent on the charity of her employers. The building is attacked, vandalized, the residents driven out. Michael K is laid off. The country is at war.

The purpose of the war, from one standpoint—that of a reasonable-minded prison-master—is "so that minorities will have a say in their destinies." This is indisputably the language of democratic idealism. In a South African context such a creed unexpectedly turns Orwellian: it means repression of the black majority by the white minority. Yet in Coetzee's tale we are not told who is black and who is white, who is in power and who is not. Except for the reference to Cape Town and to place names that are recognizably Afrikaans, we are not even told that this is the physical and moral landscape of South Africa. We remain largely uninstructed because we are privy solely to Michael K's heart, an organ that does not deal in color or power, a territory foreign to abstractions and doctrines; it knows only what is obvious and elemental. Another way of putting this is to say that—though there is little mention anywhere of piety or faith, and though it is the prison-masters alone who speak sympathetically and conscientiously of rights and of freedom— Michael K responds only to what appears to be divinely ordered, despite every implacable decree and manmade restraint. He names no tyranny and no ideal. He cares for his mother; he cares for the earth; he will learn how they come to the same in the end.

With laborious tenderness, with intelligent laboriousness—how intelligent he is!—Michael K builds a crude hand-drawn vehicle to restore his mother to a lost place that has become the frail ephemeral text of her illness, no more substantial than a vision: a bit of soil with a chicken run, where she remembers having once been happy in childhood. The town nearest this patch is only five hours away, but without a permit they may not go by train. No permit arrives. They set out clandestinely, the young man heaving the weight of his old mother in the cart, dodging military convoys, hiding, the two of them repeatedly assaulted by cold and bad weather and thugs with knives. To Michael K at the start of the journey, brutality and danger and stiffness of limb and rain seem all the same; tyranny feels as natural an ordeal as the harshness of the road.

On the road his mother deteriorates so piteously that Michael K must surrender her to a hospital. There he is shunted aside and she dies. Without consultation her body is cremated and given back to him, a small bundle of ashes in a plastic bag. He holds his mother's dust and imagines the burning halo of her hair. Then, still without permission, he returns her to the place of her illumination and buries her ashes. It is a grassy nowhere, a guess, the cloudrack of a dream of peace, the long-abandoned farm of a departed Afrikaaner family, a forgotten and unrecorded spot fallen through the brute mesh of totalitarian surveillance.

And here begins the parable of Michael K's freedom and resourcefulness; here begins Michael K's brief bliss. He is Robinson Crusoe, he is the lord of his life. It is his mother's own earth; it is his motherland; he lives in a womblike burrow; he tills the fruitful soil. Miracles sprout from a handful of discovered seeds: "Now two pale green melons were growing on the far side of the field. It seemed to him that he loved these two, which he thought of as two sisters, even more than the pumpkins, which he thought of as a band of brothers. Under the melons he placed pads of grass so that their skins should not bruise." He eats with deep relish, in the fulfillment of what is ordained: the work of his hands, a newfound sovereignty over his own hands and the blessing of fertility in his own scrap of ground. "I am becoming a different kind of man," he reflects. For the first time he is unprotected. When he has grown almost unafraid, civilization intrudes.

A whining boy who is a runaway soldier takes over the farmhouse and declares himself in need of a servant. A group of guerrillas and their donkeys pass through by night and trample the seedlings. Michael K flees; he is picked up as a "parasite " and confined to a work camp. But because he has lived in the field as a free man—in the field "he was not a prisoner or a castaway . . . he was himself'—he has learned how to think and judge. "What if the hosts were far outnumbered by the parasites, the parasites of idleness and the other secret parasites in the army and the police force and the schools and the factories and offices, the parasites of the heart? Could the parasites then be called parasites? Parasites too had flesh and substance; parasites too could be preyed upon . . ."

From the seed of freedom Michael K has raised up a metaphysics. It is not the coarse dogma of a killer-rebel or a terrorist; he does not join the guerrillas. He sees vulnerable children on all sides—the runaway who wants to be taken care of, the careless insurgents who are like "young men come off the field after a hard game," even the young camp guard with diabetes, callous and threatening, yet willing to share his food, who will end up as a prisoner himself. "How many people are there left who are neither locked up nor standing guard at the gate?"

But behind the gate Michael K cannot eat, cannot swallow, cannot get nourishment, and now Coetzee turns his parable to one of starvation. Repression wastes. Tyranny makes skeletons. Injustice will be vomited up. "Maybe he only eats the bread of freedom," says a doctor in the camp for "rehabilitation," where Michael K is next incarcerated. His body is "crying to be fed its own food, and only that." Behind the wire fences of a politics organized by curfew and restriction, where essence is smothered by law, and law is lie, Michael K is set aside as a rough mindless lost unfit creature, a simpleton or an idiot, a savage. It is a wonder, the doctor observes, that he has been able to keep himself alive. He is "the runt of the cat's litter," "the obscurest of the obscure." Thus the judgment of benevolent arrogance—or compassion indistinguishable from arrogance—on the ingenious farmer and visionary free man of his mother's field.

Coetzee is a writer of clarifying inventiveness and translucent conviction. Both are given voice gradually, seepingly, as if time itself were a character in the narrative. "There is time enough for everything." As in his previous novel, *Waiting for the Barbarians*, Coetzee's landscapes of suffering are defined by the little-by-little art of moral disclosure—his stories might be about anyone and anyplace. At the same time they defy the vice of abstraction; they are engrossed in the minute and the concrete. It would be possible, following Coetzee's dazzlingly precise illuminations, to learn how to sow, or use a pump, or make a house of earth. The grain of his sentences is flat and austere, and so purifying to the senses that one comes away feeling that one's eye has been sharpened, one's hearing vivified, not only for the bright proliferations of nature, but for human unexpectedness.

If *Life & Times of Michael K* has a flaw, it is in the density of its own interior interpretations. In the final quarter we are removed, temporarily, from the plain seeing of Michael K to the self-indulgent diary of the prison doctor who struggles with the entanglements of an increasingly abusive regime. But the doctor's commentary is superfluous; he thickens the clear tongue of the novel by naming its "message" and thumping out ironies. For one thing, he spells out what we have long ago taken in with the immediacy of intuition and possession. He construes, he translates: Michael K is "an original soul . . . untouched by doctrine, untouched by history . . . evading the peace and the war . . . drifting through time, observing the seasons, no more trying to change the course of history than a grain of sand does." All this is redundant. The sister-melons and the brother-pumpkins have already had their eloquent say. And the lip of the child kept from its mother's milk has had its say. And the man who grows strong and intelligent when he is at peace in his motherland has had his say.

Coetzee's subdued yet urgent lament is for the sadness of a South Africa that has made dependents and parasites and prisoners of its own children, black and white. (Not to mention more ambiguously imprisoned groups: Indians, "coloreds," the troubled and precarious Jewish community.) Moreover, Coetzee makes plain that the noble endurances and passionate revelations of Michael K do not mask a covert defense of terror; although he evades no horrors, existing or to come, Coetzee has not written a symbolic novel about the inevitability of guerrilla war and revolution in a country where oppression and dependency are breathed with the air. Instead, he discloses, in the language of imagination, the lumbering hoaxes and self-deceptions of stupidity. His theme is the wild and merciless power of inanity. Michael K suffers from the obdurate callowness of both sides, rulers and rebels—one tramples the vines, the other blows up the pump. At the end of the story, he dreams of drinking the living water drawn out of his mother's earth, if only drop by drop, if only from a teaspoon.

For the sake of the innocent, time is Coetzee's hope.

What Drives Saul Bellow

A concordance, a reprise, a summary, all the old themes and obsessions hauled up by a single tough rope—does there come a time when, out of the blue, a writer offers to decode himself? Not simply to divert, or paraphrase, or lead around a corner, or leave clues, or set out decoys (familiar apparatus, art-as-usual), but to kick aside the maze, spill wine all over the figure in the carpet, bury the grand metaphor, and disclose the thing itself? To let loose, in fact, the secret? And at an hour no one could have predicted? And in a modestly unlikely form? The cumulative art concentrated, so to speak, in a vial?

For Saul Bellow, at age sixty-eight, and with his Nobel speech some years behind him, the moment for decoding is now, and the decoding itself turns up unexpectedly in the shape of *Him with His Foot in His Mouth*, a volume of five stories, awesome yet imperfect, at least one of them overtly a fragment, and none malleable enough to achieve a real "ending." Not that these high-pressure stories are inconclusive. With all their brilliant wiliness of predicament and brainy language shocked into originality, they are magisterially the opposite. They tell us, in the clarified tight compass he has not been so at home in since *Seize the Day*, what drives Bellow.

What drives Bellow. The inquiry is seductive, because Bellow is Bellow, one of three living American Nobel laureates (the only one, curiously, whose natural language is English), a writer for whom great fame has become a sort of obscuring nimbus, intruding on the cleanly literary. When *The Dean's December* was published in 1982, it was not so much reviewed as scrutinized like sacred entrails: had this idiosyncratically independent writer turned "conservative"? Had he soured on Augiesque America? Was his hero, Albert Corde, a lightly masked Saul Bellow? Can a writer born into the Jewish condition successfully imagine and inhabit a WASP protagonist? In short, it seemed impossible to rid Bellow's novel of Bellow's presence, to free it as fiction.

In consequence of which, one is obliged to put a riddle: if you found this book of stories at the foot of your bed one morning, with the title page torn away and the author's name concealed, would you know it, after all, to be Bellow? Set aside, for the interim, the ruckus of advertised "models": that Victor Wulpy of "What Kind of Day Did You Have?" has already been identified as the art critic Harold Rosenberg, Bellow's late colleague at the University of Chicago's Committee on Social Thought; that the prodigy-hero of "Zetland: By a Character Witness" is fingered as the double of Isaac Rosenfeld, Bellow's boyhood friend, a writer and Reichian who died at thirty-eight. There are always antireaders, resenters or recanters of the poetry side of life, mean distrusters of the force and turbulence of the free imagination, who are ready to demote fiction to the one-on-one flatness of photo-journalism. Omitting, then, extraterritorial interests not subject to the tractable laws of fiction—omitting *gossip*—would you recognize Bellow's muscle, his swift and glorious eye?

Yes, absolutely; a thousand times yes. It is Bellow's Chicago, Bellow's portraiture—these faces, these heads!—above all, Bellow's motor. That Bellow himself may acknowledge a handful of biographical sources—"germs," textured shells—does not excite. The life on the page resists the dust of flesh, and is indifferent to external origins. Victor Wulpy is who he is as Bellow's invention; and certainly Zetland. These inventions take us not to Bellow as man, eminence, and friend of eminences (why should I care whom Bellow knows?), but to the private clamor in the writing. And it is this clamor, this sound of a thrashing soul—comic because metaphysical, metaphysical because aware of itself as a farcical combatant on a busy planet—that is unequivocally distinguishable as the pure Bellovian note. "The clever, lucky old Berlin Jew, whose head was like a round sourdough loaf, all uneven and dusted with flour, had asked the right questions"—if this canny sentence came floating to us over the waves, all alone on a dry scrap inside a bottle, who would not instantly identify it as Bellow's voice?

It is a voice demonized by the right (or possibly the right) questions. The characters it engenders are dazed by what may be called the principle of plenitude. Often they appear to take startled credit for the wild ingenuity of the world's abundance, as if they had themselves brought it into being. It isn't that they fiddle with the old freshman philosophy-course conundrum, Why is there everything instead of nothing? They ask rather: What is this everything composed of? What is it preoccupied with? They are knocked out by the volcanic multiplicity of human thought, they want to count up all the ideas that have ever accumulated in at least our part of the universe, they roil, burn, quake with cosmic hunger. This makes them, sometimes, jesters, and sometimes only sublime fools.

"What Kind of Day Did You Have?," the novella that is the centerpiece of this volume, also its masterpiece, gives us a day in the life of "one of the intellectual captains of the modern world"—Victor Wulpy, who, if love is sublime and lovers foolish, qualifies as a reacher both high and absurd. Reaching for the telephone in a Buffalo hotel, Victor calls his lover, Katrina Goliger, in suburban Chicago, and invites—commands—her to fly in zero weather from Chicago to Buffalo solely in order to keep him company on his flight from Buffalo to Chicago. "With Victor refusal was not one of her options," so Trina, sourly divorced, the mother of two unresponsive young daughters, acquiesces. Victor's egotism and self-indulgence, the by-blows of a nearly fatal recent illness and of a powerfully centered arrogance, are as alluring as his fame, his dependency, his brilliance, his stiff game leg "extended like one of Admiral Nelson's cannon under wraps," his size-sixteen shoes that waft out "a human warmth" when Trina tenderly pulls them off. Victor is a cultural lion who exacts, Trina surmises, ten thousand dollars per lecture. In Buffalo his exasperating daughter, a rabbinical school dropout who once advised her decorous mother to read a manual on homosexual foreplay as a means of recapturing Victor's sexual interest, hands him her violin to lug to Chicago for repairs; it is Trina who does the lugging. Victor is headed for Chicago to address the Executives Association, "National Security Council types," but really to be with Trina. Trina suffers from a carping angry sister, a doting hanger-on named Krieggstein, who carries guns and may or may not be a real cop, and the aftermath of a divorce complicated by psychiatric appointments, custody wrangling, greed. She is also wrestling with the perplexities of a children's story she hopes to write, if only she can figure out how to extricate her elephant from his crisis on the top floor of a department store, with no way down or out. At the same time Victor is being pursued, in two cities, by Wrangel, a white-furred Hollywood plot-concocter, celebrated maker of *Star Wars*–style films, a man hot with ideas who is impelled to tell Victor that "ideas are trivial" and Trina that Victor is a "promoter."

Meanwhile, planes rise and land, or don't take off at all; there is a bad-weather detour to Detroit and a chance for serendipitous sex in an airport hotel, and finally a perilous flight in a Cessna, where, seemingly facing death in a storm, Trina asks Victor to say he loves her. He refuses, they touch down safely at O'Hare, the story stops but doesn't exactly end. Wrangel has helped Trina dope out what to do about the trapped elephant, but Trina herself is left tangled in her troubles, submissively energetic and calculating, and with no way up or out.

What emerges from these fluid events, with all their cacophonous espousal of passion, is a mind at the pitch of majesty. The agitated, untamable, yet flagging figure of the dying Victor Wulpy, a giant in the last days of his greatness, seizes us not so much for the skein of shrewd sympathy and small pathos in which he is bound and exposed, as for the claims of these furious moments of insatiable connection: "Katrina had tried to keep track of the subjects covered between Seventy-sixth Street and Washington Square: the politics of modern Germany from the Holy Roman Empire through the Molotov-Ribbentrop Pact; what surrealist communism had really been about; Kiesler's architecture; Hans Hofmann's influence; what limits were set by liberal democracy for the development of the arts . . . Various views on the crises in economics, cold war, metaphysics, sexaphysics."

Not that particular "subjects" appear fundamentally to matter to Bellow, though they thrillingly engage him. The young Zetland, discovering *Moby-Dick*, cries out to his wife: "There really is no human life without this poetry. Ah, Lottie, I've been starving on symbolic logic." In fact he has been thriving on it, and on every other kind of knowledge. "What were we here for, of all strange beings and creatures the strangest? Clear colloid eyes to see with, for a while, and see so finely, and a palpitating universe to see, and so many human messages to give and receive. And the bony box for thinking and for the storage of thought, and a cloudy heart for feelings."

It is the hound of heaven living in the bony box of intelligence that dogs Bellow, and has always dogged him. If the soul is the mind at its purest, best, clearest, busiest, profoundest, then Bellow's charge has been to restore the soul to American literature. The five stories in *Him with His Foot in His Mouth* are the distillation of that charge. Bellow's method is to leave nothing unobserved and unremarked, to give way to the unprogrammed pressure of language and intellect, never to retreat while imagination goes off like kites. These innovative sentences, famous for pumping streetsmarts into literary blood vessels, are alive and snaky, though hot. And Bellow's quick-witted lives of near-poets, as recklessly confident in the play and intricacy of ideas as those of the grand Russians, are Russian also in the gusts of natural force that sweep through them: unpredictable cadences, instances where the senses fuse ("A hoarse sun rolled up"), single adjectives that stamp whole portraits, portraits that stamp whole lives (hair from which "the kink of high vigor had gone out"), the knowing hand on the ropes of how-things-work, the stunning catalogues of worldliness ("commodity brokers, politicians, personal-injury lawyers, bagmen and fixers, salesmen and promoters"), the boiling presence of Chicago, with its "private recesses for seduction and skuldug-gery." A light flavoring of Jewish social history dusts through it all: e.g., Victor Wulpy reading the Pentateuch in Hebrew in a cheder on the Lower East Side in 1912; or Zetland's immigrant father, who, in a Chicago neighborhood "largely Polish and Ukrainian, Swedish, Catholic, Orthodox, and Evangelical Lutheran . . . preferred the company of musical people and artists, bohemian garment workers, Tolstoyans, followers of Emma Goldman and of Isadora Duncan, revolutionaries who wore pince-nez, Russian blouses, Lenin or Trotsky beards."

What this profane and holy comedy of dazzling, beating, multiform pro-fusion hints at, paradoxically, is that Bellow is as notable for what isn't in his pages as for what is. No preciousness, of the ventriloquist kind or any other; no carelessness either (formidably the opposite); no romantic aping of archa-isms or nostalgias; no restraints born out of theories of form, or faddish tenets of experimentalism or ideological crypticness; no neanderthal flatness in the name of cleanliness of prose; no gods of nihilism; no gods of subjectiv-ity; no philosophy of parody. As a consequence of these and other salubrious omissions and insouciant dismissals, Bellow's detractors have accused him of being "old-fashioned," "conventional," of continuing to write a last-gasp American version of the nineteenth-century European novel; his omnivorous "Russianness" is held against him, and at the same time he is suspected of expressing the deadly middle class.

The grain of truth in these disparagements takes note, I think, not of regression or lagging behind, but of the condition of local fiction, which has more and more closeted itself monkishly away in worship of its own litur-gies—i.e., of its own literariness. Whereas Bellow, seeing American writing in isolation from America itself, remembered Whitman and Whitman's cornu-copia: in homage to which he fabricated a new American sentence. All this, of course, has been copiously remarked of Bellow ever since Augie March; but these five stories say something else. What Bellow is up to here is noth-ing short of a reprise of Western intellectual civilization. His immigrants and children of immigrants, blinking their fetal eyes in the New World, seem to be cracking open the head of Athena to get themselves born, in eager thirst for the milk of Enlightenment. To put it fortissimo: Bellow has brain on the brain, which may cast him as the dissident among American writers.

But even this is not the decoding or revelation I spoke of earlier. It has not been enough for Bellow simply to have restored attention to society—the density and entanglements of its urban textures, viz.: "He [Woody Selbst in "A Silver Dish"] maintained the bungalow—this took in roofing, pointing, wiring, insulation, air-conditioning—and he paid for heat and light and food, and dressed them all out of Sears, Roebuck and Wieboldt's, and bought them a TV, which they watched as devoutly as they prayed." Nor has it been enough for Bellow to have restored attention to the overriding bliss of learning: "Scholem and I [of "Cousins"], growing up on neighboring streets, attending the same schools, had traded books, and since Scholem had no trivial interests, it was Kant and Schelling all the way, it was Darwin and Nietzsche, Dostoyevsky and Tolstoy, and in our senior year it was Oswald Spengler. A whole year was invested in *The Decline of the West*."

To this thickness of community and these passions of mind Bellow has added a distinctive ingredient, not new on any landscape, but shamelessly daring just now in American imaginative prose. Let the narrator of "Cousins" reveal it: "We enter the world without prior notice, we are manifested before we can be aware of manifestation. An original self exists, or, if you prefer, an original soul . . . I was invoking my own fundamental perspective, that of a person who takes for granted distortion in the ordinary way of seeing but has never given up the habit of referring all truly important observations to that original self or soul." Bellow, it seems, has risked mentioning—who can admit to this without literary embarrassment?—the Eye of God.

And that is perhaps what his intellectual fevers have always pointed to. "Cousins" speaks of it explicitly: "As a man is, so he sees. As the Eye is formed, such are its powers." Yet "Cousins" is overtly about "the observation of cousins," and moves from cousin Tanky of the rackets to cousin Seckel whose "talent was for picking up strange languages" to cousin Motty, who, "approaching ninety, still latched on to people to tell them funny things." All this reflects a powerfully recognizable Jewish family feeling—call it, in fact, family love, though it is love typically mixed with amazement and disorder. The professor-narrator of "Him with His Foot in His Mouth"—the title story—like cousin Motty is also a funny fellow, the author of a long letter conscientiously recording his compulsion to make jokes that humiliate and destroy: putdowns recollected in tranquillity. But the inescapable drive to insult through wit is equated with "seizure, rapture, demonic possession, frenzy, *Fatum*, divine madness, or even solar storm," so this lambent set of comic needlings is somehow more than a joke, and may touch on the Eye of Dionysus. "A Silver Dish," with its upside-down echo of the biblical tale of Joseph's silver cup, concerns the companionable trials of Woody Selbst and his rogue father, the two of them inextricably entwined, though the father has abandoned his family; all the rest, mother, sisters, aunt, and ludicrous immigrant reverend uncle, are Jewish converts to evangelicalism. Woody, like Joseph in Egypt, supports them all. The Eye of God gazes through this story too, not in the bathetic converts but in the scampish father, "always, always something up his sleeve." "Pop had made Woody promise to bury him among Jews"—neglected old connections being what's up that raffish sleeve. It is Woody's "clumsy intuition" that "the goal set for this earth was that it should be filled with good, saturated with it." All the same, the commanding image in this narrative is that of a buffalo calf snatched and devoured by a crocodile in the waters of the Nile, in that alien country where Joseph footed the family bills and his father Jacob kept his wish to be buried among Jews up his sleeve almost to the end.

The commanding image of this volume—the concordance, so to speak, to all of Bellow's work—turns up in the reflections of one of the cousins, Ijah Brodsky: "'To long for the best that ever was': this was not an abstract project. I did not learn it over a seminar table. It was a constitutional necessity, physiological, temperamental, based on sympathies which could not be acquired. Human absorption in faces, deeds, bodies, drew me toward metaphysical grounds. I had these peculiar metaphysics as flying creatures have their radar."

This metaphysical radar (suspiciously akin to the Eye of God) "decodes" Saul Bellow; and these five ravishing stories honor and augment his genius.

Throwing Away the Clef:
Saul Bellow's Ravelstein

Roman à clef? Never mind. When it comes to novels, the author's life is nobody's business. A novel, even when it is autobiographical, is not an autobiography. If the writer himself leaks the news that such-and-such a character is actually so-and-so in real life, readers nevertheless have an obligation—fiction's enchanted obligation—to shut their ears and turn away. A biographer may legitimately wish to look to *Buddenbrooks*, say, to catch certain tonalities of Thomas Mann's early years; a reader is liberated from the matching game. Fiction is subterranean, not terrestrial. Or it is like Tao: say what it is, and that is what it is not. One reason to read imaginative literature is to be carried off into the strangeness of an unknown planet, not to be dogged by the verifiable facts of this one. Why should we care for blunt information—for those ephemeral figures fictional creatures are "based on"? The originals vanish; their simulacra, powerful marvels, endure. Does it matter that "The Rape of the Lock" makes sport of one Arabella Fermor and of the eminent Lord Petre? Fermor and Petre are bones. Belinda and Sir Plume go on frolicking from line to frothy line of Pope's comic ode. Who lives forever—Flimnap, the all-important treasurer of the Kingdom of Lilliput, or his sent-up model, Sir Robert Walpole, gone to dust two and a half centuries ago? Why should Philip Roth's "Philip Roth" be Philip Roth?

And why should Saul Bellow's Ravelstein be Allan Bloom? Or, to turn the question around (the better to get at an answer), why should Saul Bellow's Ravelstein not be Allan Bloom? It might be argued that Bellow has a fat track record of insinuating into his fiction the frenziedly brilliant men he has known, intellectuals given to complications: in *Humboldt's Gift*, Delmore Schwartz; in "Zetland: By a Character Witness," Isaac Rosenfeld; in "What Kind of Day Did You Have?," Harold Rosenberg. And in *Ravelstein*, Allan Bloom, Bellow's longtime colleague at the University of Chicago's School of Social Thought. But Bloom and Bellow were more entangled—more raveled—than academic colleagues usually are: they were cognitive companions, mutual brain-pickers, and, in Bloom's Platonic lingo, true friends. For Bloom especially, friendship was a calling, "the community of those who seek the truth, the potential knowers." In 1987, Bellow supplied a foreword to *The Closing of the American Mind*, Bloom's startling bestseller—startling because it was a bestseller, despite its countless invocations of Socrates, Herodotus, Nietzsche, Hobbes, Locke, Descartes, Spinoza, Bacon, Newton, and all the other denizens of the philosophical mind. Summing up Bloom, Bellow faithfully reported, "Professor Bloom is neither a debunker nor a satirist, and his conception of seriousness carries him far beyond the positions of academia"—and then ran off the Bloomian rails to tumble into engaging self-clarification. With familiar antic Bellovian bounce, Bellow wrote, "There was not a chance in the world that Chicago, with the agreement of my eagerly Americanizing extended family, would make me in its image. Before I was capable of thinking clearly, my resistance to its material weight took the form of obstinacy. I couldn't say why I would not allow myself to become the product of an environment. But gainfulness, utility, prudence, business, had no hold on me. My mother wanted me to be a fiddler, or, failing that, a rabbi." (He became, in a way, both: a fiddler with the sharps and flats of American prose, and a metaphysical ruminator.) Bloom, too, in the final pages of his book, spoke of living "independent of accidents, of circumstance"—a view, Bellow affirmed, that was "the seed from which my life grew."

Two self-propelled thinkers, freed from predictive forces. They had in common an innate longing, revealed in youth, for the bliss of Idea. Bloom, under the head "From Socrates' *Apology* to Heidegger's *Rektoratsrede*": "When I was fifteen years old I saw the University of Chicago for the first time and somehow sensed that I had discovered my life." The university, he early came to understand, "provided an atmosphere of free inquiry, and therefore excluded what is not conducive to or is inimical to such inquiry. It made a distinction between what is important and not important. It protected the tradition, not because tradition is tradition but because tradition provides models of discussion on a uniquely high level. It contained marvels and made possible friendships consisting in shared experiences of those marvels." And Bellow, spilling the beans among the wayward paragraphs of his foreword: "Reluctantly my father allowed me at seventeen to enter the university, where I was an enthusiastic (wildly excited) but erratic and contrary student. If I signed up for Economics 201, I was sure to spend all my time reading Ibsen and Shaw. Registering for a poetry course, I was soon bored by meter and stanzas, and shifted my attention to Kropotkin's *Memoirs of a Revolutionist* and Lenin's *What Is to Be Done?* . . . I preferred to read poetry on my own without the benefit of lectures on the caesura." Both young men are "wildly excited" by this opening into the seductions of ultimate meaning. One becomes an extraordinary teacher. The other becomes Saul Bellow. One writes the cardboard sentences, workmanlike and often mentally exhilarating, of the intellectual nonwriter. The other *writes*. For years, until Bloom's death, the two are true friends—a friendship bred in Chicago, with robust tendrils stretching toward ancient Athens and the dustiness of upper Broadway. Bloom, like the Ravelstein of Bellow's novel, is in thrall to Socrates. Like Ravelstein, he publishes a volume critical of the displacement of humanist liberal culture by the pieties of political cant. Like Ravelstein, he earns a fortune from his book and feels the venom of the radical left. Like Ravelstein, he is a homosexual who reveres Eros and scorns gay rights; again like Ravelstein, he has a Chinese lover. This ought to be more than enough to make the case for Ravelstein as roman à clef. But there is no case. Or: to make the case in so literal a fashion, one on one (on all fours, as lawyers put it), is to despise the idea of the novel—the principle of what a novel is—and to harbor a private lust to destroy it.

In scary-kitschy old movies, an ambition-crazed scientist constructs in his laboratory two ominously identical boxes, in the shape of telephone booths, side by side. He enters one, the door shuts, a fearful electrical buzz follows, lights flash and darken, and suddenly the first box is empty and the scientist stands, intact, in the other: a triumph of molecular disintegration and reintegration; instant transportation sans trolley or rocket. If you are ready to believe this, you will accept the notion of roman à clef—that a life is transferable from flesh to print; that since the resemblances line up ever so nicely, Ravelstein "is" Bloom. Under this persuasion, fiction is hijacked by gossip, the vapor of transience. Under this persuasion, Bellow's own admission (he has confirmed that his model was Bloom) invites the scandal of outing: Ravelstein dies of AIDS; then did Bloom, who never intimated having the disease, die of it? Under this persuasion, Andrew Sullivan, noted gay journalist and pundit, observes how salutary it is that even a conservative like Bloom can be openly gay. Bloom's politics, enemies, sexual habits, even his dying, are all freshly rehearsed—because Ravelstein is Bloom.

Ravelstein is not Bloom. To insist on it is hardly to allow Bloom to speak for himself in what is left of him. Bloom, dead, is (as a doctor once described to me the condition of a newly deceased relative) a pile of electrons. Bloom, still lively, continues his worthy arguments in teacherly discourses that, far from staling, have intensified at a time when dot-com merges with New Age. Say of Bloom what Bloom said of Leo Strauss, his venerated philosophy professor: that he "left his own memorial in the body of works in which what he understood to be his essence lives on." Say this; but not that Bellow has written Bloom. That Bellow acknowledges Bloom as his subject—acknowledges it with all the authority of the mighty *New York Times* behind him—means nothing, or almost nothing, in the kingdom of the novel. An author's extraliterary utterance (blunt information), prenovel or postnovel, may infiltrate journalism; it cannot touch the novel itself. Fiction does not invent out of a vacuum, but it invents; and what it invents is, first, the fabric and cadence of language, and then a slant of idea that sails out of these as a fin lifts from the sea. The art of the novel (worn yet opulent phrase) is in the mix of idiosyncratic language—language imprinted in the writer, like the whorl of the fingertip—and an unduplicable design inscribed on the mind by character and image. Invention has little capacity for the true-to-life snapshot. It is true to its own stirrings. The real-life Bloom, steeped in a congeries of arresting social propositions, lacked language and metaphor—which is why the legacy of his books can replicate his thought, but not the mysterious crucible of his breath.

Bellow, in going after his friend's mystery, leaves Bloom behind—just as in past novels and stories he ultimately deserts Rosenberg, Rosenfeld, and Schwartz, those latter-day piles of electrons, who, like Bloom, are obliged to live on, impressively enough, in the ink of their own fingerprints. Bellow's is an independent art. The souls who thrive or shrivel in his fiction ("soul" being his most polemical term) are not replicas; they are primal coinages, unbounded by flesh and likely to be faithless to fact. Literary verisimilitude is a chimera. Look to the "stein" in Ravelstein for a suggestive clue: the philosopher's stone that turns base metal into gold. Allan Bloom, Bellow's supremely intelligent Chicago compatriot, had the university professor's usual tin ear for prose (his own). But the philosopher's stone does not mimic or reproduce; it transmutes. Bloom's tin is Ravelstein's gold.

"Lifestyle" raised to a right equal to other human rights was what Bloom particularly excoriated; such relativism, he believed, led to "nihilism as moralism." Andrew Sullivan sizes up Bloom acutely when he remarks that "victimology never tempted him." Sullivan speculates that Bloom's homosexuality "may even have reinforced his conservatism," a striking aside—but what is it doing in the context of Bellow's novel? An essay on Bloom ought to be an essay on Bloom. It is important to repudiate the tag of roman à clef not only because it is careless and rampant, but because it reduces and despoils the afflatus—and the freedom—of the literary imagination. The clef gets stuck in the lock, and the lock attaches to fetters.

*

And so to the real Ravelstein of the novel. I am reluctant to speak of Bellow's "voice," a writerly term overgrown with academic fungus, and by now nearly useless. (Consider also the ruination by English departments of "gaze," that magical syllable, fully and foully theorized into ash.) Better to return to Bellow's mother, who hoped for a fiddling son; better to think of him as a sentence-and-paragraph fiddler, or a rabbi presiding over an unruly congregation of words. The words are unruly because they refuse to be herded into categories of style: they are high, low, shtick, soft-shoe, pensive, mystical, sermonic, eudaemonic—but never catatonic; always on the move, in the swim, bathed in some electricity-conducting effluvium. Bellow's incremental sound—or noise—rejects imitation the way the human immune system will reject foreign tissue. There are no part-Bellows or next-generation Bellows; there are no literary descendants. As for precursors, Bellow's jumpy motor has more in common (while not so fancy) with the engine that ratchets Gerard Manley Hopkins's lines—that *run-run-turn-stop!*—than with any prose ancestor. In *Ravelstein* he puts these racing weight-bearing energies to use in something that ought not to be called a "portrait." ("What an olden-days' word 'portraying' has become," says Chick, the novel's narrator.) Verbal sculpture is more like it—think of those Roman busts with strong noses and naked heads, round heavy stone on square heavy plinths. Ravelstein's head is central, tactile, dominant, and it is examined with a sculptor's or architect's eye. "On his bald head you felt that what you were looking at were the finger marks of its shaper." "This tall pin- or chalk-striped dude with his bald head (you always felt there was something dangerous about its whiteness, its white force, its dents) . . ." "He liked to raise his long arms over the light gathered on his bald head and give a comic cry." "There are bald heads that proclaim their strength. Ravelstein's head had been like that." "His big eyes were concentrated in that bald, cranial watchtower of his." "You couldn't imagine an odder container for his odd intellect. Somehow his singular, total, almost geological baldness implied that there was nothing hidden about him." "The famous light of Paris was concentrated on his bald head." And so on, image upon image. Ravelstein's is not so much a man's head as it is a lit dome: the dome (or Renaissance *duomo*) of some high-ceilinged cathedral or broad-corridored library. Ravelstein's ideas—also his gossip, his extravagant wants—are solidly housed. This head is no hotel for brief mental sojourns.

A hotel is where we first meet Abe Ravelstein—the lavish penthouse of the Hotel Crillon, in Paris, where the luxury-intoxicated humanities professor, "who only last year had been a hundred thousand dollars in debt," is reveling in the millions piled up by his cultural bestseller. Ravelstein is a sybarite. He is also a man who would know the Greek origin of that word.

His appetite for five-thousand-dollar designer suits, silk ties, gold pens, mink quilts, French crystal, smuggled Cuban cigars, Oriental carpets, antique sideboards, and all the other paraphernalia of the dedicated voluptuary, is accompanied by a philosopher's scrupulous worship of civic virtue. Ravelstein is a principled atheist, a homosexual (but quietly, privately), a bit of a matchmaker, a thinker "driven by longing"—a longing understood as Aristophanes meant it, the haunted desire for human completion. He likes puns and gags, he likes meddling in the lives of his brightest students, he likes being ahead of the news (thanks to former students now in high places); his cell phone is at the ready. Socrates is his ideal and Thucydides his immediacy, but he is as alert to current anti-Semitic subtleties and historic anti-Jewish depredations as he is to the problems of Alcibiades in the Sicilian campaign of the Peloponnesian War. Chick—the not-so-famous midlist writer who is Ravelstein's catch-as-catch-can biographer—seizes his subject at the crux: "He preferred Athens, but he respected Jerusalem greatly."

Commenting and kibitzing in the first person, Chick (a self-described "serial marrier") mostly keeps a low profile, except in the matter of his wives: Vela, the vengeful Romanian physicist who walks out on him, and Rosamund, the loyal, intelligent, empathic young woman who was once Ravelstein's student. Other characters pass, or hurtle, through Chick's recording cascades: Nikki, Ravelstein's presumed lover, "a handsome, smooth-skinned, black-haired, Oriental, graceful, boyish man," for whom Ravelstein buys a chestnut-colored BMW with kid-leather upholstery; Rachmiel Kogon, "tyrannically fixated, opinionated," a genuine ex-Oxonian don but a fake Brit, owner of complete sets of Dickens, James, Hume, and Gibbon; Morris Herbst, an observant Jew with a heart transplant obtained from the deadly crash of a goyish motorcyclist in Missouri; Radu Grielescu, a renowned Jungian mythologist and Nazi-tainted former Iron Guardist, who play-acts blameless politesse; Battle, paratrooper, pilot, ballroom dancer, Sanskrit scholar, with "the mouth of a Celtic king." They represent, in Chick's phrase, "penetrations of the external world." Accounting for them to the impatient Ravelstein—who recommends a larger concern for society and politics—Chick argues, "I had no intention . . . of removing, by critical surgery, the metaphysical lenses I was born with."

It is these powerful lenses that finally raise questions about how a novel—generically, the *novel*—is to be fathomed. Ravelstein is busy with revelatory incident but is mainly plotless: Ravelstein becomes ill, rallies, retains his acerbic nobility, declines further, and begins the slide into death. At Ravelstein's hospital bedside Chick uncovers the mundane secret of the philosopher's eloquent cranial dome. "Now and then I put my hand to my friend's bald head," he confides. ". . . I was surprised to find that there was an invisible stubble on his scalp. He seemed to have decided that total baldness suited him better than thinning hair, and shaved his head as well as his cheeks. Anyway," Chick concludes, "this head was rolling toward the grave." A mightiness theatricalized by the razor's artifice; a mightiness at last undone. Following which, Rosamund and Chick vacation in the Caribbean ("one huge tropical slum," Chick characterizes these islands), where he eats spoiled fish and nearly perishes from the effects of poisoning; Rosamund's intrepid devotion through an extended medical ordeal saves him. This final occurrence, the novel's climactic scene, seems out of kilter with the rich thick Ravelstein stew that precedes it. Chick's preoccupations veer off the Ravelsteinian tracks into the demands of his own circumstances, much as Bellow, in his foreword to Bloom's blockbuster, ran off the Bloomian rails to grapple with his own spirit. But by now Ravelstein is dead; and a novel is not a biography. Biographies are innately saddled with structure. When the biographer's subject dies, the biography comes to a close—what else can it choose to do? A novel need make no such obeisance to graph or sine curve, or to the deeper curve of death's scythe. Only the lower orders of fiction—case solved, romance consummated—abide by ordained rigidities and patterns. The literary novel (call it the artist's novel) engenders freedom, flexibility, exemption from determined outcomes; waywardness and surprise. What falls out then is not story (or not only story), but certain obstinacies and distillations, which can be inspected solely through Chick's metaphysical lenses. It can even be argued that it is only through this supra-optical equipment that fiction's necessary enactments can be prodded into lustiness.

What "metaphysical" intends is not left unspecified: it is the earthly shock of Creation's plenitude. "Ordinary daily particulars were my specialty," Chick explains. "The heart of things is shown in the surface of those things." Elsewhere he illustrates: "I carried [Rosamund] through the water, the sand underfoot ridged as the surface of the sea was rippled, and inside the mouth the hard palate had its ridges too." Out of the blue, the ridges of the hard palate! A planetary connectedness, a Darwinian propensity for minute perceiving—which Ravelstein, whose thought runs vertically through history, both marvels at and chides. Here Rosamund sides with her old teacher: "But this is how you do things, Chick: the observations you make crowd out the main point." They are discussing Grielescu, the concealed Iron Guardist. "How could such a person be politically dangerous?" Chick counters. "His jacket cuffs come down over his knuckles." An instant of comic toughness, reminiscent of the famous crack in *Augie March*: "He had rich blood. His father peddled apples." But Grielescu, a minor character, barely a walk-on, is the novel's suboceanic mover: he is like the ridges of the hard palate inside the mouth. Once you become conscious of these shallow bumps, you cannot leave off exploring them—they lead you mentally to the treacherous floor of the deepest sea. In Ravelstein's exuberant mind-roving prime, his memoirist recalls, he had been absorbed in nasty speculations about Grielescu's Nazi past: how Grielescu had been summoned to lecture in Jerusalem, and how the invitation was soon withdrawn. Weakening now, under death's lintel, Ravelstein appears to be enveloped in Jewish fate, in the twentieth century's "great evil." What was once a flicker in a crepuscular background, veiled by a Greek passion for polis and eros, invades and illumines his still pulsing intellect. "It was unusual for him these days, in any conversation, to mention Plato or even Thucydides. He was full of Scripture now," Chick records. "In his last days it was the Jews he wanted to talk about, not the Greeks."

Athens gives way to Jerusalem—but it is understood, anyhow, that Socrates had always been Ravelstein's rebbe, and Periclean Athens his yeshiva. Ravelstein's final dictum: in the wake of "such a volume of hatred and the denial of the right to live," Jews are "historically witness to the absence of redemption." For the reader looking back on Ravelstein's musings as preserved by Chick, a great totting-up looms. Of a French landlord's ancestry: "Those Gabineaus were famous Jew-haters." Of Grielescu's myth expertise: "The Jews had better understand their status with respect to myth. Why should they have any truck with myth? It was myth that demonized them." Of Jews and teaching: "We are a people of teachers. For millennia, Jews have taught and been taught. Without teaching, Jewry was an impossibility." Of a luncheon for T. S. Eliot, where the snooty hostess complains of Ravelstein's manners: "She wasn't going to let any kike behave badly at her table." And again: "And what will T. S. Eliot think of us!"

That last gibe is to the point. How would T. S. Eliot assess an American novelist (one of those "freethinking Jews" he deplored) so confident of writer's sovereignty that he can fiddle with the English language with all the freewheeling relish of an Elizabethan inventing new inflections—and in such a way as to make 'The Waste Land' (and, God knows, those solemnified essays and plays) seem lethargic? "I had a Jewish life to lead in the American language," Chick announces, "and that's not a language that's helpful with dark thoughts." But it is through Chick's dark thoughts—and not only Ravelstein's—that we are apprised, or reminded, of Lloyd George's, Kipling's, and Voltaire's hot anti-Semitism, and of "the Wehrmacht way of getting around responsibility for their crimes," and of German militarism as "the bloodiest and craziest kind of revanchist murderous zeal." This is a long way from Rachel née Rabinovitch's murderous paws, and it is also a substantial distance from the mannerly fear of nomenclature that paradoxically turned Nathan Weinstein into the ferocious Nathanael West. Sovereignty for a novelist means unleashing the language of one's marrow and—this especially—tunneling into any subject matter, however transgressive it may be of the current societal glyph. (Think of that other Bloom as *echt* Dubliner. And note that Ravelstein's snooty hostess is named Mrs. Glyph.) Hence Chick's reflections on leading a Jewish life in the American language are light-years from the rivalrous group-tenets of multiculturalism, and ought not to be mistaken for them. The reviewer who called *Ravelstein* "Bellow's most Jewish novel" is only partly right; on second thought, if he means it as essence or circumscription, he is all wrong. It is not the nature of subject matter that defines a novel. It is the freedom to be at home in any subject matter; and this holds for Louis Auchincloss as much as it holds for Saul Bellow. All subject matter is equal under the law (or democratic lawlessness) of the novel. What is a novel? A persuasion toward dramatic interiority. A word-hoard that permits its inventor to stand undefined, unprescribed, liberated from direction or coercion. Freedom makes sovereignty; it is only when the writer is unfettered by external expectations that clarity of character—Ravelstein, for instance, bald and baldly opinionated, intellectually quarrelsome, a comic epicurean, a hospitable thinker with trembling hands, a Jew tormented by evil and pedagogically fixed on virtue—can be imagined into being. When, apropos of Bloom's 1987 credo, Bellow insisted that, "I would not allow myself to become the product of an *environment*," he had a canny interest in those italics. As for the idea of roman à clef: what is it if not the product, and the imprisoning imposition, of an environment?

The Lastingness of Saul Bellow

How easy it is, and plausible, to regard a collection of letters spanning youth and old age as an approximation of autobiography: the procession of denizens who inhabit a life, the bit players with their entrances and exits, the faithful chronology of incidents—all turn up reliably in either form, whether dated and posted or backward-looking. Yet autobiography, even when ostensibly steeped in candor, tends toward reconsideration—if not revisionary paperings-over, then late perspectives and second thoughts. Whereas letters (but here let us specify a *writer*'s letters) are appetite and urgency, unmediated seizures of impulse and desire torn from the fraught and living moment. And letters—sorted, indexed, bound—are themselves a paradox: hotly alive, they claim death as a requisite. Rare and anomalous is the publisher who would prefer the correspondence of the quick, however celebrated, to the letters of the dead: the death of a writer who answers his mail, especially one possessed of a powerful fame, lengthens and amplifies the body of work.

Even so, death disports with writers more cruelly than with the rest of humankind. The grave can hardly make more mute those who were voiceless when alive—dust to dust, muteness to muteness. But the silence that dogs the established writer's noisy obituary, with its boisterous shock and busy regret, is more profound than any other. Oblivion comes more cuttingly to the writer whose presence has been *felt*, argued over, championed, disparaged—the writer who is seen to be what Lionel Trilling calls a Figure. *Lionel Trilling?* Consider: who at this hour (apart from some professorial specialist currying his "field") is reading Mary McCarthy, James T. Farrell, John Berryman, Allan Bloom, Irving Howe, Alfred Kazin, Edmund Wilson, Anne Sexton, Alice Adams, Robert Lowell, Grace Paley, Owen Barfield, Stanley Elkin, Robert Penn Warren, Norman Mailer, Leslie Fiedler, R. P. Blackmur, Paul Goodman, Susan Sontag, Lillian Hellman, John Crowe Ransom, Stephen Spender, Daniel Fuchs, Hugh Kenner, Seymour Krim, J. F. Powers, Allen Ginsberg, Philip Rahv, Jack Richardson, John Auerbach, Harvey

Swados—or Trilling himself? These names of the dead—a good number of them past luminaries, a few (Lillian Hellman, say) worthy of being forgotten—do not come randomly. They all have their fleeting turn in Saul Bellow's letters, whether vituperatively, casually, or approvingly (though scarcely ever indifferently). It is safe to say that most are nowadays not much in demand either at your local library or on Amazon, and safer yet to surmise that many have little chance of outlasting even the first third of the twenty-first century; several have barely outlasted the twentieth. Nearly all have been overtaken by newer writers lately grown familiar, vernal aspirants who crowd the horizon with their addictive clamor.

And even as these contemporary importunings swamp our perception, what can already be clearly discerned rising from this swelling armada of the twice-buried is a single exemption: Bellow. Among all the literary tumults and public roilings of the recently Famous, he alone courts lastingness, he alone escapes eclipse. To state this so bluntly is not so much a declaration as it is an inquiry. Only see how speedily the grave works its mufflings and comedowns—Ginsberg, mum; Mailer, dumb as stone. In the tracings of unassailable art, high or low, they leave improbable spoor: the poet no poet but minstrel and mountebank, the would-be immortal novelist undone by the politicized harlequin he became. Gradually they decay into symptom and artifact—documents of a receding social history—while the vestigial rustlings surrounding their names testify to nothing more memorable than outdated literary tinsel.

But Bellow stays, and why? Language—the acclaimed style—cannot be the whole of it, though its energetic capaciousness captures and capsizes American English with an amplitude and verve not heard since Whitman, and never before in prose. The mandarin-poolroom link, elevated riffs married to street vernacular, has become Bellow's signature, and attracts lovestruck imitators. Yet brilliant flourishes alone, even when embedded in galloping ambition, will not make a second Bellow. (A second Bellow? Not for a hundred years!) There is instead something else, beyond the heated braininess and lavish command of ideas: call it *feeling*. In this bountiful volume of letters, the writer's last brief words, set down fourteen months before his death, should all at once break open the hidden-in-plain-sight code that reveals why Bellow stays:

[My parents] needed all the help they could get. They were forever asking, "What does the man say?" and I would translate for them into heavy-footed English. The old people were as ignorant of English as they were of Canadian French. We often stopped before a display of children's shoes. My mother coveted for me a pair of patent-leather sandals with an *elegantissimo* strap. I finally got them—I rubbed them with butter to preserve the leather. This is when I was six or seven years old. . . . Amazing how it all boils down to a pair of patent-leather sandals.

It all boils down to a pair of patent-leather sandals. A dying old man's sentimental nostalgia, a fruitlessly self-indulgent yearning for a mother lost too soon? No; or not only. What we are hearing also is the culmination of a theory of pastness—and pastness means passage. In nine sentences, an annotated history of an immigrant family, where it settled, how it struggled, how it aspired; and a hint of the future novelist's moral aesthetic, the determination to preserve. As with the family, so with the family of man. Bellow, who as a graduate student studied anthropology, as a writer pursues the history of civilized thought—an inquisitiveness directed to the way experience (Augie) turns into a quest for philosophy (Henderson, Sammler, Herzog), sometimes via a scalding bath of comedy.

The letters are all zest and craving and demand—so many journeys, so many cities, so many liaisons, so many courtings, so many marriages and partings, so many spasms of rage, so many victories and downers, so many blue or frenetic melancholias and grievances; but cumulatively they add up to a rich montage of knowing, speckled now and again with laughter, that most metaphysical of emotions. And always, pulsing below the hungry race, the loyalty to pastness. Well into Bellow's old age, Chicago's Tuley High School held an emblematic place in his psyche. Tuley was where the excitations of intellectual ambition first encountered their kin in the formidably intelligent children of mostly working-class immigrant Jews, boys and girls drenched in ferocious bookishness and utopian politics, unselfconsciously asserting ownership of American culture at a time when it was most vigorously dominated by WASPS. Nathan Gould, Louis Lasco, Oscar Tarcov, David Peltz, Stuart Brent, Herbert Passin, Abe Kaufman, Hymen Slate, Louis Sidran, Rosalyn Tureck, Zita Cogan, Yetta Barshevsky, Sam Freifeld, and especially Isaac Rosenfeld—Bellow kept up with a surprising number of these witnesses to his early ardors, and mourned acutely when the dying of old friends began. In a letter to Nathan Gould in 1981, the Nobel five years behind him, he fell into elegy:

I attended the Tuley reunion and it was a depressing affair—elderly people nostalgic for youth and the Depression years. There seemed nothing for them (for us) to do but turn into middle-class Americans with the same phrases and thoughts from the same sources. Some came from far away . . . and some were crippled and required wheeling . . . [One] who seemed well preserved turned out to have a heredity disorder affecting his memory so that he was groping, while we talked, and his new wife was deeply uneasy . . . But my closest friends were Oscar and Isaac, dead for many years. In every decade I try to think what they might have been had they lived.

He ended with a tribute to "the old days." If as "a sort of public man" he didn't retain the old affections, he said, "I would feel alienated from my own history, *false.*"

Fifteen years later, at a memorial service for Yetta Barshevsky, who had been Tuley's class orator and radical firebrand, elegy burst into exuberant reminiscence. After reciting Yetta's street address of seven decades before (and his own, "right around the corner"), after dismissing her "spectacularly handsome" mother as an unregenerate Stalinist and describing her carpenter father's "jalopy . . . filled with saws and sawdust," he appended a tour de force of recollection:

I even came to know Yetta's grandfather, whom I often saw at the synagogue when I came to say Kaddish for my mother. He was an extremely, primitively orthodox short bent man with a beard that seemed to rush out of him and muffled his face. He wore a bowler hat and elastic-sided boots. The old women, it seems, were wildly radical communist sympathizers. The grandfathers were the pious ones.

Passages like these, with their sociohistorical notation and their indelible optical prowess—rushing beard, elastic-sided boots!—can easily be found reverberating in any of Bellow's stories and novels. And even in the very first letter in this collection, a clowning response to Yetta's having jilted him in favor of one Nathan Goldstein, Bellow at seventeen was already a conscious writer—antic, teasing, showing off, pumping adolescent brio and witty pastiche. He *felt* what he was; he was sure of what he had. Like Henry James and T. S. Eliot, those confident conquistadors of London who were his precursors in early self-knowledge, Bellow claimed recognition before he was in a position to have earned it. But London was an insular village vulnerable to conquest, and America was a continent. What could be accomplished gracefully, if cattily, in Virginia Woolf's Tavistock Square required boldness in Chicago.

In 1932, Bellow is a teenage boy writing to a teenage girl; five years on, as subeditor of an obscure Trotskyist journal, he addresses James T. Farrell in the worldly tones of a seasoned colleague—though at twenty-two he has so far published only occasional pieces. "It is peculiar," Bellow instructs Farrell, who had become his mentor, "how the Stalinites have lost central discipline by spreading themselves through liberal groups. . . . [Sydney] Harris thinks nothing of assassinating a scruple or knifing a principle if thereby he can profit." This fierce disparagement—the skewering of a now nearly forgotten journalist in that antediluvian period when "Trotskyist" and "Stalinite" were warring bywords—only intensified as Bellow aged into viewpoints adversarial to his youthful radicalism. In 1986, summing up for Karl Shapiro his impressions of an international writers' congress in New York sponsored by PEN, he dismissed a clutch of contemporary notables: "Mailer," he reported, "mostly wanted a huge media event—that's what he calls living. . . . It boggled my mind to see how greedy the radicals were for excitement 'radical-style.' I'm speaking of big-time subversives like Ginsberg, Nadine Gordimer, Grace Paley, Doctorow, and other representatives of affluent revolution." One can marvel at how the polemical voice of the mature Bellow is scarcely changed (despite the change of politics) from that of the self-assured and strenuously contentious young man of fifty years before—yet even more striking is how Bellow in his twenties is ready to pit his taste and his talent against anyone, however more established. To be famous and forceful at seventy is one thing; to believe in one's fame before it has evolved is a kind of magical faith. It was an authority—no, an authenticity—that carried him far. He had no intention (so the letters reveal) of wasting time as a novitiate pursuing deferential cultivation of influential eminences. His approach was that of an instant equal. His successful candidacy (and third try) for a Guggenheim fellowship elicited support from Farrell, Edmund Wilson, and Robert Penn Warren. He had already been in friendly correspondence with all three, and was intimate enough with Warren to know him as "Red."

Still earlier, he had quickly formed a connection with Philip Rahv of *Partisan Review,* the most imperially prestigious literary magnet of the forties. For the young Bellow, publication failed to satisfy if it fell short of widening both courage and opportunity. James Henle of Vanguard Press, who in 1944 brought out *Dangling Man,* Bellow's first published novel—later followed by *The Victim*—was soon jettisoned. To Henry Volkening, his agent, Bellow spoke of "swollen feelings," and to Henle he wrote sourly:

> I know you will accuse me again of putting off the philosopher's robe and of being too impatient, and that you will repeat that before I have published five or six books I can't expect to live by writing. But as

I write slowly I will be forty before my fifth book is ready and I don't think it is unreasonable of me to expect that the most should be made of what I do produce. When I see my chances for uninterrupted work going down the drain I can't help protesting the injustice of it. This year I have been ill and teaching leaves me no energy for writing. [Bellow at this time was assistant professor of English at the University of Minnesota.] . . . I see next year and the next and the one after that fribbled away at the university. My grievance is a legitimate one, I think. I don't want to be a commercial writer or to be taken up with money. I have never discussed money matters with you in four years, except for the letter I wrote you last spring about [*The Victim*]. You were annoyed with me . . . But now the book is out, it hasn't been badly received and already it seems to be going the way of *Dangling Man*.

The letter was not sent. But the break with Henle was carried out; it stood for more than ambition, more than a writer's nervous self-advocacy. It was clairvoyance, it was a heralding, it spoke for the cause of imagination untrammeled. Already it bristled with the thickening future. His second novel only just published, Bellow was numbering the long row of still-to-be-written novels ahead. The unsent letter was not about money—it was about freedom, it was about becoming. Even more, it was about knowing. Bellow knew what he knew, and like some youthfully anointed evangelist, he wanted what he knew to be known. The flight from Henle was the beginning of a credo.

And what was that credo? An impulse running through many of the letters discloses it: it was, plainly and unaffectedly, how to *see*; meaning, at bottom, how a novelist must think. For decades it has been common wisdom—common because Bellow himself made it so—that *Dangling Man* and *The Victim*, the pair of novels preceding *The Adventures of Augie March*, were too "Flaubertian," too controlled, pinched by the orderliness of European modernist constraint, while *Augie* was an extravagant release into the impetuous comedic buoyancy of a manifold America. Of *The Victim*, Bellow was moved to write:

Compared to what is published nowadays between boards, it is an accomplishment. By my own standards, however, it is promissory. It took hold of my mind and imagination very deeply but I know that I somehow failed to write it *freely*, with all the stops out from beginning to end . . . And I must admit that in spite of the great amount of energy I brought to the book at certain times, I was at others, for some reason,

content to fall back on lesser resources . . . But there is a certain diffidence about me . . . that prevents me from going all out. . . . I assemble
the dynamite but I am not ready to touch off the fuse. Why? Because
I am working toward something and have not arrived . . . I wanted
to write before I had the maturity to write as "high" as I wished and
so I had a very arduous and painful apprenticeship and am still undergoing it.

Or so he declared in January 1948. But by April he was disputing this
unforgiving verdict, complaining of "a rather disagreeable letter from Kurt
[Wolff] about *The Victim*. I didn't mind his criticisms of specific things but
I disliked extremely his telling me 'you aren't there *yet.*'" *The Victim*, he went
on, "is a powerful book . . . There aren't many recent books that come close
to it and I can't take seriously any opinion that doesn't begin by acknowledging that." Adding more than sixty years of reappraisal to Bellow's spare three
months, we can argue even more effectively against the notion of apprenticeship. There is by now no getting away from it: the earlier novels need not,
should not, be overshadowed or diminished by *Augie*. It is not too daring to
venture that if *Augie*—grand gusts of vitality notwithstanding—had never
come into being, Bellow would still have been Bellow: the mind, the wit, the
word, the reach; the perplexity and the delirium of the human animal. There
are whole pages in *Dangling Man* that might have been torn out of *Seize the
Day*. There are rolling tracts of dialogue in *The Victim* with telling affinities
to *Ravelstein*. The familiar metaphysical cunning is everywhere. From the
start, Bellow wrote "high." And the key to writing high, said this most intellectual of novelists, is to force intellect into hiding, to trick the explicit into
vanishing into the implicit.

To Leslie Fiedler, who accused him of "misology"—hatred of argument
and reason—he recited his unwavering principle of elasticity:

I think positions *emerge* in a work of art, and you seem to think they're
imposed. It makes small difference what the artist says he thinks, and a
"prepared" attitude is an invitation to disaster. . . . I only complain that
intelligence has become so naked.

And to Josephine Herbst:

If you think *Seize the Day* is good, I'm satisfied that I'm doing all right.
It's hard for me to know, because so much of the time I'm deaf, dumb
and blind, the slave of unknown masters.

To John Berryman:

All the formal properties have to be cracked and the simplicities released.

To Ruth Miller, who had sent him her essay on Ralph Ellison's *Invisible Man*:

Your explication is too dense, too detailed . . . Perhaps it is too much like laboratory analysis . . . You see, you have left out the literary side of the matter almost entirely, and that, to my mind, is a mistake. I myself distinguish between the parts of the novel that were *written* and those that were constructed as part of the argument; they are not alike in quality . . . your interest is in Opinion rather than Creation.

To the Guggenheim Foundation, in support of Bernard Malamud's application for a fellowship:

Imagination has been steadily losing prestige in American life, it seems to me, for a long time. I am speaking of the poetic imagination. Inferior kinds of imagination have prospered, but the poetic has less credit than ever before. Perhaps that is because there is less room than ever for the personal, the spacious, unanxious and free, for the unprepared, unorganized, and spontaneous elements from which poetic imagination springs.

To Louis Gallo, while working on *Herzog*:

You'll find the book I'm writing now less "tender," "tolerant," etc. When a writer has such feelings, however, it's his business to lead them all into the hottest fire. He must expose them to the most destructive opposites he can find and, if he wishes to be tender, confront the murderer's face. The converse, however, is equally true, for writers who believe there is a Sargasso of vomit into which we must drift are obliged to confront beauty. To deny that, you would have to deny your instincts as a writer.

To Robert Penn Warren:

Augie was very difficult for me in the last half. I suppose I succumbed to the dreadful thing I warn everyone against—seriousness . . . My slogan was "Easily or not at all," but I forgot it. Too much of a temptation to speak the last word.

To Susan Glassman:

> Somehow I've managed to do exactly what I like. There are certain phi-
> losophers (Samuel Butler, if he is one) who say we really do get what we
> want. Question: Can we bear it when we get it? That's the question
> that's the beginning of religion.

To Richard Stern:

> No amount of assertion will make an ounce of art.

But he did assert his *idea* of art—he asserted his instincts, his intuitions—and he did do exactly what he liked, at least in everything he wrote,
and he really did get what he wanted, if not sooner, then later. His sovereignty as a writer was, so to say, *built in*. And for every statement of
credo-instruction, especially when directed to other writers, he appended
generous tributes. When he was stirred to criticism, he almost always began
with self-criticism, taking on himself the very flaw he had fingered in the
other. There might be an occasional exception, most particularly if the object
of scrutiny was a fellow novelist publicly acknowledged to be on his own
team. With such confirmed colleagues he pulled no punches: he wrote
scathingly to Philip Roth, disparaging *I Married a Communist* and lecturing
him on Stalin's Western loyalists and "hatred of one's own country." He was
merciless toward Malamud's *A New Life*: "all the middle-class platitudes of
love and liberalism . . . mean and humorless." Nevertheless there was personal warmth and varying degrees of literary admiration for his confederates
in the triumvirate he parodied as "Hart, Schaffner and Marx," a quip that has
survived the decades. What reluctantly united all three—Bellow, Roth,
Malamud—was a concept imposed on them by the celebrity-sloganeering of
the journalists: "American Jewish writers." But the link was both superficial
and specious: each invented his own mythos and imagined his own republic
of letters. It was not the complexity of heritage Bellow was resisting in his
tailor-made mockery, but its reduction to a narrowing palliative, nowadays
fashionably termed "identity." In a memorial tribute to Malamud, Bellow
reiterated his ties to the old atmospherics of origins, while introducing a still
greater claim:

> We were cats of the same breed. The sons of Eastern European immi-
> grant Jews, we had gone early into the streets of our respective cities,
> were Americanized by schools, newspapers, subways, streetcars, sand-

lots. Melting Pot children, we had assumed the American program to be the real thing: no barriers to the freest and fullest American choices. Of course we understood that it was no simple civics-course matter. We knew too much about the slums, we had assimilated too much dark history in our mothers' kitchens to be radiant optimists . . . it was admiration, it was love that drew us to the dazzling company of the great masters, all of them belonging to the Protestant Majority—some of them explicitly anti-Semitic . . . But one could not submit to control by such prejudices. My own view was that in religion the Christians had lived with us, had lived in the Bible of the Jews, but when the Jews wished to live in Western history with them they were refused. As if that history was not, by now, also ours.

These words (brilliantly included among the letters) were recited on Bellow's behalf under the dim chandeliers of the meeting room of the American Academy of Arts and Letters, where the members' chairs bore brass plaques inscribed with such storied names as Henry Adams, Owen Wister, Hamlin Garland, Edwin Markham, and other venerable representatives of Bellow's capitalized Majority. And when, not yet out of their teens, he and Isaac Rosenfeld dissolved the solemn ironies of Eliot's "Love Song of J. Alfred Prufrock" into a hilariously lampooning Yiddish ditty, it may have marked the signal moment when writers born Jewish and awakened into America would refuse to be refused by Western history.

Bellow's capacity for what might (in quick march) be called Jewish intelligence summoned deeps far beyond where the journalists could follow: the literary talent that rose up, in puzzling if impressive flocks, out of what appeared to be a low immigrant culture. Bellow was distinctive in transcending—transgressing against—the archetype of the coarse and unlettered ghetto greenhorn. The greenhorns in their humble trades were aware that they were carriers of a moral civilization. ("You are too intelligent for this," Herzog protests to his vaporously overtheorizing friend Shapiro. "Your father had rich blood. He peddled apples.") Though he had repeatedly declared himself, as an American, free to choose according to will or desire, Bellow also chose not to be disaffected. He was in possession of an inherited literacy that few novelists of Jewish background, writers of or close to his generation, could match, however sophisticated otherwise they might be. His range spanned an inclusive continuum; as his eulogy for Malamud insisted, Western learning and literature had also to mean Jewish learning and literature. He was at home in biblical Hebrew, was initiated into the liturgy from early childhood, and read and spoke (always with relish) a supple Yiddish. In the letters he will now and again slide into a Yiddish word or phrase for its pungent or familial aptness where English might pale. It was Bellow who, with Irving Howe and the Yiddish poet Eliezer Greenberg standing by, translated I. B. Singer's "Gimpel the Fool," in effect creating, in a matter of hours, a modernist American writer out of what had passed, mistakenly, for an old-fashioned Yiddish storyteller. What other "American Jewish writer" could have pulled off this feat? Or would have been willing to set aside the mask of fiction to pursue—his personal viewpoint plain to see—the political culture of Israel, as Bellow did in *To Jerusalem and Back,* a book-length essay composed at the crux of churning contention? (Decades old and read today, it remains, in its candor and credibility, shatteringly up-to-date.) And finally—we are compelled to come to this—there is the strangely misunderstood question of Bellow and the Holocaust.

In a letter dated July 19, 1987, he wrote:

> It's perfectly true that "Jewish writers in America" (a repulsive category!) missed what should have been for them the central event of their time, the destruction of European Jewry. We (I speak of Jews now and not merely writers) should have reckoned more fully, more deeply with it . . . I was too busy becoming a novelist to take note of what was happening in the Forties. I was involved with "literature" and given over to preoccupations with art, with language, with my struggle on the American scene, with the claims for recognition of my talent or, like my pals at the *Partisan Review,* with modernism, Marxism, New Criticism, with Eliot, Yeats, Proust, etc.—with anything except the terrible events in Poland. Growing slowly aware of this unspeakable evasion I didn't even know how to begin to admit it into my inner life. Not a particle of this can be denied. And can I really say—can anyone say—what was to be done, how this "thing" ought to have been met? Since the late Forties I have been brooding about it and sometimes I imagine I *can* see something. But what brooding may amount to is probably insignificant. I can't even begin to say what responsibility any of us may bear in such a matter, a crime so vast that it brings all Being into Judgment.

If there appears to be a contradiction in this arresting statement, it is hardly to the point. "I was too busy becoming a novelist to take note of what was happening in the Forties" may in fact clash with "Since the late Forties I have been brooding about it," but it is the closing phrase that calls reality into question—the known reality of "the terrible events in Poland." Bellow was made fully aware of these events earlier than most, and with a close-up precision unbefogged by such grand metaphorical abstractions as "a crime so vast that it brings all Being into Judgment." The writer who could explicitly describe the particular texture of an old man's boots glimpsed seventy years before here fades into the elusiveness of high declamation. Yet a single much-overlooked biographical datum may dispute these assertions of over-riding literary distraction. In 1948, three years after the defeat of Germany and the appalling revelations of the death camps, Bellow and Anita Goshkin, the social worker who became his first wife, went with their small son Gregory to live in Paris; a Guggenheim grant made the move possible. Bellow settled in to work on a new novel, caught up in the convivial cadres of literary Americans drawn to postwar Paris, while Anita found a job with the Joint Distribution Committee. Here we must pause to take this in. The Joint, as it was called, was a privately funded American effort to salvage the broken lives of the remnant of Holocaust survivors; Anita was perforce immersed daily in freshly accumulating news of "the terrible events in Poland." Are we to believe that the wife never imparted to the husband what she learned and witnessed and felt every day, or that, detached, he took no notice of it?

But if we may not conjecture what a wife privately recounts to a hus-band—even one so alert to the historically momentous—the letters themselves, with their multiple sharp retrospections, are testimony enough. In 1978, writing to the twenty-something Leon Wieseltier ("I found I could tell you things"), Bellow responded to a pair of articles Wieseltier had sent him on the philosophic origins of Hannah Arendt's post-Holocaust thinking. "That superior Krautess," as Bellow dubbed her, had notoriously charged the European Jewish leadership with collaboration in the administration of the Nazi ghettos and deportations. "She could often think clearly," Bellow tells Wieseltier, "but to think simply was altogether beyond her, and her imagina-tive faculty was stunted." He goes on to cite the "simple facts":

I once asked Alexander Donat, author of *The Holocaust Kingdom*, how it was that the Jews went down so quickly in Poland. He said something like this: "After three days in the ghetto, unable to wash and shave, without clean clothing, deprived of food, all utilities and municipal ser-vices cut off, your toilet habits humiliatingly disrupted, you are demoralized, confused, subject to panic. A life of austere discipline would have made it possible to keep my head, but how many civilized people had such a life?" Such simple facts—had Hannah had the imagination to see them—would have vitiated her theories.

Arendt may have been a respectable if not wholly respected adversary, but the treasonous Ezra Pound was likely the most poisonous figure by whom Bellow judged both "the terrible events in Poland" and the writers who declined to face them. In 1982, addressing Robert Boyers's commiseration with what Boyers termed an "uncharitable" review of *The Dean's December* by the critic Hugh Kenner, Bellow fulminated against Kenner's "having come out openly in his Eliot-Pound anti-Semitic regalia" in defense of Pound. Infamous for his wartime broadcasts from Mussolini's Italy— tirade after tirade on Jews and "usury"—Pound had nevertheless attracted faithful literary champions. "It was that the poet's convictions could be separated from his poetry," Bellow argued. "It was thus possible to segregate the glory from the shame. Then you took possession of the glory in the name of 'culture' and kept the malignancies as a pet." A quarter of a century before, in 1956, in the most coldly furious confrontation to be found here, Bellow had already accused William Faulkner of heartlessly overlooking Pound's malevolence. As head of a presidentially appointed committee of writers "to promote pro-American values abroad," Faulkner had asked Bellow to sign on to a recommendation for Pound's release from his confinement in a hospital for the insane; though deemed a traitor, he had been spared prison. With uncommon bitterness, Bellow retorted:

> Pound advocated in his poems and in his broadcasts enmity to the Jews and preached hatred and murder. Do you mean to ask me to join you in honoring a man who called for the destruction of my kinsmen? I can take no part in such a thing even if it makes effective propaganda abroad, which I doubt. Europeans will take it instead as a symptom of reaction. In France, Pound would have been shot. Free him because he is a poet? Why, better poets than he were exterminated perhaps.
>
> Shall we say nothing in their behalf? America has dealt mercifully with Pound in sparing his life. To release him is a feeble and foolish idea. It would identify this program in the eyes of the world with Hitler and Himmler and Mussolini and genocide . . . What staggers me is that you and Mr. [John] Steinbeck who have dealt for so many years in words should fail to understand the import of Ezra Pound's plain and brutal statements about the "kikes" leading the "goy" to slaughter. Is this—from *The Pisan Cantos*—the stuff of poetry? It is a call to murder . . . The whole world conspires to ignore what has happened, the giant wars, the colossal hatreds, the unimaginable murders, the destruction of the very image of man. And we—"a representative group of American writers"—is this what we come out for, too?

In light of this uncompromising cri de coeur, and of similar mordant reflections in the novels and stories (covertly in *The Victim* and boldly elsewhere), how are we to regard Bellow's "I was too busy becoming a novelist" apologia? A false note: there was, in fact, no "unspeakable evasion"; rather, an enduring recognition of acid shame and remorse. *And can I really say— can anyone say—what was to be done?* Clearly, and from the first, he saw and he knew.

Now it may be imagined—or even insisted—that too much is being made of all this, that the emphasis here is disproportionate, and that there are other dimensions, more conspicuous and profuse, which can more readily define Bellow as writer. Or it can be said, justifiably, that he openly denigrated anything resembling special pleading—after all, hadn't he brushed off as "a repulsive category" the phrase "Jewish writers in America"? And what was this dismissal if not a repudiation of a vulgarizing tendency to bypass the art in order to laud the artist as a kind of ethnic cheerleader— much as young Jewish baseball fans are encouraged to look to Hank Greenberg for prideful self-validation. Besides, he had long ago put himself on record as freewheeling, unfettered, unprescribed, liberated from direction or coercion. In words that will not be found in the correspondence (they derive from the essays, those publicly personal letters to readers), Bellow wrote, "I would not allow myself to become the product of an *environment*"—flaunting willful italics. And though he never failed to refresh his law of the unleashed life, it rang now with a decisive coda: "In my generation, the children of immigrants *became* American. An effort was required. One made oneself, freestyle . . . I was already an American, and I was also a Jew. I had an American outlook, superadded to a Jewish consciousness." To Faulkner's indifference he could speak—powerfully, inexorably—of "my kinsmen." And to history the same.

Say, then, that he was, as he intended to be, free, unstinting in what he chose to love or mourn or recoil from. The letters tell us whom and how he loved. He loved his sons. He loved John Berryman, John Cheever, Ralph Ellison, Martin Amis. He loved Alfred Kazin (whom he mostly disliked). He loved, to the end, Janis Bellow and their little daughter, Naomi Rose. He loved, even in death, Isaac Rosenfeld, the tumultuously inspired intimate of his youth (who nastily destroyed a hoard of his old friend's letters). He revered—but not always—thought, civilization, and what he named "the very image of man," all of which could be undone. He believed in outcry, and trusted the truth of his own. He was adept at witticism and outright laughter. He was serious in invoking whatever particle of eternity he meant by soul, that old, old inkling he was fearless in calling up from contemporary disgrace.

Like the novels and stories, the letters in their proliferation and spontaneity unveil the life—those sinews of it amenable to utterance—almost to its final breath. What happened soon afterward came to something less. On September 21, 2005, five months after Bellow's death, a celebratory symposium was convened at the 92nd Street Y in New York. The participants included British writers Ian McEwen, Martin Amis, and the critic James Wood, the first two having flown from London for the occasion; William Kennedy and Jeffrey Eugenides completed the panel. Each spoke movingly in turn: joyfully reverential, heartfelt, intermittently (and charmingly) anecdotal, adoring—a density of love. There was mention of modernism, fictional digression, character, childhood, Chicago, crowded tenements, the immigrant poor. Riffing in homage, Amis delivered an imitation of Bellow's laugh, the delight and self-delight of it, the lifted chin, the head thrown back. But all this was a departure from the culminating sentiment—it *was* a sentiment, a susceptibility, a rapturous indulgence—that captivated and dominated these writerly temperaments. Wood: "I judge all modern prose by his . . . The prose comes before and it comes afterward." Amis: "His sentences and his prose were a force of nature." McEwen: "The phrase or sentence has become part of our mental furniture . . . Sentences like these are all you need to know about Saul Bellow." And so on. Understandable, plainly: superb novelists, stellar craftsmen, each one mesmerized by Bellow's unparalleled combinations.

Yet, despite these plenitudes, Saul Bellow was missing on that platform and in that auditorium teeming with admirers—as much missing there as, clothed in living flesh, he is an insistent presence in the letters. It was as if a committee of professional jewelers, loupes in place, had met to sift through heaps of gems strewn scattershot on a velvet scarf—the splendor and flash and glitter of opal and ruby and emerald, the word, the phrase, the sentence, the marvelous juxtapositions, the sublime clashes of style, the precious trove of verbal touchstones!

It was not enough. It was an abundant truth that diminished even as it aggrandized. A mammoth absence opened its jaws—where was the century, the century that Bellow's reality-stung inquisitiveness traversed almost in its entirety, from Trotsky to Wilhelm Reich to Rudolf Steiner; where was the raw and raucously shifting society he knocked about in, undermined, reveled in, and sometimes reviled? Where was his imagined Africa, where were the philosophies he devoured, where were the evanescent infatuations he pursued, where was the clamor of history, and the defiant angers, and the

burning lamentations for the beloved dead, the broken heart for Isaac Rosenfeld, whose writer's envy blazed, and for the father and brothers whose
belittlements never left off hurting? And where, during that long tribute-
laden afternoon in New York, was America itself?

Among the soon-to-be-forgotten novelists of our time, Saul Bellow stays
on. Surely it is for the kaleidoscopic astonishments of his sentences that he
lasts. But not only.

Innovation and Redemption:
What Literature Means

1. Innovation

A while ago, freed by a bout of flu from all responsibility, I became one of those nineteenth-century leisured persons we hear about, for whom the great novels are said to have been written. In this condition I came, for the first time, to the novels of Thomas Hardy. I began with *Tess of the D'Urbervilles*, and discovered this: it is possible first to ask the question "What is this novel about?" and then to give an answer. Hardy writes about—well, *life* (nowadays we are made to hesitate before daring seriously to employ this word); life observed and understood as well as felt. A society with all its interminglings and complexities is set before us: in short, knowledge; knowledge of convention and continuity; also knowledge of something real, something *there. Tess*, for instance, is thick with knowledge of Cow. What is a cow, how does it feel to lean against, how do you milk, what is the milkshed like, what is the life of a milker, who is the milker's boss, where does the milk go? To touch any element of Cow intimately and concretely is to enter a land, a society, a people, and to penetrate into the whole lives of human beings.

The world of Cow, or its current equivalents, is now in the possession of writers like Leon Uris and Harold Robbins—shadows of shadows of Hardy. Post-Joyce, the "real" writers have gone somewhere else. And though we may not, cannot, turn back to the pre-Joycean "fundamentalist" novel, it is about time it was recognized that too much "subjectivity" has led away from mastery (which so-called "experimental" novelist tells us about Cow?) and from seriousness (to which black-humorist or parodist would you entrust the whole lives of human beings?).

What is today called "experimental" writing is unreadable. It fails because it is neither intelligent nor interesting. Without seriousness it cannot be interesting, and without mastery it will never be intelligent.

353

The idea of the experimental derives from the notion of generations: a belief in replacement, substitution, discontinuity, above all repudiation. Who invented "generations," and when did they come into being? John Hollander, reflecting on children's literature, notes that the idea of "children" as a classification of fresh innocence is itself a remarkably short-lived fancy, squeezed into that brief pre-Freudian bourgeois moment that made Lewis Carroll possible; before the nineteenth century there were no children, only smaller-sized working people; and then Freud arrived to take the charm, and the purity, out of Victorian childhood.

There are, in fact, no "generations," except in the biological sense. There are only categories and crises of temperament, and these criss-cross and defy and deny chronology. The concept of generations, moreover, is peculiarly solipsistic: it declares that because I am new, then everything I make or do in the world is new.

When I was a quite young child, just beginning to write stories, I had an odd idea of time. It seemed to me that because writing signified permanence, it was necessary to address not only everyone who might live afterward, but also everyone who had ever lived before. This meant one had to keep one's eye on the ancient Greeks in particular, to write for them too; and, knowing no ancient Greek, I got around the difficulty by employing the most archaic language the Green, Yellow, Blue, Red, and Violet Fairy Books had to offer.

Now if this belief that everything counts forever, both backward and forward, is a kind of paradisal foolishness, it is no more nonsensical than the belief that nothing counts for long—the credo that the newest generation displaces the one before it. The problem with believing in generations is not only the most obvious one—that you excise history, that you cut off even the most immediately usable past—but the sense of narrow obligation it imposes on the young, a kind of prisoner's outlook no less burdensome than all the following dicta taken together:

1. That each new crop of mass births must reinvent culture.
2. That models are unthinkable.
3. That each succeeding generation is inherently brighter and more courageous than the one before.
4. That "establishments" are irreversibly closed.
5. That whatever has won success is by definition stale.
6. That "structurelessness"—i.e., incoherence—must be understood as a paradox, since incoherence is really coherence.

7. That "experiment" is endlessly possible, and endlessly positive, and that the more "unprecedented" a thing is, the better it is.
8. That "alternative forms" are salvational.
9. That irrational (or "psychedelic") states represent artistic newness.

I could make this list longer, but it is already long enough to demonstrate the critical point that more useful cultural news inhabits the Fifth Commandment than one might imagine at first glance.

The sources of these statements are of course everywhere—they are the bad breath of the times. At best, "experimental" fiction aims for parody: it turns the tables on the old voices, it consists of allusion built upon allusion, it is a choreography of ridicule and satire. It goes without saying that no literature can live without satire; satire nourishes and cleanses and resuscitates. The great satires that have survived are majestic indictments. Our attention now is assaulted by ephemeral asterisks claiming to be satire: when you follow the dim little star to its destination, what you find is another littleness—parody. Parody without seriousness, without, in the end, irony. If the writer does not know what to do with the remnants of high culture, he parodies them; if he does not know what to do with kitsch, he simply invites it in. Twenty years hence, the American fiction of parody is going to require an addendum—complete citations of the work and tone and attitude it meant to do in. Whatever seems implicit now because of its currency as memory or tradition will have to be made explicit later, for the sake of comprehension, when tradition is forgotten and memory is dead. (Compare any annotated copy of "The Rape of the Lock.") And meanwhile, the trouble with parody is that it is endlessly reflective, one parody building on a previous parody, and so on, until eventually the goal becomes ingenuity in the varieties of derivativeness, and one loses sight of any original objective notion of what literature can be about, of the real sources of literature. Redundance is all—and in the name of escape from the redundance of convention.

One of the great conventions—and also one of the virtues—of the old novel was its suspensefulness. Suspense *seems* to make us ask "What will happen to Tess next?," but really it emerges from the writer's conviction of social or cosmic principle. Suspense occurs when the reader is about to learn something, not simply about the relationship of fictional characters, but about the writer's relationship to a set of ideas, or to the universe. Suspense is the product of teaching, and teaching is the product of mastery, and mastery is the product of seriousness, and seriousness springs not from ego or ambition or the workings of the subjective self, but from the amazing permutations of the objective world.

Fiction will not be interesting or lasting unless it is again conceived in the art of the didactic. (Emphasis, however, on *art*.) The experimental is almost never the innovative. The innovative imagines something we have never experienced before: think of Tolstoy's imagining the moment of dying in "The Death of Ivan Ilych." The experimental fiddles with what has gone before, precisely and exclusively with what has gone before; it is obsessed by precedent and predecessors. The innovative, by contrast, sets out to educate its readers in its views about what it means to be a human being—though it too can fiddle with this and that if it pleases, and is not averse to unexpected seizures and tricks, or to the jarring gifts of vitality and cunning. Innovation cannot be defined through mere *method*; the experimental can be defined no other way. And innovation has a hidden subject: coherence.

An avatar of "alternative kinds of literary coherence" asks us to note how

the criteria for measuring literacy change in time, so that the body of information and ideas that seemed "literate" in the forties may, because of the sheer increase of knowledge, seem only semi-literate now. Moreover, unless older writers' minds are open enough to recognize that what a young poet learns today may be quite different from what his predecessors know, they may miss evidences of his learning . . . very rare is the literary gent over forty who can recognize, for instance, such recent-vintage ideas as say, feedback, information theory and related cybernetic concepts. This deficiency partially explains why, try as hard as we might, it is often so frustrating, if not impossible, to conduct an intelligent dialogue with older writers, the most dogmatic and semi-literate of whom are simply unable to transcend their closed and hardened ways of thought and learning. Not only do the best educated young minds seem much better educated than older intellectuals were at comparable ages, but also what a well-informed young writer knows is likely to be more relevant, not just to contemporary understanding, but also to the problems of creating literary art today.

(Surely the authors of "The Waste Land" and *Finnegans Wake*, literary and intellectual heroes of the forties, would count as "older writers"—instances, no doubt, of semi-literacy and hardened ways.)

Mindful that youth alone may not altogether make his argument, and relying on the McLuhanite vocabulary current a decade ago, the same writer offers still another variant definition of "coherence":

A truth of contemporary avant-garde esthetics is that "formless art" is either a polemical paradox or an impossible contradiction in terms, for any work that can be defined—that can be characterized in any way—is by definition artistically coherent. It follows that just because a work fails to cohere in a linear fashion need not mean that it cannot be understood; rather, as recent literature accustoms us to its particular ways of organizing expression, so we learn to confront a new work with expectations wholly different from those honed on traditional literature.

Or, history is bunk.

And just here is the danger and the grief—those "wholly different" expectations. If apprentice writers are trained to define away plain contradictions, bringing us at last to a skilled refinement of Orwellian doublethink (incoherence is coherence), if standardized new "information"—though no one doubts that "feedback, information theory and related cybernetic concepts" are the Cow of our time—is to take the place of the idiosyncratic cadences of literary imagination and integration, if "the criteria for measuring literacy" lead to the dumping of both cognition and recognition, if focus and possession are to be dissipated into the pointless distractions and distractabilities of "multimedia" and other devices, if becoming "wholly different" means the tedium of mechanical enmity toward and mechanical overthrow of "older writers," and if all this is to be programmed through hope of instantaneous dissolutions, then not only literature but *the desire to have a literature* will be subverted.

Culture is the continuity of human aspiration—which signifies a continuity of expectations. Innovation in art is not rupture. Innovation in art is not the consequence of the implantation of "wholly different" expectations. Innovation in art means the continuity of expectations.

Every new sentence, every new fragment of imaginative literature born into the world, is a heart-in-the-mouth experiment, and for its writer a profound chanciness; but the point of the risk is the continuation of a recognizably human enterprise. "Wholly different" means unrecognizable; unrecognizable means the breaking-off of a culture, and its supplanting. It cannot be true that the end of a culture is the beginning of art. When cultural continuity is broken off—as in the Third Reich—what happens is first the debasement, then the extirpation, of any recognizable human goals. First the violation of art (Mozart at the gas chamber's door), then the end of art.

Innovation in art is not the same as innovation in the human psyche; just the opposite. Innovation in art has as its motivation the extension of humanity, not a flow of spite against it. The difference between barbarian and civilized expectations is the difference between the will to dominate

357

and the will toward regeneration. To dominate you must throw the rascals out; to regenerate, you have to take them with you. Spite vandalizes. Innovation redeems.

As for who the rascals are: there is no predicament that cures itself so swiftly as that of belonging to "the young." Alice, nibbling at the mushroom, shrank so quickly that her chin crashed into her shoe: *that* fast is how we go from twenty-three to fifty-four, and from fifty-five to eighty-six. *Vita brevis!* If writers are to have a program, it ought not to be toward *ressentiment*, but toward achronology. Younger writers who resent older ones will, before they are nearly ready for it, find themselves hated by someone astonishingly recently out of the pram. Older writers who envy younger ones have a bottomless cornucopia to gorge on: the baby carriages are packed with novelists and poets. The will to fashion a literature asserts the obliteration of time. The obliteration of time makes "experiment" seem a puff of air, the faintest clamor of celestial horselaugh.

2. Redemption

At a party once I heard a gifted and respected American writer—a writer whose prestigious name almost everyone would recognize—say, "For me, the Holocaust and a corncob are the same." The choice of "corncob"—outlandish, unexpected, askew—is a sign of the strong and daring charge of his imagination, and so is its juxtaposition with the darkest word of our century. What he intended by this extraordinary sentence was not to shock the moral sense, but to clarify the nature of art.

He meant that there is, for art, no such element as "subject matter"; for art, one sight or moment or event is as good as another—there is no "value" or "worth" or "meaning"—because all are equally made up of language, and language and its patterns are no different from tone for the composer or color for the painter. The artist as citizen, the writer explained, can be a highly moral man or woman—one who would, if the Nazis came, hide Jews. But the artist as artist is not a moral creature. Within literature, all art is dream, and whether or not the artist is or is not in citizenly possession of moral credentials is irrelevant to the form and the texture of the work of art, which claims only the territory of the imagination, and nothing else.

For that writer, a phrase such as "a morally responsible literature" would be an oxymoron, the earlier part of the phrase clashing to the death with the latter part. To be responsible as a writer is to be responsible solely to the seizures of language and dream.

I want to stand against this view. The writer who says "For me, the Holocaust and a corncob are the same" is putting aside the moral sense in art, equating the moral impulse only with the sociologically real, or perhaps with the theologically ideal. In literature he judges the moral sense to be an absurd intrusion. He is in the stream that comes to us from Greece, through Walter Pater and Emerson: art for its own sake, separated from the moral life. He is mainly Greek.

For me, with certain rapturous exceptions, literature is the moral life. The exceptions occur in lyric poetry, which bursts shadowless like flowers at noon, with the eloquent bliss almost of nature itself, when nature is both benevolent and beautiful. For the rest—well, one discounts stories and novels that are really journalism; but of the stories and novels that mean to be literature, one expects a certain corona of moral purpose: not outright in the grain of the fiction itself, but in the form of a faintly incandescent envelope around it. The tales we care for lastingly are the ones that touch on the redemptive—not, it should be understood, on the guaranteed promise of redemption, and not on goodness, kindness, decency, all the usual virtues. Redemption has almost nothing to do with virtue, especially when the call to virtue is prescriptive or coercive; rather, it is the singular idea that is the opposite of the Greek belief in fate: the idea that insists on the freedom to change one's life.

Redemption means fluidity; the notion that people and things are subject to willed alteration; the sense of possibility; of turning away from, or turning toward; of deliverance; the sense that we act for ourselves rather than are acted upon; the sense that we are responsible, that there is no *deus ex machina* other than the character we have ourselves fashioned; above all, that we can surprise ourselves. Implicit in redemption is amazement, marveling, suspense—precisely that elation-bringing suspense of the didactic I noted earlier, wherein the next revelation is about to fall. Implicit in redemption is everything against the fated or the static: everything that hates death and harm and elevates the life-giving—if only through terror at its absence.

Now I know how hazardous these last phrases are, how they suggest philistinism, how they lend themselves to a vulgar advocacy of an "affirmative" literature in order to fulfill a moral mandate. I too recoil from all that: the so-called "affirmative" is simple-minded, single-minded, crudely explicit; it belongs either to journalism or to piety or to "uplift." It is the enemy of literature and the friend of coercion. It is, above all, a hater of the freedom inherent in storytelling and in the poetry side of life. But I mean something else: I mean the corona, the luminous envelope—perhaps what Henry James meant when he said "Art is nothing more than the shadow of humanity."

I think, for instance, of the literature of midrash, of parable, where there is no visible principle or moral imperative. The principle does not enter into, or appear in, the tale; it is the tale; it realizes the tale. To put it another way: the tale is its own interpretation. It is a world that decodes itself.

And that is what the "corona" is: interpretation, implicitness, the nimbus of *meaning* that envelops story. Only someone who has wholly dismissed meaning can boast that the Holocaust and a corncob are, for art, the same. The writers who claim that fiction is self-referential, that what a story is about is the language it is made out of, have snuffed the corona. They willingly sit in the dark, like the strict-constructionist Karaites who, wanting to observe the Sabbath exactly, sat in the lampless black and the fireless cold on the very day that is most meant to resemble paradise. The misuse of the significance of language by writers who most intend to celebrate the comeliness of language is like the misuse of the Sabbath by the fundamentalist Karaites: both annihilate the thing they hope to glorify.

What literature means is meaning.

But having said that, I come to something deeply perilous: and that is imagination. In Hebrew, just as there is *t'shuva*, the energy of creative renewal and turning, so there is the *yetzer ha-ra*, the Evil Impulse—so steeped in the dark brilliance of the visionary that it is said to be the source of the creative faculty. Imagination is more than make-believe, more than the power to invent. It is also the power to penetrate evil, to take on evil, to become evil, and in that guise it is the most frightening human faculty. Whoever writes a story that includes villainy enters into and becomes the villain. Imagination owns above all the facility of becoming: the writer can enter the leg of a mosquito, a sex not her own, a horizon he has never visited, a mind smaller or larger. But also the imagination seeks out the unsayable and the undoable, and says and does them. And still more dangerous: the imagination always has the lust to tear down meaning, to smash interpretation, to wear out the rational, to mock the surprise of redemption, to replace the fluid force of suspense with an image of stasis; to transfix and stun rather than to urge; to spill out, with so much quicksilver wonder, idol after idol. An idol serves no one; it is served. The imagination, like Moloch, can take you nowhere except back to its own maw. And the writers who insist that literature is "about" the language it is made of are offering an idol: literature for its own sake, for its own maw: not for the sake of humanity.

Literature is for the sake of humanity.

My conclusion is strange, and takes place on a darkling plain. Literature, to come into being at all, must call on the imagination; imagination is in fact the flesh and blood of literature; but at the same time imagination is the very force that struggles to snuff the redemptive corona. So a redemptive literature, a literature that interprets and decodes the world, beaten out for the sake of humanity, must wrestle with its own body, with its own flesh and blood, with its own life. Cell battles cell. The corona flickers, brightens, flares, clouds, grows faint. The *yetzer ha-ra*, the Evil Impulse, fills its cheeks with a black wind, hoping to blow out the redemptive corona; but at the last moment steeples of light spurt up from the corona, and the world with its meaning is laid open to our astonished sight.

In that steady interpretive light we can make distinctions; we can see that one thing is not interchangeable with another thing; that not everything is the same; that the Holocaust is different, God knows, from a corncob. So we arrive, at last, at the pulse and purpose of literature: to reject the blur of the "universal"; to distinguish one life from another; to illumine diversity; to light up the least grain of being, to show how it is concretely individual, particularized from any other; to tell, in all the marvel of its singularity, the separate holiness of the least grain.

Literature is the recognition of the particular.

For that, one needs the corona.

LOSSES

Isaac Babel and the
Identity Question

Identity, at least, is prepared to ask questions.
—LEON WIESELTIER

A year or so before the Soviet Union imploded, S.'s mother, my first cousin—whose existence until then had been no more than a distant legend—telephoned from Moscow. "Save my child!" she cried, in immemorial tones. So when S. arrived in New York, I expected a terrified refugee on the run from the intolerable exactions of popular anti-semitism; at that time the press was filled with such dire reports. For months, preparing for her rescue, I had been hurtling from one agency to another, in search of official information on political asylum.

But when S. finally turned up, in black tights, a miniskirt, and the reddest lipstick, it was clear she was indifferent to all that. She didn't want to be saved; what she wanted was an American holiday, a fresh set of boyfriends, and a leather coat. She had brought with her a sizable cosmetics case, amply stocked, and a vast, rattling plastic bag stuffed with hundreds of cheap tin Komsomol medals depicting Lenin as a boy. She was scornful of these; they were worthless, she said; she had paid pennies for the lot. Within two weeks S., a natural entrepreneur, had established romantic relations with the handsome young manager of the local sports store and had got him to set up a table at Christmas in his heaviest traffic location. She sold the tin Lenin medals for three dollars each, made three hundred dollars in a day; and bought the leather coat.

Of course she was a great curiosity. Her English was acutely original, her green eyes gave out ravishing ironic lightnings, her voice was as dark as Garbo's in *Ninotchka*, and none of us had ever seen an actual Soviet citizen up close before. She thought the telephone was bugged. She thought the supermarket was a public exhibition. Any show of household shoddiness—a lamp, say, that came apart—would elicit from her a comical crow: "Like in

Soviet!" She was, emphatically, no atheist: she had an affinity for the occult, believed that God could speak in dreams (she owned a dream book, through which Jesus often walked), adored the churches of old Russia, and lamented their destruction by the Bolsheviks. On the subject of current anti-Semitism she was mute; that was her mother's territory. Back in Moscow, her boyfriend, Gennadi, had picked her up in the subway *because* she was Jewish. He was in a hurry to marry her. "He want get out of Soviet," she explained.

At home she was a *Sportsdoktor*: she traveled with the Soviet teams, roughneck country boys, and daily tested their urine for steroids. (Was this to make sure her athletes were properly dosed?) She announced that *everybody* hated Gorbachev; only the gullible Americans liked him, he was a joke like all the others. A historically-minded friend approached S. with the earnest inquiry of an old-fashioned liberal idealist: "We all know, obviously, about the excesses of Stalinism," she said, "but what of the beginning? Wasn't Communism a truly beautiful hope at the start?" S. laughed her cynical laugh; she judged my friend profoundly stupid. "Communism," she scoffed, "what Communism? Naive! Fairy tale, always! No Communism, never! Naive!"

And leaving behind five devastated American-as-apple-pie boyfriends (and wearing her leather coat), S. returned to Moscow. She did not marry Gennadi. Her mother emigrated to Israel. The last I heard of S., she was in business in Sakhalin, buying and selling—and passing off as the real thing– ersatz paleolithic mammoth tusks.

Well, it's all over now—the Great Experiment, as the old brave voices used to call it—and S. is both symptom and proof of how thoroughly it is over. She represents the Soviet Union's final heave, its last generation. S. is the consummate New Soviet Man: the unfurled future of its seed. If there is an axiom here, it is that idealism squeezed into utopian channels will generate a cynicism so profound that no inch of human life—not youth, not art, not work, not romance, not introspection—is left untainted. The S. I briefly knew trusted nothing; in her world there was nothing to trust. The primal Communist fairy tale had cast its spell: a baba yaga's birth-curse.

In college I read the Communist Manifesto, a rapture-bringing psalm. I ought to have read Isaac Babel's *Red Cavalry* stories—if only as a corrective companion text. Or antidote. "But what of the beginning?" my friend had asked. S. answered better than any historian, but no one will answer more terrifyingly than Isaac Babel. If S. is the last generation of New Soviet Man, he is the first—the Manifesto's primordial manifestation.

That Babel favored the fall of the Czarist regime is no anomaly. He was a Jew from Odessa, the child of an enlightened family, hungry for a European education; he was subject to the *numerus clausus*, the Czarist quota that kept Jews as a class out of the universities, and Babel in particular out of the University of Odessa. As a very young writer, he put himself at risk when—to be near Maxim Gorky, his literary hero—he went to live illegally in St. Petersburg, a city outside the Pale of Settlement (the area to which Jews were restricted). What Jew would not have welcomed the demise of a hostile and obscurantist polity that, as late as 1911, tried Mendel Beiliss in a Russian court on a fantastic blood-libel charge, and what Jew in a time of government-sanctioned pogroms would not have turned with relief to forces promising to topple the oppressors? In attaching himself to the Bolshevik cause, Babel may have been more zealous than many, but far from aberrant. If the choice were either Czar or Bolshevism, what Jew could choose Czar? (A third possibility; which scores of thousands sought, was escape to America.) But even if one were determined to throw one's lot in with the Revolution, what Jew would go riding with Cossacks?

In 1920 Isaac Babel went riding with Cossacks. It was the third year of the Civil War—Revolutionary Reds versus Czarist Whites; he was twenty-six. Babel was not new to the military. Two years earlier, during the First World War, he had been a volunteer—in the Czar's army—on the Romanian front, where he contracted malaria. In 1919 he fought with the Red Army to secure St. Petersburg against advancing government troops. And in 1920 he joined ROSTA, the Soviet wire service, as a war correspondent for the newspaper *Red Cavalryman*. Poland, newly independent, was pressing eastward, hoping to recover its eighteenth-century borders, while the Bolsheviks, moving west, were furiously promoting the Communist salvation of Polish peasants and workers. The Polish-Soviet War appeared to pit territory against ideology; in reality territory—or, more precisely, the conquest of impoverished villages and towns and their wretched inhabitants—was all that was at stake for either side. Though the Great War was over, the Allies, motivated by fear of the spread of Communism, went to the aid of Poland with equipment and volunteers. (Ultimately the Poles prevailed and the Bolsheviks retreated, between them despoiling whole populations.)

In an era of air battles, Babel was assigned to the First Cavalry Army; a Cossack division led by General Semyon Budyonny. The Cossack image—glinting sabers, pounding hooves—is indelibly fused with Czarist power, but the First Cavalry Army was, perversely, Bolshevik. Stalin was in command of the southern front—the region abutting Poland—and Budyonny was in league with Stalin. Ostensibly, then, Babel found himself among men sympathetic to Marxist doctrine; yet Red Cossacks were no different from White

Cossacks: untamed riders, generally illiterate, boorish and brutish, suspicious of ideas of any kind, attracted only to horseflesh, rabid looting, and the quick satisfaction of hunger and lust. "This isn't a Marxist revolution," Babel privately noted; "it's a rebellion of Cossack wild men." Polish and Russian cavalrymen clashing in ditches while warplanes streaked overhead was no more incongruous than the raw sight of Isaac Babel—a writer who had already published short stories praised by Gorky—sleeping in mud with Cossacks.

Lionel Trilling, in a highly nuanced (though partially misinformed) landmark introduction to a 1955 edition of *The Collected Stories of Isaac Babel*—which included the Red Cavalry stories speaks of "the joke of a Jew who is a member of a Cossack regiment." A joke, Trilling explains, because

> traditionally the Cossack was the feared and hated enemy of the Jew
> . . . The principle of his existence stood in total antithesis to the principle of the Jew's existence. The Jew conceived of his own ideal character as being intellectual, pacific, humane. The Cossack was physical, violent, without mind or manners . . . the natural and appropriate instrument of ruthless oppression.

Yet Trilling supplies another, more glamorous, portrait of the Cossack, which he terms Tolstoyan: "He was the man as yet untrammeled by civilization, direct, immediate, fierce. He was the man of enviable simplicity, the man of the body—the man who moved with speed and grace." In short, "our fantasy of the noble savage." And he attributes this view to Babel.

As it turns out, Babel's tenure with Budyonny's men was more tangled, and more intricately psychological, than Trilling—for whom the problem was tangled and psychological enough—could have known or surmised. For one thing, Trilling mistakenly believed that Babel's job was that of a supply officer—i.e., that he was actually a member of the regiment. But as a correspondent for a news agency (which meant grinding out propaganda), Babel's position among the troops was from the start defined as an outsider's, Jew or no. He was there as a writer. Worse, in the absence of other sources, Trilling fell into a crucial-and surprisingly naive—second error: he supposed that the "autobiographical" tales were, in fact, autobiographical. Babel, Trilling inferred from Babel's stories, "was a Jew of the ghetto" who "when he was nine years old had seen his father kneeling before a Cossack captain." He compares this (fictitious) event to Freud's contemplation of his father's "having accepted in a pacific way the insult of having his new fur cap knocked into the mud by a Gentile who shouted at him, 'Jew, get off the pavement.'" "We might put it," Trilling concludes, that Babel rode with

Budyonny's troops because he had witnessed his father's humiliation by "a Cossack on a horse, who said, 'At your service,' and touched his fur cap with his yellow-gloved hand and politely paid no heed to the mob looting the Babel store."

There was no Babel store. This scene—the captain with the yellow glove, the Jew pleading on his knees while the pogrom rages—is culled from Babel's story "First Love." But it was reinforced for Trilling by a fragmentary memoir, published in 1924, wherein Babel calls himself "the son of a Jewish shopkeeper." The truth was that Babel was the son of the class enemy: a well-off family His father sold agricultural machinery and owned a warehouse in a business section of Odessa where numerous import-export firms were located. In the same memoir Babel records that because he had no permit allowing him residence in St. Petersburg, he hid out "in a cellar on Pushkin Street which was the home of a tormented, drunken waiter." This was pure fabrication: in actuality Babel was taken in by a highly respectable engineer and his wife, with whom he was in correspondence. The first invention was to disavow a bourgeois background in order to satisfy Communist dogma. The second was a romantic imposture.

It did happen, nevertheless, that the young Babel was witness to a pogrom. He was in no way estranged from Jewish suffering or sensibility, or, conversely, from the seductive winds of contemporary Europe. Odessa was modern, bustling, diverse, cosmopolitan; its very capaciousness stimulated a certain worldliness and freedom of outlook. Jewish children were required to study the traditional texts and commentaries, but they were also sent to learn the violin. Babel was early on infatuated with Maupassant and Flaubert, and wrote his first stories in fluent literary French. In his native Russian he lashed himself mercilessly to the discipline of an original style, the credo of which was burnished brevity, At the time of his arrest by the NKVD in 1939—he had failed to conform to Socialist Realism—he was said to be at work on a Russian translation of Sholem Aleichem.

Given these manifold intertwinings, it remains odd that Trilling's phrase for Babel was "a Jew of the ghetto." Trilling himself had characterized Babel's Odessa as "an eastern Marseilles or Naples," observing that "in such cities the transient, heterogeneous population dilutes the force of law and tradition, for good as well as for bad." One may suspect that Trilling's cultural imagination (and perhaps his psyche as well) was circumscribed by a kind of either / or: *either* worldly sophistication *or* the ghetto; and that, in linking Jewish learning solely to the ghetto, he could not conceive of its association with a broad and complex civilization. This partial darkening of mind, it seems to me, limits Trilling's understanding of Babel. An intellectual who had mastered the essentials of rabbinic literature, Babel was an educated Jew not "of the ghetto," but of the world. And not "of both worlds," as the divisive expression has it, but of the great and variegated map of human thought and experience.

Trilling, after all, in his own youth had judged the world to be rigorously divided. In 1933, coming upon one of Hemingway's letters, he wrote in his notebook:

[A] crazy letter, written when he was drunk—self-revealing, arrogant, scared, trivial, absurd; yet [I] felt from reading it how right such a man is compared to the 'good minds' of my university life—how he will pro-duce and mean something to the world . . . how his life which he could expose without dignity and which is anarchic and 'childish' is a better life than anyone I know could live, and right for his job. And how far— far—far—I am going from being a writer.

Trilling envied but could not so much as dream himself into becoming a version of Hemingway—rifle in one hand and pen in the other, intellectual Jew taking on the strenuous life; how much less, then, could he fathom Babel as Cossack. Looking only to Jewish constriction, what Trilling vitally missed was this: coiled in the bottom-most pit of every driven writer is an impersonator—protean, volatile, restless and relentless. Trilling saw only stasis, or, rather, an unalterable consistency of identity: either lucubrations or daring, never both. But Babel imagined for himself an identity so fluid that, having lodged with his civilized friend, the St. Petersburg engineer, it pleased him to invent a tougher Babel consorting underground with a "tor-mented, drunken waiter." A drunken waiter would have been adventure enough—but ah, that Dostoyevskian "tormented"!

"He loved to confuse and mystify people," his daughter Nathalie wrote of him, after decades spent in search of his character. Born in 1929, she lived with her mother in Paris, where her father was a frequent, if raffish, visitor. In 1935 Babel was barred from leaving the Soviet Union, and never again saw his wife and child. Nathalie Babel was ten when Babel was arrested. In 1961 she went to look for traces of her father in Moscow, "where one can still meet people who loved him and continue to speak of him with nostalgia. There, thousands of miles from my own home in Paris, sitting in his living room, in his own chair, drinking from his glass, I felt utterly baffled. Though in a sense I had tracked him down, he still eluded me. The void remained."

In a laudatory reminiscence published in a Soviet literary magazine in

1964—a time when Babel's reputation was undergoing a modicum of "rehabilitation"—Georgy Munblit, a writer who had known Babel as well as anyone, spoke of "this sly, unfaithful, eternally evasive and mysterious Babel"; and though much of this elusiveness was caution in the face of Soviet restriction, a good part of it nevertheless had to do with the thrill of dissimulation and concealment. In a mid-sixties Moscow speech at a meeting championing Babel's work, Ilya Ehrenburg—the literary Houdini who managed to survive every shift of Stalinist whim—described Babel as liking to "play the fool and put on romantic airs. He liked to create an atmosphere of mystery about himself; he was secretive and never told anybody where he was going."

Other writers (all of whom had themselves escaped the purges) came forward with recollections of Babel's eccentricities in risky times: Babel as intrepid wanderer; as trickster, rapscallion, ironist; penniless, slippery, living on the edge, off the beaten track, down and out; seduced by the underlife of Paris, bars, whores, cab drivers, jockeys—all this suggests Orwellian experiment and audacity. Babel relished Villon and Kipling, and was delighted to discover that Rimbaud too was an "adventurer." Amusing and mercurial, "he loved to play tricks on people," according to Lev Nikulin, who was at school with Babel and remembered him "as a bespectacled boy in a rather shabby school coat and a battered cap with a green band and badge depicting Mercury's staff."

Trilling, writing in 1955, had of course no access to observations such as these; and we are as much in need now as Trilling was of a valid biography of Babel. Yet it is clear even from such small evidences and quicksilver portraits that Babel's connection with the Cossacks was, if not inevitable, more natural than not; and that Trilling's Freudian notion of the humiliated ghetto child could not have been more off the mark. For Babel lamp-oil and fearlessness were not antithetical. He was a man with the bit of recklessness between his teeth. One might almost ask how a writer so given to disguises and role-playing could *not* have put on a Cossack uniform.

"The Rebbe's Son," one of the *Red Cavalry* tales, is explicit about this fusion of contemplative intellect and physical danger. Ilya, the son of the Zhitomir Rebbe, "the last prince of the dynasty," is a Red Army soldier killed in battle. The remnants of his possessions are laid out before the narrator:

> Here everything was dumped together—the warrants of the agitator and
> the commemorative booklets of the Jewish poet. Portraits of Lenin and
> Maimonides lay side by side. Lenin's nodulous skull and the tarnished
> silk of the portraits of Maimonides. A strand of female hair had been

placed in a book of the resolutions of the Sixth Party Congress, and in the margins of Communist leaflets swarmed crooked lines of ancient Hebrew verse. In a sad and meager rain they fell on me—pages of the Song of Songs and revolver cartridges.

Babel was himself drawn to the spaciousness and elasticity of these unexpected combinations. They held no enigma for him. But while the Rebbes son was a kind of double patriot—loyal to the God of Abraham, Isaac and Jacob, and loyal to a dream of the betterment of Russia—Babel tended toward both theological and (soon enough) political skepticism. His *amor patriae* was passionately—for the Russian mother-tongue. Before the Stalinist prison clanged shut in 1935, Babel might easily have gone to live permanently in France, with his wife and daughter. Yet much as he reveled in French literature and language, he would not suffer exile from his native Russian. A family can be replaced, or duplicated; but who can replace or duplicate the syllables of Pushkin and Tolstoy? And, in fact (though his wife in Paris survived until 1957, and there was no divorce), Babel did take another wife in the Soviet Union, who gave birth to another daughter; a second family was possible. A second language was not. (Only consider what must be the intimate sorrows—even in the shelter of America, even after the demise of Communism—of Czeslaw Milosz, Joseph Brodksy, Norman Manea, and countless other less celebrated literary refugees.) By remaining in the Soviet Union, and refusing finally to bend his art to Soviet directives, Babel sacrificed his life to his language.

It was a language he did not allow to rest. He meant to put his spurs to it, and run it to unexampled leanness. He quoted Pushkin: "precision and brevity." "Superior craftsmanship," Babel told Munblit, "is the art of making your writing as unobtrusive as possible." Ehrenburg recalled a conversation in Madrid with Hemingway, who had just discovered Babel. "I find that Babel's style is even more concise than mine . . . It shows what can be done," Hemingway marveled. "Even when you've got all the water out of them, you can still clot the curds a little more." Such idiosyncratic experiments in style were hardly congruent with official pressure to honor the ascent of socialism through prescriptive prose about the beauty of collective farming. Babel did not dissent from Party demands; instead he fell mainly into silence, writing in private and publishing almost nothing. His attempts at a play and a filmscript met convulsive Party criticism; the director of the film, an adaptation of a story by Turgenev, was forced into a public apology.

The *Red Cavalry* stories saw print, individually; before 1924. Soviet cultural policies in those years were not yet consolidated; it was a period of postrevolutionary leniency and ferment. Russian modernism was sprouting in the shape of formalism, acmeism, imagism, symbolism; an intellectual and artistic avant-garde flourished. Censorship, which had been endemic to the Czarist regime, was reintroduced in 1922, but the restraints were loose. Despite a program condemning elitism, the early Soviet leadership, comprising a number of intellectuals—Lenin, Bukharin, Trotsky—recognized that serious literature could not be wholly entrusted to the sensibilities of Party bureaucrats. By 1924, then, Babel found himself not only famous, but eligible eventually for Soviet rewards: an apartment in Moscow, a dacha in the country, a car and chauffeur.

Yet he was increasingly called on to perform (and conform) by the blunter rulers of a darkening repression: why was he not writing in praise of New Soviet Man? Little by little a perilous mist gathered around Babel's person: though his privileges were not revoked (he was at his dacha on the day of his arrest), he began to take on a certain pariah status. When a leftist Congress for the Defense of Culture and Peace met in Paris, for example, Babel was deliberately omitted from the Soviet delegation, and was grudgingly allowed to attend only after the French organizers brought their protests to the Soviet Embassy.

Certain manuscripts he was careful not to expose to anyone. Among these was the remarkable journal he had kept, from June to September 1920, of the actions of Budyonny's First Cavalry Army in eastern Poland. Because it was missing from the papers seized by the secret police at the dacha and in his Moscow flat, the manuscript escaped destruction, and came clandestinely into the possession of Babel's (second) wife only in the 1950s. Ehrenburg was apparently the journal's first influential reader, though very likely he did not see it until the 1960s, when he mentioned it publicly, and evidently spontaneously, in his rehabilitation speech:

> I have been comparing the diary of the Red Cavalry with the stories. He scarcely changed any names, the events are all practically the same, but everything is illuminated with a kind of wisdom. He is saying: this is how it was. This is how the people were—they did terrible things and they suffered, they played tricks on others and they died. He made his stories out of the facts and phrases hastily jotted down in his notebook.

It goes without saying that the flatness of this essentially evasive summary does almost no justice to an astonishing historical record set down with godlike prowess in a prose of frightening clarity. In Russia the complete text of the journal finally appeared in 1990. Yale University Press brings it to us now under the title *Isaac Babel: 1920 Diary*, in an electrifying translation, accompanied by a first-rate (and indispensable) introduction. (It ought to be added that an informative introduction can be found also in the Penguin *Collected Stories*; but the reader's dependence on such piecemeal discussions only underscores the irritating absence of a formal biography.) In 1975 Ardis Publishers, specialists in Russian studies, made available the first English translation of excerpts from the journal (*Isaac Babel: Forgotten Prose*). That such a manuscript existed had long been known in the Soviet Union, but there was plainly no chance of publication; Ehrenburg, in referring to it, was discreet about its contents.

The *Diary* may count, then, as a kind of secret document; certainly as a suppressed one. But it is "secret" in another sense as well. Though it served as raw material for the *Red Cavalry* stories, Babel himself, in transforming private notes into daring fiction, was less daring than he might have been. He was, in fact, circumspect and selective. One can move from the notes to the stories without surprise—or put it that the surprise is in the masterliness and shock of a ripe and radical style. Still, as Ehrenburg reported, "the events are all practically the same," and what is in the *Diary* is in the stories.

But one cannot begin with the stories and then move to the journal without the most acute recognition of what has been, substantively and for the most part, shut out of the fiction. And what has been shut out is the calamity (to say it in the most general way) of Jewish fate in Eastern Europe. The *Diary* records how the First Cavalry Army, and Babel with it, went storming through the little Jewish towns of Galicia, in Poland—towns that had endured the Great War, with many of their young men serving in the Polish army, only to be decimated by pogroms immediately afterward, at the hands of the Poles themselves. And immediately after that, the invasion of the Red Cossacks. The Yale edition of the *Diary* supplies maps showing the route of Budyonny's troops; the resonant names of these places, rendered half-romantic through the mystical tales of their legendary hasidic saints, rise up with the nauseous familiarity of their deaths: Brody, Dubno, Zhitomir, Belz, Chelm, Zamosc, etc. Only two decades after the Red Cossacks stampeded through them, their Jewish populations fell prey to the Germans and were destroyed. Riding and writing, writing and riding, Babel saw it all: saw it like a seer. "Ill-fated Galicia, ill-fated Jews," he wrote. "Can it be," he wrote, "that ours is the century in which they perish?"

True: everything that is in the stories is in the *Diary*—priest, painter, widow, guncart, soldier, prisoner; but the heart of the *Diary* remains secreted in the *Diary*. When all is said and done—and much is said and done in these blistering pages: pillaged churches, ruined synagogues, wild Russians, beaten

Poles, mud, horses, hunger, looting, shooting—Babel's journal is a Jewish lamentation: a thing the Soviet system could not tolerate, and Ehrenburg was too prudent to reveal. The merciless minds that snuffed the identities of the murdered at Babi Yar would hardly sanction Babel's whole and bloody truths.

Nor did Babel himself publicly sanction them. *The Red Cavalry* narratives include six stories (out of thirty-five) that touch on the suffering of Jews; the headlong *Diary* contains scores. An act of authorial self-censorship, and not only because Babel was determined to be guarded. Impersonation, or call it reckless play, propelled him at all points. The *Diary* can muse: "The Slavs—the manure of history?"—but Babel came to the Cossacks disguised as a Slav, having assumed the name K. L. Lyutov, the name he assigns also to his narrator. And in the *Diary* itself, encountering terrified Polish Jews, he again and again steers them away from the knowledge that rides in his marrow, and fabricates deliberate Revolutionary fairy tales (his word): he tells his trembling listeners how "everything's changing for the better—my usual system—miraculous things are happening in Russia—express trains, free food for children, theaters, the International. They listen with delight and disbelief. I think-you'll have your diamond-studded sky, everything and everyone will be turned upside down and inside out for the umpteenth time, and [I] feel sorry for them."

"My usual system": perhaps it is kind to scatter false consolations among the doomed. Or else it is not kindness at all, merely a writer's mischief or a rider's diversion—the tormented mice of Galicia entertained by a cat in Cossack dress. Sometimes he is recognized as a Jew (once by a child), and then he half-lies and explains that he has a Jewish mother. But mainly he is steadfast in the pretense of being Lyutov. And nervy: the *Diary* begins on June 3, in Zhitomir, and on July 12, one day before Babel's twenty-sixth birthday, he notes: "My first ride on horseback." In no time at all he is, at least on horseback, like all the others: a skilled and dauntless trooper. "The horse galloped well," he says on that first day. Enchanted, proud, he looks around at his companions: "red flags, a powerful, well-knit body of men, confident commanders, calm and experienced eyes of topknotted Cossack fighting men, dust, silence, order, brass band." But moments later the calm and experienced eyes are searching out plunder in the neat cottage of an immigrant Czech family, "all good people." "I took nothing, although I could have," the new horseman comments. "I'll never be a real Budyonny man."

The real Budyonny men are comely, striking, stalwart. Turning off a highway, Babel catches sight of "the brigades suddenly appear[ing], inexplicable beauty, an awesome force advancing." Another glimpse: "Night . . .

horses are quietly snorting, they're all Kuban Cossacks here, they eat together, sleep together, a splendid silent comradeship . . . they sing songs that sound like church music in lusty voices, their devotion to horses, beside each man a little heap—saddle, bridle, ornamental saber, greatcoat, I sleep in the midst of them."

Babel is small, his glasses are small and round, he sets down secret sentences. And meanwhile his dispatches, propaganda screeches regularly published in *Red Cavalryman*, have a different tone: "Soldiers of the Red Army, finish them off! Beat down harder on the opening covers of their stinking graves!" And: "That is what they are like, our heroic nurses! Caps off to the nurses! Soldiers and commanders, show respect to the nurses!" (In the *Diary* the dubious propagandist writes satirically, "Opening of the Second Congress of the Third International, unification of the peoples finally realized, now all is clear . . . We shall advance into Europe and conquer the world.")

And always there is cruelty, and always there are the Jews. "Most of the rabbis have been exterminated." "The Jewish cemetery . . . hundreds of years old, gravestones have toppled over . . . overgrown with grass, it has seen Khmelnitsky, now Budyonny . . . everything repeats itself, now that whole story—Poles, Cossacks, Jews—is repeating itself with stunning exactitude, the only new element is Communism." "They all say they're fighting for justice and they all loot." "Life is loathsome, murderers, it's unbearable, baseness and crime." "I ride along with them, begging the men not to massacre prisoners . . . I couldn't look at their faces, they bayoneted some, shot others, bodies covered by corpses, they strip one man while they're shooting another, groans, screams, death rattles." "We are destroyers . . . we move like a whirlwind, like a stream of lava, hated by everyone, life shatters, I am at a huge, never-ending service for the dead . . . the sad senselessness of my life."

The Jews: "The Poles ransacked the place, then the Cossacks." "Hatred for the Poles is unanimous. They have looted, tortured, branded the pharmacist with a red-hot iron, put needles under his nails, pulled out his hair, all because somebody shot at a Polish officer." "The Jews ask me to use my influence to save them from ruin, they are being robbed of food and goods . . . The cobbler had looked forward to Soviet rule—and what he sees are Jew-baiters and looters . . . Organized looting of a stationer's shop, the proprietor in tears, they tear up everything . . . When night comes the whole town will be looted—everybody knows it."

The Jews at the hands of the Poles: "A pogrom . . . a naked, barely breathing prophet of an old man, an old woman butchered, a child with fingers chopped off, many people still breathing, stench of blood, everything turned upside down, chaos, a mother sitting over her sabered son, an old woman lying twisted up like a pretzel, four people in one hovel, filth, blood under a black beard, just lying there in the blood."

The Jews at the hands of the Bolsheviks: "Our men nonchalantly walking around looting whenever possible, stripping mangled corpses. The hatred is the same, the Cossacks just the same, it's nonsense to think one army is different from another. The life of these little towns. There's no salvation. Everyone destroys them." "Our men were looting last night, tossed out the Torah scrolls in the synagogue and took the velvet covers for saddlecloths. The military commissar's dispatch rider examines phylacteries, wants to take the straps." The *Diary* mourns, "What a mighty and marvelous life of a nation existed here. The fate of Jewry."

And then: "I am an outsider." And again: "I don't belong, I'm all alone, we ride on . . . five minutes after our arrival the looting starts, women struggling, weeping and wailing, it's unbearable, I can't stand these never-ending horrors . . . [I] snatch a flatcake out of the hands of a peasant woman's little boy." He does this mechanically, and without compunction.

"How we eat," he explains. "Red troops arrive in a village, ransack the place, cook, stoves crackling all night, the householders' daughters have a hard time" (a comment we will know how to interpret). Babel grabs the child's flatcake—a snack on the fly, as it were—on August 3. On July 25, nine days earlier, he and a riding companion, Prishchepa, a loutish syphilitic illiterate, have burst into a pious Jewish house in a town called Demidovka. It is the Sabbath, when lighting a fire is forbidden; it is also the eve of the Ninth of Av, a somber fast day commemorating the destruction of the Temple in Jerusalem. Prishchepa demands fried potatoes. The dignified mother, a flock of daughters in white stockings, a scholarly son, are all petrified; on the Sabbath, they protest, they cannot dig potatoes, and besides, the fast begins at sundown. "Fucking Yids," Prishchepa yells; so the potatoes are dug, the fire to cook them is lit.

Babel, a witness to this anguish, says nothing. "I keep quiet, because I'm a Russian"—will Prishchepa discover that Lyutov is only another Yid? "We eat like oxen, fried potatoes and five tumblersful of coffee each. We sweat, they keep serving us, all this is terrible, I tell them fairy tales about Bolshevism." Night comes, the mother sits on the floor and sobs, the son chants the liturgy for the Ninth of Av—Jeremiah's Lamentations: "They eat dung, their maidens are ravished, their menfolk killed, Israel subjugated." Babel hears and understands every Hebrew word. "Dernidovka, night, Cossacks," he sums it up, "all just as it was when the Temple was destroyed. I go out to sleep in the yard, stinking and damp."

And there he is, New Soviet Man: stinking, a sewer of fairy tales, an unbeliever—and all the same complicit. Nathalie Babel said of her father that nothing "could shatter his feeling that he belonged to Russia and that he had to share the fate of his countrymen. What in so many people would have produced only fear and terror, awakened in him a sense of duty and a kind of blind heroism." In the brutal light of the *Diary*—violation upon violation—it is hard not to resist this point of view. Despair and an abyss of cynicism do not readily accord with a sense of duty; and whether or not Babel's travels with the Cossacks—and with Bolshevism altogether—deserve to be termed heroic, he was anything but blind. He saw, he saw, and he saw.

It may be that the habit of impersonation, the habit of deception, the habit of the mask, will in the end lead a man to become what he impersonates. Or it may be that the force of "I am an outsider" overwhelms the secret gratification of having got rid of a fixed identity. In any case, the *Diary* tells no lies. These scenes in a journal, linked by commas quicker than human breath, run like rapids through a gorge—on one side the unrestraint of violent men, on the other the bleaker freedom of unbelonging. Each side is subversive of the other; and still they embrace the selfsame river.

To venture yet another image, Babel's *Diary* stands as a tragic masterwork of breakneck cinematic "dailies"—those raw, unedited rushes that expose the director to himself. If Trilling, who admitted to envy of the milder wilderness that was Hemingway, had read Babel's *Diary*—what then? And who, in our generation, should read the *Diary*? Novelists and poets, of course; specialists in Russian literature, obviously; American innocents who define the world of the twenties by jazz, flappers, and Fitzgerald. And also: all those who protested Claude Lanzrnann's film *Shoah* as unfair to the psyche of the Polish countryside; but, most of all, the cruelly ignorant children of the Left who still believe that the Marxist Utopia requires for its realization only a more favorable venue, and another go.

No one knows when or exactly how Babel perished. Some suppose he was shot immediately after the NKVD picked him up and brought him to Moscow's Lyubanka prison, on May 16, 1939. Others place the date of his murder in 1941, following months of torture.* More than fifty years later, as

---

* But a letter from Robert Conquest, dated May 15, 1995, offers the following: "Babel's fate is in fact known. Arrested on 16 May 1939, he was subjected to three days and nights of intensive interrogation on 29-31 May, at the end of which he confessed. At various interrogations over the year he withdrew that part of his confession that incriminated other writers. At his secret trial on 26 January 1940, he pled not guilty on all counts. The main charges were of Trotskyism; espionage for Austria and France (the latter on behalf of Andre Malraux); and involvement in a terrorist plot against Stalin and Voroshilov by former NKVD chief Nikolai Yezhov, whose wife Babel knew. He was shot at 1:40 A.M. the next day."

if the writer were sending forth phantoms of his first and last furies, Babel's youthful *Diary* emerges. What it attests to above all is not simply that fairy tales can kill—who doesn't understand this?—but that Bolshevism was lethal in its very cradle.

Which is just what S., my ironical Muscovite cousin, found so pathetically funny when, laughing at our American stupidity, she went home to Communism's graveyard.

Of Christian Heroism

There is a story about Clare Boothe Luce complaining that she was bored with hearing about the Holocaust. A Jewish friend of hers said he perfectly understood her sensitivity in the matter; in fact, he had the same sense of repetitiousness and fatigue, hearing so often about the Crucifixion.
—HERBERT GOLD, *"Selfish Like Me"*

1

Of the great European murder of six million Jews, and the murderers themselves, there is little to say. The barbaric years when Jews were hunted down for sport in the middle of the twentieth century have their hellish immortality, their ineradicable infamy, and will inflame the nightmares—and (perhaps) harrow the conscience—of the human race until the sun burns out and takes our poor earth-speck with it. Of the murder and the murderers everything is known that needs to be known: how it was done, who did it, who helped, where it was done, and when, and why: especially why: the hatred of a civilization that teaches us to say No to hatred.

Three "participant" categories of the Holocaust are commonly named: murderers, victims, bystanders. Imagination demands a choosing. Which, of this entangled trio, are we? Which are we most likely to have become? Probably it is hardest of all to imagine ourselves victims. After all, we were here and not there. Or we were Gentiles and not Jews or Gypsies. Or we were not yet born. But if we had already been born, if we were there and not here, if we were Jews and not Gentiles . . .

"If" is the travail of historians and philosophers, not of the ordinary human article. What we can be sure of without contradiction—we can be sure of it because we are the ordinary human article—is that, difficult as it might be to imagine ourselves among the victims, it is not in us even to begin to think of ourselves as likely murderers. The "banality of evil" is a catchword of our generation; but no, it is an unusual, an exceptional, thing to volunteer for the S.S.; to force aged Jews to their knees to scrub the gutter with their beards; to empty Zyklon B canisters into the hole in the roof of the gas chamber; to enact those thousand atrocities that lead to the obliteration of a people and a culture.

The victims take our pity and our horror, and whatever else we can, in our shame, cede to their memory. But they do not puzzle us. It does not puzzle us that the blood of the innocent cries up from the ground—how could it be otherwise? Even if humanity refuses to go on remembering, the voices crushed in the woods and under the fresh pavements of Europe press upward. The new plants that cover the places where corpses were buried in mass pits carry blood in their dew. Basement-whispers trouble the new blocks of flats that cover the streets where the flaming Warsaw Ghetto fell. The heavy old sideboards of the thirties that once stood in Jewish dining rooms in certain neighborhoods of Berlin and Vienna are in Catholic and Protestant dining rooms now, in neighborhoods where there are no longer any Jews; the great carved legs of these increasingly valued antiques groan and remember the looting. The books that were thrown onto bonfires in the central squares of every German city still send up their flocks of quivering phantom letters.

All that—the looting, the shooting, the herding, the forced marches, the gassing, the torching of synagogues, the cynicism, the mendacity, the shamelessness, the truncheons, the bloodthirstiness, the fanaticism, the opportunism, the Jews of Europe as prey, their dehumanization, the death factories, the obliteration of a civilization, the annihilation of a people— all that it is possible to study, if not to assimilate. Pious Jews, poor Jews, secular Jews, universalist Jews, baptized Jews, Jews who were storekeepers, or doctors, or carpenters, or professors, or teamsters, Jewish infants and children—all annihilated. Thousands upon thousands of Jewish libraries and schools looted and destroyed. Atrocity spawns an aftermath—perhaps an afterlife. In the last four decades the documents and the testimonies have been heaped higher and higher—yet a gash has been cut in the world's brain that cannot be healed by memorial conferences or monuments. Lamentation for the martyred belongs now to the history of cruelty and to the earth. There is no paucity of the means to remember; there may be a paucity of the will to remember. Still, we know what we think of the murders and the murderers. We are not at a loss to know how to regard them.

But what of the bystanders? They were not the criminals, after all. For the bystanders we should feel at least the pale warmth of recognition—call it self-recognition. And nowadays it is the bystanders whom we most notice, though at the time, while the crimes were in progress, they seemed the least noticeable. We notice them now because they are the ones we can most readily identify with. They are the ones imagination can most readily accommodate. A bystander is like you and me, the ordinary human article—what normal man or woman or adolescent runs to commit public atrocities? The luck of the draw (the odds of finding oneself in the majority) saves the bystander from direct victimhood: the Nuremberg "racial" laws, let us say, are what exempt the bystander from deportation. The bystander is, by definition, not a Jew or a Gypsy. The bystander stays home, safe enough if compliant enough. The bystander cannot be charged with taking part in any evil act; the bystander only watches as the evil proceeds. One by one, and suddenly all at once, the Jewish families disappear from their apartments in building after building, in city after city. The neighbors watch them go. One by one, and suddenly all at once, the Jewish children disappear from school. Their classmates resume doing their sums.

The neighbors are decent people—decent enough for ordinary purposes. They cannot be blamed for not being heroes. A hero—like a murderer—is an exception and (to be coarsely direct) an abnormality, a kind of social freak. No one ought to be expected to become a hero. Not that the bystanders are, taken collectively, altogether blameless. In the Germany of the thirties it was they—because there were so many of them—who created the norm. The conduct of the bystanders—again because there were so many of them—defined what was common and what was uncommon, what was exceptional and what was unexceptional, what was heroic and what was quotidian. If the bystanders in all their numbers had not been so docile, if they had not been so conciliatory, or, contrariwise, if they had not been so "inspired" (by slogans and rabble-rousers and uniforms and promises of national glory), if they had not acquiesced both through the ballot box and alongside the parades—if, in short, they had not been *so many*—the subject of heroism would never have had to arise.

When a whole population takes on the status of bystander, the victims are without allies; the criminals, unchecked, are strengthened; and only then do we need to speak of heroes. When a field is filled from end to end with sheep, a stag stands out. When a continent is filled from end to end with the compliant, we learn what heroism is. And alas for the society that requires heroes.

Most of us, looking back, and identifying as we mainly do with the bystanders—because it is the most numerous category, into which simple demographic likelihood thrusts us; or because surely it is the easiest category, the most recognizably human, if not the most humane—will admit to some perplexity, a perplexity brought on by hindsight. Taken collectively, as I dared to do a moment ago, the bystanders are culpable. But taking human beings collectively is precisely what we are obliged not to do. Then consider the bystanders not as a group, not as a stereotype, but one by one. If the bystander is the ordinary human article, as we have agreed, what can there be to puzzle us? This one, let us say, is a good and zealous hater (no one can deny that hating belongs to the ordinary human article), encouraged by epaulets, posters, flashy rhetoric, and pervasive demagoguery. And this one is an envious malcontent, lustful for a change of leadership. And this one is a simple patriot. And this one, unemployed, is a dupe of the speechmakers. Such portraits, both credible and problematical, are common enough. But let us concede that most of the bystanders were quiet citizens who wanted nothing more than to get on with their private lives: a portrait entirely palatable to you and me. The ordinary human article seeks nothing more complex than the comforts of indifference to public clamor of any kind. Indifference is a way of sheltering oneself from evil; who would interpret such unaggressive sheltering as a contribution to evil? The ordinary human article hardly looks to get mixed up in active and wholesale butchery of populations; what rational person would want to accuse the bystander—who has done no more than avert her eyes—of a hardness-of-heart in any way approaching that of the criminals? That would be a serious lie—a distortion both of fact and of psychological understanding.

Yet it is the nature of indifference itself that bewilders. How is it that indifference, which on its own does no apparent or immediate positive harm, ends by washing itself in the very horrors it means to have nothing to do with? Hoping to confer no hurt, indifference finally grows lethal; why is that? Can it be that indifference, ostensibly passive, harbors an unsuspected robustness? The act of turning toward—while carrying a club—is an act of brutality; but the act of turning away, however empty-handed and harmlessly; remains nevertheless an act. The whole truth may be that the idea of human passivity is nothing but the illusion of wistful mortals; and that waking into the exigencies of our own time—whichever way we turn, toward or away—implies action. To be born is to be compelled to act.

One of the most curious (and mephitic) powers of indifference is its retroactive capacity: it is possible to be indifferent *nunc pro tunc*. I am thinking of a few sentences I happened to be shown the other day: they were from the pen of a celebrated author who was commenting on a piece of so-called "Holocaust writing." "These old events," he complained, "can rake you over only so much, and then you long for a bit of satire on it all. Like so many others of my generation"—he was a young adult during the forties— "who had nothing to do with any of it, I've swallowed all the guilt I can bear, and if I'm going to be lashed, I intend to save my skin for more recent troubles in the world."

Never mind the odd protestation of innocence where nothing has been charged—what secret unquiet lies within this fraying conscience? What is odder still is that a statement of retroactive indifference is represented as a commitment to present compassion. As for present compassion, does anyone doubt that there is enough contemporary suffering to merit one's full notice? Besides, a current indifference to "these old events" seems harmless enough now; the chimneys of Dachau and Birkenau and Belsen have been cold for fifty years. But does this distinguished figure—a voice of liberalism as well as noteworthy eloquence—suppose that indifference to "old events" frees one for attention to new ones? In fact, indifference to past suffering is a sure sign that there will be indifference to present suffering. Jaded feelings have little to do with the staleness of any event. To be "jaded' is to decline to feel at all.

And that is perhaps the central point about indifference, whether retroactive or current. Indifference is not so much a gesture of looking away—of choosing to be passive—as it is an active disinclination to feel. Indifference shuts down the humane, and does it deliberately, with all the strength deliberateness demands. Indifference is as determined—and as forcefully muscular—as any blow. For the victims on their way to the chimneys, there is scarcely anything to choose between a thug with an uplifted truncheon and the decent citizen who will not lift up his eyes.

2.

We have spoken of three categories: criminal, victim, bystander. There is a fourth category—so minuscule that statistically it vanishes. Fortunately it is not a category that can be measured by number—its measure is metaphysical and belongs to the sublime. "Whoever saves a single life," says the Talmud, "is as one who has saved an entire world." This is the category of those astounding souls who refused to stand by as their neighbors were being hauled away to the killing sites. They were willing to see, to judge, to decide. Not only did they not avert their eyes—they set out to rescue. They are the heroes of Nazified Europe. They are Polish, Italian, Romanian, Russian, Hungarian, French, Yugoslavian, Swiss, Swedish, Dutch, Spanish, German. They are Catholic and Protestant. They are urban and rural; educated and uneducated; sophisticated and simple; they include nuns and socialists. And whatever they did, they did at the risk of their lives.

It is typical of all of them to deny any heroism. "It was only decent," they say. But no: most people are decent; the bystanders were decent. The rescuers are somehow raised above the merely decent. When the rescuers declare that heroism is beside the point, it is hard to agree with them.

There is, however, another view, one that takes the side of the rescuers. Under the steady Jerusalem sun stands a low and somber building known as Yad Vashem: a memorial to the Six Million, a place of mourning, a substitute for the missing headstones of the victims; there are no graveyards for human beings ground into bone meal and flown into evanescent smoke. But Yad Vashem is also a grove of celebration and honor: a grand row of trees, one for each savior, marks the valor of the Christian rescuers of Europe, called the Righteous Among the Nations. Mordechai Paldiel, the director of the Department for the Righteous at Yad Vashem, writing in *The Jerusalem Post* not long ago, offered some arresting reflections on the "normality" of goodness:

> We are somehow determined to view these benefactors as heroes: hence the search for underlying motives. The Righteous persons, however, consider themselves as anything but heroes, and regard their behavior during the Holocaust as quite normal. How to resolve this enigma?
>
> For centuries we have undergone a brain-washing process by philosophers who emphasized man's despicable character, highlighting his egotistic and evil disposition at the expense of other attributes. Wittingly or not, together with Hobbes and Freud, we accept the proposition that man is essentially an aggressive being, bent on destruction, involved principally with himself, and only marginally interested in the needs of others . . .
>
> Goodness leaves us gasping, for we refuse to recognize it as a natural human attribute. So off we go on a long search for some hidden motivation, some extraordinary explanation, for such peculiar behavior.
>
> Evil is, by contrast, less painfully assimilated. There is no comparable search for the reasons for its constant manifestation (although in earlier centuries theologians pondered this issue).
>
> We have come to terms with evil. Television, movies and the printed word have made evil, aggression and egotism household terms and unconsciously acceptable to the extent of making us immune to displays of evil. There is a danger that the evil of the Holocaust will be

absorbed in a similar manner; that is, explained away as further confirmation of man's inherent disposition to wrongdoing. It confirms our visceral feeling that man is an irredeemable beast, who needs to be constrained for his own good.

In searching for an explanation of the motivations of the Righteous Among the Nations, are we not really saying: what was wrong with them? Are we not, in a deeper sense, implying that their behavior was something other than normal? . . . Is acting benevolently and altruistically such an outlandish and unusual type of behavior, supposedly at odds with man's inherent character, as to justify a meticulous search for explanations? Or is it conceivable that such behavior is as natural to our psychological constitution as the egoistic one we accept so matter-of-factly?

It is Mr. Paldiel's own goodness that leaves me gasping. How I want to assent to his thesis! How alluring it is! His thesis asserts that it is the rescuers who are in possession of the reality of human nature, not the bystanders; it is the rescuers who are the ordinary human article. "In a place where there are no human beings, be one"—it is apparent that the rescuers were born to embody this rabbinic text. It is not, they say, that they are exceptions; it is that they are human. They are not to be considered "extraordinary," "above the merely decent." Yet their conduct emphasizes—exemplifies—the exceptional.

For instance: Giorgio Perlasca, an Italian from Padua, had a job in the Spanish Embassy in Budapest. When the Spanish envoy fled before the invading Russians, Perlasca substituted the Spanish "Jorge" for the Italian "Giorgio" and passed himself off as the Spanish *charge d'affaires*. He carried food and powdered milk to safe houses under the Spanish flag, where several hundred Jews at a time found a haven. He issued protective documents that facilitated the escape of Jews with Spanish passes. "I began to feel like a fish in water," he said of his life as an impostor: the sole purpose of his masquerade was to save Jews. And he saved thousands.

Bert Berchove was a Dutch upholsterer who lived with his wife and two children in a large apartment over his shop, in a town not far from Amsterdam. At first he intended to help only his wife's best friend, who was Jewish; her parents had already been deported. Berchove constructed a hiding place in the attic, behind a false wall. Eventually thirty-seven Jews were hidden there.

In a Dominican convent near Vilna, seven nuns and their mother superior sheltered a number of Jews who had escaped from the ghetto, including some poets and writers. The fugitives were disguised in nuns' habits. The sisters did not stop at hiding Jews: they scoured the countryside for weapons to smuggle into the ghetto.

Who will say that the nuns, the upholsterer, and the impostor are not extraordinary in their altruism, their courage, the electrifying boldness of their imaginations? How many nuns have we met who would think of dressing Jewish poets in wimples? How many upholsterers do we know who would actually design and build a false wall? Who among us would dream of fabricating a fake diplomatic identity in order to save Jewish lives? Compassion, it is clear, sharpens intuition and augments imagination.

For me, the rescuers are *not* the ordinary human article. Nothing would have been easier than for each and everyone of them to have remained a bystander, like all those millions of their countrymen in the nations of Europe. It goes without saying that the bystanders, especially in the occupied lands, had troubles enough of their own, and hardly needed to go out of their way to acquire new burdens and frights. I do not—cannot—believe that human beings are, without explicit teaching, naturally or intrinsically altruistic. I do not believe, either, that they are naturally vicious, though they can be trained to be. The truth (as with most truths) seems to be somewhere in the middle: most people are born bystanders. The ordinary human article does not want to be disturbed by extremes of any kind—not by risks, or adventures, or unusual responsibility.

And those who undertook the risks, those whose bravery steeped them in perilous contingencies, those whose moral strength urged them into heart-stopping responsibility—what (despite their demurrals) are they really, if not the heroes of our battered world? What other name can they possibly merit? In the Europe of the most savage decade of the twentieth century, not to be a bystander was the choice of an infinitesimal few. These few are more substantial than the multitudes from whom they distinguished themselves; and it is from these undeniably heroic and principled few that we can learn the full resonance of civilization.

Who Owns Anne Frank?

If Anne Frank had not perished in the criminal malevolence of Bergen-Belsen early in 1945, she would have marked her seventieth birthday at the brink of the twenty-first century. And even if she had not kept the extraordinary diary through which we know her, it is likely that we would number her among the famous of the twentieth—though perhaps not so dramatically as we do now. She was born to be a writer. At thirteen, she felt her power; at fifteen, she was in command of it. It is easy to imagine—had she been allowed to live—a long row of novels and essays spilling from her fluent and ripening pen. We can be certain (as certain as one can be of anything hypothetical) that her mature prose would today be noted for its wit and acuity, and almost as certain that the trajectory of her work would be closer to that of Nadine Gordimer, say, than that of Françoise Sagan. Put it that as an international literary presence she would be thick rather than thin. "I want to go on living even after my death!" she exclaimed in the spring of 1944.

This was more than an exaggerated adolescent flourish. She had already intuited what greatness in literature might mean, and she clearly sensed the force of what lay under her hand in the pages of her diary: a conscious literary record of frightened lives in daily peril; an explosive document aimed directly at the future. In her last months she was assiduously polishing phrases and editing passages with an eye to postwar publication. *Het Achterhuis,* as she called her manuscript—"the house behind," often translated as "the secret annex"—was hardly intended to be Anne Frank's last word; it was conceived as the forerunner work of a professional woman of letters.

Yet any projection of Anne Frank as a contemporary figure is an unholy speculation: it tampers with history, with reality, with deadly truth. "When I write," she confided, "I can shake off all my cares. My sorrow disappears, my spirits are revived!" But she could not shake off her capture and annihilation, and there are no diary entries to register and memorialize the snuffing of her spirit. Anne Frank was discovered, seized, and deported; she and her

388

mother and sister and millions of others were extinguished in a program calculated to assure the cruelest and most demonically inventive human degradation. The atrocities she endured were ruthlessly and purposefully devised, from indexing by tattoo to systematic starvation to factory-efficient murder. She was designated to be erased from the living, to leave no grave, no sign, no physical trace of any kind. Her fault—her crime—was having been born a Jew, and as such she was classified among those who had no right to exist: not as a subject people, not as an inferior breed, not even as usable slaves. The military and civilian apparatus of an entire society was organized to obliterate her as a contaminant, in the way of a noxious and repellent insect. Zyklon B, the lethal fumigant poured into the gas chambers, was, pointedly, a roach poison. Anne Frank escaped gassing. One month before liberation, not yet sixteen, she died of typhus fever, an acute infectious disease carried by lice. The precise date of her death has never been determined. She and her sister Margot were among 3,659 women transported by cattle car from Auschwitz to the merciless conditions of Bergen-Belsen, a barren tract of mud. In a cold, wet autumn, they suffered through nights on flooded straw in overcrowded tents, without light, surrounded by latrine ditches, until a violent hailstorm tore away what had passed for shelter. Weakened by brutality, chaos, and hunger, fifty thousand men and women—insufficiently clothed, tormented by lice—succumbed, many to the typhus epidemic.

Anne Frank's final diary entry, written on August 1, 1944, ends introspectively—a meditation on a struggle for moral transcendence set down in a mood of wistful gloom. It speaks of "turning my heart inside out, the bad part on the outside and the good part on the inside," and of "trying to find a way to become what I'd like to be and what I could be if . . . if only there were no other people in the world." Those curiously self-subduing ellipses are the diarist's own; they are more than merely a literary effect—they signify a child's muffled bleat against confinement, the last whimper of a prisoner in a cage. Her circumscribed world had a population of eleven—the three Dutch protectors who came and went, supplying the necessities of life, and the eight in hiding: the van Daans, their son Peter, Albert Dussel, and the four Franks. Five months earlier, on May 26, 1944, she had railed against the stress of living invisibly—a tension never relieved, she asserted, "not once in the two years we've been here. How much longer will this increasingly oppressive, unbearable weight press down on us?" And, several paragraphs on, "What will we do if we're ever . . . no, I mustn't write that down. But the question won't let itself be pushed to the back of my mind today; on the contrary, all the fear I've ever felt is looming before me in all its horror . . . I've asked myself again and again whether it wouldn't have been better if we hadn't gone into hiding, if we were dead now and didn't have to go through this misery . . . Let something happen soon . . . Nothing can be more crushing than this anxiety. Let the end come, however cruel." And on April 11, 1944: "We are Jews in chains."

The diary is not a genial document, despite its author's often vividly satiric exposure of what she shrewdly saw as "the comical side of life in hiding." Its reputation for uplift is, to say it plainly, nonsensical. Anne Frank's written narrative, moreover, is not the story of Anne Frank, and never has been. That the diary is miraculous, a self-aware work of youthful genius, is not in question. Variety of pace and tone, insightful humor, insupportable suspense, adolescent love-pangs and disappointments, sexual curiosity, moments of terror, moments of elation, flights of idealism and prayer and psychological acumen—all these elements of mind and feeling and skill brilliantly enliven its pages. There is, besides, a startlingly precocious comprehension of the progress of the war on all fronts. The survival of the little group in hiding is crucially linked to the timing of the Allied invasion; overhead the bombers, roaring to their destinations, make the house quake. Sometimes the bombs fall terrifyingly close. All in all, the diary is a chronicle of trepidation, turmoil, alarm. Even its report of quieter periods of reading and study express the hush of imprisonment. Meals are boiled lettuce and rotted potatoes; flushing the single toilet is forbidden for ten hours at a time. There is shooting at night. Betrayal and arrest always threaten. Anxiety and immobility rule. It is a story of fear.

But the diary in itself, richly crammed though it is with incident and passion, cannot count as Anne Frank's story. A story may not be said to be a story if the end is missing. And because the end is missing, the story of Anne Frank in the fifty years since *The Diary of a Young Girl* was first published has been bowdlerized, distorted, transmuted, traduced, reduced; it has been infantilized, Americanized, homogenized, sentimentalized; falsified, kitschified, and, in fact, blatantly and arrogantly denied. Among the falsifiers and bowdlerizers have been dramatists and directors, translators and litigators, Anne Frank's own father, and even—or especially—the public, both readers and theatergoers, all over the world. A deeply truth-telling work has been turned into an instrument of partial truth, surrogate truth, or anti-truth. The pure has been made impure—sometimes in the name of the reverse. Almost every hand that has approached the diary with the well-meaning intention of publicizing it has contributed to the subversion of history.

The diary is taken to be a Holocaust document; that is overridingly what it is not. Nearly every edition—and there have been innumerable editions—is emblazoned with words like "a song to life," "a poignant delight in the infinite human spirit." Such characterizations rise up in the bitter perfume of mockery. A song to life? The diary is incomplete, truncated, broken off; or, rather, it is completed by Westerbork (the hellish transit camp in Holland from which Dutch Jews were deported), and by Auschwitz, and by the fatal winds of Bergen-Belsen. It is here, and not in the "secret annex," that the crimes we have come to call the Holocaust were enacted. Our entry into those crimes begins with columns of numbers: the meticulous lists of deportations, in handsome bookkeepers' handwriting, starkly set down in German "transport books." From these columns—headed, like goods for export, *"Ausgange-Transporte nach Osten"* (outgoing shipments to the east)—it is possible to learn that Anne Frank and the others were moved to Auschwitz on the night of September 6, 1944, in a collection of 1,019 *Stücke* (or "pieces," another commodities term). That same night, 549 persons were gassed, including one from the Frank group (the father of Peter van Daan), and every child under fifteen. Anne, at fifteen, and seventeen-year-old Margot were spared, apparently for labor. The end of October, from the twentieth to the twenty-eighth, saw the gassing of more than six thousand human beings within two hours of their arrival, including a thousand boys eighteen and under. In December, 2,093 female prisoners perished, from starvation and exhaustion, in the women's camp; early in January, Edith Frank expired.

But Soviet forces were hurtling toward Auschwitz, and in November the order went out to conceal all evidences of gassing and to blow up the crematoria. Tens of thousands of inmates, debilitated and already near extinction, were driven out in bitter cold on death marches. Many were shot. In an evacuation that occurred either on October 28 or November 2, Anne and Margot were dispatched to Bergen-Belsen. Margot was the first to succumb. A survivor recalled that she fell dead to the ground from the wooden slab on which she lay, eaten by lice, and that Anne, heartbroken and skeletal, naked under a bit of rag, died a day or two later.

To come to the diary without having earlier assimilated Elie Wiesel's *Night* and Primo Levi's *The Drowned and the Saved* (to mention two accounts only), or the columns of figures in the transport books, is to allow oneself to stew in an implausible and ugly innocence. The litany of blurbs—"a lasting testimony to the indestructible nobility of the human spirit," "an everlasting source of courage and inspiration"—is no more substantial than any other display of self-delusion. The success—the triumph—of Bergen-Belsen was precisely that it blotted out the possibility of courage, that it proved to be a lasting testament to the human spirit's easy destructibility. *"Hier ist kein warum,"* a guard at Auschwitz warned Primo Levi: here there is no "why," neither question nor answer, only the dark of unreason. Anne Frank's story, truthfully told, is unredeemed and unredeemable.

These are notions that are hard to swallow—so they have not been swallowed. There are some, bored beyond toleration and callous enough to admit it, who are sick of hearing—yet again!—about depredations fifty years gone. "These old events," one of these fellows may complain, "can rake you over only so much . . . If I'm going to be lashed, I might as well save my skin for more recent troubles in the world." (I quote from a private letter from a distinguished author.) This may be a popular, if mostly unexpressed, point of view, but it is not socially representative. The more common response respectfully discharges an obligation to pity: it is dutiful. Or it is sometimes less than dutiful. It is sometimes frivolous, or indifferent, or presumptuous. But what even the most exemplary sympathies are likely to evade is the implacable recognition that Auschwitz and Bergen-Belsen, however sacramentally prodded, can never yield light.

And the vehicle that has most powerfully accomplished this almost universal obtuseness is Anne Frank's diary. In celebrating Anne Frank's years in the secret annex, the nature and meaning of her death has been, in effect, forestalled. The diary's keen lens is helplessly opaque to the diarist's explicit doom—and this opacity, replicated in young readers in particular, has led to shamelessness.

It is the shamelessness of appropriation. Who owns Anne Frank? The children of the world, say the sentimentalists. A case in point, then, is the astonishing correspondence, published in 1995 under the title *Love, Otto*, between Cara Wilson, a Californian born in 1944, and Otto Frank, the father of Anne Frank. Wilson, then twelve-year-old Cara Weiss, was invited by Twentieth Century-Fox to audition for the part of Anne in a projected film version of the diary. "I didn't get the part," the middle-aged Wilson writes, "but by now I had found a whole new world. Anne Frank's diary, which I read and reread, spoke to me and my dilemmas, my anxieties, my secret passions. She felt the way I did . . . I identified so strongly with this eloquent girl of my own age, that I now think I sort of became her in my own mind."And on what similarities does Wilson rest her acute sense of identification with a hunted child in hiding?

> I was miserable being me . . . I was on the brink of that awful abyss of teenagedom and I, too, needed someone to talk to . . . (Ironically, Anne, too, expressed a longing for more attention from her father.) . . . Dad's whole life was a series of meetings. At home, he was too tired or too frustrated to unload on. I had something else in common with Anne.

We both had to share with sisters who were prettier and smarter than we felt we were . . . Despite the monumental difference in our situations, to this day I feel that Anne helped me get through the teens with a sense of inner focus. She spoke for me. She was strong for me. She had so much hope when I was ready to call it quits.

A sampling of Wilson's concerns as she matured appears in the interstices of her exchanges with Otto Frank—which, remarkably, date from 1959 until his death in 1980. For instance: "The year was 1968—etched in my mind. I can't ever forget it. Otis Redding was 'Sittin' on the Dock of the Bay' . . . while we hummed along to 'Hey Jude' by the Beatles." Or again: "What a year 1972 was! That was when I saw one of my all-time favorite movies, *Harold and Maude*, to the tune of Cat Stevens' incredible sound track . . . I remember singing along to Don McLean's 'American Pie' and daydreaming to Roberta Flack's exquisite 'The First Time Ever I Saw Your Face,' " and so on. "In 1973–74," she reports, "I was wearing headbands, pukka-shell necklaces, and American Indian anything. Tattoos were a rage"—but enough. Tattoos were the rage, she neglects to recall, in Auschwitz; and of the Auschwitz survivor who was her patient correspondent for more than two decades, Wilson remarks: "Well, what choice did the poor man have? Whenever an attack of 'I-can't-take-this-any-longer' would hit me, I'd put it all into lengthy diatribes to my distant guru, Otto Frank."

That the designated guru replied, year after year, to embarrassing and shabby effusions like these may open a new pathway into our generally obscure understanding of the character of Otto Frank. His responses—from Basel, where he had settled with his second wife—were consistently attentive, formal, kindly. When Wilson gave birth, he sent her a musical toy, and he faithfully offered a personal word about her excitements as she supplied them: her baby sons, her dance lessons, her husband's work on commercials, her freelance writing. But his letters were also political and serious: it is good, he wrote in October 1970, to take "an active part in trying to abolish injustices and all sorts of grievances, but we cannot follow your views regarding the Black Panthers." And in December 1973, "As you can imagine, we were highly shocked about the unexpected attack of the Arabs on Israel on Yom Kippur and are now mourning with all those who lost their families." Presumably he knew something about losing a family. Wilson, insouciantly sliding past these faraway matters, was otherwise preoccupied, "finding our little guys sooo much fun."

The unabashed triflings of Cara Wilson—whose "identification" with Anne Frank can be duplicated by the thousand, though she may be more audacious than most—point to a conundrum. Never mind that the intellectual distance between Wilson and Anne Frank is immeasurable; not every self-conscious young girl will be a prodigy. Did Otto Frank not comprehend that Cara Wilson was deaf to everything the loss of his daughter represented? Did he not see, in Wilson's letters alone, how a denatured approach to the diary might serve to promote amnesia of what was rapidly turning into history? A protected domestic space, however threatened and endangered, can, from time to time, mimic ordinary life. The young who are encouraged to embrace the diary cannot always be expected to feel the difference between the mimicry and the threat. And (like Cara Wilson) most do not. Natalie Portman, then sixteen years old, who in December 1997 débuted as Anne Frank in the Broadway revival of the famous play based on the diary—a play that has itself influenced the way the diary is read—was reported to have concluded from her own reading that "it's funny, it's hopeful, and she's a happy person."

Otto Frank, it turns out, is complicit in this shallowly upbeat view. Again and again, in every conceivable context, he had it as his aim to emphasize "Anne's idealism," "Anne's spirit," almost never calling attention to how and why that idealism and spirit were smothered, and unfailingly generalizing the sources of hatred. If the child is father of the man—if childhood shapes future sensibility—then Otto Frank, despite his sufferings in Auschwitz, may have had less in common with his own daughter than he was ready to recognize. As the diary gained publication in country after country, its renown accelerating year by year, he spoke not merely about but for its author—and who, after all, would have a greater right? The surviving father stood in for the dead child, believing that his words would honestly represent hers. He was not entitled to such certainty: fatherhood does not confer surrogacy. His own childhood, in Frankfurt, Germany, was wholly unclouded. A banker's son, he lived untrammeled until the rise of the Nazi regime, when he was already forty-four. At nineteen, in order to acquire training in business, he went to New York with Nathan Straus, a fellow student who was heir to the Macy's department-store fortune. During the First World War, Frank was an officer in the German military, and in 1925 he married Edith Holländer, a manufacturer's daughter. Margot was born in 1926 and Anneliese Marie, called Anne, in 1929. His characteristically secular world view belonged to an era of quiet assimilation, or, more accurately, accommodation (which includes a modicum of deference), when German Jews had become, at least in their own minds, well integrated into German society. From birth, Otto Frank had breathed the free air of the affluent bourgeoisie.

Anne's childhood, in contrast, fell into shadows almost immediately. She was four when the German persecutions of Jews began, and from then until the anguished close of her days she lived as a refugee and a victim. In 1933 the family fled from Germany to Holland, where Frank had commercial connections, and where he founded and directed a spice and pectin business. By 1940 the Germans had occupied the Netherlands. In Amsterdam, Jewish children, Anne among them, were thrown out of the public-school system and made to wear the yellow star. At thirteen, on November 19, 1942, already in hiding, Anne Frank could write:

> In the evenings when it's dark, I often see long lines of good, innocent people accompanied by crying children, walking on and on, ordered about by a handful of men who bully and beat them until they nearly drop. No one is spared. The sick, the elderly, children, babies, pregnant women—all are marched to their death.

And earlier, on October 9, 1942, after hearing the report of an escape from Westerbork:

> Our many Jewish friends and acquaintances are being taken away in droves. The Gestapo is treating them very roughly and transporting them in cattle cars to Westerbork . . . The people get almost nothing to eat, much less to drink, as water is available only one hour a day, and there's only one toilet and sink for several thousand people. Men and women sleep in the same room, and women and children have their heads shaved . . . If it's that bad in Holland, what must it be like in those faraway and uncivilized places where the Germans are sending them? We assume that most of them are being murdered. The English radio says they're being gassed.

Perhaps not even a father is justified in thinking he can distill the "ideas" of this alert and sorrowing child, with scenes such as these inscribed in her psyche, and with the desolations of Auschwitz and Bergen-Belsen still ahead. His preference was to accentuate what he called Anne's "optimistical view of life." Yet the diary's most celebrated line (infamously celebrated, one might add)—"I still believe, in spite of everything, that people are truly good at heart"—has been torn out of its bed of thorns. Two sentences later (and three weeks before she was seized and shipped to Westerbork), the diarist sets down a vision of darkness:

> I see the world being transformed into a wilderness, I hear the approaching thunder that, one day, will destroy us too, I feel the suffering of

millions . . . In the meantime, I must hold on to my ideals. Perhaps the day will come when I'll be able to realize them!

Because that day never came, both Miep Gies, the selflessly courageous woman who devoted herself to the sustenance of those in hiding, and Hannah Goslar, Anne's Jewish schoolmate and the last to hear her tremulous cries in Bergen-Belsen, objected to Otto Frank's emphasis on the diary's "truly good at heart" utterance. That single sentence has become, universally, Anne Frank's message, virtually her motto—whether or not such a credo could have survived the camps. But why should this sentence be taken as emblematic, and not, for example, another? "There's a destructive urge in people, the urge to rage, murder, and kill," Anne wrote on May 3, 1944, pondering the spread of guilt. These are words that do not soften, ameliorate, or give the lie to the pervasive horror of her time. Nor do they pull the wool over the eyes of history.

Otto Frank grew up with a social need to please his environment and not to offend it; it was the condition of entering the mainstream, a bargain German Jews negotiated with themselves. It was more dignified, and safer, to praise than to blame. Far better, then, in facing the larger postwar world the diary had opened to him, to speak of goodness rather than destruction: so much of that larger world had participated in the urge to rage. (The diary notes how Dutch anti-Semitism, "to our great sorrow and dismay," was increasing even as the Jews were being hauled away.) After the liberation of the camps, the heaps of emaciated corpses were accusation enough. Postwar sensibility hastened to migrate elsewhere, away from the cruel and the culpable. It was a tone and a mood that affected the diary's reception; it was a mood and a tone that, with cautious yet crucial excisions, the diary itself could be made to support. And so the diarist's dread came to be described as hope, her terror as courage, her prayers of despair as inspiring. And since the diary was now defined as a Holocaust document, the perception of the cataclysm itself was being subtly accommodated to expressions like "man's inhumanity to man," diluting and befogging specific historical events and their motives. "We must not flog the past," Frank insisted in 1969. His concrete response to the past was the establishment, in 1957, of the Anne Frank Foundation and its offshoot the International Youth Center, situated in the Amsterdam house where the diary was composed, to foster "as many contacts as possible between young people of different nationalities, races and religions"—a civilized and tender-hearted goal that nevertheless washed away into do-gooder abstraction the explicit urge to rage that had devoured his daughter.

But Otto Frank was merely an accessory to the transformation of the diary from one kind of witness to another kind: from the painfully revealing to the partially concealing. If Anne Frank has been made into what we nowadays call an "icon," it is because of the Pulitzer Prize-winning play derived from the diary—a play that rapidly achieved worldwide popularity, and framed the legend even the newest generation has come to believe in. Adapted by Albert Hackett and Frances Goodrich, a Hollywood husband-and-wife screenwriting team, the theatricalized version opened on Broadway in 1955, ten years after the ovens of Auschwitz had cooled; its portrayal of the "funny, hopeful, happy" Anne continues to reverberate, not only in how the diary is construed, but in how the Holocaust itself is understood. The play was a work born in controversy, and was destined to roil on and on in rancor and litigation. Its tangle of contending lawyers finally came to resemble nothing so much as the knotted imbroglio of Jarndyce vs. Jarndyce, the unending court case of *Bleak House*. "This scarecrow of a suit," as Dickens describes it, "has, in course of time, become so complicated, that no man alive knows what it means . . . Innumerable children have been born into the cause; innumerable young people have married into it; old people have died out of it." Many of the chief figures in the protracted conflict over the Hacketts' play have by now died out of it, but the principal issues, far from fading away, have, after so many decades, intensified. And whatever the ramifications of these issues, whatever perspectives they illumine or defy, the central question stands fast: who owns Anne Frank?

The hero, or irritant (depending on which side of the controversy one favors), in the genesis of the diary's dramatization was Meyer Levin, a Chicago-born novelist of the social realist school, author of such fairly successful works as *The Old Bunch*, *Compulsion*, and *The Settlers*. Levin began as a man of the left, though a strong anti-Stalinist: he was drawn to proletarian fiction (*Citizens*, about steel workers), and had gone to Spain in the thirties to report on the Civil War. In 1945, as a war correspondent attached to the Fourth Armored Division, he was among the first Americans to enter Buchenwald, Dachau, and Bergen-Belsen. What he saw there was ungraspable and unendurable. "As I groped in the first weeks, beginning to apprehend the monstrous shape of the story I would have to tell," he wrote, "I knew already that I would never penetrate its heart of bile, for the magnitude of the horror seemed beyond human register." The truest telling, he affirmed, would have to rise up out of the mouth of a victim.

His "obsession," as he afterward called it—partly in mockery of the opposition his later views evoked—had its beginning in those repeated scenes of piled-up bodies as he investigated camp after camp. From then on he could be said to carry the mark of Abel. He dedicated himself to helping the survivors get to Mandate Palestine, a goal that Britain had made illegal. In 1946, he reported from Tel Aviv on the uprising against British rule, and during the next two years he wrote and produced a pair of films on the struggles of the survivors to reach Palestine. In 1950 he published *In Search*, an examination of the effects of the European cataclysm on his experience and sensibility as an American Jew; Thomas Mann acclaimed it as "a human document of high order, written by a witness of our fantastic epoch whose gaze remained both clear and steady." Levin's intensifying focus on the Jewish condition in the twentieth century grew more and more heated, and when his wife, the novelist Tereska Torres, handed him the French edition of the diary (it had previously appeared only in Dutch), he felt he had found what he had thirsted after: a voice crying up from the ground, an authentic witness to the German onslaught

He acted instantly. He sent Otto Frank a copy of *In Search* and offered his services as, in effect, an unofficial agent to secure British and American publication, asserting his distance from any financial gain; his interest, he said, was purely "one of sympathy." He saw in the diary the possibility of "a very touching play or film," and asked Frank's permission to explore the idea. Frank at first avoided reading Levin's book, saturated as it was in passions and commitments so foreign to his own susceptibilities; but he was not unfamiliar with Levin's preoccupations. He had seen and liked one of his films. He encouraged Levin to go ahead—though a dramatization, he observed, would perforce "be rather different from the real contents" of the diary. Hardly so, Levin protested: no compromise would be needed; all the diarist's thoughts could be preserved.

The "real contents" had already been altered by Frank himself, and understandably, given the propriety of his own background and of the times. The diary contained, here and there, intimate adolescent musings—talk of how contraceptives work, and explicit anatomical description: "In the upper part, between the outer labia, there's a fold of skin that, on second thought, looks like a kind of blister. That's the clitoris. Then come the inner labia . . ." All this Frank edited out. He also omitted passages recording his daughter's angry resistance to her mother's nervous fussiness ("the most rotten person in the world"). Undoubtedly he better understood Edith Frank's protective tremors, and was unwilling to perpetuate a negative portrait. Beyond this, he deleted numerous expressions of religious faith, a direct reference to Yom Kippur, terrified reports of Germans seizing Jews in Amsterdam. It was prudence, prudishness, and perhaps his own diffidently acculturated temperament that had stimulated many of these tamperings. In 1991, eleven years after Frank's death, a "definitive edition" of the diary restored every-thing he had expurgated. But the image of Anne Frank as merry innocent and steadfast idealist—an image the play vividly promoted—was by then ineradicable.

A subsequent bowdlerization, in 1950, was still more programmatic, and crossed over even more seriously into the area of Levin's concern for uncom-promised faithfulness. The German edition's translator, Anneliese Schütz, in order to mask or soft-pedal German culpability, went about methodically blurring every hostile reference to Germans and German. Anne's parodic list of house rules, for instance, includes "*Use of language*: It is necessary to speak softly at all times. Only the language of civilized people may be spoken, thus no German." The German translation reads: "*Alle Kultur-sprachen . . . aber leise!*"—"all civilized languages . . . but softly!" "Heroism in war or when confronting Germans" is dissolved into "heroism in war and in the struggle against oppression." ("A book intended after all for sale in Ger-many," Schütz explained, "cannot abuse the Germans.") The diarist's honest cry, in the midst of a vast persecution, that "there is no greater hostility in the world than exists between Germans and Jews," became, in Schütz's ver-sion, "there is no greater hostility in the world than between *these* Germans and Jews!" Frank agreed to the latter change because, he said, it was what his daughter had really meant: she "by no means measured all Germans by the same yardstick. For, as she knew so well, even in those days we had many good friends among the Germans." But this guarded accommodationist view is Otto Frank's own; it is nowhere in the diary. Even more striking than Frank's readiness to accede to these misrepresentations is the fact that for forty-one years (until a more accurate translation appeared) no reader of the diary in German had ever known an intact text.

In contemplating a dramatization and pledging no compromise—he would do it, he told Frank, "tenderly and with the utmost fidelity"—Levin was clear about what he meant by fidelity. In his eyes the diary was con-scious testimony to Jewish faith and suffering; and it was this, and this nearly alone, that defined for him its psychological, historical, and meta-physical genuineness, and its significance for the world. With these convictions foremost, Levin went in search of a theatrical producer.

At the same time he was unflagging in pressing for publication; but the work was meanwhile slowly gaining independent notice. Janet Flanner, in her "Letter from Paris" in *The New Yorker* of November 11, 1950, noted the French publication of a book by "a precocious, talented little Frankfurt Jewess"—apparently oblivious to the unpleasant echoes, post-Hitler, of "Jewess." Sixteen English-language publishers on both sides of the Atlantic had already rejected the diary when Levin succeeded in placing it with Valentine Mitchell, a London firm. His negotiations with a Boston house were still incomplete when Doubleday came forward to secure publication rights directly from Frank. Relations between Levin and Frank were, as usual, warm; Frank repeatedly thanked Levin for his efforts to further the fortunes of the diary, and Levin continued under the impression that Frank would support him as the playwright of choice.

If a single front-page review in the *New York Times Book Review* can rocket a book to instant sanctity, that is what Meyer Levin, in the spring of 1952, achieved for *Anne Frank: The Diary of a Young Girl*. It was an assignment he had avidly gone after. But Barbara Zimmerman (afterward Barbara Epstein, a founder of *The New York Review of Books*), the diary's young editor at Doubleday, had earlier recognized its potential as "a minor classic," and had enlisted Eleanor Roosevelt to supply an introduction. (According to Levin, it was ghostwritten by Zimmerman.) Levin now joined Zimmerman and Doubleday in the project of choosing a producer. Doubleday was to take over as Frank's official agent, with the stipulation that Levin would have an active hand in the adaptation. "I think I can honestly say," Levin wrote Frank, "that I am as well qualified as any other writer for this particular task." In a cable to Doubleday, Frank appeared to agree: "DESIRE LEVIN AS WRITER OR COLLABORATOR IN ANY TREATMENT TO GUARANTEE IDEA OF BOOK." The catch, it would develop, lurked in a perilous contingency: whose idea? Levin's? Frank's? The producer's? The director's? In any case, Doubleday was already sufficiently doubtful about Levin's ambiguous role: what if an interested producer decided on another playwright?

What happened next—an avalanche of furies and recriminations lasting years—has become the subject of a pair of arresting discussions of the Frank-Levin affair. And if "affair" suggests an event on the scale of the Dreyfus case, that is how Levin saw it: as an unjust stripping of his rightful position, with implications far beyond his personal predicament. *An Obsession with Anne Frank*, by Lawrence Graver, brought out by the University of California Press in 1995, is the first study to fashion a coherent narrative out of the welter of claims, counterclaims, letters, cables, petitions, polemics, and rumbling confusions that accompany any examination of the diary's journey to the stage. *The Stolen Legacy of Anne Frank*, by Ralph Melnick, published in 1997 by Yale University Press, is denser in detail and in sources than its predecessor, and more insistent in tone. Both are accomplished works of scholarship that converge on the facts and diverge in their conclusions. Graver is reticent with his sympathies; Melnick is Levin's undisguised advocate. Graver finds no villains. Melnick finds Lillian Hellman.

Always delicately respectful of Frank's dignity and rights—and mindful always of the older man's earlier travail—Levin had promised that he would step aside if a more prominent playwright, someone "world famous," should appear. Stubbornly and confidently, he went on toiling over his own version. As a novelist, he was under suspicion of being unable to write drama. (In after years, when he had grown deeply bitter, he listed, in retaliation, "Sartre, Gorky, Galsworthy, Steinbeck, Wilder!") Though there are many extant drafts of Levin's play, no definitive script is available; both publication and performance were proscribed by Frank's attorneys. A script staged without authorization by the Israel Soldiers' Theater in 1966 sometimes passes from hand to hand, and reads well: moving, theatrical, actable, professional. This later work was not, however, the script submitted in 1952 to Cheryl Crawford, one of a number of Broadway producers who rushed in with bids in the wake of the diary's acclaim. Crawford, an eminent co-founder of the Actors Studio, was initially encouraging to Levin, offering him first consideration and, if his script was not entirely satisfactory, the aid of a more experienced collaborator. Then—virtually overnight—she rejected his draft outright. Levin was bewildered and infuriated, and from then on became an intractable and indefatigable warrior on behalf of his play—and on behalf, he contended, of the diary's true meaning. In his *Times* review he had summed it up stirringly as the voice of "six million vanished Jewish souls."

Doubleday, meanwhile, sensing complications ahead, had withdrawn as Frank's theatrical agent, finding Levin's presence—injected by Frank—too intrusive, too maverick, too independent and entrepreneurial: fixed, they believed, only on his own interest, which was to stick to his insistence on the superiority of his work over all potential contenders. Frank, too, had begun—kindly, politely, and with tireless assurances of his gratitude to Levin—to move closer to Doubleday's cooler views, especially as urged by Barbara Zimmerman. She was twenty-four years old, the age Anne would have been, very intelligent and attentive. Adoring letters flowed back and forth between them, Frank addressing her as "little Barbara" and "dearest little one." On one occasion he gave her an antique gold pin. About Levin, Zimmerman finally concluded that he was "impossible to deal with in any terms, officially, legally, morally, personally"—a "compulsive neurotic . . . destroying both himself and Anne's play." (There was, of course, no such entity as "Anne's play.")

But what had caused Crawford to change her mind so precipitately? She had sent Levin's script for further consideration to Lillian Hellman, and to the producers Robert Whitehead and Kermit Bloomgarden. All were theater luminaries; all spurned Levin's work. Frank's confidence in Levin, already much diminished, failed altogether. Advised by Doubleday, he put his trust in the Broadway professionals, while Levin fought on alone. Famous names—Maxwell Anderson, John Van Druten, Carson McCullers—came and went. Crawford herself ultimately pulled out, fearing a lawsuit by Levin. In the end—in a plethora of complications, legal and emotional, and with the vigilant Levin still agitating loudly and publicly for the primacy of his work—Kermit Bloomgarden surfaced as producer and Garson Kanin as director. Hellman had recommended Bloomgarden; she had also recommended Frances Goodrich and Albert Hackett. The Hacketts had a long record of Hollywood hits, from *Father of the Bride* to *It's A Wonderful Life*, and they had successfully scripted a series of lighthearted musicals. Levin was appalled—had his sacred vision been pushed aside not for the awaited world-famous dramatist, but for a pair of frivolous screen drudges, mere "hired hands"?

The hired hands were earnest and reverent. They began at once to read up on European history, Judaism and Jewish practice; they consulted a rabbi. They corresponded eagerly with Frank, looking to satisfy his expectations. They traveled to Amsterdam and visited 263 Prinsengracht, the house on the canal where the Franks, the Van Daans, and Dussel had been hidden. They met Johannes Kleiman, who, together with Harry Kraler and Miep Gies, had taken over the management of Frank's business in order to conceal and protect him and his family in the house behind. Reacting to the Hacketts' lifelong remoteness from Jewish subject matter, Levin took out an ad in the *New York Post* attacking Bloomgarden and asking that his play be given a hearing. "My work," he wrote, "has been with the Jewish story. I tried to dramatize the Diary as Anne would have, in her own words. . . . I feel my work has earned the right to be judged by you, the public." "Ridiculous and laughable," said Bloomgarden. Appealing to the critic Brooks Atkinson, Levin complained—extravagantly, outrageously—that his play was being "killed by the same arbitrary disregard that brought an end to Anne and six million others." Frank stopped answering Levin's letters; many he returned unopened.

The Hacketts, too, in their earliest drafts, were devotedly "with the Jewish story." Grateful to Hellman for getting them the job, and crushed by Bloomgarden's acute dislike of their efforts so far, they flew to Martha's Vineyard weekend after weekend to receive advice from Hellman. "She was amazing," Goodrich crowed, happy to comply. Hellman's suggestions—and those of Bloomgarden and Kanin—were consistently in a direction opposite to Levin's. Wherever the diary touched on Anne's consciousness of Jewish fate or faith, they quietly erased the reference or changed its emphasis. Whatever was specific they made generic. The sexual tenderness between Anne and the young Peter van Daan was moved to the forefront. Comedy overwhelmed darkness. Anne became an all-American girl, an echo of the perky character in *Junior Miss*, a popular play of the previous decade. The Zionist aspirations of Margot, Anne's sister, disappeared. The one liturgical note, a Hanukkah ceremony, was absurdly defined by local contemporary habits ("eight days of presents"); a jolly jingle replaced the traditional "Rock of Ages," with its somber allusions to historic travail. (Kanin had insisted on something "spirited and gay," so as not to give "the wrong feeling entirely." "Hebrew," he added, "would simply alienate the audience.")

Astonishingly, the Nazified notion of "race" leaped out in a line attributed to Hellman and nowhere present in the diary. "We're not the only people that've had to suffer," says the Hacketts' Anne. "There've always been people that've had to . . . sometimes one race . . . sometimes another." This pallid speech, yawning with vagueness, was conspicuously opposed to the pivotal reflection it was designed to betray:

> In the eyes of the world, we're doomed, but if after all this suffering, there are still Jews left, the Jewish people will be held up as an example. Who knows, maybe our religion will teach the world and all the people in it about goodness, and that's the reason, the only reason, we have to suffer . . . God has never deserted our people. Through the ages Jews have had to suffer, but through the ages they've gone on living, and the centuries of suffering have only made them stronger.

For Kanin, this kind of rumination was "an embarrassing piece of special pleading . . . The fact that in this play the symbols of persecution and oppression are Jews is incidental, and Anne, in stating the argument so, reduces her magnificent stature." And so it went throughout. The particularized plight of Jews in hiding was vaporized into what Kanin called "the infinite." Reality—the diary's central condition—was "incidental." The passionately contemplative child, brooding on concrete evil, was made into an emblem of evasion. Her history had a habitation and a name; the infinite was nameless and nowhere.

For Levin, the source and first cause of these excisions was Lillian Hellman. Hellman, he believed, had "supervised" the Hacketts, and Hellman was fundamentally political and inflexibly doctrinaire. Her outlook lay at the root of a conspiracy. She was an impenitent Stalinist; she followed, he said, the Soviet line. Like the Soviets, she was anti-Zionist. And just as the Soviets had obliterated Jewish particularity at Babi Yar, the ravine where thousands of Jews, shot by the Germans, lay unnamed and effaced in their deaths, so Hellman had directed the Hacketts to blur the identity of the characters in the play. The sins of the Soviets and the sins of Hellman and her Broadway deputies were, in Levin's mind, identical. He set out to punish the man who had allowed all this to come to pass. Otto Frank had allied himself with the pundits of erasure; Otto Frank had stood aside when Levin's play was elbowed out of the way. What recourse remained for a man so affronted and injured? Meyer Levin sued Otto Frank. It was as if, someone observed, a suit were being brought against the father of Joan of Arc.

The bulky snarl of courtroom arguments resulted in small satisfaction for Levin: because the structure of the Hacketts' play was in some ways similar to his, the jury detected plagiarism; yet even this limited triumph foundered on the issue of damages. Levin sent out broadsides, collected signatures, summoned a committee of advocacy, lectured from pulpits, took out ads, rallied rabbis and writers (Norman Mailer among them). He published *The Obsession*, his grandly confessional *"J'accuse,"* rehearsing, in skirmish after skirmish, his fight for the staging of his own adaptation. In return, furious charges flew at him: he was a redbaiter, a McCarthyite. The term "paranoid" began to circulate: why rant against the popularization and dilution that was Broadway's lifeblood? "I certainly have no wish to inflict depression on an audience," Kanin had argued. "I don't consider that a legitimate theatrical end." (So much for *Hamlet* and *King Lear*.)

Grateful for lightness, reviewers agreed. What they came away from was the liveliness of Susan Strasberg as a radiant Anne, and Joseph Schildkraut in the role of a wise and steadying Otto Frank, whom the actor engagingly resembled. "Anne is not going to her death; she is going to leave a dent on life, and let death take what's left," Walter Kerr, on a mystical note, wrote in the *Herald Tribune*. Variety seemed relieved that the play avoided "hating the Nazis, hating what they did to millions of innocent people," and instead left a "glowing, moving, frequently humorous" impression, with "just about everything one could wish for. It is not grim." *The Daily News* confirmed what Kanin had striven for: "not in any important sense a Jewish play . . . Anne Frank is a Little Orphan Annie brought into vibrant life." Audiences laughed and were charmed; but they were also dazed and moved.

And audiences multiplied: the Hacketts' drama went all over the world, including Israel—where numbers of survivors were remaking their lives—and was everywhere successful. The play's reception in Germany was especially noteworthy. In an impressive and thoroughgoing essay entitled "Popularization and Memory," Alvin Rosenfeld, a professor of literature at Indiana University, recounts the development of the Anne Frank phenomenon in the country of her birth. "The theater reviews of the time," Rosenfeld reports, "tell of audiences sitting in stunned silence at the play and leaving the performance unable to speak or look one another in the eye." These were self-conscious and thin-skinned audiences; in the Germany of the fifties, theatergoers still belonged to the generation of the Nazi era. (On Broadway, Kanin had unblinkingly engaged Gusti Huber, of that same generation, to play Anne Frank's mother. As a member of the Nazi Actors Guild until Germany's defeat, Huber had early on disparaged "non-Aryan artists.") But the strange muteness in theaters all over Germany may have derived not so much from guilt or shame as from an all-encompassing compassion; or call it self-pity. "We see in Anne Frank's fate," a German drama critic offered, "our own fate—the tragedy of human existence per se." Hannah Arendt, philosopher and Hitler refugee, scorned such oceanic expressions: "cheap sentimentality at the expense of a great catastrophe," she wrote. And Bruno Bettelheim, a survivor of Dachau and Buchenwald, condemned the play's most touted line: "If all men are good, there was never an Auschwitz." A decade after the fall of Nazism, the spirited and sanitized young girl of the play became a vehicle of German communal identification—with the victim, not the persecutors—and, according to Rosenfeld, a continuing "symbol of moral and intellectual convenience." The Anne Frank whom thousands saw in seven openings in seven cities "spoke affirmatively about life and not accusingly about her torturers." No German in uniform appeared onstage. "In a word," Rosenfeld concludes, "Anne Frank has become a ready-at-hand formula for easy forgiveness."

The mood of consolation lingers on, as Otto Frank meant it to—and not only in Germany, where, even after fifty years, the issue is touchiest. Sanctified and absolving, shorn of darkness, Anne Frank remains in all countries a revered and comforting figure in the contemporary mind. In Japan, because both diary and play mention first menstruation, "Anne Frank" is a code word among teenagers for getting one's period. In Argentina in the seventies, church publications began to link her with Roman Catholic martyrdom. "Commemoration," the French cultural critic Tsvetan Todorov explains, "is always the adaptation of memory to the needs of today."

But there is a note that drills deeper than commemoration: it goes to the idea of identification. To "identify with" is to become what one is not, to become what one is not is to usurp, to usurp is to own—and who, after all, in the half-century since Miep Gies retrieved the scattered pages of the diary, really owns Anne Frank? Who can speak for her? Her father, who, after reading the diary and confessing that he "did not know" her, went on to tell us what he thought she meant? Meyer Levin, who claimed to be her authentic voice—so much so that he dared to equate the dismissal of his work, however ignobly motivated, with Holocaust annihilation? Hellman, Bloomgarden,

Kanin, whose interpretations clung to a collective ideology of human inter-changeability? (In discounting the significance of the Jewish element, Kanin had asserted that "people have suffered because of being English, French, German, Italian, Ethiopian, Mohammedan, Negro, and so on"—as if this were not all the more reason to comprehend and particularize each history.) And what of Cara Wilson and the children of the world," who have reduced the persecution of a people to the trials of adolescence?

All these appropriations, whether cheaply personal or densely ideologi-cal, whether seen as exalting or denigrating, have contributed to the conversion of Anne Frank into usable goods. There is no authorized version other than the diary itself, and even this has been brought into question by the Holocaustdenial industry—in part a spinoff of the Anne Frank indus-try—which labels the diary a forgery. One charge is that Otto Frank wrote it himself, to make money. (Scurrilities like these necessitated the issuance, in 1986, of a Critical Edition by the Netherlands State Institute for War Docu-mentation, including forensic evidence of handwriting and ink—a defensive hence sorrowful volume.)

No play can be judged wholly from what is on the page; a play has evocative powers beyond the words. Still, the Hacketts' work, read today, is very much a conventionally well-made Broadway product of the fifties, alter-nating comical beats with scenes of alarm, a love story with a theft, wisdom with buffoonery. The writing is skilled and mediocre, not unlike much of contemporary commercial theater. Yet this is the play that electrified audi-ences everywhere, that became a reverential if robotlike film, that—far more than the diary—invented the world's Anne Frank. Was it the play, or was it the times?

As the Second World War and the Holocaust recede for each new gen-eration into distant fable, no different from tales, say, of Attila the Hun, Holocaust scholarship nevertheless accelerates prodigiously—survivor mem-oirs, oral histories, wave after wave of fresh documentation and analysis. Under the rubric "reception studies," Holocaust incidents and figures are being examined for how current cultural perceptions have affected them. And Stephen Spielberg's *Schindler's List*, about a Nazi industrialist as the savior of hunted Jews, has left its transformative mark. (The security guard who uncovered the Swiss banks' culpability in appropriating survivors' assets is said to have been inspired by the Spielberg film.) Unsurprisingly, the 1997 revival of the Hacketts' dramatization entered an environment psychologi-cally altered from that of its 1955 predecessor. The new version's adapter and director were far more scrupulous in keeping faith with the diary, and went out of their way to avoid stimulating all the old quarrelsome issues. Yet the later production, with its cautious and conscientious additions, leaves no trace; it is as if it never was. What continues in the public consciousness of Anne Frank is the unstoppable voice of the original play. It was always a voice of good will; it meant, as we say, well—and, financially, it certainly did well. But it was Broadway's style of good will, and that, at least for Meyer Levin, had the scent of ill. For him, and signally for Bloomgarden and Kanin, the most sensitive point—the focus of trouble—lay in the ancient dispute between the particular and the universal. All that was a distraction from the heart of the matter: in a drama about hiding, evil was hidden. History was transcended, ennobled, rarefied. And if any proof is needed that the puffery of false optimism remains uneffaced, only recall how the young lead of 1997, forty years after the furies of the Kanin-Bloomgarden-Levin conflict, saw her role as Anne: it's *funny, it's hopeful, and she's a happy person.*

Evisceration, an elegy for the murdered. Evisceration by blurb and stage, by shrewdness and naïveté, by cowardice and spirituality, by forgiveness and indifference, by success and money, by vanity and rage, by principle and passion, by surrogacy and affinity. Evisceration by fame, by shame, by blame. By uplift and transcendence. By usurpation.

On Friday, August 4, 1944, the day of the arrest, Miep Gies climbed the stairs to the hiding place and found it ransacked and wrecked. The beleaguered little band had been betrayed by an informer who was paid seven and a half guilders—about a dollar—for each person: sixty guilders for the lot. Miep Gies picked up what she recognized as Anne's papers and put them away, unread, in her desk drawer. There the diary lay untouched, until Otto Frank emerged alive from Auschwitz. "Had I read it," she said afterward, "I would have had to burn the diary because it would have been too dangerous for people about whom Anne had written." It was Miep Gies—the uncommon heroine of this story, a woman profoundly good, a failed savior—who succeeded in rescuing an irreplaceable masterwork. It may be shocking to think this (I am shocked as I think it), but one can imagine a still more salvational outcome: Anne Frank's diary burned, vanished, lost—saved from a world that made of it all things, some of them true, while floating lightly over the heavier truth of named and inhabited evil.

Primo Levi's Suicide Note

~

Primo Levi, an Italian Jewish chemist from Turin, was liberated from Auschwitz by a Soviet military unit in January of 1945, when he was twenty-five, and from that moment of reprieve (*Moments of Reprieve* was one of his titles) until shortly before his death in April of 1987, he went on recalling, examining, reasoning, recording—telling the ghastly tale—in book after book. That he saw himself as a possessed scribe of the German hell, we know from the epigraph to his final volume, *The Drowned and the Saved*—familiar lines taken from "The Rime of the Ancient Mariner" and newly startling to a merely literary reader, for whom the words of Coleridge's poem have never before rung out with such an anti-metaphorical contemporary demand, or seemed so cruel:

> Since then, at an uncertain hour,
> That agony returns,
> And till my ghastly tale is told
> This heart within me burns.

Seized by the survivor's heart, this stanza no longer answers to the status of Lyrical Ballad, and still less to the English Department's quintessential Romantic text redolent of the supernatural; it is all deadly self-portrait. In the haven of an Italian spring—forty years after setting down the somber narrative called in Italian "If This Be a Man" and published in English as *Survival in Auschwitz*—Primo Levi hurled himself into the well of a spiral staircase four stories deep, just outside the door of the flat he was born in, where he had been living with his wife and aged ailing mother. Suicide. The composition of the last Lager manuscript was complete, the heart burned out; there was no more to tell.

There was no more to tell. That, of course, is an assumption nobody can justify, and nobody perhaps ought to dare to make. Suicide is one of the mysteries of the human will, with or without a farewell note to explain it.

And it remains to be seen whether *The Drowned and the Saved* is, after all, a sort of suicide note.

Levi, to be sure, is not the first writer of high distinction to survive hell and to suggest, by a self-willed death, that hell in fact did not end when the chimneys closed down, but was simply freshening for a second run—Auschwitz being the first hell, and post-Auschwitz the second; and if "survival" is the thing in question, then it isn't the "survivor" whose powers of continuation are worth marveling at, but hell itself. The victim who has escaped being murdered will sometimes contrive to finish the job, not because he is attached to death—never this—but because death is under the governance of hell, and it is in the nature of hell to go on and on: inescapability is its rule, No Exit its sign. "The injury cannot be healed," Primo Levi writes in *The Drowned and the Saved*; "it extends through time, and the Furies, in whose existence we are forced to believe . . . perpetuate the tormentor's work by denying peace to the tormented."

Tadeusz Borowski, for instance, author of *This Way for the Gas, Ladies and Gentlemen*, eluded the gas at both Auschwitz and Dachau from 1943 to 1945; in Warsaw, in 1951, not yet thirty, three days before the birth of his daughter, he turned on the household gas. Suicide. The poet Paul Celan: a suicide. The Austrian-born philosopher Hans Mayer—another suicide—who later became Jean Améry by scrambling his name into a French anagram, was in Auschwitz together with Primo Levi, though the two never chanced on one another. Before his capture and deportation, Améry had been in the Belgian resistance and was subjected to Gestapo torture. After the war, Améry and Levi corresponded about their experiences. Levi esteemed Amery, appeared to understand him, but evidently could not like him—because, he says, Amery was a man who "traded blows." "A gigantic Polish criminal," Levi recounts, "punches [Améry] in the face over some trifle; he, not because of an animallike reaction but because of a reasoned revolt against the perverted world of the Lager, returns the blow as best he can." "'Hurting all over from the blows, I was satisfied with myself,'"Levi quotes Amery; but for himself, Levi asserts,

> "trading punches" is an experience I do not have, as far back as I can go
> in memory; nor can I say I regret not having it . . . go[ing] down onto
> the battlefield ... was and is beyond my reach. I admire it, but I must
> point out that this choice, protracted throughout his post-Auschwitz
> existence, led [Amery] to such severity and intransigence as to make
> him incapable of finding joy in life, indeed of living. Those who "trade

blows" with the entire world achieve dignity but pay a very high price for it because they are sure to be defeated.

Remarkably, Levi concludes: "Améry's suicide, which took place in Salzburg in 1978 [i.e., nine years before Levi's leap into the stairwell], like other suicides allows for a nebula of explanations, but, in hindsight, that episode of defying the Pole offers one interpretation of it."

This observation—that the rage of resentment is somehow linked to self-destruction—is, in the perplexing shadow of Levi's own suicide, enigmatic enough, and bears returning to. For the moment it may be useful to consider that Primo Levi's reputation—rather, the grave and noble voice that sounds and summons through his pages—has been consummately free of rage, resentment, violent feeling, or any overt drive to "trade blows." The voice has been one of pristine sanity and discernment. Levi has been unwilling to serve either as preacher or as elegist. He has avoided polemics; he has shrunk from being counted as one of those message-bearers "whom I view with distrust: the prophet, the bard, the soothsayer. That I am not." Instead, he has offered himself as a singular witness—singular because he was "privileged" to survive as a laboratory slave, meaning that German convenience, at least temporarily, was met more through the exploitation of his training as a chemist than it would have been through his immediate annihilation as a Jew; and, from our own point of view, because of his clarity and selflessness as a writer. It is selfless to eschew freely running emotion, sermonizing, the catharsis of anger, when these so plainly plead their case before an unprecedentedly loathsome record of criminals and their crimes. Levi has kept his distance from blaming, scolding, insisting, vilifying, lamenting, crying out. His method has been to describe—meticulously, analytically, clarifyingly. He has been a Darwin of the death camps: not the Virgil of the German hell but its scientific investigator.

Levi himself recognizes that he has been particularly attended to for this quality of detachment. "From my trade," he affirms in *The Drowned and the Saved*,

I contracted a habit that can be variously judged and defined at will as human or inhuman-the habit of never remaining indifferent to the individuals that chance brings before me. They are human beings but also "samples," specimens in a sealed envelope to be identified, analyzed, and weighed. Now, the sample book that Auschwitz had placed before me was rich, varied, and strange, made up of friends, neutrals, and enemies, yet in any case food for my curiosity, which some people, then and later, have judged to be detached . . . I know that this "naturalistic" attitude does not derive only or necessarily from chemistry, but in my case it did come from chemistry.

Whatever its source—chemistry, or, as others have believed, a lucent and humane restraint—this "naturalistic" approach has astonished and inspired readers and critics. Irving Howe speaks of Levi's "unruffled dignity" and "purity of spirit," James Atlas of his "magisterial equanimity." Rita Levi-Montalcini, a recipient of the 1986 Nobel Prize in Medicine and a fellow Turinese, devotes an epilogue in her memoir, *In Praise of Imperfection*, to Levi's "detachment and absence of hatred." You, she addresses Levi, have "come out of the most atrocious of all experiences with an upright forehead and a spirit pure."

A temperament so transparent, so untainted, so unpolemical (indeed, so anti-polemical)—so like clear water—has, however, also provided a kind of relief, or respite, for those who hope finally to evade the gravamen of Levi's chronicle. The novelist Johanna Kaplan sets it out for us: *"Oh, that? Oh, that again?* . . . Because by now, after all the powerful, anguished novels . . . after all the simple, heartrending documentary accounts, the stringent, haunting historians' texts, the pained and arduous movies—that shocking newsreel footage . . . after all the necessary, nightmare lists of involuntary martyrology, by now our response to the singular horrific barbarity of our time is—just the tiniest bit dutiful." This desire to recoil may describe all of us; and yet we—some of us—drag through these foul swamps, the documents, the films, the photos, the talks, the tales, the conferences, year after year, taking it in and taking it in: perhaps because we are dutiful, perhaps because the fury of outrage owns us, more likely because we are the children of mercy and will not allow the suffering to recede into mere past-ness, a time not ours, for which we are not responsible. We press on with the heartsick job of assimilating the imagination of savagery because in some seizure of helplessly belated justice we want to become responsible for the murdered. In short, guilt: in one form or another we are wounded by conscience. Either, as Jews, we were not there with the others who stood in for us as victims, or, as Christians, we were too much there, represented by the familiar upbringing of the criminals, with whose religious inheritance we have so much in common. Guilt in our absence, guilt in our presence. Jewish guilt; Christian guilt; English, French, Italian, Croatian, Ukrainian, American guilt. Guilt of the Germans whose patriotism gave birth to the criminals. Guilt of the Irish and the Swedes who hid behind neutrality. Guilt over zeal, guilt over apathy.

All of this Levi as naturalist skirts. He appears to have nothing to do with any of it. He is not in favor of a generalized anguish. His aim has been to erect a principled barrier against any show of self-appointed fanaticism, from any direction. Book after book has shied away from the emotive accusatory issues. Above all, Levi is careful not to blur victim and victimizer. He is wary of the sentimentalizers, preeners, hypothesizers: "I do not know," he writes, "and it does not much interest me to know, whether in my depths there lurks a murderer, but I do know that I was a guiltless victim and not a murderer . . . to confuse [the murderers] with their victims is a moral disease or an aesthetic affectation or a sinister sign of complicity." He is a stringent taxonomist, on the side of precision: the crimes and the criminals have an identifiable habitation and name. This may be one reason—it is not the only one—it has been possible to read Levi with soul's pain (how could this be otherwise?), but without guilt. It is not that Levi absolves; rather, he mutes the question of absolution—a question always in the forefront for messengers as radically different from each other as, say, Elie Wiesel and Raul Hilberg. Hilberg's investigations in particular, coolly data-obsessed as they are, have erased the notion of "bystander" status in Nazi Germany. Levi has devoted himself less to social history and psychological motivation than to the microscope, with its exactingly circumscribed field of vision. Society-as-organism is not the area under his scrutiny, as it is for Hilberg; neither is suffering as metaphor, as with Wiesel's emblematic mourning madmen.

The advantage, for many of Levi's readers, has been—dare one say this?—a curious peacefulness: the consequence of the famous "detachment." Levi is far from being a peaceful witness, but because he has not harassed or harangued or dramatized or poetized or shaken a fist or shrieked or politicized (a little of the last, but only a little), because he has restricted himself to observation, notation, and restraint, it becomes alarmingly easy to force him into a false position. If it was futile for him to plead, as he once did, "I beg the reader not to go looking for messages," it is nevertheless disconcerting that of all the various "lessons" that might have been drawn from Levi's penetrations, the one most prevalent is also the coarsest and the most misleading: uplift. Rarely will you come on a publisher's jacket blare as shallow as the one accompanying *The Drowned and the Saved*: "a wondrous celebration of life . . . a testament to the indomitability of the human spirit and humanity's capacity to defeat death through meaningful work, morality and art." Contemptible puffery, undermining every paragraph of the text it ostensibly promotes; and if it is designed to counter "*Oh, that? Oh, that again?*" then it is even more contemptible. Celebration of life? Defeat of death? *Meaningful* work? Morality? Art? What callousness, what cravenness, before the subject at hand! In the Lager world, Levi tells us again and again, "work" was pointless, and deliberately so, in order to intensify torment; morality was reduced to staying alive as long as possible, and by any means; and art was non-existent. Applied to a place where murder claimed daily dominion, "celebration of life" can only be a mockery, or—if that phrase is meant to describe Levi's intent as witness—a double mockery: his intent is to let us see for ourselves the nature, extent, and depth of the German crime.

Yet "celebration of life," that falsifying balm, is hardly untypical of the illusory—or self-deluding-glow of good feeling (or, at worst, absence of bad feeling) that generally attaches to Levi's name. Of the scribes of the Holocaust, Levi appears to be the one who least troubles, least wounds, least implicates, the reader. A scientific or objective attitude will inform, certainly, but declines any show of agitation. What we have had from Levi, accordingly, is the portrait of a psychological oxymoron: the well-mannered cicerone of hell, mortal horror in a decorous voice. "Améry called me 'the forgiver,'" Levi notes. "I consider this neither insult nor praise but imprecision. I am not inclined to forgive, I never forgave our enemies of that time . . . because I know no human act that can erase a crime; I demand justice, but I am not able, personally"—here again is this insistent declaration of refusal—"to trade punches or return blows." All the same (untenable as he might consider it), Levi is widely regarded, if not quite as "the forgiver," then as the survivor whose books are, given their subject matter, easiest to take; one gets the impression (and from Levi's own pages) that he has been read in Germany far more willingly than have some others. He writes, as his countrywoman remarked, in the "absence of hatred."

And so it has seemed until this moment. *The Drowned and the Saved* reveals something else. It is a detonation, all the more volcanic because so unexpected. Yet "detonation" is surely, at least from Levi's point of view, the wrong word: concussion is an all-of-a-sudden thing. In *The Drowned and the Saved*, the change of tone is at first muted, faint. Gradually, cumulatively, rumble by rumble, it leads to disclosure, exposure—one can follow the sizzle flying along the fuse; by the last chapter the pressure is so powerful, the rage so immense, that "detachment" has long given way to convulsion. What was withheld before is now imploded in these pages. *The Drowned and the Saved* is the record of a man returning blows with all the might of human fury, in full knowledge that the pen is mightier than the fist. The convulsions of rage have altered the nature of the prose, and—if we can judge by Levi's suicide—the man as well. Almost no one, interestingly, has been disposed to say of Levi's final testimony that it is saturated in deadly anger—as if it would be too cruel to tear from him the veil of the spirit pure. It may be cruel; but it is Levi's own hand that tears away the veil and sets the fuse.

The fuse is ignited almost instantly, in the Preface. "No one will ever be able to establish with precision how many, in the Nazi apparatus, could *not not know* about the frightful atrocities being committed, how many knew something but were in a position to pretend they did not know, and, further, how many had the possibility of knowing everything but chose the more prudent path of keeping their eyes and ears (and above all their mouths) well shut." Here is the heralding of the indictment that will emerge: it is the German people whom Levi subjects to judgment, which may account for his rarely shrinking from the use of "German," where, nowadays, "Nazi" is usually the polite, because narrower, term. In the Preface also may be found the single most terrible sentence ever offered on the issue of what is variously called "restitution," "changed attitudes," "the new generation," and all the rest: "The crematoria ovens themselves were designed, built, assembled, and tested by a German company, Topf of Wiesbaden (it was still in operation in 1975, building crematoria for civilian use, and had not considered the advisability of changing its name)." *Had not considered the advisability of changing its name*: this applies equally to Krupp, notorious for slave labor, and, in its most celebrated incarnation, to Hitler's "people's car," the ubiquitous Volkswagen, driven unselfconsciously by half the world. (An unselfconscious irony, by the way, that Levi, or his admirable translator, should fall into the phrase "civilian use," meaning, one supposes, the opposite of official governmental policy—i.e., ordinary funerals employing cremation. But who else other than "civilians" were annihilated in the Lager?)

When Levi comes to speak of shame, it is nevertheless not the absence of shame among Germans he invokes, though he condemns the "complicity and connivance" of the "majority of Germans" just before and during the Hitler years; rather, it is the loss of shame in the victims of the Lager, dispossessed of any civilizing vestige, reduced to the animal. The Lager "*anus mundi*," dominated "from dawn to dusk by hunger, fatigue, cold, and fear," "ultimate drainage site of the German universe," was a condition without reciprocity, where you sought to succor and relieve only yourself, to take care of yourself alone. Shame returned with the return of freedom, retrospectively. In the "gray zone" of Lager oppression, contaminated victims collaborated with contaminating persecutors. Arrival at Auschwitz meant "kicks and punches right away, often in the face; an orgy of orders screamed with true or simulated rage; complete nakedness after being stripped; the shaving off of all one's hair; the outfitting in rags," and some of these depredations were conducted by fellow victims appointed as functionaries. Again and again

Levi emphasizes the diminishment of every human trait, the violated modesty, the public evacuation, the satanically inventive brutality, the disorientation and desperation. He describes the absolute rule of "small satraps"—the common criminals who became Kapos; the wretched *Bettnachzieher*, whose sole job was to measure the orderliness of straw pillows with a maniacal string and who had the power to punish "publicly and savagely"; the overseers of the "work that was purely persecutory"; the "Special Squads" that operated the crematoria for the sake of a few weeks more of life, only to be replaced and thrown into the fire in turn. These squads, Levi explains, "were made up largely of Jews. In a certain sense this is not surprising, since the Lager's main purpose was to destroy Jews, and, beginning in 1943, the Auschwitz population was 90–95 percent Jews." (Here I interrupt to remind the reader of William Styron's choice in *Sophie's Choice*, wherein we are given, as the central genocidal emblem of Lager policy in those years, a victim who is not a Jew.*) "From another point of view," Levi continues, "one is stunned by this paroxysm of perfidy and hatred: it must be the Jews who put the Jews into the ovens; it must be shown that the Jews, the sub-race, the sub-men, bow to any and all humiliation, even to destroying themselves." Levi admits that merely by virtue of his having stayed alive, he never "fathomed [the Lager] to the bottom." The others, the "drowned," he maintains, those who went down to the lees of suffering and annihilation, were the only true fathomers of that perfidy and hatred.

Levi's reflections appear to be fathomings enough. *The Drowned and the Saved* is much less a book of narrative and incident than it is of siftings of the most sordid deposits of the criminal imagination—the inescapable struggle of a civilized mind to bore through to the essence and consequence of degradation and atrocity. Levi is not the first to observe that "where violence is inflicted on man it is also inflicted on language," though he may be among the first to inform us of the life-or-death role of language in the Lager. Simply, not to understand German was to go under at once: "the rubber truncheon was called *der Dolmetscher*, the interpreter: the one who made himself understood to everybody." Levi had studied some German at the

---

* Let no one misconstrue this remark. The point is not that Jews suffered more than anyone else in the camps, or even that they suffered in greater numbers; concerning suffering there can be no competition or hierarchy. To suggest otherwise would be monstrous. Those who suffered at Auschwitz suffered with an absolute equality, and the suffering of no one victimized group or individual weighs more in human anguish than that of any other victimized group or individual. But note: Catholic Poland, for instance (language, culture, land), continues, while European Jewish civilization (language, culture, institutions) was wiped out utterly—and that, for Jewish history, is the different and still more terrible central meaning of Auschwitz. It is, in fact, what defines the Holocaust, and distinguishes it from the multiple other large-scale victimizations of the Nazi period.

university to prepare himself as a chemist. He learned more in Auschwitz—grotesquely distorted barbarisms which he deliberately held on to years later, "for the same reason I have never had the tattoo removed from my left arm." As for the tattoo itself—"an autochthonous Auschwitzian invention," "gratuitous, an end in itself, pure offense," "a return to barbarism"—Levi, a secular Jew, is careful to note that Leviticus 19:28 forbids tattooing "precisely in order to distinguish Jews from the barbarians." Even newborn babies, he reports, were tattooed on arrival in Auschwitz.

All this, and considerably more, Levi gathers up under the chilling heading of "Useless Violence," which he defines as "a deliberate creation of pain that was an end in itself." What else was the purpose of the vindictive halt of a boxcar of Jews at an Austrian railroad station, where, while the guards laughed, "the German passengers openly expressed their disgust" at "men and women squatting wherever they could, on the platforms and in the middle of the tracks"? What else was the purpose of emptying out nursing homes filled with elderly sick people already near death and hauling them off to Auschwitz to be gassed? Or forcing grown men to lap up soup like dogs by depriving them of spoons (of which there were tens of thousands at Auschwitz)? Or using human ash from the crematoria to make "gravel" paths for the SS village that ruled the camp? Or selling human hair to the German textile industry for mattress ticking? Or locking human beings into decompression chambers "to establish at what altitude human blood begins to boil: a datum that can be obtained in any laboratory at minimum expense and without victims, or even can be deduced from common tables"?

A sparse sampling from Levi's meditation on the German abominations, some familiar, some not. Cardinal John O'Connor's theologizing not long ago—which led him to identify the torments of Auschwitz as a Jewish gift to the world—is no doubt indisputably valid Roman Catholic doctrine concerning the redemptive nature of suffering; but, much as the observation was intended to confer grace on the victims, it strikes me as impossible, even for a committed Christian, even for an angel of God, to speak of redemption and Auschwitz in the same breath. What we learn overwhelmingly from Levi is this: if there is redemption in it, it cannot be Auschwitz; and if it is Auschwitz, it is nothing if not unholy. Let no one mistake Primo Levi. If an upright forehead and a spirit pure mean forgoing outrage for the sake of one lofty idea or another—including the renunciation of hatred for the designers of the crematoria—then Primo Levi is as sullied as anybody else who declines to be morally neutered in the name of superior views.

He is in fact not morally neutered, and never was. He is not a "forgiver" (only someone with a clouded conscience would presume to claim that right on behalf of the murdered), and he is not dedicated, as so many believe, to an absence of rancor toward the strategists of atrocity and their followers. He is, as he asserts, a scientist and a logician: nowhere in Levi's pages will you find anything even remotely akin to the notion of "hate the sin, not the sinner." He is not an absurdist or a surrealist; nowhere does he engage in such a severance. On the contrary, his pre-eminent theme is responsibility: "The true crime, the collective, general crime of almost all Germans of that time, was that of lacking the courage to speak." One thinks, accordingly, of those unmoved German citizens waiting for a train on a station platform, compelled to hold their noses in revulsion as the freight cars, after passing through miles of unpeopled countryside, disgorge their dehumanized prey—a "relief stop" conceived in malice and derision. In his final chapter, "Letters from Germans," Levi quotes a correspondent who pleads with him "to remember the innumerable Germans who suffered and died in their struggle against iniquity." This letter and others like it bring Levi to the boiling point. He scorns the apologists, the liars, the "falsely penitent." He recalls his feelings when he learned that *Survival in Auschwitz* would be published in Germany:

> yes, I had written the book in Italian for Italians, for my children, for those who did not know, those who did not want to know, those who were not yet born, those who, willing or not, had assented to the offense; but its true recipients, those against whom the book was aimed like a gun, were they, the Germans. Now the gun was loaded . . . I would corner them, tie them before a mirror . . . Not that handful of high-ranking culprits, but them, the people, those I had seen from close up, those from among whom the SS militia were recruited, and also those others, those who had believed, who not believing had kept silent, who did not have the frail courage to look into our eyes, throw us a piece of bread, whisper a human word.

He quotes from *Mein Kampf*; he reminds his "polite and civil interlocutors, members of a people who exterminated mine," of the free elections that put Hitler into office, and of *Kristallnacht*; he points out that "enrollment in the SS was voluntary," and that heads of German families were entitled, upon application, to receive clothing and shoes for both children and adults from the warehouses at Auschwitz. "Did no one ask himself where so many children's shoes were coming from?" And he concludes with a *j'accuse* directed toward "that great majority of Germans who accepted in the beginning, out of mental laziness, myopic calculation, stupidity, and national pride, the 'beautiful words' of Corporal Hitler."

The Drowned and the Saved is a book of catching-up after decades of abstaining. It is a book of blows returned by a pen on fire. The surrender to fury in these burning chapters does not swallow up their exactness—the scientist's truthful lens is not dissolved—but Levi in the violated voice of this last completed work lets fly a biblical ululation that its predecessors withheld: *thy brother's blood cries up from the ground.* I do not mean that Levi has literally set down those words; but he has, at long last, unleashed their clamor.

And what of the predecessor-volumes? What of their lucid calm, absence of hatred, magisterial equanimity, unaroused detachment? Readers have not misconstrued Levi's tone, at least not until now. *The Drowned and the Saved* makes it seem likely that the restraint of forty years was undertaken out of a consistent adherence to an elevated *idée fixe,* possibly to a self-deception: a picture of how a civilized man ought to conduct himself when he is documenting savagery. The result was the world's consensus: a man somehow set apart from retaliatory passion. A man who would not trade punches. A transparency; a pure spirit. A vessel of clear water.

I spoke earlier of creeping fuses, mutedness, the slow accretion of an insurmountable pressure. "The Furies . . . perpetuate the tormentor's work by denying peace to the tormented." But all that was subterranean. Then came the suicide. Consider now an image drawn from Primo Levi's calling. Into a vessel of clear water—tranquil, innocuous—drop an unaccustomed ingredient: a lump of potassium, say, an alkali metal that reacts with water so violently that the hydrogen gas given off by the process will erupt into instant combustion. One moment, a beaker of unperturbed transparency. The next moment, a convulsion: self-destruction.

The unaccustomed ingredient, for Levi, was rage. "Suicide," he reflects in *The Drowned and the Saved*—which may be seen, perhaps and after all, as the bitterest of suicide notes—"is an act of man and not of the animal. It is a meditated act, a noninstinctive, unnatural choice." In the Lager, where human beings were driven to become animals, there were almost no suicides at all. Améry, Borowski, Celan, and ultimately Levi did not destroy themselves until some time after they were released. Levi waited more than forty years; and he did not become a suicide until he let passion in, and returned the blows. If he is right about Améry—that Améry's willingness to trade punches is the key to his suicide—then he has deciphered for us his own suicide as well.

What we know now—we did not know it before *The Drowned and the Saved*—is that at bottom Levi could not believe in himself as a vessel of clear water standing serenely apart. It was not detachment. It was dormancy, it was latency, it was potentiality; it was inoperativeness. He was always con-scious of how near to hand the potassium was. I grieve that he equated rage—the rage that speaks for mercifulness—with self-destruction. A flawed formula. It seems to me it would not have been a mistake—and could not have been misinterpreted—if all of Primo Levi's books touching on the German hell had been as vehement, and as pointed, as the last, the most remarkable.

The Posthumous Sublime

There is almost no clarifying publisher's apparatus surrounding *The Emigrants*, W. G. Sebald's restless, melancholy, and (I am almost sorry to say) sublime narrative quartet. One is compelled—ludicrously, clumsily—to settle for that hapless term (what is a "narrative quartet"?) because the very identity of this work remains murky. Which parts of it are memoir, which fiction—and ought it to matter? As for external facticity, we learn from the copyright page that the original German publication date is 1993, and that the initials W. G. represent Winfried Georg. A meager paragraph supplies a handful of biographical notes: the author was born in Wartach im Allgäu, Germany; he studied German literature in Freiburg (where, one recalls, Heidegger's influence extended well into the 1970s), and later in Francophone Switzerland and in Manchester, England, where he began a career in British university teaching. Two dates stand out: Sebald's birth in 1944, an appalling year for all of Europe, and for European Jews a death's-head year; and 1970, when, at the age of twenty-six, Sebald left his native Germany and moved permanently to England.

It cannot be inappropriate to speculate why. One can imagine that in 1966, during the high period of Germany's "economic miracle," when Sebald was (as that meagerly informative paragraph tells us) a very young assistant lecturer at the University of Manchester—a city then mostly impoverished and in decline—he may have encountered a romantic attachment that finally lured him back to Britain; or else he came to the explicit determination, with or without any romantic attachment (yet he may, in fact, have fallen in love with the pathos of soot-blackened Manchester), that he would anyhow avoid the life of a contemporary German. "The life of a contemporary German": I observe, though from a non-visitor's distance, and at so great a remove now from those twelve years of intoxicated popular zeal for Nazism, that such a life is somehow still touched with a smudge, or taint, of the old shameful history; and that the smudge, or taint—or call it, rather, the little tic of self-consciousness—is there all the same, whether it is regretted or repudiated, examined or ignored, forgotten or relegated to a principled indifference. Even the youngest Germans traveling abroad—especially in New York— know what it is to be made to face, willy-nilly, a history of national crime, however long receded and repented.

For a German citizen to live with 1944 as a birth date is reminder enough. Mengele stood that year on the ramp at Auschwitz, lifting the omnipotent gloved hand that dissolved Jewish families: mothers, babies, and the old to the chimneys, the rest to the slave labor that temporarily fore-stalled death.—Ah, and it is sentences like this last one that present-day Germans, thriving in a democratic Western polity, resent and decry. A German professor of comparative literature accused me not long ago— because of a sentence like that—of owning a fossilized mind, of being unable to recognize that a nation "develops and moves on." Max Ferber, the painter-protagonist of the final tale in Sebald's quartet, might also earn that professor's fury. "To me, you see," Sebald quotes Ferber, "Germany is a country frozen in the past, destroyed, a curiously extraterritorial place." It is just this extra-territorialism—this ineradicable, inescapable, ever-recurring, hideously retrievable 1944—that Sebald investigates, though veiled and at a slant, in *The Emigrants*. And it was, I suspect, not the democratic Germany of the economic miracle from which Sebald emigrated in 1970; it may have been, after all, the horribly frozen year of his birth that he meant to leave behind.

That he did not relinquish his native language or its literature goes with-out saying; and we are indebted to Michael Hulse, Sebald's translator (himself a poet), for allowing us to see, through the stained glass of his con-summate Englishing, what must surely be the most delicately powerful German prose since Thomas Mann. Or, on second thought, perhaps not Mann really, despite a common attraction to the history-soaked. Mann on occasion can be as heavily ornate as those carved mahogany sideboards and wardrobes—vestiges of proper German domesticity abandoned by the fleeing Jews—which are currently reported to add a certain glamorous middle-thirties tone to today's fashionable Berlin apartments. Sebald is more trans-lucent than Mann; he writes as Turner paints: "To the south, lofty Mount Spathi, two thousand meters high, towered above the plateau, like a mirage above the flood of light. The fields of potatoes and vegetables across the broad valley floor, the orchards and clumps of other trees, and the untilled land, were awash with green upon green, studded with the hundreds of white sails of wind pumps." Notably, this is not a landscape viewed by a fresh and naked eye. It is, in fact, a verbal rendering of an old photograph— a slide shown by a projector on a screen.

An obsession with old photographs is what separates Sebald from traces of Mann, from Turner's hallucinatory mists, from the winding reflections of Proust (to whom, in his freely searching musings and paragraphs wheeling cumulatively over pages, Sebald has been rightly and repeatedly compared), and even from the elusively reappearing shade of Nabokov. The four narratives recounted in *The Emigrants* are each accompanied by superannuated poses captured by obsolete cameras; in their fierce time-bound isolations they suggest nothing so much as Diane Arbus. Wittingly or not, Sebald evokes Henry James besides, partly for his theme of expatriation, and partly on account of the mysterious stillness inherent in photography's icy precision. In the 1909 New York Edition of his work, James eschewed illustration, that nineteenth-century standby, and turned instead to the unsentimental fixity of photography's Time and Place, or Place-in-Time. In Sebald's choosing to incorporate so many photos (I count eighty-six in 237 pages of text)—houses, streets, cars, headstones, cobblestones, motionless schoolchildren, mountain crevasses, country roads, posters, roofs, steeples, hotel postcards, bridges, tenements, grand and simple rooms, overgrown gardens—he, like James with his 1909 frontispieces, is acknowledging the uncanny ache that cries out from the silence of solid things. These odd old pictures attach to Sebald's voice like an echo that cannot be heard, no matter how hard one strains; they lie in the crevices of print with a terrible helplessness—deaf-mutes without the capacity to sign.

The heard language of these four stories—memories personal, borrowed, invented—is, as I noted earlier, sublime; and I wish it were not—or, if that is not altogether true, I admit to being disconcerted by a grieving that has been made beautiful. Grief, absence, loss, longing, wandering, exile, home-sickness—these have been made millennially, sadly beautiful since the *Odyssey*, since the *Aeneid*, since Dante ("You shall come to know how salt is the taste of another's bread"); and, more venerably still, since the Psalmist's song by the waters of Babylon. Nostalgia is itself a lovely and piercing word, and even more so is the German *Heimweh*, "home-ache." It is art's sacred ancient trick to beautify pain, to romanticize the shadows of the irretrievable. "O lost, and by the wind grieved, ghost, come back again"—Thomas Wolfe, too much scorned for boyishness, tolls that bell as mournfully as anyone; but it is an American tolling, not a German one. Sebald's mourning bell is German, unmistakably German; when it tolls the hour, it is almost always 1944. And if I regret the bittersweet sublime Turner-like wash of Beauty that shimmers over the whole of this volume, it is because sublime grieving is a category of yearning, fit for that which is irretrievable. But 1944 is always, always retrievable. There stands Mengele on the ramp, forever lifting his gloved hand; and there, sent off to the left and the right, are the Jews, going to the left and the right forever. Nor is this any intimation of Keats's urn—there are human ashes in it. The posthumous sublime is discordant; an oxymoron. Adorno told us this long ago: after Auschwitz, no more poetry. We resist such a dictum; the Psalmist by the waters of Babylon resisted it; the poet Paul Célan resisted it; Sebald resists it. It is perhaps natural to resist it.

So, in language sublime, Sebald is haunted by Jewish ghosts—Europe's phantoms: the absent Jews, the deported, the gassed, the suffering, the hidden, the fled. There is a not-to-be-overlooked irony (a fossilized irony, my professor-critic might call it) in Sebald's having been awarded the Berlin Literature Prize—Berlin, the native city of Gershom (né Gerhardt) Scholem, who wrote definitively about the one-sided infatuation of Jews in love with high German culture and with the *Vaterland* itself. The Jewish passion for Germany was never reciprocated—until now. Sebald returns that Jewish attachment, although tragically: he is too late for reciprocity. The Jews he searches for are either stricken escapees or smoke. Like all ghosts, they need to be conjured.

Or, if not conjured, then come upon by degrees, gradually, incrementally, in hints and echoes. Sebald allows himself to discover his ghosts almost stealthily, with a dawning notion of who they really are. It is as if he is intruding on them, and so he is cautious, gentle, wavering at the outer margins of the strange places he finds them in. In "Dr. Henry Selwyn," as the first narrative is called, the young Sebald and his wife drive out into the English countryside to rent a flat in a wing of an overgrown mansion surrounded by a neglected garden and a park of looming trees. The house seems deserted. Tentatively, they venture onto the grounds and stumble unexpectedly on a white-haired, talkative old man who describes himself as "a dweller in the garden, a kind of ornamental hermit." By the time we arrive at the end of this faintly Gothic episode, however, we have learned that Dr. Henry Selwyn was once a *cheder-yingl*—a Jewish schoolchild—named Hersch Seweryn in a village near Grodno in Lithuania. When he was seven years old, his family, including his sisters Gita and Raya, set out for America, like thousands of other impoverished shtetl Jews at the beginning of the century; but "in fact, as we learnt some time later to our dismay (the ship having long since cast off again), we had gone ashore in London." The boy begins his English education in Whitechapel in the Jewish East End, and eventually wins a scholarship to Cambridge to study medicine. Then, like a proper member of his adopted milieu, he heads for the Continent for advanced training, where he becomes enamored—again like a proper

Englishman—with a Swiss Alpine guide named Johannes Naegeli. Naegeli tumbles into a crevasse and is killed; Dr. Selwyn returns home to serve in the Great War and in India. Later he marries a Swiss heiress who owns houses in England and lets flats. He has now completed the trajectory from Hersch Seweryn to Dr. Henry Selwyn. But one day, when the word "homesick" flies up out of a melancholy conversation with Sebald, Selwyn tells the story of his childhood as a Jewish immigrant.

The American term is immigrant, not emigrant, and for good reason, America being the famous recipient of newcomers: more come in than ever go out. Our expatriates tend to be artists, often writers: hence that illustrious row of highly polished runaways, James, Eliot, Pound, Wharton, Gertrude Stein, Hemingway. But an expatriate, a willing (sometimes temporary) seeker, is not yet an emigrant. And an emigrant is not a refugee. A *cheder-yingl* from a shtetl near Grodno in a place and period not kind to Jews is likely to feel himself closer to being a refugee than an emigrant: our familiar steerage image expresses it best. Sebald, of course, knows this, and introduces Dr. Selwyn as a type of foreshadowing. Displaced and homesick in old age for the child he once was (or in despair over the man he has become), Dr. Selwyn commits suicide. And on a visit to Switzerland in 1986, Sebald reads in a Lausanne newspaper that Johannes Naegeli's body has been found frozen in a glacier seventy-two years after his fall. "And so they are ever returning to us, the dead," Sebald writes.

But of exactly what is Dr. Selwyn a foreshadowing? The second account, entitled "Paul Bereyter," is a portrait of a German primary-school teacher— Sebald's own teacher in the fifties, "who spent at least a quarter of all his lessons on teaching us things that were not on the syllabus." Original, inventive, a lover of music, a scorner of catechism and priests, an explorer, a whistler, a walker ("the very image . . . of the German *Wandervogel* hiking movement, which must have had a lasting influence on him from his youth"), Paul Bereyter is nevertheless a lonely and increasingly aberrant figure. In the thirties he had come out of a teachers' training college (here a grim photo of the solemn graduates, in their school ties and rather silly caps) and taught school until 1935, when he was dismissed for being a quarter-Jew. The next year his father, who owned a small department store, died in a mood of anguish over Nazi pogroms in his native Gunzenhausen, where there had been a thriving Jewish population. After the elder Bereyter's death, the business was confiscated; his widow succumbed to depression and a fatal deterioration. Paul's sweetheart, who had journeyed from Vienna to visit him just before he took up his first teaching post, was also lost to him: deported, it was presumed afterward, to Theresienstadt. Stripped of father, mother, inheritance, work, and love, Paul fled to tutor in France for a time, but in 1939 drifted back to Germany, where, though only three-quarters Aryan, he was unaccountably conscripted. For six years he served in the motorized artillery all over Nazi-occupied Europe. At the war's end he returned to teach village boys, one of whom was Sebald.

As Sebald slowly elicits his old teacher's footprints from interviews, reconstructed hints, and the flickering lantern of his own searching language, Paul Bereyter turns out to be that rare and mysterious figure: an interior refugee (and this despite his part in the German military machine)— or call it, as Sebald might, an internal emigrant. After giving up teaching—the boys he had once felt affection for he now began to see as "contemptible and repulsive creatures"—he both lived in and departed from German society, inevitably drawn back to it, and just as inevitably repelled. All his adult life, Sebald discovers, Paul Bereyter had been interested in railways. (The text is now interrupted by what appears to be Paul's own sketch of the local *Bahnhof*, or train station, with the inscription *So ist es seit dem* 4.10.49: This is how it has looked since the fourth of October 1949.) On the blackboard he draws "stations, tracks, goods depots, and signal boxes" for the boys to reproduce in their notebooks. He keeps a model train set on a card table in his flat. He obsesses about timetables. Later, though his eyesight is troubled by cataracts, he reads demonically—almost exclusively the works of suicides, among them Wittgenstein, Benjamin, Klaus Mann, Koestler, Zweig, Tucholsky. He copies out, in shorthand, hundreds of their pages. And finally, on a mild winter afternoon, he puts on a windbreaker that he has not worn since his early teaching days forty years before, and goes out to stretch himself across the train tracks, awaiting his own (as it were) deportation. Years after this event, looking through Paul's photo album with its record of childhood and family life, Sebald again reflects: "it truly seemed to me, and still does, as if the dead were coming back"—but now he adds, "or as if we were on the point of joining them." Two tales, two suicides. Yet suicide is hardly the most desolating loss in Sebald's broader scheme of losses. And since he comes at things aslant, his next and longest account, the history of his aunts and uncles and their emigration to the United States in the twenties—a period of extreme unemployment in Germany—is at first something of a conundrum. Where, one muses, are those glimmers of the Jewish ghosts of Germany, or any inkling of entanglement with Jews at all? And why, among these steadily rising German-American burghers, should there be? Aunt Fini and Aunt Lini and Uncle Kasimir, Aunt Theres and Cousin Flossie, "who later became a secretary in Tucson, Arizona, and learnt to belly dance when she was in her fifties"—these are garden-variety acculturating American immigrants; we know them; we know the smells of their kitchens; they are our neighbors. (They were certainly mine in my North Bronx childhood.) The geography is familiar—a photo of a family dinner in a recognizable Bronx apartment (sconces on the wall, steam-heat radiators); then the upwardly mobile move to Mamaroneck, in Westchester; then the retirement community in New Jersey. To get to Fini and Kasimir, drive south from Newark on the Jersey Turnpike and head for Lakehurst and the Garden State. In search of Uncle Adelwarth in his last years: Route 17, Monticello, Hurleyville, Oswego, Ithaca. There are no ghosts in these parts. It is, all of it, plain-hearted America.

But turn the page: here are the ghosts. A photo of Uncle Kasimir as a young man, soon after his apprenticeship as a tinsmith. It is 1928, and only once in that terrible year, Kasimir recounts, did he get work, "when they were putting a new copper roof on the synagogue in Augsburg." In the photo Kasimir and six other metal workers are sitting at the top of the curve of a great dome. Behind them, crowning the dome, are three large sculptures of the six-pointed Star of David. "The Jews of Augsburg," explains Kasimir, "had donated the old copper roof for the war effort during the First World War, and it wasn't till '28 that they had the money for a new roof." Sebald offers no comment concerning the fate of those patriotic Jews and their synagogue a decade on, in 1938, in the fiery hours of the Nazis' so-called *Kristallnacht*. But Kasimir and the half-dozen tinsmiths perched against a cluster of Jewish stars leave a silent mark in Sebald's prose: what once was is no more.

After the roofing job in Augsburg, Kasimir followed Fini and Theres to New York. They had been preceded by their legendary Uncle Ambros Adelwarth, who was already established as a majordomo on the Long Island estate of the Solomons family, where he was in particular charge of Cosmo Solomons, the son and heir. Adelwarth helped place Fini as a governess with the Seligmans in Port Washington, and Theres as a lady's maid to a Mrs. Wallerstein, whose husband was from Ulm in Germany. Kasimir, meanwhile, was renting a room on the Lower East Side from a Mrs. Litwak, who made paper flowers and sewed for a living. In the autumn succahs sprouted on all the fire escapes. At first Kasimir was employed by the Seckler and Margarethen Soda and Seltzer Works; Seckler was a German Jew from Brünn, who recommended Kasimir as a metal worker for the new yeshiva on Amsterdam Avenue. "The very next day," says Kasimir, "I was up on the top of the tower, just as I had been on the Augsburg Synagogue, only much higher."

So the immigrants, German and Jewish, mingle in America much as Germans and Jews once mingled in Germany, in lives at least superficially entwined. (One difference being that after the first immigrant generation the

German-Americans would not be likely to continue as tinsmiths, just as Mrs. Litwak's progeny would hardly expect to take in sewing. The greater likelihood is that a Litwak daughter is belly-dancing beside Flossie in Tucson.) And if Sebald means for us to feel through its American parallel how this ordinariness, this matter-of-factness, of German-Jewish coexistence was brutally ruptured in Germany, then he has succeeded in calling up his most fearful phantoms. Yet his narrative continues as impregnable here as polished copper, evading conclusions of any kind. Even the remarkably stoic tale of Ambros Adelwarth, born in 1896, is left to speak for itself—Adelwarth who, traveling as valet and protector and probably lover of mad young Cosmo Solomons, dutifully frequented the polo grounds of Saratoga Springs and Palm Beach, and the casinos of Monte Carlo and Deauville, and saw Paris and Venice and Constantinople and the deserts on the way to Jerusalem. Growing steadily madder, Cosmo tried to hang himself and at last succumbed to catatonic dementia. Uncle Adelwarth was obliged to commit him to a sanatorium in Ithaca, New York, where Cosmo died—the same sanatorium to which Adelwarth, with all the discipline of a lifetime, and in a strange act of replication, later delivered himself to paralysis and death.

The yeshiva on Amsterdam Avenue, the Solomons, Seligmans, Wallersteins, Mrs. Litwak and the succahs on the Lower East Side—this is how Sebald chooses to shape the story of the emigration to America of his Catholic German relations. It is as if the fervor of Uncle Adelwarth's faithful attachment to Cosmo Solomons were somehow a repudiation of Gershom Scholem's thesis of unrequited Jewish devotion; as if Sebald were casting a posthumous spell to undo that thesis.

And now on to Max Ferber, Sebald's final guide to the deeps. Ferber was a painter Sebald got to know—"befriended" is too implicated a term for that early stage—when the twenty-two-year-old Sebald came to study and teach in Manchester, an industrially ailing city studded with mainly defunct chimneys, the erstwhile black fumes of which still coated every civic brick. That was in 1966; my own first glimpse of Manchester was nine years before, and I marveled then that an entire metropolis should be so amazingly, universally charred, as if brushed by a passing conflagration. (Later Sebald will tell us that in its bustling heyday Lodz, in Poland—the site of the Lodz Ghetto, a notorious Nazi vestibule for deportation—was dubbed the Polish Manchester, at a time when Manchester too was booming and both cities had flourishing Jewish populations.) At eighteen Ferber arrived in Manchester to study art and thereafter rarely left. It was the thousands of Manchester smokestacks, he confided to the newcomer Sebald, that prompted his belief that "I had found my destiny." "I am here," he said, "to serve under the chimney." In those early days Ferber's studio, as Sebald describes it, resembled an ash pit: "When I watched Ferber working on one of his portrait studies over a number of weeks, I often thought that his prime concern was to increase the dust . . . that process of drawing and shading [with charcoal sticks] on the thick, leathery paper, as well as the concomitant business of constantly erasing what he had drawn with a woollen rag already heavy with charcoal, really amounted to nothing but a steady production of dust."

And in 1990, when Sebald urgently undertook to search out the life of the refugee Max Ferber and the history of his lost German Jewish family, he seemed to be duplicating Ferber's own pattern of reluctant consummation, overlaid with haltings, dissatisfactions, fears, and erasures: "Not infrequently I unravelled what I had done, continuously tormented by scruples that were taking tighter hold and steadily paralyzing me. These scruples concerned not only the subject of the narrative, which I felt I could not do justice to, no matter what approach I tried, but also the entire questionable act of writing. I had covered hundreds of pages . . . By far the greater part had been crossed out, discarded, or obliterated by additions. Even what I ultimately salvaged as a 'final' version seemed to me a thing of shreds and patches, utterly botched."

All this falls out, one imagines, because Sebald is now openly permitting himself to "become" Max Ferber—or, to put it less emblematically, because in these concluding pages he begins to move, still sidling, still hesitating, from the oblique to the headon; from intimation to declaration. Here, terminally—at the last stop, so to speak—is a full and direct narrative of Jewish exile and destruction, neither hinted at through an account of a loosely parallel flight from Lithuania a generation before, nor obscured by a quarter-Jew who served in Hitler's army, nor hidden under the copper roof of a German synagogue, nor palely limned in Uncle Adelwarth's journey to Jerusalem with a Jewish companion.

Coming on Max Ferber again after a separation of twenty years, Sebald is no longer that uncomprehending nervous junior scholar fresh from a postwar German education—he is middle-aged, an eminent professor in a British university, the author of two novels. Ferber, nearing seventy, is now a celebrated British painter whose work is exhibited at the Tate. The reunion bears unanticipated fruit: Ferber surrenders to Sebald a cache of letters containing what is, in effect, a record of his mother's life, written when the fifteen-year-old Max had already been sent to safety in England. Ferber's father, an art dealer, and his mother, decorated for tending the German wounded in the First World War, remained trapped in Germany, unable to obtain the visas that would assure their escape. In 1941 they were deported from Munich to Riga in Lithuania, where they were murdered. "The fact is,"

Ferber now tells Sebald, "that that tragedy in my youth struck such deep roots within me that it later shot up· again, put forth evil flowers, and spread the poisonous canopy over me which has kept me so much in the shade and dark." Thus the latter-day explication of "I am here to serve under the chimney," uttered decades after the young Sebald loitered, watchful and bewildered, in the exiled painter's ash-heaped studio.

The memoir itself is all liveliness and light. Sebald recreates it lyrically, meticulously—from, as we say, the inside out. It begins with Luisa and Leo Lanzberg, a little brother and sister (reminding us of the brother and sister in *The Mill on the Floss*) in the village of Steinach, near Kissingen, where Jews have lived since the 1600s. ("It goes without saying," Sebald interpolates—it is a new note for him—"that there are no Jews in Steinach now, and that those who live there have difficulty remembering those who were once their neighbors and whose homes and property they appropriated, if indeed they remember them at all.") Friday nights in Steinach juxtapose the silver Sabbath candelabrum with the beloved poems of Heine. The day nursery, presided over by nuns, excuses the Jewish children from morning prayers. On Sabbath afternoons in summer, before the men return to the synagogue, there is lemonade and challah with corned beef. Rosh Hashana; Yom Kippur; then the succah hung with apples and pears and chains of rosehips. In winter the Jewish school celebrates both Hanukkah and the Reich. Before Passover "the bustle is dreadful." Father prospers, and the family moves to the middle-class world of Kissingen. (A photo shows the new house: a mansion with two medieval spires. Nevertheless several rooms are rented out.) And so on and so on: the blessing of the ordinary. Luisa grows into a young woman with suitors; her Gentile fiancé dies suddenly, of a stroke; a matchmaker finds her a Jewish husband, Max's father. "In the summer of 1921," Ferber's mother writes, "soon after our marriage, we went to the Allgäu . . . where the scattered villages were so peaceful it was as if nothing evil had happened anywhere on earth." Sebald, we know, was born in one of those villages. In 1991—fifty years after the memoirist was deported to Riga—Sebald visits Steinach and Kissingen. (I almost want to say revisits, so identified has he become with Ferber's mother's story.) In the old Jewish cemetery in Kissingen, "a wilderness of graves, neglected for years, crumbling and gradually sinking into the ground amidst tall grass and wild flowers under the shade of trees, which trembled in the slight movements of the air," he stands before the gravestones and reads the names of the pre-Hitler dead, Auerbach, Grunwald, Leuthold, Seeligmann, Goldstaub, Baumblatt, Blumenthal, and thinks how "perhaps there was nothing the Germans begrudged the Jews so much as their beautiful names, so intimately bound up with the country they lived in and with its language." He finds a more recent marker: a relative of Max Ferber's who, in expectation of the outcome, took her own life. (The third suicide in Sebald's quartet.) And then he flees: "I felt increasingly that the mental impoverishment and lack of memory that marked the Germans, and the efficiency with which they had cleaned everything up were beginning to affect my head and my nerves." A sign on the cemetery gates warns that vandals will be prosecuted.

The Emigrants (an ironically misleading title) ends with a mental flash of the Lodz Ghetto—the German occupiers feasting, the cowed Jewish slave laborers, children among them, toiling for their masters. In the conqueror's lens, Sebald sees three young Jewish women at a loom, and recalls "the daughters of night, with spindle, scissors and thread." Here, it strikes me, is the only false image in this ruthlessly moving and profoundly honest work dedicated to the recapture of phantoms. In the time of the German night, it was not the Jews who stood in for the relentless Fates, they who rule over life and death. And no one understands this, from the German side, more mournfully, more painfully, than the author of *The Emigrants*.

Love and Levity at
Auschwitz: Martin Amis

She was coming back from the Old Town with her two daughters, and
they were already well within the Zone of Interest. Up ahead, waiting to
receive them stretched an avenue—almost a colonnade—of maples,
their branches and lobed leaves interlocking overhead. A late afternoon
in midsummer, with minutely glinting midges . . . Tall, broad, and full,
and yet light of foot, in a crenellated white ankle-length dress and a
cream-colored straw hat with a black band, and swinging a straw bag
(the girls, also in white, had the straw hats and the straw bags), she
moved in and out of pockets of fuzzy, fawny, leonine warmth. She
laughed—head back, with tautened neck.

So begins "First Sight," the opening chapter of *The Zone of Interest*,
Martin Amis's provocatively titled fourteenth novel—but where, then, are we
really? The Old Town, after all, might be anywhere in the old world of
romantic allusiveness. *A late afternoon in midsummer:* isn't that where we
first discover Isabel Archer, yet another enchanting figure seen within a ver-
dant vista? Or might this radiant painterly vision—the white dress, the
dappled path, the insouciant tread—reflect Leonard Woolf's rapturous first
glimpse of Virginia Stephen, also in white dress and round hat, "as when in
a picture gallery you suddenly come face to face with a great Rembrandt
or Velasquez"?

As for the Zone of Interest, this too can be found anywhere, including
the erotic turf of the psyche—and isn't instant infatuation frequently fiction's
particular zone of interest? Here, though, the phrase will shock a knowing
ear—it is, in its original German, the *Interessengebiet* of a sprawling Third
Reich death camp: an area cleared of its native residents to accommodate
workaday camp administration, storage for gas cylinders, barracks for the
lesser SS, and housing for the officers and their families. The laughing, light-
footed young woman who so quickly captivates the narrator is Frau Hannah

Doll, the wife of Kommandant Paul Doll, the man chiefly responsible for the efficient running of the murder factory. And Golo Thomsen, her love-struck observer, is himself an officer charged with slave labor operations at the adjacent I. G. Farben Buna-Werke. It is he who will argue over how much brute hunger a slave worker can endure before he grows useless and is shot or sent to the gas. He also has the distinction of being the nephew of Martin Bormann, Hitler's private secretary, confidant, and trusted deputy.

The leafy idyll, it turns out, is a sham, the artful novelist's Potemkin village masking rot. Hence the publisher's absurdist blast: *love in a concentration camp*. And love, moreover, not among the sexless doomed, but in the privileged quarters of the masters of death—yet another upstairs-downstairs drama, upstairs as usual plush and advantaged and lavishly expressive of feeling; downstairs a hill of skulls. *Anus mundi* as viewed not by the broken and the damned, but by their shatterers. A satire, then? A bitter comedy?

By now, seventy years after the closing of the camps, *The Zone of Interest,* however else it is perceived, must be regarded as a historical novel, a literary convention by its nature inexorably tethered to verifiable events. All the same, it remains a novel, with fiction's primal freedom to invent its own happenings, both the plausible and the implausible, the sympathetic along with the repellent, the antic embedded in the unspeakable. Imagination is sovereign. Characters are at liberty to contemplate their lives and shape and assess them as they wish. Interior thought is rampant. We are privy to all things hidden: rivalry, vanity, deception, jealousy, lust.

Scripture, which purports to be history, is mainly impatient with interiority. It is God, we are told, who hardens Pharaoh's heart, and after this no more need be said. Pharaoh's wickedness is absolute, dyed in the marrow, opaque; no light can be leached from it. We are not permitted to know more than the intractable breadth and depth of this wickedness—nothing of Pharaoh's psychology, nothing of his inner musings, nothing of his everyday, how he was appareled, whether he was sometimes tipsy, or if he bantered with his courtiers, how often he summoned women of the palace, or of the brickworks, to his bed; or if he ever faltered in remorse. God is a judge, not a novelist; this is the meaning of a God-hardened heart: the deed's the thing.

Novelists, mini-gods though they may be, do not harden hearts, and inner musings are their métier. A deed, however foul, has an origin, or call it a backstory, and every backstory is a kind of explanation, and every explanation is on its way to becoming, if not quite an absolution, then certainly a diagnosis. And then the evildoer (if such an absolutist term is admissible), having been palpated for diagnosis, is reduced from zealous criminal to one possessed of a "condition" not of his own making—insanity, perhaps, or the inevitable outcome of an ideological rearing. In literary fiction (here we naturally exclude comic strips and melodrama) there are no outright villains, and even a pharaoh would be interestingly introspective.

In an afterword both bibliographical and discursive—itself an anomaly in a novel—Amis grapples with the monstrous question of such explanatory mitigations: monstrous because it teeters perilously over the filthy chasm of exculpation. In support of the novelist's right to imagine the inmost workings of evil's agents, he cites, reverently, a passage from Primo Levi:

> Perhaps one cannot, what is more one must not, understand what happened, because to understand is almost to justify. Let me explain: "understanding" a proposal or human behavior means to "contain" it, contain its author, put oneself in his place, identify with him. Now no normal person will ever be able to identify with Hitler, Himmler, Goebbels, Eichmann, and endless others. This dismays us, and at the same time gives us a sense of relief, because perhaps it is desirable that their words (and also, unfortunately, their deeds) cannot be comprehensible to us. They are non-human words and deeds, really counter-human . . . There is no rationality in Nazi hatred; it is a hate that is not in us; it is outside man.

A hate that is outside man. It would appear on the face of it that Levi's insight is nothing if not instinctively biblical: hearts so hardened, and deeds so inhumanly wicked, that only God can fathom them. Yet Amis comes away from these seemingly transparent reflections with the sense of having been granted permission, or even a blessing. "Historians," he begins, "will consider this more an evasion than an argument," and goes on to remind us that Levi was also a novelist and a poet, placing him "very far from hoisting up the no-entry sign demanded by the sphinxists, the anti-explainers." Instead, Amis oddly insists (against Levi's plain language) that it is Levi himself who is "pointing a way in."

And Amis's way in to the hate that is outside man is fully and unstintingly the novelist's way. If the deed's the thing, it's not the only thing. Soliloquies that tunnel into minds to expose their folly or their intransigence or their delusions, and sometimes their disillusions. The permutations of plot, the rise and fall of ambition and hope, whether in the rivalrous bureaucracy of death-making or in the chancy living and automated dying of the doomed. And of course the tentative strivings of the well-advertised *love in a concentration camp*. The camp is, after all, a hierarchical society; a kind of village, a veritable *Middlemarch* of Nazidom; or better yet, given its dense though highly transient population, a bustling, busy city with recurring traffic bottlenecks, especially at the ramp, where the selections take place. In cinematic mode, there are scenes outdoors and indoors. Outdoors: always the ramp looming over its thickened plaza of human detritus, the *Stücke* ("pieces," as one speaks of inanimate cargo) just disgorged from the freight cars; and the tragic Szmul, the most pitiable of the doomed, the grieving overseer of a vast heaving meadow of human ash, a *Sonderkommando* fated to escort the unsuspecting victims to their end.

And indoors: The SS bigwigs and their wives at the theater (the *Interessengebiet* is not without *Kultur*), or enjoying a concert, or a ballet where the young principal dancer is one of the *Häftlinge*. Ilse Grese, a sadistic and lecherous female guard seen in her private billet—her surname that of a notorious SS *Helferin* tried after the war and hanged for savagery, her Christian name invoking Ilse Koch of human-skin lampshade infamy. Martin Bormann at home *en famille,* his wife Gerda perpetually and aspiringly pregnant (each of her nine surviving children named for yet another prominent Nazi), hoping to receive a coveted award for Aryan fertility. The charming villa of Paul and Hannah Doll, with its garden and pet tortoise, its *Häftling* Polish gardener, a former professor of zoology, and its *Häftling* housemaid, a compliant Jehovah's Witness suitably called Humilia. The pampered Doll daughters, cosseted in the routines of a normal childhood (their mother duly accompanies them to school and sees to their proper bedtime), perturbed by their sickly pony, brokenhearted over the killing of their tortoise, yet oblivious to the hourly killing all around. The unfortunate Alisz, widow of a German soldier, herself only recently welcome at the dinner table, now a subhuman confined in a solitary cell, tainted by the discovery of her Sinti (Gypsy) blood. And pervasively, both indoors and out: the relentlessly inescapable smell of burning human flesh.

"My own inner narrative," Amis notes, "is one of chronic stasis . . . I first read Martin Gilbert's *The Holocaust: the Jewish Tragedy* in 1987; in 2011 I read it again, and my incredulity was intact and entire—it was wholly undiminished." The phrase "chronic stasis," even removed from the intent of its context and on its own, is remarkable for what it imparts. *The Zone of Interest* is not Amis's first venture into the deadly morass of assembly-line Jew-killing. It was preceded two decades earlier by *Time's Arrow,* an Ezekiel-inspired vision of reversed chronology: the bony dead refreshed into bloom. Clearly, Amis is possessed by these smoldering particulars; he is not among those worldly sick-and-tired-of-hearing-about-it casuists for whom the Holocaust has gone stale to the point of insult. In a novel so hotly close to the rind of history, he is scrupulously faithful to the findings of the scholars and committed to a flawless representation of place, time, and event. Most telling is his admission of a single purposeful deviation: "My only conscious liberty with the factual record was in bringing forward the defection to the USSR of Friedrich Paulus (the losing commander at Stalingrad) by about seven months." The confession attests to the novelist's aversion to manipulative fakery.

The facts, accordingly, are meticulously attended to; but then, as mockery follows mockery, come the voices with their slyly revealing ironies that turn self-deception into satire, and self-appraisal into stinging disclosure. Kommandant Doll is frequently the butt of these unwitting sallies, as when, contemplating his personal nature, he declares himself "a normal man with normal feelings. When I'm tempted by human weakness, however, I simply think of Germany and of the trust reposed in me by her Deliverer, whose visions, whose ideals and aspirations, I unshakably share." And here Amis may be lampooning Hannah Arendt's inflammatory thesis of the "banality" of a murderous SS zealot—as if he were to ask, what could be more commonplace, more *normal,* than full-bore fanaticism?

But ridicule finds a still ampler berth: Doll, questioning Prufer, his second-in-command and "an unimpeachable Nazi," is eager to learn how the siege of Stalingrad is proceeding.

"Oh, we'll carry the day, mein Kommandant," he said over lunch in the Officers' Mess. "The German soldier scoffs at the objective conditions."

"Yes, but what *are* the objective conditions?"

"Well, we're outnumbered. On paper. Ach, any German is worth 5 Russians. We have the fanaticism and the will. They can't match us for merciless brutality."

". . . Are you sure about that, Prufer?" I asked. "Very stubborn resistance." . . .

"With our zeal? Victory's not in doubt. It'll just take a little longer."

"I hear we're undersupplied. There are shortages."

"True. There's hardly any fuel. Or food. They're eating the horses."

"And the cats, I heard."

"They finished the cats."

The absurdity builds: dysentery, lice, frostbite, dwindling ammunition, encirclement; and finally surrender. And still the clownish back-and-forth of illusory confidence: "The German ranks are impregnable." "Besides, privation presents no problem to the men of the Wehrmacht." "For a German soldier, these difficulties are nothing." "How can we go down to a rabble of Jews and peasants? *Don't* make me laugh."

A pair of buffoons. Abbott and Costello in Nazi dress.

Doll, meanwhile, is regarded as an incompetent fool even by his confederates. His peroration on the ramp—following the usual reassuring litany of disinfection, showers, hot soup afterward—is a failure, since it introduces what is instantly suspect: *"But if there's anything you especially treasure and can't afford to be without, then pop it in the barrel at the end of the ramp."* "You don't deceive them any more," they chide him. ". . . There are some very unpleasant scenes nearly every time . . . You sound so insincere. As if you don't believe it yourself." To which Doll indignantly responds, "Well, of course I don't believe it myself . . . How could I? You think I'm off my head?"

Arendt, so proudly sealed in intellect that nothing could penetrate the armor of her synthesis, ended less in condemnation than in mitigation—her neutered Eichmann is a weak-kneed pharaoh, scarcely worth all those plagues. History as comedy has a parallel effect: it trivializes the unconscionable. The blood the clown spills is always ketchup.

Hannah Doll is not trivialized. She baits her husband, she withholds sex, she listens to subversive enemy radio; and, as we eventually discover, she has privately given the Kommandant a black eye. To hide the shame of it, he pins the blame on the Polish *Häftling* and his shovel. And to add to the gardener's fabricated culpability, it is Doll himself who smashes the tortoise so prized by his young daughters. As penalty, his hapless victim is swiftly dispatched to his death. Throughout all this grim chaos, Amis means us to view Hannah as an internal dissident, a melancholy prisoner of circumstance: perhaps even as a highly privileged quasi-*Häftling* powerless to rebel. Though seeing through Doll's cowardice and deception, she conforms, however grumblingly, to bourgeois life among the chimneys—the dinners, the playgoing, the children's indulgences. Her own indulgence: cigarettes, the lesser reek intended to overcome the greater. Her open derision, seen by Doll's colleagues as a wifely nuisance, is pointless; the fake showerheads continue to spew their poison. Her needling humiliations of Doll affect nothing; the daily business of the ramp prevails.

In the historic facticity of the camps, does Hannah Doll have a real-life counterpart? And does it matter if she does or doesn't? The women of the camps have left a substantial record, not only the grisly SS *Helferinnen* with their uniforms and whips, but the SS wives in their well-appointed villas, shamelessly flaunting rings and necklaces seized from the doomed. The base activities of many such women are documented in Wendy Lower's *Hitler's Furies: German Women in the Nazi Killing Fields,* a volume not included among Amis's acknowledgments—though Hannah is proof of his copious knowledge of these spousal miscreants: she is their purposefully contrapuntal projection.

"What is especially striking about these wives," Lower writes, "is that . . . they were not officially given any direct role in the division of labor that made the Holocaust possible. Yet their proximity to the murderers and their own ideological fanaticism made many of them into potential participants." She instances Erna Petri, the wife of Horst Petri—an SS officer attached to the Race and Settlement Office (a euphemism for the mass annihilation of Jews)—who found cowering at a roadside six half-naked little boys somehow escaped from a death-bound freight car. She took them home, fed them, and then, one by one, shot each child in the back of the neck. Liesel Willhaus, another SS wife and a crack shot, delighted in picking off Jews from her balcony. SS honeymooners celebrated their love in the midst of deportations and mass executions. All in all, exemplars of SS wives reveling in atrocities abound—and still this heinous chronicle yields not a single Hannah Doll.

Golo Thomsen, Hannah's aspiring lover, is made of the same exceptionalism. From his position defending slow starvation of the Buna slave laborers—against a proposal that a few more daily calories would speed the work—he at length comes to welcome Germany's defeat. So much so that, calling on the little English he can muster, he quietly joins a British prisoner of war in reciting "Rule Britannia"—even as he recognizes that the man is a likely Buna saboteur. (As it happens, not an ounce of the synthetic rubber vaunted by the Germans ever emerged from the Buna-Werke.) That an SS official, the nephew of Martin Bormann, a Nazi of such elevated rank that he dines with the Führer at his gilded mountain retreat, should end as a turncoat in the harshest hour of Germany's eastern Blitzkrieg . . . ah, but isn't this the very conundrum woven by the twining of history and fiction? Has a believably disaffected Golo Thomsen ever been known to recant in an actual Zone of Interest? Do the oceanic testimonies of this fraught period throw up any evidence of even one SS officer who, while within earshot of the cries of the doomed, decried those cries? And if not, it must be asked again: does it matter?

History commands communal representation—nations, movements, the reigning Zeitgeist. Fiction champions the individuated figure. Bovary is Bovary, not an insubstantiation of the overall nature of the French bourgeoisie. Characters in novels (unless those novels are meant to be allegories) are no one but themselves, not stand-ins or symbols of societies or populations. History is ineluctably bound to the authenticity of documents; but all things are permitted to fiction, however contradictory it may be of the known record. It is this freedom to posit redemptive phantoms that justifies the historic anomalies that are Hannah Doll and Golo Thomsen. And further: no literary framework is more liberated from obligation to the claims of history than comedy, with its manifold jesters: parody, satire, farce, caricature, pratfall. All these are entertainments—and so it is that we are frankly entertained by Kommandant Doll, even as he stands "with sturdy fists planted on jodhpured hips" on the murderous ramp. And still further: something there is in the resistance to parody that is obtuse, dense, dully unread. What of Gulliver, what of Quixote? To resist the legacy of their majestic makers is to deny literature itself. Then why resist Amis, their daringly obsessed if lesser colleague? And why pursue skepticism of *love in a concentration camp*? Or of latecomer dissidents who nevertheless eat and drink in comfort on the lip of the merciless inferno?

Read beforehand, as one is tempted to do, Amis's afterword becomes the novel's mentor and conscience. In it he echoes Paul Celan's "coldly muted" naming of the Holocaust as "that which happened"—a phrase again reminiscent of the biblical refusal of elaboration—and adds, "I am reminded of W. G. Sebald's dry aside to the effect that no serious person ever thinks of anything else." In this way the afterword, in combination with *Sonderkommando* Szmul, the novel's third interior voice, repudiates and virtually annuls all other voices, the farcical with the ahistorical; and nearly erases also the dominating voice of the novel itself. For Szmul, no suspension of disbelief, fiction's busy handmaiden, is required, and no element of caricature can touch him. He alone is immune to the reader's skepticism, he alone is safe from even the possibility of diminishment through parody; and this holds both within the novel's pliancy and in the tougher arena of historical truth.

It is Szmul who speaks of "the *extraterritorial* nature of the Lager": "I feel we are dealing with propositions and alternatives that have never been discussed before, have never needed to be discussed before—I feel that if you knew every minute, every hour, every day of history, you would find no exemplum, no model, no precedent." His macabre task ("the detail," as he obliquely calls it) is to shepherd the doomed to the gas, and then to dispose of their close-packed corpses first to the ovens, and then to the limitless and undulating fields of ash. As a secret-bearing witness, he will soon be consumed by the very fire that he himself facilitated:

> When squads of heavily armed men come to the crematoria and this or
> that section of the detail knows that it is time, the chosen Sonders take
> their leave with a nod or a word or a wave of the hand—or not even

that. They take their leave with their eyes on the floor. And later, when I say Kaddish for the departed, they are already forgotten.

Szmul is one of the chosen—chosen by the power of the jackboot to be the servant of these gruesome rites. Ruth Franklin, reviewing the novel in the *New York Times,* describes the "crematory ravens" of the *Sonderkommando* as "the nadir of degradation," "a portrait of depravity." But Amis's Szmul is a presence of lacerating pathos and unrelenting mourning. In a brittle tone so colloquially matter-of-fact as to shatter its burden, he ruminates, "I used to have the greatest respect for nightmares—for their intelligence and artistry. Now I think nightmares are pathetic. They are quite incapable of coming up with anything as remotely terrible as what I do all day." He recalls a time at Chelmno when the quantities of carcasses were so overwhelming that the SS "selected another hundred Jews to help the Sonders drag the bodies to the mass grave. This supplementary Kommando consisted of teenage boys. They were given no food or water, and they worked for twelve hours under the lash, naked in the snow and the petrified mud." Szmul's two sons were among them; and in this plainspoken account we can perhaps hear (yet only if we are open to it) a judgment on the omnipresent misuse and abuse of "that which happened." Amis's crematory raven flies out from the novel as its single invincibly convincing voice.

Despite the afterword's dismissal of "the sphinxists, the anti-explainers," it is they, knowing what is at stake, who are finally in the right. And what is at stake is the conviction that premeditated and cocksure evil is its own representation, sealed and sufficient. A hardened heart needs no reason beyond its own opacity. The ripened deed is all; to riff on it is to veil it. This is not to say that *The Zone of Interest* ought never to have departed the wilder precincts of Amis's cunning imaginings. It is good to have this fractious novel. It makes the best argument against itself.

LIFE AND LOVE

A Drug Store Eden

In 1929 my parents sold their drug store in Yorkville—a neighborhood comprising Manhattan's East Eighties—and bought a pharmacy in Pelham Bay, in the northeast corner of the Bronx. It was a move from dense city to almost country. Pelham Bay was at the very end of a relatively new stretch of elevated train track that extended from the subway of the true city all the way out to the small-town feel of little houses and a single row of local shops: shoemaker's, greens store, grocery, drug store, bait store.

There was even a miniature five-and-ten where you could buy pots, housedresses, and thick lisle stockings for winter. Three stops down the line was the more populous Westchester Square, with its bank and post office, which old-timers still called "the village"—Pelham Bay had once lain outside the city limits, in Westchester County.

This lost little finger of the borough was named for the broad but mild body of water that rippled across Long Island Sound to a blurry opposite shore. All the paths of Pelham Bay Park led down to a narrow beach of rough pebbles, and all the surrounding streets led, sooner or later, to the park, wild and generally deserted. Along many of these streets there were empty lots that resembled meadows, overgrown with Queen Anne's lace and waist-high weeds glistening with what the children termed "snake spit"; poison ivy crowded between the toes of clumps of sky-tall oaks. The snake spit was a sort of bubbly botanical excretion, but there were real snakes in those lots, with luminescent skins, brownish-greenish, criss-crossed with white lines. There were real meadows, too: acres of downhill grasses, in the middle of which you might suddenly come on a set of rusty old swings—wooden slats on chains—or a broken red-brick wall left over from some ruined and forgotten Westchester estate.

The Park View Pharmacy—the drug store my parents bought—stood on the corner of Colonial Avenue, between Continental and Burr: Burr for Aaron Burr, the Vice President who killed Alexander Hamilton in a duel. The neighborhood had a somewhat bloodthirsty Revolutionary flavor. Not far away you could still visit Spy Oak, the venerable tree on which captured Redcoats had once been hanged; and now and then Revolutionary bullets were churned up a foot or so beneath the front lawn of the old O'Keefe house, directly across the street from the Park View Pharmacy. George Washington had watered his horses, it was believed, in the ancient sheds beyond Ye Olde Homestead, a local tavern that, well after Prohibition, was still referred to as the "speak-easy." All the same, there were no Daughters of the American Revolution here: instead, Pelham Bay was populated by the children of German, Irish, Swedish, Scottish, and Italian immigrants, and by a handful of the original immigrants themselves. The greenhorn Italians, from Naples and Sicily, kept goats and pigs in their back yards, and pigeons on their roofs. Pelham Bay's single Communist—you could tell from the election results that there was such a rare bird—was the Scotsman who lived around the corner, though only my parents knew this. They were privy to the neighborhood's opinions, ailments, and family secrets.

In those years a drug store seemed one of the world's permanent institutions. Who could have imagined that it would one day vanish into an aisle in the supermarket, or re-emerge as a kind of supermarket itself? What passes for a pharmacy nowadays is all open shelves and ceiling racks of brilliant white neon suggesting perpetual indoor sunshine. The Park View, by contrast, was a dark cavern lined with polished wood cabinets rubbed nearly black and equipped with sliding glass doors and mirrored backs. The counters were heaped with towering ziggurats of lotions, potions, and packets, and under them ran glassed-in showcases of the same sober wood. There was a post office (designated a "substation") that sold penny postcards and stamps and money orders. The prescription area was in the rear, closed off from view: here were scores of labeled drawers of all sizes, and rows of oddly shaped brown bottles. In one of those drawers traditional rock candy was stored, in two flavors, plain and maple, dangling on long strings. And finally there was the prescription desk itself, a sloping lecternlike affair on which the current prescription ledger always lay, like some sacred text.

There was also a soda fountain. A pull at a long black handle spurted out carbonated water; a push at a tiny silver spout drew out curly drifts of whipped cream. The air in this part of the drug store was steamy with a deep coffee fragrance, and on wintry Friday afternoons the librarians from the Traveling Library, a green truck that arrived once a week, would linger, sipping and gossiping on the high-backed fountain chairs, or else at the little glass-topped tables nearby, with their small three-cornered seats. Everything was fashioned of the same burnished chocolate-colored wood; but the fountain counters were heavy marble. Above the prescription area, sovereign over all, rose a symbolic pair of pharmacy globes, one filled with red fluid, the other with blue. My father's diploma, class of 1917, was mounted on a wall; next to it hung a picture of the graduates. There was my very young father, with his round pale eyes and widow's peak—a fleck in a mass of black gowns.

Some time around 1937, my mother said to my father, "Willie, if we don't do it now, we'll never do it."

It was the trough of the Great Depression. In the comics, Pete the Tramp was swiping freshly baked pies set out to cool on windowsills; and in real life, tramps (as the homeless were then called) were turning up in the Park View nearly every day. Sometimes they were city drunks—"Bowery bums"—who had fallen asleep on the subway downtown and had ended up in Pelham Bay. Sometimes they were exhausted Midwesterners who had been riding the rails, and had rolled off into the obscuring cattails of the Baychester marsh. But always my father sat them down at the fountain and fed them a sandwich and soup. They smelled bad, these penniless tramps, and their eyes were red and rheumy; often they were very polite. They never left without a meal and a nickel for carfare.

No one was worse off than the tramps, or more desolate than the family who lived in an old freight car on the way to Westchester Square; but no one escaped the Depression. It stalked the country, it stalked Pelham Bay, it stalked the Park View. Drugstore hours were famously long—monstrously long: seven days a week the Park View opened at nine a.m. and closed at two the next morning. My mother scurried from counter to counter, tended the fountain, unpacked cartons, climbed ladders; her varicose veins oozed through their strappings. My father patiently ground powders, and folded the white dust into translucent paper squares with elegantly efficient motions. The drug store was, besides, a public resource: my father bandaged cuts, took specks out of strangers' eyes, and once removed a fishhook from a man's cheek—though he sent him off to the hospital, on the other side of the Bronx, immediately afterward. My quiet father had cronies and clients, grim women and voluble men who flooded his understanding ears with the stories of their sufferings, of flesh or psyche. My father murmured and comforted, and later my parents would whisper sadly about who had "the big C," or, with an ominous gleam, they would smile over a geezer certain to have a heart attack: the geezer would be newly married to a sweet young thing. (And usually they were right about the heart attack.)

Yet no matter how hard they toiled, they were always in peril. There were notes to pay off; they had bought the Park View from a pharmacist named Robbins, and every month, relentlessly, a note came due. They never fell behind, and never missed a payment (and, in fact, were eventually awarded a certificate attesting to this feat); but the effort—the unremitting pressure, the endless anxiety—ground them down. "The note, the note," I would hear, a refrain that shadowed my childhood, though I had no notion of what it meant.

What it meant was that the Depression, which had already crushed so many, was about to crush my mother and father: suddenly their troubles intensified. The Park View was housed in a building owned by a catlike woman my parents habitually referred to, whether out of familiarity or resentment, only as Tessie. The pharmacy's lease was soon to expire, and at this moment, in the cruelest hour of the Depression, Tessie chose to raise the rent. Her tiger's eyes narrowed to slits: no appeal could soften her.

It was because of those adamant tiger's eyes that my mother said, "Willie, if we don't do it now, we'll never do it."

My mother was aflame with ambition, emotion, struggle. My father was reticent, and far more resigned to the world as given. Once, when the days of the Traveling Library were over, and a real library had been constructed at Westchester Square—you reached it by trolley—I came home elated, carrying a pair of books I had found side by side. One was called *My Mother Is a Violent Woman*; the other was *My Father Is a Timid Man*. These seemed a comic revelation of my parents' temperaments. My mother was all heat and enthusiasm. My father was all logic and reserve. My mother, unrestrained, could have run an empire of drug stores. My father was satisfied with one.

Together they decided to do something revolutionary; something virtually impossible in those raw and merciless times. One street over—past McCardle's sun-baked gas station, where there was always a Model-T Ford with its hood open for repair, and past the gloomy bait store, ruled over by Mr. Isaacs, a dour and reclusive veteran of the Spanish-American War who sat reading military histories all day under a mastless sailboat suspended from the ceiling—lay an empty lot in the shape of an elongated lozenge. My parents' daring plan—for young people without means it was beyond daring—was to buy that lot and build on it, from scratch, a brand-new Park View Pharmacy.

They might as well have been dreaming of taking off in Buck Rogers' twenty-fifth-century rocket ship. The cost of the lot was a stratospheric $13,500, unchanged from the Boom of 1928, just before the national wretchedness descended; and that figure was only for the land. After that would come the digging of a foundation and the construction of a building. What was needed was a miracle.

One sad winter afternoon my mother was standing on a ladder, concentrating on setting out some newly arrived drug items on a high shelf. (Although a typical drug store stocked several thousand articles, the Park View's unit-by-unit inventory was never ample. At the end of every week I would hear my father's melodious, impecunious chant on the telephone, ordering goods from the jobber: "A sixth of a dozen, a twelfth of a dozen . . .") A stranger wearing a brown fedora and a long overcoat entered, looked around, and appeared not at all interested in making a purchase; instead he went wandering from case to case, picking things up and putting them down again, trying to be inconspicuous, asking an occasional question or two, all the while scrupulously observing my diligent and tireless parents. The stranger turned out to be a mortgage officer from the American Bible Society, and what he saw, he explained afterward, was a conscientious application of the work ethic; so it was the American Bible Society that supplied the financial foundation of my parents' Eden, the new Park View. They had entertained an angel unawares.

The actual foundation, the one to be dug out of the ground, ran into instant trouble. An unemployed civil engineer named Levinson presided over the excavation; he was unemployed partly because the Depression had dried up much of the job market, but mostly because engineering firms in those years were notorious for their unwillingness to hire Jews. Poor Levinson! The vast hole in the earth that was to become the Park View's cellar filled up overnight with water; the bay was near, and the water table was higher than the hapless Levinson had expected. The work halted. Along came Finnegan and rescued Levinson: Finnegan the plumber, who for a painful fee of fifty dollars (somehow squeezed out of Levinson's mainly empty pockets) pumped out the flood.

After the Park View's exultant move in 1939, the shell of Tessie's old place on Colonial Avenue remained vacant for years. No one took it over; the plate-glass windows grew murkier and murkier. Dead moths were heaped in decaying mounds on the inner sills. Tessie had lost more than the heartless increase she had demanded, and more than the monthly rent the renewed lease would have brought: there was something ignominious and luckless—tramplike—about that fly-specked empty space, now dimmer than ever. But within its freshly risen walls, the Park View Redux gleamed. Overhead, fluorescent tubes—an indoor innovation—shed a steady white glow, and a big square skylight poured down shifting shafts of brilliance. Familiar objects appeared clarified in the new light: the chocolate-colored fixtures, arranged in unaccustomed configurations, were all at once thrillingly revivified. Nothing from the original Park View had been left behind—everything was just the same, yet zanily out of order: the two crystal urns with their magical red and blue fluids suggestive of alchemy; the entire stock of syrups, pills, tablets, powders, pastes, capsules; tubes and bottles by the hundreds; all the contents of all the drawers and cases; the fountain with its marble top; the prescription desk and its sacrosanct ledger; the stacks of invaluable cigar boxes stuffed with masses of expired prescriptions; the locked and well-guarded narcotics cabinet; the post office, and the safe in which the post office receipts were kept. Even the great, weighty, monosyllabically blunt hanging sign—"DRUGS"—had been brought over and rehung, and it too looked different now. In the summer heat it dropped its black rectangular shadow over Mr. Isaacs' already shadowy headquarters, where vials of live worms were crowded side by side with vials of nails and screws.

At around this time my mother's youngest brother, my uncle Rubin, had come to stay with us—no one knew for how long—in our little house on Saint Paul Avenue, a short walk from the Park View. Five of us lived in that house: my parents, my grandmother, my brother and I. Rubin, who was called Ruby, was now the sixth. He was a bachelor and something of a family enigma. He was both bitter and cheerful; effervescence would give way to lassitude. He taught me how to draw babies and bunnies, and could draw anything himself; he wrote ingenious comic jingles, which he illustrated as adroitly, it struck me, as Edward Lear; he cooked up mouth-watering corn fritters, and designed fruit salads in the shape of ravishing unearthly blossoms. When now and then it fell to him to put me to bed, he always sang the same heartbreaking lullaby: "Sometimes I fee-eel like a motherless child, a long, long way-ay from ho-ome," in a deep and sweet quaver. In those days he was mostly jobless; on occasion he would crank up his Tin Lizzie and drive out to upper Westchester to prune trees. Once he was stopped at a police roadblock, under suspicion of being the Lindbergh baby kidnapper—the back seat of his messy old Ford was strewn with ropes, hooks, and my discarded baby bottles.

Ruby had been disappointed in love, and was somehow a disappointment to everyone around him. When he was melancholy or resentful, the melancholy was irritable and the resentment acrid. As a very young man he had been single-minded in a way none of his immigrant relations, or the snobbish mother of the girlfriend who had been coerced into jilting him, could understand or sympathize with. In Czarist Russia's restricted Pale of Settlement, a pharmacist was the highest vocation a Jew could attain to. In a family of pharmacists, Ruby wanted to be a farmer. Against opposition, he had gone off to the National Farm School in New Jersey—one of several Jewish agricultural projects sponsored by the German philanthropist Baron

Maurice de Hirsch. Ruby was always dreaming up one sort of horticultural improvement or another, and sometimes took me with him to visit a certain Dr. McClain, at the Bronx Botanical Gardens, whom he was trying to interest in one of his inventions. He was kindly received, but nothing came of it. Despite his energy and originality, all of Ruby's hopes and strivings collapsed in futility.

All the same, he left an enduring mark on the Park View. It was a certain circle of stones—a mark more distinctive than his deserted bachelor's headstone in an overgrown cemetery on Staten Island.

Ruby assisted in the move from Tessie's place to the new location. His presence was fortuitous—but his ingenuity, it would soon develop, was benison from the goddess Flora. The Park View occupied all the width but not the entire depth of the lot on which it was built. It had, of course, a welcoming front door, through which customers passed; but there was also a back door, past a little aisle adjoining the prescription room in the rear of the store, and well out of sight. When you walked out this back door, you were confronted by an untamed patch of weeds and stones, some of them as thick as boulders. At the very end of it lay a large flat rock, in the center of which someone had scratched a mysterious X. The X, it turned out, was a surveyor's mark; it had been there long before my parents bought the lot. It meant that the property extended to that X and no farther.

I was no stranger either to the lot or its big rock. It was where the neighborhood children played—a sparse group in that sparsely populated place. Sometimes the rock was a pirate ship; sometimes it was a pretty room in a pretty house; in January it held a snow fort. But early one summer evening, when the red ball of the sun was very low, a little girl named Theresa, whose hair was as red as the sun's red ball, discovered the surveyor's X and warned me against stamping on it. If you stamp on a cross, she said, the devil's helpers climb right out from inside the earth and grab you and take you away to be tortured. "I don't believe that," I said, and stamped on the X as hard as I could. Instantly Theresa sent out a terrified shriek; chased by the red-gold zigzag of her hair, she fled. I stood there abandoned—suppose it was true? In the silence all around, the wavering green weeds seemed taller than ever before.

Looking out from the back door at those same high weeds stretching from the new red brick of the Park View's rear wall all the way to the flat rock and its X, my mother, like Theresa, saw hallucinatory shapes rising out of the ground. But it was not the devil's minions she imagined streaming upward; it was their very opposite—a vision of celestial growths and fragrances, brilliant botanical hues, golden pears and yellow sunflower-faces, fruitful vines and dreaming gourds. She imagined an enchanted garden. She imagined a secret Eden.

Ruby was angry at my mother; he was angry at everyone but me: I was too young to be held responsible for his lost loves and aspirations. But he could not be separated from his love of fecund dirt. Dirt—the brown dirt of the earth—inspired him; the feel and smell of dirt uplifted him; he took an artist's pleasure in the soil and all its generative properties. And though he claimed to scorn my mother, he became the subaltern of her passion. Like some wizard commander of the stones—they were scattered everywhere in a wild jumble—he swept them into orderliness. A pack of stones was marshaled into a low wall. Five stones were transformed into a perfect set of stairs. Seven stones surrounded what was to become a flower bed. Stones were borders, stones were pathways, stones—placed just so—were natural sculptures.

And finally Ruby commanded the stones to settle in a circle in the very center of the lot. Inside the circle there was to be a green serenity of grass, invaded only by the blunders of violets and wandering buttercups. Outside the circle the earth would be a fructifying engine. It was a dreamer's circle, like the moon or the sun; or a fairy ring; or a mystical small Stonehenge, miniaturized by a spell.

The backyard was cleared, but it was not yet a garden. Like a merman combing a mermaid's weedy hair, my uncle Ruby had unraveled primeval tangles and brambles. He had set up two tall metal poles to accommodate a rough canvas hammock, with a wire strung from the top of one pole to the other. Over this wire a rain-faded old shop-awning had been flung, so that the hammock became a tent or cave or darkened den. A backyard hammock! I had encountered such things only in storybooks.

And then my uncle was gone. German tanks were biting into Europe. Weeping, my grandmother pounded her breast with her fist: the British White Paper of 1939 had declared that ships packed with Jewish refugees would be barred from the beaches of Haifa and Tel Aviv and returned to a Nazi doom. In P.S. 71, our neighborhood school, the boys were drawing cannons and warplanes; the girls were drawing figure skaters in tutus; both boys and girls were drawing the Trylon and the Perisphere. The Trylon was a three-sided obelisk. The Perisphere was a shining globe. They were already as sublimely legendary as the Taj Mahal. The official colors of the 1939 World's Fair were orange and blue—everyone knew this; everyone had ridden in noiselessly moving armchairs into the Fair's World of Tomorrow, where the cloverleaf highways of the impossibly futuristic 1960s materialized among inconceivable suburbs. In the magical lanes of Flushing you could watch yourself grin on a television screen as round and small as the mouth of a teacup. My grandmother, in that frail year of her dying, was taken to see the Palestine Pavilion, with its flickering films of Jewish pioneers.

Ruby was drafted before the garden could be dug. He sent a photograph of himself in Army uniform, and a muffled recording of his voice, all songs and jolly jingles, from a honky-tonk arcade in an unnamed Caribbean town.

So it was left to my mother to dig the garden. I have no inkling of when or how. I lived inside the hammock all that time, under the awning, enclosed; I read and read. Sometimes, for a treat, I would be given two nickels for carfare and a pair of quarters, and then I would climb the double staircase to the train and go all the way to Fifty-ninth Street: you could enter Bloom-ingdale's directly from the subway, without ever glimpsing daylight. I would run up the steps to the book department on the mezzanine, moon over the Nancy Drew series in an agony of choosing (*The Mystery of Larkspur Lane*, *The Mystery of the Whispering Statue*, each for fifty cents), and run down to the subway again, with my lucky treasure. An hour and a half later, I would be back in the hammock, under the awning, while the afternoon sun broiled on. But such a trip was rare. Mostly the books came from the Traveling Library; inside my hammockcave the melting glue of new bindings sent out a blissful redolence. And now my mother would emerge from the back door of the Park View, carrying—because it was so hot under the awning—half a cantaloupe, with a hillock of vanilla ice cream in its scooped-out center. (Have I ever been so safe, so happy, since? Has consciousness ever felt so steady, so unimperiled, so immortal?)

Across the ocean, synagogues were being torched, refugees were in flight. On American movie screens Ginger Rogers and Fred Astaire whirled in and out of the March of Time's grim newsreels—Chamberlain with his defeatist umbrella, the Sudetenland devoured, Poland invaded. Meanwhile my mother's garden grew. The wild raw field Ruby had regimented was rip-ening now into a luxuriant and powerful fertility: all around my uncle's talismanic ring of stones the ground swelled with thick savory smells. Corn tassels hung down over the shut greenleaf lids of pearly young cobs. Fat tomatoes reddened on sticks. The bumpy scalps of cucumbers poked up. And flowers! First, as tall as the hammock poles, a flock of hunchbacked sunflowers, their heads too weighty for their shoulders—huge heavy heads of seeds, and a ruff of yellow petals. At their feet, rows of zinnias and mari-golds, with tiny violets and the weedy pink buds of clover sidling between.

Now and then a praying mantis—a stiffly marching fake leaf—would rub its skinny forelegs together and stare at you with two stern black dots. And butterflies! These were mostly white and mothlike; but sometimes a great black-veined monarch would alight on a stone, in perfect stillness. Year by year the shade of a trio of pear trees widened and deepened.

Did it rain? It must have rained—it must have thundered—in those successive summers of my mother's garden; but I remember a perpetual sunlight, hot and honeyed, and the airless boil under the awning, and the heart-piercing scalliony odor of library glue (so explicit that I can this minute re-create it in my very tear ducts, as a kind of mourning); and the fear of bees.

Though I was mostly alone there, I was never lonely in the garden. But on the other side of the door, inside the Park View, an unfamiliar churning had begun—a raucous teeming, the world turning on its hinge. In the aftermath of Pearl Harbor, there were all at once jobs for nearly everyone, and money to spend in any cranny of wartime leisure. The Depression was receding. On weekends the subway spilled out mobs of city picnickers into the green fields of Pelham Bay Park, bringing a tentative prosperity to the neighborhood—especially on Sundays. I dreaded and hated this new Sunday frenzy, when the Park View seemed less a pharmacy than a carnival stand, and my own isolation grew bleak. Open shelves sprouted in the aisles, laden with anomalous racks of sunglasses, ice coolers, tubes of mosquito repellent and suntan lotion, paper cups, colorful towers of hats—sailors' and fishermen's caps, celluloid visors, straw topis and sombreros, headgear of every conceivable shape. Thirsty picnickers stood three deep at the fountain, clamoring for ice-cream cones or sodas. The low, serious drug-store voices that accompanied the Park View's weekday decorum were swept away by revolving laughing crowds—carnival crowds. And at the close of these frenetic summer Sundays, my parents would anxiously count up the cash register in the worn night of their exhaustion, and I would hear their joyful disbelief: unimaginable riches, almost seventy-five dollars in a single day!

Then, when the safe was locked up, and the long cords of the fluorescent lights pulled, they would drift in the dimness into the garden, to breathe the cool fragrance. At this starry hour the katydids were screaming in chorus, and fireflies bleeped like errant semaphores. In the enigmatic dark, my mother and father, with their heads together in silhouette, looked just then as I pictured them looking on the Albany night boat, on June 19, 1921, their wedding day. There was a serial photo from that long-ago time I often gazed at—a strip taken in an automatic-photo booth in fabled, faraway Albany. It showed them leaning close, my young father quizzical, my young mother trying to smile, or else trying not to; the corners of her lips wandered toward one loveliness or the other. They had brought back a honeymoon souvenir: three sandstone monkeys joined at the elbows: see no evil, hear no evil, speak no evil. And now, in their struggling forties, standing in

Ruby's circle of stones, they breathed in the night smells of the garden, onion grass and honeysuckle, and felt their private triumph. Seventy-five dollars in eighteen hours!

No one knew the garden was there. It was utterly hidden. You could not see it, or suspect it, inside the Park View, and because it was nested in a wilderness of empty lots all around, it was altogether invisible from any surrounding street. It was a small secluded paradise.

And what vegetable chargings, what ferocities of growth, the turbulent earth pushed out! Buzzings and dapplings. Birds dipping their beaks in an orgy of seed-lust. It was as if the ground itself were crying peace, peace; and the war began. In Europe the German death factories were pumping out smoke and human ash from a poisoned orchard of chimneys. In Pelham Bay, among bees and white-wing flutterings, the sweet brown dirt pumped ears of corn.

Nearly all the drug stores—of the old kind—are gone, in Pelham Bay and elsewhere. The Park View Pharmacy lives only in a secret Eden behind my eyes. Gone are Bernardini, Pressman, Weiss, the rival druggists on the way to Westchester Square. They all, like my father, rolled suppositories on glass slabs and ground powders with brass pestles. My mother's garden has returned to its beginning: a wild patch, though enclosed now by brick house after brick house. The houses have high stoops; they are city houses. The meadows are striped with highways. Spy Oak gave up its many ghosts long ago.

But under a matting of decayed pear pits and thriving ragweed back of what used to be the Park View, Ruby's circle of stones stands frozen. The earth, I suppose, has covered them over, as—far off in Staten Island—it covers my dreaming mother, my father, my grandmother, my resourceful and embittered farmer uncle.

The Seam of the Snail

In my Depression childhood, whenever I had a new dress, my cousin Sarah would get suspicious. The nicer the dress was, and especially the more expensive it looked, the more suspicious she would get. Finally she would lift the hem and check the seams. This was to see if the dress had been bought or if my mother had sewed it. Sarah could always tell. My mother's sewing had elegant outsides, but there was something catch-as-catch-can about the insides. Sarah's sewing, by contrast, was as impeccably finished inside as out; not one stray thread dangled.

My uncle Jake built meticulous grandfather clocks out of rosewood; he was a perfectionist, and sent to England for the clockworks. My mother built serviceable radiator covers and a serviceable cabinet, with hinged doors, for the pantry. She built a pair of bookcases for the living room. Once, after I was grown and in a house of my own, she fixed the sewer pipe. She painted ceilings, and also landscapes; she reupholstered chairs. One summer she planted a whole yard of tall corn. She thought herself capable of doing anything, and did everything she imagined. But nothing was perfect. There was always some clear flaw, never visible head-on. You had to look underneath, where the seams were. The corn thrived, though not in rows. The stalks elbowed one another like gossips in a dense little village.

"Miss Brrrrooooobaker," my mother used to mock, rolling her Russian r's, whenever I crossed a *t* she had left uncrossed, or corrected a word she had misspelled, or became impatient with a *v* that had tangled itself up with a *w* in her speech. ("V*v*ventriloquist," I would say. "V*v*ventriloquist," she would obediently repeat. And the next time it would come out "wiolinist.") Miss Brubaker was my high school English teacher, and my mother invoked her name as an emblem of raging finical obsession. "Miss Brrrrooooobaker," my mother's voice hoots at me down the years, as I go on casting and recasting sentences in a tiny handwriting on monomaniacally uniform paper. The loops of my mother's handwriting—it was the Palmer Method—were as big

454

as soup bowls, spilling generous splashy ebullience. She could pull off, at five minutes' notice, a satisfying dinner for ten concocted out of nothing more than originality and panache. But the napkin would be folded a little off center, and the spoon might be on the wrong side of the knife. She was an optimist who ignored trifles; for her, God was not in the details but in the intent. And all these culinary and agricultural efflorescences were extracurricular, accomplished in the crevices and niches of a fourteen-hour business day. When she scribbled out her family memoirs, in heaps of dog-eared notebooks, or on the backs of old bills, or on the margins of last year's calendar, I would resist typing them; in the speed of the chase she often omitted words like "the," "and," "will." The same flashing and bountiful hand fashioned and fired ceramic pots, and painted brilliant autumn views and vases of imaginary flowers and ferns, and decorated ordinary Woolworth platters with lavish enameled gardens. But bits of the painted petals would chip away.

Lavish: my mother was as lavish as nature. She woke early and saturated the hours with work and inventiveness, and read late into the night. She was all profusion, abundance, fabrication. Angry at her children, she would run after us whirling the cord of the electric iron, like a lasso or a whip; but she never caught us. When, in seventh grade, I was afraid of failing the Music Appreciation final exam because I could not tell the difference between "To a Wild Rose" and "Barcarole," she got the idea of sending me to school with a gauze sling rigged up on my writing arm, and an explanatory note that was purest fiction. But the sling kept slipping off. My mother gave advice like mad—she boiled over with so much passion for the predicaments of strangers that they turned into permanent cronies. She told intimate stories about people I had never heard of.

Despite the gargantuan Palmer loops (or possibly because of them), I have always known that my mother's was a life of—intricately abashing word!—excellence: insofar as excellence means ripe generosity. She burgeoned, she proliferated; she was endlessly leafy and flowering. She wore red hats, and called herself a gypsy. In her girlhood she marched with the suffragettes and for Margaret Sanger and called herself a Red. She made me laugh, she was so varied: like a tree on which lemons, pomegranates, and prickly pears absurdly all hang together. She had the comedy of prodigality.

My own way is a thousand times more confined. I am a pinched perfectionist, the ultimate fruition of Miss Brubaker; I attend to crabbed minutiae and am self-trammeled through taking pains. I am a kind of human snail, locked in and condemned by my own nature. The ancients believed that the moist track left by the snail as it crept was the snail's own essence, depleting its body little by little; the farther the snail toiled, the smaller it became, until it finally rubbed itself out. That is how perfectionists are. Say to us Excellence, and we will show you how we use up our substance and wear ourselves away, while making scarcely any progress at all. The fact that I am an exacting perfectionist in a narrow strait only, and nowhere else, is hardly to the point, since nothing matters to me so much as a comely and muscular sentence. It is my narrow strait, this snail's road; the track of the sentence I am writing now; and when I have eked out the wet substance, ink or blood, that is its mark, I will begin the next sentence. Only in treading out sentences am I perfectionist; but then there is nothing else I know how to do, or take much interest in. I miter every pair of abutting sentences as scrupulously as Uncle Jake fitted one strip of rosewood against another. My mother's worldly and bountiful hand has escaped me. The sentence I am writing is my cabin and my shell, compact, self-sufficient. It is the burnished horizon—a merciless planet where flawlessness is the single standard, where even the inmost seams, however hidden from a laxer eye, must meet perfection. Here "excellence" is not strewn casually from a tipped cornucopia, here disorder does not account for charm, here trifles rule like tyrants.

I measure my life in sentences pressed out, line by line, like the lustrous ooze on the underside of the snail, the snail's secret open seam, its wound, leaking attar. My mother was too mettlesome to feel the force of a comma. She scorned minutiae. She measured her life according to what poured from the horn of plenty, which was her own seamless, ample, cascading, elastic, susceptible, inexact heart. My narrower heart rides between the tiny twin horns of the snail, dwindling as it goes.

And out of this thinnest thread, this ink-wet line of words, must rise a visionary fog, a mist, a smoke, forging cities, histories, sorrows, quagmires, entanglements, lives of sinners, even the life of my furnace-hearted mother: so much wilderness, waywardness, plenitude on the head of the precise and impeccable snail, between the horns. (Ah, if this could be!)

The Ladle

I came late to the ladle. For years it lay in a kitchen drawer, its wooden handle split—from age, not use. A practical friend's practical gift, for which I felt no gratitude. The truth is I have no affinity for pans and colanders and other culinary devices; my friendliest utensils have always been a trustworthy can opener screwed to the wall and a certain ancient red-handled wrench designed to twist the covers off recalcitrant grocery jars. The ladle, I believed, was a serious instrument for serious cooks, an accessory to the fact of real soups and real stews. I saw no need for it.

Yet the first time I dipped the ladle into a stew-laden pot (a real stew, finally, but by then my hair had turned white), I knew its value. The ladle, though made of commonplace stainless steel, was pure gold. I had all along been feebly spooning things out; but in the depth of a true stew a spoon is an inept, lazy, shallow fellow, poor kin to a ladle. Your spoon will bring up a pair of peas in a mild flat puddle—a spoon is nearly as feckless as a sieve. But your ladle is a powerful radar-equipped submarine churning into the wild deeps of an undertow, capable of trawling the sea-floor, a driving authentic vessel that will raise a rich authentic freight.

A spoon is an effete and timid little mouth, good enough for teacups and sweet puddings. A ladle is a great guzzling inebriate, given to gargantuan draughts; a swiller of oceanic wassail; a diver into densest abysses.

It is no surprise, then, to look up to the sea of stars—the well of infinity that is the sky at night—and find there two ladles, one Big, one Little. The Big Dipper's seven stars are hitched to the nearby constellations of Draco and Leo; the hollow of its ladle has been transformed into a kind of Cinderella-coach driven not by mice but by a dragon and a lion. The Little Dipper, in contrast, is the perfected form of the purified, unmetaphoricized ladle; it is the very incarnation of a Platonic notion of a ladle. (That the ancients should have seen it as Ursa Minor, a small bear, is no credit to them. But of

457

course eyeglasses, never mind the telescope, hadn't yet been invented, so let it pass.)

As a reward for such precision of celestial engineering, a divine Hand long ago placed a diamond at the tip of the Little Dipper's handle. The diamond is called Polaris: the North Star, which connects the sky's seas with the earth's seas. For thousands of years before there were compasses, sailors fixed on Polaris to map the way from here to there, and back again. Without the ladle there would have been no navigation, no trade, no cross-culturalization. Without the ladle, how would Greece have learned geometry from Egypt? How would the alphabet have voyaged from the land of the Semites across the Mediterranean to Europe? How would Marco Polo have met the silkworm in China?

The ladle is, after all, the ultimate cosmic receptacle. It dips into knowledge and brings up wisdom, in the shape of a hundred images. The ladle is image: it is configuration in all its variety. It is the world's well. "Very deep is the well of the past. Should we not call it bottomless?" Thomas Mann asks in *Joseph and His Brothers*. Leave off the handle on occasion, or attach it afterward if you like, and you have scooped up a universe of stories. For Joseph, the ladle had no handle; it was a pit, out of which he rose to sit at the right hand of Pharaoh. For Joseph's father, Jacob, the ladle kept its handle, and went down into the bucket that Rachel drew up from the well in Haran to water Jacob's sheep and win his strenuous love. Isaac, Jacob's father, dug three wells—their names were Esek, Sitnah, and Rehoboth—in remembrance of the wells his father Abraham had dug a generation before. With its handle attached, the ladle is always activist: it will delve, scoop, dip, gouge, shovel, excavate. It will fetch up a mess of vegetables from the maw of a stewpot. Or an archaeological plinth; or a shard of what was itself once a Middle Bronze dipper.

Without its handle, the ladle can be laid-back, hammocklike, a cradle (the rhyme is, at least in the etymology of the psyche, plainly no accident): it can be the cavity of a crescent moon for Wynken, Blynken, and Nod to lie in. It can be civilized or primitive, enameled or rough, utilitarian or luxuriant. It can be tank, vat, barrel, keg, cask, or stoup; it can be urn or calabash shell, bowl or basin, silver salver or Shaker firkin, Roman simpulum or Greek kyathos. It can be Ali Baba's jars to catch forty thieves in. It can be Tom Sawyer's scary cave. It can be the tunnel of love. Hook the handle on again, and it can become the long haft of a fountain pen terminating in a well of black ink.

And just here we come (though for most of us the fountain pen has been superseded by the compact cavern of the computer, with its interior cybernetic cosmos)—we come to the ladle's deepest work: deeper than the ocean floor, deeper than the reach of the heavenly Dippers, deeper, in a way, than history itself. This is the ladle as it dips down, down, down into memory and imagination, into the bottomlessness of the word. It is the enchanted ladle that storytellers and writers grasp, or hope to grasp. Its handle (or hilt) is as long as the record of human habitation on our planet—or, some might wish to say, as long as thought and insight, as long as music and mathematics and science and art. And at the end of this longest handle of all is the dipper, the scoop, the vessel that raises up from the poet's or the philosopher's well something deeper, and higher, than we knew we knew.

Once upon a time there really used to be an inkwell and a dipper; I recollect it myself. In my childhood every elementary-school desk had, in its upper right corner, a round hole into which would fit a round glass cup. The ink monitor—generally a self-important factotum—filled the cup weekly, from a large glass bottle. Invariably the ink would spill and stain the wooden desk. We pupils dipped our pens (metal nibs in wooden slots) and were drilled in "penmanship," and dipped our pens again. Every few words necessitated a fresh dip. The inkwell was not deep—yet every year, as the grades ascended, it deepened. It deepened with *Travels with a Donkey*; it deepened with "Ode to the West Wind"; it deepened with Ichabod Crane.

And the well of sensibility goes on deepening, the ladle goes on dipping. A month or so ago I heard a man my own age, a brilliant editor—of books, and also of a famous magazine—scoop up out of his mind a lifetime's worth of ecstatic reading, novel after novel. His brain was mobbed with literature; the remembering dipper fetched and fetched. What a pity, he said at last, that all this joyful mental stock is impermanent; ephemeral; it will go to waste; it will vanish when I vanish.

That same week I saw a newborn infant, and marveled at how perfectly it was formed, a complete human simulacrum; but it had no mental stock at all. It was a freshly made ladle: a replenishing ladle ready soon enough to dip into pictures and melodies and rhymes. The well of stories and ideas is eternal. But the ladle must be renewed. So decrees the Hand that put the diamond on the Little Dipper.

North

One dark wet November afternoon a few years ago, I flew in a small plane from Copenhagen to Aarhus, Jutland, and landed in a cold and pelting storm. The wind drove more powerfully than any wind I had ever known before; it struck with a mythic moan, like that of the wind in the nursery rhyme: *The North Wind will blooowww, and soon we'll have snooowww*. Afterward, shivering over tea in the refuge of a snug little hotel, I looked around the dining room, all shining mahogany, and felt myself a desolate stranger. I was traveling alone. The hotel had once been a way station for missionaries heading for foreign parts; no New Yorker, I thought, could be at ease in such a place. I was banished, lost. I ached with forlornness. The people in the dining room seemed enviably at home. They shuffled their newspapers and hardly spoke, and when they did, the alien syllables shut me decisively out.

And suddenly, just then, I found myself assaulted by a brilliant eeriness; enchantment swept me through and through. It was very nearly a kind of seizure: an electrifying pang that shook me to tears of recognition. It was, to choose the palest term for it, a moment of *déjà vu*, but also something vaster, more tumultuous, bottomless. Though I was incontrovertibly new to this wind-ghosted place, it came to me all at once that north was where I had once belonged, north was the uncanny germ of my being.

Northernness—the shrouded poetry of northernness—is why we crave the Scandinavian autumn and winter. It may be that July and August beam down on Copenhagen, Stockholm, Oslo, and Helsinki as attractively as they do elsewhere—who can doubt it? But say it outright: summer in Sweden is for the homebody Swedes. The imagination of a Stockholm-bound traveler is transfixed by a crystal dream of low, cold, tilted light.

We go north "enamored of a season . . . cold, spacious, severe, pale and remote," misted over by "trouble, ecstasy, astonishment"—C. S. Lewis's apparition of Northernness, drawn from childhood susceptibility, and from the icy glimmer of Norse fable. We go north to reclaim something buried, clouded, infiltrating, unsure, or else as sure as instantaneous sensation.

For me, it was, I think, a grain of historical memory in the gleam of that little hotel, a secret idiosyncratic autobiographical Jutland jot: a thousand ancestral years lived to the east, just across the Baltic, along the same latitude, in old Russia's Minsk province. But there are more universal reasons to seek out the north when it is most northern in aspect. The blinding late-October sun-slant on Copenhagen walks; the pewter pavements of Stockholm under a days-long autumn rain—in all of that there lurks a time-before, whirling up from storybooks and pictures and legends, and from some idea we have of our hot inward life set against a rind of frosted light.

Mystically, in sheets of clarified air, the north reminds.

The Shock of Teapots

One morning in Stockholm, after rain and just before November, a mysteriously translucent shadow began to paint itself across the top of the city. It skimmed high over people's heads, a gauzy brass net, keeping well above the streets, skirting everything fabricated by human arts—though one or two steeples were allowed to dip into it, like pens filling their nibs with palest ink. It made a sort of watermark over Stockholm, as if a faintly luminous river ran overhead, yet with no more weight or gravity than a vapor.

This glorious strangeness—a kind of crystalline wash—was the sunlight of a Swedish autumn. The sun looked *new*: it had a lucidity, a texture, a tincture, a position across the sky that my New York gape had never before taken in. The horizontal ladder of light hung high up, higher than any sunlight I had ever seen, and the quality of its glow seemed thinner, wanner, more tentatively morning-brushed; or else like gold leaf beaten gossamer as tissue—a lambent skin laid over the spired marrow of the town.

"Ah yes, the sun *does* look a bit different this time of year," say the Stockholmers in their perfect English (English as a second first language), but with a touch of ennui. Whereas I, under the electrified rays of my whitening hair, stand drawn upward to the startling sky, restored to the clarity of childhood. The Swedes have known a Swedish autumn before; I have not.

Travel returns us in just this way to sharpness of notice; and to be saturated in the sight of what is entirely new—the sun at an unaccustomed slope, stretched across the northland, separate from the infiltrating dusk that always seems about to fall through clear gray Stockholm—is to revisit the enigmatically lit puppet-stage outlines of childhood: those mental photographs and dreaming woodcuts or engravings that we retain from our earliest years. What we remember from childhood we remember forever—permanent ghosts, stamped, imprinted, eternally seen. Travelers regain this ghost-seizing brightness, eeriness, firstness.

They regain it because they have cut themselves loose from their own

462

society, from every society; they are, for a while, floating vagabonds, like astronauts out for a space walk on a long free line. They are subject to preternatural exhilarations, absurd horizons, unexpected forms and transmutations: the matter-of-fact (a battered old stoop, say, or the shape of a door) appears beautiful; or a stone that at home would not merit the blink of your eye here arrests you with its absolute particularity—just because it is what your hand already intimately knows. You think: a stone, a stone! They have stones here too! And you think: how uncannily the planet is girdled, as stone-speckled in Sweden as in New York. For the vagabond-voyeur (and for travelers voyeurism is irresistible), nothing is not for notice, nothing is banal, nothing is ordinary: not a rock, not the shoulder of a passerby, not a teapot.

Plenitude assaults; replication invades. Everything known has its spooky shadow and Doppelganger. On my first trip anywhere—it was 1957 and I landed in Edinburgh with the roaring of the plane's four mammoth propellers for days afterward embedded in my ears—I rode in a red airport bus to the middle of the city, out of which ascended its great castle. It is a fairy-book castle, dreamlike, Arthurian, secured in the long-ago. But the shuddery red bus—hadn't I been bounced along in an old bus before, perhaps not so terrifically red as this one?—the red bus was not within reach of plain sense. Every inch of its interior streamed with unearthliness, with an undivulged and consummate witchery. It put me in the grip of a wild Elsewhere. This unexceptional vehicle, with its bright forward snout, was all at once eclipsed by a rush of the abnormal, the unfathomably Martian. It was the bus, not the phantasmagorical castle, that clouded over and bewildered our reasoned humanity. The red bus was what I intimately knew: only I had never seen it before. A reflected flicker of the actual. A looking-glass bus. A Scottish ghost.

This is what travelers discover: that when you sever the links of normality and its claims, when you break off from the quotidian, it is the teapots that truly shock. Nothing is so awesomely unfamiliar as the familiar that discloses itself at the end of a journey. Nothing shakes the heart so much as meeting—far, far away—what you last met at home. Some say that travelers are informal anthropologists. But it is ontology—the investigation of the nature of being—that travelers do. Call it the flooding-in of the real.

There is, besides, the flooding-in of character. Here one enters not landscapes or streetlit night scenes, but fragments of drama: splinters of euphoria that catch you up when you are least deserving. Sometimes it is a jump into a pop-up book, as when a cockney cabdriver, of whom you have asked directions while leaning out from the curb, gives his native wink of blithe goodwill. Sometimes it is a mazy stroll into a toy theater, as when, in a museum, you suddenly come on the intense little band following the lecturer on Mesopotamia, or the lecturer on genre painting, and the muse of civilization alights on these rapt few. What you are struck with then—one of those mental photographs that go on sticking to the retina—is not what lies somnolently in the glass case or hangs romantically on the wall, but the enchantment of a minutely idiosyncratic face shot into your vision with indelible singularity, delivered over forever by your own fertile gaze. When travelers stare at heads and ears and necks and beads and mustaches, they are—in the encapsuled force of the selection—making art: portraits, voice sonatinas, the quick haiku of a strictly triangular nostril.

Traveling is seeing; it is the implicit that we travel by. Travelers are fantasists, conjurers, seers—and what they finally discover is that every round object everywhere is a crystal ball: stone, teapot, the marvelous globe of the human eye.

How I Got Fired from
My Summer Job

The summer after graduate school, when I was twenty-two years old, I wanted to get a job. I had just come back from Ohio State University in Columbus, Ohio, at that time a hotbed of the New Criticism, where I had completed a fat M.A. thesis on the later novels of Henry James. In those distant days, an M.A. was like a mini-Ph.D.; I had even had to endure a grilling by a committee of three professors. It was important not to go after a Ph.D., though, because it meant you were not in earnest about becoming a writer; it was, in fact, an embarrassment, a cowardly expedient that could shame you. The models for the young of my generation, after all, Hemingway and Faulkner and Willa Cather, had rushed straight into life. Yet when the chairman of the English Department summoned me into his office, I was certain that he was going to urge me to continue. To forestall him, I instantly offered my confession: I was not planning to stick around for a higher degree. I expected him to say, "But you did so nicely with Henry James, so you *must* stay." Instead he said, "Well, right, you should go home and get married." I was hurt; I didn't want to marry anyone; what I really wanted was to write a metaphysical novel.

But first I wanted a summer job.

Even though I was not serious about a Ph.D., I was very serious about the New Criticism. Its chief tenet was that you could pry meaning out of any sort of mysterious parlance, especially if Ezra Pound had written it. Ezra Pound and T. S. Eliot were the New Criticism's archbishops (and faith and mystery were what kept it going), but *A Theory of Literature*, by René Wellek and Austin Warren—"Wellek-and-Warren" for short—was its Bible. Piously, I carried Wellek-and-Warren with me everywhere, and it was on my desk the very first day of my summer job. I had answered an ad by Margate, Haroulian, a firm of accountants. What had attracted me was its location: a short walk from Bryant Park, the green rectangle behind the Forty-second Street Library. I plotted lunch hours on a bench under a hot and dreamy city sun, eating a sandwich out of a paper bag and inhaling the philosophical fragrance of Wellek-and-Warren.

The man who interviewed me was neither Mr. Margate nor Mr. Haroulian. He introduced himself as George Berkeley, Mr. Haroulian's second-in-command. Disciplined blond wisps were threaded across his red-dish scalp, and his mouth made a humorless line. He was dry and precise and acutely courteous. Though I had no previous office experience, he seemed pleased with my credentials.

"So you've got a Master's," he said. "What in?"

"English," I said.

"That's fine. That's all right," he said, and asked if I could type. I said I could, and he explained what the work would require. I was to copy lists of numbers onto different printed forms, with three sets of carbons. He showed me my desk and the forms, each with its vertical rows of small oblong boxes. He opened a drawer filled with carbon paper and staples. "That's all you'll need," he said.

"But your *name*," I marveled. "It's so thrilling to have a name like that!"

"I don't see anything special about my name."

"George Berkeley—Bishop Berkeley, the eighteenth-century idealist! He said no existence is conceivable that isn't conscious spirit. He believed in Universal Mind. He's the one that infuriated Samuel Johnson so much that Dr. Johnson kicked a stone and said 'I refute it *thus*.'"

"I don't think we're related," George Berkeley said, and disappeared into an inner office. It was Mr. Haroulian's office. I never saw Mr. Margate, who seemed to have no office.

I put my sandwich into the drawer with the carbons and arranged my desk. First I placed Wellek-and-Warren next to the typewriter, so as to remind me of the nature of my soul. Then I plucked up three sheets of carbon paper and three sheets of blank paper, and stacked them behind one of the forms, and got ready to begin. I had a page of numbers to copy from—clusters of numbers: some had six digits, some four, some ten, and each set of digits had to be typed into an oblong box. It was hard to keep track, and I discovered in alarm that I had typed the same group of digits twice. I found a typewriter eraser (a stiff round thing, with a miniature whiskbroom at one end) and tried to erase the mistake on the form, but the eraser scraped the paper and almost tore it through; it made an unsightly translucent lozenge. Worse, I had forgotten about the carbons underneath. When I inspected them, they were hopelessly smudged. There was nothing to do but toss the whole mess into the trash and start over. I started over many times.

"How're you doing?" George Berkeley asked, passing by.

"I'm afraid I've wasted some forms."

"Not to worry, you'll get the hang of it," he said. "The girl you're replacing didn't have a Master's, believe me."

At lunchtime I walked to Bryant Park with my sandwich, and rapturously mooned through the densities of Wellek-and-Warren. Summer in the city! Pigeons preened in the grass; young women in white sandals and light skirts sauntered by; the shoulders of the great Library baked serenely in the heat; an ice-creamwagon floated out its jolly carillon.

But by the end of that first day—it was Monday—I still had not managed to type the right numbers into the right boxes on a single form.

"Now I don't want you to get discouraged," George Berkeley said. "All this is routine stuff, and I know you've been dealing with things a whole lot more complicated than a bunch of figures. I notice you're doing some studying on the side, and that's what I call desirable. I've been waiting a long while to get hold of someone like you, a smart girl who thinks about more than the color of her nail polish. It struck me right away that you don't wear any nail polish, and that's why I hired you—that and the fact that you lug that book around and keep up with your studying. I expect you to get somewhere with this firm. I give myself credit for being a pretty fair judge of people. I can spot someone who's going to go far with us. Potential," he said, "that's what I'm interested in."

He dragged a chair over from a nearby desk, and settled himself just opposite me; he was all earnestness. We were sitting almost knee to knee, with his big milky face so close to mine that I could see the pores, large and clean, in the wings of his nostrils. Healed pockmarks ran up the sides of his cheeks. He looked scrubbed and tidy, and it came to me that he might be the kind of man who went to bed under a framed slogan, like those I had seen in landladies' rooming houses in Columbus: BLESS THIS HOME, or GOD LOVES ME, or the pure-hearted TRUTH MAY BE BLAMED, BUT CANNOT BE SHAMED. The truth was that just then, in the middle of a peroration intended for my improvement, I was feeling considerably shamed. I had been taken into Margate, Haroulian under false colors; I had committed a lie of omission. George Berkeley, himself in a position of permanent allegiance to Margate, Haroulian, assumed I was what he termed "entry-level," a young person in pursuit of advancement in business. I did not disabuse him.

"Now let me tell you something about all these lists of figures," he went on. "They may not seem very glamorous, but they are our lifeline. They are the lifeline of our country. A really intelligent person can see right through to what these lists of figures actually stand for, and just as soon as you get the gist of all that, I have every confidence you'll be as impressed as I am with how figures like ours keep this country safe and strong. Some people may think that keeping the books the way we do it around here is the exact opposite of the sort of charge a person like you gets out of . . . well, let's say poetry, a poem like 'The Midnight Ride of Paul Revere,' let's say. Well, I get the same charge out of business that you get out of . . . that's Henry Wordsworth Longfellow, isn't it?"

There was no way out. "Henry *Wadsworth* Longfellow," I said weakly. "Wordsworth is a different poet."

"That's fine," he said, "that's very good. I like it that you're enthusiastic that way, and by this time tomorrow, watch and see, you'll be just as expert with our figures. Now here's my suggestion. Suppose instead of going out to lunch tomorrow, you join me in Mr. Margate's office. I'll order in some sandwiches and we can have a talk about books—I'm a book lover myself. I'll bring in a couple to show you that've been helpful to me in my career here. You might find them just as useful as I have."

I said, "I didn't know Mr. Margate had an office."

"Mr. Margate passed away eight years ago. It's my office now, but we still call it Mr. Margate's office. Mr. Margate was the founder of this firm, and even though he got to be very old, he was remarkable to the end. He could carry columns and columns of figures in his head. One look at a column of figures and Mr. Margate *had* them. Mr. Haroulian is certainly a brilliant man, but Mr. Margate was a genius. He was married to an authoress—she passed on right after he did. It was Mr. Margate who gave me these books I'm going to lend you, and believe me they had an effect on my whole attitude and behavior in the office. One of them was written by Mrs. Margate herself."

I was reluctant to give up my Bryant Park lunch hour to sit in Mr. Margate's office with George Berkeley. Besides, I was discovering that my lie had a living pulse in it, and was likely to go on ticking: it appeared to be leading me to a future in accounting. That future was visible in George Berkeley, but it was still more visible in Mr. Haroulian, even though Mr. Haroulian was a kind of apparition. His door was always shut; whatever he did behind it was secret, significant, worldly. But several times a day a small bony man with copper-penny eyes and a domelike head would glide by, expressionlessly, monarchically, caressing his mustache and speaking to no one. Once or twice he halted in front of my wastebasket and stared down into the crumpled heap of my discards and sad mistakes.

On Tuesday at twelve-thirty, a delivery boy carried in a cardboard tray with two lettuce-and-tomato sandwiches on it, and two paper cups filled with a urine-yellow liquid, which proved to be apple juice. George Berkeley, it developed, was a vegetarian and a health theorist.

He asked where I had eaten lunch the day before.

"On a bench in the park," I said.

"Not in the sun?" he said. "You should keep out of the sun. It affects the nerves. And I hope you didn't have meat or cheese. My rule is, if it comes from anything that has a head on it, don't eat it."

He reached into Mr. Margate's desk drawer and brought out two well-worn books. It was plain that they had been zealously read and reread. One was *How to Win Friends and Influence People*, by Dale Carnegie. The full title of the other, by Bertha N. Margate, was *Changing Losses into Bosses: A Handbook for Talented and Ambitious Young People Who Feel They Have Come to a Dead End Yet Wish to Succeed in the Business World*.

"Mrs. Margate knew whereof she wrote. According to what she says here, when she met Mr. Margate he was making fifteen dollars a week, but with her on board to inspire him he ended up on top. Look at this! Solid mahogany!" He slapped the ruddy flanks of Mr. Margate's glossy desk. "You just take these couple of books and look them through, and you'll feel the difference they make. But whatever you do, don't skip Mrs. Margate's Chapter Six, the one called 'Inspiration Increaseth Potential.' You'll notice she uses biblical language all through. Now tell me," he finished, "how did it go this morning? How're you doing?"

"A little better," I fibbed, and opened to Mrs. Margate's Table of Contents.

"That's fine, that's just fine," George Berkeley said in his flat way. I wondered whether he was putting to instant use Mrs. Margate's Chapter Twelve: "A Cheerful Word Encourageth Subordinates." He wrapped his sandwich crumbs in a paper napkin, made a little wad of it, and threw the wad into Mr. Margate's otherwise pristine wastebasket with a force that startled me. Under all that restraint and hollow optimism, something boiled; behind those nondescript syllables what unknown yet colorful life lay in passionate ambush? Perhaps the god of figures did not suffice. I wanted to romanticize George Berkeley, but all at once he romanticized himself: he turned inquisitive, peering over the bow of Margate, Haroulian into the uncharted sea beyond. "I'm interested in that kick," he said. "What's that name again, the fellow who kicked the stone?"

"Dr. Johnson? Who refuted Bishop Berkeley?"

"That's the one. Well, I don't see it. How did that settle anything?"

"Berkeley insisted that matter wasn't real, only mind was real. So Dr.

Johnson kicked the stone to prove the reality of matter. Or you could say to prove the falsity of the invisible."

"Lost his temper and let go, I can understand a thing like that. Whose side are you on?"

I was astonished. It was a question no graduate student would think to ask; I had never before considered it. But wasn't *A Theory of Literature* on the side of the invisible?

"I guess I'm with Berkeley," I said.

"Well, I'm the Berkeley who's with the fellow who did the kicking. Is that what that book you're studying's about?"

"No, it isn't," I said. Here was an embarrassment: how to explain Wellek-and-Warren to the man who bore the name of a classical idealist, yet was deaf to the cry of eternals and universals? "It's about a way of reading and analyzing what you read. It's called the New Criticism. You're supposed to read without being influenced by history or biography or psychology. As if the words were immutable. You're supposed to . . . well, you just concentrate on the language, and leave out everything to do with . . . I don't know, external entanglements. Human relations."

"The New Criticism," George Berkeley repeated. The white tract of his forehead slowly flooded pink. "Seems to me they're teaching the wrong things in the colleges nowadays. You'll never get ahead based on that kind of idea. You'd do a lot better, believe me, with Dale Carnegie and Mrs. Margate." Though I was careful to set Dale Carnegie and Mrs. Margate on top of Wellek-and-Warren on the corner of my desk next to the typewriter, I did not do well the rest of that day.

Wednesday was the same. And again Mr. Haroulian slid silently out, circling and circling the narrow space in which I toiled and failed, toiled and failed. Again he looked into my wastebasket—that wild surf, all those ruined and wrinkled forms, those smudged and spoiled and torn tropisms of my despair.

At noon I left Wellek-and-Warren behind and took Mrs. Margate, along with my salami sandwich, to Bryant Park. The midtown heat sizzled in the path. Even the pigeons confined their pecking to random blots of shade eked out by a few dangling dry leaves, or the edge of a bench, or a knot of men with briefcases standing fixed in conversation, sweltering in their puckered seersucker jackets. The brightness dazzled and dazed; pinpoints of painful light glanced out of the necklaces and wristwatches of passers-by. George Berkeley had warned that the sun would trouble my nerves; or perhaps it was Mrs. Margate who was endangering the motionless sticky air. A dread fell over me. I could never live up to her ardor:

Chapter Nine

WHAT IS EXPECTED OF YOUNG WOMEN IN BUSINESS

When the Psalmist saith, "Judge me, O Lord, for I have walked in my integrity," surely he is looking ahead to the conduct of young women in business offices today. When we speak of integrity in this connection, we must always remember that it behooves young women to be accommodating, never condescending; to accept the meanest drudgery of paperwork with humble mien, for this is the instrument of your future ascent; and to treat with superintendents and superiors as with representatives of the power of aspiration. I well recall the case of Miss M.W., an attractive girl of twenty, who considered herself "spunky," and who consistently contradicted her employers, until one day she learned to her dismay that what she regarded as "courageous" was viewed by others as "impudent." Woe to the pert young woman in a busy office! (Young men, do not suppose that this advice does not apply to YOU!)

I noticed that Mrs. Margate's handbook was dated 1933, and was self-published. Probably Mr. Margate himself had footed the bill.

On Thursday morning George Berkeley approached my desk.

The shallow cheeriness was drained out of him. It was as if the engines of Margate, Haroulian had without warning changed course; he looked like a man dizzied by a wheeling horizon. Two thin streams of sweat voyaged down the immaculate gullies that lay between his little tight nostrils and the flat string that was his mouth. I saw the throb of his throat. On the broad windowsills a pair of electric fans turned sluggishly against an overcast cityscape; it was going to rain.

"Mr. Haroulian wants to see you right away," he said. He did not ask me how I was doing; he did not egg me on to loftier achievement.

"I'll just finish this sheet," I said. I was close to the bottom of the page, and was afraid of losing my place in the march of numbers.

"Right away! Get into Mr. Haroulian's office this minute, will you? I've had enough chewing out from Mr. Haroulian over the likes of you."

Mr. Haroulian began at once to tell me about Lillian, his daughter. Since I had never heard him speak, his voice was a surprise: it ran loud and fast, like a motorcycle. Lillian, he boomed, was twenty-two; a student at Juilliard; a superlative violinist. When Lillian wasn't at school she was practicing—she hardly had a minute, not even to pick up her music. All her time was admirably occupied.

"Schirmer's on East Forty-third Street. Shake a leg and get over there,"

Mr. Haroulian growled. He handed me his daughter's shopping list; fleet-ingly, I took in flashes of Mozart, Beethoven, Sibelius. Lillian's photograph was on Mr. Haroulian's desk. A bony royal snippet, heir to the throne, eyes as round as coins—just like Mr. Haroulian himself. All that was missing was Mr. Haroulian's gray imperious mustache, which at that moment appeared to be sweeping me out of his sight like a diminutive but efficient broom. I under-stood that in Mr. Haroulian's opinion, my time was not so admirably occupied.

Walking uptown to Schirmer's in the thick late-June air, with big rain-drops darkening the pavement, I thought of "The Changeling," a story by Mary Lamb that I remembered from childhood. A nurse, ambitious for her offspring, switches two infants in their cradles. One is her own; the other is the daughter of her aristocratic employers. The nurse's natural child, dull and with no talent at all, is lovingly reared by the cultivated aristocratic family, though they are quietly disappointed in the undistinguished girl. Meanwhile their real child, brought up by the nurse, is deprived for years of the development of her innate musical gifts. When the ruse is discovered and the musical daughter is at last restored to her rightful parents, she is showered with music lessons and flourishes. Mr. Haroulian, I felt, in sending me on this humiliating errand, could not recognize that his daughter—exactly my age, after all—might be the inauthentic one, while I, plodding onward in rain-soaked shoes in service to her, might secretly be the genuine article. It hardly lessened my bitterness that Wellek-and-Warren was a thou-sand times more to me than any violin.

That was Thursday. On Friday morning my work on the forms unexpect-edly improved. As George Berkeley had promised—before the great wave of his disappointment in the New Criticism—I was starting to get the hang of it, and the rows of digits were finally jumping into their proper boxes. Not all of them, to be sure; for every form I struggled to complete, two or three ruined ones went into the wastebasket. Yet even this minor accomplishment depended on my mastery of the typewriter eraser; I had learned, for example, to erase each carbon separately.

Ten minutes before the lunch hour George Berkeley came to collect Dale Carnegie and Mrs. Margate. "You won't be needing these," he said, and swooped them away. That left Wellek-and-Warren exposed on the corner of my desk; he rested his palm on it. "Dale Carnegie may be a bit more famous, but he doesn't hold a candle to Mrs. Margate. I don't suppose you've even looked into her."

"Yes, I have," I said.

"And what did you think?"

I hesitated: my "spunky" might just turn out to be his "pert." The best answer, I speculated, would be to return diligently to the typewriter.

"Well, never mind. No one here cares what you think. Stop typing," he ordered.

I stopped.

"I've always had Mr. Haroulian's perfect confidence—I've had it right along. It's your sort of thinking that's put me in trouble with him. I've been on the telephone with Mr. Haroulian, and we've both decided that you ought to spend the rest of the afternoon just as you please. And you don't need to come back on Monday. Mr. Haroulian's attending his daughter's concert today, or he would be telling you this himself."

I knew he felt betrayed; he had put his trust in higher education.

Then, as if he were handling an unfamiliar and possibly harmful small animal, George Berkeley picked up Wellek-and-Warren and carefully placed it on the floor. He loosened his tie, something I had never seen him do. His damp neck glowed. "And by the way," he said politely, "here's what we here at Margate, Haroulian think of the New Criticism."

With one crisp thwack of his foot he sent *A Theory of Literature* hurtling against the wall.

I crossed the room, retrieved the sacred text, and escaped into the somnolent molasses sunlight of a New York summer afternoon—a failure and an incompetent, and not a changeling at all

Washington Square, 1946

ॐ

. . . this portion of New York appears to many persons the most delec-
table. It has a kind of established repose which is not of frequent
occurrence in other quarters of the long, shrill city; it has a riper,
richer, more honorable look than any of the upper ramifications of the
great longitudinal thoroughfare—the look of having had something
of a social history.
HENRY JAMES, *Washington Square*

I first came down to Washington Square on a colorless February morning in
1946. I was seventeen and a half years old and was carrying my lunch in a
brown paper bag, just as I had carried it to high school only a month before.
It was—I thought it was—the opening day of spring term at Washington
Square College, my initiation into my freshman year at New York University.
All I knew of N. Y. U. then was that my science-minded brother had gone
there; he had written from the Army that I ought to go there too. With
master-of-ceremonies zest he described the Browsing Room on the second
floor of the Main Building as a paradisal chamber whose bookish loungers
leafed languidly through magazines and exchanged high-principled witti-
cisms between classes. It had the sound of a carpeted Olympian club in
Oliver Wendell Holmes's Boston, Hub of the Universe, strewn with leather
chairs and delectable old copies of *The Yellow Book*.

On that day I had never heard of Oliver Wendell Holmes or *The Yellow
Book*, and Washington Square was a faraway bower where wounded birds
fell out of trees. My brother had once brought home from Washington
Square Park a baby sparrow with a broken leg, to be nurtured back to flight.
It died instead, emitting in its last hours melancholy faint cheeps, and leaving behind a dense recognition of the minute explicitness of mortality. All
the same, in the February grayness Washington Square had the allure of the
celestial unknown. A sparrow might die, but my own life was luminously
new: I felt my youth like a nimbus.

Which dissolves into the dun gauze of a low and sullen city sky. And here I am flying out of the Lexington Avenue subway at Astor Place, just a few yards from Wanamaker's, here I am turning the corner past a second-hand bookstore and a union hall; already late, I begin walking very fast toward the park. The air is smoky with New York winter grit, and on clogged Broadway a mob of trucks shifts squawking gears. But there, just ahead, criss-crossed by paths under high branches, is Washington Square; and on a single sidewalk, three clear omens; or call them riddles, intricate and redolent. These I will disclose in a moment, but before that you must push open the heavy brass-and-glass doors of the Main Building, and come with me, at a hard and panting pace, into the lobby of Washington Square College on the earliest morning of the freshman year.

On the left, a bank of elevators. Straight ahead, a long burnished corridor, spooky as a lit tunnel. And empty, all empty. I can hear my solitary footsteps reverberate, as in a radio mystery drama: they lead me up a short staircase into a big dark ghost-town cafeteria. My brother's letter, along with an account of the physics and chemistry laboratories (I will never see them), has already explained that this place is called Commons—and here my heart will learn to shake with the merciless newness of life. But not today; today there is nothing. Tables and chairs squat in dead silhouette. I race back through a silent maze of halls and stairways to the brass-and-glass doors—there stands a lonely guard. From the pocket of my coat I retrieve a scrap with a classroom number on it and ask the way. The guard announces in a sly croak that the first day of school is not yet; come back tomorrow, he says.

A dumb bad joke: I'm humiliated. I've journeyed the whole way down from the end of the line—Pelham Bay, in the northeast Bronx—to find myself in desolation, all because of a muddle: Tuesday isn't Wednesday. The nimbus of expectation fades off. The lunch bag in my fist takes on a greasy sadness. I'm not ready to dive back into the subway—I'll have a look around.

Across the street from the Main Building, the three omens. First, a pretzel man with a cart. He's wearing a sweater, a cap that keeps him faceless—he's nothing but the shadows of his creases—and wool gloves with the fingertips cut off. He never moves; he might as well be made of papier-mache, set up and left out in the open since spring. There are now almost no pretzels for sale, and this gives me a chance to inspect the construction of his bare pretzel poles. The pretzels are hooked over a column of gray cardboard cylinders, themselves looped around a stick, the way horseshoes drop around a post. The cardboard cylinders are the insides of toilet paper rolls.

The pretzel man is rooted between a Chock Full o' Nuts (that's the second omen) and a newsstand (that's the third).

The Chock Full: the doors are like fans, whirling remnants of conversation. *She will marry him. She will not marry him.* Fragrance of coffee and hot chocolate. *We can prove that the senses are partial and unreliable vehicles of information, but who is to say that reason is not equally the product of human limitation?* Powdered doughnut sugar on their lips.

Attached to a candy store, the newsstand. Copies of *Partisan Review*: the table of the gods. Jean Stafford, Mary McCarthy, Elizabeth Hardwick, Irving Howe, Delmore Schwartz, Alfred Kazin, Clement Greenberg, Stephen Spender, William Phillips, John Berryman, Saul Bellow, Philip Rahv, Richard Chase, Randall Jarrell, Simone de Beauvoir, Karl Shapiro, George Orwell! I don't know a single one of these names, but I feel their small conflagration flaming in the gray street: the succulent hotness of their promise. I mean to penetrate every one of them. Since all the money I have is my subway fare—two nickels—I don't buy a copy (the price of *Partisan* in 1946 is fifty cents); I pass on.

I pass on to the row of houses on the north side of the Square. Henry James was born in one of these, but I don't know that either. Still, they are plainly old, though no longer aristocratic: haughty last-century shabbies with shut eyelids, built of rosy-ripe respectable brick, down on their luck. Across the park bulks Judson Church, with its squat squarish bell tower; by the end of the week I will be languishing at the margins of a basketball game in its basement, forlorn in my blue left-over-from-high-school gym suit and mooning over Emily Dickinson:

> There's a certain Slant of light,
> Winter Afternoons—
> That oppresses, like the Heft
> Of Cathedral Tunes—

There is more I don't know. I don't know that W. H. Auden lives just down *there*, and might at any moment be seen striding toward home under his tall rumpled hunch; I don't know that Marianne Moore is only up the block, her doffed tricorn resting on her bedroom dresser. It's Greenwich Village—I know *that*—no more than twenty years after Edna St. Vincent Millay has sent the music of her name (her best, perhaps her only, poem) into these bohemian streets: bohemia, the honey pot of poets.

On that first day in the tea-leafed cup of the town I am ignorant, ignorant! But the three riddle-omens are soon to erupt, and all of them together will illumine Washington Square.

Begin with the benches in the Park. Here, side by side with students and their loose-leafs, lean or lie the shadows of the pretzel man, his creased ghosts or doubles: all those pitiables, half-women and half-men, neither awake nor asleep, the discountable, the repudiated, the unseen. No more notice is taken of any of them than of a scudding fragment of newspaper in the path. Even then, even so long ago, the benches of Washington Square are pimpled with this hell-tossed crew, these Mad Margarets and Cokey Joes, these volcanic coughers, shakers, groaners, tremblers, droolers, blasphemers, these public urinators with vomitous breath and rusted teeth-stumps, dead-eyed and self-abandoned, dragging their makeshift junkyard shoes, their buttonless layers of raggedy ratfur. The pretzel man with his toilet paper rolls conjures and spews them all—he is a loftier brother to these citizens of the lower pox, he is guardian of the garden of the jettisoned. They rattle along all the seams of Washington Square. They are the pickled City, the true and universal City-below-Cities, the wolfish vinegar-Babylon that dogs the spittled skirts of bohemia. The toilet paper rolls are the temple-columns of this sacred grove.

Next, the whirling doors of Chock Full o' Nuts. Here is the marketplace of Washington Square, its bazaar, its roiling gossip parlor, its matchmaker's office and arena—the outermost wing, so to speak, evolved from the Commons. On a day like today, when the Commons is closed, the Chock Full is thronged with extra power, a cello making up for a missing viola. Until now, the fire of my vitals has been for the imperious tragedians of the *Aeneid*; I have lived in the narrow throat of poetry. Another year or so of this oblivion, until at last I am hammer-struck with the shock of Europe's skull, the bled planet of death camp and war. Eleanor Roosevelt has not yet written her famous column announcing the discovery of Anne Frank's diary. The term "cold war" is new. The Commons, like the college itself, is overcrowded, veterans in their pragmatic thirties mingling with the reluctant dreamy young. And the Commons is convulsed with politics: a march to the docks is organized, no one knows by whom, to protest the arrival of Walter Gieseking, the German musician who flourished among Nazis. The Communists—two or three readily recognizable cantankerous zealots—stomp through with their daily leaflets and sneers. There is even a Monarchist, a small poker-faced rectangle of a man with secretive tireless eyes who, when approached for his views, always demands, in perfect Bronx tones, the restoration of his king. The engaged girls—how many of them there seem to be!—flash their rings and tangle their ankles in their long New Look skirts. There is no feminism and no feminists; I am, I think, the only one. The Commons is a tide: it washes up the cold war, it washes up the engaged girls' rings, it washes up the several philosophers and the numerous poets. The philosophers are all Existentialists; the poets are all influenced by "The Waste Land." When the

Commons overflows, the engaged girls cross the street to show their rings at the Chock Full.

Call it density, call it intensity, call it continuity: call it, finally, society. The Commons belongs to the satirists. Here, one afternoon, is Alfred Chester, holding up a hair, a single strand, before a crowd. (He will one day write stories and novels. He will die young.) "What is that hair?" I innocently ask, having come late on the scene. "A pubic hair," he replies, and I feel as Virginia Woolf did when she declared human nature to have "changed in or about December 1910"—soon after her sister Vanessa explained away a spot on her dress as "semen."

In or about February 1946 human nature does not change; it keeps on. On my bedroom wall I tack—cut out from *Life* magazine—the wildest Picasso I can find: a face that is also a belly. Mr. George E. Mutch, a lyrical young English teacher twenty-seven years old, writes on the blackboard: "When lilacs last in the dooryard bloom'd," and "Bare, ruined choirs, where late the sweet birds sang," and "A green thought in a green shade"; he tells us to burn, like Pater, with a hard, gemlike flame. Another English teacher—his name is Emerson—compares Walt Whitman to a plumber; next year he will shoot himself in a wood. The initial letters of Washington Square College are a device to recall three of the Seven Deadly Sins: Wantonness, Sloth, Covetousness. In Commons they argue the efficacy of the orgone box. Eda Lou Walton, sprightly as a bird, knows all the Village bards, and is a Village bard herself. Sidney Hook is an intellectual rumble in the logical middle distance. Homer Watt, chairman of the English Department, is the very soul who, in a far-off time of bewitchment, hired Thomas Wolfe.

And so, in February 1946, I make my first purchase of a "real" book— which is to say, not for the classroom. It is displayed in the window of the secondhand bookstore between the Astor Place subway station and the union hall, and for weeks I have been coveting it: *Of Time and the River.* I am transfigured; I am pierced through with rapture; skipping gym, I sit among morning mists on a windy bench a foot from the stench of Mad Margaret, sinking into that cascading syrup: "Man's youth is a wonderful thing: It is so full of anguish and of magic and he never comes to know it as it is, until it is gone from him forever . . . And what is the essence of that strange and bitter miracle of life which we feel so poignantly, so unutterably, with such a bitter pain and joy, when we are young?" Thomas Wolfe, lost, and by the wind grieved, ghost, come back again! In Washington Square I am appareled in the "numb exultant secrecies of fog, fog-numb air filled with solemn joy of nameless and impending prophecy, an ancient yellow light, the old smoke-ochre of the morning . . ."

The smoke-ochre of the morning. Ah, you who have flung Thomas Wolfe, along with your strange and magical youth, onto the ash heap of juvenilia and excess, myself among you, isn't this a lovely phrase still? It rises out of the old pavements of Washington Square as delicately colored as an eggshell.

The veterans in their pragmatic thirties are nailed to Need; they have families and futures to attend to. When Mr. George E. Mutch exhorts them to burn with a hard, gemlike flame, and writes across the blackboard the line that reveals his own name,

The world is too much with us; late and soon, Getting and spending, we lay waste our powers,

one of the veterans heckles, "What about getting a Buick, what about spending a buck?" Chester, at sixteen, is a whole year younger than I; he has transparent eyes and a rosebud mouth, and is in love with a poet named Diana. He has already found his way to the Village bars, and keeps in his wallet Truman Capote's secret telephone number. We tie our scarves tight against the cold and walk up and down Fourth Avenue, winding in and out of the rows of secondhand bookshops crammed one against the other. The proprietors sit reading their wares and never look up. The books in all their thousands smell sleepily of cellar. Our envy of them is speckled with longing; our longing is sick with envy. We are the sorrowful literary young.

Every day, month after month, I hang around the newsstand near the candy store, drilling through the enigmatic pages of *Partisan Review*. I still haven't bought a copy; I still can't understand a word. I don't know what "cold war" means. Who is Trotsky? I haven't read *Ulysses*; my adolescent phantoms are rowing in the ablative absolute with *pius* Aeneas. I'm in my mind's cradle, veiled by the exultant secrecies of fog.

Washington Square will wake me. In a lecture room in the Main Building, Dylan Thomas will cry his webwork syllables. Afterward he'll warm himself at the White Horse Tavern. Across the corridor I will see Sidney Hook plain. I will read the Bhagavad Gita and Catullus and Lessing, and, in Hebrew, a novel eerily called *Whither*? It will be years and years before I am smart enough, worldly enough, to read Alfred Kazin and Mary McCarthy.

In the spring, all of worldly Washington Square will wake up to the luster of little green leaves.

The Question of Our Speech: The Return to Aural Culture

When I was a thirteen-year-old New Yorker, a trio of women from the provinces took up, relentlessly and extravagantly, the question of my speech. Their names were Miss Evangeline Trolander, Mrs. Olive Birch Davis, and Mrs. Ruby S. Papp (pronounced *pop*). It was Mrs. Papp's specialty to explain how to "breathe from the diaphragm." She would place her fingers tip-to-tip on the unyielding hard shell of her midriff, hugely inhaling: how astonishing then to see how the mighty action of her lungs caused her fingertips to spring apart! This demonstration was for the repair of the New York voice. What the New York voice, situated notoriously "in the throat," required above everything was to descend, pumping air, to this nether site, so that "Young Lochinvar came out of the WEST" might come bellowing out of the pubescent breast.

The New York palate, meanwhile, was consonantally in neglect. *T*'s, *d*'s, and *l*'s were being beaten out against the teeth, European-fashion—this was called "dentalization"—while the homeless *r* and *n* went wandering in the perilous trough behind the front incisors.

There were corrective exercises for these transgressions, the chief one being a liturgical recitation of "Tillie the Toiler took Tommy Tucker to tea," with the tongue anxiously flying up above the teeth to strike precisely on the lower ridge of the upper palate.

The diaphragm; the upper palate; and finally the arena in the cave of the mouth where the vowels were prepared. A New Yorker could not say a proper *a*, as in "paper"—this indispensable vibration was manufactured somewhere back near the nasal passage, whereas civility demanded the *a* to emerge frontally, directly from the lips' vestibule. The New York *i* was worst of all: how Mrs. Davis, Mrs. Papp, and Miss Trolander mimicked and ridiculed the New York *i*! "Oi loik oice cream," they mocked.

All these emendations, as it happened, were being applied to the entire population of a high school for girls in a modest Gothic pile on East Sixty-eighth Street in the 1940s, and no one who emerged from that pile after four years of daily speech training ever sounded the same again. On the eve of graduation, Mrs. Olive Birch Davis turned to Mrs. Ruby S. Papp and said: "Do you remember the *ugliness* of her *diction* when she came to us?" She meant me; I was about to deliver the Class Speech. I had not yet encountered Shaw's *Pygmalion*, and its popular recrudescence in the form of *My Fair lady* was still to occur; all the same, that night, rehearsing for commencement, I caught in Mrs. Davis and Mrs. Papp something of Professor Higgins's victory, and in myself something of Eliza's humiliation.

Our teachers had, like young Lochinvar, come out of the West, but I had come out of the northeast Bronx. Called on to enunciate publicly for the first time, I responded with the diffidence of secret pleasure; I liked to read out loud, and thought myself not bad at it. Instead, I was marked down as a malfeasance in need of overhaul. The revisions and transformations that followed were not unlike an evangelical conversion. One had to be willing to be born again; one had to be willing to repudiate wholesale one's former defective self. It could not be accomplished without faith and shame: faith in what one might newly become, shame in the degrading process itself—the dedicated repetition of mantras. "Tillie the Toiler took Tommy Tucker to tea," "Oh! young LOCHinvar has come out of the WEST, Through all the wide BORDer HIS steed was the BEST." All the while pneumatically shooting out one's diaphragm, and keeping one's eye (never one's *oi*) peeled for the niggardly approval of Miss Evangeline Trolander.

In this way I was, at an early age, effectively made over. Like a multitude of other graduates of my high school, I now own a sort of robot's speech—it has no obvious native county. At least not to most ears, though a well-tutored listener will hear that the vowels hang on, and the cadence of every sentence has a certain laggardly northeast Bronx drag. Brooklyn, by contrast, is divided between very fast and very slow. Irish New York has its own sound, Italian New York another; and a refined ear can distinguish between Bronx and Brooklyn Irish and Bronx and Brooklyn Jewish: four separate accents, with the differences to be found not simply in vowels and consonants, but in speed and inflection. Nor is it so much a matter of ancestry as of neighborhood. If, instead of clinging to the green-fronded edge of Pelham Bay Park, my family had settled three miles west, in a denser "section" called Pelham Parkway, I would have spoken Bronx Jewish. Encountering City Island, Bronx Jewish said Ciddy Oilen. In Pelham Bay, where Bronx Irish was almost exclusively spoken in those days, it was Ciddy Allen. When Terence Cooke became cardinal of New York, my heart leaped up: Throggs Neck! I had assimilated those sounds long ago on a pebbly beach. No one had ever put the cardinal into the wringer of speech repair. I knew him through and through. He was my childhood's brother, and restored my orphaned ear.

Effectively made over: these noises that come out of me are not an overlay. They do not vanish during the free play of dreams or screams. I do not, cannot, "revert." This may be because Trolander, Davis, and Papp caught me early; or because I was so passionate a devotee of their dogma.

Years later I tried to figure it all out. What did these women have up their sleeves? An aesthetic ideal, perhaps: Standard American English. But behind the ideal—and Trolander, Davis, and Papp were the strictest and most indefatigable idealists-there must have been an ideology; and behind the ideology, whatever form it might take, a repugnance. The speech of New York streets and households soiled them: you could see it in their proud pained meticulous frowns. They were intent on our elevation. Though they were dead set on annihilating Yiddish-derived "dentalization," they could not be said to be anti-Semites, since they were just as set on erasing the tumbling consonants of Virginia Greene's Alexander Avenue Irish Bronx; and besides, in our different styles, we all dentalized. Was it, then, the Melting Pot that inspired Trolander, Davis, and Papp? But not one of us was an "immigrant"; we were all fully Americanized, and our parents before us, except for the handful of foreign-born "German refugees." These were marched off to a special Speech Clinic for segregated training; their *r*'s drew Mrs. Davis's eyes toward heaven, and I privately recognized that the refugees were almost all of them hopeless cases. A girl named Hedwig said she *didn't care*, which made me conclude that she was frivolous, trivialized, not serious; wasn't it ignominious enough (like a kind of cheese) to be called "Hedwig"?

Only the refugees were bona fide foreigners. The rest of us were garden-variety subway-riding New Yorkers. Trolander, Davis, and Papp saw us nevertheless as tainted with foreignness, and it was the remnants of that foreignness they meant to wipe away: the last stages of the great turn-of-the-century alien flood. Or perhaps they intended that, like Shaw's Eliza, we should have the wherewithal to rise to a higher station. Yet, looking back on their dress and manner, I do not think Trolander, Davis, and Papp at all sought out or even understood "class"; they were reliably American, and class was nothing they were capable of believing in.

What, then, did these ferrywomen imagine we would find on the farther shore, once we left behind, through artifice and practice, our native speech? Was it a kind of "manners," was it what they might have called "breeding"? They thought of themselves as democratic noblewomen (nor did they suppose this to be a contradiction in terms), and they expected of us, if not the same, then at least a recognition of the category. They trusted in the power of models. They gave us the astonishing maneuvers of their teeth, their tongues, their lungs, and drilled us in imitation of those maneuvers. In the process, they managed—this was their highest feat—to break down embarrassment, to deny the shaming theatricality of the ludicrous. We lost every delicacy and dignity in acting like freaks or fools while trying out the new accent. Contrived consonants began freely to address feigned vowels: a world of parroting and parody. And what came of it all?

What came of it was that they caused us—and here was a category *they* had no recognition of—they caused us to exchange one regionalism for another. New York gave way to Midwest. We were cured of Atlantic Seaboard, a disease that encompassed north, middle, and south; and yet only the middle, and of that middle only New York, was considered to be on the critical list. It was New York that carried the hottest and sickest inflammation. In no other hollow of the country was such an effort mounted, on such a scale, to eliminate regionalism. The South might have specialized in Elocution, but the South was not ashamed of its idiosyncratic vowels; neither was New England; and no one sent missionaries.

Of course this was exactly what our democratic noblewomen were: missionaries. They restored, if not our souls, then surely and emphatically our *r*'s—those *r*'s that are missing in the end syllables of New Yorkers, who call themselves Noo Yawkizz and nowadays worry about muggizz. From Boston to New York to Atlanta, the Easterner is an Eastinna, his mother is a mutha, his father a fahtha, and the most difficult stretch of anything is the hahd paht; and so fawth. But only in New York is the absent *r*—i.e., the absent *aw*—an offense to good mannizz. To be sure, our missionaries did not dream that they imposed a parochialism of their own. And perhaps they were right not to dream it, since by the forties of this century the radio was having its leveling effect, and Midwest speech, colonizing by means of "announcers," had ascended to the rank of standard speech.

Still, only forty years earlier, Henry James, visiting from England after a considerable period away, was freshly noticing and acidly deploring the pervasively conquering *r*:

> . . . the letter, I grant, gets terribly little rest among those great masses of our population that strike us, in the boundless West especially, as, under some strange impulse received toward consonantal recovery of balance, making it present even in words from which it is absent, bringing it in everywhere as with the small vulgar effect of a sort of morose grinding of the back teeth. There are, you see, sounds of a mysterious intrinsic meanness, and there are sounds of a mysterious intrinsic

frankness and sweetness; and I think the recurrent note I have
indicated—fatherr and motherr and otherr, waterr and matterr and scat-
terr, harrd and barrd, parrt, starrt, and (dreadful to say) arrt (the repetition
it is that drives home the ugliness), are signal specimens of what becomes
of a custom of utterance out of which the principle of taste has dropped.

In 1905, to drop the r was to drop, for the cultivated ear, a principle of
taste; but for our democratic noblewomen four decades on, exactly the
reverse was true. James's New York/Boston expectations, reinforced by
southern England, assumed that Eastern American speech, tied as it was to
the cultural reign of London, had a right to rule and to rule out. The history
and sociolinguistics governing this reversal is less pressing to examine than
the question of "standard speech" itself. James thought that "the voice *plus*
the way it is employed" determined "positively the history of the national
character, almost the history of the people." His views on all this, his alarms
and anxieties, he compressed into a fluid little talk ("The Question of Our
Speech") he gave at the Bryn Mawr College commencement of June 8,
1905—exactly one year and two days before my mother, nine years old,
having passed through Castle Garden, stood on the corner of Battery Park,
waiting to board the horsecar for Madison Street on the Lower East Side.

James was in great fear of the child waiting for the horsecar. "Keep in
sight," he warned, "the so interesting historical truth that no language, so far
back as our acquaintance with history goes, has known any such ordeal, any
such stress or strain, as was to await the English in this huge new community it was to help, at first, to father and mother. It came *over*, as the phrase
is, came over originally without fear and without guile—but to find itself
transplanted to spaces it had never dreamed, in its comparative humility, of
covering, to conditions it had never dreamed, in its comparative innocence,
of meeting." He spoke of English as an "unfriended heroine," "our transported medium, our unrescued Andromeda, our medium of utterance, . . .
disjoined from all the associations, the other presences, that had attended
her, that had watched for her and with her, that had helped to form her manners and her voice, her taste and her genius."

And if English, orphaned as it was and cut off from its "ancestral circle,"
did not have enough to contend with in its own immigrant situation, arriving
"without fear and without guile" only to be ambushed by "a social and political order that was both without previous precedent and example and
incalculably expansive," including also the expansiveness of a diligent public
school network and "the mighty maniac" of journalism—if all this was not
threatening enough, there was the special danger my nine-year-old mother

posed. She represented an unstable new ingredient. She represented violation, a kind of linguistic Armageddon. She stood for disorder and promiscuity.
"I am perfectly aware," James said at Bryn Mawr,

> that the common school and the newspaper are influences that shall
> often have been named to you, exactly, as favorable, as positively and
> actively contributive, to the prosperity of our idiom; the answer to
> which is that the matter depends, distinctively, on what is meant by
> prosperity. It is prosperity, of a sort, that a hundred million people, a few
> years hence, will be unanimously, loudly—above all loudly, I think!—
> speaking it, and that, moreover, many of these millions will have been
> artfully wooed and weaned from the Dutch, from the Spanish, from the
> German, from the Italian, from the Norse, from the Finnish, from the
> Yiddish even, strange to say, and (stranger still to say), even from the
> English, for the sweet sake, or the sublime consciousness, as we may
> perhaps put it, of speaking, of talking, for the first time in their lives,
> really at their ease. There are many things our now so profusely import-
> ant and, as is claimed, quickly assimilated foreign brothers and sisters
> may do at their ease in this country, and at two minutes' notice, and
> without asking any one else's leave or taking any circumstance whatever
> into account—any save an infinite uplifting sense of freedom and facil-
> ity; but the thing they may best do is play, to their heart's content, with
> the English language, or, in other words, dump their mountain of pro-
> miscuous material into the foundation of the American.

"All the while we sleep," he continued, "the vast contingent of aliens
whom we make welcome, and whose main contention, as I say, is that, from
the moment of their arrival, they have just as much property in our speech
as we have, and just as good a right to do what they choose with it . . . all
the while we sleep the innumerable aliens are sitting up (*they* don't sleep!) to
work their will on their new inheritance." And he compared the immigrants'
use of English to oilcloth—"highly convenient . . . durable, tough, cheap."

James's thesis in his address to his audience of young aristocrats was
not precisely focused. On the one hand, in describing the depredations of
the innumerable sleepless aliens, in protesting "the common schools and
the 'daily paper,'" he appeared to admit defeat—"the forces of looseness are
in possession of the field." Yet in asking the graduates to see to the perfection
of their own speech, he had, he confessed, no models to offer them. Imitate,
he advised—but whom? Parents and teachers were themselves not watchful. "I am at a loss to name you particular and unmistakable, edifying and

illuminating groups or classes," he said, and recommended, in the most general way, the hope of "encountering, blessedly, here and there, articulate individuals, torch-bearers, as we may rightly describe them, guardians of the sacred flame."

As it turned out, James not only had no solution; he had not even put the right question. These young women of good family whom he was exhorting to excellence were well situated in society to do exactly what James had described the immigrants as doing: speaking "*really* at their ease," playing, "to their heart's content, with the English language" in "an infinite uplifting sense of freedom and facility." Whereas the "aliens," hard-pressed by the scramblings of poverty and cultural confusions, had no notion at all of linguistic "freedom and facility," took no witting license with the English tongue, and felt no remotest ownership in the language they hoped merely to earn their wretched bread by. If they did not sleep, it was because of long hours in the sweatshops and similar places of employment; they were no more in a position to "play" with English than they were to acquire bona fide *Mayflower* ancestry. Ease, content, facility—these were not the lot of the unsleeping aliens.

To the young people of Bryn Mawr James could offer nothing more sanguine, nothing less gossamer, than the merest metaphor —"guardians of the sacred flame." Whom then should they imitate but himself, the most "articulate individual" of them all? We have no record of the graduates' response to James's extravagant "later style" as profusely exhibited in this address: whatever it was, they could not have accepted it for standard American. James's English had become, by this time, an invention of his own fashioning, so shaded, so leafy, so imbricated, so brachiate, so filigreed, as to cast a thousand momentary ornamental obscurities, like the effect of the drill-holes in the spiraled stone hair of an imperial Roman portrait bust. He was the most eminent torchbearer in sight, the purest of all possible guardians of the flame—but a model he could not have been for anyone's everyday speech, no more than the Romans talked like the Odes of Horace. Not that he failed to recognize the exigencies of an active language, "a living organism, fed by the very breath of those who employ it, whoever these may happen to be," a language able "to respond, from its core, to the constant appeal of time, perpetually demanding new tricks, new experiments, new amusements." He saw American English as the flexible servant "of those who carry it with them, on their long road, as their specific experience grows larger and more complex, and who need it to help them to meet this expansion." And at the same time he excluded from these widened possibilities its slangy young native speakers and the very immigrants whose educated children would enrich and re-animate the American language (eight decades later we may judge how vividly), as well as master and augment its literature.

Its literature. It is striking beyond anything that James left out, in the course of this lecture, any reference to reading. Certainly it was not overtly his subject. He was concerned with enunciation and with idiom, with syllables, with vowels and consonants, with tone and inflection, with *sound*—but he linked the American voice to such "underlying things" as "proprieties and values, perfect possessions of the educated spirit, clear humanities," as well as "the imparting of a coherent culture." Implicit was his conviction that speech affects literature, as, in the case of native speakers, it inevitably does: naturalism in the dialogue of a novel, say, is itself always a kind of dialect of a particular place and time. But in a newly roiling society of immigrant speakers, James could not see ahead (and why should he have seen ahead? Castle Garden was unprecedented in all of human history) to the idea that a national literature can create a national speech. The immigrants who learned to read learned to speak. Those who only learned to speak did not, in effect, learn to speak.

In supposing the overriding opposite—that quality of speech creates culture, rather than culture quality of speech—James in "The Question of Our Speech" slighted the one formulation most pertinent to his complaints: the uses of literature. Pressing for "civility of utterance," warning against "influences round about us that make for . . . the confused, the ugly, the flat, the thin, the mean, the helpless, that reduce articulation to an easy and ignoble minimum, and so keep it as little distinct as possible from the grunting, the squealing, the barking or roaring of animals," James thought it overwhelmingly an issue of the imitation of oral models, an issue of "the influence of *observation*," above all an issue of manners—"for that," he insisted, "is indissolubly involved." How like Mrs. Olive Birch Davis he is when, at Bryn Mawr, he hopes to inflame his listeners to aspiration! "At first dimly, but then more and more distinctly, you will find yourselves noting, comparing, preferring, at last positively emulating and imitating." Bryn Mawr, of course, was the knowing occasion, not the guilty target, of this admonition—he was speaking of the young voices he had been hearing in the street and in the parlors of friends, and he ended with a sacred charge for the graduates themselves: "you may, sounding the clearer note of intercourse as only women can, become yourselves models and missionaries [sic], perhaps even a little martyrs, of the good cause."

But why did he address himself to this thesis exclusively in America? Could he not, even more emphatically, have made the same declarations, uttered the same dooms, in his adopted England? No doubt it would not have been seemly; no doubt he would have condemned any appearance of ingratitude toward his welcoming hosts. All true, but this was hardly the reason the lecture at Bryn Mawr would not have done for Girton College. In Britain, regionalisms are the soul of ordinary English speech, and in James's time more than in our own. Even now one can move from hamlet to hamlet and hear the vowels chime charmingly with a different tone in each village. Hull, England, is a city farther from London in speech—though in distance only 140 miles to the north—than Hull, Massachusetts, is from San Francisco, 3,000 miles to the west. Of England, it is clear, James had only the expectations of class, and a single class set the standard for cultivated speech. Back home in America, diversity was without enchantment, and James demanded a uniform sound. He would not have dreamed of requiring a uniform British sound: English diversity was *English* diversity, earned, native, beaten out over generations of the "ancestral circle"—while American diversity meant a proliferating concatenation of the innumerable sleepless aliens and the half-educated slangy young. With regard to England, James knew whence the standard derived. It was a quality—an emanation, even— of those who, for generations, had been privileged in their education. As Virginia Woolf acknowledged in connection with another complaint, the standard was Oxbridge. To raise the question of "our" speech in England would have been a superfluity: both the question and the answer were self-evident. In England the question, if anyone bothered to put it at all, was: Who sets the standard? And the answer, if anyone bothered to give it at all, was: Those who have been through the great public schools, those who have been through either of the great pair of ancient universities—in short, those who run things.

This was perhaps what led James, in his American reflections, to trip over the issues, and to miss getting at the better question, the right and pertinent question: *the* question, in fact, concerning American speech. In Britain, and in the smaller America of his boyhood that strained to be a mirror of the cousinly English culture, it remained to the point to ask who sets the standard. And the rejoinder was simple enough: the people at the top. To risk the identical question in the America of 1905, with my mother about to emerge from Castle Garden to stand waiting for the horsecar on the corner of Battery Park, was unavoidably to hurtle to the very answer James most dreaded and then desperately conceded: the people at the bottom.

The right and pertinent question for America was something else. If, in politics, America's Enlightenment cry before the world was to be "a nation of laws, not of men," then it was natural for culture to apply in its own jurisdiction the same measure: unassailable institutions are preferable to models or heroes. To look for aristocratic models for common speech in the America of 1905 was to end exactly where James *did* end: "I am at a loss to name you particular and unmistakably edifying and illuminating groups or classes." It could not be done. As long as James believed—together with Trolander, Davis, and Papp, his immediate though paradoxical heirs: paradoxical because their ideal was democratic and his was the-people-at-the-top—as long as he believed in the premise of "edifying and illuminating" models, his analysis could go nowhere. Or, rather, it could go only into the rhapsody of vaporous hope that is the conclusion of "The Question of Our Speech"— "become yourselves models and missionaries, even a little martyrs, of the good cause." Holy and resplendent words I recognize on the instant, having learned them-especially the injunction to martyrdom-at the feet of Trolander, Davis, and Papp.

No, it was the wrong question for America, this emphasis on *who*; the wrong note for a campus (however homogeneous, however elite) just outside Philadelphia, that Enlightenment citadel, whose cracked though mighty Bell was engraved with a rendering of the majestic Hebrew word *dror*: a word my nine-year-old mother, on her way to Madison Street, would have been able to read in the original, though presumably James could not—a deprivation of literacy my mother might have marked him down for. "All life," James asserted on that brilliant June day (my mother's life was that day still under the yoke of the Czar; the Kishinev pogrom, with its massacre and its maimings, had occurred only two years earlier), "all life comes back to the question of our speech, the medium through which we communicate with each other; for all life comes back to the question of our relations with each other." And: "A care for tone is part of a care for many things besides; for the fact, for the value, of good breeding, above all, as to which tone unites with various other personal, social signs to bear testimony. The idea of good breeding . . . is one of the most precious conquests of civilization, the very core of our social heritage."

Speech, then, was *who*; it was breeding; it was "relations"; it was manners; and manners, in this view, make culture. As a novelist, and particularly as a celebrated practitioner of "the novel of manners" (though to reduce James merely to this is to diminish him radically as a recorder of evil and to silence his full moral genius), it was requisite, it was the soul of vitality itself, for James to analyze in the mode of *who*. But for a social theorist—and in his lecture social theory was what James was pressing toward—it was a failing and an error. The absence of models was not simply an embarrassment; it should have been a hint. It should have hinted at the necessary relinquishment of *who* in favor of *what*: not who appoints the national speech, but what creates the standard.

If, still sticking to his formulation, James had dared to give his private answer, he might have announced: "Young women, I, Henry James, am that august Who who fixes the firmament of our national speech. Follow me, and you follow excellence." But how had this vast substantial Who that was Henry James come to be fashioned? It was no Who *he* followed. It was instead a great cumulative corporeal What, the voluminous and manifold heritage of Literature he had been saturated in since childhood. In short, he read: he was a reader, he had always read, reading was not so much his passion or his possession as it was his bread, and not so much his bread as it was the primordial fountain of his life. Ludicrous it is to say of Henry James that he read, he was a reader! As much say of Vesuvius that it erupted, or of Olympus that it kept the gods. But reading—just that, *what is read*—is the whole, the intricate, secret of his exemplum.

The vulgarity of the low press James could see for himself. On the other hand, he had never set foot in an American public school (his education was, to say the least, Americanly untypical), and he had no inkling of any representative curriculum. Nevertheless it was this public but meticulous curriculum that was to set the standard; and it was a curriculum not far different from what James might have found for himself, exploring on his own among his father's shelves.

A year or so after my mother stepped off the horsecar into Madison Street, she was given Sir Walter Scott's "The Lady of the Lake" to read as a school assignment. She never forgot it. She spoke of it all her life. Mastering it was the triumph of her childhood, and though, like every little girl of her generation, she read *Pollyanna,* and in the last months of her eighty-third year every word of Willa Cather, it was "The Lady of the Lake" that enduringly typified achievement, education, culture.

Some seventy-odd years after my mother studied it at P.S. 131 on the Lower East Side, I open "The Lady of the Lake" and take in lines I have never looked on before:

> Not thus, in ancient days of Caledon,
>> Was thy voice mute amid the festal crowd,
> When lay of hopeless love, or glory won,
>> Aroused the fearful, or subdued the proud.
> At each according pause was heard aloud
>> Thine ardent symphony sublime and high!
> Fair dames and crested chiefs attention bowed;

For still the burden of thy minstrelsy
Was Knighthood's dauntless deed, and Beauty's matchless eye.

O wake once more! how rude soe'er the hand
    That ventures o'er thy magic maze to stray;
O wake once more! though scarce my skill command
    Some feeble echoing of thine earlier lay;
Though harsh and faint, and soon to die away,
    And all unworthy of thy nobler strain,
Yet if one heart throb higher at its sway,
    The wizard note has not been touched in vain.
Then silent be no more! Enchantress, wake again!

My mother was an immigrant child, the poorest of the poor. She had come in steerage; she knew not a word of English when she stepped off the horsecar into Madison Street; she was one of the innumerable unsleeping aliens. Her teachers were the entirely ordinary daughters of the Irish immigration (as my own teachers still were, a generation on), and had no special genius, and assuredly no special training (a certain Miss Walsh was in fact ferociously hostile), for the initiation of a Russian Jewish child into the astoundingly distant and incomprehensible premises of such poetry. And yet it was accomplished, and within the briefest period after the voyage in steerage.

What was accomplished was not merely that my mother "learned" this sort of poetry—i.e., could read and understand it. She learned what it represented in the widest sense—not only the legendary heritage implicit in each and every word and phrase (to a child from Hlusk, where the wooden sidewalks sank into mud and the peasants carried water buckets dangling from shoulder yokes, what was "minstrelsy," what was "Knighthood's dauntless deed," what on earth was a "wizard note"?), but what it represented in the American social and tribal code. The quickest means of stitching all this down is to say that what "The Lady of the Lake" stood for, in the robes and tapestries of its particular English, was the received tradition exemplified by Bryn Mawr in 1905, including James's presence there as commencement speaker. The American standard derived from an American institution: the public school, free, democratic, open, urgent, pressing on the young a program of reading not so much for its "literary value," though this counted too, as for the stamp of Heritage. All this James overlooked. He had no firsthand sense of it. He was himself the grandson of an ambitiously money-making Irish immigrant; but his father, arranging his affluent life as a meta physician,

Cynthia Ozick

had separated himself from public institutions—from any practical idea, in fact, of institutions *per se*—and dunked his numerous children in and out of school on two continents, like a nomad in search of the wettest oasis of all. It was hardly a wonder that James, raised in a self-enclosed clan, asserted the ascendancy of manners over institutions, or that he ascribed to personal speech "positively the history of the national character, almost the history of the people," or that he spoke of the "ancestral circle" as if kinship were the only means to transmit that national character and history.

It was as if James, who could imagine nearly everything, had in this instance neglected imagination itself: kinship as construct and covenant, kinship imagined—and what are institutions if not invented kinship circles: society as contract? In the self-generating Enlightenment society of the American founding philosophers, it was uniquely the power of institutions to imagine, to create, kinship and community. The Constitution, itself a kind of covenant or imaginatively established "ancestral circle," created peoplehood out of an idea, and the public schools, begotten and proliferated by that idea, implemented the Constitution; and more than the Constitution. They implemented and transmitted the old cultural mesh. Where there was so much diversity, the institution substituted for the clan, and discovered—through a kind of civic magnetism—that it could transmit, almost as effectively as the kinship clan itself, "the very core of our social heritage."

To name all this the principle of the Melting Pot is not quite right, and overwhelmingly insufficient. The Melting Pot called for imitation. Imagination, which is at the heart of institutionalized covenants, promotes what is intrinsic. I find on my shelves two old textbooks used widely in the "common schools" James deplored. The first is *A Practical English Grammar*, dated 1880, the work of one Albert N. Raub, A.M., Ph.D. ("Author of 'Raub's Readers,' 'Raub's Arithmetics,' 'Plain Educational Talks, Etc.'"). It is a relentless volume, thorough, determined, with no loopholes; every permutation of the language is scrutinized, analyzed, accounted for. It is also a commonplace book replete with morally instructive quotations, some splendidly familiar. Each explanatory chapter is followed by "Remarks," "Cautions," and "Exercises," and every Exercise includes a high-minded hoard of literary Remarks and Cautions. For instance, under Personal Pronouns:

Though the mills of God grind slowly,
    yet they grind exceedingly small;
Though with patience He stands waiting,
    with exactness grinds He all.

This above all, to thine own self be true,
And it must follow, as the night the day,
Thou canst not then be false to any man.

These are thy glorious works, Parent of good,
    Almighty! Thine this universal frame.

Alas! they had been friends in youth,
But whispering tongues can poison truth;
And constancy lives in realms above,
And life is thorny, and youth is vain;
And to be wroth with one we love
Doth work like madness on the brain.

So much for Longfellow, Shakespeare, Milton, and Coleridge. But also Addison, Cowper, Pope, Ossian, Scott, Ruskin, Thomson, Wordsworth, Trollope, Gray, Byron, Whittier, Lowell, Holmes, Moore, Collins, Hood, Goldsmith, Bryant, Dickens, Bacon, Franklin, Locke, the Bible—these appear throughout, in the form of addenda to Participles, Parsing, Irregular Verbs, and the rule of the Nominative Independent; in addition, a handful of lost presences: Bushnell, H. Wise, Wayland, Dwight, Blair, Mrs. Welby (nearly the only woman in the lot), and Anon. The *content* of this volume is not its subject matter, neither its syntactic lesson nor its poetic maxims. It is the voice of a language; rather, of language itself, language as texture, gesture, innateness. To read from beginning to end of a schoolbook of this sort is to recognize at once that James had it backwards and upside down: it is not that manners lead culture; it is culture that leads manners. What shapes culture—this is not a tautology or a redundancy—is culture. "Who makes the country?" was the latent question James was prodding and poking, all gingerly; and it was the wrong—because unanswerable—one. "What kind of country shall we have?" was Albert N. Raub's question, and it *was* answerable. The answer lay in the reading given to the children in the schoolhouses: the institutionalization, so to say, of our common speech at its noblest.

My second text is even more striking: *The Etymological Reader*, edited by Epes Sargent and Amasa May, dated 1872. "We here offer to the schools of the United States," begins the Preface, "the first systematic attempt to associate the study of etymology with exercises in reading." What follows is a blitz of "vocabulary," Latin roots, Saxon roots, prefixes, and suffixes, but these quickly subside, and nine-tenths of this inventive book is an anthology engaging in its richness, range, and ambition. "Lochinvar" is here; so are the

Declaration of Independence and selections from Shakespeare; so is Shelley's "To a Skylark"; so is the whole "Star-Spangled Banner." But also: "Description of a Bee Hunt," "Creation a Continuous Work," "The Sahara," "Anglo-Saxon and Norman French," "Conversation," "Progress of Civilization," "Effects of Machinery," "On the Choice of Books," "Our Indebtedness to the Greeks," "Animal Heat," "Corruptions of Language," "Jerusalem from the Mount of Olives," "On the Act of Habeas Corpus," "Individual Character," "Going Up in a Balloon," and dozens of other essays. Among the writers: Dickens, Macaulay, Wordsworth, Irving, Mark Twain, Emerson, Channing, John Stuart Mill, Carlyle, De Quincey, Tennyson, Mirabeau, and so on and so on.

It would be foolish to consider *The Etymological Reader* merely charming, a period piece, "Americana"—it is too immediately useful, too uncompromising, and, for the most part, too enduring to be dismissed with condescension.

It was one of those heads which Guido has often painted—mild, pale, penetrating, free from all commonplace ideas of fat, contented ignorance, looking downward upon the earth; it looked forward, but looked as if it looked at something beyond this world. How one of his order came by it, Heaven above, who let it fall upon a monk's shoulders, best knows; but it would have suited a Brahmin, and had I met it upon the plains of Hindostan, I had reverenced it.

To come upon Sterne, just like this, all of a sudden, for the first time, pressed between Southey's sigh ("How beautiful is night!") and Byron's "And the might of the Gentile, unsmote by the sword, / Hath melted like snow in the glance of the Lord"—to come upon Sterne, just like that, is to come upon an unexpected human fact. Such textbooks filled vessels more fundamental than the Melting Pot—blood vessels, one might venture. Virtuous, elevated, striving and stirring, the best that has been thought and said: thus the voice of the common schools. A fraction of their offerings had a heroic, or monumental, quality, on the style perhaps of George Washington's head. They stood for the power of civics. But the rest were the purest belles-lettres: and it was belles-lettres that were expected to be the fountainhead of American civilization, including civility. Belles-lettres provided style, vocabulary, speech itself; and also the themes of Victorian seriousness: conscience and work. Elevated literature was the model for an educated tongue. Sentences, like conscience and work, were demanding.

What did these demanding sentences do in and for society? First, they demanded to be studied. Second, they demanded sharpness and cadence in writing. They promoted, in short, literacy—and not merely literacy, but a vigorous and manifold recognition of literature as a *force*. They promoted an educated class. Not a hereditarily educated class, but one that had been introduced to the initiating and shaping texts early in life, almost like the hereditarily educated class itself.

All that, we know, is gone. Where once the *Odyssey* was read in the schools, in a jeweled and mandarin translation, Holden Caulfield takes his stand. He is winning and truthful, but he is not demanding. His sentences reach no higher than his gaze. The idea of belles-lettres, when we knock our unaccustomed knees against it, looks archaic and bizarre: rusted away, like an old car chassis. The content of belles-lettres is the property of a segregated caste or the dissipated recollections of the very old.

Belles-lettres in the schools fashioned both speech and the art of punctuation—the sound and the look of nuance. Who spoke well pointed well; who pointed well spoke well. One was the skill of the other. No one now punctuates for nuance—or, rather, whoever punctuates for nuance is "corrected." Copy editors do not know the whole stippled range of the colon or the semicolon, do not know that "O" is not "oh," do not know that not all juxtaposed adjectives are coordinate adjectives; and so forth. The degeneration of punctuation and word-by-word literacy is pandemic among English speakers: this includes most poets and novelists. To glimpse a typical original manuscript undoctored by a copy editor is to suffer a shock at the sight of ignorant imprecision; and to examine a densely literate manuscript after it has passed through the leveling hands of a copy editor is again to suffer a shock at the sight of ignorant imprecision.

In 1930 none of this was so. The relentlessly gradual return of aural culture, beginning with the telephone (a farewell to letterwriting), the radio, the motion picture, and the phonograph, speeded up by the television set, the tape recorder, and lately the video recorder, has by now, after half a century's worth of technology, restored us to the pre-literate status of face-to-face speech. And mass literacy itself is the fixity of no more than a century, starting with the advancing reforms following the industrial revolution—reforms introducing, in England, the notion of severely limited leisure to the classes that formerly had labored with no leisure at all. Into that small new recreational space fell what we now call the "nineteenth-century novel," in both its supreme and its lesser versions. The act of reading—the *work*, in fact, of the act of reading—appeared to complicate and intensify the most ordinary intelligence. The silent physiological translation of letters into sounds, the leaping eye encoding, the transmigration of blotches on a page into the story of, say, Dorothea Brooke, must surely count among the most intricate of biological and transcendent designs. In 1930 the so-called shopgirl, with her pulp romance, is habitually engaged in this electrifying webwork of eye and mind. In 1980 she reverts, via electronics, to the simple speaking face. And then it is all over, by and large, for mass literacy. High literacy has been the province of an elite class since Sumer; there is nothing novel in having a caste of princely readers. But the culture of mass literacy, in its narrow period from 1830 to 1930, was something else: Gutenberg's revolution did not take effect in a popular sense—did not properly begin—until the rise of the middle class at the time, approximately, of the English Reform Act of 1832. Addison's *Spectator*, with its Latin epigraphs, was read by gentlemen, but Dickens was read by nearly everyone. The almost universal habit of reading for recreation or excitement conferred the greatest complexity on the greatest number, and the thinnest sliver of history expressed it: no more than a single century. It flashed by between aural culture and aural culture, no longer-lived than a lightning bug. The world of the VCR is closer to the pre-literate society of traveling mummers than it is to that of the young Scott Fitzgerald's readership in 1920.

When James read out "The Question of Our Speech" in 1905, the era of print supremacy was still in force, unquestioned; the typewriter and the electric light had arrived to strengthen it, and the telephone was greeted only as a convenience, not a substitute. The telephone was particularly welcome—not much was lost that ought not to have been lost in the omission of letters agreeing to meet the 8:42 on Tuesday night on the east platform. Since then, the telephone has abetted more serious losses: exchanges between artists and thinkers; documents of family and business relations; quarrels and cabals among politicians; everything that in the past tended to be preserved for biographers and cultural historians. The advent of the computer used as word processor similarly points toward the wiping out of any *progressive* record of thought; the grain of a life can lie in the illumination of the crossed-out word.

But James, in the remoteness of post-Victorian technology, spoke unshadowed by these threatened disintegrations among the community of the literate; he spoke in the very interior of what seemed then to be a permanently post-aural culture. He read from a manuscript; later that year, Houghton, Mifflin published it together with another lecture, this one far more famous, "The Lesson of Balzac." We cannot hear his voice on a phonograph record, as we can hear his fellow self-exile T. S. Eliot's; and this, it might be said, is another kind of loss. If we cherish photographs of Henry James's extraordinarily striking head with its lantern eyes, we can regret the loss of a filmed interview of the kind that nowadays captures and delivers into the future Norman Mailer and John Updike. The return to an aural culture is, obviously, not *all* a question of loss; only of the most significant loss of all: the widespread nurture by portable print; print as water, and sometimes wine. It was, in its small heyday (we must now begin to say was), the most glorious work of the eye-linked brain.

And in the heyday of that glorious work, James made a false analysis. In asking for living models, his analysis belonged to the old aural culture, and he did not imagine its risks. In the old aural culture, speech was manner, manner *was* manners, manners did teach the tone of the civilized world. In the new aural culture, speech remains manner, manner becomes manners, manners go on teaching the tone of the world. The difference is that the new aural culture, based, as James urged, on emulation, is governed from below. Emulation as a principle cannot control its sources. To seize on only two blatancies: the guerrilla toy of the urban underclass, the huge and hugely loud portable radio—the "ghetto blaster"—is adopted by affluent middle-class white adolescents; so is the locution "Hey, man," which now crosses both class and gender. James worried about the replacement in America of "Yes" by "Yeah" (and further by the comedic "Yep"), but its source was the drawl endemic to the gilt-and-plush parlors of the upper middle class. "Yeah" did not come out of the street; it went into the street. But it is also fairly certain that the "Yeah"-sayers, whatever their place in society, could not have been strong readers, even given the fissure that lies between reading and the style of one's talk. The more attached one is to the community of readers, the narrower the fissure. In a society where belles-lettres are central to education of the young, what controls speech is the degree of absorption in print. Reading governs speech, governs tone, governs manner and manners and civilization. "It is easier to overlook any question of speech than to trouble about it," James complained, "but then it is also easier to snort or neigh, to growl or 'meaow,' than to articulate and intonate."

And yet he overlooked the primacy of the high act of reading. No one who, in the age of conscience and work, submitted to "The Lady of the Lake," or parsed under the aegis of Albert N. Raub, or sent down a bucket into *The Etymological Reader*, was likely to snort or neigh or emit the cry of the tabby. Agreed, it was a more publicly formal and socially encrusted age than ours, and James was more publicly formal and socially encrusted than many of his contemporaries: he was an old-fashioned gentleman. He had come of age during the Civil War. His clothes were laid out by a manservant. His standard was uncompromising. All the same, he missed how and where his own standard ruled. He failed to discover it in the schoolhouses, to which it had migrated after the attenuation of the old aural culture. To be sure, the school texts, however aspiring, could not promise to the children of the poor, or to the children of the immigrants, or to the children of working men, any hope of a manservant; but they *did* promise a habit of speech, more mobilizing and organizing, even, than a valet. The key to American speech was under James's nose. It was at that very moment being turned in a thousand locks. It was opening gate after gate. Those who could read according to an elevated standard could write sufficiently accomplished sentences, and those who could write such sentences could "articulate and intonate."

"Read, read! Read yourself through all the stages of the masters of the language," James might have exhorted the graduates. Instead, he told them to seek "contact and communication, a beneficent contagion," in order to "bring about the happy state—the state of sensibility to tone." It offended him, he confessed, that there were "forces assembled to make you believe that no form of speech is provably better than another." Forty years on, Trolander, Davis, and Papp set their own formidable forces against the forces of relativism in enunciation. Like James, they were zealous to impose their own parochialisms. James did not pronounce the *r* in "mother"; it was, therefore, vulgar to let it be heard. Our Midwestern teachers *did* pronounce the *r*; it was, therefore, vulgar *not* to let it be heard. How, then, one concludes, is any form of speech "provably better than another"? In a relativist era, the forces representing relativism in enunciation have for the moment won the argument, it seems; yet James has had his way all the same. With the exception of the South and parts of the East Coast, there is very nearly a uniform *vox Americana*. And we have everywhere a uniform "tone." It is in the streets and in the supermarkets, on the radio and on television; and it is low, low, low. In music, in speech, in manner, the upper has learned to imitate the lower. Cheapened imprecise speech is the triumph of James's tribute to emulation; it is the only possible legacy that could have come of the principle of emulation.

Then why did James plead for vocal imitation instead of reading? He lived in a sea of reading, at the highest tide of literacy, in the time of the crashing of its billows. He did not dream that the sea would shrink, that it was impermanent, that we would return, through the most refined technologies, to the aural culture. He had had his own dealings with a continuing branch of the aural culture—the theater. He had written for it as if for a body of accomplished readers, and it turned on him with contempt. "Forget not," he warned in the wake of his humiliation as a playwright, "that you write for the stupid—that is, your maximum of refinement must meet the minimum of intelligence of the audience—the intelligence, in other words, of the biggest ass it may conceivably contain. It is a most unholy trade!" He was judging, in this outcry, all those forms that arrange for the verbal to bypass the eye and enter solely through the ear. The ear is, for subtlety of interpretation, a coarser organ than the eye; it follows that nearly all verbal culture designed for the ear is broader, brighter, larger, louder, simpler, less intimate, more insistent—more *theatrical*—than any page of any book.

For the population in general, the unholy trades—they are now tremendously in the plural, having proliferated—have rendered reading nearly obsolete, except as a source of data and as a means of record-keeping—"warehousing information."' For this the computer is an admittedly startling advance over Pharaoh's indefatigably meticulous scribes, notwithstanding the lofty liturgical poetry that adorned the ancient records, offering a tendril of beauty among the granary lists. Pragmatic reading cannot die, of course, but as the experience that feeds *Homo ridens*, reading is already close to moribund. In the new aural culture of America, intellectuals habitually define "film" as "art" in the most solemn sense, as a counterpart of the literary novel, and ridicule survivors of the age of "movies" as naifs incapable of making the transition from an old form of popular entertainment to a new form of serious expression meriting a sober equation with written art—as if the issue had anything to do with what is inherently complex in the medium, rather than with what is inherently complex in the recipient of the medium. Undoubtedly any movie is more "complicated" than any book; and also more limited by the apparatus of the "real." As James noted, the maker of aural culture brings to his medium a "maximum of refinement"—i.e., he does the best he can with what he has to work with; sometimes he is even Shakespeare. But the job of sitting in a theater or in a movie house or at home in front of a television set is not so reciprocally complex as the wheels-within-wheels job of reading almost anything at all (including the comics). Reading is an act of imaginative conversion. That specks on a paper can turn into tale or philosophy is as deep a marvel as alchemy or wizardry. A secret brush construes phantom portraits. In the proscenium or the VCR everything is imagined *for* one: there is nothing to do but see and hear, and what's there is what is literally there. When film is "poetic," it is almost never because of language, but rather because of the resemblance to paintings or engravings—one thinks of the knight on a horse in a field of flowers in Bergman's *The Virgin Spring*. Where film is most art, it is least a novelty.

The new aural culture is prone to appliance-novelty—a while ago who could have predicted the video recorder or the hand-held miniature television set, and who now knows what variations and inventions lie ahead? At the same time there is a rigidity to the products of the aural culture—like those static Egyptian sculptures, stylistically unaltered for three millennia, that are brilliantly executed but limited in imaginative intent.

In the new aural culture there is no prevalent belles-lettres curriculum to stimulate novel imaginative intent, that "wizard note" of the awakened Enchantress; what there is is replication—not a reverberation or an echo, but a copy. The Back to Basics movement in education, which on the surface looks as if it is calling for revivification of a belles-lettres syllabus, is not so much reactionary as lost in literalism, or *trompe l'oeil*: another example of the replication impulse of the new aural culture, the culture of theater. Only in a *trompe l'oeil* society would it occur to anyone to "bring back the old values" through bringing back the McGuffey Reader—a scenic designer's idea, and still another instance of the muddle encouraged by the notion of "emulation." The celebration of the McGuffey Reader can happen only in an atmosphere where "film," a copyist's medium, is taken as seriously as a book.

A book is not a "medium" at all; it is far spookier than that, one of the few things-in-themselves that we can be sure of, a Platonic form that can inhabit a virtual infinity of experimental incarnations: any idea, any story, any body of poetry, any incantation, in any language. Above all, a book is the riverbank for the river of language. Language without the riverbank is only television talk—a free fall, a loose splash, a spill. And that is what an aural society, following a time of complex literacy, finally admits to: spill and more spill. James had nothing to complain of: he flourished in a period when whoever read well could speak well; the rest was provincialism—or call it, in kindness, regional exclusiveness. Still, the river of language—to cling to the old metaphor—ran most forcefully when confined to the banks that governed its course. But we who come after the hundred-year hegemony of the ordinary reader, we who see around us, in all these heaps of appliances (each one a plausible "electronic miracle"), the dying heaves of the caste-free passion for letters, should know how profoundly—and possibly how irreversibly—the mummers have claimed us.

Old Hand As Novice

I remember precisely the moment I knew I wanted to write a play: it was in an out-of-the-way theater, the Promenade, on Broadway in the seventies, somewhere in the middle of the second act of *The Common Pursuit*, a melancholic comedy by the British playwright Simon Gray. The play was a send-up of the passionate Cambridge cenacle attached to *Scrutiny*, that fabled literary periodical presided over by F. R. Leavis, an eminent critic of forty years ago; it followed the rise and fall and erotic history of its madly literary protagonists from cocky youth to sour middle age. Madly literary myself, I sat electrified in the seductive dark of the Promenade, flooded by an overpowering wish: Some day! And I remember precisely the moment I discovered the first sinister fumes brewed up by those liars and obfuscators who dare to term themselves "revisionists," but are more accurately named Holocaust deniers. It was the late summer of 1961. My husband and I had just rented an apartment in a building so new that the fresh plaster, not yet fully dried, was found to be congenial to a repulsive army of moisture-seeking insects rather prettily called silverfish. How to rid ourselves of this plague? Off we went to the town library, to look for a book on household infestation. The helpful volume we hit on happened to be translated, and very nicely so, from the German. It recommended a certain gas with a record of remarkable success in the extermination of vermin. An asterisk led to a slyly impassive footnote at the bottom of the page, utterly deadpan and meanly corrupt: "Zyklon B, used during the Second World War."

How the delectable theatrical dark came to be entangled with the dark of Zyklon B, the death-camp gas, I can hardly fathom; but when, after years of feeling unready, I did finally undertake to write a play, it turned out to be tempestuously and bitterly political—nothing in the least like that dream of literary laughter the Promenade had inspired long before. Its salient theme was Holocaust denial: a trap contrived out of cunning, deceit, and wicked surprise. Yet a not inconsequential literary issue stuck from the start to the outer flanks of my play, and continued to dog it: the ill-humored question of the playwright's credentials.

Of course there is nothing new in a writer's crossing from one form into another; no one is startled, or aggrieved, by a novelist turned essayist, or by a poet who ventures into fiction. The radical divide is not in the writer, but in the mode, and mood, of reception. Reading is the expression of a profound social isolation. As in getting born or dying, you are obliged to do it alone; there is no other way. Theater—like religion, its earliest incarnation— is a communal rite. Study a row of faces transfixed in unison by a scene on a stage, and you will fall into a meditation on anatomical variety irradiated by a kind of dramaturgical monotheism: the infusion of a single godly force into so many pairs of luminously staring eyes.

Theater is different from fiction, yes; an untried genre for the novice playwright, a dive into strangeness: that mysterious hiatus in the dark, that secret promissory drawing of breath just before the stage lights brighten. Nevertheless a novice is not the same as an amateur. An amateur worships— is glamorized by—the trappings of an industry, including the excitements of being "inside." Theater industry (or call it, as anthropologists nowadays like to do, theater culture), with all its expertise, protocol, hierarchy, jargon, tradition, its existential hard knocks and heartbreak, its endemic optimism and calloused cynicism, its experience with audiences, its penchant for spectacle, still cannot teach a writer the writer's art—which is not on the stage, but in the ear and in the brain. Though a novice playwright will certainly be attentive to "technique," to "knowhow," real apprenticeship is ultimately always to the self; a writer's lessons are ineluctably internal. As a beginning novelist long ago, I learned to write dialogue not in a fiction workshop ruled by a sophisticated "mentor," but by reading Graham Greene's *The Heart of the Matter* over and over again. There were uncanny reverberations in those short, plain sentences, and a peculiarly suspenseful arrest of a character's intent. The perfected work was the mentor.

Let me not arrogantly misrepresent. There is plenty for an uninitiated playwright to learn from the living air of a reading, a rehearsal, a developing performance in the theater itself; and from an actor's cadence or lift of the eyelid; and from an impassioned talk with a seasoned playwright (and no one is more openly generous than lifelong playwrights, who are a band of mutually sympathizing cousins); and above all from a trusted and trusting director who recognizes the writer *as writer*. Besides, a novelist's perspective is hardly akin to a playwright's. Novels are free to diverge, to digress, to reflect, to accrete. Proust is a gargantuan soliloquizer. Tolstoy encompasses whole histories. George Eliot pauses for psychological essays. A novel is like the physicist's premise of an expanding universe—horizon after horizon, firmament sailing past firmament. But a play is just the reverse: the fullness of the universe drawn down into a single succinct atom—the all-consuming compactness and density of the theorist's black hole. Everything converges in the dot that is the stage. A novelist seeking to become a playwright will uncover new beauty—structure and concision; the lovely line of the spine and the artfully integrated turn of each vertebra.

Yet always a gauntlet is thrown down before the newcomer playwright (especially one who has arrived from the famously sequestered craft of fiction), and that is the many-fingered image of "collaboration." I want to say quickly—against all the power and authority of theatrical magnates and magi, against the practice and conviction of all those who know more and better than an uninformed interloper like myself—that the term "collaboration," as I have heard it used again and again, is a fake, a fib, and a sham. The truth stands clarified: no matter what the genre, a writer is necessarily an autonomous, possessed, and solitary figure generating furies. Imagination is a self-contained burning, a fire that cannot be fed from without. The idea of a "collaborative art" is an idea out of Oz—i.e. it supplies you with a phony wizard haranguing into a megaphone. No one can claim ascendancy over a writer's language or imagination, and anyone who tries—and succeeds—is an invader, an editor, or just a run-of-the-mill boss. Writers cloutless and consequently docile will likely acquiesce—but what will come out of it is what editors and bosses always get: something edited, something obliging. An artificial voice. A dry wadi where the heart of a river might have roiled. In the name of a putative collaborative art, a novice playwright (even if an old hand as a writer) will be manipulated by the clever, patronized by the callow, humiliated by the talentless. Generations of cliches will pour down. To become master over a writer is not, as it happens, to become a master of writing.

But if the notion of a collaborative art is simply authoritarian make-believe, the experience of *skills* in collaboration is the rapt and gorgeous satisfaction of theater—the confluence of individual artists, each conceptually and temperamentally singular. The brainy director's orchestral sensibility; the actors' transformative magickings (a gesture over nothingness will build you the solidest phantom table conceivable); dramatic sculptures hewn of purest light; inklings sewn into a scene by the stitch of a tiny sound; a dress that is less a costume than a wise corroboration; a set that lands you unerringly in the very place you need to be; and the sine qua non of the producers' endlessly patient acts of faith—all these carry their visionary plenitude.

Novice playwrights—and veterans, too, I believe-will fall on their knees in gratitude.

To return to the matter of credentials. A bird can fly over any continent you choose; it's the having wings that counts. A writer can be at home in novel, story, essay, or play; it's the breathing inside a blaze of words that counts. However new to theater culture, a writer remains exactly that—the only genuine authority over the words and the worlds they embody.

And if the play should vanish away without being realized in a theater before an audience (nine times out of ten, plays are snowflakes in July), the disappointed scribbler will peacefully turn back to the blessed privacy of a secluded desk—where the writer not only acts all the roles, wears all the costumes, and dreams all the scenery, but is both determined producer and tireless director, unwaveringly committed to fruition; and where there is no mistaking who is sovereign.

Lovesickness

1.

Once, when I had already been married for a time, I went to a friend's wedding and fell in love with the bridegroom. It happened out of the blue, in an instant, as unexpectedly as a sneeze. I was not responsible for it; it came upon me; it was an incursion, an invasion—a possession, like that of a dybbuk. Or it was what diplomats call an "intervention," an intact sovereign tract subjected without warning to military fire. Or it was a kind of spell, the way the unearthly music of a fairy-tale pipe casts a helpless enchantment, so that, willy-nilly, you are compelled to dance and dance without surcease.

The bride had a small head and a Cheshire-cat smile. I had known her since childhood. Together, under the heavy-hanging trees, we had gathered acorns and pretended to dine on them. But we were not confidantes; we were not close. We had differing temperaments. She was humorous: her jokiness cut with an icy ironic blade. I was naïve and grave and obtuse. She was diligent at the violin and played it well. I hid when the piano teacher rang the doorbell. She was acutely and cleverly mathematical. I was an arithmetical imbecile. She was tall and I was short: we were seriously divided by our arms' reach. Often I felt between us a jealous tremor. I was jealous because she was almost two years younger, and even in girlhood I lamented the passing of my prime. At eleven, I scribbled a story and appended a lie: "By the Young Author," I wrote, "Age Nine."

The bride was standing under the wedding canopy in a white dress, her acorn head ringed by a wreath, when lovesickness struck. The venerable image of arrow or dart is crucially exact. Though I had met the bridegroom once before, in the long green darkening tangle of a meadow at dusk—it was a game of Frisbee—I had been unmoved. His thighs were taut, his calf-sinews thick; he had the inky curly hair of a runner on a Greek amphora. The white plastic disk arced into a blackening sky, along the trajectory of an invisible yet perfect night-rainbow. He sprinted after it; his catch was deft, like the pluck of a lyre. He was an Englishman. He was a mathematician. He was nothing to me.

But when I saw him under the wedding canopy next to my childhood friend, I was seized and shaken by a dazing infatuation so stormy, so sibyl-line, so like a divination, that I went away afterward hollowed-out. Infatuation was not an added condition: it was loss—the strangeness of having lost what had never been mine.

The newly married pair departed for England, by sea, in a sluggishly churning vessel. A shipboard postcard arrived: on the one side a view of the ship itself, all serene white flanks pocked by portholes, and on the other an unfamiliar script. It was the new husband's. I studied his handwriting— examined its loops and troughs, the blue turns of ink where they thickened and narrowed, the height of the *l*'s and *d*'s, the width of the crossbars, the hillocks of the *m*'s and *n*'s, the connecting tails and the interrupting gaps. The sentences themselves were sturdy and friendly, funny and offhand— entirely by-the-by. Clearly, composing this note was a lunch-table diversion. "You do it," I imagined the new wife telling the new husband. In a minute and a half it was done.

For weeks I kept the card under my eye; it was as if the letters of each word were burning, as if the air above and below the letters were shuddering in an invisible fire. The words, the sentences, were of no moment; I hardly saw them; but the letters crazed me. They were the new husband's nerves, they were the vibrations of his pulse, his fingers' pressure, his most intimate mark. They were more powerful than the imprint of his face and shoulders, which had anyhow begun to fade. What I remembered was the hand leaping up into the dark to snatch the Frisbee out of the sky. That same hand had shaped these intoxicating yet regimented letters. A mathematician's letters: as upright and precise as numbers.

Infatuation has its own precision. It focuses on its object as directly and sharply as sunlight through a magnifying glass: it enlarges and clarifies, but it also scorches. What we call lovesickness, or desire, is deliberate in that way—the way of exactitude and scrupulous discrimination—and at the same time it is wildly undeliberate, zigzag, unpremeditated, driven, even loony.

What I finally did with—or *to*—that postcard was both meticulously focused and rapaciously mad.

It was the hand that my desire had fixed on—or, rather, the force and the brain that flowed from that hand. I wanted to get into that hand—to become it, to grow myself into its blood vessels, to steal its fire. I had already felt the boil of that fire under my own hand: the phosphorescent threads of the letters, as blue as veins, bled hotly into the paper's grain.

And I knew what I would do. I took my pencil and slowly, slowly traced over the letters of the first word. Slowly, slowly. The sensation was that of a novice dancer mimicking the movements of a ballet master; or of a mute mouth speaking through a ventriloquist; or of a shadow following a light; or of a mountain climber ascending the upward slope of a *t*, stopping to rest on the horizontal shelf of the crossbar, again toiling upward, turning, again resting on a ledge, and then sliding downward along a sheerly vertical wall.

Letter by letter, day by day, I pressed the point of my pencil into the fleshly lines of the sea-borne bridegroom's pen; I jumped my pencil over his jumps and skips, those minute blank sites of his pen's apnea.

In a week or so it was finished. I had coupled with him. Every word was laboriously Siamese-twinned. Each of the letters bore on its back the graphite coat I had slowly, slowly laid over it. Breath by breath, muscle by muscle, nerve by nerve, with the concentration of a monkish scribe, with the dedication of a Torah scribe, I had trod in his tracks and made his marks. Like a hunter, I had pursued his marks; I had trapped and caged them. I was his fanatical, indelible Doppelgänger. And a forger besides.

2.

All this was done in secret: lovesickness is most often silent, private, concealed. But sometimes it is wily and reckless, thrusting itself into the world like a novelist on the loose. To wit: I once observed an illustrious young professor of philosophy swinging a small boy between his knees. The child was rapturous; the man went on teasing and swinging. He had a merry, thin, mobile face—not at all professorial. And yet his reputation was dauntingly fierce: he was an original; his famous Mind crackled around him like an electric current, or like a charged whip fending off mortals less dazzlingly endowed. It was said that his intellectual innovations and uncommon insights had so isolated him from ordinary human pursuits, and his wants were so sparse, that he slept on a couch in his mother's apartment in an outer borough. And here he was, laughing and swinging—himself a boy at play.

The blow of lovesickness came hammering down. I had no connection of any kind with this wizard of thought. It was unlikely that I could ever aspire to one.

But I had just then been reading Peter Quennell's biography of Lord

Byron, and was captivated by its portrait of Lady Caroline Lamb, a married flirt who had seduced and conquered Byron (or vice-versa—both were mercurial and inclined toward escapades). Quennell described Lady Caroline as a volatile woman in search of "some violent, self-justificatory explosion, some crisis in which she could gather up the spasmodic and ill-directed energies that drove her . . . The fever of Romanticism was in her blood." She delighted in spats and subterfuges and secret letters delivered to her lover by a page, who turned out to be Lady Caroline in disguise. It was she who invented Byron's most celebrated epithet—*Mad, bad, and dangerous to know.* This would do admirably for Lady Caroline.

Certainly Byron found her dangerous to know. When, exasperated, he tired of her, he discovered she was impossible to get rid of. He called her "a little volcano," and complained that her fascination was "unfortunately coupled with a total want of common conduct." In the end she became a pest, an affliction, a plague. In vindictive verses he pronounced her a fiend. She was a creature of ruse and caprice and jealousy; she would not let him go. She chased after him indefatigably, she badgered him, she burned him in effigy, she stabbed herself. And she wrote him letters.

The fever of Romanticism was in my blood; I had been maddened by a hero of imagination, a man who could unravel the skeins of logic that braid human cognition. Byron had his club-foot; my philosopher was still spending his nights on his mother's couch. Byron spoke of his pursuer as a volcano; I could at least leak quantities of epistolary lava. And so, magnetized and wanting to mystify, I put on a disguise and began my chase: I wrote letters. They were love letters; they were letters of enthrallment, of lovesickness. I addressed them to the philosopher's university and signed them all, in passionately counterfeit handwriting, "Lady Caroline Lamb."

3.

But what of lovesickness in reverse? The arrow not suffered but inadvertently shot? The wound not taken but blindly caused?

The Second World War was just over; the college cafeteria swarmed with professed Communists, grim veterans on the G.I. Bill, girls flaunting Edwardian skirts down to their ankles in the New Look style, and a squat square mustached fellow who, when anyone inquired after his politics, insisted he was a monarchist working for the restoration of his dynasty. There was, in addition, an aristocratic and very young Turkish boy, a prodigy, whose father was attached to the United Nations and whose mother wore the veil. The Turkish boy and I studied Latin together, and sometimes spoke of *amor intellectualis*—but intellectual love rooted in a common admiration of Catullus's ode to kissing was too heated, or not heated enough. In the cafeteria I was often ambushed by spasms of bewitchment—over a green-eyed sophomore, for instance, with a radio-announcer voice, who was himself in love with a harpist called Angel. I waited for him at the foot of a certain staircase, hoping he might come down it. I cultivated one of his classmates in the expectation that I might learn something intimate about my distant love, and I did: his nickname, I was told, was Beanhead. "Beanhead, Beanhead," I would murmur at the bottom of the stairs. All my loves at that time were dreamlike, remote, inconclusive, evanescent.

But one afternoon in winter, a foreign-seeming young man (I had noticed him in the cafeteria, curled over a notebook) followed me home. What made him appear foreign was his intensity, his strict stride, his unembarrassed persistence; and also the earnest luster of his dangling black bangs, which shielded his eyes like a latticed gate, and freed him to gaze without moderation. Following me home was no easy journey—it was a long, long subway ride to the end of the line. Despite that curtained look, I saw in his face an urgency I knew in myself. Unaccountably, I had become his Beanhead, his Byron, his bridegroom. I pleaded with him not to undertake the trek to the northeast Bronx—what, I privately despaired, would I *do* with him?

He filled an underground hour by explaining himself: he was a Persian in command of the history and poetry of his beautiful country, and with my permission, because at this moment he was unluckily without a nosegay (he was prone to words like nosegay, garland, attar), he would offer me instead a beautiful poem in Arabic. He drew out his notebook and a pen: from its nib flowed a magical calligraphy.

"This is my poem, my original own," he said, "for you," and folded the sheet and slipped it into my copy of Emily Dickinson, exactly at the page where I had underlined "There's a certain Slant of light / On winter afternoons."

"You don't really want to ride all this distance," I said, hoping to shake him off. "Suppose you just get out at the East 86th Street express stop and go right back, all right?"

"Ah," he said, "will the moon abandon the sun?"

But the third time he demanded to come home with me, it was the sun who abandoned the moon. I had had enough of lovelorn importuning. He accepted his dismissal with Persian melancholy, pressing on me yet another poem, his original own, that he had set down in those melodious, undulating Scheherazadean characters. At the entrance to the subway, forbidden to go farther, he declaimed his translation: "There is a garden, a wall, a brook. You are the lily, I am the brook. O wall, permit me to refresh the lily!"

No one is crueler than the conscious object of infatuation: I blew back the black veil of hair, looked into a pair of moonstruck black eyes, and laughed. Meanly, heartlessly.

4.

And once I made a suitor cry. He was, I feared, a genuine suitor. By now the war had long been over, and nearly all the former G.I.s had gladly returned to civilian life. My suitor, though, was still in uniform; he was stationed at an army base on an island in the harbor. He had a tidy blond head on which his little soldier's cap rested; he had little blunt fingers; everything about him was miniature, like a toy soldier. He was elfin, but without elfishness: he was sober, contained, and as neutral as khaki. He put me in mind of a drawing in a children's coloring book: those round clear pale eyes anticipating blueness, that firm outline beyond which no crayon would ever stray. He had a kind of blankness waiting to be filled in. On weekends, when he was free, he came to call with a phonograph record under his arm. We sat side by side, sternly taking in the music. We were two sets of blank out-lines. The music was coloring us in.

One Sunday he brought Richard Strauss's *Death and Transfiguration*. The jacket supplied the title in German, *Tod und Verklärung*, and a description—tone poem. But it was "transfiguration" that held me. Transfiguration! Would the toy soldier be transformed into live human flesh and begin to move and think on his own?

When he returned to his island, I put *Death and Transfiguration* on the record player and, alone, listened to it over and over again. It colored the empty air, but I saw there would be no transfiguration. Stasis was the toy soldier's lot.

The next Sunday, I piled all the records that had been his gifts into his arms. "At least keep this one. You liked it," he said dolefully: it was *Tod und Verklärung*. But I dropped it on top of the farewell pile and watched him weep, my marble heart immune to any arrow.

5.

Not long afterward, a young man whose eyes were not green, who inspired nothing eccentric or adventurous, who never gave a thought to brooks and lilies or death and transfiguration, who never sought to untangle the knots in the history of human thought, began, with awful consistency, to bring presents of marzipan. So much marzipan was making me sick—though not lovesick.

Ultimately the philosopher learned the true identity of the writer of those love letters; it was reported that he laughed. He is, I believe, still sleeping on his mother's couch.

I never saw the bridegroom again. He never sent another postcard. I suppose he is an unattractive old man by now. Or anyhow I hope so.

The marzipan provider? Reader, I married him.

The Synthetic Sublime

ᴑ

1.

More than any other metropolis of the Western world, New York disappears. It disappears and then it disappears again; or say that it metamorphoses between disappearances, so that every seventy-five years or so another city bursts out, as if against nature—new shapes, new pursuits, new immigrants with their unfamiliar tongues and worried uneasy bustle. In nature, the daffodil blooms, withers, vanishes, and in the spring returns—always a daffodil, always indistinguishable from its precursor. Not so New York, preternatural New York! Go to Twenty-third Street and Eighth Avenue: where is the Grand Opera House, with its statuary and carvings, its awnings and Roman-style cornices? Or reconnoiter Thirteenth Street and Broadway: who can find Wallack's Theatre, where the acclaimed Mrs. Jennings, Miss Plessy Mordaunt, and Mr. J. H. Stoddart once starred, and where, it was said, "even a mean play will be a success"? One hundred years ago, no one imagined the dissolution of these dazzling landmarks; they seemed as inevitable, and as permanent, as our Lincoln Center, with its opera and concerts and plays, and its lively streaming crowds.

In Archaeology 101 they tell a New York joke. It is the year 3000. Archaeologists are sifting through the rubble of over-grown mounds, searching for relics of the lost city that once flourished on this brambly wild site. They dig here and there without reason for excitement (beer cans, a plastic sherd or two, unbiodegradable grocery bags), until at last they uncover what appears to be a primitive concourse of some kind, along which is placed, at surprisingly even intervals, a row of barbaric-looking poles. The poles are molded of an enduring ancient alloy, and each one is topped by a head with a single glass eye and an inch of crude mouth. "Identical sacrificial cultic stands in homage to the city's divinity-king," the archaeologists conclude.

What they have found are Second Avenue parking meters: the Ozymandias of the late twentieth century.

The joke may apply to other modern societies (no contemporaneous city, after all, was as modern as Nebuchadnezzar's Babylon), but New York eludes such ironies. New York will never leave town. It will never sink into a desert waste. Catapult us forward a thousand years, and we won't recognize the place; yet it is certain to be, uninterruptedly, New York, populous, evolving, faithfully inconstant, magnetic, man-made, unnatural—the synthetic sublime. If you walk along Lexington Avenue, say, it isn't easy to be reminded that Manhattan is an island, or even that it lies, like everything else, under an infinitude of sky. New York's sky is jigsawed, cut into geometric pieces glimpsed between towers or caught slantwise across a granite-and-glass ravine. There is no horizon; the lucky penthouses and fifteenth-floor apartments and offices may have long views, but the streets have almost none. At night the white glow that fizzes upward from the city—an inverted electric Niagara—obscures the stars, and except for the Planetarium's windowless mimicry, New York is oblivious of the cosmos. It is nearly as indifferent, by and large, to its marine surround. Walt Whitman once sang of the "tall masts of Mannahatta" and of the "crested and scallop-edg'd waves," but the Staten Island ferry and the Circle Line beat on mastless, and the drumming ribbon of the West Side Highway bars us from the sound and smell of waters rushing or lapping. New York pretends that it is inland and keeps dry indoors and feels shoreless; New York water means faucets and hidden pipes and, now and then, a ceiling leak or the crisis of a burst main. Almost in spite of itself, Riverside Drive looks out on the Hudson, and can, if it likes, remember water. On Manhattan's other flank, the F.D.R. Drive swims alongside the East River like a heavy-chuffing landlubber crocodile, unmindful of the moving water nearby. And here come the bridges, the Queensboro, the Manhattan, the Williamsburg, and finally the Brooklyn, Hart Crane's fabled "harp and altar." These varied spans, squat or spidery—together with the grand George Washington to the north and west—may cry out their poetry of arch and tide and steely ingenuity; but when you ride across in car or bus they are only, again, urban roadways. The tunnels are the same, with their line of lights perpetually alert under the river's tonnage. New York domesticates whatever smacks of sea. And when the two rivers, the Hudson and the East, converge and swallow each other at the Battery's feet, it is the bays alone, the Upper and the Lower, that hurry out to meet the true deep. New York turns its back on the Atlantic. The power and the roar New York looks to are its own.

And if New York is to be misinterpreted and misunderstood, it will not be by future antiquarians, but by its present-day citizens. The Village stymies Wall Street. Chinatown is Greek to Washington Heights. Harlem and Tribeca are mutual enigmas. Neighborhoods are sealed off from one another by the border police of habit and mindset and need and purpose. And there is another border, even more rigid, and surely more disconsolate, than geography: the divide between then and now, a gash that can occur in a single lifetime. Fourth Avenue, masquerading as Park Avenue South, has lost its venerable name; Sixth Avenue—despite its rebirth, half a century ago, as Avenue of the Americas—has not. Where are the hotels of yesteryear? The Astor, the Chatham, the Savoy-Plaza? The Biltmore and its legendary clock? Where are the rows and rows of second-hand book stores that crept northward from Astor Place to Fourteenth Street? Where are Klein's and Wanamaker's and Gimbel's and Ohrbach's? Where are those urban walkers and scribes—Joseph Mitchell, Meyer Berger, Kate Simon, Alfred Kazin? Where is that cloud of gray fedoras that made men in crowds resemble dandelions gone to seed? When, and why, did New York hats give up the ghost? And who was the last to dance in the Rainbow Room?

The Russian poet Joseph Brodsky—born in Leningrad, exiled to New York, buried in Venice—used to say that he wrote to please his predecessors, not his contemporaries. Often enough New York works toward the opposite: it means to impress the here-and-now, which it autographs with an insouciant wrecking ball. Gone is the cleaner-and-dyer; gone is the shoe-repair man. In their stead, a stylish boutique and a fancy-cookie shop. To see—close at hand—how the present is displaced by a newer present, how streets long confident of their particularity can rapidly molt into streets of a startlingly unexpected character, is to be a bit of a god: what is Time, what is Change, to the gods? For New Yorkers, a millennium's worth of difference can be encompassed in six months. Downtown lofts on spooky dark blocks that once creaked under the weight and thunder and grime of industrial machinery are suddenly filled with sofas upholstered in white linen and oak bars on wheels and paintings under track lighting and polyurethaned coffee tables heaped with European magazines. Bryant Park, notorious shady hang-out, blossoms into a cherished noonday amenity. Or else the deserted tenements along the Metro-North line, staring out eyeless and shamefaced at the commuters' train down from Stamford, will, overnight, have had their burnt-out hollows covered over with painted plywood—*trompe l'oeil* windows and flower pots pretending, Potemkin-like, and by municipal decree, that human habitation has resumed.

Yet despite New York's sleight-of-hand transmutations and fool-the-eye pranks, the lady isn't really sawed in half; she leaps up, alive and smiling. If physical excision is the city's ongoing principle, there are, anyhow, certain surprising tenacities and keepsake intuitions. Wait, for instance, for the downtown No. 104 at the bus stop on Broadway and Seventy-second Street, look across the way, and be amazed—what Renaissance palazzo is this? A tall facade with draped female sculptures on either side, arched cornices, patterned polychrome bricks: ornamental flourish vying with ornamental flourish. And then gaze down the road to your right: one vast slab after another, the uncompromising severity of straight lines, brilliantly winking windows climbing and climbing, not a curve or entablature or parapet or embrasure ruffling the sleek skin of these new residential monoliths. In sharp winter light, a dazzling juxtaposition, filigreed cheek by modernist jowl. The paradox of New York is that its disappearances contain constancies— and not only because some buildings from an earlier generation survive to prod us toward historical self-consciousness. What is most steadfast in New York has the fleet look of the mercurial: the city's persistent daring, vivacity, enchantment, experiment; the marvel of new forms fired by old passions, the rekindling of the snuffed.

The Lower East Side, those tenement-and-pushcart streets of a century ago, once the venue of synagogues and succahs and religious-goods stores and a painful density of population, and later the habitat of creeps and druggies, is now the neighborhood of choice for the great-grandchildren of earlier tenants who were only too happy to escape to the Bronx. The talismanic old Rainbow Room has shut its doors? Never mind: its drama and urgent charm have migrated south. The downtown bands and their girl singers have a different sound, but the bands are there, and the girl singers too. At the Knitting Factory and other clubs—with names like Arlene Grocery, Luna Lounge, Baby Jupiter—you may catch up with Motel Girl, a band specializing in "Las Vegas stripper noir": avant-garde jazz described as jarring, seedy, sexy, Movietone-violent, dark. Even Ratner's on Delancey, the destination of senior citizens with an appetite for potato pancakes and blintzes, has succumbed to bands and poetry readings. Many of the singers and musicians live in the old tenement flats (toilet down the hall) on Avenue B, with monthly rents as high as a thousand dollars. Broadway and Prince, where Dean & DeLuca boasts three hundred varieties of cheese, was home to a notions shop two generations ago; not far away, on Orchard Street, the Tenement Museum stands as an emblem of nostalgic consecration, ignored by its trendy neighbors. You can still buy pickles out of the barrel at Guss's, but the cutting-edge young who come down to Ludlow and Stanton for the music or the glitz rarely find those legendary greenhorn warrens of much historic interest; their turf is the East Village. The Lower East Side's current inhabitants, despite their fascination with the louche, are educated and middle-class, with mothers back on Long Island wishing their guitar-playing daughters had gone to medical school. What these seekers on A, B, and C are after—like Scott and Zelda plunging into fountains to jump-start the Jazz Age—is New York's insuperable constant: the sense of belonging to the glamorous marrow of one's own time.

Uptown's glamour drive is more domestic. On the Upper West Side, the bodegas and the little appetizing and hardware stores on Amsterdam, Columbus, and Broadway are long gone, and the great style emporia dominate, behemoths of food, cooking devices, leather accessories, "natural" cosmetics, no-color cotton sheets, Mission furniture, Zabar's, the Fairway, Barney Greengrass, Citarella, H & H Bagels—dizzyingly flooded with epicurean getters and spenders—harbor prodigalities of dimpled breads, gourmet coffees, the right kind of polenta, the right kind of rice and salsa, the right kind of coffeemaker and salad-spinner. Body Works offers soaps and lotions and oils, Godiva's chocolates are set out like jewels, Gracious Home dazes with kitchenware chic. There is something of a puzzle in all this exuberant fashionableness and household seductiveness, this bean-grinding, face-creaming, bed-making: where are the political and literary intellectuals the Upper West Side is famous for, why are the conversations about olives and fish?

Across town, the Upper East Side seems, in contrast, staid, reserved, nearly quiet. The streets are less peopled. The wind is colder. A hauteur lurks in the limestone. If the West Side is a roiling marketplace, the East Side is a marble lobby presided over by a monarchical doorman. Fifth Avenue can be tacky here and there, but Madison grows more and more burnished, New York's version of the Rue du Faubourg St. Honoré. Here march the proud shops of the élite European designers, whose names make tailors' music: Yves St. Laurent, Versace, Gucci, Valentino, Giorgio Armani, Prada, Missoni, Dolce & Gabbana. Here is the Tiffany's of greengrocers, where Mozart is played and a couple of tomatoes will cost as much as a movie ticket. Here are L'Occitane for perfumes and Bulgari for diamonds. On Park and Madison affluence reigns, and with it a certain neighborhood serenity—a privacy, a regal seclusion. (Over on Lexington and Third, the city's rush begins again.)

Posh East and extravagant West dislike each other, with the ingrained antipathy of restraint and profusion, calm and bustle; nor are they likely, except for an audacious handful of crosstown adventurers, to rub elbows in the shops. A silent cold war chills Manhattan. Its weapons are Zabar's in the West, Versace in the East. There is no hot line between them.

2.

Who lives in New York? E. B. White, mulling the question fifty years ago, imagined "a farmer arriving from Italy to set up a small grocery in a slum, or a young girl arriving from a small town in Mississippi to escape the indignity of being observed by her neighbors, or a boy arriving from the Corn Belt with a manuscript in his suitcase and a pain in his heart." This has a musty if sweetish scent for us now—eau de Jimmy Stewart, perhaps. The circumstances of the arrivals were generally not so benign; nor was their reception. In a 1922 address before the New York-based American Academy of Arts and Letters, Owen Wister, the author of *The Virginian*, said of the newcomers, "Recent arrivals pollute the original spring . . . It would be well for us if many recent arrivals would become departures." He meant the immigrants who were just then flooding Castle Garden; but the children of those immigrants would soon be sorting out the dilemmas of welcome and unwelcome by other means.

I remember a ferocious street game that was played in the northeast Bronx long ago, in the neighborhood known as Pelham Bay. It was called "War," and it was exclusively a girls' game. With a piece of colored chalk you drew a small circle, in which you placed a pink rubber ball. Then you drew a second circle around it, concentric but far larger. This second circle you divided into as many pie-slices as there were players. Each player was assigned a pie-slice as her designated territory and wrote in it the name of a country she felt to be her own. So it went like this: Peggy Scanlon chose Ireland; Dorothy Wilson, Scotland; Hilda Weber, Germany; Carolyn Johnson, Sweden; Maria Viggiano (whose Sicilian grandmothers yearly wrapped their fig trees in winter canvas), Italy; Allegra Sadacca (of a Sephardic family recently from Turkey, a remnant of the Spanish Jews exiled by Ferdinand and Isabella in 1492), Spain; Madge Taylor (an immigrant from Iowa), America; and I (whose forebears had endured the despots of Russia for nearly a thousand years), Palestine. So much for the local demographics. Immediately after these self-defining allegiances were declared, someone would shriek "War!" and the asphalt mayhem of racing and tackling and tumbling would begin, with the pink rubber globe as prize. I don't suppose little girls anywhere in

New York's boroughs nowadays play this disunited nations game; but if they do, surely the pie-slices are chalked up with preferences for Trinidad, Jamaica, Haiti, Puerto Rico, the Dominican Republic, Colombia, Mexico, Peru, Greece, Lebanon, Albania, Pakistan, India, China, and of course—for antecedents who were never willing immigrants—Africa. In New York, origins still count, and not always benevolently.

3.

The poor of New York occupy streets only blocks away from the palaces. There are cities where such matters are handled otherwise. In Paris some time ago, heading for the Louvre—a row of former royal palaces—I passed a pitiful maternal scene: a dark-eyed young woman half-reclining on the pavement, with a baby in the crook of her arm and a sad-faced little girl huddled against her. The infant's only covering was a newspaper. "Gypsies," someone explained, in a tone that dismissed concern. "By the end of the day, when she's collected her hoard of francs, her husband comes to fetch her in a white limousine." Behind this cynicism lay a social reality. The woman and her children had to be taken, however sardonically, for canny entrepreneurs, not outcasts begging for pennies. The outcasts were elsewhere. They were not in the shadow of the Louvre; they were in the suburbs. In New York lingo, "suburbs" evokes green lawns and commuters of middling affluence. But the great European cities—Paris, Stockholm—have cordoned off their needy, their indigent, their laboring classes. The habitations of the poor are out of town, away from the central brilliance, shunted off and invisible. In New York you cannot lose sight of the poor—the workfare leaf-rakers in the parks, the ragged and piebald homeless, who appear on nearly every corner, some to importune, some to harass, and the pressing mass of the tenement poor, whose eager children fill (as they always have) the public schools. The vivid, hectic, noisily dense barrio, bouncy and bedraggled, that is West 155th Street leads straight across northern Broadway to that austerely resplendent Venetian palace, designed by McKim, Mead, and White, where Owen Wister inveighed against the intruders. But New York, like the stories of O. Henry (one of its early chroniclers), is pleased to spring ironic endings—so there stands the noble Academy, far uptown's distinguished monument to Arts and Letters, surrounded now by poor immigrants, an emerald's throw from the buzz and dust of Broadway's bazaar, where rugs and pots and plastic gewgaws clutter the teeming sidewalks. In New York, proletarian and patrician are neighbors.

4.

As for the upper crust in general, it is known to run New York. This stratum of the social order was once dubbed the Four Hundred, but New York's current patriciate, however it may have multiplied, escapes being counted—though it counts as heavily as ever and remains as conscientiously invisible. Elitism of this kind is rarely political; it almost never becomes mayor. In a democratic ambiance New York's potentates and nabobs have no easy handle; no one names them, not even in tabloid mockery. Then let us call them, collectively, by what they possess: Influence. Influence is financial, corporate, loftily and discreetly legal; Influence is power and planning and money. And money is the armature on which the mammoth superstructure that is New York is sculpted: architecture and philanthropy, art galleries and libraries and foundations, zoos and conservatories and museums, concert halls and universities and houses of worship. The tallest buildings—the Chrysler, the Empire State, the risen polyhedrons of Rockefeller Center, the Twin Towers, assorted old spires—all have their ankles in money. Influence *means* money, whether in the making of it, the spending, or the giving. Influence is usually private and guarded; it may shun celebrity; it needs no public face; its precincts are often reclusive. You are not likely to follow Influence in its daily maneuvers—though you can, all week long, observe the subway riders as they patiently swarm, intent on getting in and getting out and getting there. The jerky cars grind out their wild sawing clamor; locked inside the racket, the passengers display a Buddhist self-forgetfulness. Noiseless Influence, meanwhile, is driven in smoked-glass limousines, hidden, reserved, arcane. If all the rest of the citizenry were carted off, and only Influence were left, the city would be silent. But if Influence were spirited away in some grand and ghostly yacht, a kind of Flying Dutchman, say, the men in their dinner jackets, the women in their gowns, what would happen to New York? The mysterious and mazy coursings of money would dry up. The city would come to a halt.

Old money (old for us, though it was new then) made the palaces. Here is James D. McCabe, Jr., writing in 1872 of the transport cathedral, in Second Empire style, that was the brain-child of Cornelius Vanderbilt, the railway magnate:

> One of the most imposing buildings in the city is the new Grand Central Depot, on Forty-second street and Fourth Avenue. It is constructed

of red brick, with iron trimmings painted white, in imitation of marble. The south front is adorned with three and the west front with two massive pavilions. The central pavilion of each front contains an illuminated dock . . . The car-shed is covered with an immense circular roof of iron and glass . . . It is lighted from the roof by day, and at night large reflectors, lighted by an electrical apparatus, illuminate the vast interior.

And here again, in 1948, is E. B. White (a man who knew how to catch the beat of what he called "Manhattan's breathing"), describing his own encounter with the Depot's successor, built in 1913 on the same site:

Grand Central has become honky-tonk, with its extradimensional advertising displays and its tendency to adopt the tactics of a travel broker. I practically lived in Grand Central Terminal at one period (it has all the conveniences and I had no other place to stay) and the great hall seemed to me one of the more inspiring interiors in New York, until Lastex and Coca-Cola got into the temple.

Kodak got in, too, and honky-tonk turned into logo. Like some painted colossus, Kodak's gargantuan sign, in flaming color (it was named the Colorama), presided for years over the criss-crossing rush-hour flow—a fixture of the terminal's contemporary identity. The gilded constellations on the vaulted horizon dimmed to an undifferentiated gray; no one troubled to look up at blinded Orion. A gluey grime thickened the interstices of the marble balustrades. Frankfurter wrappings and sticky paper soda cups littered the public telephones. Commuters in need of a toilet knew what to avoid and went next door to the Grand Hyatt. The temple had become a routinely seedy train station.

And then New York, the Eraser and the Renewer, with a sweep of its resuscitating will, cleansed the temple's degradation. What old money brought into being, new money, along with civic determination, has refurbished. The theme is artful mirroring: the existing grand stair engenders an answering grand stair on the opposite end of the great concourse. The gawky advertising signs are banished and the heavens scrubbed until their stars glitter. Below and behind, the secret ganglia of high-tech engineering and up-to-date lighting may snake and throb, but all across the shining hall it is Commodore Vanderbilt's ghost who walks. Grand Central has no fear of the ornamental; it revels in breadth and unstinting scale; it *intends* to inspire. The idea of the publicly palatial—unashamed lavishness—has returned.

And not only here. Follow Forty-second Street westward to Fifth Avenue and enter the most illustrious temple of all, the lion-sentried Library, where the famed third-floor Reading Room has just undergone its own rebirth—both in homage to, and in dissent from, the modern. Card catalogues have descended into the dustbin of antiquated conveniences. Electrical outlets accommodate laptops; rows of computers parade across the vast polished tables under a gilded rococo ceiling, a Beaux-Arts confection frosted with floral arabesques. Whatever the mavens may say, and however the critics may scowl, New York (in at least one of its multiple manifestations) thirsts for intimations of what the Victorians did not hesitate to invoke: Noble Beauty. New York has learned to value—though never to venerate—its old robber-baron muses, not for their pre-income-tax devourings, but for their appetite for the baronial: the Frick Collection, the Morgan Library, the Cooper-Hewitt (housed in Andrew Carnegie's sixty-four-room mansion). The vanished Pennsylvania Station, the original—razed a generation ago as an elaborate eyesore, now regretted, its bargain-basement replacement a daily discouragement—will soon rise again, in the nearby body of the superannuated General Post Office (Roman, kingly, columned). Fancy, then, a soaring apparition of the Metropolitan Museum of Art, that prototype of urban palace, and of its philosophical rival, the Museum of Modern Art, hovering over the city, scanning it for symptoms of majesty—the Met and MOMA, joined by spectral flights of the City Ballet, the serious little theaters, and Carnegie Hall, all whispering "Aspire, aspire!"

Susurrations of grandeur.

5.

But grandeur on this style is a neighborhood of the mind, and a narrow one at that. Real neighborhoods and psychological neighborhoods may, in fact, overlap—literary Greenwich Village being the most storied case in point. In the Village of the psyche, the outré is always in, and it is safely conventional to be bizarre. Writers once looked for cheap rent in these streets, after which it began to feel writerly to live in the Village, within walking distance of the fountain in Washington Square. The earlier luminaries who resided here are the more enshrined—Washington Irving, James Fenimore Cooper, Louisa May Alcott, Mark Twain, Edgar Allan Poe, O. Henry, Horace Greeley, Walt Whitman, Theodore Dreiser, Bret Harte, Sinclair Lewis, Sherwood Anderson, Upton Sinclair, Willa Cather; and, in a later generation, Thomas Wolfe, e. e. cummings, Richard Wright, Djuna Barnes, Edmund Wilson, Elinor Wylie, Hart Crane, James Agee, Marianne Moore, W. H. Auden! Yet fame re-enacted can become parody as well as homage, and there was a touch of in-your-face déjà vu in the 1950s, when Allen Ginsberg, Jack Kerouac, and LeRoi Jones (afterward known as Amiri Baraka) established the then new-born East Village as a beatnik redoubt. Nowadays it would be hard to discover a writers' roster equal to those of the past, and West Village literari-ness hangs as a kind of tattered nimbus not over the old (mostly temporary) residences of the celebrated but over the bars, cellars, and cafés they once frequented. The Saturday night hordes that flow through Bleecker Street are mostly from New Jersey. ("The bridge-and-tunnel crowd," sniffs the East Village of the hour.)

Neighborhoods of the mind, though, are rarely so solidly placed in a single location. Of actual neighborhoods (or "sections," in moribund New Yorkese)—Soho, Little Italy, Chelsea, Gramercy Park, Murray Hill, South Street Seaport, and all the rest—only a few are as determinedly self-defined as the Village. But a courageous denizen of any of them (despite home-grown inhibitions of boundary and habit) can venture out to a collectivity of taste and imagination and familiarity unconstrained by geography. Jazz and blues and nightlife aficionados, movie buffs, gays, rap artists, boxing and wrestling zealots, singles, esoteric-restaurant habitués, Central Park joggers, marathon runners, museum addicts, lovers of music or theater or dance, lonely-hearts, shoppers, hotel weekenders, barflies, churchgoers, Talmud enthusiasts, Bronx-born Tibetan Buddhists, students of Sufism, kabbalists, theosophists, voice or ski coaches, SAT and LSAT crammers, amateur paint-ers, union members, members of boards and trustees, Internet devotees, fans of the Yankees or the Mets or the Jets or the Knicks, believers in psy-chics and tea-leaves readers, streetwalkers and their pimps, antiques fanciers, art collectors, philanthropists, professors of linguistics, lexicogra-phers, copy editors, librarians, kindergarten teachers, crossing guards, wine votaries, storefront chiropractors, Chinese or Hebrew or Arabic calligra-phers—all these, and inconceivably more, can emerge from any locality to live, if only for a few hours, in a sympathetic neighborhood of affinity. Exper-tise and idiosyncrasy and bursting desire burn and burn in New York: a conflagration of manifold, insatiable, tumultuous will.

6.

I was born in a brownstone on East Eighty-eighth Street, between First and York Avenues—but both the latter avenue and the area have since altered their designations and their character. York was once Avenue A, and the neighborhood, populated largely by German immigrants, was called Yorkville. It was in Yorkville before my birth that my infant brother was kidnapped by a madwoman. The story as it was told to me is set in a certain year, but not in any special weather; it seems to me that it must have been summer. I see my mother, hot, sleeveless, breathless, frantic, running through the night streets of Yorkville to find the kidnapper and snatch her baby back. He had been sleeping in his wicker carriage in a nook among rows of brown bottles and drawers filled with maple-flavored rock candy on strings, not four yards from where my young father in his pharmacist's jacket, a fountain pen always in its pocket, stood tending to his mortar and pestle, working up a medicinal paste. Into my parents' drug store the madwoman flew, seizing baby and carriage and all, and out into the dark she fled, only to be discovered some hours later in nearby Carl Schurz Park, disheveled and undone by furious infantile howls, and grateful to relinquish the captive screamer.

In my half-dreaming re-creation of this long-ago scene—the stolen child, the fleeing madwoman—why must it be summertime? I think I know why. New York in summer is another sort of city; in mood and weight it has nothing in common with wintry New York. A New York summer is frenetic, syncopated, blistered, frayed, dusty. There is a desperation in its heat, and a sense of letdown, despite relief, in its air-conditioned indoors. Melting squads of tourists, in shorts and open shirts or halters, sweat pooling under their camera straps, their heads swiveling from one gaudy carnival sight to the next, push through Times Square in anxious quick-march. Smells of perspiring hot dogs under venders' grease-lined umbrellas mingle with the exhaust fumes of heaving buses. There is nothing relaxed about the summer city. New York's noise is louder, New York's toughness is brasher, New York's velocity is speedier. Everything—stores, offices, schedules, vacations, traffic—demands full steam ahead; no one can say that the livin' is easy. New York in July is out of synch, not quite itself, hoping for ransom, kidnapped by midsummer frolicking: picnickers awaiting free twilight performances of Shakespeare in Central Park; street parades of night-time swelterers along Museum Mile, where tappers and clappers gather before the Jewish Museum to salute the tootling klezmer players; breakdancers down from Harlem, twelve-year-olds effortless and expert and little and lithe, who spin on their heels across from the hive of Madison Square Garden. In the American heartland in summer, babies fall down wells and pipes, and that is news. In New York—fidgety, frittering, frenzied, boiling New York— summer itself is news.

The true city is the winter city. The woolly enchantment of a population swaddled and muffled, women and men in long coats, eccentric boots, winding scarves; steam sculptures forming out of human breath; hushed streets; tiny white electric points on skeletal trees! The icy air like a scratch across a sheet of silver, the smoky chestnut carts, the foggy odor of hot coffee when you open a door, a bakery's sweet mist swirling through its transom, a glimpse of rosy-nosed skaters in the well of the Rockefeller stelae, the rescuing warmth of public lobbies—New York in January is a city of grateful small shocks. And just as in an antiquated English novel of manners, New York has its "season"—lectures, readings, rallies, dinner parties, chamber music in someone's living room. While in summer you cannot rely on the taxis to turn on their air-conditioning, in winter each yellow capsule is a hot little bullet; the driver in his turban remembers his subcontinental home. There is no dusk like a New York winter dusk: the blurry gray of early evening, when the lone walker, ferried between day and night, jostled by strangers in packs, feels most desolate, and when the privacy of burrowing into a coat collar brings on a nameless loss. At such a moment the forest of flowering lights (a brilliance suddenly apprehended) makes its cheering claim: that here, right here, is importance, achievement, delight in the work of the world; that here, right *here*, is the hope of connection, and life in its fulfillment. In a gregarious New York winter, especially in restaurants at eight o'clock, you will hear jokes, stories with amazing climaxes, futures plotted out, jealousies retailed, gossip above all: who's up, who's down, what's in, what's out. Central heating never abolished the theory and practice of the fireside.

7.

What Manhattan talks about, obliquely or openly—what it thinks about, whatever the season—is ambition. Europeans always make much of this: how *hard* New Yorkers work, the long days, the paltry vacations, the single-minded avarice for status, the obsessiveness, the terrible drive. What? No *dolce far niente*? But only an outsider would remark on the city's striving; for New Yorkers it is ingrained, taken for granted, valued. Unlike Bartleby, downtown's most distinctive imaginary inhabitant, New York never prefers not to. New York prefers and prefers and prefers—it prefers power and scope to tranquility and intimacy, it prefers struggle and steel to acquiescence and cushions. New York is where you go to seize the day, to leave your mark, to live within the nerve of your generation. Some might say that there is nothing new in this—why else did Willa Cather begin in Red Cloud, Nebraska, and end on Bank Street? Why else did Jackson Pollock, born in Cody, Wyoming, land in New York?

Yet there is a difference. New York ambition has changed its face. Fifty years ago, when postal clerks and bank tellers wearing vests were what was still called "family men," the hankering young were on the lowest rung of any hierarchy. Their patience was commanded; their deference was expected. It was understood that power and position were the sovereign right of middle age, and that a twenty-three-year-old would have to wait and wait. Opportunity and recognition were light-years away. A few—writers mostly—broke out early: Mary McCarthy at twenty-two, Norman Mailer at twenty-five, Philip Roth and John Updike at twenty-six. Leonard Bernstein and Bobby Fischer were youthful stars. Still, these were all prodigies and exceptions. In the run-of-the-mill world of getting ahead, the young were at the bottom, and stayed there until judged—by their elders at the top—to be sufficiently ripe. The Information Age, with its ear to the ground, reverses all that. The old ways are undone. A twenty-something young woman in publishing keeps a television set on in her office all day, monitoring possible acquisitions: what sells, who's cool. The auditory and the visual, in whatever mode, belong almost exclusively to the newest generation. Everywhere in New York the knowledgeable young are in charge of the sound, the image, the latest word; ambition need no longer stand in line and wait its graying turn. (Fifty-somethings, their passion still unspent, and recalling the slower passages of long ago, may be a little wistful.)

In a city always relinquishing, always replacing, always on the wing, mores close down and expectations alter; milestones fade away; landmarks vanish. In its shifting primordial constancy, New York is faithful to loss and faithful to change. After the hullabaloo over the demise of Books & Company on Madison and Shakespeare & Company on upper Broadway, some still mourn those small principalities of letters. But does anyone born since the Second World War miss the intellectual newsstand next to the Chock Full O' Nuts across from Washington Square, or the Forty-second Street Automat, where you could linger over your teacup and read your paper all afternoon?

Now and then, heartstruck, I pass the crenellated quasi-Gothic building that once housed my high school, where latecomers, myself among them, would tremble before its great arched doorway, fearing reprimand; but the reprimanders are all dead. My Latin teacher is dead. My German teacher is dead. My biology teacher is dead. It is only the city itself that lives on, half-amnesiac, hardly ever glancing back, re-inventing its fabric, insisting on being noticed for what it is now. There is no grief for what precedes the common memory, and ultimately the fickle urban tide, as immutable as the Nile, accommodates every disappearance.

8.

In May of 1860, when Frederick Law Olmsted's Central Park was just in the making, a forty-year-old Wall Street lawyer named George Templeton Strong recorded in his diary his own preference:

> The park below the reservoir begins to look intelligible. Unfinished still, and in process of manufacture, but shewing the outline now of what it is to be. Many points are already beautiful. What will they be when their trees are grown and I'm dead and forgotten?
>
> One thinks sometimes that one would like re-juvenescence, or a new birth. One would prefer, if he could, to annihilate his past and commence life, say in this A.D. 1860, and so enjoy longer acquaintance with this era of special development and material progress, watch the splendid march of science on earth, share the benefits of the steam engine and the electric telegraph, and grow up with this park—which is to be so great a fact for the young men and maidens of New York in 1880, if all goes well and we do not decompose into anarchy meanwhile . . . Central Park and Astor Library and a developed Columbia University promise to make the city twenty years hence a real center of culture and civilization, furnishing privileges to youth far beyond what it gave me in my boyhood.

A century and a half on, Strong's "era of special development and material progress" may seem quaint to us, for whom fax and e-mail and jets and microwaves are everyday devices, and whose moonwalkers are already old men. By now the park below the reservoir, the library on Fifth Avenue, and the university on Morningside Heights are seasoned inheritances—established components of the city's culture and civilization. But even standing as we do on the lip of the new millennium, who can resist falling into George Templeton Strong's wishful dream of a new birth and a longer acquaintance? His New York of steam engine and telegraph, as ephemeral as the May clouds of 1860, has ceased to be. Our New York, too, will disappear, and a renewed and clarified city will lift out of the breathing breast of the one we know. New York, Enemy of the Merely Picturesque, Headquarters of Misery and Marvel, Eraser and Renewer, Brain and Capital of the Continent!

The immigrants will come—what language will they speak? The towers will climb to the sky—what shapes will they have? The crowds will stream in the streets—what thoughts will they think? Will they think our outworn thoughts, or imaginings we cannot imagine?

LASTLY

"It Takes a Great Deal of History to Produce a Little Literature"

H. G. Wells once accused Henry James of knowing practically nothing. In the Jamesian novel, Wells charged, "you will find no people with defined political opinions, no people with religious opinions, none with clear partisanships or with lusts or whims, none definitely up to any specific impersonal thing." Wells concluded: "It is leviathan retrieving pebbles."

James was desperately wounded. He was at the close of his great span of illumination—it was less than a year before his death—and he was being set aside as useless, "a church lit but without a congregation." Replying to Wells, he defended himself on the question of the utility of art. Literature, he asserted, is "for use": "I regard it as relevant in a degree that leaves everything behind." There followed the famously characteristic Jamesian credo, by now long familiar to us. "It is art," he wrote, "that *makes* life, makes interest, makes importance . . . I know of no substitute whatever for the force and beauty of its process." And though he was speaking explicitly of the novel's purpose as "the extension of life, which is the novel's great gift," there is evidence enough that he would not have excluded the literary essay, of which he was equal master, from art's force and beauty. Thus, what Henry James knew.

To which Wells retorted: "I had rather be a journalist, that is the essence of it."

In the quarrel between Wells and James, James's view has been overtaken by times and habits far less elevated in their literary motives (and motifs) than his own, and by radical changes in the aims of education and in the impulses that drive the common culture. What James knew was the nobility of art—if, for him, the novel and the literary essay were not splendors just short of divine, then they were, anyhow, divining rods, with the capacity to quiver over the springs of discovered life. What Wells knew was something else—the future; us; what we are now. He welcomed the germinating hour of technology's fecundity, and flourished in it. James, we recall, switched from pen and ink to the typewriter, not because he was attracted to machines—he was not—but because he suffered from writer's cramp. He never learned to type himself; instead, he dictated to a typist—a technological regression, in a way, to the preliterate oral; or else an ascendance to the dominant priestly single voice. Wells, by contrast, was magnetized by the machine-world. Imagine him our contemporary: his study is mobbed by computer, printer, modem, e-mail, voice-mail, photocopier, fax, cable—the congeries and confluence of gadgets and conveniences that feed what the most up-to-date colleges advertise as "communications skills."

The truth of our little age is this: nowadays no one gives a damn about what Henry James knew. I dare to say our "little" age not to denigrate (or not only to denigrate), but because we squat now over the remnant embers of the last diminishing decade of the dying twentieth century, possibly the rottenest of all centuries, and good riddance to it (despite modernism at the start and moonwalking near the middle). The victories over mass murder and mass delusion, West and East, are hardly permanent. "Never again" is a pointless slogan: old atrocities are models (they give permission) for new ones. The worst reproduces itself; the best is singular. Tyrants, it seems, can be spewed out by the dozens, and their atrocities by the thousands, as by a copy machine; but Kafka, tyranny's symbolist, is like a fingerprint, or like handwriting, not duplicatable. This is what Henry James knew: that civilization is not bred out of machines, whether the machines are tanks or missiles, or whether they are laser copiers. Civilization, like art its handmaid (read: hand-made), is custom-built.

Let this not be mistaken for any sort of languorous pre-Raphaelite detachment from science or technology, or, heaven forfend, as a complaint against progress and its reliefs. Gratitude for anaesthesia and angioplasty and air travel, and for faxes and computers and frozen food and the flush toilet and all the rest! Gratitude, in truth, for Mr. Gradgrind and the Facts, and for those who devise the Facts—especially when those facts ease the purely utilitarian side of life. What distinguishes the data of medicine and science is precisely that they *can* be duplicated: an experiment that cannot be repeated will be discarded as an unreliable fluke, or, worse, as a likely forgery. In the realm of science, what is collective has authority. It is the same with journalism: if two reporters witness an incident, and the two accounts differ, one must be wrong, or must at least promote distrust. A unique view, uncorroborated, is without value. Wells, in discrediting James, was in pursuit of public and collective discriminations, as opposed to the purely idiosyncratic; he was after consensus-witnessing, both in science and society, and a more recognizable record, perhaps, even of lust and whim. Defined political and religious opinions, clear partisanships, persons definitely up to some specific impersonal thing.

Defined, definite, specific—how, what, when, where: the journalist's catalogue and catechism. Naming generates categories and headings, and categories and headings offer shortcuts—like looking something up in the encyclopedia, where knowledge, abbreviated, has already been codified and collected. James's way, longer and slower, is for knowledge to be detected, inferred, individually, laboriously, scrupulously, mazily—knowledge that might not be found in any encyclopedia.

"I had rather be a journalist, that is the essence of it"—hark, the cry of the common culture. Inference and detection (accretion heading toward revelation) be damned. What this has meant, for literature, is the eclipse of the essay in favor of the "article"—that shabby, team-driven, ugly, truncated, undeveloped, speedy, breezy, cheap, impatient thing. A while ago, coming once again on Robert Louis Stevenson's "Virginibus Puerisque"—an essay not short, wholly odd, no other like it, custom-made, soliciting the brightness of full attention in order to release its mocking charms—I tried to think of a single periodical today that might be willing to grant print to this sort of construction. Not even "judicious cutting," as editors like to say, would save Stevenson now. Of course there may be an instantly appropriate objection to so mildewed an observation. Stevenson is decidedly uncontemporary—the tone is all wrong, and surely we are entitled to our own sounds? Yes, the nineteenth century deserves to be read—but remember, while reading, that it is dead.

All right. But what of the "clear partisanship" of a book review encountered only this morning, in a leading journal dedicated to reviews? "Five books, however rich and absorbing, are a hefty number for the reader to digest," the reviewer declares, commenting on Leon Edel's multivolume biography of Henry James; "a little amateur sleuthing some years ago suggested to me that the number of people who bought Mr. Edel's quintet bore little relation to the number who succeeded in battling their way through them." (Amateur sleuthing may be professional gall. "Succeeded in battling," good God! Is there a paragraph in Edel's devoted work, acclaimed as magisterial by two generations, that does not seduce and illuminate?) Edel, however, is not under review; he is only a point of contrast. The book in actual question, a fresh biography of James—in one volume—is, among other merits, praised for being admirably "short." It is attention span that is victor, even for people who claim to be serious readers.

And writers may give themselves out as a not dissimilar sample. Now and then you will hear a writer (even one who does not define herself as a journalist) speak of her task as "communication," as if the meticulous making of a sentence, or the feverish uncovering of an idea, or the sting of a visionary jolt delivered by what used to be called the Muse, were no more artful than a ten-minute telephone conversation. Literature may "communicate" (a redundancy, even a tautology), but its enduring force, well past the routine of facile sending and receiving, is in the consummation, as James tells us, of life, interest, importance. Leviathan rises to kick away the pebble of journalism.

Yet the pebble, it seems, is mightier than leviathan. The ten-minute article is *here*, and it has, by and large, displaced the essay. The essay is gradual and patient. The article is quick, restless, and brief. The essay reflects on its predecessors, and spirals organically out of a context, like a green twig from a living branch. The article rushes on, amnesiac, despising the meditative, reveling in gossip and polemics, a courtier of the moment. Essays, like articles, can distort and lie, but because essays are under the eye of history, it is a little harder to swindle the reader. Articles swindle almost by nature, because superficiality is a swindle. Pessimists suppose that none of this is any longer reversible. That the literary essay survives in this or that academic periodical, or in a handful of tiny quarterlies, is scarcely to the point. It has left the common culture.

Some doubt whether there is a common culture now at all, whether it is right to imagine that "the West" retains any resonance of worthy meaning; or even that it should. To claim commonality is, paradoxically, to be written off as elitist. Politically, through exploration, exploitation, and contempt, the West has spread elitism and exclusion; but it has also spread an idea of democratic inclusiveness so powerful—all of humanity is made in the image of the One Creator—that it serves to knock the politics of contempt off its feet all over the world. The round earth, like an hourglass, is turned upside down these days, spilling variegated populations-in-motion into static homogeneous populations, south into north, east into west; the village mentality, with its comfortable reliance on the familiar, is eroded by the polychrome and polyglot. America, vessel of migrations, began it. Grumbling, Europe catches up. While the kaleidoscope rattles and spins, and tribe assaults tribe, no one can predict how all this will shake itself out; but the village mentality is certainly dead. The jet plane cooked its goose.

Between the last paragraph and this one, I took a quick trip to Paris. This is not the sort of thing a hermitlike scribbler usually does; generally it is a little daunting for me to walk the three short blocks to Main Street. But the rareness of such a plummeting from one society into another, perhaps because one's attention becomes preternaturally heightened, somehow illumines the notion of commonality. I crossed an ocean in an airplane and found, on the opposite shore, almost exactly what I left behind: the same congeries of concerns. The same writers were being talked about, the same world news (starvation, feuding, bombing) was being deplored; only the language was different. So there really *is* a "West"—something we mostly forget as we live our mostly Main Street lives. Suppose, then, the language were not different but the same?

And if "commonality" requires more persuasive evidence than a transoceanic flight, there is, after all, the question (the answer, rather) of English—setting aside Shaw's quip about America and Britain being separated by a common language. The mother-tongue, as the sweet phrase has it, is a poet's first and most lasting home, his ineradicable patriotism.* In my teens I read Katherine Mansfield: what did a New York-born Jewish girl whose family had fled the boot of the Russian Czar have in common with a woman born in New Zealand forty years earlier? And what did this woman of the farthest reaches of the South Pacific have in common with an island off the continent of Europe? How rapidly the riddle is undone: Keats and Shelley and Coleridge and Wordsworth, to begin with. The great tree-trunk of English literature . . . no, that grand image ought to give way to something homelier. Call it the drawstring of English letters, which packs us all into the same sack, at the bottom of which—as we tumble around all mixed up down there, North Americans, Australians, Nigerians, South Africans, Jamaicans, numbers of Indians, and on and on—lies a hillock of gold.

The gold is the idea (old-fashioned, even archaic, perhaps extinct) of belles-lettres. Some will name it false gold, since English, as language and as literature, came to the Caribbean, and to New York, and to all those other places, as the spoor of empire. (Spooky thought: if not for the Czar of All the Russias, and if not for mad King George III, and if not for their anachronistic confluence, I would not now be, as I am, on my knees before the English poets. Also: no native cadences of Hawthorne, Melville, Emerson, Thoreau, Dickinson, Faulkner, Mark Twain, Cather!) *A Shropshire Lad* for a while

---

* I know a European writer of genius, in love with his language, whose bad luck it was to have been born just in time to suffer two consecutive tyrannies. It is a wonder that this writer lived past childhood. At the age of five, under Hitler, he was torn from his home and shipped to a concentration camp. Having survived that, he was spiritually and intellectually crushed by the extremes of Communist rule, including a mindless and vicious censorship. Currently, after the fall of the dictator, and having emigrated to America, he is being vilified in the press of his native land for having exposed one of its national heroes as a programmatic anti-Semite. After so much brutalization by the country of his birth, it would be difficult to expect him to identify himself as a patriot. But that is what he is. He is a patriot of his mother-tongue, and daily feels the estrangement of exile. *Pro patria dulce mori!*

bestrode the world, and was welcome nowhere. But Milton and Mill and Swift and George Eliot and E. M. Forster came along as stowaways— "Areopagitica," and *A Vindication of the Rights of Woman*, and "A Modest Proposal," and *Daniel Deronda*, and *A Passage to India*. These hardly stand for the arrogance of parochialism—and it is just this engagement with belles-lettres that allows parochialism to open its arms, so that the inevitable accompaniment of belles-lettres is a sense of indebtedness. "It takes a great deal of history to produce a little literature," James noted; everything that informs belles-lettres is in that remark, and also everything that militates against the dismissal of either the term or the concept.

If I began these reflections in curmudgeonly resentment of the virtual annihilation of what Henry James knew—of the demise of the literary essay—it is only to press for its rescue and reclamation. Poetry and the novel will continue to go their own way, and we can be reasonably confident that they will take care of themselves. But the literary essay needs and merits defense: defense and more—celebrants, revivification through performance. One way or another, the literary essay is connected to the self-conscious progression of a culture, whereas the essay's flashy successor—the article, or "piece"—is in every instance a pusher of Now, a shaker-off of whatever requires study or patience, or what used to be called, without prejudice, ambition. The essayist's ambition is no more and no less than that awareness of indebtedness I spoke of a moment ago—indebtedness to history, scholarship, literature, the acutest nuances of language.

Is this what is meant by "elitism"? Perhaps. I think of it as work, if work is construed (as it ought to be) as "the passion for exactitude and sublimity." The latter phrase I borrow from a young essayist in London—my daughter's age exactly—who, because of a driven Parnassian ardor and because he is still in his twenties, has, I trust, the future of belles-lettres secreted in his fountain pen. In the newest literary generation, the one most assailed by the journalist's credo of Now, it is a thing worth marveling at: this determination to subdue, with exactitude and sublimity, the passionless trivia of our time.

The Boys in the Alley,
the Disappearing Readers,
and the Novel's Ghostly Twin

"On or about December 1910," Virginia Woolf wrote more than one hundred years ago, "human character changed." The phrase has come down to us mockingly, notoriously, but also with the truth-like endurance of a maxim. By a change in human character, Woolf meant modernism, and by modernism she meant the kind of overt self-consciousness that identifies and interrogates its own motions and motives. Set forth in "Character in Fiction," an essay arguing for innovation in the novel, it was an aesthetic rather than an essentialist proposition. The change—a new dispensation of premise and utterance—had been wickedly heralded two years before, on an August afternoon in 1908, when Lytton Strachey happened to notice a stain on Woolf's sister's skirt. "Semen?" Strachey inquired, as definitively as the final squeal of a hinge: a door flung shut for the last time. Behind that door lurked the muzzled premodern, and before it swarmed what modernism has long since made of us (and postmodernism even more so): harriers of the hour, soothsayers and pulse-takers, augurs and dowsers, examiners of entrails. Literary entrails especially: many are the stains subject to writerly divination.

And so it was that on or about April 1996, Jonathan Franzen published a manifesto on the situation of the contemporary novelist (with himself as chief specimen and proof text), and the character of bookish querulousness changed. What had been muttered mutely in cenacles and bars erupted uninhibitedly in print, as flagrante delicto as any old spot of early-twentieth-century semen. *The Corrections,* Franzen's ambitious and celebrated literary bestseller, had not yet appeared; he was still a mostly obscure fiction writer whose two previous novels, though praised by reviewers, had slid into the usual quicksand of forgotten books. When a little-known writer undertakes a manifesto—a statement, after all, of sober purpose and principle—it is likely also to be a cri de coeur, and its reasoned argument will derive from the intimate wounds of autobiography. "I'd intended to provoke; what I got instead,"

Franzen said of his first novel, "was sixty reviews in a vacuum." Even sixty reviews, he made plain, was not sufficient: it was not equivalent to a public event, attention was not being paid, certainly not in the coin of genuine Fame, and the vacuum in question was the airlessness of writer's depression.

It was a brave stand, then, to issue a manifesto in the form of a turbulent confluence of introspective memoir and cultural analysis; nor was it a career move, despite its publication in a major magazine. Literary essays are generally well beneath popular notice, and Franzen's piece, though pumped up by anecdote ("When I got off the phone, I couldn't stop laughing") and political apocalypse ("the United States seemed to me . . . terminally out of touch with reality"), aroused its expected flurry among the literati, but was overlooked by Oprah. It took *The Corrections* to catch the eye, and then the ire, of television's latter-day publishing goddess, and Franzen's fame was confirmed. Retrospectively, if the success of *The Corrections* had not catapulted Franzen into precisely those precincts of the literary stratosphere he had so ringingly and publicly coveted, his declaration might have disintegrated, like all other articles of passing faith, into a half-remembered bleat.

This has not happened—partly because Franzen continues as a noted writerly presence, and partly because his observations of nearly twenty years ago have failed to escape the transience of mere personal complaint. There were many such ventings, embedded in irritating and by now obsolete trivia, to wit: ". . . even as I was sanctifying the reading of literature, I was becoming so depressed that I could do little after dinner but flop in front of the TV. Even without cable, I could always find something delicious: Phillies and Padres, Eagles and Bengals, *M*A*S*H, Cheers, Homicide*." Still more grumbling followed, about the discouraging fate of a second novel: "But the result was the same: another report card with A's and B's from the reviewers who had replaced the teachers whose approval, when I was younger, I had both craved and taken no satisfaction from; decent sales; and the deafening silence of irrelevance"—all this as if private grievance could rise to societal position-taking. Yet the deafening silence of irrelevance was, finally, the undergirding of Franzen's point: that the common culture has undermined the novelist's traditional role as news-bringer. Novelists, he said, "do feel a responsibility to dramatize important issues of the day, and they now confront a culture in which almost all the issues are burned out almost all of the time." They are burned out by the proliferating, instantaneous, and superior technological sources of what Franzen calls "social instruction."

His subject, in short, was the decline of reading in an electronic age when scores of plots, shocks, titillations, and unfolding dramatic disclosures, shot out daily by the reality machines of radio, television, the Internet, endlessly evolving apps, and the journalist's confiding up-to-the-nanosecond cell phone and Twitter appear to supply all the storytelling seductions anyone might thirst after. Franzen was hardly the first writer to notice this; he acknowledged that Philip Roth, three decades earlier, was already despairing of the novel's viability in the face of mad actuality's pervasive power. Franzen's thesis was not fresh, but neither was it stale. What *was* new was his linking the question of public literacy with marketplace lust, with—in an idiom Norman Podhoretz made famous nearly forty years ago—Making It. Having confessed to a blatant desire for success ("the dirty little secret"), Podhoretz was roundly excoriated, so much so that if flogging had been legal, the reigning literary-intellectual tribe of that period would have come after him with a forest of cat-o'-nine-tails. It was a time, moreover, when the publication of a serious literary novel was an exuberant communal event; only recall how *The Naked and the Dead,* or *The Adventures of Augie March,* was received. And it was a time, paradoxically, when serious writers looked down on the wider publishing marketplace and were sedulously detached from it: "popular" novelists were scorned. No one spoke of the decline of reading because it had not yet occurred.

All that is nowadays extinct. Ambition, even of the kind termed naked, no longer invites elitist denunciation. Writers who define themselves by the loftiest standards of literary art are happy to be counted as popular; the lucky ones gratefully, not to say covetously, accept the high advances that signify the hope for a six-digit readership. But fifty years ago, Lionel Trilling, the paramount critic of the American midcentury, inveighed against the democratic wider audience, and the "big advertising appropriation" that accompanied it, as corrupting forces—even as he worshiped Hemingway, who had the largest readership of any serious novelist then writing. In an essay titled "The Function of the Little Magazine" (referring to the literary quarterlies that once occupied the pinnacle of intellectual prestige), Trilling recommended, and extolled, the most ideal readership of all, no matter how closed or small or invisible or abstract or imaginary. "The writer must define his audience by its abilities, by its perfections," he insisted. "He does well, if he cannot see his right audience within immediate reach of his voice, to direct his words to his spiritual ancestors, or to posterity, or even, if need be, to a coterie."

A coterie! Spiritual ancestors! Posterity! Such martyred satisfactions are a long way from Franzen's appetite, or the appetite of his contemporaries. Trilling demanded a self-denying purity; purity for the sake of a higher purity. Franzen, more pragmatic and businesslike, talks numbers. "The educated single New Yorker who in 1945 read twenty-five serious novels in a year today has time for maybe five," he writes. "That hard core is a very small prize to be divided among a very large number of working novelists," and he tots up the few who, back in 1996, "actually hit the charts": "Annie Proulx's *The Shipping News* has sold nearly a million copies in the last two years; the hardcover literary bestseller *The Crossing,* by Cormac McCarthy, came in on the *Publishers Weekly* annual best seller list." (Up there in Paradise, among his spiritual ancestors, one can hear Trilling's fastidious sighs.) By now, Franzen has caught up with, or perhaps surpassed, those impressive sales figures of twenty years ago. And if Trilling cannot be Franzen's spiritual ancestor (he once tried out the purity path, he tells us), it is because our world has left reticence behind: a reticence that, for Franzen, has come to resemble "an estrangement from humanity." He calls it that; but what he *means* is being "known," and escape from the confinements of a small readership, and finally that desirable state, or trait, that goes by the name of "accessibility." All the same, the terminology of publishing success has grown softer with the years. Instead of the brash Making It, there is the melancholy worry over the silence of irrelevance. Almost no one, least of all Franzen, is asking for invisible, unheard coteries.

Yet in October of 2005 Trilling (or his proselytizing shade) made an unexpected comeback, in the form of an answering manifesto that challenged Franzen's. Under a gaudy banner—"Why Experimental Fiction Threatens to Destroy Publishing, Jonathan Franzen, and Life as We Know It," slyly subtitled "A Correction"—Ben Marcus, Franzen's dedicated antagonist, undertook, Trilling-like, to prescribe the nature of his ideal reader. Marcus's reader was not Franzen's. Franzen had identified the born reader as a "social isolate" in childhood, an insight supplied to him by a practicing sociologist. Marcus's own definition was derived from the fairy realm of elixirs and transmutations. "A writer might be forgiven," he said, "for wishing to slip readers enhancements to their Wernicke's areas [the segment of the human brain responsible for language], doses of a potion that might turn them into fierce little reading machines, devourers of new syntax, fluent interpreters of the most lyrical complex grammar, so that the more difficult kind of sense writing might strive to make could find its appropriate Turing machine, and would be revealed to the reader with the delicacy the writer intended . . . But these enhancements to Wernicke's areas in fact already exist, and they're called books."

As this wishful casting of spells may intimate, the books Marcus speaks of are not the kinds of books Franzen might champion: conventional social narratives promising pleasure sans difficulty. Ultimately Franzen's credo, as he expressed it nine years before Marcus threw down the gauntlet, is the need to attract and please readers. A declared enemy of "audience-friendly writing," Marcus is fearlessly on the side of difficulty: "entirely new syntactical byways," "a poetic aim that believes in the possibility of language to create ghostly frames of sense." Gertrude Stein, Samuel Beckett, and William Gaddis are among his older models, and these he opposes to a "narrative realist mode, which generally builds linearly on what has gone before, subscribes to cinematic verisimilitude, and, when it's not narrating, slaps mortar into an already stable fictional world." Accordingly, he bludgeons Franzen relentlessly: "Language is a poor medium for the kinds of mass entertainment that Franzen seems interested in." And: "He wants literary language to function as modestly as spoken language." And: "He seems desperately frustrated by writers who don't actively court their audiences, who do not strive for his specific kind of clarity, and who take a little too much pleasure in language."

So it is a fight rather than an argument, really—a fight over complexity versus ease, a fight that mostly mimics gang war, which is not so much a vigorous instance of manly bloodletting (though it is that too) as a dustup over prestige: who has the prior right to swagger in public. It cannot be an argument these two are having—meaning a debate between fundamentally differing positions—because both Franzen and Marcus are in stringent agreement. What they are in agreement about is the necessity of having a readership. Franzen's is large, Marcus's is decidedly smaller—a coterie perhaps, drawn to entirely new syntactical byways and similar hurdles. Each scorns the other's audience; each is content with his own. And both are preoccupied with the recitation of numbers—Franzen earnestly, with those bestseller millions, Marcus derisively, with something called "the Fog Index point spread." The Fog Index, he explains, provides statistical proof that Franzen's vocabulary beats Gaddis's by several school grades: Franzen's fog is even thicker than Gaddis's! Then there is the "Lexile Framework for Reading," according to which, Marcus points out, Gaddis's prose in *A Frolic of His Own* is "just slightly more readable than the Harry Potter series," while Franzen's far higher readability score is on a par with the abstrusely specialized vocabulary of a manual on how to lay brick. All this recondite mathematical taunting appears in an ample footnote designed to mock Franzen's commitment to popularity and his flaunted disdain for difficulty. Still, it is Gaddis, Marcus gloats, who, for all his simpler words and shorter sentences, remains the more complex writer. So: a punch in the eye for Franzen! The Cripps and the Bloods would feel right at home in this alley.

Out of the alley and along the culture's main concourse, both Franzen and Marcus have stumbled into the same deep public ditch—a nearly vacant trench in need of filler. Never mind that one believes in diversion and the other dreams of potions. If the two of them are equally touchy and contentious and competitive, what has made them so is the one great plaint they have in common: *the readers are going away.* Whether they are readers to be lured to Marcus's putative avant-garde experiments, or to Franzen's entertainments, it hardly matters. The readers are diminishing, they are going away.

Denis Donoghue, in an essay titled "The Defeat of Poetry," tells where they are going. An eminent literary scholar, and for thirty years a university professor, Donoghue is here speaking of American undergraduates: the newest crop of potential readers that novelists will try to harvest. "When I started teaching, at University College, Dublin many years ago," he reports,

> I urged students to believe that the merit of reading a great poem, play, or novel consisted in the pleasure of gaining access to deeply imagined lives other than their own. Over the years, that opinion, still cogent to me, seems to have lost much of its persuasive force. Students seem to be convinced that their own lives are the primary and sufficient incentive. They report that reading literature is mainly a burden. Those students who think of themselves as writers and take classes in "creative writing" to define themselves as poets or fiction writers evidently write more than they read, and regard reading as a gross expenditure of time and energy. They are not open to the idea that one learns to write by reading good writers.
>
> In class, many students are ready to talk, but they want to talk either about themselves or about large-scale public themes, independent of the books they are supposedly reading. They are happy to denounce imperialism and colonialism rather than read "Heart of Darkness," *Kim,* and *A Passage to India* in which imperialism and colonialism are held up to complex judgment. They are voluble in giving you their opinions on race and its injustices, but they are tongue-tied when it is a question of submitting to the language of *The Sound and the Fury, Things Fall Apart,* and *A Bend in the River.* They find it arduous to engage with the styles of *Hard Times* and *The Wings of the Dove,* but easy to say what they think about industrialism, adultery, and greed.

So is that where the readers of the next generation are going: to the perdition of egotism and moralizing politicized self-righteousness? The case can be made—Franzen surmised this almost two decades ago—that these students will never evolve into discriminating readers; or, as Marcus would have it, their Wernicke's areas have been rendered infertile. Then where are they going, if not to Faulkner and Achebe and Naipaul? The answer is almost too hackneyed. To the movies; to television (hours and hours); to Googling obsessively (hours and hours), to tweeting and blogging and friending and texting (hours and hours); and undoubtedly also, when at the dentist's, to *People* magazine, where the celebrity photos outnumber the words. While concentrating on dispraising audience-friendliness, Marcus seems to have overlooked, or thinks it not worth mentioning (as Gertrude Stein, his predecessor in autonomous art, once put it): *there is no there there.* The audience, or most of it, has gone the way of the typewriter and the telephone booth and fedoras and stockings with seams.

Then what is to be done about the making, and the taking in, of literature—specifically, in our time, the serious literary novel? Is Franzen right to blame popular electronic seductions for the novelist's problems? Is Marcus justified in rating the wizardry of language juxtaposition over the traditional novel's long heritage of "deeply imagined lives"? Is the realist novel, as he claims, merely a degraded device whereby "language is meant to flow, predigested, like liquid down a feeding tube"? (Does this, by the way, characterize any novel by Nabokov or Bellow?) As it turns out, Marcus does not altogether denigrate realism—he pauses to laud its "deep engineering" as a "brilliant feat"—but he faults it, in furious italics, because *it has already been accomplished.* According to this thesis, nothing is worth doing unless it has never been done before. But we have heard, and from a master, that ripeness—not newness—is all. Besides, why should one literary form lust to dispossess another? Why must there be a hierarchy, Experimentalism (pushing the envelope) on top, Realism (old hat) below? Mozart and jazz, for instance, live honorably together on the same planet. Marcus describes the style of writing he admires as "free of coherence, so much more interested in forging complex bursts of meaning that are expressive rather than figurative, enigmatic rather than earthly, evasive rather than embracing." He concludes: "I find it difficult to discover literary tradition so warmly embraced and coddled, as if artists existed merely to have flagrant intercourse with the past, guaranteed to draw a crowd, but also to cover that crowd in an old, heavy breading." Ah, now we are back at the old gang rumble. At Marcus's end of the alley, though, something smells stale, like old heavy breading. "Expressive rather than figurative," "enigmatic rather than earthly," "free of coherence," and all the rest: *it has already been accomplished.* The avant-garde's overused envelope was pushed long ago, and nothing is more exhaustedly old hat than the so-called experimental. Hoary superannuated abstract painting, consisting chiefly of colors and planes, practiced by Mondrian, born 1872; by

Kandinsky, also born 1872; by Delaunay, born 1885. Experimental music, micro-macrocosmic rhythmic structure à la John Cage, born 1912. Experimental writing, as in Dadaism, a movement begun in 1916. And here comes Ben Marcus, self-styled enigmatic experimentalist innovator, born 1967.

All the foregoing may be mesmerizing for those in the book business who are drawn to the spectacle of writerly acrobatics—to the shifting highs and lows of publicity—but it is beside the point and misleading. Except for the few pre-eminent novelists who have earned, via stature and money, the power to stand aloof, serious fiction writers *are* pressed by elements external to the imagination's privacies, and external also to the secrets of language (including the clarinet that attends the semicolon). But in searching for the key to the Problem of the Contemporary Novel (or Novelist), there are cupboards where it is useless to look. And there are reasons that do not apply: writers vying for the highest rung of literary prestige; potential readers distracted by the multiplicity of storytelling machines. Feuds and jealousies are hardly pertinent, and the notorious decline of reading, while incontrovertible, may have less to do with the admittedly shaky situation of literary fiction than many believe.

The real trouble lies not in what is happening, but in what is not happening.

What is not happening is literary criticism.

But wait. Why should the novel care about that? Novels *will* be written, whatever the conditions that roil around them. The novel is an independent art, secretive in its gestation, a living organism subject to a hundred protean characterizations. Of all its touted representations, the most irritable is Henry James's "loose baggy monster," while the most insistently self-proclaiming is Flaubert's "*Madame Bovary, c'est moi.*" The scholar-critic Robert Alter, if less succinct, is more suggestive: "In the novel," he writes, "the possibility always exists, and is often exploited, to zigzag rapidly between different narrative stances, voices, styles, to improvise and jiggle with new options of narration, to flaunt the mechanisms of narration as they are deployed and invented." He goes on to cite "the elaborately decorous omniscient narrator of *Tom Jones* . . . the nested first-person narrations of *Wuthering Heights,* the purportedly impassive narratorial manipulator of *style indirect libre* in *Madame Bovary,* the shifting verbal vaudeville of *Ulysses.*" (A definition as capacious as this one should go far to reconcile the boys in the alley.)

The novel, then, in all its forms and freedoms, is not in danger; nor is the born novelist—dwindling audiences and the intrusions of pixels notwithstanding. The next Saul Bellow may at this moment be playing patty-cake in his crib—or we may have to wait another two hundred years or so for a writer equal in intellect and vivacity and breadth to turn up. It hardly matters. The "fate of the novel," that overmasticated, flavorless wad of old chewing gum, is not in question. Novels, however they may manifest themselves, will never be lacking. What is missing is a powerfully persuasive, and pervasive, intuition for how they are connected, what they portend in the aggregate, how they comprise and color an era. A novel, it goes without saying, is an idiosyncrasy: it stands alone, it intends originality—and if it is commandeered by genius, it will shout originality. Yet the novels that crop up in any given period are like the individual nerves that make up a distinct but variegated sensation, or act in chorus to catch a face or a tone. What is missing is an undercurrent, or call it, rather (because so much rests on it), an infrastructure, of serious criticism.

This does not mean reviews. A reviewer is not the same as a critic; a case can be made (I will try to make it) that a reviewer is, in effect, the *opposite* of a critic, in the way that an architect is different, not in degree but in kind, from a mason, or in the way that a string theorist is different, though both employ mathematics, from a bookkeeper. Neither masons nor bookkeepers are likely to feel disparaged by this observation. Reviewers may be stung. Reviews, after all, are the sustenance of publishing. Reviews are indispensable: a book that goes unreviewed is a dud to its publisher, and a grief to its author. Besides, reviews through their ubiquity simulate the skin of a genuine literary culture—rather like those plastic faux-alligator bags sold everywhere, which can almost pass for the real thing. In newspapers and magazines, both print and electronic, in book clubs and blogs, in television interviews and in radio format, reviews proliferate more freely than ever before. And they have the advantage of accelerating and multiplying through undreamed-of new venues open to nonprofessionals. The book clubs, for instance. Book club reviewers are characterized, by and large, by earnestness and eagerness, and by a sort of virtuous communal glow: they are "amateur" in its root meaning—they are lovers, lovers of books. Some, or perhaps many, may also be amateur in the sense of being unskilled; but they practice reviewing privately, in the secluded warmth of a living room, within a circle of friends, hence innocently. That these clubs are too often caught in a kind of Möbius spiral, or chicken-and-egg conundrum, is an ongoing curiosity: because they choose to read mainly bestsellers (e.g., *The Hunger Games,* or *Fifty Shades of Grey,* or whatever currently tops the list), they appear simultaneously to *create* these bestsellers.

Less innocent is the rise of the nonprofessional reviewer on Amazon—though "rise" suggests an ascent, whereas this computerized exploitation, through commerce and cynicism, of typically unlettered exhibitionists signals a new low in public responsibility. Unlike the valued book club reviewer, who may be cozily challenged by companionable discourse, Amazon's "customer reviewer" goes uncontested and unedited: the customer is always right. And the customer, the star of this shoddy procedure, controls the number of stars that reward or denigrate writers. Amazon's unspoken credo is that anyone, or everyone, is well suited to make literary judgments—so that a reader of chick lit (the term defines the reader), perhaps misled by ad hype (the term defines book marketing), will howl with impatience at any serious literary fiction she may have blundered into. Here is "Peggy of Sacramento (*see my other reviews*)" grudgingly granting one ill-intentioned star to a demanding contemporary novel: "boring slowness, hard going, characters not even a mother could love." Or Tim: "A thoroughly depressing book. The home life was not a pleasant atmosphere in which to raise children." Most customer reviewers, though clearly tough customers when it comes to awarding stars, are not tough enough—or well-read enough—for tragic realism or psychological complexity. Amazon encourages naïve and unqualified readers who look for easy prose and uplifting endings to expose their insipidities to a mass audience. It is true that one can, on occasion, find on Amazon a literate, lively, penetratingly intelligent response: an artful golden minnow in a fetid sea, where both praise and blame are leveled by tsunamis of incapacity.

(Academic theorists equipped with advanced degrees, who make up yet another species of limited reviewers, are worthy only of a parenthesis. Their confining ideologies, heavily politicized and rendered in a kind of multi-syllabic pidgin, have for decades marinated literature in dogma. Of these inflated dons and doctors it is futile to speak, since unlike the hardier customer reviewers, they are destined to vanish like the fog they evoke.)

And what of the professional reviewers? They count as writers, certainly; but few writers of fiction can be found among them. It may be that novelists wish to stick to writing novels, uninterrupted; or that competitiveness toward other people's books engenders a sour reluctance to celebrate a rival; or simply that reviewing is a skill antithetical to the fictive talent; or, less simply, that the reviewer's more modest stitches will not satisfy the wider ambition of the tapestry weaver who hopes to cover a wall. For all these reasons, and possibly more, most novelists, especially as they mature, tend to eschew reviewing. A good thing, too. The literary judgments even of novelists of consequence can be capricious—Virginia Woolf dismissing James Joyce, for example, or, more recently, V. S. Naipaul dissing Henry James:

> The worst writer in the world actually [Naipaul told an interviewer in Britain's *Literary Review*]. He never went out into the world . . . He

never risked anything . . . He never thought he should mingle in the crowd and find out what they were there for, or how they behaved. He did it all from the top of a carriage or the top of a coach. A lot of his writing is like that. And he exalts his material because he thinks this subject matter he alighted on—the grandeur of Europe and the grandeur of new American money—is unbeatable.

For generations of readers of *The Golden Bowl* and *The Princess Casamassima,* that Jamesian subject *has* been unbeatable, and is as worldly as the range of an expansively inquisitive mind can be; so it is a relief to know that Sir Vidia is not an incessant reviewer of his lowly contemporaries. And a relief also to recognize that though reviewers are, in their fashion, writers, they are not often Nobel-winning novelists.

Frequently they are publishers. In fact, a book's publisher is its first and perhaps most influential reviewer. How a book is "positioned"—i.e., described to the sales staff and in catalogues and flap copy—can nearly seal its fate, or at least condition its reception. In the case of a literary novel (the term intends a dangerous elitism), in-house positioning can snuff it with a word. That word is "midlist"; whoever coined it merits hanging. It emits defeatism. It promises failure. An emblem of noblesse oblige, it reminds publishers that they still owe a modicum of responsibility to the higher literary culture. But what executive editor or vice president will want to back, with dollars and fanfare, a novel tainted by the whisper of midlist? Even so, the writer privileged to be included in this doubtful category is a thousand times more fortunate than the serious literary novelist who is not likely to be published at all. A publishing house is not an eleemosynary organization: who today would publish Proust? (An inapt question, since no mainstream press was willing to publish Proust *then:* initially he paid out of his own pocket to get his work into print; and nowadays, with digital self-publishing readily available, it's every writer his own Proust.) Besides, your typical publisher as first-stage reviewer is more prone to favor treacle—to treat an uplifting pedestrian fiction as a genuine literary novel—than to honor the real right thing. Or, on the other hand, to gussy up the real right thing with commerce-pleasing fakery: only imagine *Pride and Prejudice* hyped, in suitable shiny jacket, as a bodice ripper. Still, in crannies here and there (the golden minnow factor), and again in the larger houses, there remain editors possessed by the old calling—the bringing to light of darker worlds, heretical glimpses, adamantine art.

I stand accused, nevertheless, of misleading. Book club members, Amazon customers, postcolonialist English departments, canny publishing executives—are these what we mean when we speak of reviewers? Aren't the *real* reviewers the people who do it for a living, the talented hired hands who write regularly for a single periodical, or the diligent scattershot freelancers? In brief, that body of readers-by-occupation whose expertise, we feel, ought to make up, collectively, a society's cultural temperament. Were there space enough and time, it might be so—this notion of a powerful undercurrent of literary intelligences, streams crossing streams, all flowing out of one great governing critical headwater; but it is not so. The professional reviewer, given fifteen hundred words or fewer to consider a work of fiction, must jump in and jump out again: an introductory paragraph, sometimes thematic though often not, a smattering of plot, a lick at idea (if there is one), and then the verdict, the definitive cut—yes or no. A sonnet, with worse constraints, or a haiku's even tinier confines, can conjure philosophies and worlds. A review, whose nature is prose, is not permitted such legerdemain. Nor is criticism. Yet what separates reviewing from criticism—pragmatically—are the reductive limits of space; the end is always near. What separates criticism from reviewing—intrinsically—is that the critic must summon what the reviewer cannot: horizonless freedoms, multiple histories, multiple libraries, multiple metaphysics and intuitions. Reviewers are not merely critics of lesser degree, on the farther end of a spectrum. Critics belong to a wholly distinct phylum.

This is a phylum that, at present, hardly exists. When, a few years ago, and in the mode of a social experiment, the *New York Times Book Review* asked a pool of writers to name the best novel of the past twenty-five years, the results were partly predictable and considerably muddled. Toni Morrison's *Beloved,* a tale of slavery and its aftermath, won the most votes. Philip Roth, John Updike, Don DeLillo, and Cormac McCarthy were substantially represented. In an essay musing on the outcome of an exercise seemingly more quixotic than significant, A. O. Scott, a *Times* reviewer, noted that the choices gave "a rich, if partial and unscientific picture of American literature, a kind of composite self-portrait as interesting perhaps for its blind spots and distortions as for its details." Or call it flotsam and jetsam. You could not tell, from the novels that floated to the top, and from those bubbling vigorously below, anything more than that they were all written in varieties of the American language. You could not tell what, taken all together, they intimated in the larger sense—the tone of their time. A quarter century encompasses a generation, and a generation does have a composite feel to it. But here nothing was composite, nothing joined these disparate writers to one another—only the catchall of the question itself, dipping like a fishing net into the sea of fiction and picking up what was closest to the surface, or had already prominently surfaced. All these novels had been abundantly reviewed—piecemeal. No reviewer had thought to set *Beloved* beside Philip Roth's *The Plot Against America* (both are political novels historically disguised) to catch the cross-reverberations. No reviewer had thought to investigate the possibly intermarried lineage of any of these works: what, for instance, has Nick in DeLillo's *Underworld* absorbed from the Nick of Fitzgerald's *The Great Gatsby*? The novels that rose up to meet the *Book Review*'s inquiry had never been suspected of being linked, whether horizontally or vertically. It was as if each one was a wolf-child reared beyond the commonality of a civilization; as if there was no recognizable thread of literary inheritance that could bind, say, Mark Helprin to Raymond Carver. Or if there was, no one cared to look for it. Nothing was indebted to nothing.

Many readers shrugged off this poll as entertaining trivia, or as run-of-the-mill editorial attention-seeking. Yet something culturally important came of it. It revealed, blazingly, what was missing, and has long been missing, in American letters: criticism that explains, both ancestrally and contemporaneously, not only how literature evolves, but how literature influences and alters the workings of human imagination. Here, to illustrate, is Harold Bloom, avatar and prescient forerunner, tracing—via Walt Whitman's *Song of Myself*—just such a pattern of cross-generational transfusion:

> Like its major descendants—T. S. Eliot's *The Waste Land,* Hart Crane's *The Bridge,* Wallace Stevens's *Notes Toward a Supreme Fiction,* William Carlos Williams's *Paterson,* Conrad Aiken's *The Kid,* A. R. Ammons's *Sphere,* John Ashbery's *A Wave—Song of Myself* is an internalized quest-romance, whose antecedents include the long English Romantic tradition of falling in love with the poet's failure. That tradition goes from Wordsworth's *The Excursion* and Coleridge's nightmare *Rime of the Ancient Mariner* on through Shelley's *Alastor* and Keats's *Endymion* to Browning's ruined questers and the daemonic defeats of poets by their antithetical muse in Yeats.

This is Bloom's familiar messianism at work: the dazing fulfillment of a desired critical project before it has properly begun. And here also is James Wood, elucidating the design of that desire, not in one of his grand critical essays but merely in a short public letter making the case for Flaubert as the founder of the modern novel:

> Our indebtedness, whether we like it or not, extends to, among other things: the fetishizing of visual detail; the inverted relationship between background and foreground detail (or habitual and dynamic detail); the

sacralization of art; the privileging of the music of style over the recalcitrance of "unmusical" subject matter (Flaubert's famous desire to write
a book about nothing); the agonizing over aesthetic labor—all this looks
pretty new, and different in many ways from Balzac's great achievements and solutions, not least because these new Flaubertian anxieties
cannot be solutions. You might say that Flaubert founds realism and
simultaneously destroys it, by making it so aesthetic: fiction is real and
artificial at once. And I could have added two other elements of modernity: the refinement of "free indirect style"; and the relative plotlessness
of Flaubert's novels. All this is why different writers—realists, modernists and postmodernists—from Stephen Crane to Ian McEwan, from
Kafka to Nabokov to Robbe-Grillet, all owe so much to Flaubert.

The key, then, is indebtedness. The key is connectedness. If Wood
cannot read Flaubert without thinking of McEwan, neither can he read
McEwan without thinking of Flaubert. In this single densely packed paragraph (though he is not usually so compact), Wood reflects on how scenes
are constructed; how art imitates faith; how aesthetics can either combine
with or annihilate what passes for the actual world. And also: the relation of
story to the language that consumes it, and the descent of literature not only
from one nation to another, but from one writer to another—all the while
clinging to a unitary theme, the origin and nature of the modern. Such an
imperial analysis has both a Darwinian and a biblical flavor: evolution mixed
with Genesis.

Perhaps because Wood is partial to realism (though not to "magical"
or—his term—"hysterical" realism), he is sometimes faulted for narrow sympathies, and for deprecating those styles and dispositions that escape the
bounds of his particular credo. Yet a critic is nothing without an authoritative
posture, or standard, or even prejudice, against which an opposing outlook or
proposition can be tested. To keep to a point of view is itself a critical value.
The grand historic example of critical authority is Samuel Johnson, whose
unyielding mastery of a position was such that to affirm it wholly was never
easy, while to dissent from it was still more difficult—but the assertion itself
roused the mind. In just this sense of instigating counterbalance, Wood is a
necessary contemporary goad.

For an extended period—an anomaly in a culture of kaleidoscopically
rapid shifts—he stood alone, a promontory of notice and prestige. A stimulus
and a goad, yes, but companionless. On the American scene, from the New
England Transcendentalists to the Southern Agrarians to the New Critics to
the New York Intellectuals, linkages and public movements have been more

nearly the norm. At least part of the reason for isolated renown may be what has come to be called a "platform"—the critic's identification with a single journal. George Steiner's hierarchical elitism, for instance, once dominated the *New Yorker,* defining for its readers what criticism ought to do. Consistency of this order has its public benefit (steady access to a singular mind), but after a time an evolving disadvantage creeps in: the pace, the voice, the tone, the habits of phrasing, have grown too familiar. (And also the occasional verbal tic: older readers may recall Steiner's evocation of lofty models, such as "an Aristotle," "a Mozart," as if there might be several of each to choose from.) Where dazzlement is routinely expected, it ceases to dazzle. A critic is fresher when less territorial, a restless pilgrim bird with multiple nests.

And the contrapuntal—contrapuntal, that is, to Wood's prevailing clef—has begun to assert itself, as will happen when a notable critic commands an overriding baton. A case in point: as long ago as 1925, Edmund Wilson, in an essay on Henry James, took issue with Van Wyck Brooks, a leading critic of that burgeoning if quarrelsome era. Wilson's subject, it turned out, was not so much James as it was Brooks's influence on the critical idiom of the hour. Brooks had disparaged James as "an enchanted exile in a museum-world"—a fore-echo of Naipaul's "from the top of a carriage or the top of a coach" (that oddly redundant vehicular sneer). "The truth is," Wilson wrote, "Mr. Brooks cannot help expecting a really great writer to be a stimulating social prophet." And again: "It is precisely because Mr. Brooks's interest is all social and never moral that he has missed the point of James's art." In arguing that James eschewed overt societal indictment because he was "preoccupied simply with the predilection of moral character," Wilson was intending to unseat Brooks's position as arbiter of what a significant literature should properly pursue: Brooks, he insisted, was a "preacher." Certainly Wilson was pushing against a view that in the following decade would support the rise of the blunt and blatant proletarian novel. And whether or not it was Wilson's dissent, in combination with gathering mutations of taste, that finally deposed him, the fading of Brooks as a pre-eminent critic was such that today he is mainly forgotten. Not, however, that Brooks was deprived of an ironic victory. Wilson in all his expansiveness went on to become, among manifold other literary paths zealously trod, a conscious social critic. And as a multivalent pundit, he argued with Nabokov over the nuances of Russian translation, popularized the complex history of the Dead Sea Scrolls, and wrote reverberatingly about everything from burlesque shows to the stock market crash to what he termed "the special psychology of reviewers."

Wilson-versus-Brooks represents a purposeful clash of differing temperaments; but the contrapuntal critic can also turn up in the absence of deliberate opposition, out of the communal air, out of contrasting literary intuitions that begin now to be widely heard—and unlike Wilson, with no intent to diminish a lauded critic. The contrapuntals have, finally, appeared; they are here, and Wood is no longer lonely in his eminence. For Wood, the animating force, his engine of origins, is the crisis of belief and unbelief, of reality and sham: a metaphysical alertness. And something else, unspoken but speaking for itself: the conviction that criticism must be able to stand as literature in its own right.

The contrapuntals I have in mind (because they are visible everywhere, winging from nest to nest) are Adam Kirsch and Daniel Mendelsohn. Like Wood, each comes from—as in the ideologically minded exploratory phrase "Where are you coming from?"—a background of early, and deeply embedded, preoccupation. Mendelsohn is that uncommon contemporary presence, a master of the literature of ancient Greece. Kirsch is a poet, and more than that: he is in serious possession of the very thing that long ago alarmed John Blackwood, George Eliot's publisher, when, on first reading *Daniel Deronda,* he unhappily discovered "the Jewish element." (Kirsch is also in possession of what might be termed "the George Eliot element," the capacity to embrace intellectually, and inhabit sympathetically, discrete yet crucially intertwined cultures.) Both Kirsch and Mendelsohn follow Wilson in breadth, ranging at will beyond the immediately literary, Mendelsohn more peripatetically than Kirsch. Kirsch is closer to Wood in scrupulous attention to language, as one would expect of a poet, particularly one of formal inclination. Mendelsohn's paragraphs will freely employ relaxed popular speech, sometimes even tending toward the breezy, while at the same time tightly analytical. Having fully assimilated the postmodernist leveling of high and low, he approaches film and television with the same brio as he might bring to a play by Euripides; or he will mingle the current with the classical, pointing out parallels (viz. "As *Seinfeld* and Aristotle both knew . . ."). Neither Mendelsohn nor Kirsch is as fierce a close reader as Wood, or drills into the work under inspection with the same fanatical eye. Kirsch has undertaken to penetrate the oceanic pages of the Talmud (albeit in English translation), *daf* by patient *daf.* He has published a biography of Disraeli and a comprehensive study of Lionel Trilling: impossible to conceive of Wood's being drawn to either figure. (Kirsch has, in fact, been described as Trilling's heir.) And Mendelsohn is the author of *The Lost,* a moving, exhaustive, and revelatory history of his family's Holocaust-devoured Polish branch that stands starkly apart from the critic's role.

In an analogy that is certainly inexact as to particulars, but nevertheless interestingly suggestive of how oddly and unexpectedly forked a life can be, Mendelsohn brings to mind the career of A. E. Housman, who as a ferociously contentious dry-as-dust Latin scholar was devoted, among others, to Manilius, a minor and mostly overlooked Roman poet and astrologer. All that side of Housman is half obliterated; what lasts are the lyrically bucolic verses that erupted from an unsuspected and yearningly tender inwardness. And for Mendelsohn, a disciplined early immersion in the rigor of the classics has somehow drawn out an appetite for the most tumultuous, even circus-like, aspects of the present scene: from Sophocles and Aristophanes, say, to *Mad Men* and *Downton Abbey*. Yet while this exuberant transmutation from one species of perception to another can never be predictable or stodgy, it can sometimes come at the cost of depth. The commanding if graver Kirsch, meanwhile, has moved with conceptual agility from the innate structural enclosures of the poem to elasticity, history, connectedness; and to steadfast literary authority fed by a sympathetic intellect. His ability to enter into the political, the societal, the moral—to leap from Reinhold Niebuhr to Harper Lee—distances his reach from the narrower channels of most contemporary critics.

Wellsprings are not always signposts; sometimes they are mazes. A classicist becomes a ringmaster of all the arts. A poet—a man of subtle letters—becomes a cultural interpreter.

But where, in all this, is Susan Sontag, who before her death at seventy-one was for more than forty years an inescapable omnipresence, named by the *New York Review of Books* as "one of the most influential critics of her generation"? She took the compliment as too easily obvious, and also obtuse; she preferred to think of herself as primarily a novelist: "I'm a storyteller," she proclaimed. Wood, skeptical of the historical novel as a form, lauded her final work of historical fiction, *In America,* as a successful exception. (His seemingly spirited endorsement, caught between a principle and its exemption, somehow ends feeling tacitly lukewarm.) Yet because Sontag was, incontrovertibly, that marmoreal edifice, a Public Intellectual, her self-recognition as such lofted her stature well above her plentiful essays, and surely beyond her four novels: it could not be said that she strove in the common critical stewpot. She knew herself to be royalty; she was no one's counterpart, and no one, she made plain, was her peer: she countenanced neither her like nor her unlike. She organized her own exile by ordering her burial in the venerable Père Lachaise cemetery in Paris, where Balzac, Proust, Colette, Gertrude Stein, and countless legendary luminaries are interred. And having lived as an American lioness of unsparing ambition, she willed herself to end as a foreigner in a foreign land: a literary, perhaps also a political, declaration. To formulate—to contribute to—a viable critical infrastructure, one must first be willing to be a part of it.

If Sontag—neither critical competitor nor critical confrere—made certain to steer clear of the hope for such an infrastructure, Leon Wieseltier has been its tutelary spirit and facilitator. As literary editor of the *New Republic* for more than three decades (until its transmigration into a digital afterlife), he presided over the magazine's matchless book section, inviting largeness and depth, imposing no constraints on space or theme. Himself a distinctive stylist and a revivifying cultural critic, he gave a moral shape to questions of aesthetics, and brought humanist perspectives to political thought. Under his influence, the critical essay flourished, whether touching on literature or philosophy or history or painting or music. It was under Wieseltier's eye that Kirsch started out, and it was Wieseltier who recruited Wood—then chief critic for the London *Guardian*—and introduced him to American readers.

As more and more review journals give up the ghost or, like the *New Republic*, turn cybernetically anti-literary, the shallower digital venues proliferate. There, where the long essay makes for uneasy reading, and reviews are mostly random and trivial and shrunk to fit the hither-and-yon notice of cafeteria-style readers, what chance is there for the notion of a serious and sustained critical surround? Yet large projects do not relate to chance, nor are they prone to be stymied by prevailing circumstances. Instead, they germinate out of necessity and will.

Begin with necessity. What is essential is a critical mass of critics pursuing the kind of criticism that can define, or prompt, or inspire, or at least intuit, what is happening in a culture in a given time frame. What is needed are critics who can tease out hidden imperatives and assumptions held in common, and who will create the fertilizing conditions that underlie and stimulate a living literary consciousness. In this there is something almost ceremonial, or ceremoniously slow: unhurried thinking, the ripened long (or sidewise) view, the gradualism of deliberate shading. And here the critic comes closest to the historian by preparing the historian's path. When we speak of an era, an age, a period, a "climate of opinion" (as, in relatively recent times, the Georgian, the Edwardian, the twenties, the thirties, and so on), what is meant is a distillation of the insights, arguments, intimations, and even ideas of taste that the critics, in unintended concert, have amassed.

As for will—that conjoined sibling of necessity—much depends on the individual critic's perception of his task and its motives. In an essay reflecting on his own credo, Kirsch writes: "The critic participates in the world of literature not as a lawgiver or a team captain for this or that school of writing, but as a writer, a colleague of the poet and the novelist. Novelists interpret experience through the medium of plot and character, poets through the medium of rhythm and metaphor, and critics through the medium of other texts. This," he adds, "is my definition of 'serious criticism,' and I think it's essentially the same today as it was fifty years ago: a serious critic is one who says something true about life and the world." For Kirsch, lambent poet and discerning modulator, it is hardly a misstep to allow literary criticism to stand as an equal beside the novel and the poem, those deeply susceptible manifestations of the free imagination—since, after all, criticism too can be the source of the visual, the tactile, the emotive; but as a principle it may turn perilous. When the critic ventures too near the mode of the novel, aspiring to fathom the psyche of the author under review, or when he verges still more dangerously on the poet's power of metaphor, criticism then becomes akin to usurpation: to soul-snatching. Serious criticism is surely a form of literature, but the critic is not an artist with the artist's freedom of play. A critic is, at bottom, a judge, and judgment ought not to be tentative, or it is flat and useless. Neither ought it to be definitive in the way of drawing out a rounded, completed character that does not exist. And metaphor, when applied as personification, can be either revelation—or lie.

So, in asking for a broad infrastructure of critics and criticism to support and confirm a maturing literary organism, there will be caveats and skepticism. Still, should such an authentically engaged infrastructure ever come into being—or, rather, return, since (at least in our backward-looking trustfulness) it once prospered in large enough numbers to make a recognizable literary force—what would change? Professional reviewers, those hemmed-in heralds of the new, would trudge on as before, useful as always. Prudent publishers would go about their business of expediently touting the sentimental or the shocking while marginally tolerating the serious. Readers would continue to drift away, seduced and socialized by the ever-breeding pixels. The boys in the alley—sophisticated armies on a darkling plain— would continue to clash over accessibility and iconoclasm. But for unfulfilled readers and writers who fret over the neglect of the literary novel, something instinctually different might begin to hover: a hint of innate kinship, a backdrop, the white noise of the era that claims us all. In times that are made conscious of the air they breathe—a consciousness that only a critical infrastructure can supply—the varieties of literary experience become less antagonistic than inquisitively receptive. In the age we have learned to call Victorian, Disraeli and Oscar Wilde, novelists (and spirits) as unlike as can be imagined, evince a certain virtuoso interplay: we know this because criticism has taught us how to see it.

When Lionel Trilling reigned at Columbia, Edmund Wilson, Irving Howe, and Alfred Kazin enlivened the magazines, decade upon decade. Today there are inklings of who might constitute a potential critical aggregate, beginning with the legacy of John Updike, pressing on with essay after essay for forty years: self-evidently, the prophetic Harold Bloom, the scholar-poet Geoffrey Hartman, the formidably rounded and witty Joseph Epstein, the exquisitely indispensable Helen Vendler, the philosopher of literature Bernard Harrison; also Dana Gioia, Edward Mendelson, Richard Howard, Robert Alter, Morris Dickstein, Joyce Carol Oates, Laura Miller, Edward Alexander, Sven Birkerts, Martin Rubin, Michael Dirda, Linda Hall, Christopher Beha, William Giraldi, William Deriesewicz, Thomas Mallon, Wyatt Mason, Ruth Franklin, Louis Menand, Jed Perl, Phillip Lopate, Camille Paglia, Michael Gorra, Arthur Krystal—a range of status, age, consistency of publication, breadth of attentiveness, depth of desire, level of pugnacity. These, and others I have failed to mention, some perhaps in embryo, a few busy elsewhere as poets or novelists—not even these are enough. Passions and principles are copious beyond the anxieties of Franzen and Marcus, whose chief urgencies appear to be who will read. The better question is not who will read, or how they will read, but *why*.

And why really? To catch hold of the tincture and pitch of the hour, the why of the moment, the why of what led to the moment, the why of what may come of the moment, the frights and the fads, the hue and the cry, the why of what is honorable and what is not, the why of what is true and what is lie. It is the *why* that implicates and judges readers, and reviewers, and publishers, and bestseller lists; and novelists. *No novel is an island, entire of itself*. And it is again the *why* that tells us how superior criticism—the novel's ghostly twin—not only unifies and interprets a literary culture, but has the power to imagine it into being.

The Novel's Evil Tongue

When the world was just new, Story came into being, and it came with the beguilements of gossip, and talebearing, and rumor.

Most pressingly, it came through truth-telling. After all, the garrulous serpent was no liar when he told Eve the secret of the Tree of the Knowledge of Good and Evil. Eat of it, he whispered, and "your eyes shall be opened, and ye shall be as God, knowing good and evil." Ever since Genesis, no story has been free of gossip, and how unreasonable it is that gossip has its mischief-making reputation. Had Eve not listened, had she been steadfast in the face of so unverifiable a proposition, what barrenness! Eden would still be what it was, a serene and tedious nullity, a place where nothing happens: two naked beings yawning in their idleness, innocent of what mutual nakedness might bring forth. No Cain and Abel, then no crime novels and Hitchcock thrillers. No Promised Land, then no Young Men From the Provinces setting out on aspiring journeys. No Joseph in Egypt, then no fraught chronicles of travail and redemption. In the absence of secrets revealed—in the absence also of rumor and repute and misunderstanding and misdirection—no Chaucer, no Boccaccio, no Boswell, no Jane Austen, no Maupassant, no Proust, no Henry James! The instant Eve took in that awakening morsel of serpentine gossip, Literature in all its variegated forms was born.

Scripture too teems with stories, including tales of envy, murder, adultery, idolatry, betrayal, lust, deceit. Yet its laws of conscience relentlessly deplore gossip, the very engine that engenders these narratives of flawed mortals. Everything essential to storytelling is explicitly forbidden: *Keep your tongue from speaking evil*, no *bearing false witness*, no *going up and down as a talebearer among your people*. The wily tongue itself is a culprit deserving imprisonment: There it is, caged by the teeth, confined by the lips, squirming like a serpent in its struggle to break free. Harmful speech has been compared in its moral injury to bloodshed, worship of false gods, incest and adultery; but what novelist can do without some version of these fundamentals of plot?

Gossip is the steady deliverer of secrets, the necessary divulger of who thinks this and who does that, the carrier of speculation and suspicion. The gossiper is often a grand imaginer and, like the novelist, an enemy of the anthill. The communitarian ants rush about with full deliberation, pursuing their tasks with admirable responsibility, efficiency, precision. Everything in their well-structured polity is open and predictable—every gesture, every pathway. They may perish by the hundreds (step on an anthill and precipitate a Vesuvius); the survivors continue as prescribed and do not mourn. And what a creaturely doom it is, not to know sorrow, or regret, or the meaning of death; to have no memory, or wonder, or inquisitiveness, never to go up and down as a talebearer, never to envy, never to be seduced, never to be mistaken or guilty or ashamed. To be destined to live without gossip is to forfeit the perilous cost of being born human—gossip at its root is nothing less than metaphysical, Promethean, hubristic. Or, to frame it otherwise: To choose to live without gossip is to scorn storytelling. And to scorn storytelling is to join the anthill, where there are no secrets to pry open.

Why is it needful to penetrate the labyrinth of hidden things, to go up and down among your people as a detective spilling hypotheses? Not unlike the philosophers, the gossiper strives to fathom the difference between appearance and reality, and to expose the gap between the false and the genuine. Even something so private as rumination is a mode of gossip, whereby the newsmonger is on the lookout for motive and character: every prober her own Proust. And since gossip peers through the keyhole of unsuspecting humanity, how can Emma Woodhouse not be compelled to reflect on Mrs. Elton, the young vicar's newly arrived bride?

"She did not really like her. She would not be in a hurry to find fault, but she suspected that there was no elegance; ease, but not elegance. She was almost sure that for a young woman, a stranger, a bride, there was too much ease. Her person was rather good; her face not unpretty; but neither feature, nor air, nor voice, nor manner were elegant. Emma thought at least it would turn out so. . . . She had a quarter of an hour of the lady's conversation to herself, and could composedly attend to her; and the quarter of an hour quite convinced her that Mrs. Elton was a vain woman, extremely well satisfied with herself, and thinking much of her own importance; that she meant to shine and be very superior, but with manners which had been formed in a bad school, pert and familiar; that all her notions were drawn from one set of people, and one style of living; that if not foolish she was ignorant, and that her society would certainly do Mr. Elton no good."

We too do not like Mrs. Elton, nor are we intended to like her; but oh, what nasty pleasure we take in making her acquaintance! And must Jane Austen be admonished, by the strictures of biblical fiat, to keep her tongue from speaking acidly? Interior gossip of this kind, not yet spoken aloud or acted out, is certainly not the most cutting, though elsewhere Jane Austen can do better (by doing far worse).

Evolutionary biologists tell us that the history of gossip—of which their formulations are now inevitably a part—begins with primates grooming primates, where "grooming" means the practice of apes companionably picking unwelcome bits of foreign matter from one another's fur. Nothing will illustrate the plausibility of this predecessor thesis more than the exchange, bitter rather than obliging, that unfolds within the affluently appointed walls of Dr. Sloper's house in fashionable Washington Square. Mrs. Penniman, the doctor's sister, has been zealously promoting her unprepossessing niece's choice of suitor. "Allow me to say," the doctor rebukes her, "that it is extremely indiscreet of you to form secret alliances with young men; you don't know where they may lead you."

But Mrs. Penniman will persist. She retails what she thinks she knows. She slyly weaves tangles that cannot be undone. She is the incarnation of the primordial go-between: She is Pandarus, she is Iago, she turns up in Chaucer's pageant of schemers, and before that as the clever manipulator of the early French fabliaux, those bawdy comic tales in verse of thwarted lovers and their eager helpers. And while Emma as busybody is dangerously intelligent, Mrs. Penniman is self-importantly foolish:

"'I don't know what you mean by an alliance,' said Mrs. Penniman. 'I take a great interest in Mr. Townsend; I won't conceal that. But that's all.'

"'Under the circumstances, that is quite enough. What is the source of your interest in Mr. Townsend?'

"'Why,' said Mrs. Penniman, musing, and then breaking into her smile, 'that he is so interesting!'

"The doctor felt that he had need of his patience. 'And what makes him interesting? His good looks?'

"'His misfortunes, Austin.'

"'Ah, he has had misfortunes? That, of course, is always interesting. Are you at liberty to mention a few of Mr. Townsend's?'

"'I don't know that he would like it,' said Mrs. Penniman. 'He has told me a great deal about himself—he has told me, in fact, his whole history. But I don't think I ought to repeat those things. He would tell them to you, I am sure, if he thought you would listen to him kindly. With kindness you may do anything with him.'

"The doctor gave a laugh. 'I shall request him very kindly, then, to leave Catherine alone.'"

There is a recognizable cruelty in Dr. Sloper's laugh; his laugh is that of the tongue that speaks evil. He is cruel to his silly sister, to his lovesick yearning daughter, to her opportunistic fortune-hunting suitor. It is the same species of cruelty Henry James uncovers in Gilbert Osmond, the sinister aesthete Isabel Archer weds; it is the anguish George Eliot imposes on Dorothea in her horribly mistaken marriage to the withered Casaubon. And all of it comes about through the novelist's transgressive devisings; these go where prudent moral restraint forbids.

Gossip at its inquisitive heart is heartless interrogation, and will sometimes push on to extremes: as in Oscar Mandel's *Otherwise Fables*, where verity and piercing cynicism mingle; as in "In the Reign of Harad IV," Steven Millhauser's ingenious inquiry into ultimate miniaturization, the nature of the least particle of being; as in Chaim Grade's fiery "My Quarrel With Hersh Rasseyner," where two survivors of the German hell argue bitterly over God's faithfulness or faithlessness; as in Philip Roth's *American Pastoral*, with its pricking of pride and its punishing fall; as in the unforgiving thunder of Dostoyevsky's Grand Inquisitor.

Under the influence of the evil tongue, 10,000 stories and novels, before and since, have insinuated themselves into our sin-seeking world. They proliferate in their scores of languages, out of continents leafy or arid, out of furious histories and agitated moral persuasions. They are made by go-betweens, by whisperers and tattletales, by ironists and miscreants, by jesters and mourners, and always by the fevered bearers of false witness.

Yet even Solomon's Proverbs, that ancient well of prudence, in one of its seemingly admonitory homilies, reveals—against its intent —a fierce intuition for the shattering force of storytelling: "The words of a gossip are like choice morsels; they go down to a man's innermost parts."

A man's innermost parts! A woman's innermost parts! Interpret this as you will, it all comes down to the self-conscious and vulnerable organ that humanity once dared (defiantly, subversively) to call Soul—where gossip longs to tread.

No gossip, no interiority. No interiority, the anthill.

Afterword

by
Cynthia Ozick

"Selected Essays" instigates a primal question: selected by whom? To cull is to design, and to design is to color, and to color is to assert one's temperament, and to assert one's temperament is to own, in the realm of letters, the stigmata of the artist. We are obliged (in our more objective moods) to recognize Death as the ultimate artist, the culler and colorist *par excellence*, the selector who is also a universal collector. And that is why Death—as editor—deserves our indifference: there will be no engagement between sifter and subject. Often enough, though, it is living writers themselves who choose what to keep and what to set aside, what to value and what to dismiss. Over every volume of essays there hovers always the ghosts of essays either not ventured, or, in the case of a selection, sequestered for another day, or simply doomed to oblivion. And then the quarreling begins, the uproar and the enmity, self contending with self, the war of will against nil. And nothing resembling coherent dialogue.

Here, for instance, is Henry James afflicting himself with doubts and regrets in his 1890 preface to his self-chosen travel essays:

> Many things come back to me on reading my pages over—such a world of reflection and emotion as I can leave unmentioned nor yet, in this place, weigh them down with the full expression of. . . . Not one of these small chapters but suggests to me a regret that I might not, first or last, have gone farther, penetrated deeper, spoken oftener—closed, in short, more intimately with the great general subject; and I mean, of course, not in such a form as the present, but in many another, possible and impossible.

"Many another, possible and impossible." The melancholia of the might-have-been. Still, a preface by a contemporary editor of James's travel writings might take a less dissatisfied and more sympathetic view, and certainly one that would consider the changes in France and Italy, and in Europe overall, since James imbibed his Paris and his Rome: the "feel" of the Continent following the two World Wars, the rise and fall of Nazism and Communism, the founding of the European Union, the current political and cultural upheavals in the wake of tens of thousands of inrushing migrants. To contemplate a group of essays is to enter into a conversation, or sometimes an argument, or even a kind of know-it-all chiding: "Look," the writer of such a preface might say, "how naive you were, how romantic, all your pretty verbal pictures, your sensitive observations! Only see what has become of your luminous Europe!" Or (forgetting the Dreyfus Affair, which tore apart French society only four years after James confessed his writerly regrets), she might express her envy of a more serene and peaceable age.

All the portentous foregoing applies far more intimately—and certainly more modestly and lightly—to the selected essays gathered here. If dialogue counts (and it does!), then the dialogue between the essayist and her editor has been in progress for years, and the sifting of fifty-odd pieces from a little over one hundred is not without its earlier resonances.

But first let us note who and what, exactly, is the editor of these essays. To begin with, he is an agent, or, in fancier lingo, a "literary representative"— which in actuality means that he is one of those heroic midwives (like Puah and Shifra, who saved the Hebrew babies from the Nile) who keeps writers from drowning; who inspires, who lifts morale, who makes connections not merely in a worldly way, but in E. M. Forster's more ardent sense. And then—passionately, inevitably, drivenly—he is a reader, even an evangelist of reading, for whom Conrad, say, and Ibsen (and Muriel Spark and Ford Madox Ford and Shirley Hazzard and Javier Marias and V. S. Pritchett) are bread and wine, transubstantiations of word into life. And *then,* the hidden having been revealed, he is a novelist: a writer of unshowy feeling and immaculate clarity of language—so that he can, as Conrad says, make you *see*. But also: he is a wit and a great laughter and a mischief-maker (mostly the mischief is no different from hilarious insight, the mockery that illumines). He wryly notes—leaving the arithmetic perilously to me—that when he was eleven, I was, um, forty-eight? So we meet, or collide, somewhere along Nature's continuum: testimony to the truth (or is it merely a wistful hypothesis?) that there are no generations, only temperaments that flow largely in the same direction. And finally, *nota bene!* As a student at Cambridge, this book-besotted youth majored (as we say in America) not in Literature, but in God.

And why, you will ask, am I telling all this? To describe David Miller—to make you *see* him—is the very point. His is the organizing mind, his the discriminating sieve, his the dominating tone; his is the artist's will. If I, or anyone else, had picked out some four or five dozen essays from the six original collections, it would in every instance have resulted in a different book. In configuring the order and groupings of these pieces, and in choosing the rubrics that announce them, he has in effect transfigured their contents. In tune with the alliterative ampersanding alphabet soup of my own long-ago titles for individual volumes (*Art & Ardor, Metaphor & Memory, Fame & Folly, Quarrel & Quandary*) he lands on the letter L—what better letter for the life of letters? And here, on behalf of transfiguration, is a case in point: under Literature, the former divinity student lists

. . . no, not Tolstoy or James or Forster or Woolf or Wharton, as you might expect, but Job and Ruth and Existence and Scripture, with Chekhov thrown in to further perplex you. Make of this what you will; only remember that you are now in the hands of an intellectual tease who is likely to dizzy you out of your preconceptions.

Nor is it easy to resist him. Yet *Seizing Freedom*, the title he originally chose for this volume (you will see that he likes it so well that he is keeping it for himself), strikes an American ear—though possibly not a British ear—as an inadvertent purloining of a noble phrase. I had used it narrowly, in a writerly and feminist sense, in homage, in a way, to Edmund Waller's seventeenth-century "My Mind to Me a Kingdom Is," a poem declaring sovereign ownership of inner freedom despite any societal circumscription. I meant simply—repressive regimes aside—that no one can stop a writer from writing, and to claim otherwise is cant. But for anyone who witnessed the tumult and anguish of the Civil Rights Movement, the words "seizing freedom," together with "We shall overcome," rightly belong to that cause alone.

So the struggle for a title went on, and many were the "L"s that leaped up, only to be laid low. A legal dictionary came sympathetically to the rescue: *A letter of intent stipulates the argument presented by the writer in favor of a position, while at the same time remaining open to negotiation and opposition.* Which is precisely the role of the essay: a back-and-forth interchange, not always a quarrel, on occasion even an affirmation, between writer and reader. Hence the title: *Letters of Intent.*

But there is more to it than that—not so much what is present here as what is not. This book is an odd sort of palimpsest, in which the earlier inkings are fully visible, while the editor's superimposed ministrations seem, in their generosity, to enlarge (hugely) what is inscribed beneath. Yet every writer's harvest has survived a winnowing, and even what remains can't escape regret. Convictions are mercurial, ideas are fickle, feelings set in stone melt. A closer look at the sweepings on the threshing floor would reveal the stale, the accommodating, the superfluous, the forced, the heedless, the angry polemical, the ephemeral (journalism, letters-to-the-editor): the product of a mostly obscure writer, once young but then not so young, willing to write anything anywhere, if only to see coveted print. And meanwhile toiling in solitude over vast unrealizable novels. Letters of intent, then, do not always deserve to be sent.

The editor in his introduction, rife with brio and warmth, remembers, as I do, a golden afternoon in Notting Hill ("and here is where Orwell lived"), and an antic evening in a Manhattan restaurant when a rose in a fluted flask was beginning, touchingly, to die before our very eyes. And I remember something else: walking along with the editor on a London street noisy with the chatter of passers-by and the groans of bus engines, and then turning into a neighborhood grocery to fetch one or two last-minute items for dinner, and now the voice of the cashier and the editor's "Thank you," and off again into the London welter to catch the bus home. Yet all through this busy companionable quarter-hour, I was, in fact, not in London but in faraway New York, and how could that be? Ah, the mundane cell phone: David Miller had me in his pocket. He kept me there while he paid the cashier, and took me out again afterward.

In this book too I am in his pocket, and he carries me away, wherever he means to go.

New York
January 23, 2016

Additional collections of essays by Cynthia Ozick are available online

Index

Index

Index

"Thoughts After Lambeth" 210
tie to England 208–11
"Tradition and the Individual Talent" 201, 203
Vivien's influence on poetry 225–7
"The Waste Land" 196, 200, 212, 213, 226,
    227–8, 232–3
and Woolf 218, 219
emigrant experience, German 420–30
Emmet, Richard Stockton 40
Empson, William 198
exogamy 252–3
experimental writing 353–4, 355, 356
explication de texte 202

fairy tales 153
faith 246
fanatics and fanaticism 180–1
Farrell, James T. 341
Faulkner, William 349
feminism 49, 58, 61, 75, 142–3
Fet, Afanasy 305
Fiedler, Leslie 343
films 499
First World War 61, 71, 95, 102, 146, 208, 394
Fischer, Bobby 525
Fitzgerald, F. Scott 31, 65
Flanner, Janet 399–400
Fletcher, Valerie 222, 224, 225
Florence 42, 43
Fog Index, the 541
Forster, E. M. 33, 66, 123, 142–3, 145, 151–61,
    162–6, 562
    A Passage to India 155, 160, 162, 164–5, 165–6
    A Room with a View 155, 156, 157
    Aspects of the Novel 155, 274–5
    on characters 155
    death 161
    essays 162
    ethics of privacy 165
    Howards End 152–3, 154, 157, 163
    life 151–2
    The Longest Journey 151, 152, 154, 155, 157,
      158
    Maurice 152–61, 163, 165–6
    and personal relationships 162–6
Fourier, Charles 290
Fox, Everett 273–4
Frank, Anne 388–407
    appropriations 392–407
    death 389
    diary 388–407
    diary editions 390
    German edition of diary 399
    Hackett play 402–7
    idealism and spirit 394–5
    message 396
    status 390–1
    subversion of 390

transfer to Bergen-Belsen 391–2
transportation to Auschwitz 391
upbeat view 394
vision of darkness 395–6
on writing 388–9
Frank, Edith 391, 394
Frank, Joseph 292, 296
Frank, Otto 392–7, 398, 400, 401, 404, 405, 406,
    407
Franklin, Ruth 439
Franzen, Jonathan, *The Corrections* 534–41, 556
freedom 336
Freud, Sigmund 4, 5, 75, 134, 298, 354
    Civilization and Its Discontents 191
Frisch, Shelley 109
Frost, Robert 188, 211
Fry, Roger 133
Fullerton, Morton 22, 62, 67, 70, 73

Gaddis, William 541
Gallo, Louis 344
Gardner, Isabella Stewart 214, 215
Gelernter, David 286
generations 354–5
genocide 304, 305
German emigrant experience 420–30
Germany, Nazi 128–9, 204, 382, 431–9
Gertler, Mark 147
ghost stories 5
Gielgud, John 48
Gies, Miep 396, 407
Gieseking, Walter 477
Gilbert, Martin, *The Holocaust: the Jewish Tragedy*
    434
Ginsberg, Allen 77, 175, 187
    "Howl" 232
Glassman, Susan 345
God 237, 238, 240, 240–3, 244, 244–6, 281
goodness, normality of 385–6
Goodrich, Frances 397, 402–7
Gordimer, Nadine 78
Gordon, Lyndall 226
    Eliot's Early Years 205–6
    Eliot's New Life 206
    *A Private Life of Henry James: Two Women and
      His Art* 35–6, 38–44
Goslar, Hannah 396
gossip 557–60
Gould, Nathan 339–40
Grant, Duncan 133
Grant, Richard E. 48
Graver, Lawrence 400
Gray, John Chipman 39
Gray, Simon, *The Common Pursuit* 501
Great Depression, the 445–6, 447
Greenberg, Eliezer 347
Greene, Graham, *The Heart of the Matter* 502
Gualdo, Luigi 27

568

Index

Index